Golf
ALL-IN-ONE

FOR

DUMMIES®

Golf
ALL-IN-ONE
FOR
DUMMIES®

by Gary McCord, Shirley Archer,
LaReine Chabut, Georg Feuerstein, PhD,
Michael Kernicki, Liz Neporent,
Larry Payne, PhD, Suzanne Schlosberg,
Michael Patrick Shiels, and John Steinbreder

WILEY

John Wiley & Sons, Inc.

30692 8209

L

Golf All-in-One For Dummies®

Published by
John Wiley & Sons, Inc.
111 River St.
Hoboken, NJ 07030-5774
www.wiley.com

For general information on our other products and services, please contact our Customer Care Department within the U.S. at 877-762-2974, outside the U.S. at 317-572-3993, or fax 317-572-4002.

For technical support, please visit www.wiley.com/techsupport.

Wiley publishes in a variety of print and electronic formats and by print-on-demand. Some material included with standard print versions of this book may not be included in e-books or in print-on-demand. If this book refers to media such as a CD or DVD that is not included in the version you purchased, you may download this material at http://booksupport.wiley.com. For more information about Wiley products, visit www.wiley.com.

Library of Congress Control Number: 2012930550

ISBN 978-1-118-11504-6 (pbk); ISBN 978-1-118-20632-4 (ebk); ISBN 978-1-118-20633-1 (ebk); ISBN 978-1-118-20634-8 (ebk)

Manufactured in the United States of America

10 9 8 7 6 5 4 3 2 1

WILEY

About the Authors

Gary McCord: McCord is a player, television announcer, instructor, author, and speaker. He's well known for enduring 23 years and 422 tournaments on the PGA Tour without nabbing a single victory. For 25 years, McCord has provided color commentary for CBS golf events. When he isn't broadcasting or playing golf, McCord keeps busy with myriad other projects. He portrayed himself in and served as technical director for the golf movie *Tin Cup,* starring Kevin Costner. In addition to writing *Golf For Dummies* (Wiley), he's the author of a collection of essays about his life on tour, *Just a Range Ball in a Box of Titleists.* His bestselling *Golf For Dummies* was released in DVD form in 2004. Gary brings a sense of fun to everything he does and never takes himself too seriously. He and his wife, Diane, share the "ups and downs" of a busy life together at their homes in Scottsdale and Denver.

Shirley Archer: Archer is a former New York City attorney who traded the fast life for the fit life. A survivor of Chronic Fatigue Syndrome from stress and overworking, her recovery helped her become a champion of fitness for health and to live fully in body, mind, and spirit. A coauthor of *Weight Training For Dummies* (Wiley), she is a health educator and fitness specialist at the Health Improvement Program at Stanford University School of Medicine in Palo Alto, the author of ten fitness and wellness books, an international trainer of fitness instructors, and a frequently quoted media spokesperson worldwide. Archer believes that healthy bodies come in all shapes and sizes, and that you can live a longer, happier, and better life by choosing fitness every day.

LaReine Chabut: A fitness and lifestyle expert, model, and mom, Chabut is also the author of *Exercise Balls For Dummies* (Wiley), *Core Strength For Dummies* (Wiley), *Stretching For Dummies* (Wiley), and *Lose That Baby Fat!* (M.Evans). Chabut is a leading contributing fitness expert for *Shape* and *Fit Pregnancy* magazines and is most recognized as the lead instructor for America's popular exercise video series, *The Firm* (with more than three million copies sold worldwide). She has appeared on *Dr. Phil, Chelsea Lately* on E!, CNN, ABC, FOX News, *EXTRA, Access Hollywood, Good Day LA,* and KABC. To read more about LaReine Chabut, log on to her website at www.lareine chabut.com.

Georg Feuerstein, PhD: A practitioner of Buddhist Yoga, Feuerstein has been studying and practicing Yoga since his early teens. He is internationally respected for his contribution to Yoga research and the history of consciousness and has been featured in many national magazines both in the United States and abroad. The coauthor of *Yoga For Dummies* (Wiley), Feuerstein has authored over 40 books, including *The Yoga Tradition, The Shambhala Encyclopedia of Yoga,* and *Yoga Morality.* Since his retirement in 2004, he has designed and tutored several distance-learning courses on Yoga philosophy for Traditional Yoga Studies, a Canadian company founded and directed by his wife, Brenda (visit www.traditionalyogastudies.com).

Michael Kernicki: A PGA member for over 25 years, Kernicki has spent most of his career as a Head Golf Professional and General Manager at some of America's finest golf clubs. He has served as a member of the PGA of America National Board of Directors and on the Rules of Golf Committee, where he has administered the rules at 13 PGA Championships, and he is a coauthor of *Golf's Short Game For Dummies* (Wiley). Today, Kernicki is the Head Golf Professional at one of the nation's most prominent country clubs, Indian Creek Country Club in Miami Beach, Florida. His primary objective is for his students to enjoy the game while they improve and make golf a game for a lifetime.

Liz Neporent: Before becoming a well-known corporate fitness consultant, designing and managing fitness centers worldwide, Neporent was a personal trainer, received a master's degree in exercise physiology, and was certified by the American College of Sports Medicine, National Strength and Conditioning Association, American Council of Exercise, and the National Academy of Sports Medicine. She was named *Club Industry Magazine*'s Woman Entrepreneur of the Year and was appointed to the board of directors and faculty of the American Council on Exercise. She is coauthor and author of several books, including *Weight Training For Dummies* (Wiley), *Fitness For Dummies* (Wiley), and *Fitness Walking For Dummies* (Wiley), and writes frequently for the *New York Times, Family Circle, Shape,* and others.

Larry Payne, PhD: Payne is an internationally prominent Yoga teacher, author, workshop leader, and pioneer in the field of Yoga therapy since 1980. He is co-founder of the Yoga curriculum at the UCLA School of Medicine. Payne was named "One of America's most respected Yoga teachers" by the *Los Angeles Times,* and was selected as a leading Yoga expert by Dr. Mehmet Oz, *Reader's Digest,* Web-MD, Rodale Press, and the *Yoga Journal.* In Los Angeles, Payne is founding director of the Yoga Therapy Rx and Prime of Life Yoga certification programs at Loyola Marymount University. He is coauthor of five books, including *Yoga For Dummies* (Wiley), and is featured in the DVD series *Yoga Therapy Rx* and *Prime of Life Yoga.* His website is www.samata.com.

Suzanne Schlosberg: A contributing editor to *Shape and Health* magazine, Schlosberg is the coauthor of *Weight Training For Dummies* (Wiley) and *Fitness For Dummies* (Wiley) and the author of *The Ultimate Workout Log.* She is also an instructor in the UCLA Extension Certificate in Journalism program. Always happy when she has a barbell in hand, Schlosberg has lifted weights in Zimbabwe, Morocco, Iceland, and Micronesia, among other locales. She is the women's record holder in the Great American Sack Race, a quadrennial event held in Yerington, Nevada, in which competitors must run 5 miles while carrying a 50-pound sack of chicken feed. Schlosberg also has bicycled across the United States twice and cycles about 200 miles a week near her home in Los Angeles.

Michael Patrick Shiels: *Golf's Short Game For Dummies* (Wiley) was Shiels' fifth book. The *Los Angeles Times* called his *Good Bounces & Bad Lies,* written with Emmy Award-winning golf announcer Ben Wright, "perhaps the best sports book ever," and a *Washington Times* review sardonically compared Shiels and Wright to Ernest Hemingway and F. Scott Fitzgerald. His travel articles have appeared in publications such as *Golf Magazine, Travel + Leisure Golf,* www.pgatour.com, and *Sports Illustrated,* and he's written scripts for The Golf Channel and ESPN. Shiels has traveled the world — from Thailand to the Middle East to his beloved ancestral Republic of Ireland — in search of rich stories to tell. You can contact Shiels at Mshiels@aol.com.

John Steinbreder: A senior writer for *Golfweek* magazine, Steinbreder is the author of six books, including *Golf Rules & Etiquette For Dummies* (Wiley). A former reporter for *Fortune* magazine and writer/reporter for *Sports Illustrated,* he has been honored by the Golf Writers Association of America for his work and has had his writing published in a number of top periodicals, including *The New York Times Magazine, Forbes FYI, Time, The Wall Street Journal,* and *Sky.* Steinbreder also served for a time as a special contributor to ESPN Television and is a contributing editor to *Met Golfer, Sporting Classics,* and *Chief Executive* magazines. An avid golfer who carries a 5 handicap (most of the time), he lives in Easton, Connecticut, with his daughter, Exa.

Publisher's Acknowledgments

We're proud of this book; please send us your comments at http://dummies.custhelp.com. For other comments, please contact our Customer Care Department within the U.S. at 877-762-2974, outside the U.S. at 317-572-3993, or fax 317-572-4002.

Some of the people who helped bring this book to market include the following:

Acquisitions, Editorial, and Vertical Websites

Compilation Editor: Connie Isbell

Senior Project Editor: Victoria M. Adang

Acquisitions Editor: Stacy Kennedy

Copy Editor: Megan Knoll

Assistant Editor: David Lutton

Editorial Program Coordinator: Joe Niesen

Technical Editor: Derek Carlson

Editorial Manager: Michelle Hacker

Editorial Assistants: Rachelle S. Amick, Alexa Koschier

Art Coordinator: Alicia B. South

Cover Photos: © iStockphoto.com/Anne Clark, Andrew Penner, and vm

Cartoons: Rich Tennant (www.the5thwave.com)

Composition Services

Project Coordinator: Nikki Gee

Layout and Graphics: Claudia Bell, Mark Pinto

Proofreaders: Laura Albert, Melissa D. Buddendeck

Indexer: Steve Rath

Publishing and Editorial for Consumer Dummies

    Kathleen Nebenhaus, Vice President and Executive Publisher

    Kristin Ferguson-Wagstaffe, Product Development Director

    Ensley Eikenburg, Associate Publisher, Travel

    Kelly Regan, Editorial Director, Travel

Publishing for Technology Dummies

    Andy Cummings, Vice President and Publisher

Composition Services

    Debbie Stailey, Director of Composition Services

Contents at a Glance

Table of Contents

Book II: Focusing on Fairway Fitness 85

Chapter 1: Figuring Out Your Fitness Level 87

Chapter 2: Stretching: Flexibility and the Golfer 107

Introduction

∙ ∙

*W*elcome to *Golf All-in-One For Dummies,* your guide to everything you need to know to be a great golfer. If you're simply thinking about embarking on your journey into the world of golf, you've come to the right place. If you're one of the millions and millions of people who play golf but can't quite master the game, you've also come to the right place. (You folks know who you are — the type who throws clubs and/or tantrums after a bad moment or day on the course.)

Although we've written this book for beginners, we've made sure that the chapters within offer something for golfers at every level. From expert tips on technique and form to anecdotes from veterans such as Gary McCord, this book has something for everyone.

About This Book

Golf All-in-One For Dummies isn't your average book about golf. We go beyond the mechanics of the swing to present the big picture of golf. Read the chapters on fitness to get yourself in shape and not only improve your swing and your score but also keep your body from falling prey to pain and injury. Check out the chapters on gear, lessons, and course choices to save yourself from wasting time and money on clubs, instruction, and green fees you don't need. And because a good portion of the game of golf is played in your head, we offer solid guidance about keeping your nerves calm and your mental game strong.

Of course, the way you swing a club *is* important, so we dissect and highlight the grips, stances, and strokes you need to get started. But we also go farther and cover the finer points of the short game — strokes and strategies that help keep your scores down and your opponents impressed. Plagued by slices, shanks, and hooks? No worries. This book also offers fixes and solutions to those and many of the other common problems faced by frustrated golfers.

The exercises, tips, drills, games, and other tidbits of advice in *Golf All-in-One For Dummies* get you started on the path to great golf and also bring you back for quick refreshers along the way on your journey to golf greatness.

Conventions Used in This Book

To make the text even more accessible, we've used some handy conventions throughout the book:

- New words or terms are formatted in *italics* and accompanied by a definition.
- **Bold** text denotes the specific steps of processes that we've spelled out. It also highlights keywords in bulleted lists.
- We've used `monofont` for web addresses. When this book was printed, some web addresses may have needed to break across two lines of text. If that happened, rest assured that we didn't put in any extra characters (like a hyphen) to indicate the break. When using one of these web addresses, type exactly what you see on the page, pretending that the line break doesn't exist.

What You're Not to Read

We've put this book together with your convenience in mind, including highlighting the stuff you don't have to read to understand golf. These sidebars, which are shaded boxes of text, are added attractions. We've tried to make them fun and informative, but they aren't crucial to the rest of the book. Feel free to skip them.

Foolish Assumptions

In writing this book, we have made some assumptions about you, the reader:

- You're interested in golf.
- You're not already a great golfer.

    ✔ You've played golf before, but you're looking for ways to improve your game.

    ✔ You prefer straight talk over jargon.

If any or all of these statements describe you, keep reading!

How This Book Is Organized

Golf All-in-One For Dummies is organized into six books that lead you through the process of becoming a golfer. Beginners need many questions answered as they navigate through the steps of preparing for and learning the game. These divisions help you take those steps one at a time and let you flip to them anytime for quick reference. Here are the books and what you can find in them.

Book I: Getting Started with Golf

You say you're ready for tee time? Stop and think about that for a minute. First you need clubs and gear. Then you need to know how to swing those clubs. You may want to take a lesson to see whether you really like the game and then find golf clubs that fit you. In this book, we sort through the choices in clubs and give you helpful tips on the questions to ask before you make a purchase. We also give you the lowdown on the types of golf courses and ways to save money on green fees. If you're embarking on your golf journey, this book is a good place to start.

Book II: Focusing on Fairway Fitness

This book explains how to tune your most important piece of golf equipment: your body. In this book, we cover the keys to getting into shape for golf, with chapters on stretching, core strength, and weight training. Whether you're a fitness freak, a bit out of shape, or a lot out of shape, this book is an important stop along your journey. In it, you find exercises that improve your swing, help prevent injury, and may help you avoid the aches and pains that come when you're hitting the course.

Golfers are crazy about golf, but a bad day on the course can also make a golfer crazy. This book also covers some exercises, visualization methods, and breathing tips to help with your mental game.

Book III: Playing Golf: The Swing and the Short Game

This book gets right to the point: We present you with a close look at the workings of the golf swing: the grip, the strokes, the stance, all of it. You also get a good look at the *short game* (everything within 70 yards of the hole), where most of your scoring takes place. We show you how to refine your pitch shot and your chip shot. We outline techniques for blasting your way out of bunkers, and we show you how to develop a sound putting stroke.

Book IV: Rules and Etiquette

In this book, we offer some great insider information about the rules of the game. You discover how to conduct yourself on the golf course, cope with penalty shots, and handle the fine art of betting. You even get the do's and don't of golf-course etiquette, both for players and for fans. With the info in this book under your belt, you can walk onto any golf course and look like you know what you're doing — because you do.

Book V: Hitting the Course

Okay, now you're ready to hit the course. Get started on the right foot by following our routine for limbering up before that first swing. Check out tactics for teeing off like a pro, and do it all without losing your composure along the way. Think you don't need to practice? Think again. This book outlines the importance of practicing; we even provide you with some great games that make practicing less of a chore.

Book VI: Easy Fixes for Common Faults

In this book, we tackle the tough shots — the terrible tees, slices, hooks, and more — and offer advice to help you deal with bad luck, bad moods, and bad weather. You'll develop many faults during your golfing life, and this book tells you how to fix most of them. You also find a glossary of golf terms in this book to help you decipher any jargon you may not be familiar with yet.

Icons Used in This Book

The following icons appear throughout this book and point you toward valuable advice and hazards to watch out for.

This icon flags quick, easy ways to improve your game.

This icon marks moves or myths that can derail your golf game. Be careful!

This icon alerts you to missteps that may cause you physical harm.

When you see this icon, be on the lookout for Gary McCord's recommendations and personal stories from his years of playing and covering professional golf.

This icon flags information that's important enough to repeat.

Where to Go from Here

Feel free to flip through this book. It isn't designed to be read like a novel from cover to cover. If you're a complete novice, you may want to start at the very beginning. If you're a little more advanced and need help with a specific aspect of your game or swing, you can find that information in Book III. Have some skills but need help navigating the social nuances of the game? Head to Book IV, which covers the rules of the game and the finer points of etiquette. The rest of the book helps you make that vital jump from golf novice to savvy golfer.

Book I
Getting Started with Golf

The 5th Wave — By Rich Tennant

"Betty, you're not going to embarrass me at the club by wearing that hat, are you?"

In this book . . .

*B*ook I explores the basics of golf. We show you how
to buy clubs and accessories that can help make
you play and look like a pro. We take a look at the many
options for learning the game of golf, from evaluating your
beginner skills and making the most of your lessons to
using books, magazines, and technology to improve your
game. We describe a typical golf course and give you a
whirlwind tour of playing space options, from the driving
range all the way up to a full 18-hole course, including the
penthouse of golf: the private country club.

Here are the contents of Book I at a glance.

Chapter 1

Choosing Your Golf Gear

· ·

· ·

*B*ritain's great prime minister Winston Churchill once griped that golf was "a silly game played with weapons singularly ill-suited to the purpose." Today's clubs are unrecognizable compared to the rather primitive implements used by Young Tom Morris (one of the game's early pioneers) and his Scottish buddies in the late 19th century, or even by Churchill half a century later. Yes, early golf equipment had more romantic names: Niblick, brassie, spoon, driving-iron, mashie, and mashie-niblick are more fun than 9-iron, 3-wood, 1-iron, 5-iron, and 7-iron. But today's equipment is much better suited to the purpose: getting the ball down the fairway to the green and then into the hole.

Nowadays, you have no excuse for playing with equipment ill-suited to your swing, body, and game. There's too much information out there to help you. And that's the purpose of this chapter — to help you get started as smoothly as possible.

Getting a Handle on Cost

Take one look at a shiny, new driver made of super-lightweight alloys and other space-age materials. Beautiful, isn't it? Now peek at the price tag. Gulp! Each year, the hot new drivers seem to cost a few dollars more — many now retail for $400 and up. And that's just one club. You're going to need 13 more to fill up your golf bag, and the bag itself can set you back another $100 or more. Sure, Bill Gates and Donald Trump are avid golfers, but do you have to be a billionaire to play?

Not at all. Just as you can get a golf ball from the tee into the hole in countless ways, you can get the equipment you need, including the ball, in just as many ways.

Going the budget route

Bear in mind that getting the most out of today's highest-priced equipment takes a pretty good player. Just as a student driver doesn't need a Maserati, beginning golfers can get their games in gear with the golf equivalent of a reliable clunker. In the old days, many golfers started out with hand-me-down clubs. They may have been Dad's or Mom's old set cut down for Junior to try. The young phenom may have graduated to a full set found at a garage sale, and if those clubs happened to fit the young whippersnapper's swing and physique, Junior may have made the school team.

Today's version of the old garage sale, of course, is that virtual marketplace called the Internet. (We discuss many of the best golf websites later in this chapter.) When you know what to look for (and you can discover that information throughout this chapter), you can find precisely what you need, either online or in a golf shop — often for a fraction of what *Messrs* Gates and Trump would pay. If you really keep an eye on costs, you can get started in this game for as little as $100.

Moving on up: Upscale equipment

You may be planning to spend thousands of dollars getting started in this game. If so, let us have a word with you: Don't.

Of course, you can purchase a gleaming, new set of clubs custom-fit to suit your swing. But if you're a beginning golfer, your swing is sure to change as you become more acquainted with this great game. A top-of-the-line set can cost more than a used car — why pay through the nose when your progress will soon render your custom fit obsolete? You can also opt for the high-tech golf balls that tour pros use — the professionals get them free, but a dozen can cost you about $50. Again, that's a needless expense if you're a beginner.

Spending doesn't guarantee success. For that, you need a good swing. Still, you can rest assured that when and if you do shell out your hard-earned cash for today's name-brand golf gear, you aren't getting cheated. Golf equipment has never been better suited to its purpose.

Knowing Which Clubs to Pack

In the game's early centuries, players could carry as many clubs as they liked. Since 1938, however, 14 clubs has been the limit. Those clubs come in several varieties:

- ✓ **Driver:** The *driver,* the big-headed club with the longest shaft, is what you use to drive the ball off the tee on all but the shortest holes.

- ✓ **Woods:** *Woods* are lofted clubs (*loft* is the angle at which a clubface is angled upward) that got their names because they used to have wooden clubheads. These clubs are numbered, from the 2-wood and 3-wood up to more-lofted 9- and even 11-woods. Today almost all woods have steel or titanium heads.

- ✓ **Irons:** *Irons* are generally more lofted than most woods; you most commonly use them to hit shots from the fairway or rough to the green. These include *wedges* for hitting high shots from the fairway, *rough* (long grass), or sand.

- ✓ **Hybrids:** *Hybrids,* sometimes called *utility* or *rescue* clubs, are like a cross between a wood and an iron.

- ✓ **Putter:** You reach for your *putter* to roll the ball into the hole.

For more details on what specific clubs can do (a 9-iron versus a 5-iron, for example, or a driver versus a wedge), check out Tables 1-1 and 1-2 later in this chapter.

Deciding which clubs to put in your golf bag can be as simple or as complicated as you want to make it. You can go to any store that doesn't have a golf pro, pick a set of clubs off the shelf, and then take them to the tee. You can go to garage sales or order clubs online. You can check with the pro at your local municipal course. Any or all of these methods can work. But your chances of choosing a set with the correct loft, lie, size of grip, and all the other stuff involved in club fitting are pretty low.

Having said that, it wasn't so long ago that *unsophisticated* was a fair description of every golf-club buyer. Even local champions could waggle a new driver a few times and "know" that it wasn't for them — hardly the most scientific approach! The following sections show you some options for putting together your set of clubs.

If you're just starting out in golf, keep in mind that you may discover that this game isn't for you. So you should start with rental clubs at a driving range. Most driving ranges rent clubs for a few dollars apiece. Go out and test-wield these weapons to get a feel for what you need. You can always buy your own clubs when the time comes.

Women and juniors should beware of swinging clubs made for men, which may be too long or too heavy for them. That only makes golf more frustrating! Juniors should start out with junior clubs, women with women's clubs.

Find an interim set of clubs

In your first few weeks as a golfer (after you've swung rental clubs for a while), find cheap clubs to use as an interim set during your adjustment period. You're learning the game, so you don't want to make big decisions about what type of clubs to buy yet. If you keep your ears open around the golf course or driving range, you may hear of someone who has a set that he or she is willing to sell. You can also ask whether people have any information on clubs that you can get cheaply. Many garage sales and yard sales offer golf clubs. And, of course, you can check the Internet — the fastest-growing marketplace in golf. (More on that later in this chapter.) You can become your own private investigator and hunt down the best buy. Buy cheap for now, but pay close attention to proper length and weight of the golf club — you've got plenty of time for bigger purchases.

You're in your experimental stage, so try all sorts of clubs — ones with steel shafts, graphite shafts (which are lighter and therefore easier to swing), big-headed clubs, *investment-cast clubs* (made by pouring hot metal into a mold), *forged clubs* (made from a single piece of metal), and *cavity-backed clubs* (ones that are hollowed out in the back of the iron). You have more choices than your neighborhood Baskin-Robbins.

Don't be afraid to ask your friends if you can try their clubs on the range, especially when a new product comes out. Try out these clubs and judge for yourself whether they feel good. But if you don't like the club that you just tried, don't tell the person who loaned it to you that the club stinks — that's not good golf etiquette. Simply hand the club back and say thanks.

Consider getting fitted for clubs

Today, club fitting is big business. Tour pros and average amateur golfers have access to the same club-fitting technology and information. It's important for all golfers — male and female — to use the right equipment for their body types and physical conditions. For instance, many manufacturers of golf clubs specialize in creating clubs for women that have softer shafts, which are lighter and more flexible.

Here are some factors every golfer should consider:

- ✔ **The grip:** Determine how thick the grip on your clubs should be. Grips that are too thin encourage too much hand action in your swing; grips that are too thick restrict your hand action. Generally, the proper-sized grip should allow the middle and ring fingers on your left hand to barely touch the pad of your thumb when you hold the club. If your fingers don't touch your thumb, the grip is too thick; if your fingers dig into the pad, the grip is too thin.

- ✔ **The shaft:** Consider your height, build, and strength when you choose a club. If you're really tall, you need longer (and probably stiffer) shafts.

What does your swing sound like? If your swing makes a loud *swish* noise and the shaft is bending like a long cast from a fly-fishing rod at the top of your swing, you need a very strong shaft. If your swing makes no noise and you could hang laundry on your shaft at the top of your swing, you need a regular shaft. Anybody in between needs a regular to stiff shaft.

- ✔ **Loft:** Think about your typical ball flight and then how you can enhance it with club loft. If you slice, for example, you can try clubs with less loft — or perhaps offset heads — to help alleviate that common problem. Keep in mind, though, that lower-lofted clubs are longer and harder to hit when you're first beginning. For more information about slicing, see Chapter 1 of Book VI.

- ✔ **The clubhead:** Consider the size of the clubhead. Today, you can get standard, midsize, and oversize heads on your clubs. The biggest are a relatively mammoth 460 cubic centimeters. We recommend bigger clubheads for your early days of playing golf. They're more forgiving — your mishits go longer and straighter. A big clubhead can help psychologically, too. With some of today's jumbo drivers, your swing thought may well be, "With this thing, how can I miss?"

- ✔ **The iron:** Advanced players choose irons that are perfectly suited to their swings. Forged, muscle-backed irons are for elite players who hit the ball on the clubface precisely. Cavity-backed irons (also called *perimeter-weighted*) are for players who hit the ball all over the clubface.

The bigger the clubface, the more room for error — hence the bigger-headed metal woods that are popular today for all the wild swingers out there. They're more forgiving on mishits.

Because of all the technology that's available, purchasing golf clubs nowadays is like buying a computer: Whatever you buy may be outdated in six months. So be frugal and shop for your best buy. When you get a set that fits you and you're hitting the ball with consistency, stick with that set. Finding a whole set of clubs that matches the temperament of your golf swing is hard. Find the ones that have your fingerprints on them and stick with 'em.

Eleven questions to ask before you buy

✔ **Do you have a club-fitting program?** If your local PGA professional doesn't have a club-fitting program, he can direct you to someone in the area who does. After you've started this game and found you like it enough to continue playing, choosing the right equipment is the biggest decision you have to make. Don't leave your PGA golf pro out of that decision.

✔ **What's the price of club fitting?** Don't be too shy to ask this question. Club fitting can be expensive. You should be the judge of how much you can afford.

✔ **What shaft length do I need for my clubs?** Golfers come in different heights and builds. Some are tall with short arms, and some are short with long arms. People have different postures when they bend over to address the golf ball, and they need different shaft lengths to match those postures. This issue is where PGA golf professionals can really help; they're trained to answer questions like these and can make club fitting very easy.

✔ **How about shaft flex?** Most golfers should use clubs with regular flex, signified by an *R* on the shaft. Don't let your ego spur you to ask for a stiff shaft unless you're strong enough to generate a lot of clubhead speed. Most female players should use a whippier shaft that requires less strength — look for an *L* for "ladies" on the shaft.

✔ **What lie angle do I need on my clubs?** Here's the general rule: The closer you stand to the ball, the more upright your club needs to be. As you get farther from the ball, the lie angle of your clubs should be flatter.

✔ **What grip size do I need?** The bigger your hands are, the bigger grip you need. If you have a tendency to slice the ball, you can try smaller grips that help your hands work faster. If you tend to hook the ball, you can use bigger grips that slow down your hands.

✔ **What material — leather, cord, all-rubber, half-rubber — do you recommend for my grips?** Leather is the most expensive and the hardest to maintain. It's for accomplished players; we recommend that beginners stick to an all-rubber grip and get new grips every year if they play at least once a week.

✔ **What kind of irons should I buy — investment-cast, forged, oversized, or cavity-backed?** The best advice is to look for an investment-cast, cavity-backed, oversized golf club. For beginners, this choice is simply the best.

✔ **Should I use space-age materials like boron, titanium, or graphite in my shafts? Or should I go with steel?** Steel shafts are the cheapest; all the others are quite a bit more expensive, so keep your budget in mind. Test some of these other shafts to see how they compare with steel, which is still very good and used by most of the players on tour. In general, you want the lightest shaft you can swing effectively. And don't be intimidated if you see that tricky word *kickpoint*. Think of it this way: kickpoint = trajectory. If you want to hit the ball lower, try a shaft with a low kickpoint; to hit the ball higher, get one with a higher kickpoint.

✔ **What type of putter should I use: center-shafted or end-shafted? Do I want a mallet putter, a belly putter, or a long putter?** The last few years have seen an explosion of putter technology. You can try out the result at the golf course where you play. Just ask the pro whether you can test one of the putters on the rack. If you have a friend or playing partner who has a putter you think you may like, ask to try it.

↙ **If you're buying new clubs, ask the pro whether you can test them for a day.** Most of the time, someone who's trying to make a sale will give you every opportunity to try the clubs. Golf pros are just like car dealers; they let you test-drive before you buy.

Build your own set of clubs

Here's the ultimate in custom fitting: You can literally build your own set of clubs to your own specifications. You just have to do some homework first. A lot of people are building their own clubs, judging by the success of firms like Golfsmith. And DIY clubs are cheaper than the ones you can buy off the shelf.

Although building your clubs requires time and effort, the end result can be rewarding. A hobby to go with your favorite new sport! You can get catalogs from component companies, call their toll-free numbers, or visit their websites (see the nearby "DIY club-building resources" sidebar). Component companies offer grip tape, solvents, clamps, epoxy, shaft-cutting tools, shaft extensions, grip knives, and every kind of shaft, head, and grip imaginable. You name it, they've got it. If you're not sure, order a club-making video or book first. You never know — you may end up a golfsmith yourself.

Giving Loft a Look

Short game equipment runs the gamut from irons and wedges to putters. And a key consideration is the loft of each club (see Table 1-1). *Loft* refers to the angle of the clubface. A steeper face angle (more degrees of loft) means more lift when you strike the ball. But the loft of each club actually affects two important aspects of the short-game shot:

↙ How far the ball travels

↙ How high the ball travels

Check out Table 1-1 for a rundown of the more common clubs and their typical lofts.

DIY club-building resources

If you're up for the challenge of building your own clubs, the following component supply companies are a good place to start:

Golfsmith
11000 N. 1H-35
Austin, TX 78753
Phone 800-813-6897 (toll-free) or 512-837-4810
Website golfsmith.com

The GolfWorks
P.O. Box 3008
Newark, OH 43023
Phone 800-848-8358 (toll-free) or 740-328-4193
Website golfworks.com

Hireko Golf
16185 Stephens St.
City of Industry, CA 91745

Phone 800-367-8912
Website hirekogolf.com

Hornung's Pro Golf Sales, Inc.
815 Morris St.
Fond du Lac, WI 54936
Phone 800-323-3569 (toll-free) or
920-922-2640
Website hornungs.com

Wittek Golf Supply
3865 Commercial Ave.
Northbrook, IL 60062
Phone 800-869-1800 (toll-free) or 847-943-2399
Website wittekgolf.com

Table 1-1	The Loft of Common Clubs
Club	*Loft*
Driver	8.5 to 11.5 degrees
3-wood	16 degrees
5-wood	21 degrees
3-iron	22 degrees
4-iron	25 degrees
5-iron	28 degrees
6-iron	32 degrees
7-iron	36 degrees
8-iron	40 degrees
9-iron	44 degrees
Pitching wedge	45 to 50 degrees
Gap wedge	50 to 54 degrees
Sand wedge	54 to 56 degrees
Lob wedge	58 or 60 degrees

What you don't see in Table 1-1 is a column listing average distances you can expect to get from each club. Assigning "average distances" to clubs can make folks feel like something's wrong with their game if they don't meet the average. You shouldn't try to measure up to some predetermined "average." Whatever club works for you from a distance is fine. But if you're interested in such averages, head to Table 1-2 later in this chapter. Of course, if you want to take a snapshot of where your game is at in terms of distances, head to the range and work your way through your bag of clubs.

Sorting Through the Short-Game Sticks

The rules of golf dictate that you can carry only 14 clubs in your bag during a round. The typical set you buy from a retailer consists of three woods and nine irons (including two wedges). Throw in the requisite putter that players often purchase separately, and you're up to 13 of your 14-club limit.

But no rule states which 14 clubs you can or should carry. And just because certain clubs come in a set doesn't mean you can't mix and match to customize your golf bag with clubs you see fit to carry.

Irons range from the 1-iron up to the 9-iron and from a lob wedge to a pitching wedge, and you choose what club to hit depending on how far and how high you want to hit the ball. The 1-iron, in theory, provides the lowest and longest flight path, and a lob wedge (60 degrees) or sand wedge provides the highest and shortest trip. (Very few average golfers ever carry a 1- or 2-iron because it takes great skill to hit these low-lofted clubs consistently well.)

Irons perform differently for every player, but you can assume about a 15-yard difference in length as you work your way up the iron scale. A well-struck 8-iron should make the ball fly 15 yards farther than a similarly struck 9-iron, and so forth.

Unlike the standard variances in the angle of the blade in irons, individual wedges come in many different degrees of loft, and those degrees allow for much more precise distance than the 15 yards between the irons.

You can find wedges with blades that feature 45 degrees of loft all the way up to 62 degrees — and everything in between (see Figure 1-1). You can buy a wedge or have one custom made at almost any launch angle you prefer.

Figure 1-1:
Wedges
typically
range in
launch
angle from
48 to 60
degrees.

Pumping irons

Wedges aren't the only "short irons." The 7-, 8-, and 9-irons are also among the family of short irons. How and when you use these clubs is a matter of preference, but fundamentally speaking, you typically use a 7- or 8-iron to chip (see Chapter 5 of Book III) and the 9-iron and pitching wedge for pitches with higher trajectory and shorter distance (see Chapter 4 of Book III), along with their normal full-swing uses, of course.

Weighing wedges

Before golf equipment makers starting adding varied wedges, they produced only pitching wedges (PW) and sand wedges (SW) with every set of irons they made. Equipment makers and players never thought about offering or carrying wedges with varied degrees of angle and loft.

But as players became increasingly skilled and golf club technology improved, player demand, plus the opportunity for more product and profit, caused golf club manufacturers to create more clubs with varying degrees of loft. Now *wedges* is a generic term.

In the following sections, we provide you with some background information on four of the more common wedges, and in the "Matching Your Clubs to Your Game" section later in this chapter, we help you make some decisions about what to stick in your bag.

Pitching wedge

A typical male player of average skill can expect to hit a pitching wedge 90 to 110 yards at the longest (it's about 10 yards shorter for the typical female player of average skill), but you can, of course, shorten your swing to hit much shorter shots when necessary.

The pitching wedge, the next step beyond a 9-iron, is typically lofted between 45 and 50 degrees. The club also has a *bounce,* or flange, that runs across the bottom of the blade to give it weight. Because the face is angled so much, the club has more room on the bottom edge for a flange.

The pitching wedge should produce a high, arching shot. High wedge shots roll forward a very short distance after they hit the green and sometimes, especially when hit with high swing speeds and by skilled players, spin back from the spot where they land if they hit the green with enough backspin (see Chapter 4 of Book III for pitching mechanics).

The club produces backspin when the ball rides up the clubface. The grooves in the wedge help to impart backspin as the ball stays on the face longer, and the ball stays on the face longer when the angle of attack is steeper — more vertical and striking down on the ball. As for club speed, you want to maximize the time that the ball spends riding up the face when you want to create maximum backspin. A slower but consistent speed with the club at the correct angle is the best way for most golfers to produce backspin.

Sand wedge

You use the sand wedge, in its most literal purpose, to extract the golf ball from sand bunkers (see Chapter 7 of Book III). But many golfers use the sand wedge just as they use any lofted wedge, from greenside rough or even the fairway.

Enough practice with the sand wedge can give you confidence with it from anywhere, but practicality and simplicity dictate limiting its use. Better to choose a club of appropriate loft for the yardage needed than to try to force or muscle a sand wedge.

The sand wedge has a very short shaft and is usually the heaviest of the short irons, weighing nearly 40 ounces. Sand wedges have a typical loft angle of 54 to 56 degrees. The blade of a sand wedge splashes through the sand and through grassy lies, sending the ball a short distance on a high trajectory.

Lob wedge

Lob wedges have extremely angled blades and typical lofts of 58 or 60 degrees. (Some touring professionals actually have wedges with more loft than that!) Striking the ball with this club causes it to "lob" up high, travel only a short distance, and fall steeply onto the target.

A lob wedge comes in handy when you need to hit a high shot that travels a short distance and stops quickly, such as when you're greenside and you have a bunker between your ball and the hole and you don't see enough room on the green for the ball to roll to the hole.

You may want to leave the lob wedge to advanced or highly skilled players unless you have the time to practice with one and really get to know it. The margin for error (and the margin of success) with a lob wedge is very small because the face angle is severe and because the ball doesn't roll much after it lands. The flop shot, which we describe in Chapter 2 of Book VI, often requires a lob wedge.

If you decide to add a lob wedge to your golf bag — and to your golf game — consider doing so only after you feel comfortable with your pitching wedge and the other short irons.

Most golf retailers allow you to hit the various lob wedges they sell into a practice net or on a range. Just as with choosing any club, hit some of them until you find one that looks good, feels good, and gives you the results you like — a confident, effective shot.

Gap wedge

Because pitching wedges typically have a loft from 45 to 50 degrees and sand and lob wedges go from 54 to 60, the gap wedge poetically fills the "gap" in loft. Again, it all depends on which wedges you carry and what loft they offer, but if you feel the need to have a short iron with a loft in between those that you already have, you can select a gap wedge to bridge that distance.

You have to be an excellent short-game player with terrific awareness of how far and high you hit the ball to require wedges with "in-between" lofts. Work hard enough on your short game, and you can gain the feel, touch, and imaginative shot-making that make a gap wedge useful to you.

Golf retail shops and your golf club's PGA professional can show you gap wedges with varying degrees of loft. After you run the numbers and figure out what degree of loft you want your wedge to be, choosing one is a matter of preference and performance.

Calling all putters

More than any club in your bag, the type of putter you use is a personal choice. Although you see many brands of drivers and irons available on the market, most manufacturers turn out woods and irons that all have essentially the same look, shape, and specifications. Putters, however, come in all shapes, sizes, styles, weights, and lengths.

Putters are designed to put a good, straight roll on the ball, and when it comes to physics, they essentially accomplish that when the face strikes the ball. But the way you grip them, their length, how heavy they are, the manner in which you swing them, and the way they look vary wildly. Some putters seem expressive, some look classic, some are very futuristic, and some are very plain. Some even sport school colors or personalized logos. You can splurge on an expensive putter, or you can settle on one for as little as $10. But whether it looks like a spaceship or a mallet, choose the putter that works best for you.

If you're new to the game, using a putter with a line indicator on the top may make aiming down the target line easier for you.

The traditional putter

The earliest putters in golf's modern era (say, starting in the 1960s) were all very similar. They had comparable lengths, looks, styles, and weights. The shaft was upright and attached to the *hosel,* which connects the near end of the putterhead. The putterhead was typically a *blade,* which is to say the putter looked very much like any of the irons, only with a steep face designed to roll the ball on the ground.

The traditional putter is the most popular, conventional type of putter and is widely used among average players and touring professionals alike. These putters become the shortest club in your bag — rivaled only by the lob wedge. Traditional putters are steel-shafted, and their putterheads can be made of any number of materials, including wood, aluminum, copper, and stainless steel. They can be metallic and unfinished in appearance, or they can look like smooth, shiny metal. Sometimes they come painted, and sometimes they have materials inserted into the sweet spot of the face to help the player feel the ball make contact and set the ball rolling properly.

The blade and the mallet putters are two of the traditional-length putters:

- **Blade putter:** Golf's original *blade putter* is still in wide use, although, in most cases, manufacturers have thickened and widened the blade and put a line across the top to aid in alignment. Phil Mickelson, playing on the PGA Tour, uses a putter similar to the original blade putter — very minimalist. Tiger Woods, on the other hand, uses a traditional-style blade putter that he has modified (or modernized) and milled to be thicker, heavier, and sometimes perimeter weighted.

✔ **Mallet putters:** Putters of traditional length may not always be blade putters. Mallet-shaped putters, and modernized variations of them (see Figure 1-2), have become popular. Like blade putters, mallet putters spring from the earliest golf clubs, but instead of being modeled after the irons, mallet putters closely resemble woods. The putterhead is rounded in the back and has some heft behind the face. Imagine a tiny 5-wood, and you essentially picture a mallet putter.

The modernized versions of the mallet putter are produced in various shapes, and many of them use various measures to balance the putter — sometimes resulting in a futuristic appearance. The ball "pops" more strongly off a mallet putter than it does off a blade putter because of the extra weight behind the blade. With larger putterheads, club makers have more flexibility in moving around the club's center of gravity.

Figure 1-2: Hitting the green with a traditional mallet putter.

The long putter

The *long putter* has been a subject of controversy from the very beginning of its existence. Instead of being the shortest club in the bag, the "broom handle" or "polecat" long putter is the longest club in the bag — longer even than the driver! (See Figure 1-3 for a glimpse at its length.)

Form follows function, the end justifies the means, and demand creates supply. So what's the purpose of the long putter? Golfers have various reasons for preferring the long putter, ranging from steadying their nerves to taking stress off their backs.

Some players turn to the long putter because they can putt — and practice putting — without having to bend over. The upright position puts less strain on the back, which appeals to older golfers with back concerns.

Other players turn to the long putter because they struggle with their nerves — especially over short putts. Players who are too "wristy" with their putting stroke or suffer from the *yips* (a putting condition) find that the grip needed to swing the long putter stabilizes their wrists and arms and allows them to swing the putter in a pendulum fashion. You can't really swing the long putter without letting it flow freely, and that free motion eliminates pulled or pushed putts.

Book I

Getting Started with Golf

Figure 1-3: Long putters keep your shoulders from turning and allow the putterhead to swing along the putting line in a pendulum fashion.

Because the long putter is so tall, the most popular way to grip it is to anchor the top, butt-end of the putter to your chest with your left hand (for righties) and then lightly grip the putter farther down below with the right hand (see Figure 1-3). The weight of the putterhead can swing almost freely and directly back and forth on the line of the putt, almost like the pendulum on a grandfather clock. Your shoulders have a difficult time turning, and you don't provide a chance for your wrists, elbows, or lower body to affect the stroke and the swing path of the blade.

Because the long putter is legal and accepted by golf's governing bodies, the United States Golf Association (or USGA, in the United States) and the Royal and Ancient Golf Club (or R&A, in the rest of the world), the real question isn't whether they create an unfair advantage (see the "Considering the long-debated controversy" sidebar), but rather whether they're sensible and to *your* advantage to use. The long putter is definitely worth a try for older players or players who suffer from the yips or nervous maladies.

Rocco Mediate was the first player to win on the PGA Tour with the long putter when he won at Doral. It was a tender back that drove Mediate to the long putter, and he later stated that if the long putter were really an easier and better way to putt, everyone on tour would use it. As of now, only a handful of players in the top 500 in the world employ it. Some of the touring professionals are simply wary of the stigma of stocking such an unconventional putter, because others may view it as a concession to weakness. Others, of course, are just so nimble and skilled that they don't need to use the long putter.

The belly putter

The *belly putter* is golf's latest, greatest idea — a compromise between the advantage of the long putter and the practicality of the traditional putter. The belly putter is longer than the traditional putter and shorter than the long putter.

You grip the belly putter, just as you may imagine by the image the name conjures up, by anchoring the top, butt end of the club literally into your belly (see Figure 1-4). By doing so, the motion of the stroke becomes simpler and more reliable — a pendulum effect, just as with the long putter.

Vijay Singh popularized the belly putter more than any other player. Ironically, Singh took the top ranking from Tiger Woods not long after he (Singh) had switched back from a long spell with a belly putter to a traditional putter. (Even one of the top golfers in the world overanalyzes sometimes!)

Considering the long-debated controversy

The controversy about the long putter being a fair piece of golf equipment continues, and some have called for the United States Golf Association (USGA) to ban it from tournament play. Players and critics often cite two reasons:

✔ **Unusual equipment:** Some see it as unusual equipment because of its unconventional design and how far removed it is from the intended spirit of putting. After all, golfers can't putt croquet-style by swinging a putter between their legs, nor can they use the putter like a pool cue, so why should they be able to simplify their putting stroke to the degree that most of the challenge and skill is removed? Anchoring part of the club to your body, some argue, is unfair and defies the spirit of the golf stroke.

✔ **Extra relief:** Another reason that the USGA regularly considers banning the long putter is because it can help in the application of a completely unrelated rule. When taking relief from an unplayable lie, hazard, ground under repair, or other situation from which relief is allowed, players are granted, depending on the situation, one or two club-lengths of relief (no nearer the hole). Any player who carries a long putter (whether he actually putts with it or not) can use it to measure off two club-lengths of relief, which is an advantage over anyone else in the field who doesn't carry the long putter. (Most drivers, however, are roughly within an inch or two in length.)

Figure 1-4:
The belly putter encourages a reliable pendulum putting motion, which even entices younger golfers.

Matching Your Clubs to Your Game

The benefit of not having to carry 14 particular clubs is that you get to match the composition of your set to your strengths and weaknesses. We're assuming that you're going to carry a driver, a 3-wood, a putter, and irons 4 through 9. Nearly everyone does. So you have five clubs left to select. The first thing you need to know, of course, is how far you're likely to hit each club. After you know that, you can look into plugging the gaps. Those gaps are most important at the short end of your set.

Table 1-2 shows how far the average golfer generally hits with each club when he or she makes solid contact. When you start to play this game, you probably won't attain these yardages, but as you practice, you'll get closer.

Table 1-2	Which Club Should You Use?	
Club	**Men's Average Distance**	**Women's Average Distance**
Driver	230 yards	200 yards
3-wood	210 yards	180 yards
2-iron	190 yards	Not recommended; 4-wood or hybrid = 170 yards
3-iron	180 yards	Not recommended; 5-wood or hybrid = 160 yards
4-iron	170 yards	150 yards (consider a hybrid instead)
5-iron	160 yards	140 yards
6-iron	150 yards	130 yards
7-iron	140 yards	120 yards
8-iron	130 yards	110 yards
9-iron	120 yards	100 yards
Pitching wedge	110 yards	90 yards
Sand wedge	90 yards	80 yards
Lob wedge	65 yards	60 yards

You should know your average. The best way to find out is to hit, oh, 50 balls with each club. Eliminate the longest five and the shortest five and then pace off to the middle of the remaining group. That's your average yardage. Use your average yardage to gauge which club to use on each shot.

I recommend that you carry three wedges, each with a different loft. That's what I do. I use a 48-degree pitching wedge, a 53-degree sand wedge, and a 58-degree lob wedge. I hit them 125 yards (pitching wedge), 105 yards (sand wedge), and 85 yards (lob wedge). That way, the yardage gap between them isn't significant. If I carried only the 125-yard wedge and the 85-yard wedge, that would leave a gap of 40 yards — too much. If I leave myself with a shot of about 105 yards, right in the middle of my gap, I've got problems. Carrying the 105-yard wedge plugs that gap. If I didn't have it, I'd be forced to manufacture a shot with a less-than-full swing. And that's too hard, especially under pressure. Full swings, please!

Okay, that's 12 clubs taken care of. You have two left. We recommend carrying at least one lofted wood or hybrid club. Make that two. Low-numbered irons are too unforgiving. So give yourself a break. Carry a 5-wood and even a 7-wood. These clubs are designed to make it easy for you to get the ball up in the air. They certainly achieve that more quickly than a 2-iron.

Another option is the hybrid. It's a fairly recent entry — a forgiving club that gets the ball airborne in a hurry and can be wonderful out of the rough. You can even use it for chipping, as Todd Hamilton did on a shot that clinched the 2004 British Open. Hybrid clubs, which come in different lofts, are getting more popular every day. You should swing a few, and consider carrying a hybrid rather than that 7-wood, 5-wood, or maybe even your 4-iron.

Figure 1-5 shows the clubs that I have in my bag. You can see I have 15 clubs! Depending on the course and weather, I leave one out when I play — probably the 3-iron or 5-wood.

Caring for Your Clubs

You've put a good deal of time, energy, and money into your clubs, so it makes good sense to care for them properly. Each club is a valuable member of your team, but the putter and driver are the clubs that receive the most attention — the stars of the team, if you will. If your driver is like a baseball team's home run slugger, your putter is like an ace closer. The driver gets attention for belting the ball a long way, but the putter comes in and does the precision work to close out the hole or save par. So you should give your putter the star treatment.

Handle with care

Missed shots, especially short putts, can cause a lot of frustration. Do what you can to resist the temptation to take out your anguish on your clubs. Tossing, flipping, or ramming your putter back down into your golf bag can damage it, as can the time-honored tradition of bending or breaking it over your knee. Remember that, according to the rules, you can no longer use a club that you bend or alter during play. Too much "putter punishment" may leave you without a putter to finish the round! (But in case you succumb to temptation as many a golfer has, check out Chapter 8 of Book III, where we give you some pointers on how to putt when you suddenly find yourself without a putter.)

Cover it up

A headcover, which slips easily on and off the clubhead during a round, helps protect your club. Covers are soft and padded with fluffy insides, which help them serve a dual purpose: They clean and dry your clubhead each time you slide the snug cover back on the club (helping to ward off rust), and they help prevent nicking and chipping caused by other clubs in the golf bag.

Some covers come with the club upon purchase, but you can also buy them at golf courses and resorts. Golfers have a wide range to choose from. You have your cuddly-animal devotees. Other players like to be identified with a particular golf club, university, or sports team. Some are content merely to advertise the manufacturer of the club they're using. Whatever you choose, club covers can be nice souvenirs that put a little color and expression into your golf bag!

Give your putter a home of its own

Some players take the extra precaution of keeping the putter in a separate part of the golf bag or even outside the golf bag. Some newer golf bags have an individual compartment designed to hold just the putter. Some golf bags even have a clip on the outside that secures the putter for easy removal. This spares the putter shaft from all the abrasive action of removing and replacing woods and irons from the bag during the course of a round and from the clanging abuse you or the golf cart can cause.

Keep them clean and dry

Take measures to keep your clubs clean and dry. Sometimes golf club staffers give your clubs a swiping with a towel following a round, but you should give your clubs some special attention from time to time. Make certain you properly clean and polish them. Depending on the design of the club, water and a mild detergent or soap usually does the job. Be sure to dry the clubhead thoroughly after washing.

Get a grip

You should replace the rubber or leather grips of your woods and irons on a regular basis — how often is a matter of how much use they get and how they stand up to the elements. Give the same attention to your putter when you feel the time is right. Of course, touch is so important when it comes to putting that you may get comfortable with the feel of an old, worn grip, but if the putter grip feels hard and dried out or slippery, you should consider a new grip.

Go to a golf shop and take the time to try out and evaluate the many types, shapes, and sizes of putter grips available, just as you did when choosing your putter. You can find rubber, leather, wrapped, round, paddle, corded, and other types of grips available in all sizes and thicknesses. Your PGA professional and your own good sense of touch and feel help you choose the grip that best suits you.

Be careful of unusual or larger putter grips. They're heavier and make the putter have a totally different swing weight, which makes the putter feel different while swinging.

Checking out Golf Balls

Many technological advances have occurred in golf over the years, but perhaps nothing has changed more than the ball. It's no coincidence that the USGA and R&A keep a tight rein on just how far a ball can go nowadays. If the associations didn't provide regulations, almost every golf course on the planet would be reduced to a pitch and putt. Everyone would be putting through windmills just to keep the scores up in the 50s.

All golf balls are created equal

For the record, here are the specifications the USGA imposes on Titleist, Callaway, TaylorMade, and the rest of the ball manufacturers:

- **Size:** A golf ball may not be smaller than 1.68 inches in diameter. The ball can be as big as you want, however. Just don't expect a bigger ball to go farther — it doesn't. We've never seen anyone use a ball bigger than 1.68 inches in diameter.

- **Weight:** The golf ball may not be heavier than 1.62 ounces.

- **Velocity:** The USGA has a machine for measuring how fast a ball comes off the face of a club. That's not easy, because impact lasts only 450 millionths of a second, and a good ball can zoom off the club at more than 170 miles per hour. When long-driving champion Jamie Sadlowski creams a drive, the ball takes off at an amazing 218 miles per hour!

  No legal ball may exceed an initial velocity of 250 feet per second at a temperature between 73 and 77 degrees Fahrenheit. A tolerance of no more than 2 percent is allowed, which means an absolute max of 255 feet per second. This rule ensures that golf balls don't go too far. (In addition to balls, the USGA now tests bouncy-faced drivers to keep a lid on distance.)

- **Distance:** Distance is the most important factor. For years the standard was the USGA's "Iron Byron" robot (named for sweet-swingin' Byron Nelson). No ball struck by Iron Byron could go farther than 280 yards. A tolerance of 6 percent was allowed, making 296.8 yards the absolute farthest the ball could go. Today the robot has some help from high-tech ball launchers in the USGA labs, and the upper limit has risen to 317 yards.

Yeah, right. Iron Byron, meet the PGA Tour! Guys like Tiger Woods, Bubba Watson, Dustin Johnson, and their buddies just aren't normal — they regularly blast drives past 350 and even 400 yards!

✔ **Shape:** A golf ball must be round. An anti-slice ball on the market a few years ago was weighted on one side and failed this test. Nice try, though!

Who do I take to the ball? Choosing the best beginner's golf ball

Even with the regulations listed in the preceding section, take a look around any golf professional's shop and you see many different ball brands. And upon closer inspection, you notice that every type of ball falls into one of two categories: The manufacturer claims either that its ball goes farther and straighter than any other ball in the cosmos or that its ball gives you more control.

Try not to get overwhelmed. Keep in mind that golf balls come in three basic types: one-piece, two-piece, and three-piece. (TaylorMade now offers a five-piece ball, the Penta.) You can forget one-piece balls — they tend to be cheap and nasty and found only on driving ranges. So that leaves two-piece and three-piece balls.

Don't worry; deciding on a type of ball is still easy. You don't even have to know what a two-piece or three-piece ball contains or why it has that many "pieces." Leave all that to the scientists. And don't fret about launch angle or spin rate, either. Today's balls are technological marvels, designed to take off high and spin just enough to go as straight as possible.

Go with a two-piece ball. I don't recommend a three-piece ball to a beginning golfer. Tour pros and expert players use such balls to maximize control. As a beginner, you need a reliable, durable ball. Unless you have very deep pockets, go the surlyn, two-piece route. (*Surlyn* is a type of plastic — the same stuff bowling pins are covered with — developed by the Dupont Corporation.) Most beginners use this type of ball. A surlyn-covered ball's harder cover and lower spin rate give you less *feel* — the softness that gives better players tactile feedback telling them how well they've struck the ball — which is why better players tend not to use them. But assuming you don't whack them off the premises, they last longer. They just may roll farther, too.

Golf balls used to come in three compressions: 80, 90, or 100. The 80-compression ball was the softest, and the 100 the hardest. You may think that the harder the ball (100 compression), the farther it goes. Not the case. All balls go far when hit properly, but each one feels a little different. How hard or soft you want the ball to feel has to do with your personal preference. These days, you needn't worry about compression.

Here's a rule of thumb: If you hit the ball low and want to hit it higher, switch to a softer cover. Your drives will spin more and soar toward the stratosphere. If you hit the ball too high, switch to a ball labeled "low-trajectory."

Take all the commercial hype with a grain (make that a bowl) of salt. The most important factors you need to know when buying golf balls are your own game, tendencies, and needs. Your local PGA professional can help you choose the golf ball best suited to you.

Debating the Technological Advances of Golf Gear

Technology is the guiding light of fundamental change that is inherent to a capitalistic society in search of a more expensive way to hit the #$&!?*@ ball farther.*

—Quote on the bathroom wall of the Wayward Soul Driving Range in Temecula, California

Is technology threatening the game? Is the ball too hot? Are big-headed titanium drivers giving the golf ball too much rebound? Is Phil Mickelson left-handed? Most players would answer these questions in the affirmative. Should golfers take a stance in the battle between tradition and technology? Most would say, "Probably not."

To see where golf is today, you have to examine its past; you can then try to predict the game's future. This section helps you gaze into the future.

Testing out high-tech clubs and balls

Many clubs these days are made of titanium and other composite metals. These clubs allegedly act like a spring that segments of the golfing populace believe propels the ball — also enhanced by state-of-the-art materials and designs — distances it was never meant to travel. This phenomenon is called the *trampoline effect,* which some folks may mistake for a post-round activity for reducing stress. In fact, this effect is the product of modern, thin-faced metal clubs.

This phenomenon has fueled a debate pitting the forces of technology (golf's Dr. Frankensteins) against those of tradition (gents in tweed jackets and tam-ó-shanters). Equipment that makes the game easier for the masses helps the game grow, the techno-wizards say. Traditionalists fret that classic courses are becoming obsolete, that the need for new super-long courses may make the game cost more in both time and money, and that golf may become too easy for elite players. Regardless of which side you're on (you may, indeed, back both camps), one fact is undeniable: Golf equipment has been improving ever since the game began.

People have been developing the golf ball and clubs for centuries. In the last 100 years, however, science has played an increasing role in golf-club development, with a strong influence coming from research into new metals, synthetic materials, and composites. Other developments worth noting include the following:

- The introduction of the casting method of manufacturing clubheads in 1963.
- The introduction of graphite for use in shafts in 1973.
- The manufacture of metal woods in 1979 (first undertaken by TaylorMade). This last creation rendered persimmon woods obsolete, although a small number are still crafted.

Titanium clubheads raised the bar in technological development (yet again). Lighter than previous materials yet stronger than steel, titanium allows club makers to create larger clubheads with bigger sweet spots that push the legal limit of 460 cubic centimeters. Such clubs provide high-handicap golfers a huge margin for error — nothing feels quite like having a mishit ball travel 200 yards! But it's golf balls flying in excess of 300 yards that raise suspicions that these new clubs are making the ball too "excitable."

Golf balls have been under scrutiny for much longer, probably because each new generation of ball has had an ever greater impact on the game. Modern balls tout varied dimple patterns, multiple layers, and other features that attempt to impart a certain trajectory, spin, greater accuracy, and better feel, as well as the ever-popular maximum distance allowed under the Rules of Golf established by the USGA. A recent change in the Rules added more than 20 yards to the old maximum of 296.8 yards. But even way back in 1998, John Daly averaged 299.4 yards on his measured drives on the PGA Tour. By 2004, the leader averaged 314, and in 2010 the best average poke was up two more yards.

Looking to the future

The rest of the 21st century likely won't come close to rivaling the recent era for technological impact or dramatic innovation. Why? For one thing, scientists are running out of new stuff they can use to make clubheads — at least stuff that isn't edible. An expedition to Saturn may yield possibilities. Metallurgists are going to be challenged, although so far they're staying ahead of the game. New entries in the substance category include beta titanium, maraging steel, graphite in clubheads, and liquid metal, all purportedly better than current club materials.

Dick Rugge, Senior Technical Director for the USGA, is one of the prominent folks standing in the way of radical equipment enhancement. His job is to regulate the distance a golf ball should travel, yet he doesn't want to stifle technology altogether. The goal is to give the average golfer an advantage (whether it comes from the equipment itself or the joy of having better equipment) while keeping the game a challenge for the top players. The USGA demonstrated this approach in 2010 when it banned the U-shaped grooves (often called *square grooves*) on clubfaces that helped pros make their approach shots stop and back up on the greens. Those grooves were banned for the pros only — amateurs who like the clubs they've got can keep using them until at least 2024!

Still, manufacturers keep trying to build a better mousetrap. And although everyone thinks about distance and spin, the most revolutionary equipment innovations will likely come in putter designs. On average, the USGA approves more than one new putter every day, and many of the new ones look like something out of the *Transformers* movies. But no one has yet invented a yip-proof blade. When somebody does, that genius is going to make a fortune.

The ball may also see changes — although, again, dramatic alterations in ball design are unlikely. Customizing may become more commonplace. You may also find more layering of golf-ball materials to help performance. After the Penta, can an octoball be far behind?

Not to be discounted are improvements in turf technology — an overlooked area boasting significant breakthroughs in the last 20 years. For example, in 1977, the average Stimpmeter reading for greens around the country was 6.6. (The *Stimpmeter* measures the speed of a putting surface — or any surface on a course.) This number means that a ball rolled from a set slope traveled 6½ feet. Today, the average is closer to 9 feet.

But the biggest breakthroughs of all will probably come from humans. Physiological improvement and psychological refinement may be the surest paths to more distance and lower scoring. So go to the gym, take up Pilates, hit your sports psychologist's couch, get in touch with your inner self, eat bran and all the protein bars you can stand, drink green tea, and take a stab at self-hypnotism if you have to.

If all that fails to add 10 yards off the tee, you can try a different ball. Ain't innovation grand?

Dressing the Part: Golf Clothes

The easiest way to date an old picture of a golfer, at least approximately, is by the clothes he or she is wearing. Sartorially, the game has changed enormously since the Scots tottered around the old links wearing jackets, shirts, and ties.

Back at St. Andrews, the restraint of the clothing affected the golf swing. Those jackets were tight! In fact, that was probably the single biggest influence on the early golf swings. A golfer had to sway off the ball and then let his left arm bend on the backswing to get full motion. Also, he had to let go with the last three fingers of his left hand at the top of the swing. It was the only way to get the shaft behind his head. Put on a tweed jacket that's a little too small and try to swing. You'll see what the early golfers had to go through.

Fabrics have changed from those days of heavy wool and restricted swings. Light cotton is what the splendidly smart golfer wears today — if he or she hasn't switched to one of the new, high-tech fabrics that wick perspiration away from the body. Styles have changed, too. In the early 1970s, polyester was the fabric of choice. Bell-bottoms and bright plaids filled golf courses with ghastly ridicule. We've evolved to better fabrics — and a softer, more humane existence on the course. Some guys on tour now wear expensive pants with more-expensive belts. And a few, like Rickie Fowler and Ian Poulter, are more colorful than golfers were back in the '70s! (Though we can't recall seeing any diamond-encrusted skull belt buckles like Rory Sabbatini's back in the day.) But most players wear off-the-rack clothes provided by clothing manufacturers.

Women have undergone an enormous fashion transformation on the course, too. Years ago, they played in full-length skirts, hats, and blouses buttoned up to the neck. Sounds pretty restrictive, no? Now, of course, they're out there in shorts and pants.

For today's golfer, the most important point is to dress within your budget. This game can get expensive enough; you don't need to out-dress your playing partners. A good general rule is to aim to dress better than the *starter* at the course (the person in charge of getting everyone off the first tee). The starter's style is usually a reflection of the dress standards at that particular golf course. If you're unsure about the style at a particular course, give the pro shop a call to find out the dress code.

The bottom line is to dress comfortably and look good. If you dress well, you may appear as if you can actually play this game with a certain amount of distinction. People can be fooled. You never know!

Golf shoes are the final aspect of a golfer's ensemble. Shoes can be a fashion statement in alligator or ostrich. They can be comfortable — tennis shoes or sandals with spikes. They can take on the lore of the Wild West in the form of cowboy boots with spikes or even be military combat boots.

What's on the bottom of the shoe is all the rage now. Except for a few top tour pros who swing so hard they need to stay anchored to the ground, everyone plays in *soft spikes*. Soft spikes reduce spike marks and wear and tear on the greens. They're also easier on the feet. If the style of shoes is worthy, you can even go directly from the golf course to the nearest restaurant without changing shoes. The golf world is becoming a simpler place to live.

Accessorizing Like a Pro

When it comes to accessories, you can find a whole subculture out there. By accessories, we mean things such as

- Covers for your clubs (see "Caring for Your Clubs" earlier in this chapter)
- Plastic tubes that you put in your bag to keep your shafts from clanging together
- Tripod tees to use when the ground is hard, or "brush" tees to aid your drive's aerodynamics
- Telescoping ball retrievers to scoop your lost ball from a water hazard
- Rubber suction cups that allow you to lift your ball from the hole without bending down

You can even get a plastic clip that fits to the side of your bag so that you can "find" your putter quickly. You know the sort of things. Most accessories appear to be good ideas, but then you often use them only once.

The place to find this sort of stuff is in the back of golf magazines, but don't go rushing for your credit card just yet. Real golfers — and you want to look and behave like one — don't go in for tchotchkes. Accessories are very uncool. The best golf bags are Spartan affairs and contain only the bare essentials:

- About six balls
- A few wooden tees

- A couple of gloves
- Headcovers for your clubs
- A rain suit
- A pitch-mark repair tool
- A few small coins (preferably foreign) for markers
- Two or three pencils
- A little bag (leather is cool) for your wallet, money clip, loose change, car keys, rings, cellphone (turned off!), and so on.

Your bag should also have a towel (a real, full-sized one) hanging from the strap. Use your towel to dry off and clean your clubheads. Keep a spare towel in your bag. If it rains, you can't have too many towels.

As for your golf bag, you don't need a large tour-sized monstrosity with your name on the side. Pros have them because someone pays them to use their equipment. But you should go the understated route. Especially if you're going to be carrying your bag, go small and get a stand bag — the kind with legs that fold down automatically to support the bag. That way your bag stays on its feet, even on hot August days when you feel like collapsing.

Buying Golf Gear Online

The Internet is a valuable resource for those looking to buy anything associated with golf. Every major manufacturer (and even some unusual minor ones) has a presence on the web, so don't hesitate to check out such sites as `CallawayGolf.com`, `NikeGolf.com`, `Ping.com`, `TaylorMadeGolf.com`, and `Titleist.com`. The following sites specialize in bringing you good prices on brand-name new and used products.

A visit to a PGA professional is probably the most reliable way to get properly fitted clubs. Many PGA pros offer good deals, and some will match competitors' prices.

- **eBay:** The giant web marketplace has become one of the hubs of equipment sales. At eBay's golf section (`shop.ebay.com/Golf`), you find not only tons of golf balls and clubs (often at great prices) but also clothing, carts, games, and memorabilia, not to mention golf-themed humidors, candles, hip flasks, and plenty of other stuff you never knew existed.
- **Dick's Sporting Goods:** Head to `dickssportinggoods.com` and click on the *GOLF* tab for a vast array of golf gear, much of it at bargain prices,

at the web HQ of Dick's Sporting Goods. A full-service chain with stores in 40 states and counting, Dick's is where you may find a hot new driver for $100 less than you'd pay elsewhere or a dozen premium balls for half the sticker price.

✔ **GolfDiscount.com:** With a home page so busy it may give you eyestrain, `GolfDiscount.com` practically shouts "Value!" For more than 30 years, this online bazaar has helped golfers buy equipment at low, low prices. The site even dedicates a blog page to feedback from satisfied customers. With great prices on all the top brands and an online golf expert for recommendations, questions, and prices, GolfDiscount.com is hard to beat.

✔ **Edwin Watts Golf:** The site for the popular Edwin Watts stores in Texas and the southeastern United States (`Edwinwatts.com`) offers deals on all sorts of gear, including high-quality used clubs.

Chapter 2

Looking into Golf Lessons

. . . .

In This Chapter

▶ Identifying your strengths and weaknesses

▶ Examining your options for lessons

▶ Approaching your golf lesson with the right attitude

▶ Taking advantage of other useful instructional sources

▶ Tuning in to pro golfers

. . . .

Say you just started to play golf. Your friends took you over to the driving range at lunch; you launched a couple of balls into the sunshine and thought you may actually want to learn the game. What next?

✔ **You can get instruction from friends.** Most golfers start out this way, which is why they develop so many swing faults. Friends' intentions are good, but their teaching abilities may not be.

✔ **You can learn by hitting balls.** A lot of golfers who study this way go to the driving range and hit balls day and night to watch how the pure act of swinging a golf club in a certain way makes the ball fly in different trajectories and curves. This process is a very slow one because you have to learn by trial and error.

✔ **You can study books.** You can find many books on golf instruction that can lead you through the fundamentals of the game. But you can go only so far by teaching yourself from a book.

✔ **You can take lessons from a PGA professional.** This option is the most expensive and most efficient way to learn the game. Lessons can cost as little as $8 an hour and as much as $300 or more. The expensive guys are the ones you read about in *Golf Digest* and *Golf Magazine* and see on TV. But any golf professional can help you with the basics of the game.

In this chapter, we help you figure out where to turn for golf lessons and what to expect from those lessons. And if your scheduled lessons aren't enough to fuel your passion for golf, we also include other sources you can look to for further instruction.

Eleven things your teaching pro should have

Not all teaching pros are created equal. Look for these criteria when choosing an instructor:

- Plenty of golf balls
- Plenty of sunblock
- Plenty of patience
- A sense of humor
- Enthusiasm

- An ability to teach players at all levels
- An ability to explain the same thing in ten different ways
- An upbeat manner
- A teaching method that he or she believes in
- An ability to adapt that method to your needs
- More golf balls

Doing a Pre-Lesson Evaluation

Keep a record of how you've played for a few weeks before your first lesson. And we're not just talking about recording your scores. Keep accurate counts of

- How often you hit your drive into the fairway.
- How often you reach the green *in regulation;* that is, how often you get to the green in two fewer shots than that hole's par (for example, you hit the green of a par-5 in three shots). It won't be many, at least at first.
- How many putts you average.
- How many strokes you usually take to get the ball into the hole from a greenside bunker.

Tracking so many things may seem like overkill, but it's invaluable to your pro because it helps him or her quickly detect tendencies or weaknesses in your game. Then the pro knows how to help you improve. Figure 2-1 shows how to keep track of all those numbers on your scorecard.

Deciding Where to Go for Lessons

Golf lessons are available almost anywhere balls are hit and golf is played: driving ranges, public courses, resorts, private clubs, and so on. The price usually increases in that order — driving-range pros usually charge the least. As for quality, if the pro is PGA qualified — look for the term *PGA professional* posted in the pro shop or on his or her business card — you can be reasonably sure you'll get top-notch instruction. If not, the pro may still know a lot about the game, but proceed with caution.

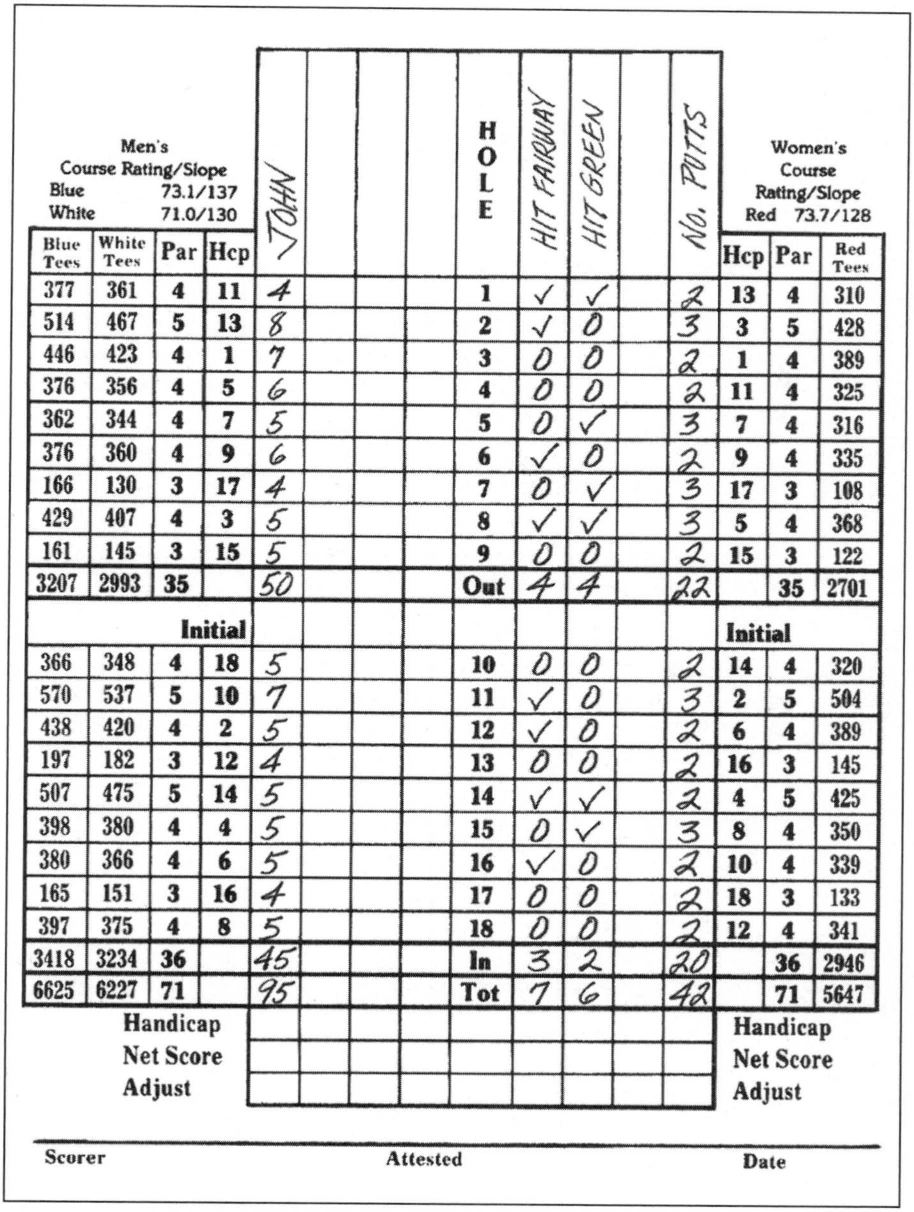

Blue Tees	White Tees	Par	Hcp	JOHN				HOLE	HIT FAIRWAY	HIT GREEN	NO. PUTTS	Hcp	Par	Red Tees
Men's Course Rating/Slope Blue 73.1/137 White 71.0/130												Women's Course Rating/Slope Red 73.7/128		
377	361	4	11	4				1	✓	✓	2	13	4	310
514	467	5	13	8				2	✓	0	3	3	5	428
446	423	4	1	7				3	0	0	2	1	4	389
376	356	4	5	6				4	0	0	2	11	4	325
362	344	4	7	5				5	0	✓	3	7	4	316
376	360	4	9	6				6	✓	0	2	9	4	335
166	130	3	17	4				7	0	✓	3	17	3	108
429	407	4	3	5				8	✓	✓	3	5	4	368
161	145	3	15	5				9	0	0	2	15	3	122
3207	2993	35		50				Out	4	4	22		35	2701
Initial												**Initial**		
366	348	4	18	5				10	0	0	2	14	4	320
570	537	5	10	7				11	✓	0	3	2	5	504
438	420	4	2	5				12	✓	0	2	6	4	389
197	182	3	12	4				13	0	0	2	16	3	145
507	475	5	14	5				14	✓	✓	2	4	5	425
398	380	4	4	5				15	0	✓	3	8	4	350
380	366	4	6	5				16	✓	0	2	10	4	339
165	151	3	16	4				17	0	0	2	18	3	133
397	375	4	8	5				18	0	0	2	12	4	341
3418	3234	36		45				In	3	2	20		36	2946
6625	6227	71		95				Tot	7	6	42		71	5647
Handicap Net Score Adjust												Handicap Net Score Adjust		

Scorer   Attested   Date

Figure 2-1: Recording your golf stats.

A qualified PGA teaching professional may charge as little as $25 or as much as $100 (or more) per session, which can range from 30 minutes to an hour. A professional has a good sense of how much to tell you and at what rate of speed; not all lessons require a specific amount of time. The following sections give you the lowdown on some potential lesson options.

When checking out places that offer golf lessons, ask whether they have video-analysis capabilities. When you're able to watch yourself on video, you and your instructor can pinpoint problem areas for improvement. If nothing else, a video record is a great way to track and monitor your progress as you build your fundamental skills.

Golf schools

No matter where you live in the United States, a golf school should be fairly close by. Golf schools serve all levels of players, and many are designed for those just learning the game. (The sidebar "School days" contains a list of recommended golf schools.)

Golf schools are great for beginners. You find yourself in a group from 3 to 20 strong, which is perfect for you — the safety in numbers is reassuring. You discover that you're not the only beginner. And you never know: Watching others struggle with their own problems may help you with *your* game.

Most of the better golf schools advertise in golf magazines. Be warned, though. These schools tend to be expensive. They did very well in the '80s and early '90s, when the economy was perceived to be strong and people had more disposable income. Since then, however, golf schools have been less successful. Golf-school lessons are big-ticket items, which makes them among the first things people omit from their yearly budgets.

Many people still attend golf schools, though. Why? Because they work. You get, on average, three days of intensive coaching on all aspects of the game from a good teacher. Because groups are usually small, you get lots of one-on-one attention, too. And you can pick up a lot by listening to what your fellow students are being told.

Even though you're at golf school, don't feel you have to be hitting shots all the time. Take regular breaks — especially if you're not used to hitting a lot of balls — and use the time to learn. Try to analyze other players' swings. Soak up all the information you can. Besides, regular breaks are the best way to avoid those blisters you see on the hands of golf-school students!

School days

Looking to attend golf school? Some states are more golf oriented than others, but you can find golf schools all over the country and the world. If you can't find one that suits you here, search for "golf schools" on the Internet.

Some of the addresses listed here are the headquarters for chains of schools. Many chain golf schools have seasonal instruction in the northern states; call their headquarters to find out which have programs near you.

Aviara Golf Academy
7447 Batiquitos Dr.
Carlsbad, CA 92011
Phone 760-438-4539
Website aviaragolfacademy.com

Barton Creek Golf Academy
Barton Creek Resort
8212 Barton Club Dr.
Austin, TX 78735
Phone 512-329-4000 or 866-572-7369 for reservations
Website bartoncreek.com/golf/academy.cfm

Ben Sutton Golf Schools
P.O. Box 9199
Canton, OH 44714
Phone 800-225-6923 (toll-free) or 330-548-0043
Website golfschool.com

Boyne Golf Schools
Boyne Highlands Resort
600 Highland Dr.
Harbor Springs, MI 49740
Phone 800-462-6963
Website boyne.com/golf/Instruction/Adult.html

Classic Swing Golf School
1500 Legends Dr.
Myrtle Beach, SC 29579
Phone 800-827-2656
Website classicswing.com

Dave Pelz Scoring Game School
20308 State Hwy. 71 W, Suite 7
Spicewood, TX 78669
Phone 800-833-7370 (toll-free) or 512-264-6800
Website pelzgolf.com

David Leadbetter Golf Academy
1410 Masters Blvd.
Champions Gate, FL 33896
Phone 888-633-5323 (toll-free) or 407-787-3330
Website leadbetter.com or davidleadbetter.com

Golf Digest Schools
7825 E. Redfield Rd., #E
Scottsdale, AZ 85260
Phone 800-875-4347 (toll-free) or 480-998-7430
Website golfdigestschool.com

Grayhawk Learning Center
8620 E. Thompson Peak Pkwy.
Scottsdale, AZ 85255
Phone 480-502-1800
Website www.grayhawkgolf.com/grayhawk_learning_center/

Jim McLean Golf School
4440 NW 87th Ave.
Miami, FL 33178
Phone 305-592-2000
Website doralresort.com/golf

John Jacobs' Golf Schools
6210 E. McKellips Rd.
Mesa, AZ 85215
Phone 800-472-5007 (toll-free) or 480-991-8587
Website jacobsgolf.com

Kapalua Golf Academy
1000 Office Rd.
Lahaina, Maui, HI 96761
Phone 800-527-2582 (toll-free) or 808-665-5445
Website kapalua.com/index.php/kapaluagolf/kapalua-golf-academy-instruction

(continued)

(continued)

The Kingsmill Golf School
The Kingsmill Resort and Spa
1010 Kingsmill Rd.
Williamsburg, VA 23185
Phone 800-832-5665 (toll-free) or 757-253-1703
Website `kingsmill.com/golf/academy/`

PGA Tour Academy Golf Schools
220 Ponte Vedra Park Dr., Suite 260
Ponte Vedra Beach, FL 32082
Phone 800-766-7939 (toll-free) or 904-285-3700
Website `pgatourexperiences.com`

Phil Ritson–Mel Sole Golf School
P.O. Box 2580
Pawleys Island, SC 29585
Phone 800-624-4653 (toll-free) or 843-237-4993
Website `ritson-sole.com`

Pinehurst Golf Academy
One Carolina Vista Dr.
Pinehurst, NC 28374
Phone 866-291-4427
Website `pinehurst.com/golf-schools/about-golf-academies.php`

Randy Henry's Dynamic Golf School
Coeur d'Alene Resort
115 S. Second St.
Coeur d'Alene, ID 83814
Phone 800-688-5253 (toll-free) or 208-765-4000
Website `www.cdaresort.com/golf`

Sugarloaf Golf Club & School
Sugarloaf USA
5092 Access Rd.
Carrabassett Valley, ME 04947
Phone 800-843-5623 (toll-free) or 207-237-2000
Website `www.sugarloaf.com/GolfSchool/`

Vermont Golf School
Stratton Mountain Resort
R.R. 1, Box 145
Stratton Mountain, VT 05155
Phone 800-787-2886
Website `www.stratton.com/golf_at_stratton_vermont`

Wintergreen Golf Academy
Wintergreen Resort
Route 664
Wintergreen, VA 22958
Phone 434-325-8250
Website `wintergreenresort.com/Golf-Academy/`

Country clubs

Even if you're not a country club member, you can usually take a lesson from the local club pro. He or she likely charges more than a driving-range pro (see the following section), but the facilities are better. Certainly, the golf balls are. And chances are you have access to a putting green and a practice bunker so that you can get short-game help, too.

Driving ranges

Driving ranges vary widely as far as size and quality. Many are very sophisticated, with two or three tiers and balls that pop out of the floor already teed up. Some offer putting greens; some have miniature golf courses attached to them. Quite a few talented (and a few not-so-talented) instructors work at these facilities. Most of them can show you the basics of the swing and get you off on the right foot.

Group clinics

Try taking lessons in a group setting called a *clinic.* Most professionals will offer group clinics to similarly skilled golfers. Check out `www.playgolf america.com` for local courses that offer a variety of programs at all price levels. Also, Get Golf Ready is a great program designed to give beginner golfers all they need to play golf in five days for only $99.

A playing lesson

A *playing lesson* is just what it sounds like: You hire a professional to play any number of holes with you. This theme has three main variations:

- ✔ **You do all the playing.** The professional walks along, observes your strategy, swing, and style, and makes suggestions as you go. This approach works if you're the type of person who likes one-on-one direction.

- ✔ **You both play.** That way, you get instruction as well as the chance to observe an expert player in action. If you typically learn more by watching and copying what you see, this type of lesson is the way to go. Pay particular attention to the rhythm of the pro's swing, the way he or she manages his or her game, and how you can incorporate both into your own game.

- ✔ **The pro creates on-course situations for you to deal with.** For example, the pro may place your ball behind a tree, point out your options, and then ask you to choose one. Your choice and subsequent advice from the pro help make you a better player. He or she may give you two escape routes — one easy, one hard. All the easy one involves is a simple chip shot back to the fairway. Trouble is, you may feel like you're wasting a shot. The difficult shot — through a narrow gap in the branches — is tempting because the reward will be much greater. But if you hit the tree, you may take nine or ten shots on the hole. Decisions, decisions! That's what golf is all about.

Gary's favorite teachers

Many famous teachers will teach absolutely anybody who wants to be taught — male or female, young or old. They're expensive — $100 to $400 an hour and up. Some teach at schools, and some are multimedia phenomena. Here are some of the best:

✔ **Mike Bender:** Mike Bender Golf Academy in Lake Mary, Florida (phone 407-321-0444; website mikebender.com

✔ **Sean Foley:** Orange County National Golf Center in Winter Garden, Florida (phone 888-727-3672 or 407-656-2626; website ocngolf.com)

✔ **Hank Haney:** Hank Haney Golf Academy in McKinney, Texas (phone 972-346-2180; e-mail sjohnson@hankhaney.com, website hankhaney.com)

✔ **Butch Harmon:** Butch Harmon School of Golf in Las Vegas, Nevada (phone 888-867-3226; e-mail info@butch harmon.com, website butchharmon.com)

✔ **Peter Kostis:** CBS Golf, the Golf Channel, Golf.com — just about anywhere good golf thinking goes on

✔ **David Leadbetter:** David Leadbetter Golf Academy in Orlando, Florida (phone 888-633-5323 or 407-787-3330; e-mail info@ davidleadbetter.com, website davidleadbetter.com)

✔ **Jim McLean:** Jim McLean Golf Schools in Miami, Florida (phone 800-723-6725; website jimmclean.com)

✔ **Dave Pelz:** Dave Pelz Scoring Game Schools in Austin, Texas (phone 800-833-7370 or 512-264-6800; website pelzgolf.com)

✔ **Rick Smith:** Rick Smith Golf Academy at Treetops Resort in Gaylord, Michigan (phone 888-873-3867; Website rick smith.com) and Rick Smith Golf Academy at Tiburón in Naples, Florida (phone 877-464-6531; website ricksmith.com)

✔ **Stan Utley:** Grayhawk Learning Center in Scottsdale, Arizona (phone: 480-502-2656; e-mail info@stanutley.com, website stanutley.com)

Maximizing Your Lessons

Much has been written about the relationship between Nick Faldo and his former teacher, David Leadbetter. Under Leadbetter's guidance, Faldo turned himself from a pretty good player into a great one. In the process, Leadbetter — quite rightly — received a lot of praise and attention. More recently, Tiger Woods switched teachers and retooled his game. After Woods won the 2005 Masters and British Open, his teacher, Hank Haney, got some of the credit. Five years later, Woods and Haney split as Woods struggled with personal and professional setbacks.

Ultimately, the teacher is only as good as the pupil. Faldo, with his extraordinary dedication and total belief in what he was told, may have been the best pupil in the history of golf. Tiger at his best is nothing less than the best (and most focused) golfer of our time.

Which leads to the most important question of all: What kind of golf student are you? Are you willing to put your faith in your instructor and do the work required to improve your game, or do you expect the pro to tap you on the head with a magic golf club and miraculously fix your flaws? The following sections give you some pointers on taking full advantage of your golf lessons.

When you take lessons, you need to keep the faith in your instructor. There's no point in sticking with someone you don't believe in. If you find yourself doubting your teacher, you're wasting everybody's time. Change instructors if that happens — that is, if your instructor doesn't tell you where to go first.

Be honest

Okay, now you're on the lesson tee with your pro. The first thing you need to be is completely honest. Tell your instructor your problems (your golf problems, that is), your goals, and the shots you find difficult. Tell him or her what style of learning — visual, auditory, or kinesthetic — you find easiest. For example, do you like to be shown how to do something and then copy it? If so, you're a *visual learner.* Do you prefer to have that same something explained (making you an *auditory learner*)? Or do you prefer to repeat the motion until it feels natural (which makes you a *kinesthetic learner*)?

No matter which learning technique you prefer, the instructor needs to know what it is. How else can he or she be effective in teaching you? You should also be sure to mention any physical limitations you have because of injury, illness, or other causes.

The bottom line is that the pro needs to know anything that helps create an accurate picture of you and your game. Don't be shy or embarrassed. Believe me, you can't say anything that your instructor hasn't heard before!

Listen carefully

After you've done some talking, let your teacher reciprocate. Listen to what the pro has to say. After the pro has evaluated you and your swing, he or she can give you feedback on where you should go from there. Feedback is part of every good lesson. So keep listening. Take notes if you have to.

Don't rate the success or failure of a session on how many balls you hit. You can hit very few shots and still have a great lesson. The number of shots you hit depends on what you need to work on. An instructor may have you repeat a certain swing in an attempt to develop a *swing thought,* or feel. You'll notice when the suggested change becomes part of your swing.

Too many golfers swing or hit while the pro is talking. Don't do it! Instead, imagine that you're a smart chicken crossing the road: Stop, look, and listen!

Keep an open mind

Five minutes into every lesson, you're going to have doubts. The pro changes something in your swing, grip, or stance, and you feel weird. Well, think about it this way: You *should* feel weird. What you've been doing wrong has become so ingrained that it feels comfortable. Change what's wrong for the better, and of course it feels strange at first. That's normal. Embrace the change!

Trust your professional more than you trust your friends or even loved ones, at least with your golf game. Countless pros have heard the line, "My husband told me to do it this way," and bitten their lips to keep from asking, "How much does he get paid for teaching golf?"

Don't panic. You'll probably get worse before you get better. You're changing things to improve them, not just for the heck of it. So give what you're told to do a proper chance. Changes rarely work in five short minutes. Give them at least a couple of weeks to take effect. More than two weeks is too long; go back for another lesson.

Meanwhile, practice! If you don't work between lessons on what you've learned, you're wasting the pro's time — not to mention your time and money.

Ask questions

The pro is an expert, and you're paying good money, so take advantage of the pro's knowledge while he or she belongs to you. Don't worry about sounding stupid. Again, your question won't be anything the pro hasn't heard a million times before. Besides, what's the point of spending good money on something you don't get?

The professional is trained to teach, so he or she knows any number of ways to say the same thing. One of those ways is sure to push your particular button. But if you don't share your impressions, the pro doesn't know whether the message is getting through. So speak up!

Golf-lesson do's and don'ts

Here are some tips on making the most of your lesson:

- ✔ **Find a good teacher and stick with that person.**

- ✔ **Follow a timetable.** Discipline yourself to work on what the instructor tells you.

- ✔ **Don't let your mind wander.** *Concentrate!*

- ✔ **Learn from your mistakes.** You'll make them, so you may as well make them work for you.

- ✔ **Don't tense up.** Relax, and you'll learn and play better.

- ✔ **Practice the shots you find most difficult.**

- ✔ **Set goals.** Golf is all about shooting for targets.

- ✔ **Stay positive.** Golf is hard enough — a bad attitude only hurts you.

- ✔ **Don't keep practicing if you're tired.** That's when sloppy habits begin. *Quality* practice matters more than quantity.

- ✔ **Evaluate yourself after each lesson.** Are you making progress? Do you know what you need to practice before your next lesson?

Keep your cool

Finally, stay calm. Anxious people make lousy pupils. Look on the lesson as the learning experience that it is, and don't get too wrapped up in where the balls are going. Again, the pro is aware of your nervousness. Ask him or her for tips on swinging smoothly. Nervous golfers tend to swing too quickly, so keep your swing smooth. What's important at this stage is that you make the proper moves in the correct sequence. Get those moves right and understand the order, and the good shots will come.

Turning to Other Sources

The golf swing is the most analyzed move in all of sports. As such, more has been written — and continues to be written — about the swing than just about any other athletic move. Take a look in any bookstore under "Golf," and you can see what we mean. Maybe you have, because you're reading this book. (Nice choice!) And books are just the beginning; the following sections show you some of the outlets you can peruse for golf instruction.

GARY SAYS

Ten great golf-instruction books

An amazing number of books have been written on golf. Historians have tried to document every hook and slice throughout golf's existence. Many have tracked the footsteps of the great players throughout their careers.

Instruction is the main vein nowadays, so here are ten great golf-instruction books, listed alphabetically by author. I've tried to help by reducing the list to my ten favorites, but I could include many more.

- *How to Play Your Best Golf All the Time* by Tommy Armour (Simon & Schuster, 1953)

- *On Learning Golf* by Percy Boomer (Knopf, 1992)

- *Search for the Perfect Swing* by A.J. Cochran and John Stobbs (Triumph, 2005)

- *Natural Golf* by John Duncan Dunn (Putnam's, 1931)

- *The Mystery of Golf* by Arnold Haultain (Houghton Mifflin Co., 1908; Nabu Press, 2010 — reissued in paperback after 102 years!)

- *Five Lessons: The Modern Fundamentals of Golf* by Ben Hogan (Barnes, 1957)

- *Swing the Clubhead* by Ernest Jones (Dodd, Mead, 1952)

- *The Physics of Golf* by Theodore P. Jorgensen (Springer, 1999)

- *Golf My Way* by Jack Nicklaus (Simon & Schuster, 1974)

- *Harvey Penick's Little Red Book* by Harvey Penick (Simon & Schuster, 1992)

Golf books

So where should you go for written advice? Some of the golf books out there are quite good. But most, sad to say, are the same old stuff regurgitated over and over. *Remember:* This game was centuries old in the 18th century!

HAZARD

Here's another secret: Don't expect too much from books "written" by the top players. The information they impart isn't inherently flawed, but if you think you're going to get some stunning insight into how your favorite PGA Tour star plays, think again. In all likelihood, the celebrity author has had little to do with the text. Exceptions exist, of course, but the "name" player's input is often minimal. Some of the most famous athletes have actually claimed they've been misquoted *in their own books.* And another thing: The world's greatest golfers aren't necessarily the best teachers. In fact, some of them have no idea how hard the game can be.

Golf magazines

The monthly magazines *Golf Digest, Golf Magazine,* and *Golf Tips* owe most of their popularity to their expertise in the instructional field. Indeed, most people buy these magazines because they think the articles can help them play better. The magazines all do a good job of covering each aspect of the game every month. If you're putting badly, for example, every month you can find a new tip (or two or three) to try. Best of all, these magazines use only the best players and teachers to write their stories.

But is the information in golf magazines the best? Sometimes. The key is to sift through what you read and subsequently take to the course. The great teacher Bob Toski once said, "You cannot learn how to play golf from the pages of a magazine." And he was right. Use these publications as backups to your lessons — nothing more.

Keep in mind that magazine articles are general in nature. They aren't aimed specifically at *your* game. Of course, some of them may happen to work for you. But most won't. You have to be able to filter out those that don't.

Instructional gadgets

A look at the back of any golf magazine or the home page of many websites proves that instructional doodads aren't in short supply. Most aren't very good. Some are okay. And a few can work wonders. In Table 2-1, I outline my favorites for you. Figure 2-2 shows a picture of one of the more interesting of these gadgets — the Tour Striker.

Figure 2-2:
The Tour
Striker
keeps your
hands
ahead of
the ball.

Table 2-1	Gary's Favorite Instructional Gadgets	
Gadget	*Function*	*Where to Get It*
A 2-x-4 board	Lies on the ground to aid your alignment.	Hardware store or lumberyard
Alignment sticks	Flexible fiberglass sticks, usually orange or yellow, that you can poke into the ground or lay flat to aid alignment. An improvement on the old 2-x-4.	Hardware store or online
Camcorder	Probably the best instructional gizmo of all. Have a friend record your swing, and then make sure it looks like the photos in this book.	Department store, electronics store, or online
Chalk line	A builder's tool that can help your putting stroke. The line is caked in chalk. You snap it to indicate the line you want to the hole. Many tour pros swear by this technique.	Hardware store or online
Flammer	A harness across your chest with an attachment for a shaft in the middle. When you turn as if to swing, your arms and body move together as a telescopic rod connects the club to your chest.	A few sites online
The Perfect Swing Trainer	A large, circular ring that helps keep your swing on plane.	theperfect swingtrainer. com
Putting Professor	An inclined panel to use on the practice green — it keeps your stroke consistent.	Several sites online
Swing straps	Hook them to your body to keep your arms close to your sides during the swing.	Most golf shops or online
The Tour Striker	A modified club that teaches ordinary golfers to make contact with the shaft leaning forward, like the pros do.	Tourstriker. com

GARY SAYS

Gary's top instructional DVDs

A bountiful supply of golf DVDs ranges from Tim Conway's hilarious *Dorf on Golf* to sophisticated features on the do's and don'ts of your golf swing. Here are some of my favorites:

✔ **Hank Haney's Essentials:** A four-disk set from a modern master.

✔ **David Leadbetter** *Interactive:* Four instructional DVDs plus one with software that can analyze your swing and offer drills.

✔ **David Leadbetter's** *$10,000 Lesson:* And the DVD only costs $19.99!

✔ **Gary McCord's** *Golf For Dummies* **DVD:** How could I resist? The same solid, fun instruction as in this book, plus you get to see me move!

✔ **Phil Mickelson: Secrets of the Short Game:** He even shows you how to hit his patented flop shot.

✔ **Harvey Penick's Little Red Video:** Still available only on VHS, at least until someone puts this classic on DVD.

✔ **Women's Golf Instruction, with Donna White and Friends:** Simple, easy to follow.

DVDs: A visual approach

Instructional DVDs convey movement and rhythm so much better than their print counterparts do, so they're perfect for visual learners. Indeed, watching a top teacher or tour professional hitting balls before you leave for the course isn't a bad idea. The smoothness and timing in an expert's swing has a way of rubbing off on you.

You can buy instructional DVDs at thousands of outlets, including video stores and golf shops, and you can order many of them online or from your favorite golf magazines.

Online golf wisdom (now available in the palm of your hand)

The latest form of golf instruction may one day be the best — websites and apps for your smartphone or other interactive gizmo. (For those not technologically inclined, *app* is short for *web application,* a bit of software that runs on a personal electronic device.) See the nearby sidebar "Golfers, click here" for more on great web resources — instructional and otherwise — to meet your golfing needs.

Golfers, click here

The Internet offers a nearly infinite array of golf stuff. But if you surf the Net aimlessly, you'll only drown in a digital deluge. So here's a quick look at some of my favorite golf sites.

- **PGATour.com:** Millions of golf fans rely on the PGA Tour's site (pgatour.com) for news, stats, player profiles, and (perhaps most important of all) up-to-the-minute tournament coverage. At this site, you can follow your favorite players as they compete, drilling down into their stats and even looking at their scorecards. And to the delight of hardcore fans, the site now offers Shot Tracker, an interactive feature that crunches stats and allows users to get an inside look at every shot by every player only nanoseconds after it happens. You can even play fantasy golf to win golf goodies.

- **LPGA.com:** The official site of the women's tour, lpga.com, is similar to PGATour. com, if not nearly as lavish. You can find stats, profiles, and live tournament updates from the Ladies Professional Golf Association.

- **Golf.com:** Combining the resources of *Golf Magazine* and *Sports Illustrated*, Golf. com has become the industry leader it is by developing a potent mix of tour coverage, equipment reviews, travel features, and commentary from some of the game's best-known writers and personalities. It also offers loads of instruction and a new club fitting feature called See-Try-Buy.

- **GolfObserver.com:** One of the sport's most addictive sites features an amazing amount of information and opinion every day, updated faster than you can say "Fore!" At GolfObserver.com, you find headlines, stats, smart columnists, tournament previews and reviews, and the invaluable Golf Notebook.

- **ESPN.com:** At the channel's golf page (ESPN.com/golf), you can check out schedules, statistics, and player rankings for the PGA, LPGA, Champions, Nationwide, and European tours, along with the game's top headlines. You also find extras like contests, polls, and columnists that make this stop one of the hottest golf sites on the web.

- **Thegolfchannel.com:** The only TV network devoted to golf 24/7 has changed its name to Golf Channel — no *the* anymore — but its site, Thegolfchannel.com, is the same as ever. Only better. Check live leader boards, Golf Channel schedules, photo galleries, and video after video; play trivia games; and read up-to-date features from Golf Channel personalities.

- **PGA.com:** PGA.com/home, the official site of the Professional Golfers' Association of America (not the PGA Tour; see the earlier bullet for PGATour.com), features the headlines and industry news, as well as current tour schedules and standings. Plan a golf vacation, enter to win cool golf stuff, or check out other PGA-recommended golf links. This site is definitely the place to be during the annual PGA Championship.

- **GolfDigest.com:** In collaboration with its weekly sister publication, *GolfWorld*, America's premier golf magazine has created one of the best sites on the web. GolfDigest.com is chock-full of insightful commentary, interesting stories, and professional instruction. You can also find an equipment hotline, view swing sequences of great players, search for specific tips, browse back issues of the magazine, and sign up for instant instruction with a new feature, Golf Digest On Demand.

Many course guides and instructional programs are already available as apps, and others soon will be. But the field is growing so fast that picking the best ones is hard. You can find some rotten apps in the orchard, as well as tasty ones that still have a few bugs in them, and ten more will pop up by the time you finish reading this sentence. One we're partial to: the *Basic Golf For Dummies* app (Wiley), of course.

Knowing What to Watch for on TV

By all means, enjoy the physical beauty of golf on television. But pay attention to the players, too. You can learn a lot from watching not only their swings but also their whole demeanor on the course. Listen to the language, the jargon, the parlance being used.

Watch the players carefully. Pay attention to the rhythms of their swings and to their mannerisms — the way they *waggle* the club (make preshot miniswings), the way triggers set their swings in motion, the way they putt, the way they set their feet in the sand before they play from bunkers, the way they stand on uphill and downhill lies. In other words, watch everything! Soak it all in. Immerse yourself in the atmosphere and ambience of golf. You'll soon be walking the walk and talking the talk. And don't discount the importance of osmosis: You can improve your own game just by watching great golf swings.

That's the big picture. But what about you, specifically?

Watching the pros is a good idea for every golfer. But most people can only learn so much from certain players. Pay particular attention to someone like Michelle Wie if you happen to be tall and slim. But if you happen to be shorter and more heavyset, you need to look elsewhere. Find someone whose body type approximates your own.

Then watch how that person stands to the ball at *address* (the point right before the swing). See how his arms hang or how much she flexes her knees. Golfers who are taller have much more flex in their knees than their shorter counterparts.

Watch how "your pro" swings the club. Do his arms move away from his body as the club moves back? How much does she turn her shoulders? How good is his balance? Does she have a lot of wrist action in her swing, or does she unwind her torso for explosive power?

Catching what most viewers miss

The players who get the most airtime are the leaders and the stars. No telecast is going to waste valuable minutes on someone who's 20 strokes out of the lead. (Unless, of course, it's Tiger Woods, Phil Mickelson, or Michelle Wie.) Viewers want to watch the tournament being won and lost, so those players shooting the lowest scores are the ones you see most on TV. Here's what to look for in some of the stars you'll see on TV.

- ✔ **Tiger Woods:** Look at his virtuosity in every aspect of the game. He has left no stone unturned in his pursuit of perfection. His stalking of Jack Nicklaus's record of 18 major wins is his driving force, providing his will to succeed. Plus, in 2010, personal strife and swing changes gave him new motivation.

- ✔ **Phil Mickelson:** With four major victories under his belt (as of this writing), look for Phil to take advantage of his precise short game and really focus on the majors for the rest of his career. He gives golf fans all over the country a role model they love to root for.

- ✔ **Ernie Els:** Now in his 40s, the Big Easy has a golf swing that still brings glimpses of the legendary Sam Snead, with a demeanor made for greatness. Burn that smooth swing into your memory banks the next time you see it on TV.

- ✔ **Dustin Johnson:** This young PGA Tour star came within a whisker of winning the 2010 U.S. Open and PGA Championship. Keep an eye on him, particularly super-slo-mo replays that show how he generates power.

- ✔ **Fred Couples:** The Champions Tour's "young" star still has the easy motion that made "Boom-Boom" Couples the model of effortless power. Watch him walk down the fairway after a drive as if he didn't have a care in the world. Fred has had his share of troubles through the years, including a bad back that may have ended other careers, but he's still smiling . . . and winning.

- ✔ **Rory McIlroy:** Young Rory, born in 1989 in Holywood, Northern Ireland, may be the most exciting young player since Tiger. After a final-round meltdown at the 2011 Masters, he bounced back to win that year's U.S. Open, his first major title. Watch how he swings hard, believes every putt's going in, and radiates pleasure in playing the game.

- ✔ **Michelle Wie:** This young lady, who turned 22 in 2011, has the potential to dominate the LPGA. Michelle turned pro late in 2005, fought injuries and great expectations, and struggled. But she has more talent than anyone we've seen come up in a long time. Winless until 2009, Michelle worked hard with coach David Leadbetter on her long, fluid swing. She had two LPGA victories going into spring 2011, with many more to come.

Taking notes from the stars

You can learn to play and think like the stars. This section identifies a few of the greats and their specific strengths and gives you to pointers to re-create their magic.

Getting a feel like Seve Ballesteros

Seve Ballesteros was a dashing young Spaniard when he splashed onto the scene as a teenager and began playing professionally in 1974. By the time his full-time playing career started to wind down, Ballesteros had become the first player to pass the $3 million mark on the European Tour and had won 87 titles worldwide.

Ballesteros began teaching himself to play golf at age 7 by hitting balls at the beach on the Bay of Santander in Spain with a single club — a cut-down 3-iron his brother gave him. The result of hitting shots of all length, trajectory, and shape with that single club was Ballesteros's great sense of touch and feel.

His intelligence and feel served him well when he turned professional, and those attributes gave him a reputation as a magician. He began wowing the world at the 1976 British Open at Royal Birkdale, where he hit a crafty chip shot on the 18th hole that dissected two bunkers and settled one yard from the cup. He finished in second place, but he was only 19 at the time!

His decisive birdie putt to win the 1984 British Open at St. Andrews was thrilling, as was an amazing bunker shot he struck with a 3-wood on the way to beating Fuzzy Zoeller at the Ryder Cup one year earlier (see Chapter 8 of Book III for tips on executing unconventional shots).

Ben Crenshaw said of the Spaniard, "Seve plays shots I don't even see in my dreams!" Be like Seve Ballesteros:

- **Imagine** different types of shots in different situations.
- **Develop touch and feel** by hitting different shots with the same club.
- **Feel** the clubhead making contact with the ball.
- **Practice** trouble shots from treacherous positions.

Escaping bunkers like Gary Player

A poor, 18-year-old South African golfer a long way from home, Gary Player spent long nights sleeping in the bunkers of Scottish golf courses when he turned pro in 1953. Player went on to win 163 tournaments worldwide over six decades, including nine majors. He was only the third man in history to win the career grand slam: the Masters, U.S. Open, British Open, and PGA Championship.

Few ever imagined that the 5-foot-7-inch, 146-pound Player could enjoy such success, but he made up for any deficiencies with a sterling short game — especially from the bunkers. He aggressively attacked bunker shots because he had no fear of playing from the sand and was confident that he could get up and down from anywhere.

Player believed that the harder he practiced, the luckier he became. Close examination of Player's technique, and attention to the times he has talked about it over the years, reveals that, unlike many others, he doesn't "blast" the ball out of the sand; instead, he focuses on accelerating his clubhead through the sand and lifting the ball into the air. To keep from swaying, he puts his weight on his front side and keeps his head still throughout the shot. His swing is smooth and his finish high.

Player, a member of the World Golf Hall of Fame, has delivered elegant bunker shots under pressure for over half a century. Be like Gary Player:

- **Practice,** practice, practice.

- **Accelerate** through the sand. Think "splash," not "blast."

- **Be still** and keep your weight on your front side to avoid swaying.

- **Have confidence** in your bunker play. This attitude makes you fearless when hitting approach shots, because, like Player, you know you can make the best of being in a bunker.

Living hard and playing soft like John Daly

He's been called a redneck and a drunk . . . been through rehab . . . been married four times . . . been forced off an airplane for misbehavior . . . broken his putter in anger . . . scored an 18 on a hole during a PGA Tour event . . . fought with a spectator . . . been disqualified . . . been suspended . . . been fired . . . lost millions gambling in casinos . . . lost and gained large amounts of weight . . . thrown his putter into a water hazard . . . and despite, and maybe for, these antics, golf fans unabashedly love him.

John Daly, who turned professional in 1987, has won nine tournaments worldwide, including the 1991 PGA Championship at Crooked Stick in Indianapolis and the 1995 British Open at St. Andrews. He also shot a course record 62 at TPC at The Canyons in the 2001 Las Vegas Invitational.

Everyone knows John Daly as a big hitter — at one point, his average drive on the PGA Tour was 314 yards! Big John's driving accuracy, however, was only 49.7 percent. Enter the short game: "Any time you win a tournament, you win with your short game. Whether it is chipping or putting, you win tournaments with your short game," Daly said.

Daly is a big, hardened man with soft hands. Be like John Daly:

- ✔ **Enjoy belting big drives,** but take pride in the magic and beauty of an impressive short game, too.

- ✔ **Keep a light touch with soft hands,** because Big John may "grip it and rip it" with the driver, but he keeps a very light grip when chipping or pitching. Make certain you don't squeeze the handle when you play a short-game shot.

- ✔ **Limit** your booze intake the night before and during a golf round.

Scrambling like Lee Trevino

Lee Trevino is an entirely self-taught golfer. Unlike many silver-spoon professionals raised at golf clubs, Trevino honed his skills at Hardy's Driving Range in Dallas and served a stint in the Marines before he turned professional in 1960. Learning to play golf in Texas winds on hardscrabble conditions made Trevino one of the toughest shot-shapers in the history of golf. Trevino doesn't believe a player can have a "natural touch." He believes touch is something you create by hitting millions of golf balls.

Trevino won the Vardon Trophy for the lowest scoring average on tour five times. He won 29 times on the PGA Tour, including two U.S. Opens, two PGA Championships, and two British Opens.

Trevino was so competitive that, when he arrived early at a PGA Tour stop, he went into the clubhouse, sought out the club champion, and asked him to play for money. Be like Lee Trevino:

- ✔ **Practice** in all types of conditions, including heavy wind.

- ✔ **Expect to hole** every single shot you hit. Trevino made his goal and expectation the same: to be a gunslinger and shoot for the pin on every shot. When your short game's that good, fire up those six-guns.

- ✔ **Never give up** on a hole — even when it looks grim and your temper starts to get the best of you.

- ✔ **Be tough.** Trevino survived a lightning strike on the golf course at the 1975 Western Open in Chicago.

Putting like Ben Crenshaw

Ben Crenshaw putted his way into the World Golf Hall of Fame. Known as Gentle Ben, the Texan has won 19 times on the PGA Tour, including two Masters titles, and captained the 1999 Ryder Cup team to its first win since 1993.

With a trusty putter named "Little Ben" that he's owned since he was a teenager, Crenshaw addresses the ball slightly forward in his stance and, with his hands a bit ahead of the ball, rotates very slowly from his shoulders to produce a wristless, soft putt that dies at the hole.

Crenshaw's love for putting is evident. When asked about the greens at The Country Club in Brookline, Massachusetts, before the 1999 Ryder Cup, he said, "I think they're beautiful. They're beautifully shaped. They're sufficiently undulating with some puzzling rolls in them. You've got to know where and where not to put the ball. They're beautiful greens — a good test of putting." Be like Ben Crenshaw:

- ✔ **Study** the subtle breaks, hills, dips, and valleys of every green from different angles.

- ✔ **Play** the ball in the front of your stance and, with your hands forward, make a smooth, slow putting stroke.

- ✔ **Practice** hitting putts that die at the hole and not short of it.

- ✔ **Fall in love** with a putter . . . and be loyal to it!

Finishing like Annika Sorenstam

Annika Sorenstam was born in Sweden in 1970, started playing golf at the age of 12, and became an LPGA player in 1994. Less than 10 years later, she had qualified for the LPGA Tour and World Golf Hall of Fames. In 2002, she won 11 LPGA Tournaments in one season — a feat only one person, Mickey Wright in 1964, had ever accomplished.

So prolific was Sorenstam that in 2003, she even played in a PGA Tour event — the Colonial National Invitational — against an all-male field! Later that season, she played in the Skins Game against Fred Couples, Phil Mickelson, and Mark O'Meara. She holed a 39-yard bunker shot for an eagle to win $175,000 on the first day — the most money ever won on the first day of the Skins Game.

To enjoy such consistent success no matter the circumstances, a player must own a world-class short game. Sorenstam: check. One of the most noticeable features of Sorenstam's short game is the way she finishes her pitches, chips, bunker shots, and putts. At the end of her stroke, long after the ball has gone, she keeps the clubhead frozen at the finish. Her tempo is even and smooth, as if she swings the club without even hitting a ball. Sorenstam looks up to watch the ball go to the hole, but only after the ball is well gone and she fully completes her stroke. Her concentration allows her to be consistent and relaxed during any type of shot. Be like Annika Sorenstam:

- ✔ **Hold the club still** at the top of your follow-through or at the end of your putting stroke.

- ✔ **Only look up** to see where the ball goes after you fully complete the stroke.

- ✔ **Listen** for the putt to go in instead of hurrying to watch it.

- ✔ **Only lower the club** after the ball comes to a complete stop.

Yipping like Johnny Miller

Johnny Miller is best known now as a controversial television golf analyst who pulls no punches, but the man was once the game's golden boy, anointed by critics as "the next Nicklaus."

Miller turned professional in 1969 and won 25 times on the PGA Tour. People will always remember his playing career for two things: the 63 he shot in the final round to win the 1973 U.S. Open at Oakmont and the yips that effectively ended his competitive career. (The *yips* are a nervous golf condition that affects how smoothly golfers putt.) Miller last won at Pebble Beach in 1994 when he was 46 years old, but he jabbed and stabbed his way to that win while holding his breath over every little putt.

Don't yip putts like Johnny Miller:

- ✔ **Practice** regularly. Turn to Chapter 6 of Book III to find out more about the yips and how to banish them!
- ✔ **Be confident** when you hit your putts.
- ✔ **Putt in the subconscious** without fretting over the result.
- ✔ **Stroke** putts instead of hitting them. You want to roll the ball, not skip it.

Chapter 3

Exploring the World of Golf Courses

. . . .

In This Chapter

▶ Getting the big picture of a golf course

▶ Golfing at driving ranges, public courses, country clubs, and resorts

▶ Uncovering bargains on memberships or green fees

▶ Knowing the ropes at country clubs and golf resorts

▶ Checking out some of the best courses the world

. . . .

*G*olfers play in three main settings: at public facilities, private clubs, and on resort courses. In this chapter, we tell you the basics about all three, from the most basic driving range to the fanciest country club. We also share tips on how to fit in wherever you play — how to walk, talk, and tip like a *real* golfer. We also share some info on some of the world's most spectacular courses.

Breaking Down a Typical Course

Most golf courses have 18 holes, although a few, usually because of a lack of money or land, have only 9. The *19th hole* is golfspeak for the clubhouse bar — the place where you can reflect on your game over a refreshing beverage of your choice. Courses beside the sea are called *links,* in honor of the parts of Scotland where the game began. (They were the link between beach and farmland.) Many people use "links" to mean any golf course, but we purists stick to the correct usage: A links is a course by the water.

Knowing the distance

Most golf courses are between 5,500 and 7,000 yards. A few monsters are longer, but leave those courses to the pros you see on TV. Start at the low end of that scale and work your way up.

Every hole is a par-3, a par-4, or a par-5. (Par-2s are for minigolf courses; the exceedingly rare par-6s tend to be gimmicks.) *Par* is the number of strokes a competent golfer should take to play a particular hole. For example, on a par-5 hole, a regulation par may consist of a drive, two more full swings, and two putts. Two putts is the standard on every green.

Three putts are too many. One putt is a bonus. The bottom line is that in a perfect round of par golf, half the allocated strokes should be taken on the greens. That premise makes putting crucial. (We talk about how to putt in Chapter 6 of Book III.)

Obviously, a par-5 is longer than a par-4 (two full swings, two putts), which in turn is longer than a par-3 (one full swing, two putts). With rare exceptions, par-3s are from 100 to 250 yards in length; par-4s are from 251 to 470 yards long, barring severe topography; and par-5s are from 471 to 690 yards.

Many courses in the United States have a total par of 72, consisting of ten par-4s (40), four par-3s (12), and four par-5s (20). But you can find golf courses with total pars of anywhere from 62 to 74. Almost anything goes. Table 3-1 lists the yardages that determine par on a hole, for men and women. It's worth noting that these guidelines don't always refer to precise yardages, but rather to what the United States Golf Association (USGA) calls a hole's "effective playing length." A 460-yard hole that goes straight uphill, for example, may be a par-5 for men.

Table 3-1	Regulation Yardages	
	Women	**Men**
Par-3	210 yards or less	250 yards or less
Par-4	211 to 400 yards	251 to 470 yards
Par-5	401 to 575 yards	471 to 690 yards
Par-6	More than 575 yards	More than 690 yards

Source: United States Golf Association

Choosing your starting tee

You often find several different teeing areas on each hole so you can play the hole from different lengths based on your level of skill. The vast majority of holes have more than one teeing area — usually four. Some courses have as many as six different tees on one hole. Deciding which tee area to use can make you silly. To help you out, some tee areas are marked with color-coded tees that indicate ability. However, those colors may vary from course to course, so check at the golf shop before you play to be sure:

- ✔ The **gold tees** are invariably the back tees and are for long-ball strikers or lower handicap players only.

- ✔ The **blue tees** are usually slightly ahead of the gold and make the holes shorter but still plenty hard. Club competitions are played from these tees.

- ✔ The **white tees** are for everyday, casual play and are the right choice for most men, beginning golfers, and capable senior players. Stray from the white tees at your peril.

- ✔ The **red tees** are traditionally used by women or by junior golfers, although many women use the same tees as men.

Course Insight: Planning a Smart Game

Simply stated, the goal of golf is to get the ball into each of 18 holes in succession with the fewest number of shots, using no more than 14 clubs. After you hit the ball into all the holes, you add up your scores from each hole. The lower your total score, the better. That's it.

The game's charm lies in the journey. As you play, you find countless ways to get the ball into the hole in as few strokes as possible. Many outside stimuli — and many more inside your head — make golf one of the most interesting, maddening, thrilling, and just plain *fun* endeavors you'll ever find.

The best advice is to relax on the course. Stay calm, make prudent decisions, and never hit a shot while contemplating other matters. You should play golf with complete concentration and no ego. The game tempts you to try feats of derring-do. To play your best, you must judge your talents and abilities honestly. You alone determine your success or failure: Should you try to make it over the water and go for the green that's 240 yards away? Or play it safe?

Don't get greedy — play the game one step at a time. Figure 3-1 shows a smart course of action. You start at the tee and hit your drive to Point A. From there, it's 240 yards to the green, with a watery grave lurking to the left.

So you lay up to Point B and go from there to the green via C. This approach doesn't always work — you may *aim* for Point B and still yank your second shot into the pond — but it's the smart play. And that's the key to good golf.

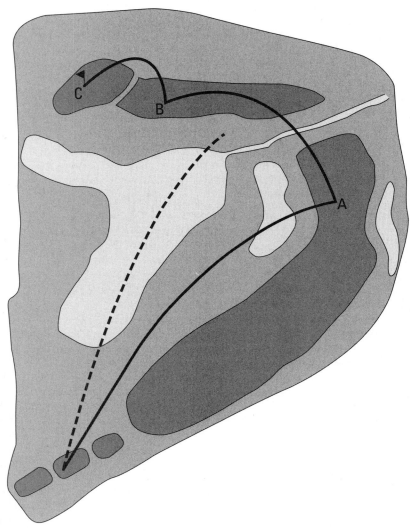

Figure 3-1:
A
reasonable
plan for
playing a
golf hole.

Score is everything. As you see in Chapters 4 through 7 of Book III, the most pivotal shots occur within 80 yards of the hole. If you can save strokes there, your score will be lower than that of the player whose sole purpose in life is to crush the ball as far as possible. So practice your putting, sand play, chips, and pitches twice as much as your driving. Your hard work will pay off, and your friends will be the ones dipping into their wallets (assuming you're wagering — see Chapter 3 of Book IV).

Looking Into Your Course Options

Start with the basics: Where in the world can you play golf?

Some courses have only 9 holes, while a few resorts offer half a dozen 18-hole courses, or even more. At the famous Pinehurst Resort in North Carolina, you can find eight great 18-hole layouts, including Pinehurst No. 2, one of the finest in the world. (Check out this chapter's "Perusing Some Great Courses" for more on this and other amazing courses.) China's gigantic Mission Hills Golf Club, the world's largest, features a dozen courses — that's 216 chances to drive yourself nuts!

A good way to gauge the difficulty of a course is to find the *course rating* and *slope*. These two numbers allow golfers to determine how difficult a course is and how much terrain there is on each course. A course rating number is normally around or below the par for the course. Anything above par, and you're getting into a more challenging golf course. The slope rating takes into account the terrain of the course, how much water is on the course, and the width of the fairways. The higher this number, the more difficult the course. Normal or average course slopes are in the 110 to 125 range.

You can also hit balls at driving ranges, which is how you should start, and gradually work up to a par-3 course, building your confidence level before you play a regulation 18-hole course. If you rush to the nearest course for your first try at golf, tee off, and then spend most of the next few hours missing the ball, you won't be very popular with your fellow golfers. They'd rather enjoy a cool beverage in the clubhouse than watch you move large clumps of earth with every swing.

Driving ranges

Driving ranges are basically large fields stretching as far as 400 yards in length. Driving ranges are fun. You can make all the mistakes you want. You can miss the ball, slice it, duff it, top it — do anything. The only people who know are the ones next to you, and they're probably making the same mistakes.

Because driving ranges are often quite long, even Tiger Woods or long-drive king Jamie Sladowski can "let the shaft out" and swing for the fences. But you don't have to hit your driver. Any good driving range has signs marking off 50 yards, 100 yards, 150 yards, and so on. You can practice hitting to these targets with any club.

Many driving ranges lend or rent you clubs, though some expect you to bring your own. As for balls, you purchase bucketfuls for a few dollars — how *many* dollars depends on where you are. In some parts of the United States, you can still hit a bucket of balls for a dollar. But on weekends at the Golf Club at Chelsea Piers in New York City, hitting balls costs a lot more: up to 25 times as much. (At least you get a great view of New Jersey. . . .)

Public courses

As you'd expect from their name, public courses are open to anyone who can afford the *green fee,* or the cost to play a round of golf (commonly, but incorrectly, known as the *greens fee*). They tend to be busy, especially on weekends and holidays. At premier public courses like New York's Bethpage Black, the site of the 2009 U.S. Open, some golfers sleep in their cars overnight so they can be first in line for a tee time the next morning.

The 21st century is proving to be a great time for public courses. Chambers Bay, a spectacular new facility near Tacoma, Washington, will host the 2015 U.S. Open, joining Bethpage Black and another famous municipal course, San Diego's venerable Torrey Pines, in the Open rotation.

Green fees

As for cost, the price depends on the course and its location. Some humble rural courses charge as little as $10 — and you pay on the honor system, dropping your money into a box! The best public courses can be hard to get on, and they aren't cheap, but most players will tell you they're worth the effort and expense. Upscale public facilities, even those with no hope of ever hosting a U.S. Open, routinely charge $100 and up. Green fees at Chambers Bay, for example, range from $89 to $175. At gorgeous Pebble Beach Golf Links in California, where the green fee way back in the 1950s was a bargain at $5, it's now $495! At least they give you free tees.

Tee-time policies

Each course has its own tee-time rules. Many let you book a time weeks in advance, and many offer convenient online scheduling. Others follow a strange rule: You must show up at a designated time midweek to sign up for weekend play. And some courses you can't book at all — you just show up and take your chance (hence, the overnight gang sleeping in their cars). Some simple advice: Phone ahead and find out the policy at the course you want to play.

GARY SAYS

Getting on the course like a pro

Here's what I do when I'm playing in a pro event: I get to the course one hour before my starting time. I go to the putting green and practice short shots — chip shots and short pitches. (Chapters 4 and 5 of Book III cover these shots in detail.) Doing so gives me an idea how fast the greens are and loosens me up for full-swing shots. *Tip:* Make sure that you're allowed to pitch to the practice green on your course — some courses prohibit it.

Then I wander over to the practice tee and loosen up with some of the exercises that I describe in Book III. Start with the wedges and work your way up to the driver. Next, I hit my 3-wood (some players call this titanium club the *3-metal* — a more accurate term, but it clangs in my ears). Then I proceed to bomb the driver.

Immediately after hitting practice drives — ten balls at most — I hit some short sand-wedge shots to slow down my metabolism.

I revisit the putting green next, usually 15 minutes before I tee off. (See Chapter 6 of Book III for more about putting.) I start with simple 2- to 3-foot putts straight up a hill, to build my confidence. Then I proceed to very long putts — aiming not for the hole, but for the far fringe of the green. I do that because I don't want to become target-conscious on long putts. Putting the ball to the fringe lets me work on speed. It's the last thing I do before going to the tee. (Well, if it's a big tournament and my knees are shaking, I may make a detour to the restroom.)

I'm here! Now what?

You've jumped through whatever hoops are necessary to establish a tee time (see the preceding section) and you know when you're supposed to play. So you pull into the parking lot about an hour before your tee time. That way, you have time to stretch and warm up before you play. What next? Most courses feature a clubhouse. You may want to stop inside to change clothes and maybe buy something to eat or drink.

TIP

By all means, make use of the clubhouse, but don't change your shoes in there. If you're already dressed to hit the greens, put on your golf shoes in the parking lot. Then throw your street shoes into the trunk. Don't worry about looking goofy as you lace those spikes with your foot on the car bumper. It's a golf tradition!

The first thing to do at the clubhouse is to find the pro shop. Confirm your time with the pro or *starter* (the person sending groups off from the first tee), and then pay for your round. The pro is sure to be in one of two places: teaching on the practice range or hanging out in the pro shop. If the pro doesn't collect your money, the starter adjacent to the first tee usually does.

After the financial formalities are out of the way, hit some balls on the driving range to warm up those creaky joints of yours.

Country clubs

In your early days as a golfer, you probably won't play much at country clubs. If you *do* play at a country club — maybe a friend who's a member invites you — it can be intimidating! But don't panic. You're still playing golf; the "goal posts" have just shifted slightly.

To avoid committing any social faux pas, remember a few formalities:

- ✔ **Before you leave home, make sure you're wearing the right clothes.** Those cutoff jeans or a sweatshirt announcing you as an avid follower of the Chicago Bulls doesn't work in this environment. Wear a shirt with a collar; if shorts are allowed, go for the tailored variety that stops just short of your knees. Short-shorts are a no-no at most country clubs. In the fall and winter, slacks are acceptable for women. In the summer, shorts cut just above the knees are fine. When in doubt, call the club and ask.

- ✔ **Get good directions to your destination.** A stressful journey full of wrong turns doesn't do your heart rate or your golf game any good.

- ✔ **Time your arrival so you have just an hour to spare before you tee off.** When you drive your car up the road toward the clubhouse, don't make the simple mistake of turning sharply into the parking lot. Go right up to the clubhouse. Look for a sign that reads "Bag Drop." A person is no doubt waiting to greet you. Acknowledge his cheery hello as if you're doing something you do every day. Tell him who you're playing with (the club member who's hosting you). Then get out of your car, pop the trunk, remove your spikes, and hand him your keys. Tip him a few bucks (or a $5 bill at a fancy club like Trump International), and stroll into the clubhouse.

  Don't worry about your car or your clubs. The car will be parked for you, and the clubs will either be loaded onto a cart or handed to a caddie.

- ✔ **Don't try to pay for your round**. Most country clubs won't take your money. The club member who's hosting you signs for everything except tips and pro-shop merchandise. Of course, you're free to settle up with him or her on your own — that's between the two of you.

- ✔ **After you're inside the clubhouse, head for the locker room.** Drop your street shoes off next to your host's locker and then ask for directions to the bar, or to wherever your host is waiting. Don't offer to buy your host a drink. Your host most likely signs the tab and gets billed at the end of the month. (The one place where your cash or plastic is accepted is the pro shop.) The pro will sell you anything,

✔ **If you have a caddie, remember that he or she is there to help you.** Trust your caddie's advice — he or she knows the course better than you do. Caddie fees at fancy clubs average about $50, which is added to your green fee. You should tip your caddie half the caddie fee at the end of the round, so that's another $25. (Savvy golfers sometimes tip the caddie master before a round — slipping him a $10 bill can get you the best caddie he's got.)

✔ **On the course, be yourself.** And don't worry about shooting the best round of golf you've ever played. Your host doesn't expect that. Even if you happen to play badly, he won't be too bothered as long as you look like you're having fun and keep trying. Just don't complain or make excuses. Nobody likes a whiner.

✔ **After your round, your clubs will probably disappear again, but don't worry: They'll be waiting at the bag drop when you finish your post-round beverage.** Don't forget to tip the bag handlers. Again, a few bucks is usually fine, but be generous if your clubs have been cleaned.

✔ **When you change back into your street shoes, you'll often find them newly polished — that means another few dollars to tip the locker-room attendant.** And when you leave, your golf shoes will have been done, too. Aren't country clubs grand?

✔ **One more tip to go: Give a few bucks to the person who delivers your car back to you and loads your clubs into the trunk.**

Resort courses

You're on vacation, and you're dying to play golf. Where to go? To a resort course, of course. Some pro favorites are Kapalua Resort (Maui, Hawaii), Doral Golf Resort & Spa (Miami, Florida), and Sea Pines Resort (Hilton Head Island, South Carolina).

The great thing about resort courses is that you don't have to be a member or even have one in tow. The only problem arises when you aren't staying in the right place. Some courses are for certain hotel guests only. And again, prices vary, depending on the course and its location. Generally, though, resort courses cost a good deal more than public courses.

Phone ahead of time to find out when you can play.

Resort courses are a lot like public courses, but some have bag handlers and other employees who expect a tip. Tip as you would at a country club (see the preceding section).

You probably have to rent a cart, too. Carts are mandatory at most resort golf courses. So enjoy the ride! You can drive to your drive and then hop back behind the wheel and putt-putt to your putt.

Let's Make a Deal: Lowering Membership and Green Fees

Back in the go-go 1990s, hardly anyone thought to ask, "Can I get a discount on that country-club membership?" That'd be like asking for a free air-freshener in a new Lamborghini. But times change, and when the economy slows down, the prices of upscale items like club memberships and resort-course green fees sometimes come down, too. That can work to the advantage of you, the smart golfer. Read on in the following sections for some insight into scoring deals on playing golf.

Saving at public courses and resorts

The same belt-tightening that squeezes country clubs hits golf resorts and high-end public courses, too. So when you call to arrange a tee time, don't hesitate to haggle. You may say, "I'm bringing two foursomes. Can you give us a price break?" Or, "I'd love to play there, but your green fees are a little high for me."

Asking (politely) never hurts. Even if the answer is no, you can ask, "Can you steer me to a nice course that's a little more affordable?" You may discover a hidden gem. Most courses these days offer online discounts for green fees, which is another way to look for a bargain.

Most public facilities and resorts offer *twilight rates*. You tee off in the late afternoon, paying half to two-thirds the usual green fee. Even if you don't finish before dark, you experience a course you may want to play again.

Making the club scene more affordable

The game's most elite clubs never seem to suffer. You don't see members complaining about the cost of belonging to Augusta National, where the pros play the Masters every spring, or Sebonack Golf Club in Southampton, New York, where joining may set you back a cool $1 million. But at other clubs, including some terrific ones, tougher times bring opportunity. Several years ago, the beautiful Newport Beach Country Club in southern California cut its initiation fee from $42,000 to $5,000 for players between 21 and 37 years old. The club wanted to attract younger members who'd keep coming back for decades, and it worked.

Many other clubs reduced their initiation fees from $5,000, $10,000, or even more to nothing. That's right — you could join for free, as long as you paid your monthly dues of a few hundred dollars.

You see, country clubs rely on much more than upfront fees. They need to sell clubs, balls, and shirts in the pro shop; burgers in the grill room; and drinks in the bar. Their caddies need bags to carry.

And this area is one in which golf, which is often seen as the preserve of old white men, may be changing for the better. Many clubs are more eager than ever to welcome younger, minority, and female players.

So if you're thinking of joining a country club, shop around. Don't be afraid to ask whether you can get reduced or waived initiation fees. Tough economic times affect almost everybody — they may just smile and say, "Join the club."

Fitting In on the Course

It all starts at the first tee. Book IV covers the rules and etiquette of the game, but you should know some other things about playing nicely with others.

If you're playing with friends, you don't need any help. You know them, and they know you. You should be able to come up with a game by yourselves. And you can say anything to them, with no risk of offending anyone.

That's not the case if you show up looking for a game. Say you're at a public course and you've asked the starter to squeeze you in (a few bucks in the starter's hand may get you going sooner rather than later). Tell the starter your skill level — and be honest. If you're a beginner, you don't want to be thrown in with three low-handicap players; you'll feel intimidated, probably won't enjoy the round as well, and may even slow up the pace of play. Forget all that talk about how golf's handicap system allows anyone to play with anyone. That propaganda doesn't take human nature into account. (Flip to Chapter 1 of Book IV for more on the handicap system.)

Golf, like life, has its share of snobs. And some of the worst are single-digit handicappers. Most of them have no interest in playing with a mere beginner. They may say they do, but they're lying. They see 18 holes with someone who can't break 100 as four to five hours of torture. The same is true on the PGA Tour. Some pros genuinely enjoy the Wednesday pro-ams — Mark O'Meara comes to mind — but many would gladly skip them if they could. (They can't, because the tour requires pros to show up for *pro-ams,* tournaments where pros play with amateurs.) That may seem like a rotten attitude, but it's a fact of golfing life. No one will actually *say* anything to you (golf pros are generally much too polite), but the attitude is there. Get used to it.

This assessment may come off as a little harsh, but most golfers would agree that the typical golfer is more comfortable playing with his "own kind." Watch a few groups play off the first tee, and you soon spot a trend. Almost every foursome consists of four players of relatively equal ability. That happens for a reason. Make that two reasons: No one wants to be the weak link in the chain. And no one wants to play with "hackers who can't keep up." Of course, a beginner *can* play as quickly as an expert golfer, but that's not a challenge you need at this stage.

So say the starter groups you with Gary, Jack, and Arnold. Introduce yourself calmly but quickly. Tell them what you normally shoot, if and when they ask, and make it clear that you're a relatively new golfer. This fact is impossible to conceal, so don't try. But don't volunteer any further information. Save that for during the round. Besides, you find that most golfers are selfish — they really don't care about your game. They make polite noises after your shots, but that's the extent of their interest. You'll soon be that way, too. Nothing — *nothing* — is more boring than listening to tales about someone else's round or game. Of course, boring your buddies that way is part of the social order of this game. Golf stories are endless, and most are embellished, but they promote the bonding done over beers in the clubhouse bar.

Beginners sometimes do things that mark them as misfits on the course. Avoid these blunders at all costs:

- **Don't carry one of those telescoping ball retrievers in your bag.** It suggests that you're planning to hit balls in the water.
- **Don't wear your golf cap backward.** Ever. No exceptions.
- **Don't do stretching exercises on the first tee.** Find a place a few yards away, where you don't look like you're auditioning for *The Biggest Loser.*
- **Don't dawdle — when it's your turn to hit, be ready!**

Perusing Some Great Courses

The longer you play golf, the more courses you visit. Although every tennis court, basketball court, or football field is pretty much the same, every golf course is different from every other. Some are along the ocean, and others are in the desert. Many have trees that frame your every shot. Others have no trees and a horizon that seems to stretch on forever.

Limitless features attach themselves to each golf course — that's what makes each one a separate journey. Golf architects such as Robert Trent Jones, Pete Dye, Jack Nicklaus, Tom Fazio, and Tom Doak have put their fingerprints on the map of American golf. The following sections give you a peek at some of the world's greatest courses as seen by pro golfer and golf commentator Gary McCord, as well as some courses that will put your short game to the test.

Gary's ten favorite courses

You see a wide variety of golf courses in your golfing life. These ten courses are my favorites. I based my choices for this list on the courses' challenge and beauty. Royal Melbourne is one that I haven't even played. Greg Norman told me that Royal Melbourne is in his top three, so who am I to argue?

Four of these courses are private, but six are open to everyone who can pay their (steep) green fees: Pebble Beach, Royal County Down, Pinehurst No. 2, Pacific Dunes, Cape Kidnappers, and the Straits course at Whistling Straits.

Pebble Beach (Monterey, California)

Pebble Beach is an extraordinary place to do anything. Golf has made it popular, but the land has made it legendary. Robert Louis Stevenson called this stretch of shoreline "the greatest meeting of land and sea in the world." Pebble Beach is blessed with two of my favorite courses in the world: Pebble Beach and Cypress Point, which I cover in the following section.

I've been playing Pebble Beach Golf Links since I was 15 years old. We used to play the California state amateur on these storied links. We'd round up ten guys and rent a motel room together. We based the sleeping arrangements on how well we'd played that day: Low round got his pick of the two beds. High round got the other bed — we figured he needed some sleep with all the swinging he did that day. Everybody else grabbed some floor. Those were the fun days, when golf was a twinkle in your eye, and innocence made the game seem easy.

Cypress Point (Monterey, California)

Cypress Point is a course of such beauty and solitude, you'd think it had holy qualities. From the quaint pro shop to the confining locker room and dusty rooms that perch atop the clubhouse, Cypress Point is a memory-maker.

The course winds from the pines into the sand dunes. Deer caper everywhere, often dodging errant tee shots. You can see the turbulent Pacific on a few holes going out and then again on most of the back nine, including the famous 16th — a gorgeous and scary par-3 that must be seen to be believed.

Pine Valley (Clementon, New Jersey)

Pine Valley is the greatest course without an ocean view. If you have a week to hang with your friends and play golf, Pine Valley is the place. The grounds are spectacular. Cottages house overnight guests, and a great dining room is full of golf memorabilia. The walls are saturated with tall tales of Pine Valley's golf history. Best of all, most of the tall tales are true.

The course is one of the great designs in the world. Builder George Crump bought this stretch of New Jersey land in 1912 and got input on the course design from great architects including C. B. Macdonald, Harry Colt, Alister MacKenzie, Donald Ross, and A. W. Tillinghast. You measure a golf course by how many holes you can remember after playing one round on it, and this course is instantly etched in your mind — every hole, every tree, and every bunker. I'm in total fascination when I walk through Pine Valley's corridor of perfectly maintained grass. This course is a place that breathes with the true spirit of golf.

Royal County Down (Newcastle, Northern Ireland)

In recent years, more and more golfers making pilgrimages to the game's ancestral home in Scotland have detoured to Ireland, where some of the best links in the world are starting to get the attention they deserve. First and foremost among these is Royal County Down. It's rugged, tricky (with blind shots all over the place), and altogether magnificent.

Originally laid out by Old Tom Morris in the 1880s and redesigned by immortals including Harry Vardon and Harry Colt, this place is one of the most beautiful, memorable courses on earth. No one who plays there ever forgets his or her day at County Down.

Pinehurst No. 2 (Pinehurst, North Carolina)

Pinehurst No. 2 is a masterpiece of design. Perhaps the most famous course designed by the great Donald Ross, it hosted the U.S. Open in 1999 and 2005. Hidden in the pines of Pinehurst, the course combines every facet of the game and boasts some of the best-designed greens in the world.

This entire complex at Pinehurst takes you back half a century with its rustic, Southern motif. Golf courses are everywhere — there are eight at the Pinehurst Resort and many others nearby — and golf is the central theme of the town.

We used to play a tour event at Pinehurst No. 2 every year, and we'd get into a golf frenzy weeks before our arrival. Pinehurst No. 2 is second to none in the Southeast, a challenge to be revered and enjoyed. And in 2014, the course gains a distinction no other venue has ever boasted: It plays host to the U.S. Open, followed a week later by the U.S. Women's Open!

Royal Melbourne (Melbourne, Australia)

My information about Royal Melbourne comes from the Aussies I know on tour. Greg Norman and Steve Elkington rave about the greens, which are said to be among the fastest in the world. The tournament course dates back to 1891, when the club hired Alister MacKenzie to come down from Scotland to oversee the design. The modern course is made up of 18 holes out of the 36 it has on site. I walked Royal Melbourne during the 2002 Presidents Cup and found that the Aussies were right: The course is gorgeous, with large eucalyptus trees standing sentinel over the scene.

Pacific Dunes (Bandon, Oregon)

In 1999, an exciting new golf course opened on a remote stretch of Oregon coastline. The architect was David McLay Kidd, a Scotsman who put a remarkable, seemingly all-natural layout on a bluff above the Pacific. In 2001, Pacific Dunes, a new course designed by Tom Doak, earned rave reviews, and 2005 brought a third natural beauty, Bandon Trails, designed by Ben Crenshaw and Bill Coore. A fourth course, called Old Macdonald in honor of pioneering player and architect C.B. Macdonald, opened in 2010.

Mentioning them here is my way of applauding all four courses. Still, if I had to choose just one of these jewels for my last round ever, I'd tee it up at Doaks's minimalist, magnificent Pacific Dunes.

Shinnecock Hills (Southampton, New York)

Eighty years after its founding, Shinnecock is still America's premier Scottish-style links course. At this course, you play the game as it was designed to be played — along the ground when the wind blows. The world's best players saw how tough that could be during the 2004 U.S. Open at Shinnecock.

From the porch of the nation's oldest clubhouse all the way out to the Atlantic Ocean, Shinnecock Hills is an American-bred beauty. Wind and golf course are meshed into your being as you stroll through this green treasure.

Cape Kidnappers (Hawke's Bay, New Zealand)

Remote? Hey, it's only 1,000 miles from Tasmania!

Here's another Tom Doak course arrayed on a spectacular site: a stretch of New Zealand's North Island, where fingers of land reach toward the South Pacific atop cliffs that plunge 500 feet to the surf. One of the most scenic venues any sport has ever seen, Cape Kidnappers is eye candy to golf photographers and a once-in-a-lifetime treat for golfers of any hemisphere.

Whistling Straits — Straits Course (Kohler, Wisconsin)

Whistling Straits opened in 1998 but really grabbed everyone's attention when it hosted the 2004 PGA Championship. Pete Dye took a flat wasteland on Wisconsin's lakefront and turned it into a rugged roller coaster of a course that evokes Scotland at every turn. You find grassy dunes and deep pot bunkers on the Straits Course, as well as stone bridges and even Scottish sheep standing almost sideways on hillsides.

When the wind whistles off Lake Michigan, this course can be a terror track. But the greens are large enough that if you play from the set of tees that matches your skill level, you have a chance to score.

Ten great short-game golf courses

Because golf balls fly farther and big drivers loaded with springlike faces launch balls like never before, some courses are finding that their designs are too short. However, equipment promising all the distance in the world doesn't help the short game, which remains the most elegant and important aspect of golf. The golf courses we highlight in this section are exciting not for their lengths, which they may or may not have, but for the short-game challenges of their intriguing designs.

Many of these courses host televised tournaments, including R&A, PGA, LPGA, and Champions Tour events. If you want to pick up some short-game strategy or just catch some exciting action, tune in when you see these courses on the dial (or, better yet, attend the tournament). And if you have the time and resources, get out there and test your short game on these courses!

The Old Course at St. Andrews (Fife, Scotland)

The birthplace of golf, where the game was invented more than 500 years ago, is a cherished antique that golfers all over the globe make a pilgrimage to. Every six years or so (including in 2010), the Old Course hosts the British Open Championship — the oldest golf championship on record. The Old

Course is a links course; its seaside location means that the wind blows more often than not. Crafty Scots realized that wind is bad for a golf ball flying through the air, so they started perfecting low-running pitches and chips.

The Old Course, which was designed more by nature than man, offers plenty of opportunity to be imaginative with pitch and run shots. The short grass and open fronts to greens even encourage you to use a putter from as far as 20 paces off the green. The Old Course also has giant double greens that serve two holes at once, so players often face cross-country putts.

Players must beware of the menacing, deep, sod-faced bunkers (with names such as Principal's Nose and Hell Bunker) that suck in wayward shots. So severe are these bunkers, which were originally dug by sheep looking for escape from the wind, that players sometimes resign themselves to playing shots out sideways rather than toward the hole just to have a fighting chance at a respectable score.

Pinehurst No. 2 (Pinehurst, North Carolina)

Pinehurst No. 2 (also featured in "Gary's ten favorite courses") is part of the famed, eight-course Pinehurst Resort, which opened in 1895 and retains much of its old-fashioned charm — especially its old-fashioned design. No. 2 looms large because of its undulating, crowned greens and strategically placed bunkers. Putts misdirected with too much bravado can roll right off the green and into a bunker.

Stadium Course, TPC at Sawgrass (Ponte Vedra Beach, Florida)

The Tournament Players Club at Sawgrass is the home of The Players Championship — the richest tournament on the PGA Tour — and boy, do the players earn their money that week! Golf course architect Pete Dye took Florida swampland between Jacksonville and St. Augustine and created 18 snarling holes that seem to rise from the wetlands just enough to allow the passage of play. Wooden bulkheads hold back the swamp on most holes.

The 132-yard, par-3 17th hole is one of the most famous in golf because its green literally rests on an island — a small patch of land in the middle of an alligator-filled pond that claims thousands of mishit golf balls each year.

Dye also punctuated his TPC course with waste bunkers that line one side or another on most every hole. The greens are undulated and speedy, and most of them are perched on severe slopes with thatched rough, meaning players who miss the green often have awkward stances and bad lies. The course also has quirky moguls and difficult mounds to play from, beside and behind the greens, that Dye inserted to make the flat land more punishing. You can't find anything subtle about the TPC at Sawgrass Stadium Course — you have to play do-or-die, target golf.

Ballybunion Old Course (County Kerry, Ireland)

In early 1897, an article in the *Irish Times* dismissed Ballybunion's Old Course as "a rabbit warren below the village, where a golfer requires limitless patience and an inexhaustible supply of golf balls." And only 12 holes existed at the time! Now Ballybunion Golf Club offers 18 of the most memorable holes you may ever play. With fairways less than 30 yards wide and tiny greens perched in towering sea-smashed sand dunes, Ballybunion is a roller coaster.

The wild and wooly golf links run alongside the Atlantic Ocean between castle ruins and a trailer park. Ballybunion begins its daring dance with craggy clifftops that slide into the ocean and sends golfers through passages in wind-blown dunes that block the sun. Tangled rough, grass bunkers, and gaping sod-faced bunkers seem to creep closer to the green as you look over your shot.

If you get a chance to play this bracing, natural masterpiece, follow the poetic and sometimes amusing advice of the Irish caddies when reading the tricky greens, which have quizzical breaks and head-scratching invisible undulations. Reaching a green at Ballybunion is only the beginning of playing the hole! Ballybunion requires precision to reach the green . . . and precision after you reach the green. The course is simply a beautiful puzzle.

Threetops at Treetops Resort (Gaylord, Michigan)

Threetops is a 9-hole collection of par-3s at Treetops Resort in Northern Michigan. Although the resort features four regulation golf courses, Threetops enjoys the most popularity because of its distinction as the most picturesque and enjoyable par-3 course in the world.

The holes range from 100 to 180 yards, but they have elevation changes of as much as 170 feet from tee to green. Deciding on a club to use is tricky with that kind of elevation change, but you can play most holes with a mid or short iron. Plenty of bunkers guard the steeply undulated greens.

Threetops, designed by teaching guru and architect Rick Smith, is cut through lush forest above the Pigeon River Valley. Each year the course plays host to the $1 million Par-3 Shootout, a televised skins game tournament that offers a cool million for an ace. Lee Trevino cashed in once.

Strategic Fox, Fox Hills Golf Club (Plymouth, Michigan)

The Strategic Fox Golf Course opened in 2001 as part of the Fox Hills golf complex just west of Detroit. When noted architect Ray Hearn designed the course, he sought to create a short-game course that would appeal to beginners and skilled players looking to hone their short games. In fact, Strategic

Fox also offers an extensive practice facility designed with a short-game emphasis — for before or after the round!

The 18-hole course begins with a user-friendly 105-yard opening hole and then increases in intensity and challenge along the way. Strategic Fox plays to a yardage of 2,554 yards, and its longest hole is its last — the 195-yard 18th.

Hearn designed the holes so that players can choose between pitch and run shots and high lob-wedge pitches. Players have to carry plenty of bunkers and water hazards. Some of the greens have as much as three feet of break, and the holes can be visually deceptive. The greens have false fronts and close-cut collections areas, as well as grass bunkers.

Indian Creek Country Club (Miami Beach, Florida)

Built in 1927 by golf course architect William Flynn, this classical timepiece of a golf course sits on a private island in Biscayne Bay between Miami Beach and Miami proper. Former Masters champion and short-game expert Raymond Floyd used to live on the island, and he calls Indian Creek one of William Flynn's finest works.

At Indian Creek, Flynn spiced up the flat tropical terrain with 124 large, sculpted sand bunkers that flash up the sides of the raised greens. Indian Creek's greens are built so that the ball will roll off the edges into bunkers or down a steep slope. Some of the bunkers appear to be in front of the green but actually cozy up along the entire side of the green. The holes are cut to penalize aggressive shots.

On top of that, South Florida's Bermuda grass has a pronounced grain to it. When the grain runs away from you, the ball rolls faster. When the grain leans toward you, the greenside grass can catch and stop your ball.

The Ocean Course at Kiawah Island Golf Resort (Charleston, South Carolina)

The Ocean Course has been much talked about since the day it was built to host the 1991 Ryder Cup Matches, which are known as the "War by the Shore." Pete Dye designed the course along nearly three miles of pristine Atlantic property in the Carolina low country. Kiawah's Ocean Course throws windy conditions at you, but it also allows you to negotiate the terrain with a variety of short-game options and necessities. The greens are undulating and well guarded. Deep bunkers line the course and provide visually intimidating approach shots. The bunkers, rough, and scrub that lurk around the greens inflict severe punishment on players who miss the green. All 18 holes offer views of the ocean, and the course plays mean and tough to a length of nearly 7,300 yards.

Augusta National Golf Club (Augusta, Georgia)

Although the highly private nature of Augusta National (and its short season —
the club opens from October to May only) makes it unlikely that you'll ever
play there, the world gets a peek inside the gates of the club each year during
the Masters. Whether you're lucky enough to score a ticket or you watch the
highest-rated tournament on television, you can see that the course Alister
MacKenzie and Robert Tyre Jones Jr. designed in the late 1920s is a short-
game challenge.

Designers have recently lengthened Augusta National and added a thin cut of
light rough, but they shouldn't worry too much about technology ruining this
gem: The speedy and undulating greens have undone some of the world's
greatest players, including Greg Norman. The greens weren't designed to be
as fast and severe as they are now, but modern land-management advance-
ments, plus the change from Bermuda grass to slippery, fast-running bent
grass on the greens, have prompted some players to dub the Masters
Tournament "the Augusta National Putting Contest."

What you can't see on TV is how hilly Augusta National really is and just how
sloped its greens are. The 9th green, for instance, slopes so severely from
back to front that players must hit their approach shots beyond the hole to
avoid having the ball run off the front of the green and back down into the
fairway.

Perhaps the most delicate and terrifying shot on the golf course is in the
heart of what is known as "Amen Corner." The 155-yard, par-3 12th hole,
the shortest hole on the course, is known as the "Golden Bell." The shallow,
sloped green lies in what looks like a giant flowerbed behind Rae's Creek.
Shots hit into bunkers behind the green must be blasted out with the touch
of a surgeon to avoid running the shot over the front of the green, down the
hill, and into the creek.

Club de Golf Valderrama (San Roque, Cadiz, Spain)

Designed by the late Robert Trent Jones, Valderrama is known as the Augusta
National of Spain because of its fast greens, lovely setting, and brilliant con-
ditioning. The 6,356-meter (6,951-yard) golf course has hosted Ryder Cup
Matches, World Golf Championships, and the Volvo Masters Tournament.
The course attracts such events because it's rich in shot values.

Valderrama's 17th hole, a par-5 named "Los Gabiones," gives even the professional players fits. In 1999, Tiger Woods hit a shot into the slippery, tilted
green that spun from the back of the green beyond the hole all the way back
off the front and into the water. The club has since changed the hole and
lowered some of the mounds that one of the players referred to as "dead ele-
phants." Cork trees planted throughout the course complicate matters. You

must carefully position the ball to the openings in front of the greens to have favorable short-game situations.

Surveying online course guides

If you don't have the time or money to play all the world's great courses, don't fret. The web can take you to them for free. Websites carry descriptions, layouts, and scorecards for countless courses around the world, from Alabama to Zimbabwe.

Take, for example, the website for golf's oldest and greatest course: the Old Course at St Andrews, Scotland (Standrews.org.uk). From this site, you can view historical information about the course, feast your eyes on a wonderful photo gallery, make hotel and tee-time reservations, and even play a virtual round. Similar sites cover other famous courses and resorts — often with gorgeous photos — from Pebble Beach (Pebblebeach.com) to PGA West (Pgawest.com) to Bandon Dunes (Bandondunesgolf.com).

Here's a look at some of the best sites that specialize in giving golfers an up-close-and-virtual look at courses nation- and worldwide.

About.com: The course-guide helper

This handy site provides links to several prominent websites devoted to courses. Start by visiting golf.about.com. Scroll down a bit to the *Browse Topic* area to the left of the page; click on *Golf Courses* and then *Find a Golf Course.* From there, you can make your way to just about any tee or green on earth.

Worldgolf.com

Feel like exploring the wide world of golf? Tootle on over to Worldgolf.com, an international golf and travel guide. It features numerous links that let you bounce easily from one continent to another. You can make reservations at St. Andrews in Scotland and then view pictures of desert courses in Palm Springs. Easy to navigate, with dozens of departments, Worldgolf.com lets you check worldwide weather and tap into links to a slew of local golf-course guides.

Golf.com's Courses and Travel Page

Rankings, a course finder, travel blogs, satellite photos, and more, all presided over by gallivanting guru Travelin' Joe Passov — that's what you find at one of the most popular golf-travel pages. Go to Golf.com, click on the *Courses & Travel* tab, and you're on your way.

Travelandleisure.com

The late, lamented magazine *Travel & Leisure Golf* is no more, but its spirit lives on at a site that boasts a unique blend of upscale travel and discount deals. It's not the easiest page to find from the Travel & Leisure home page, so go straight to travelandleisure.com/ideas/golf.

Fore! Reservations

Getting tee times just got a lot easier. The old information superhighway has an on-ramp called Fore! Reservations. To get there, go to Teeitup.com. This nationwide reservation system provides you with direct access to thousands of courses at the click of a button. Just choose a state, and a list of courses appears. Double-click the course you're interested in, and — voilà! — you're on your way.

Golfclubatlas.com

You don't find course discounts or a tee-time locator here — just the smartest, most passionate discussion of the merits of the world's golf courses you're likely to find anywhere. The brainchild of founder Ran Morrissett, Golfclubatlas.com is dedicated to all things having to do with golf-course design. Explore information about famous architects and their work, see photos of noteworthy holes, and spend hours online kicking opinions around with some highly knowledgeable folks — including some of the architects themselves. But be warned: When you click on *Discussion Group,* you may find an irresistibly addictive feature.

Book II
Focusing on Fairway Fitness

The 5th Wave   By Rich Tennant

@RICHTENNANT

"I really have to exercise more. I went from yelling 'Fore' in my 20s to yelling 'Wow' in my 30s to yelling 'Ow' in my 50s."

In this book . . .

In Book II, we discuss how to get into physical shape for good golf. Your fitness level plays a large role in how well — or how poorly — you play golf; golf is a sport, after all. This book includes tests that you can use to evaluate how physically fit you are before you begin a training program. We cover how you can use stretching, core strengthening, and weight training to increase your flexibility and power and prevent injury. In this book, we also offer tips about how to use yoga exercises to calm your mind and improve your mental game.

Here are the contents of Book II at a glance.

Chapter 1

Figuring Out Your Fitness Level

G olf is a hard game to master, yet 28 million Americans participate in the sport. If you take it too seriously, especially in the beginning, it frustrates you enough that you start wearing your shoes backward. Also, any pain you have while playing hurts your chances of playing well, discourages you, and sends you to the snack bar to pick up an adult beverage more often than you should.

If you're going to have fun playing this game, you have to get your body ready to play golf for a lifetime. This chapter helps you evaluate your fitness level. The other chapters in Book II give you specific exercises to incorporate into your fitness routine.

Understanding the Five Elements for Success

Here's a list of five things that are vital to good performance in anything you do (yes, anything!):

✔ A customized and sport-specific physical training program

✔ Professional instruction

✔ Proper mental skills

✔ Training equipment

✔ Talent to enjoy the sport

When those five elements are part of your plan, that's *integrated performance enhancement*.

To play on the highest level, you need some combination of talent, physical conditioning, mental awareness, instruction, and good ol' perseverance. Simply going out and buying new drivers that are touted to hit the ball 50 yards farther isn't going to cut it. **Remember:** You need mental as well as physical skills. We promise you'll use them.

Today's golfers are in far better shape than the roundbellies I grew up with. Gary Player was the first guy on the tour who I saw preaching the benefits of being in good shape. Even as he approached 75 years old, a milestone he reached in November 2010, Player could do most things the kids on the PGA Tour can do, short of catching some big air on a snowboard.

Tiger Woods and other pros are into rigorous physical-exercise programs that will keep them strong into the later stages of the tour schedule, when other players tire from so much wear and tear. Tiger's work ethic in the weight room used to be unusual; now it's the norm for tour pros under 40. These days, you often see more players on the 50-and-over Champions Tour in the gym than in the bar. That's quite a change from the old days when some pros shot par through rain, wind, and raging hangovers.

Figuring Out the Keys to Golf Fitness

After you're familiar with the elements of integrated performance enhancement in the preceding section, take a look at three concepts that are crucial to any good training program: structure, physical training, and customization.

Structure governs function

This heading, simply put, translates to "Your physique affects the way you play this game." If your range of motion is like the Tin Man's, your golf swing doesn't look very athletic and may actually rust. Oil those muscles with physical conditioning. It's that simple.

Here are five areas to address:

- ✔ Balance
- ✔ Control
- ✔ Flexibility
- ✔ Posture
- ✔ Strength

If you're deficient in any of these areas, you may develop bad habits in your golf swing to compensate. Not only does your golf game suffer, but your body may also break down from bad swing mechanics. Fix it now or fix it later; it's your choice.

Several factors can cause structural imbalances. They include inherited body characteristics and the natural aging process. Imbalance can increase over time because of consistent thumping of the golf ball.

No matter what causes your imbalances, the connective-tissue system in your body, called the *fascial system,* can develop restrictions that compress and/or pull on muscles, tendons, ligaments, nerves, bones — basically, everything. Left uncorrected, these imbalances in your connective tissue leave you in a mangled mess and adversely affect your performance as you start to compensate for them. Avoid these problems by seeing a health and performance expert trained to work with golfers, and cut out the middleman: bad golf.

Book II

Focusing on Fairway Fitness

Physical training improves structure

This point is a must for prospective golfers: Enhance your structure and boost your game! How can you improve your structure to play better, safer golf? Start with a quick physiology lesson:

Earlier, we mentioned fascia, your body's connective tissue, which contributes to your flexibility, mobility, posture, and function. Connective tissue is everywhere; it's the net that holds your body together.

Connective tissue's main job is to retain your body's normal shape, providing resistance to various stresses. In order to change your body structure and improve your ability to play golf, you benefit most by following a specific sequence of physical training, called "Release, Reeducate, and Rebuild":

- **Release:** First, you have to release your connective-tissue restrictions. Specially designed flexibility exercises reduce tension in the inelastic portion of the connective-tissue system that resists lengthening. You have to do these stretching exercises at low intensity but for a prolonged period — many people with tightness need to sustain a single flexibility exercise for a minimum of three to five minutes before the layers of tissue begin to relax. Gentle, sustained stretching is more effective than a quick, intense stretch because it more effectively and permanently lengthens the tough connective tissue of the body.

- **Reeducate:** As your tissue's restrictions decrease, you need to reeducate your structure with specialized exercises aimed at improving posture, balance, stability, and control. These reeducation exercises help you capitalize on your improved flexibility by teaching you how to feel the positions in which your body moves most efficiently. The goal for each golfer should be to develop a new postural identity: good athletic posture at *address* (the point before you strike the ball), including proper spine angle, plus swing mechanics that are safe, efficient, reproducible, and highly effective.

✔ **Rebuild:** Last comes a program of rebuilding exercises designed to solidify and then reinforce your physical structure and dynamic swing motion. These exercises can also improve your swing speed for added distance and improve muscular endurance for better swing control and performance toward the end of a round and/or during longer practice sessions.

Exercise programs must be golf-specific and, ideally, customized

For an exercise program to be most helpful, it must be golf-specific and personalized. Warming up by throwing a javelin doesn't help your golf game. Fitness programs for other sports aren't designed around the specific muscles, movement patterns, and physical-performance factors that support the golf swing.

Customized fitness training is equally important. If you start an exercise program that isn't designed around your own physical weaknesses, tailored to the special demands of golf, and formulated to accomplish your personal performance goals, you're wasting your time.

Find a specialist to work with and ask what sort of initial physical performance he or she uses to design your program. The elements of any evaluation should include at least the following:

✔ Health history, pain problems, injuries related to golf, and so on

✔ Tests to identify postural, structural, or biomechanical imbalances that may interfere with your ability to swing

✔ Balance assessment

✔ Muscle and joint flexibility testing

✔ Muscle strength, endurance, and control testing

✔ Biomechanical video analysis of the golf swing

✔ Golf skills evaluation (measurement of current swing and scoring performance potential, including elements of the swing such as clubhead speed, swing path, impact position, and launch angle, as well as driving distance, greens and fairways in regulation, handicap, and so on)

✔ Goals assessment (evaluation of performance goals, reasons for playing golf, and deadlines for reaching goals)

Following these steps helps you and your specific golf muscles perform better, and it beats watching talk shows all day. Your physical abilities and conditioning will merge, and you'll become a force to be reckoned with out on the course. Enjoy your new, improved golf game!

Tests and Simple Exercises to Improve Your Golf Fitness

Here's a sample test before you tackle the initial performance tests we recommend in the preceding section. These tests tell you how much serious conditioning you need. If you find that the answer to that question is "a lot," never fear; the remainder of Book II provides you with exercises that can help improve your performance.

Please remember, if you're unable to perform any portion of these simple tests (or exercises in the following chapters) easily and comfortably, you're not alone. Go slowly, and if you can't perform one or the other, stop and turn on *The Ellen DeGeneres Show*. Just don't dance along with Ellen until you loosen up.

In all seriousness, consult your physician before trying any of the exercises suggested in this book. Though these exercises are generally safe for most people, if you notice *any* discomfort while performing them, stop and consult your physician *immediately* before continuing.

Test 1: Club behind the spine

This test is a helpful evaluation tool because it can identify several areas of physical weakness and/or imbalance. First, you know that having enough rotation flexibility in your spine is vital for a good golf swing. The area of the spine that should rotate the most is the middle section, the *thoracic spine.* To have maximum flexibility to turn during the swing, you need the physical potential to achieve a straighter thoracic spine at address (see Figure 1-1a). A bent thoracic spine at address blocks your ability to turn (as shown in Figure 1-1b). Therefore, one purpose of this test is to determine your ability to achieve and maintain the ideal, straighter angle through chest and middle-spine flexibility.

In addition, this test measures (to a degree) the muscle strength of your lower abdominals, hips, thighs, middle and upper back, and shoulder blades — all essential to achieving and maintaining proper posture at address. It can also identify tightness in the *hamstring muscles* in the backs of your legs.

Figure 1-1:
A straight thoracic spine gives you flexibility; a bent thoracic spine hinders your ability to turn.

To perform the club-behind-the-spine test, follow these steps:

1. **Stand upright while holding a golf club behind your back.**

2. **Hold the head of the club flat against your tailbone with one hand and the grip of the club against the back of your head with the other, as shown in Figure 1-2a.**

3. **Bend your hips and knees slightly (10 to 15 degrees) and contract your lower abdominal muscles enough to press the small of your back into the shaft of the club.**

4. **While keeping your lower back in contact with the clubshaft, straighten the middle and upper portions of your spine and neck.**

   The goal is to make complete contact between the shaft and the entire length of your spine and back of your head. (See Figure 1-2b.)

5. **Try to bend forward from your hips and proportionately from your knees while maintaining club contact with your spine and head.**

   Keep bending until you're able to comfortably see a spot on the ground in front of you where the golf ball would normally be at address. (See Figure 1-3.)

Figure 1-2:
Keep as much of your spine and back of your head in contact with the clubshaft as possible.

Figure 1-3:
Look for the spot on the ground where the ball would be at address.

6. **Remove the club from behind your back and grip it with both hands in your normal address position, trying to maintain all the spine, hip, and knee angles that you just created (see Figure 1-4).**

Figure 1-4:
The ideal
address
position.

If you execute it properly, the club-behind-the-spine test positions you so you feel comfortably balanced over the ball in an athletic position with the appropriate muscle activity in your lower abdominals, thighs, hips, upper back, and shoulder blades. You achieve a straighter, more efficient thoracic-spine angle and a neutral, more powerful pelvic position with proper degrees of hip and knee bend. In other words, you achieve a posture at address with the most potential for producing a safe, highly effective golf swing.

If you're unable to achieve the positions of this test easily and comfortably, the next three simple exercises may help.

Exercise 1: Recumbent chest-and-spine stretch

The recumbent chest-and-spine stretch can help you with the release part of physical training that we discuss in the "Physical training improves structure" section earlier in the chapter. This exercise releases the tightness in your chest, the front of your shoulders, and your lower back. After you've mastered the stretch, you should have the flexibility to nail the club-behind-the-spine test and improve your posture at address.

To perform this releasing exercise, follow these steps:

1. **Lie on a firm, flat surface with your hips and knees bent at a 90-degree angle and rest your lower legs on a chair, couch, or bed, as shown in Figure 1-5a.**

   Depending on the degree of tightness in your chest, spine, and shoulders, you may need to begin this exercise on a softer surface (an exercise mat, blankets on the floor, or your bed), and place a small pillow or rolled-up towel under your head and neck to support them in a comfortable, neutral position. You may also need to place a small towel roll under the small of your back.

2. **As shown in Figure 1-5b, bend your elbows to approximately 90 degrees and position your arms 60 to 80 degrees away from the sides of your body so you begin to feel a comfortable stretch in the front of your chest and shoulders.**

   This arm position looks like a waiter's arms when he carries a tray in each hand.

   If you feel any pinching in your shoulders, try elevating your arms and resting them on a stack of towels or a small pillow so your elbows are higher than your shoulders.

Figure 1-5: The goal of this exercise is to feel a comfortable stretch in your chest and spine.

3. **Relax into this comfortable stretch position for at least three to five minutes or until you experience a complete release of the tightness in your chest, front of your shoulders, and lower back.**

   You're trying to get your back, spine, and shoulders completely flat on the floor.

Repeat this exercise daily for five to ten days until you can do it easily, with no lingering tightness in your body.

You may want to increase the degree of stretch in your body by removing any support or padding from under your body and/or arms — or by adding a small towel roll under the middle portion of your spine (at shoulder-blade level) perpendicular to your spine (see Figure 1-6). Remember *always* to keep the degree of stretch comfortable and to support your head, neck, spine, and arms so you don't put too much stress on those structures during the stretch.

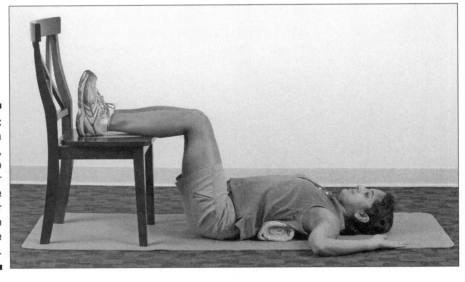

Figure 1-6:
Place a small, rolled-up towel under the middle of your spine to increase the stretch.

Exercise 2: Recumbent abdominal-and-shoulder-blade squeeze

The recumbent abdominal-and-shoulder-blade squeeze is designed to help reeducate your golf posture and begin rebuilding two key areas of muscle strength necessary for great posture at address: your lower abs and your shoulder-blade muscles.

Perform this reeducation and rebuilding exercise as follows (and see the earlier "Physical training improves structure" section for more on these aspects of training):

1. **Assume the same starting position as for the recumbent chest-and-spine stretch (refer to Figure 1-5a).**

2. **Contract the muscles of your lower abdominals and middle and lower shoulder-blade regions so you feel the entire length of your spine, neck, and shoulders flattening firmly to the floor.**

   If you're performing this exercise properly, you should feel a comfortable degree of muscle contraction while you maintain a normal, relaxed breathing pattern (see Figure 1-7).

Book II

Focusing on Fairway Fitness

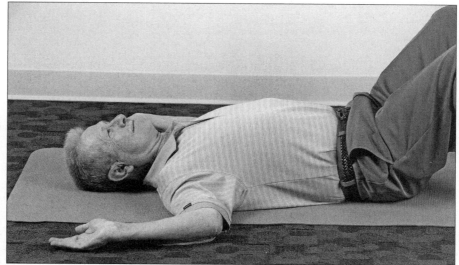

Figure 1-7: Make sure you feel a comfortable degree of stretch and can breathe normally.

3. **Hold this contraction for three to five breaths, relax, and then repeat the exercise.**

Perform this exercise at least once every other day for two to three weeks, starting with one set of 10 repetitions and building up gradually to one set of 50 repetitions.

Exercise 3: Prone torso lift

You can further challenge your abdominal, spine, and shoulder-blade muscles with the prone torso lift. This exercise provides the same golf-specific benefits as the preceding exercise but to a more advanced degree.

Perform this exercise as follows:

1. **Lie on your stomach with several large pillows under your body and place your arms in the double tray position (from the recumbent**

chest-and-spine stretch) with your forehead resting on a towel roll, as shown in Figure 1-8.

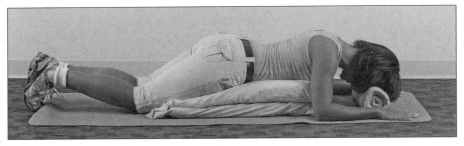

Figure 1-8:
Lie on your stomach with your forehead on a towel roll.

2. **Perform a pelvic tilt by squeezing your lower abdominal muscles and rotate your pelvis forward.**

3. **Keeping your neck long and your chin tucked, lift just your upper torso comfortably off the pillows until your spine is straight (see Figure 1-9).**

   Be sure to keep your neck tucked in and your lower back flat by contracting your lower abdominal muscles. Remember to breathe comfortably.

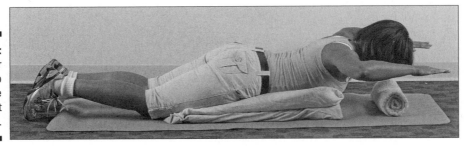

Figure 1-9:
Lift your upper torso to achieve a straight spine.

4. **Hold the lift for three to five breaths and then slowly relax and repeat.**

Do this exercise at least every other day for one to two sets of 8 to 12 repetitions, and for about two to three weeks or until it becomes easy.

Test 2: Standing balance sway

After posture, the golf swing's next most important physical characteristic is balance. The purpose of the standing balance-sway test is to help you identify muscle and connective-tissue tightness that may be pulling you out of ideal standing posture and balance, which interferes with your posture and balance at address and during your swing.

Follow these steps to tackle the standing balance-sway test:

1. **Remove your shoes and stand on a level surface with your arms hanging relaxed by your sides.**

2. **Close your eyes and relax your body; try to feel which direction your body would tend to drift, tip, or sway if you let it.**

3. **After five to ten seconds, open your eyes and identify the predominant direction of sway.**

4. **Repeat Steps 1 through 3 several times to determine whether you have a consistent direction of sway.**

Book II

Focusing on Fairway Fitness

Much like a tent's center pole leaning toward a support wire that's staked into the ground too tightly, your first and/or strongest direction of sway is probably caused by connective tissue and muscle tightness pulling your body in that direction. If left uncorrected, this tightness pulls you out of posture and balance at address as well as during your swing. Any attempts to correct your swing motion without first reducing the physical causes of your posture and balance dysfunction can lead to inconsistent performance or injury.

Exercise 4: Single-leg balance drill

Many exercises can improve your standing balance as a golfer. Here's a simple balance reeducation drill:

1. **Stand on a firm, flat surface.**

2. **Place a club behind your spine as though you were trying to perform the earlier "Test 1: Club behind the spine" (refer to Figure 1-2).**

3. **With your eyes open, lift your left knee to approximately 90 degrees so your left thigh is parallel to the floor (see Figure 1-10) and try to maintain your balance in that position for 10 to 15 seconds.**

4. **Repeat Steps 1 through 3 with your left leg down, lifting your right knee to 90 degrees.**

Perform this exercise 10 to 20 times with each leg at least once each day for two to three weeks or until you do it without losing your balance on one foot for 15 seconds.

Figure 1-10:
Try to balance for 10 to 15 seconds.

To increase the difficulty of this exercise and improve your golf balance even more, try the exercise with your eyes closed! You can imagine how much more balanced you feel at address and throughout your full swing when you can master this exercise with your eyes both open and closed.

Test 3: Seated trunk rotation

This test and the one in the following section can help you evaluate your rotation flexibility in the spine and hips. This flexibility is essential for great (and safe) golf. Without it, you can't make a complete, well-balanced swing, and you're prone to making compensations that force swing flaws such as *reverse pivots* (transferring weight forward during the backswing), *lateral sways* (moving your center of gravity off the ball), and *coming over the top* (an "outside-in" swing that causes slices). These compensations can also stress other body parts that aren't designed to rotate. If left uncorrected, this physical limitation can eventually spell disaster.

To perform this test, follow these steps:

1. **Sit forward in a stiff-backed, nonswiveling chair so your spine isn't touching the back of the chair.**

2. **Place a golf club across the front of your chest and shoulders (at the collarbone level) and hold the club securely by crossing both hands in front of you, as shown in Figure 1-11a.**

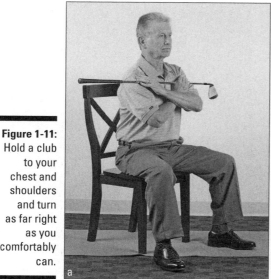

Figure 1-11: Hold a club to your chest and shoulders and turn as far right as you comfortably can.

Book II

Focusing on Fairway Fitness

3. **Sit as tall as possible in the chair, with your feet flat on the floor and both knees pointing straight ahead, and turn your upper torso as far as comfortably possible to the right (see Figure 1-11b).**

4. **When you've turned completely, look over your right shoulder, mentally mark where the end of the club is pointing, and estimate the number of degrees of rotation that you've turned to the right.**

5. **Slowly return to the neutral starting position and then repeat Steps 3 and 4 to the left.**

Repeat this test in both directions three to five times to get a good estimate of the amount of trunk rotation in each direction — and which direction you can rotate farther or more easily.

Exercise 5: Supine trunk-rotation stretch

The supine trunk-rotation stretch can help improve your ability to complete a stress-free backswing and follow-through. If the seated trunk-rotation test in this section identified rotation limitations in one or both directions, this exercise can help you gain flexibility in the proper region of your spine and enable a better turn. This stretch helps create the 90-degree turn away from the golf ball to promote maximum distance. Here's how to do it:

1. **Lie on your back with your hips and knees bent so your feet are flat on the floor and your arms rest comfortably away from your sides in the double tray position from the earlier recumbent chest-and-spine stretch (see Figure 1-12).**

Figure 1-12:
Lie on your back with your knees bent and your arms in the double tray position.

2. **Gently squeeze your shoulder blades and flatten your neck to the floor while you slowly and gently rotate your legs to the left.**

3. **Continue to slowly twist, keeping your right shoulder blade and forearm flat to the floor until you begin to feel a comfortable stretch in your spine and possibly your right hip and the front of your right shoulder (see Figure 1-13).**

4. **Hold this position for three to five minutes or until you feel a complete release of the gentle stretch in your body.**

   You can enhance the stretch in this position by bringing your left hand down from the tray position and gently pressing down on your right thigh, as shown in Figure 1-13.

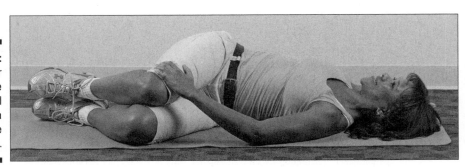

Figure 1-13:
Twist your legs to the left until you feel a comfortable stretch.

5. **Slowly return to the neutral starting position and then repeat Steps 2 through 4, rotating your legs to the right.**

Practice this exercise at least once a day for two to three weeks until you can stretch equally well in both directions. If your spine was stiffer when turning to your right during the seated trunk-rotation test, spend more time initially rotating your legs to the left, and vice versa. Your goal is balanced rotation in both directions.

Test 4: Seated hip rotation

The seated hip-rotation test is designed to measure the relative degree of rotation flexibility in your hips. It can show whether you have significant tightness in one or both hips that may be interfering with your ability to rotate them during your swing. Poor hip rotation is one of the prime causes of low-back pain for golfers and can cause poor full-swing performance.

To perform the seated hip-rotation test, follow these steps:

1. **Sit forward in a chair so your spine isn't touching the back of the chair; sit as tall as possible with your spine straight.**

2. **Cross your left leg over your right knee so the outer part of your left ankle rests on the top of your right knee, as shown in Figure 1-14a.**

Figure 1-14: Rest the outer part of your left ankle on your right knee and gently push your left knee toward the floor.

3. **Without losing your sitting posture, take both hands and gently apply downward pressure to the top of your left knee until you can't comfortably push your shin any closer to a position parallel to the floor (see Figure 1-14b).**

4. **When you've reached the limit of stretch for your left hip, observe your relative difficulty in achieving this position, the location and degree of tightness in your body, and the relative angle of your left shin to the floor.**

5. **Slowly release your left knee and repeat Steps 2 through 4 with your right ankle resting on your left knee.**

6. **Compare the results of testing both hips and determine whether one or both hips have rotation-flexibility limitations.**

Exercise 6: Supine hip-rotation stretch

The supine hip-rotation stretch can help you reduce hip-rotation tightness and therefore improve your ability to make a full turn around your hips during a full golf swing.

To perform this releasing exercise, follow these steps:

1. **Lie on your back near a wall; place both feet on the wall so your hips and knees are bent about 90 degrees (see Figure 1-15a).**

Figure 1-15:
Put your feet against a wall with your knees bent, cross your foot over your knee, and apply pressure on your knee until you feel a light stretch.

2. **Cross your right foot over your left knee and rest both hands on your right knee.**

3. **Gently apply pressure to your right knee with your hands in a direction down and away from your right shoulder (see Figure 1-15b) until you feel a light, comfortable stretch in the outer part of your right hip and/or groin.**

4. **Hold this stretch for three to five minutes or until you feel a complete release of the original stretch in your right hip.**

5. **After the stretch is complete, slowly release the pressure on your right knee and repeat Steps 2 through 4 on your left hip.**

Practice this releasing exercise at least once a day for two to three weeks or until you can stretch equally well in both hips. If you find one hip to be tighter than the other during the seated stretch, spend more time stretching the tighter hip. Your ultimate goal is balanced rotation for both hips. Only by achieving complete and balanced hip rotation can you achieve a full backswing and follow-through with each and every swing.

After you're balanced, you can advance this stretch by moving your body closer to the wall at the start. This change allows your hips and knees to bend at an angle greater than 90 degrees for more stretch in your hips.

Book II

Focusing on Fairway Fitness

Chapter 2

Stretching: Flexibility and the Golfer

*T*hink for a moment about an unbelievable hole-in-one or an amazing 18-foot putt. These feats require a combination of power, agility, and coordination. And yet if golfers, or any athletes for that matter, didn't have the flexibility to reach and stretch their bodies that last little bit, they wouldn't be able to make the play. If they weren't extremely limber, reaching to the utmost limit would most likely cause an injury.

Stretching is a powerful tool that you can always have access to and that requires only a few simple movements. And the results can be just like magic: new ease of movement, an increase in your physical capabilities, and deep composure that requires you to do nothing more than breathe.

Whether you're a professional golfer or a weekend warrior, you can benefit from stretching, which is the key not only to enhanced performance but also to long-term, injury-free fun.

Knowing the Benefits of Stretching

Go ahead — ask your doctor, your trainer, your physical therapist, or your chiropractor whether you should stretch. Get ready to hear the exact same answer from all of them: a resounding *yes*. Even though they don't make a dime giving such advice, why would all these professionals so enthusiastically recommend stretching? The long list of amazing answers follows in this section.

You have better posture and alignment

Correct posture not only makes you look taller and thinner but also allows your body to perform the way it was meant to. What's more, good posture helps facilitate free and effective breathing. Proper posture is a fundamental part of the golf swing; if your posture is off, you can't achieve the right setup position. Your shoulders, hips, and feet should all be aligned.

So where does stretching fit in? The main enemy of good posture is tight muscles. Stretching can help you correct muscular imbalances that lead to incorrect skeletal alignment. One cause of this kind of imbalance is using one side of your body more than the other, such as when you always sleep on the same side or carry your bag on the same shoulder.

Such chronic imbalances can rob you of energy and efficiency in movement, or even result in back pain. So switch it up, and stretch regularly to help balance out these bad habits.

You feel looser and improve range of motion

Over time, muscles naturally tend to shorten and become tight. So as you age, your ability to fully utilize movement in your body becomes compromised. Think about it: If a muscle is already in a chronically shortened state, it can never attain its full power potential when you try to contract it because it's already semicontracted. A tight muscle limits your range of motion, and you can easily hurt yourself, whether you're playing golf or any other sport.

Stretching increases your ability to function daily — called *functional flexibility.* This flexibility helps dramatically increase the range of motion in your joints, which helps in your everyday life by allowing you to reach higher or lower, bend farther, and reduce nagging aches and pains from tight, tense muscles.

This increased range of motion improves your ability to twist, and the better you can twist, the better your golf game will be. You need to have a separation between your lower body and your upper body to create torque in your backswing. Simply stated, your upper body should turn while your lower body stays stable. If a flexibility issue causes both to move together, you lose swing power.

You help nip injuries in the bud

Numerous studies claim that stretching exercises increase flexibility and decrease the severity of and recovery time for injuries. Stretching can reduce the chance of being injured in the first place, too!

Stretching before your round reduces muscle sprain or joint strain in case you accidentally overstretch your muscles or joints during play. In short, although nothing can prevent injury completely, stretching can be a very low-cost, long-term insurance policy for your body. For more on preventing injuries, head to the later section "Stretching Correctly to Prevent Injury."

Book II

Focusing on Fairway Fitness

You keep stress at bay

Of course, stretching can help individual muscles release and relax, but the deep, regular breathing that's so important to effective stretching can also oxygenate your blood and reduce overall stress and anxiety. What's more, the slow, meticulous movements in a good flexibility program can provide a meditative effect, helping you clear your mind of distractions and mentally focus on your upcoming round.

You keep the aches and pains away

Current research suggests that stretching can reduce that post-exercise tight, tender feeling. For decades many people thought this achy feeling was the result of lactic acid buildup in the tissues of your muscles. (*Lactic acid* is a normal byproduct of the chemical reaction of muscle contraction during exercise.)

Newer thinking attributes this discomfort to tiny tears in muscle fibers caused by the requirements of unfamiliar training. By ensuring that your muscles are elastic and you have full range of motion in your joints, stretching protects you from sustaining the microscopic injuries caused by newly intense levels of exercise.

Stretching Correctly to Prevent Injury

You may think that the idea of a "stretching injury" sounds ridiculous, but like any physical activity, you need to follow a few simple guidelines before you stretch, such as staying relaxed and comfortable. The strategies and techniques in the following sections ensure that you take care of your body, prevent injuries, and get the most out of your flexibility training.

Warm up

The number-one rule with stretching is to warm up *before* you stretch! Many people think that stretching and warming up are synonymous, but stretching involves lengthening your muscles, while *warming up* means that you're elevating your core body temperature.

A muscle can't stretch properly if it's cold. Elevating your body temperature makes the process of extending and lengthening your muscles and the connective tissue around your muscles easier. These lengthenings and extensions reduce the chances of injury and actually increase the effectiveness of the stretch.

Here are some simple five-minute exercises to get those muscles warmed up:

- Performing jumping jacks
- Jumping rope
- Jogging in place

You can warm up without stretching, but you should never stretch without warming up.

Go slowly

When you stretch, you should move slowly; breathe and hold the stretch for 30 seconds. At first, you may actually need to watch a clock to know how long 30 seconds is, but as you get more comfortable with stretching and more in tune with your body, you instinctively know how long to hold the stretch. For many, 30 seconds is about four or five deep breaths. Keep your mind focused on the stretch and on breathing slowly and deeply.

Don't bounce

Bouncing during your stretching actually causes damage to the muscle. Stretching a muscle quickly or forcefully makes your body kick into a natural protective mechanism called the *stretch reflex* — a nerve response to stress that tells the muscle to contract to protect itself. In other words, bouncing to help your muscles relax and let go can actually cause them to contract and get tighter.

Every time you forcefully bounce while in a stretch, you create microscopic tears in the muscle fibers. You may feel like bouncing increases your flexibility immediately, but that's only because you've damaged the muscle. In the end, your body heals those little tears with scar tissue, which decreases your long-term flexibility because scar tissue is far less flexible than muscle.

Progress through the stretch

Think of each stretch progressing through three different zones:

1. **Comfort zone:** The first 10 to 15 seconds

   This term describes the initial period of the stretch where you find a comfortable position, give yourself a body check, and make sure your alignment is good. You should also feel a mild tension in the muscle group that you're stretching.

2. **Relaxation zone:** The next 5 to 15 seconds

   This period in the stretch focuses on your breathing and relaxation — letting stress and tension melt away from both your body and mind. You may feel the stretch deepen slightly.

3. **Deep stretch zone:** The last 5 to 10 seconds

   You've now held the stretch for 20 to 30 seconds. Your body is relaxed, and you know that you're in correct position because you feel a slight tension precisely in the intended area. Remember, you want to feel slight discomfort, not pain!

Book II

Focusing on Fairway Fitness

Approach all the stretches in this chapter in this progressive fashion. Never try to begin a stretch fully extended. Take your time and slowly and gradually move deeper with each breath, allowing the muscle to relax and giving your body the time to produce the correct neuromuscular response.

Remember to breathe

During a stretch (especially a hard one), you focus so hard that you tend to hold your breath and forget to breathe. The only way to stretch a muscle fully is to relax and practice slow, rhythmic breathing. To simplify things, try to remember to exhale so your body automatically inhales.

Recognize your limits

Stretching is supposed to be energizing and relaxing, not painful. Never do anything that hurts! You may not believe it right now, but flexibility training should *not* be painful. In fact, if you feel pain of any kind, let up on the stretch immediately.

Rounding out your stretching regimen

In addition to following the stretching guidelines in the preceding sections, keep these pointers in mind when you're trying to increase your flexibility:

- **Create a stretching routine:** Many trainers tell you to stretch first thing in the morning, at the end of the day, or both. However, the rule of thumb is that you may stretch any time as long as you warm up your muscles first (see "Warm up" earlier in this chapter). Find a time of day that's most convenient for you and make that your special time for stretching; your body will thank you for the regular routine, and you'll soon see results.

- **Stretch daily:** To increase flexibility in a muscle, generally you should stretch that muscle at least once a day. Elite athletes stretch even more than that — two to three times a day. But the majority of people aren't professional athletes, so finding the time to stretch that much can be difficult.

- **Hold each stretch for 30 seconds:** Studies demonstrate that the optimum effectiveness of a stretching exercise is reached after holding that stretch for approximately 30 seconds (see this chapter's "Go slowly"). So stick with the 30-second rule, which equates to four to five slow, deep breaths.

- **Don't overdo the stretch:** A stretch should feel no more than slightly uncomfortable. When you reach the point of resistance in your muscle, hold that stretch. In a few more days of stretching that muscle, you'll be able to comfortably move past that point.

The old cliché "no pain, no gain" is dead wrong for stretching. In fact, pain is the most precise indicator of a stretch that has gone too far in degree or in duration. If you're stretching to the point where your muscle is quivering or you actually find that you're becoming less flexible, back off. If you force a stretch, the strain can only set you back farther than you were when you started.

Knowing the two types of stretches

Stretching always bears the same concepts: to lengthen muscles and improve the range of motion in joints. But just like ice cream, stretching comes in different flavors. The two main categories of stretching techniques are dynamic stretches and static stretches. *Dynamic stretches* involve movement, whereas *static stretches* are held steadily.

✔ **Static stretches:** Static stretching involves stretching to the farthest point you comfortably can and then holding the stretch (usually for 30 seconds).

✔ **Dynamic stretches:** Simply put, dynamic stretching is a stretching technique that involves movement. When performing a dynamic stretch, you simply use the weight of a portion of your body, such as a limb, to help overcome inertia in a tight muscle. You gently control the twisting of your torso or the swinging of your arms or legs in a movement that approaches the limit of your range of motion. The key word is *control;* dynamic stretches shouldn't be executed by bouncing or jerking. Think of your twisting or swinging motions as purposeful movements, almost like choreography.

You can do these types of dynamic stretches with a couple of clubs on the range before the round. Put the golf clubs across your shoulders and twist your torso with the added weight of the clubs to stretch the muscles. Another dynamic motion is to rotate the club in a circular motion with each arm to loosen the shoulders and arms.

Book II

Focusing on Fairway Fitness

Testing Your Flexibility

Some people are fast runners; some people are good singers. Some people are flexible, and some people aren't. This section includes a flexibility test, which can help you determine how flexible you really are and which areas of your body need the most attention so you can become as flexible as can be in your golf game.

Unlike other tests, this test isolates individual muscles to give you the most useful information possible to design your own customized stretching program. At first, the following sections of stretches may seem like a lot, but unfortunately, there's no such thing as just a few moves to determine flexibility.

After you've completed the self-test, you know exactly what muscles in your body need the most attention. At that point, you can head to the sections of stretches in this chapter that contain specific stretches for the areas you want to work and then choose those stretches that feel most comfortable for your body.

Take the results of your flexibility self-test to your golf instructor. Any imbalances you discover in the flexibility test will lead to compensations in your golf swing.

Preparing to test yourself

The very best motivation to stick with an exercise program is seeing results, which is why you should consider taking the flexibility self-test we outline here. The test helps you accomplish two important goals:

✔ **Indicates where you're tight and where your imbalances may be so you know where to focus your stretching program:** For example, by doing this self-test, you may discover that your *quadriceps* (muscles in the front of your thigh) are tight but that you have a healthy range of motion in your *hamstrings* (muscles in the back of your thigh). Eventually, the imbalance between these two opposing muscle groups may lead to an injury.

Another common imbalance that leads to injury or postural problems is being tighter on one side of your body than the other. That's why in this self-test you document your range of motion on both the right and left sides of your body. If you discover that your left shoulder has more range of motion than your right shoulder, you can put a little more time into stretching your right shoulder.

✔ **Records and tracks your increases in flexibility over time:** The only way to tell how far you've come is to know precisely where you started. Performing this self-test before you begin your flexibility training gives you a good idea of your initial flexibility level; retesting your progress regularly (every six weeks) will help you monitor your improvement as it happens.

The self-test takes about 20 minutes to complete. As you continue to test yourself over time and get more familiar with the stretches, the time required will decrease. To get started, you need the following:

✔ Comfortable, loose-fitting clothes.

✔ Mat or carpeted floor. You need a space large enough to lie down comfortably.

✔ Firm chair or exercise bench.

✔ Stretching table or your bed.

✔ Flexibility Self-Evaluation Worksheet (included later in the chapter).

✔ Pen or pencil.

✔ A small bath or gym towel. *Note:* The models in this chapter's figures use a stretching strap rather than a towel, but it performs the same function as the towel.

Before you start the test, check out a few a few pointers:

- ✔ You get better results if you warm up before you attempt these tests.

- ✔ When you retest to check your progress, make sure that you always test in similar situations: time of day, amount of warm-up, workout schedule, and so on.

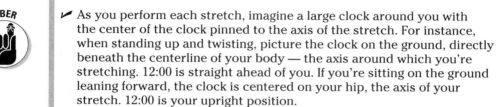

- ✔ As you perform each stretch, imagine a large clock around you with the center of the clock pinned to the axis of the stretch. For instance, when standing up and twisting, picture the clock on the ground, directly beneath the centerline of your body — the axis around which you're stretching. 12:00 is straight ahead of you. If you're sitting on the ground leaning forward, the clock is centered on your hip, the axis of your stretch. 12:00 is your upright position.

- ✔ Because this is only an assessment, not an attempt to increase your range of motion, don't hold the stretches for an extended period of time. Just get into the correct position, inhale deeply, make a note of your clock position as you exhale, and write that number down on your worksheet.

Neck

The chin-to-chest neck stretch gives you an idea of how tight the muscles are in your neck. To test the muscles in this area, stretch following these steps:

1. **Sit up tall in a chair with your back straight, your arms at your sides, and your shoulders down.**

   Don't round your back forward.

2. **Inhale; as you exhale, drop your chin down toward your chest, as shown in Figure 2-1.**

3. **Make a note on your Flexibility Self-Evaluation Worksheet where on the clock face the top of your head points.**

   Imagine that the clock face is centered on the outside of your left shoulder.

   - 1:00 is tight.
   - 2:00 is a healthy range of motion.
   - 3:00 is very flexible.

Shoulders

The shoulders and back are what move the club away from the ball. Any loss of motion leads to rounded shoulders at *address* (the position of your body just before starting your swing), which makes it harder to get turned behind the golf ball. The following simple movements can tell you a lot about the range of motion in your shoulders.

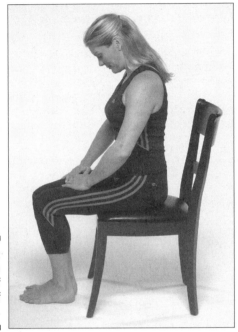

Figure 2-1:
Testing the flexibility of the back of your neck.

To do this test stretch, follow these steps:

1. **Stand up tall with your back straight, your abdominals lifted, your shoulders down, and your arms to your sides.**

2. **Inhale; as you exhale, lift your right arm straight forward, moving it as far overhead as you can (Figure 2-2).**

   Remember to keep your shoulders down, and don't let your back arch. Stop moving if you feel pain in your shoulder.

3. **Make a note on your Flexibility Self-Evaluation Worksheet where on the clock face your hand points.**

   - 10:00 is tight.
   - 12:00 is a healthy range of motion.
   - 1:00 is very flexible.

Figure 2-2:
A flexibility test for your shoulders.

4. **Repeat this stretch with your left arm and mark your results on the worksheet.**

   • 2:00 is tight.

   • 12:00 is a healthy range of motion.

   • 11:00 is very flexible.

Chest

Flexibility in your chest helps widen the *arch* in the golf swing (the distance between your hands and your chest), and a wider arch leads to longer shot distances. To test the flexibility of your chest, follow these steps:

1. **Stand up tall with your back straight, your abdominals lifted, your shoulders down, and your arms at your sides.**

2. **Inhale and bring your arms straight out in front of you at chest height.**

3. **Exhale and open your arms to the sides (palms facing forward) as far as you can without arching your back (see Figure 2-3).**

Keep your shoulder blades down and stable.

4. **Make a note on your worksheet where on the clock your hands point.**

   - 10:00 and 2:00 are tight.
   - 9:00 and 3:00 are a healthy range of motion.
   - 8:00 and 4:00 are very flexible.

Figure 2-3:
The flexibility test for your chest.

Trunk

A healthy back has a balanced range of motion in four directions: forward, side, rotation, and back. Isolating the muscles of your trunk can be difficult because many muscles are involved in the complex movement of your spine; therefore, this section contains four test stretches to measure the range of motion in your trunk as a whole.

Good trunk flexibility is a must in your golf swing. The trunk controls the rotation of the golf swing on the way back and on the way through.

Seated rotation

To do this test stretch, follow these steps:

1. **Sit up tall in a chair with your back straight, your abdominals lifted, and your shoulders down.**

2. **Place your left arm on the outside of your right thigh and your right hand on the back seat of your chair.**

   This position helps you turn your upper body at the waist in Step 3.

3. **Inhale; as you exhale, twist at your waist as if you were trying to look behind you.**

   Figure 2-4 shows this position. Remember to keep both shoulders down and to look out in front of you, not at the floor.

Figure 2-4: Testing your flexibility with the seated rotation.

4. **Make a note on your Flexibility Self-Evaluation Worksheet where on the clock your chest faces.**

   - 1:00 is tight.
   - 2:00 is a healthy range of motion.
   - 3:00 is very flexible.

5. **Repeat this stretch by rotating to your left side and record the results on your worksheet.**

   - 11:00 is tight.
   - 10:00 is a healthy range of motion.
   - 9:00 is very flexible.

Standing side bend

To do this test stretch, follow these steps:

1. **Stand with your feet hip-width apart and your back straight, your abdominals lifted, and your shoulders down (see Figure 2-5a).**

2. **Place your right hand overhead and your left arm to your side.**

3. **Inhale; as you exhale bend to the left side, reaching the fingers on your left hand down the side of your leg (Figure 2-5b).**

   Try to keep your shoulders and hips facing the front, avoiding even the slightest rotation in the spine.

Figure 2-5: Flexibility test for lateral trunk movement.

a

b

4. **Make a note on your Flexibility Self-Evaluation Worksheet where on the clock face the top of your head points to.**

- 1:00 is tight.

- 2:00 is a healthy range of motion.

- 3:00 is very flexible.

5. **Repeat this stretch on your other side (to stretch the left side).**

- 11:00 is tight.

- 10:00 is a healthy range of motion.

- 9:00 is very flexible.

Seated forward bend

A tight upper or lower back limits your range of motion. To do this test stretch, follow these steps:

1. **Sit on a chair with your feet flat on the floor (see Figure 2-6a).**

2. **Inhale; as you exhale, round forward as far as you comfortably can, bending at your hips (Figure 2-6b).**

3. **Make a note on your Flexibility Self-Evaluation Worksheet where on the clock face the back of your head points to.**

- 1:00 is tight.

- 2:00 is a healthy range of motion.

- 3:00 is very flexible.

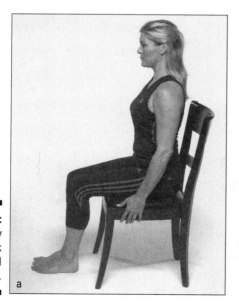 

Figure 2-6: Flexibility test for trunk forward flexion.

a

b

Standing back extension

You may have tight abdominals if this stretch is difficult. To do this test stretch, follow these steps:

1. **Stand up tall with your back straight, your abdominals lifted, and your shoulders down with your arms to your sides and your feet apart.**

2. **Inhale; as you exhale, move your shoulders back, lifting your chest and eyes toward the ceiling without compressing your lower back.**

   Think of keeping your spine long. Figure 2-7 shows you how to keep from compressing your back. You can also put your hands on your lower back for support.

Figure 2-7:
Using
the back
extension
to test your
trunk's
flexibility.

3. **Make a note on your worksheet where on the clock your head stops moving.**

   • Between 12:00 and 11:00 is tight.

   • Between 11:00 and 10:00 is a healthy range of motion.

   • Between 10:00 and 9:00 is very flexible.

Quadriceps

This stretch tests the flexibility in your quadriceps. Knowing where your tightness lies allows you to focus on stretches that improve your range of motion in this muscle group.

All lower-body flexibility exercises are important to your golf swing because the lower body is the base of the swing. The base must stay stable and level to create solid contact with the golf ball.

To stretch your quads, follow these steps:

1. **Stand up tall and place your left hand on a stable surface.**

   Your surface can be a chair, wall, doorway, or fence — anything that's sturdy and helps you keep your balance in the next steps.

2. **Inhale and lift your right foot behind you; grab hold of your ankle or the top of your foot with your right hand (see Figure 2-8).**

Book II

Focusing on Fairway Fitness

Figure 2-8: A flexibility test for your quads.

3. **Exhale and gently move your knee back, trying to line it up next to your left knee.**

   Don't force your heel to touch your right buttocks.

4. **Make a note on your Flexibility Self-Evaluation Worksheet where on the clock your knee points.**

   - 8:00 is very tight.

   - 7:00 is tight.

   - 6:00 is good flexibility.

5. **Repeat this stretch on your left side.**

Hamstrings

To do this test stretch, you grab your towel. Then follow these steps:

1. **Lie down on the floor with your legs straight out in front of you and your arms to your sides.**

2. **Bring your right foot toward your chest and wrap the towel around the arch of your foot (see Figure 2-9); don't extend your leg yet.**

Figure 2-9:
The flexibility test for your hamstrings.

3. **Inhale; as you exhale, extend your right leg toward the ceiling, as shown in Figure 2-9.**

   Try to keep your right leg as straight as possible and your hips on the floor. You can bend your left leg so your foot is on the floor if that's more comfortable for you, but try to keep your right leg straight, even if it's not straight up to the ceiling. Remember, you're only evaluating your flexibility, so your leg doesn't have to go very high. Keep working at it and stretch regularly, and you'll soon see improvement.

4. **Make a note on your worksheet where on the clock your foot stops.**

- 10:00 is tight.
- 12:00 is a healthy range of motion.
- 1:00 is very flexible.

5. **Repeat this stretch with your left leg and record those results on your worksheet, too.**

Groin

Groin pulls are often related to improper stretching or tight *adductors* (inner thigh muscles), and this test reflects your flexibility in your adductors.

This area is often tighter in men than in women because women usually have broader and shallower hips, which give them a potential for greater range of motion in this area.

To do this test stretch, follow these steps:

1. **Lie down on the floor with your legs straight out in front of you and your arms to your sides.**

2. **Inhale; as you exhale, move your legs out to the sides as far as you comfortably can.**

   Remember when you were little (okay, or last winter) and you made snow angels? You move your legs out like you were making an angel but without moving your arms. See Figure 2-10 for additional help.

Figure 2-10: The lying groin flexibility test.

3. **Make a note on your worksheet where on the clock your feet point.**
   - 7:00 and 5:00 are tight.
   - 8:00 and 4:00 are a healthy range of motion.
   - 9:00 and 3:00 are very flexible.

Buttocks

The buttocks, primarily composed of the gluteus maximus and gluteus medius, play a critical role in the golf swing. These muscles, which are largely underdeveloped by a general population that sits all day, help a golfer maintain lower body stability during a swing.

To do this test stretch of the buttocks, follow these steps:

1. **Sit up tall in a chair with your back straight, your abdominals lifted, and your shoulders down.**

2. **Place your left ankle on your right quad just above your knee and gently press your knee toward the floor with your left hand as you bend forward at the hip and tilt your pelvis back.**

   Check out Figure 2-11 if you need help visualizing this stretch. Remember to keep your opposite hip on the seat of your chair and your back straight. Look out at the floor in front of you, not at your feet.

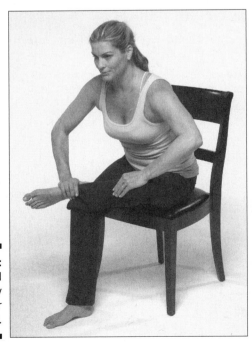

Figure 2-11:
The seated flexibility test for buttocks.

3. **Make a note on your worksheet where on the clock face your knee stops moving.**

   - 1:00 is tight.

   - 2:00 is a healthy range of motion.

   - 3:00 is very flexible.

4. **Repeat this stretch with your right leg.**

   - 11:00 is tight.

   - 10:00 is a healthy range of motion.

   - 9:00 is very flexible.

Calves

Having tight calf muscles can affect not only your range of motion in your ankle but also your walking stride. If your calf muscles are tight and you can't get full range of motion in your ankles with this test stretch, this lack of motion may have a negative effect on your form in your hip during walking. Of course, you can rent a cart to avoid walking problems on the golf course, but this imbalance may eventually lead to chronic pain or injury to your knees, hips, or even lower back.

To do this test stretch, follow these steps:

1. **Sit on the floor with your right leg straight out in front of you and your left leg bent so the bottom of your left foot rests against the inside thigh of your right leg.**

2. **Wrap a towel around the ball of your right foot and gently pull your foot toward you so your toes move toward your knee.**

   Look at Figure 2-12 if you need help. Also make sure to keep your back straight; don't lean forward at your hip. Try to move only your ankle and foot.

Figure 2-12:
The
flexibility
test for your
calves.

   3. **Make a note on your Flexibility Self-Evaluation Worksheet where on
      the clock your toes point.**

      • 1:00 is tight.

      • 12:00 is a healthy range of motion.

      • 11:00 is very flexible.

   4. **Repeat this stretch with your left foot.**

Flexibility Self-Evaluation Worksheet

When you finish each test stretch in the preceding "Testing Your Flexibility"
section, record your progress in the *Clock Position* column in the evaluation
sheet in Table 2-1. Use the description column to record any information you
want to note about the stretch, such as level of difficulty or any discomfort
you may feel.

Don't forget to make several photocopies of the worksheet so you can repeat these stretches and record your results about every six weeks. Over time, you'll see how much you've improved. Not only will you feel better, but you'll also have proof that you're getting more flexible.

Table 2-1	Flexibility Self-Evaluation Worksheet		
Exercise	*Side of Body*	*Clock Position*	*Description*
Neck	Right		
	Left		
Shoulders	Right		
	Left		
Chest	N/A		
	N/A		
Trunk (four stretches)			
Seated rotation	Right		
	Left		
Standing side bend	Right		
	Left		
Seated forward bend	Right		
	Left		
Standing back extension	Right		
	Left		
Quadriceps	Right		
	Left		
Hamstrings	Right		
	Left		
Groin	Right		
	Left		
Buttocks	Right		
	Left		
Calves	Right		
	Left		

Book II

Focusing on Fairway Fitness

Stretching Moves for Success

No matter where you're tight or which muscles you feel may be holding you back on the golf course, you can find a stretch that's right for you in this section. Working your way from head to toe, you hit upon stretches for your neck, shoulders, chest, upper back, and arms. Then you get a rundown on some functional stretches that keep your core (your center) flexible and strong. You also find directions on how to stretch your lower back and discover stretches for your legs, hips, and buttocks.

Working on the upper body

Your upper body does a lot of stretching, twisting, and reaching during a round of golf, so you need to have full range of motion in your neck, upper back, arms, and chest to prevent injury and play a better game. When your shoulders and torso are stretched effectively, you maximize your golf swing.

To get the most out of your upper body stretches, first locate the muscle that you're stretching by taking a look at the anatomy drawing in Figure 2-13. This picture gives you a visual reference of where the muscle is located and where it attaches so you can stretch it more effectively. When you perform a stretch, picture the muscle from the drawing in your mind and feel it in your body.

Lateral head tilt

The lateral head tilt stretches the muscles that run along the sides of your neck: anterior, middle, and posterior scalenes. These muscles attach to the upper rib cage, so to get an effective stretch, you have to anchor your shoulder blades down as you tilt your head to the side.

To do this stretch, follow these steps:

1. **Inhale as you lift your shoulders up to your ears with your arms straight down at your sides.**

2. **Exhale; lower your shoulders and anchor your shoulder blades in place to provide a firm foundation for the stretch.**

3. **Tilt your head to the left side, moving your left ear toward your left shoulder (see Figure 2-14), being very careful not to lift your right shoulder.**

Imagine that you're holding a very heavy book in your hand as you tilt your head to the opposite side. This thought may help you keep your right shoulder down and allow you to feel the stretch more.

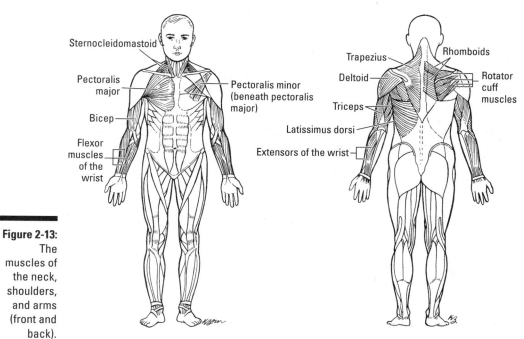

Figure 2-13:
The muscles of the neck, shoulders, and arms (front and back).

Sternocleidomastoid

Pectoralis major

Bicep

Flexor muscles of the wrist

Pectoralis minor (beneath pectoralis major)

Trapezius

Deltoid

Triceps

Latissimus dorsi

Extensors of the wrist

Rhomboids

Rotator cuff muscles

Note: Sternocleidomastoid muscle has 2 parts as indicated.

Figure 2-14:
The lateral head tilt stretches the muscles at the side of the neck.

4. **Hold the stretch for two or three deep breaths and then lift your head back to center.**

5. **Inhale as you lift your shoulders again; exhale as you lower your shoulders.**

6. **Repeat the stretch on the right side.**

Neck rotation with tilt

REMEMBER

You can do this stretch sitting or standing, but keep in mind that to effectively stretch this area, you must anchor your shoulder blades or keep them still to provide a solid foundation for the stretch.

To do this stretch, follow these steps:

1. **Find a stable, flat chair that you can sit comfortably in and position yourself in an upright, military-type posture.**

2. **Slowly rotate your head to the right approximately 45 degrees and slowly lean forward and drop your head slightly (see Figure 2-15).**

   You should begin to feel tension build lightly over the right shoulder and neck.

3. **Hold this position, maintaining the light to medium stretch for at least one *full* minute.**

4. **Repeat the stretch on the other side.**

Neck rotation

The primary muscle that turns your head side-to-side is your *sternocleido-mastoid*. No, you don't have to know how to spell it, but take a look at Figure 2-13 to see where it's located. Keeping this area flexible is important because many of the movements on the golf course require you to turn your head. Every time you look over your shoulder, you use this muscle.

Perform the following steps for this exercise:

1. **Inhale and make sure that your shoulders are down, your chest is lifted, and your abdominals are in.**

2. **As you exhale, slowly turn your head to the right (see Figure 2-16).**

3. **Find a focal point to stare at and hold this position for five seconds.**

4. **Inhale and release back to center.**

5. **As you exhale, turn your head again in the same direction and find another focal point a little farther than the first.**

6. **Hold this stretch for five seconds and release back to center.**

7. **Repeat the series, looking in the other direction.**

Figure 2-15:
The neck rotation with tilt is great for relieving stress in your neck.

Figure 2-16:
The neck rotation.

Middle of shoulder stretch

If you want to know what your deltoid muscle does, just lift your arm in any direction. Try moving your arm forward or back, overhead, in a circular motion, or just straight up and down. None of these movements is possible without your deltoid doing most of the work, so obviously your deltoids really get a workout when you're out on the course.

The following stretch is specifically for the middle part of your deltoid. This stretch can be done sitting, standing, or lying down. Just make sure to maintain good posture so you feel the full effectiveness of the stretch.

To do this stretch, follow these steps:

1. **Sit up straight with your feet flat on the floor and your abdominals lifted.**

2. **Lift your right arm across your chest and hook your left arm under your right arm (see Figure 2-17a).**

   If your shoulders are extremely stiff or tight and you find hooking one arm underneath the other difficult, try the stretch lying on your back. Just drape your arm across your body and let gravity do the work. You may find this position more comfortable.

3. **Now, gently lower your right shoulder so it's even with your left shoulder (see Figure 2-17b).**

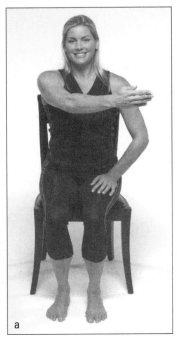

Figure 2-17: Middle of shoulder stretch.

a

b

4. **Inhale; as you exhale, use your left arm to gently pull your right arm across your body.**

5. **Hold the stretch for 30 seconds or four to five slow, deep breaths.**

6. **Repeat the stretch with the left arm.**

Back of shoulder stretch

This stretch is specifically for the back part of your deltoid; you can perform it either sitting or standing. Just remember to keep your core stable and supported.

To do this stretch, follow these steps:

Book II

Focusing on Fairway Fitness

1. **Sit or stand up straight with your feet flat on the floor and contract your abdominals.**

2. **Place your right arm straight out in front of you so it's level with your chest.**

3. **Bend your elbow so your hand moves upward and is level with your chin.**

4. **Bring your left arm under your right and intertwine your forearms with your palms facing out (see Figure 2-18a).**

Don't worry if you can't get your arms completely intertwined. Just cross your arms at your elbows and lift. As you get more flexible, you may notice a greater range of motion.

5. **Inhale; as you exhale, lift both elbows about an inch (see Figure 2-18b).**

6. **Hold for 30 seconds or four to five slow, deep breaths.**

7. **Repeat this stretch with your right arm under your left.**

Shoulder rotation stretch

You'll feel this stretch all around your shoulders because it targets the smaller, deeper muscles known as your rotator cuff and the front part of your deltoid. You can use a golf club or towel for this stretch.

To do this stretch, follow these steps:

1. **Stand up very tall with your feet about hip-width apart.**

2. **Grab each end of your towel or club with your palms down and resting in front of your thighs (see Figure 2-19a).**

3. **Straighten your arms and inhale as you raise your arms overhead (see Figure 2-19b).**

4. **Exhale and take your arms farther behind your head without arching your back.**

5. **Hold the stretch for 30 seconds or for four to five slow, deep breaths.**

Figure 2-18:
Back of
shoulder
stretch.

Supported upper back stretch

The supported upper back stretch is easy to do at the gym, at home, or outdoors. Just find a sturdy support that is about hip height. Be creative — if you're outdoors, use the back of a park bench or even a tree. If you're at home, use the kitchen counter or table or a chair.

To do this stretch, follow these steps:

1. **Stand with your feet about hip-width apart and place your hands on a sturdy surface for support.**

2. **Move your feet back far enough that you can extend your arms as you move your chest toward the floor (see Figure 2-20).**

3. **Exhale and get a deep stretch by pressing your chest toward the floor and your hips toward the ceiling so you have a slight arch in your back.**

Figure 2-19: Shoulder rotation stretch.

Figure 2-20: Supported upper back stretch.

4. **Hold the stretch for 30 seconds or four to five slow, deep breaths.**

Standing chest stretch

This simple chest stretch can be done anywhere. It helps keep your chest muscles from tightening up and can prevent that hunched-over look. Being hunched over at address makes it difficult to set up correctly with your shoulders pointed at the target.

To do this stretch, follow these steps:

1. **Stand up tall and clasp your hands together by your buttocks and behind your back (see Figure 2-21a).**

   If you have difficulty getting your hands together behind your back, try holding the ends of a small towel or your golf club.

2. **Take a deep breath; as you exhale, gently straighten your arms and lift your hands up toward the ceiling and away from your back (see Figure 2-21b).**

   Lift as high as you can while still standing tall. Be sure not to bend over.

3. **Hold this stretch for 30 seconds.**

Figure 2-21: Standing chest stretch.

a

b

Wrist stretch on hands and knees

The wrist and hands are important in controlling the clubface throughout the golf swing. If your grip is too tight or your wrist isn't flexible, the clubface won't be positioned correctly. Keeping the muscles of the wrists and fore-arms flexible is also extremely important in preventing repetitive motion injuries. If these areas are tight, the muscles and tendons can be forced beyond their natural range of movement.

If you have or think you may have carpal tunnel syndrome, you may want to skip this stretch.

To do this stretch, follow these steps:

1. **Kneel on all fours with most of your weight on your knees.**
2. **Turn the wrist of your left hand so your fingers point toward your knees and your palm is toward the floor (see Figure 2-22a).**
3. **Inhale; as you exhale, gently lower the palm of your hand to the floor as you shift your hips toward your heels.**

   You should feel the stretch in the palm of your hand and forearm.
4. **Hold the stretch for 30 seconds or four to five slow, deep breaths.**
5. **Release the stretch and lift your left hand off the floor and turn your wrist so the back of your hand is now on the floor with your fingers toward your knees (see Figure 2-22b).**
6. **Inhale; as you exhale gently move your wrist toward the floor and your hips toward your heels.**
7. **Hold for 30 seconds or four to five slow, deep breaths.**
8. **Repeat these two stretches on your other wrist.**

Figure 2-22: Wrist stretch on hands and knees.

If you want this stretching action at the course but don't want to plop down on the ground, you can simply place the palm of your left hand against the back of your right hand and push gently so your right hand bends at the wrist. Repeat on the left side.

Limbering up your lower back

Lower back pain is no fun. It can be especially troublesome when the sun is shining, a light breeze is blowing, and your golf buddies are calling. If you take some time each week to stretch your lower back, you increase your range of motion, which will improve your golf game, and you reduce your chance of injury.

The lower back is made up of five vertebrae that carry the weight of your entire upper body, as well as turn, twist, and bend. You also have nine fused vertebrae.

The spine is stabilized primarily by a large muscle group that runs on either side of the spine, known as the *erector spinae* (shown in Figure 2-23), and by your abdominals. Because no other muscles in your body are capable of such a wide range of movements while supporting such a large weight, they're uniquely susceptible to tension and strain — both enemies of the golfer. Use the following exercises to keep your lower back in tip-top shape.

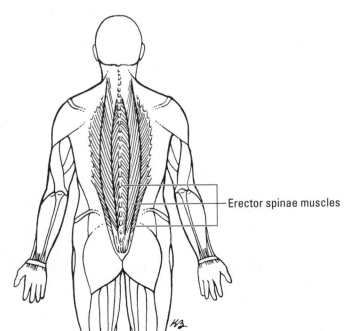

— Erector spinae muscles

Figure 2-23:
The erector
spinae
muscles
support the
spine.

Seated forward bend

You should feel this stretch along the length of your entire back — specifically the erector spinae. You may hold tension in both your upper and lower back, and because this stretch involves the *entire* back, it can really help you find where you hold tension in your back. This stretch not only helps you increase flexibility in your back but can also provide a long-term prescription for back health.

To do this stretch, follow these steps:

1. **Sit on a chair with your feet flat on the floor and your abdominal muscles pulled in.**

   To help you find and control your abdominals, imagine a string attached to your bellybutton. The string pulls back so your bellybutton moves toward your spine. Keep that string tight and your bellybutton pulled in throughout the entire exercise (see Figure 2-24a).

2. **Inhale; as you exhale, bend forward at the hips as far as you can comfortably stretch, letting your arms hang down toward the ground (see Figure 2-24b).**

3. **Hold this stretch for 30 seconds or four to five slow, deep breaths.**

4. **Place your hands on your thighs and slowly roll up one vertebra at a time until you come back to a sitting position.**

TIP

To feel a little more stretch in your lats and the middle of your back, after you perform Steps 1 and 2, try to twist your spine slightly so both arms move toward the outside of your right leg. Hold the stretch for 30 seconds and then repeat on your left side.

Figure 2-24: Stretching in the seated forward bend.

Alternating knee hugs

This exercise is a rhythmic stretch designed to help you gently stretch your lower back and hamstrings while loosening the hip joint. It's an easy way to slowly get your lower back to release and let go. Your hips start your down-swing in golf, so if they aren't flexible, your whole body will rotate and pull the club across the target line, and you won't strike the ball solidly.

To do this exercise, follow these steps:

1. **Lie on your back with your knees bent and your feet flat on the floor.**

2. **Inhale deeply; as you exhale, bring your right knee up toward your chest, placing your hands behind your knee for guidance and assistance (see Figure 2-25).**

   Don't hold your kneecap — doing so can cause pressure on and pain in your knee joint.

Figure 2-25:
A stretch for your back that involves lying on your back and alternating your knees to your chest.

3. **Hold this stretch for 30 seconds.**

4. **Lower your leg back to the beginning position and repeat the stretch with your left leg.**

5. **Alternate right and left leg stretches for eight to ten repetitions, keeping the movement slow and controlled.**

Loosening up your lower body

The muscles of your lower body — your hips, buttocks, thighs, calves, ankles, and feet — all work together like the many different instruments in an orchestra (see Figure 2-26). When they're all doing their part, they make beautiful music together, but when one of them is out of tune, the entire performance suffers.

For example, tight muscles in the lower body affect all aspects of a golfer's swing. A tight lower back and hips work together as one; in the golf swing, you want them to be able to work independently to create torque in the swing, which leads to clubhead speed and shot distance.

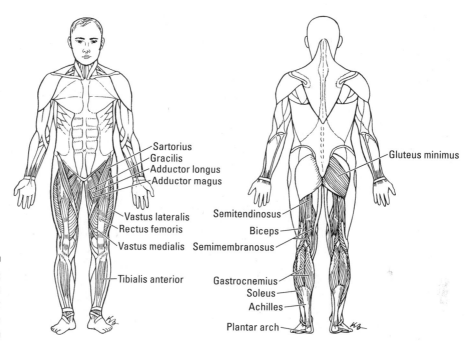

Figure 2-26:
The muscles
of your
lower half.

Sartorius
Gracilis
Adductor longus
Adductor magus
Vastus lateralis
Rectus femoris
Vastus medialis
Tibialis anterior

Gluteus minimus
Semitendinosus
Biceps
Semimembranosus
Gastrocnemius
Soleus
Achilles
Plantar arch

Standing quad stretch

The front of your thigh is made up of four muscles known as the quadriceps. You probably know them as the "quads." To stretch these muscles, follow these steps:

1. **Stand up tall with your right hand on a sturdy chair or wall.**

2. **Bend your left knee and raise your heel toward your buttocks.**

3. **Reach with your left hand and grab hold of your heel (see Figure 2-27a).**

4. **Inhale deeply; as you exhale, slowly lower your bent knee until it's even or side by side with your other knee (see Figure 2-27b).**

Try to keep the inside of your thighs touching and focus on moving your knee back, not forcing your foot to touch your buttocks. To really feel this stretch correctly, try to tuck your pelvis under and think about your tailbone moving toward the floor.

5. **Hold this stretch for 30 seconds or about four to five slow, deep breaths.**

6. **Repeat the same stretch on your right leg.**

To make this stretch more challenging, let go of the chair or wall; you'll be improving your balance while you stretch your quads.

Figure 2-27:
Standing quad stretch with support.

Hamstring stretch

To complete this hamstring stretch, you can use a chair or bench or even a fence. Just make sure that where you place your foot is no higher than your hips.

To do this stretch, follow these steps:

1. **Stand up straight with your feet flat on the floor and your abdominals lifted.**

2. **Lift your right leg and rest it on a chair or bench straight in front of you.**

   Keep your hips squared to the front and both legs straight (see Figure 2-28a).

3. **Inhale; as you exhale, lean forward from your hips and feel the stretch deepen in the back of your thigh (see Figure 2-28b).**

   Avoid rounding or bending your back.

4. **Hold the stretch for 30 seconds or four to five slow, deep breaths.**

5. **Repeat this stretch on the other leg.**

Book II

Focusing on Fairway Fitness

 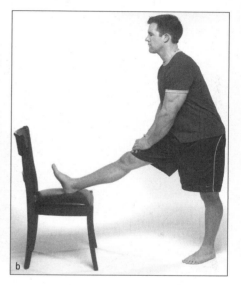

Figure 2-28:
Stretching
your
hamstrings
in a more
comfortable
position.

a

b

Standing calf stretch

Standing for long periods of time can tighten and shorten your calf muscles, which over time can cause lower back pain. This stretch helps keep you limber. Try to find a moment several times during the day to stretch your calves.

To do this exercise, follow these steps:

1. **Face a wall or sturdy surface and stand one foot away with your feet together.**

2. **Lean forward and place your hands directly on the wall in front of you.**

3. **Move your left foot back as far as you can while still keeping your heel on the floor.**

4. **Bend your right knee slightly but keep your left knee straight.**

   Try to keep your toes pointing directly forward in line with your heel. The more you turn your toes outward, the less effective the stretch is for your calf.

5. **Inhale deeply; as you exhale, gently press your hips forward, keeping your left heel on the ground (see Figure 2-29a).**

6. **Hold the stretch for several deep breaths and then slightly bend your left knee without lifting your heel off the floor (see Figure 2-29b).**

   By bending your knee, you stretch an additional muscle in your calf, which is important for ankle flexibility.

7. **Repeat this stretch with your right leg.**

Figure 2-29: Relieving calf pain with the standing calf stretch.

Achilles tendon stretch on one knee

One of the more common severe injuries of the weekend golf warrior is a torn or ruptured Achilles tendon. This tendon is a player in your golf swing as well as in your ability to walk a course. An Achilles injury can only be treated with surgery and/or prolonged immobilization in a cast. Neither option is any fun. Keeping this area flexible and strong is a good preventive approach to keep the injuries and the doctors away.

To do this stretch, follow these steps:

1. **Kneel on one knee with your hips back on your heel and your other foot flat on the floor next to your knee (see Figure 2-30a).**

2. **Place your hands on the floor in front of you and inhale; as you exhale, shift your body weight forward, keeping your heel on the floor as you lean forward (see Figure 2-30b).**

   You should feel the stretch in your Achilles tendon in your front leg.

3. **Hold this stretch for 30 seconds or four to five slow, deep breaths.**

4. **Repeat this stretch on your other leg.**

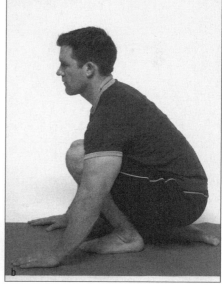

Figure 2-30: The Achilles tendon stretch on one knee.

Chapter 3

Core Strength for a Better Golf Game

*T*he human body has a miraculous capability to become stronger, tapping into the amazing power located in the abs and back, or core — the key areas associated with the force behind a spectacular golf swing. Before you can use this amazing power, however, you need to understand how it works, how to strengthen it, and how to maintain it.

Your *core* is made up of the muscles of your back, abs, hips, and — well, anything from the top of your rib cage to the bottom of your hips. Because these core muscles all work together to support your spine, they're the foundation of every movement you do throughout your day, as well as your movements in sports and other activities. So whether you're teeing off, putting, gardening, or reaching for something on the top shelf, every movement actually begins with your core.

Because of your body's connection to its core, core training has become very popular and is the foundation of any good fitness program. This chapter outlines some basic core exercises (such as crunches) and a few back strengtheners to make sure everything is working together, giving you the strongest foundation possible.

Knowing the Benefits of Core Training

Your core is the engine that runs your golf swing, so core strength is a great asset for a golfer. A strong core makes a good golf swing easier because you have the strength to hold positions throughout the swing without losing your form.

More specifically, here are some of the benefits of core training:

- Helps you get in touch with your body and tap into your inner core strength
- Increases your performance in whatever sports you choose to do
- Prevents injury because it increases strength and stamina
- Whittles down midsection fat, making you look better on the course and increasing your health and chances at living longer
- Improves posture and balance
- Increases the range of motion in your joints, which enhances your golf performance and reduces nagging aches and pains from weak muscles
- Decreases the severity of and recovery time for injuries
- Promotes relaxation not of only your body but also your mind

So, in addition to what core-strengthening can do for your muscles and your golf score, a regular program of core exercises can elevate the level of your overall health. Pretty amazing, isn't it?

Core stabilization is the expression that denotes how the muscles in your trunk keep your spine and your body stable. Core stabilization helps you stay balanced when you move.

Locating Your Core

Golfing (along with sports like running and biking) requires one characteristic: good core strength. You can hit farther, run longer, and pedal faster with core training because a stronger core means a stronger body. But training your core is hard if you're not sure what it is, so here we unveil the mystery of your core muscles.

The core is so much more than the abs and back. It also contains all the muscles from the hips (pelvis) all the way up to and including the neck and shoulders, including those that lie deep within the midsection or torso.

In the following list, we describe three of the most important core stabilizing muscles to give you an example of what they are and how they assist your core (see Figure 3-1 to get a better idea of where these muscles are located). There are many more core muscles, but these are the main ones to exercise because they make a big difference in how your core looks and feels — strong!

- ✔ **Rectus abdominus:** The *rectus abdominus* is actually a long, flat muscle that extends across the entire length of the front of the abdomen. It is separated in the middle by the *linea alba,* which is translated as "white line."

  Most commonly referred to as "abs," the rectus abdominus is the muscle responsible for flexing the lumbar spine when doing a sit-up. Terms such as *six-pack* and *washboard abs* apply to the rectus abdominus muscle.

- ✔ **Latissimus dorsi:** Want a tiny waist? Work your *latissimus dorsi,* better known as *lats.* The latissimus dorsi is the back area that looks bumpy when women wear their bras too tightly. It runs from your armpit to your butt and also incorporates your midback for doing exercises targeted at the lats.

- ✔ **Gluteus maximus:** The *gluteus maximus,* better known as *glutes,* is one of the largest and strongest muscles in the body. It starts at the pelvic bone and attaches to the rear side of the femur. The glutes are made up of three muscles, actually: the maximus, the medius, and the minimus. The medius and the minimus both lie directly underneath the maximus. (All sounds so Latin, doesn't it?) And the medius and the minimus both start at the same point as the maximus but (no pun intended!) attach to the side of the femur instead of the rear of the femur.

  Definitely the powerhouse of the body, the butt, the glutes, the booty — whatever you want to call it — is a strong muscle to help with core stabilization.

Book II

Focusing on Fairway Fitness

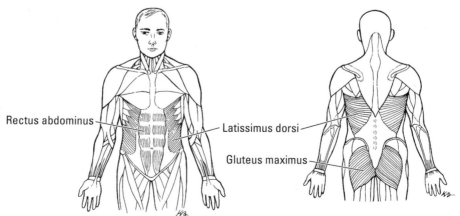

Figure 3-1: Muscles used for assisting core training.

Rectus abdominus

Latissimus dorsi

Gluteus maximus

Testing Your Core Strength

The very best motivation to stick with an exercise program is to see results. The self-test in this section simply and easily accomplishes two important goals:

- ✔ Gives you a good indication of where you're weak and where your imbalances may be in your core so you know where to focus your strengthening program.
- ✔ Tracks and records your increases in strength over time so you can see how far you've come.

Getting ready to test your core

When you first do this self-test, it'll probably take you about 15 minutes or so to complete. Eventually, after you've begun core training and come back to it, you'll be more familiar with the exercises and with using proper form, so it'll take you less time.

To get started, use the following:

- ✔ Comfortable, breathable, loose-fitting clothes.
- ✔ An exercise mat or carpeted floor. You need a space large enough to lie down comfortably.
- ✔ Firm chair or exercise bench.
- ✔ Sturdy pair of tennis shoes.
- ✔ A pair of five- to ten-pound dumbbells.

You'll have better results if you're warm before you attempt the test exercises later in this section. Head to Chapter 2 of Book II for more on warming up.

Taking the test: From the top

The following tests take you through each exercise so you can plainly see which areas of your body need the most attention. After you've completed the tests in this section, you can move on to the exercises that follow. If you find weaknesses in any particular core areas — for example, if you're unable to complete the exercise for the suggested amount of repetitions or time — pay extra attention to the exercises that address those muscle groups.

T-raises: Testing your upper back and chest

Testing your strength in your upper back and chest to see whether you have what it takes to start core training is so important because these muscles help stabilize the golf club at all points through the swing. Your upper back and chest muscles have a direct effect on the clubface, which also has a direct impact on the flight of the ball.

This test exercise requires you to pull your weights straight up directly through the centerline or midsection of your body. It tests the strength in your chest, arms, shoulders, and upper back as well. Don't forget to pull in your abdominal muscles before trying this one.

To do this test exercise, follow these steps:

1. **Standing tall and holding your weights down at your sides, slowly raise your weights until they're straight out in front of you at chest level (as shown in Figure 3-2a).**

2. **Move your arms out to either side of your body like an airplane or a _T_ (see Figure 3-2b).**

3. **Return to starting position by bringing your arms back into the centerline of your chest before lowering your weights back down to your sides.**

Book II

Focusing on Fairway Fitness

Figure 3-2: T-raises to test chest and upper-back core strength.

a

b

Seated core rotation: Testing the trunk or midsection

Isolating the muscles of your trunk is difficult because many muscles are involved in the complex movement of your spine. That's why strong abdominal muscles mean stronger back muscles: These muscle groups work together to form the core of the body. Therefore, this test exercise measures the range of motion you have in your trunk as a whole.

The seated core rotation increases the rotational movement in your spine, which in turn helps you acquire strength and flexibility in your trunk by stretching out your lower-back muscles. The biggest benefit to having strong lower-back muscles is being less prone to injury.

Being able to rotate your midsection away from the golf ball without moving your lower body helps get your weight and shoulder behind the golf ball. This position adds more power to your swing.

To do this test core exercise, follow these steps:

1. **Sit up tall on a sturdy chair with your feet flat on the floor and close together and your knees at a right angle.**

2. **Anchor your right hand on the side of the chair as you place your left hand on the outside of your right thigh (see Figure 3-3a).**

3. **Inhale; as you exhale, twist your torso to the right and look over your right shoulder (see Figure 3-3b).**

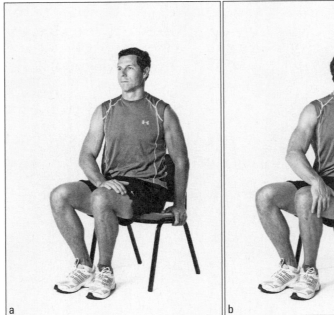

Figure 3-3:
Seated core rotation.

4. **Hold the exercise for about 10 seconds.**

   Try to make a mental note of a stationary object you see that's at about eye level.

5. **Release and come back to center.**

6. **Inhale again; as you exhale, repeat on the opposite side.**

   Find the same object you were looking at on the other side and then find another object that's past it (without straining).

Back and butt extensions: Testing the buttocks

Your buttock muscles, combined with the back muscles, pelvis, and hips, are the powerhouses of core stabilizers. Core stabilization strengthens the muscles of the buttocks and teaches you to use the inner muscles before you start to move with the outer muscles. When doing butt exercises, the focus becomes smooth, coordinated movement of those muscles along with the muscles of your back.

This back and butt test exercise seems simple, yet it's a powerful and effective back and butt strengthener. It targets the lower back and your butt when you squeeze it tight to keep your core lifted off the floor. Your downswing starts with your rotating your hips to the target, so having a strong lower back and buttocks is important for a proper swing.

To do this test exercise, follow these steps:

1. **Using a mat or towel, lie on your stomach, placing your arms at your sides with palms facing up (see Figure 3-4a).**

2. **Pulling in or contracting your abdominal muscles, lift your chest a few inches off the floor without cocking your head back (see Figure 3-4b).**

3. **Hold for a few seconds before lowering your chest back toward the ground.**

   Repeat this test a few times.

Covering Core-Training FAQs

You may be wondering how you're going to set your core-training plan into action. Following the exercises in this chapter is the first step, and lucky for you, we've also included the following commonly asked questions, which give you all the answers you need to get the job done.

🖊 **How often should I exercise to strengthen my core?** To increase core strength in your abs and back muscles, the general rule is to do strengthening exercises at least three to five times a week. Elite athletes exercise more than that — two or even three times a day, but you don't need that level of physical training.

Figure 3-4:
Core test
for buttocks
and back.

🖊 **How long should I exercise each time I work out my core?** You're going to love this answer, because less is more! Studies have demonstrated that the optimum effectiveness of an exercise is reached after your heart rate is elevated for approximately 20 to 30 minutes. Train less, and you don't really give your body time to adapt properly to your new elevated heart rate; train more, and you risk what we call the burnout factor. Moderation is the key to everything in life, so stick with the 20- to 30-minute rule before you increase the length of your workouts.

🖊 **How intense should the exercise feel?** If you're exercising to the point of pain, your muscles are quivering, or you find that you're becoming less able to hold the position you're doing, back off. A core exercise should feel no more than slightly uncomfortable. When you reach the point of resistance in your abdominals, stay there and hold it for a moment before relaxing and taking a few breaths. You'll find that you can increase your repetitions after a while or perhaps in a few days; if you force the issue, though, you only set yourself back farther than you were when you started.

✔ **Should I see a doctor before I begin a core-strengthening program?** Always consult a physician before embarking on any new fitness program, even a seemingly low-impact program such as core training. If you have back problems or an injury that hasn't healed completely, you should absolutely speak to your healthcare professional before undertaking a regular core exercise program. Your doctor can advise you about specific exercises to focus on or avoid and can help customize a core-training program to meet your unique needs.

Book II

Focusing on Fairway Fitness

Dipping into Beginner Core Exercises

The world's top golfers now understand that the core muscles are the key to increasing power while reducing the risk of lower-back injury. This knowledge is the most important advancement in golf fitness of the past 50 years. As Tiger Woods and every other strong young golfer has proved, a full, powerful rotation of the core muscles is the ultimate key to the power and precision that make great golf possible. In the following sections, we offer nine basic exercises that strengthen your core when you do them on a regular basis.

Lying pelvic tilts

Pelvic tilts done lying down loosen up your hip and core area and get your circulation flowing so everything moves more freely. Take your time with this movement, and don't forget to breathe!

To do this exercise, follow these steps:

1. **Lie on your back with your knees bent and feet hip-width apart.**

   Keep your feet flat on the floor and make sure your spine is in the neutral position (see Figure 3-5a).

2. **Keeping your back on the floor, slowly exhale as you roll your hips forward or up toward the ceiling until your lower back is pressed flat on the floor.**

3. **Inhale as you return to the starting position, and then roll your hips backward until your lower back arches slightly (see Figure 3-5b; the model's arm is hiding the arch in her back, but trust us, it's there).**

4. **Repeat ten times.**

Figure 3-5:
Lying pelvic
tilts.

Hip lifts with knees together

The lying pelvic tilts (see the preceding section) warm you up; this exercise focuses on loosening you up. To avoid stress on your lower back, use a smaller range of motion or don't lift your hips too high off the ground.

To do this exercise, follow these steps:

1. **Lie flat on your back, keeping your knees bent and tight together, your feet flat on the floor, and your arms at your sides.**

   Keeping your spine neutral, pull your bellybutton in toward your spine (see Figure 3-6a).

2. **Raise your arms straight up and slowly lift your hips toward the ceiling, allowing your butt and lower back to lift off the floor (see Figure 3-6b); hold for three to five seconds.**

3. **Slowly lower your hips back down, allowing your back to return to neutral position and keeping your knees pressed tight. Lower your arms.**

4. **Repeat ten times.**

Figure 3-6:
Hip lifts
with knees
together.

Book II

Focusing
on Fairway
Fitness

Both these hip lifts and the earlier pelvic tilts are important to help hold your lower body stable on the backswing and rotate your lower body toward the target on the downswing.

Crunches

The simplest way to gain strength in your core and endurance is to do crunches. However, be sure to progress slowly. When you first try this exercise, place your fingertips behind your ears and your elbows bent and out to the sides. Then you can try crossing your arms in front of your chest, which adds extra weight and a degree of difficulty to this exercise.

1. **Lie on your back with your knees bent and fingertips behind your neck for support.**

   Your feet should be flat on the ground (see Figure 3-7a). Be sure to keep a space between your chin and chest as you're looking up toward the ceiling.

2. **Raise your chest until your shoulder blades lift off the floor (as shown in Figure 3-7b).**

3. **Slowly lower back to the floor.**

4. **Repeat five to ten times, gradually progressing to more repetitions when you feel comfortable.**

Figure 3-7: Crunches.

If the preceding crunch proves to be too difficult, try placing your hands palm down on the floor right next to your hips. Slide your fingertips about 3 inches toward your feet by using your abdominals to lift your shoulders off the ground. Hold briefly and then return to the starting position.

Side crunch

The side lying crunch is a great addition to your beginner abdominal program because it also helps target the side muscles or obliques. It can feel a bit awkward at first, but try it a few times; after you get the hang of it, you'll see a smaller waist along with a stronger core!

To do this exercise, follow these steps:

1. **Lying on the floor or on a mat, bend your knees and place your free hand behind your neck (see Figure 3-8a).**

2. **Lifting your upper torso, raise yourself slightly off the floor by using your waist muscles or obliques (as shown in Figure 3-8b).**

   Bring your elbow toward your feet to target the waist.

3. **Return to the floor; repeat the exercise ten times and then switch sides.**

Figure 3-8:
Side crunch.

Side planks

The side plank strengthens your obliques. This beginner's version has you using bent knees rather than having your legs straight out to support your body weight — you can always work up to that more difficult position as you gain strength in your core.

To perform a side plank, follow these steps:

1. **Lie on your left side, propping up your body on your left elbow; place your elbow directly beneath your shoulder.**

   Bend both of your knees at a 90-degree angle, stacking your thighs on top of each other (Figure 3-9a illustrates the more advanced straight-legged version.). Place your right hand on the floor in front of your body for support. Ensure that your body is in a straight line from your head to your knees (or your toes if you're doing the more advanced version) with a neutral spine.

2. **Lift your hips so your torso comes off the ground and your body is in a straight line from your head to your knees (or toes).**

   If you can, take your right hand off the floor and place it alongside your body. Try to hold this position for 15 to 30 seconds (see Figure 3-9b).

3. **Repeat for three repetitions and increase reps as the exercise becomes easier.**

Figure 3-9:
Beginning
side plank.

Bicycles

Hands down, this exercise is the best core exercise for targeting the waist, obliques, and abs. The twisting and pulling motion you do with your knees and upper body is perfect for getting your core in shape fast!

All core abdominal exercises help create stability and strength throughout your golf swing. Weak abdominals typically lead you to rely too heavily on your arms for your swing, dramatically reducing clubhead speed and centeredness of impact.

To do this exercise, follow these steps:

1. **Lie on your back with your knees bent, your thighs perpendicular to the floor, and your fingers just behind your ears.**

2. **Lift your shoulders off the floor as you straighten your left leg; bring your right knee in toward your left armpit (see Figure 3-10a).**

3. **Without relaxing your torso or returning your shoulders to the floor, repeat the exercise on the other side by straightening your right leg and pulling your left knee in toward your right armpit (as shown in Figure 3-10b).**

   Alternate the legs in a slow bicycling movement.

4. **Repeat 15 times on each side.**

Figure 3-10: Bicycle for the waist and abs.

Push-ups on knees

You may be wondering what push-ups have to do with your core. After all, haven't you always been told to do push-ups to tone your upper body? Although push-ups have traditionally been the go-to exercise for upper-body toning, push-ups on your knees are a good way to strengthen your belly and core area. When you do a push-up, you recruit your core muscles to help keep your back straight and assist you in pulling your bellybutton in toward your spine. You can progress to push-ups on your toes as you get stronger; however, always keep in mind that your back should remain straight and shouldn't buckle from the weight of your body, even when supported by your knees.

Keeping your knees on the ground with a towel beneath them eases the harshness of the floor and provides better support for your body.

To do this exercise, follow these steps:

1. **Kneel and place your hands on the floor in front of you, shoulder width apart (as shown in Figure 3-11a).**

   Make sure that your hands are directly below your shoulders.

2. **Lower your upper body toward the floor, bending your elbows out to the side (see Figure 3-11b).**

3. **Straighten your elbows and exhale as you press back up into the starting position.**

4. **Complete ten repetitions.**

   You can increase the number of repetitions as the exercise becomes easier.

Figure 3-11: Push-ups on knees.

Back extensions

This seemingly simple exercise is a powerful and effective back strengthener. It also targets the lower back, so if you have lower-back problems, you may want to skip this exercise.

To do this exercise, follow these steps:

1. **Using a mat or towel, lie on your stomach and place your arms at your sides with the palms facing up (see Figure 3-12a).**

2. **Pulling in or contracting your abdominal muscles, lift your chest a few inches off the floor without cocking your head back (see Figure 3-12b).**

3. **Hold for a few seconds before lowering your chest back toward the ground.**

4. **Repeat this exercise three to five times.**

   You can increase the number of reps as the exercise becomes easier.

Figure 3-12: Back extensions.

Plank

The plank is another top core exercise that targets the abdominals and back muscles. Stay strong and lifted during this exercise and maintain a long, straight back. Strong back muscles lead to correct posture and alignment on the course and off. If your back is weak, you'll have trouble maintaining the correct posture through your swing.

To do this exercise, follow these steps:

1. **Lie face down, resting your forearms flat on the floor and keeping your elbows directly below your shoulders.**

   Your feet should be no more than an inch apart (see Figure 3-13a).

2. **Lift your body off the floor by using your forearms and toes, keeping your body as straight as possible.**

   Maintain this position for as long as possible, and challenge yourself as you build up to longer periods in the plank position (see Figure 3-13b). Shoot for 10 to 15 seconds in the plank as you're getting started.

Figure 3-13:
Plank.

Core Exercises for More Power

Here are six core exercises designed to enhance specific golf movements. These exercises complement the other exercises in this chapter, adding core strength and stability to the posture and hip and spine flexibility you've (hopefully) already developed.

To complete these maneuvers, you need some equipment:

- ✔ Exercise ball
- ✔ Soccer ball, volleyball, or kickball
- ✔ Weighted medicine ball
- ✔ Fitness tubing with handles

Downward belly burners

Downward belly burners can improve your core muscle strength, promote your ability to achieve and maintain an optimal spine angle at address and throughout your full swing, and provide significant increases in swing speed that translate into increased power.

Follow these steps to take on this exercise:

1. **Kneel on a padded surface and rest both forearms on an exercise ball (see Figure 3-14a).**

   Keep your back straight enough that a golf club can touch your lower back, upper back, and the back of your head.

Figure 3-14: Kneel against an exercise ball and then shift forward.

2. **Keeping your pelvis stable and with a natural curve of the lower spine, exhale and slowly roll the ball forward, extending your hips and shoulders equally as far as possible until you feel a strong but comfortable abdominal, chest, and shoulder muscle contraction (see Figure 3-14b).**

3. **Inhale as you slowly roll the ball and pull your body back to the starting position.**

   Do one to three sets of 10 to 15 repetitions one to three times per day.

Superman

The superman drill improves your core strength, posture, and balance control, and strengthens your upper back and shoulders. It also improves your ability to maintain a proper spine angle, to stay balanced over the ball, and to make a consistent, full swing.

To perform this exercise,

1. **Lie face down over an exercise ball and do a neutral pelvic tilt while holding a club in the tray position (see Figure 3-15a).**

   We describe the tray position in Chapter 1 of Book II.

Figure 3-15:
From the tray position, bring your arms up and then back down.

2. **Maintain the pelvic tilt and then retract your shoulder blades together and reach your arms over your head with your elbows as straight as possible (see Figure 3-15b); hold this position for one breath and then bring your arms back to the tray position.**

   Do 10 to 30 repetitions of this exercise one to three times a day. When you've mastered it, increase the difficulty by holding hand weights rather than the club.

Russian twists

Russian twists improve your upper and oblique abdominal muscle strength. They also help you fully turn your shoulders without turning your lower body, which improves your swing speed and your power and distance off the tee.

To perform this exercise,

1. **Lie on your back over an exercise ball with a soccer ball, volleyball, or kickball between your knees.**

2. **Hold a weighted medicine ball in your hands with your arms pointed straight up from your chest toward the ceiling.**

3. **As you exhale, slowly rotate your upper torso as far as possible in one direction, keeping your arms in front of your chest as shown in Figure 3-16.**

   Then slowly rotate your upper torso as far as possible in the opposite direction. Do one to three sets of 10 to 15 repetitions one to three times a day. When you're ready to advance, increase the weight of the medicine ball and/or the speed of your upper body rolls.

Figure 3-16:
Rotate as far as possible in one direction.

Seated torso rotations

Seated torso rotations can improve your posture, balance, and core muscle strength. They can help you make a more complete shoulder turn in your full swing and improve your ability to maintain arm and club connection in front of your body throughout the full swing. Equally important, they can reduce stress and injury potential to your neck, shoulders, arms, and lower back when you play golf. Here's how they work:

1. **Attach fitness tubing with handles around a fixed pole (or in a closed door) and position an exercise ball so the tubing is at chest height as you sit on the ball, with no slack in the tubing.**

   You want the tubing at an approximately 30- to 45-degree angle to your left. Make sure your exercise ball is inflated so your hips and knees are bent to 90 degrees when you sit on it.

2. **Hold both handles of the tubing with your arms pulled to the center of your chest as shown in Figure 3-17a.**

Figure 3-17: Hold the tubing in front of your chest and then rotate.

3. **Sit tall and perform a neutral pelvic tilt, squeezing your shoulder blades together and, as you exhale, slowly rotating your upper torso as far as possible to the right (see Figure 3-17b).**

4. **Hold this rotated position for one breath and then inhale as you relax your upper torso back to the starting position.**

   Perform one to three sets of 10 to 15 repetitions in both directions one to three times per day. When you're ready to do more, stretch the tubing farther to add stretch resistance to the tubing, or invest in tubing with greater resistance.

As you gain flexibility, you can advance this exercise by extending your arms in front of your chest at the end of your full shoulder turn. You can also perform the exercise while standing.

Bow-and-arrow twister

The bow-and-arrow twister can improve the strength of your core, hips, chest, shoulders, arms, hands, and spine-rotation muscles, as well as your ability to maintain a proper spine angle during your swing. It can also help you make a more powerful shoulder turn during your backswing and follow-through while reducing muscle stress and the risk of injury.

To perform this exercise, follow these steps:

1. **Attach fitness tubing with handles in a low position around a fixed pole (or in a closed door) and stand in your golf address position with your hands in front of your body (as shown in Figure 3-18a) so the tubing angles up approximately 45 to 60 degrees with no slack.**

Figure 3-18: From your address position, pull back and rotate your shoulders.

2. **Slowly pull one hand toward your body, rotating your spine and shoulders as far as possible while keeping your hips and legs stable (see Figure 3-18b).**

   You should feel like you're pulling the string back on a bow to shoot an arrow. Hold this position for one breath and then inhale as you relax back to your starting position. Do one to three sets of 10 to 15 repetitions in both directions one to three times a day. To add difficulty, stretch the tubing farther, or invest in more-resistant tubing.

Medicine ball twists

Medicine ball twists can improve your core and spinal-rotation strength as well as your posture and balance control. They can also strengthen your arms, shoulders, hips, and legs and improve your ability to maintain a proper spine angle, which creates greater stability over the ball and a more consistent swing path. They can even help you add clubhead speed for more distance.

To try this exercise, check out the following steps:

1. **Assume your normal posture at address while holding a weighted medicine ball.**

2. **Perform a neutral pelvic tilt and shoulder-blade squeeze and slowly rotate your spine and torso to the right, keeping the medicine ball in front of your chest throughout the full turn as you see in Figure 3-19.**

Figure 3-19: Rotate while keeping the medicine ball in front of your chest.

3. **Hold this fully rotated position for one breath and then slowly rotate as far as you can to the left.**

   Perform 10 to 30 repetitions one to three times per day. When you're ready to do more, gradually increase the weight of the medicine ball. Other ways to advance this exercise are to

   • Increase the speed of your torso rotations.

   • Stand on half-foam rolls or any other unstable base — but be sure you maintain a stable lower body.

Taking the Senior Core Challenge

People over 65 represent the most rapidly growing group in the population, and the degrees of health and fitness of these folks vary wildly. Nevertheless, senior golfers must strengthen their core muscles to help prevent injury. The following sections give you some pointers on core strengthening for this age group as well as some senior-approved core exercises.

Going about core exercises safely

When it comes to core-strength training as you age, you should follow these guidelines to ensure your workouts are safe as well as effective:

Book II

Focusing on Fairway Fitness

- ✔ **Talk to your doctor first.** As with any new form of exercise, consult your doctor before you begin a workout program. Seniors with certain conditions, such as diabetes and coronary heart disease, may have to take a *Graded Exercise Test* (GXT) in which they get on a stationary bicycle or treadmill while their physician monitors their blood pressure and heart rate.

- ✔ **Do moderate workouts for 30 to 60 minutes at least twice a week on nonconsecutive days.** The American College of Sports Medicine suggests this guideline, which basically means making sure that you have at least one full day of rest between workout sessions.

- ✔ **Target all your major muscle groups during your twice-weekly workouts.**

- ✔ **Do 10 to 15 repetitions of each exercise, using a moderate level of intensity.** A *moderate level of intensity* equals 70 percent of the amount of weight you can lift in a single effort. Making a 70 percent effort in your workout should feel challenging but not exhausting to your muscles or require labored breathing. In other words, exercising shouldn't be painful in any way. That being said . . .

- ✔ **Begin gradually and increase the number of repetitions over time as you get stronger.** Because seniors are more prone to health concerns when working out, begin gradually by using small movements with whatever exercise you choose to do, and stop immediately if you feel fatigued or short of breath. Of course, for seniors who are severely out of shape, the less-is-more approach is always better because you can strain muscles and injure yourself by overdoing it.

- ✔ **Determine the role of weights in your workout.** Depending on your level of fitness, it's perfectly fine to start with no weights at all. Because starting with weights that are too heavy can cause injuries, using the resistance of your own body weight is a great way to start. As you build your strength and stamina, you'll be able to progress to using weights — but do it gradually. Keep in mind, slow and steady wins the race!

Buddy system

As you get older, losing your balance and your confidence when trying new things is easy to do. Having a workout partner can help you gain back your confidence and boost your self-esteem by having someone else to share in your enthusiasm about your new workout experience; having someone else around can also help you avoid injury. Plus, exercising is just a lot more fun when you do it in pairs. Getting motivated to go to the gym or simply leave the house and take a walk is much easier if you know someone is waiting and depending on you. So take your partner or pick a friend and use the buddy system when you exercise to help motivate you and keep you safe at the same time.

Always work up slowly and stop immediately if you feel light-headed or experience any type of pain.

Core routine to help maintain balance

The following exercises are specifically designed to be accessible to anyone — even someone with physical limitations because of age or injury. None of these moves requires you to get down on the ground or to assume complicated positions. These full-body exercises are simple and straightforward to help increase your range of motion from your head to your toes.

Before you begin, remember these tips for keeping your balance:

- ✔ **Ask someone to exercise along with you or just watch you the first few times (just in case you lose your balance).**
- ✔ **Use a chair, table, couch, or other piece of heavy furniture for balance.**
- ✔ **After you're comfortable and steady, try using only one finger to hold on as you exercise.** When you feel comfortable with one fingertip, try the following exercises without holding anything. Build your confidence slowly and take your time . . . and most of all, have fun!

Hip extension
Starting with the hips and lower back, this core strengthener is a good exercise to help keep you balanced. You can use a chair or the back of a couch for assistance — just like ballet dancers do when they warm up at a ballet barre.

1. **Stand about a foot away from a chair and keep your feet slightly apart as you stand tall.**

2. **Bend forward at your hips until you're at a 45-degree angle as you hold onto the chair for balance (as shown in Figure 3-20a).**

3. **Slowly extend or raise one leg behind you without bending your knee.**

   Point your toe like a dancer and keep your upper body at a 45-degree angle with the floor. Don't bend any farther when you raise your leg (see Figure 3-20b). Hold your leg and upper-body position for one second.

4. **Slowly lower your leg before repeating on the other side.**

   Alternate your legs until you have done eight to ten repetitions on each side.

Figure 3-20: Hip extension.

a

b

Hip flexion

This exercise works the back, hips, and legs. It's simple and effective for strengthening your core. The rule is simple: Any time you lift your leg or foot off the ground, you call on your core muscles to keep you from falling. You can try this move with or without holding onto something, depending on your individual level of fitness and comfort.

To do this exercise, follow these steps:

1. **Stand up tall and as straight as possible.**

   If you need to, hold onto a table or chair for balance.

2. **Slowly bend one knee up and toward your chest without bending at your waist or hips.**

   Your arms should be in the airplane position out to your sides for balance; you can also modify the exercise and support your leg with your hands (see Figure 3-21). After you become more advanced, you can place both hands on your hips.

3. **Hold your bent knee up for one second before slowly lowering your leg all the way down.**

4. **Repeat with the other leg.**

   Alternate legs until you've completed eight to ten repetitions on each leg.

Figure 3-21:
Hip flexion.

Side leg raises

Side leg raises work your lower-back and hip muscles and make your legs feel stronger, too. You need a chair or a heavy piece of furniture to hold onto for this exercise.

To do this exercise, follow these steps:

1. **Stand up straight directly behind a chair (for support) with your feet slightly apart (see Figure 3-22a).**

   Make sure the chair is sturdy and stable. (Don't pick one that's unbalanced or has wheels!)

2. **Slowly lift one leg out to the side about 8 to 12 inches.**

   You want your back and both legs straight (as shown in Figure 3-22b). Keep your toes pointing forward during this exercise, and don't let your leg turn out.

3. **Slowly lower your leg back down to the ground before repeating with the other leg.**

   Alternate legs until you've completed eight to ten repetitions on each leg.

Book II

Focusing on Fairway Fitness

Figure 3-22: Side leg raises.

Standing core release

Using the back of a chair for support in the standing core release allows you to reach the oblique muscles and back muscles that are difficult to release without lying on the floor. You can feel the release in your back, abs, and even the top part of your hip.

To do this stretch, follow these steps:

1. **Stand with the back of your chair about a foot from your right side.**

2. **Place your right hand on the top of the back of the chair.**

3. **Stand with your feet about 1 foot apart, your knees slightly bent, and your toes pointing forward (see Figure 3-23a).**

4. **Inhale and reach your left arm directly overhead with your palm facing inward.**

   Use the muscles in your upper back to keep your shoulder blade down. Doing so should keep space between your shoulder and ear.

5. **As you exhale, lean to the right, keeping your right hand on the back of the chair for support and your hip and leg anchored to the floor (see Figure 3-23b).**

6. **Hold this stretch for 30 seconds or four to five slow, deep breaths.**

7. **Repeat on the other side.**

If you notice tension in your shoulders, keep your elbow bent instead of reaching with a straight arm. The movement should come from your waist, not your shoulder.

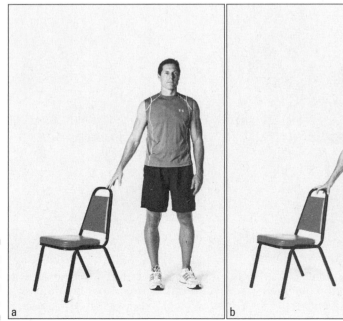

Figure 3-23:
Standing
core
release.

a   b

Seated core routine for strong abs

These three exercises modify some very popular abdominal and core exercises, making them perfect for older adults. Grab a chair and give them a try.

Seated sit-up

Doing seated sit-ups is a good way to work on your abdominals and lower back as well as your quadriceps, butt, and hamstrings without having to lie on the floor and do a sit-up! Actually, anyone can do this exercise; it's not just for seniors. It helps you strengthen your core and get up and down from a seated position without losing your balance.

To do this exercise, follow these steps:

1. **Sit tall in a chair (see Figure 3-24a).**

2. **Tighten your abdominals and extend your arms in front of you before pressing through with your heels as you straighten your legs and straighten up to a standing position (refer to Figure 3-24b).**

3. **Hold for a few seconds before sitting back down in the chair as you keep your core muscles tight and engaged.**

   Repeat eight to ten times.

Book II

Focusing on Fairway Fitness

Figure 3-24: Seated sit-up.

Seated core rotation

As we note earlier in the chapter, the biggest benefit to having strong lower-back muscles is that you're less prone to injury. Now that's good news for anyone, young or old. Both the seated core rotation and the seated core stretch (see the following section) benefit the abdominal and back muscle groups for seniors. With these two exercises, you increase the flexibility in your spine, which in turn helps prevent injuries and makes everyday movements easier.

To do the seated core rotation, follow the steps in the earlier section "Seated core rotation: Testing the trunk or midsection."

Seated core stretch

Tight chest muscles cause a lot of older adults to round their shoulders and hunch over. Increasing flexibility in the chest and upper body guarantees more freedom of movement as you age. Try this core exercise to help stretch out your chest and shoulders.

To do this stretch, follow these steps:

1. **Sit up tall on the front edge of a chair with your arms out to the side at shoulder height (see Figure 3-25a).**

2. **Reach behind your back with both arms and link your forearms (see Figure 3-25b).**

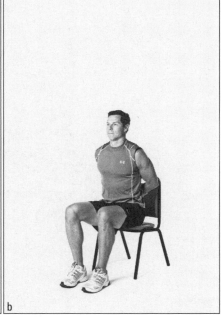

Figure 3-25:
Seated core stretch.

a

b

3. Inhale; as you exhale, squeeze your shoulder blades together.

4. Hold the pose for about 30 seconds or four to five slow, deep breaths.

5. Repeat the same exercise with the other hand on top.

If your range of motion is limited in your shoulders and/or you feel pain or discomfort, try performing this core stretch one arm at a time. Instead of grabbing both elbows at the same time, reach only one arm across the midline of your back and grab hold of your wrist or forearm with your other hand.

Book II

Focusing
on Fairway
Fitness

Chapter 4

Weight Training for Golfers

*W*hether you're a beginner golfer who wants to incorporate weight training into your new fitness routine or a golf veteran who wants to perfect certain aspects of your performance, weight training improves your current condition and helps you improve your game.

Strong muscles help you move better and avoid pain and injury at all stages of life. Weight training provides the following benefits:

✔ Increased strength and endurance

✔ Improved sleep

✔ Reduced stress

✔ Reduced risk of falls

✔ Strengthened bones

✔ Boosted metabolism for more energy burn around the clock

Because weight training strengthens your muscles and improves your muscular endurance, you'll naturally have more energy to be more active throughout the day, whether you're on the course or off.

Minimizing Post-Workout Soreness

Even though weight training is safe, you may feel occasional muscle soreness — especially if you're new to weights or haven't worked out in a while. A little bit of post-workout soreness is okay; chances are, you'll feel tightness or achiness

24 to 48 hours after your workout rather than right away. But you can reduce your amount of discomfort so you can be a normal, functioning human being after your workout. The following guidelines can help you keep this soreness to a minimum.

You don't have to build big, bulky muscles to become strong. Golf core strength is the key, and you always want to maintain flexibility when weight training.

Warming up before you lift

Before you start your training session, warm up your body with at least five minutes of easy aerobic exercise. Your warm-up increases circulation to and the temperature of your working muscles, making them more pliable and less susceptible to injury.

Walking, jogging, stairclimbing, and stationary biking are excellent aerobic warm-up activities for the muscles south of your waistline. But to prepare your upper body muscles, you need to add extra arm movements to these activities.

- ✔ Vigorously swing your arms as you walk, jog, or use the stairclimber.
- ✔ When you ride the stationary bike, gently roll your shoulders, circle your arms, and reach across the center of your body.
- ✔ Use an aerobic machine that exercises your entire body, such as a rower, cross-country ski machine, or stationary bike with arm handles.

Starting with lighter weights

If you're planning to do more than one set of an exercise, start by performing eight to ten repetitions with a light weight. A warm-up set is like a dress rehearsal for the real thing — a way of reminding your muscles to hit their marks when you go live.

If you get too cocky and head straight for the heavy weights, you risk injuring yourself. Be smart and start with lighter weights — weights that you can lift for more reps before you reach fatigue.

In addition, lifting weights too quickly doesn't challenge muscles effectively and is a pretty reliable way to injure yourself. Take at least two seconds to lift a weight and two to four seconds to lower it. Some experts feel that you should move even more slowly than that.

Was that a rep or a set? Weight training jargon

You don't need to be fluent in the language spoken at bodybuilding competitions to get going in weight training, but having a basic comprehension of a few terms can help you build an effective workout.

✔ **Repetition:** This term, often shortened to *rep,* refers to a single rendition of an exercise. For example, pressing two dumbbells straight above your head and then lowering them back down to your shoulders constitutes one complete repetition.

✔ **Set:** A *set* is a group of consecutive reps that you perform without resting. When you've done 12 repetitions of the dumbbell shoulder press and then put the weights down, you've completed one set. If you rest

for a minute and then perform 12 more repetitions, you've done two sets.

✔ **Recovery:** At the end of a set, you need to *recover,* or rest, before you can challenge that muscle to work again. This time is also referred to as the *rest period.*

✔ **Routine:** This term encompasses virtually every aspect of what you do in one weight lifting session, including the type of equipment you use; the number of exercises, sets, and repetitions you perform; and the order in which you do your exercises. Your routine (also referred to as your *program* or *workout*) can change from one exercise session to the next, or it can stay the same over a period of weeks or months.

Breathing properly

Breathing is often the most overlooked and least understood component of weight training. Relaxed breathing while exercising is the best technique. Definitely don't hold your breath.

Using proper form

In addition to heeding the general safety tips we present here, be sure to follow the specific guidelines we give you for each exercise. Even subtle form mistakes, such as overarching your back or cocking your wrist the wrong way, can lead to injury.

Follow these suggestions:

✔ Don't jerk or bounce any weight around.

✔ Don't be afraid to ask for help while you're in the gym.

✔ Follow a beginners' weight lifting routine consistently for two to three months before moving on to more challenging exercises.

Water, water everywhere: Drink it!

Drink at least two 8-ounce glasses of water before starting your weight lifting routine and two to four glasses while working out. In order to move your muscles, you need water. Muscle is considered an active tissue, which is where water is found in the highest concentrations. Your muscles are 72 percent water, so even if your body is only slightly dehydrated, your performance will decline.

Proper posture is an important part of good form because people's posture often goes down the tubes when they focus on lifting and lowering a weight. Unfortunately, good posture isn't automatic for most folks, so give yourself frequent reminders to align your ears, shoulders, hips, knees, and ankles. And if you exercise with correct posture, you'll train your muscles to hold themselves correctly in everyday life.

Cooling down

If you've done a fairly fast-paced weight workout, complete the workout with five minutes of slow, aerobic exercise. The aerobic cool-down gives your pulse, blood pressure, and breathing a chance to slow down before you hit the showers. If you've been lifting weights at more of a plodding pace, with plenty of rest between sets, a few minutes of stretching suffices as a cool-down. Ending your workout with an easy set also helps you cool down.

It's very important to stretch after weight training to maintain flexibility for the golf swing.

Resting your muscles

You can lift weights on consecutive days — just don't exercise the *same muscle* two days in a row. Forty-eight hours is usually the ideal waiting period before exercising the same muscle group again. Lifting weights tears apart your muscle cells. Your muscles need a day or two to rest and repair so they come back even stronger.

Considering Weight Training Injuries

Nothing is inherently unsafe about weight machines or barbells. It's what you *do* with these contraptions that can leave you with smashed toes, ripped hamstrings, and torn tendons. If you pay attention, use proper form, and don't get too gung-ho about how much weight you lift, you can go for years without even a minor injury. In fact, one of the best reasons to lift weights in the first place is to *reduce* your risk of injury both in daily life and on the golf course by strengthening your muscles and bones. However, accidents happen, even to careful lifters, so here's a primer on weight training injuries in case you do run into one.

When you *strain* or *pull* a muscle, you actually overstretch or tear the *tendon,* the tough, cordlike tissue at the end of the muscle where the muscle tapers off and attaches to the bone. A strain can happen when you push up the bar too forcefully during the bench press or stand up too quickly out of the squat. Strains are often accompanied by a sudden, sharp pain and then a persistent ache.

A *sprain* is something different altogether. This injury happens not to a muscle but to a joint, such as your ankle or wrist. When you sprain a joint, you've torn or overstretched a *ligament,* the connective tissue that attaches one bone to another. You may feel pain and throbbing and notice some swelling and bruising. You can sprain just about any joint in your body; ankles and wrists seem to take the most beating.

Depending on the severity of the injury, the healing process may take anywhere from a couple of days to a couple of months. If your injury doesn't appear to be healing, see your doctor. Some of the common injuries caused by lifting weights include the following:

- ✔ **Torn rotator cuff:** The muscles of your rotator cuff are often injured during bench presses and shoulder presses.

- ✔ **Sore knees:** Pinpointing the source of the problem can be difficult with knee injuries because the injury can come in so many varieties and have so many different causes. Runners, walkers, and cyclists can ward off many common knee injuries by performing quadriceps exercises.

- ✔ **Sore wrists:** Some people injure their wrist muscles by bending their wrists too much when they lift weights, so pay attention when we describe the proper wrist position for various exercises.

- ✔ **Lower-back pain:** If you have a history of back problems, you can just as easily throw out your back reaching for an apple in the fridge as you can pumping iron. But because using weights constantly challenges your ability to stabilize your spine and maintain good form, it increases the risk of triggering an old injury — or developing a new one.

RICE and easy: Overcoming injuries

We don't yet have a cure for the common cold, but we do have a reliable remedy for most minor sprains and strains: RICE, an acronym for Rest, Ice, Compression, and Elevation. RICE includes the following four components:

- **Rest:** Stop performing activities that aggravate your injury. Wait until you've had two completely pain-free days before doing exercises that involve the injured area.

- **Ice:** Contrary to popular belief, ice, not heat, helps reduce the pain and swelling of most common injuries. Ice your injury for 15 to 20 minutes, 3 or 4 times a day, for as long as you feel pain.

- **Compression:** Put pressure on the injury to keep the swelling down. Use a damp elastic bandage or buy a special brace or wrap for your knee, elbow, or wrist. Wrap the bandage tightly enough that you feel some tension but not so firmly that you cut off your circulation or feel numb.

- **Elevation:** Elevating your injured body part drains away fluids and waste products so swelling goes down. If you've hurt your ankle, you don't need to lift it up over your head. You only need to elevate it higher than your hip so gravity assists the blood flow downward.

RICE is most effective if you begin the process within 48 hours of injuring yourself. Sometimes, however, RICE isn't enough to treat an injury. If the pain is truly excruciating or is bothersome for more than a few days, your injury probably needs more aggressive treatment and possibly medical attention.

Building a Routine that Works

If an orchestra were to play Vivaldi's *Four Seasons* minus the string section, the piece would lack a certain vitality and depth. Likewise, if you leave out a key element of your weight training workout, you may end up with disappointing results. For example, you can't develop a well-toned body without chest exercises. But you can pick from a whole variety of chest exercises. You can do them sitting, standing, or lying down. You can use dumbbells, barbells, or no equipment at all. As you design your weight training routine, check out the guidelines in this section.

When you think about implementing your weight training routine, you may wonder whether you need any special equipment. The only equipment you need is an exercise bench and a few dumbbells, which provide resistance as you perform the exercises. *Resistance* is an opposing force, like a weight or gravity; in order for your muscles to get stronger, you must work against resistance. You won't use barbells in every exercise because you can build muscle without using weights at all. Your own body weight provides effective resistance in a number of exercises, such as the squat and lunge.

Working all your major muscle groups

Be sure that your routines include at least one exercise for each of the following muscle groups.

- ✔ Butt or buttocks (glutes)
- ✔ Front thighs (quadriceps)
- ✔ Rear thighs (hamstrings)
- ✔ Calves
- ✔ Chest (pecs)
- ✔ Back
- ✔ Abdominals (abs) (Chapter 3 of Book II has all the moves you need for your abdominals)
- ✔ Shoulders (delts)
- ✔ Front of upper arm (biceps)
- ✔ Rear of upper arm (triceps)

Book II

Focusing on Fairway Fitness

If you neglect any of these muscle groups, you'll have a gap in your strength and may set yourself up for injury. Figures 4-1 and 4-2 show you the major muscle groups in your body.

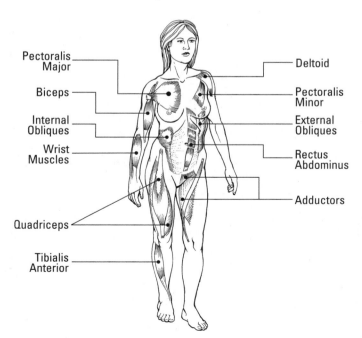

Pectoralis Major

Biceps

Internal Obliques

Wrist Muscles

Quadriceps

Tibialis Anterior

Deltoid

Pectoralis Minor

External Obliques

Rectus Abdominus

Adductors

Figure 4-1: A front view of your muscles.

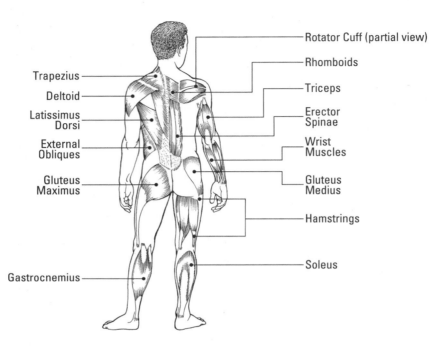

Rotator Cuff (partial view)

Rhomboids

Trapezius

Triceps

Deltoid

Latissimus Dorsi

Erector Spinae

External Obliques

Wrist Muscles

Gluteus Maximus

Gluteus Medius

Hamstrings

Soleus

Gastrocnemius

Figure 4-2: Your muscles from the back.

Doing exercises in the right order

In general, work your large muscles before your small muscles. This practice ensures that your larger muscles — such as your butt, back, and chest — are challenged sufficiently.

On occasion, however, you may specifically want to target a smaller muscle group, like your shoulders, because they're lagging behind in development compared to other parts of your body. If that's the case, you may want to design a program where you do shoulder exercises first one or two days a week for several weeks to build them up.

When choosing the sequence of a workout, imagine your body splitting into three zones: upper, middle, and lower. Within each zone, do your exercises in the following order. Feel free to mix exercises from the upper and lower body.

Upper body

1. Chest and back (the order doesn't matter)

2. Shoulders

3. Biceps and triceps (the order doesn't matter)

4. Wrists

Lifting into the golden years

Many of the things people formerly associated with aging have turned out to be simply a result of disuse. Although training provides a host of benefits for older adults (such as relief from arthritis and help with balance, in addition to the advantages listed at the beginning of the chapter), a more conservative approach is recommended for those over 50. If you've trained regularly over the course of a lifetime, you may be chronologically 50 but have the biological health of someone who is more like a 40-year-old. If that's the case, make your personal adjustments accordingly. Here are important safety guidelines for weight training and older adults:

✔ Get the approval of your healthcare provider first.

✔ Train a minimum of two days per week.

✔ Include a slightly longer warm-up, up to 10 minutes, and gentle stretches.

✔ Do one set of eight to ten exercises that challenge all the major muscle groups.

✔ Do 10 to 15 repetitions per set.

✔ Do each exercise in a slow and controlled manner.

✔ Incorporate balance exercises.

✔ Don't do any exercise that causes pain.

Middle body

You can perform your abdominal and lower-back muscle exercises in any order you want.

Lower body

1. Butt
2. Thighs
3. Calves

Following instructions

If we tried to show you every exercise in existence, this chapter would be thicker than the unabridged edition of the *Oxford English Dictionary*. Therefore, we've chosen to present the most common, basic exercises — classic moves that not only are safe and appropriate for beginners but also are standard moves for veteran exercisers.

For every muscle group presented (such as back, chest, or shoulders), we feature instructions for nonmachine exercises — moves involving dumbbells, barbells, or no equipment at all. If you work out at a gym, you'll find weight machines that will guide you through similar exercises.

At the end of each exercise, the variation describes a different version of the workout. Some of the options are easier than the basic version, requiring less coordination or strength. Others are tougher. Some options simply work the muscle from a different angle.

Focusing on Your Upper Back

Whatever upper back exercises you're performing, remind yourself that these exercises first and foremost strengthen your back muscles, not your arms. Think of your arms merely as a link between the bar and your back muscles, which should do the bulk of the work.

All the following back exercises are great to help strengthen the back and will help stabilize the golf club during the back swing. Even though back exercises may not seem critical, they are very important to overall health and strength.

One-arm dumbbell row

The one-arm dumbbell row targets your back but also emphasizes your biceps and shoulders. Be careful with this exercise if you have lower-back problems.

Follow these steps to perform the one-arm dumbbell row:

1. **Stand to the right of your weight bench and hold a dumbbell in your right hand with your palm facing in.**

2. **Pull your abdominals in and bend forward from your hips so your back is arched naturally and roughly parallel with the floor.**

   Bend your knees slightly. Place your left hand on top of the bench in line with your left shoulder for support and let your right arm hang down underneath your right shoulder. Tilt your chin toward your chest so your neck is in line with the rest of your spine. See Figure 4-3a.

3. **Pull your right arm up, keeping it in line with your shoulder and parallel to the ceiling.**

   Lift your arm until your hand brushes against your waist.

4. **Lower the weight slowly back down.**

   See Figure 4-3b.

5. **Repeat until you've done 10 to 12 reps.**

6. **Repeat Steps 1 through 5 with the other arm.**

Figure 4-3:
Focus
on using
your back
muscles
rather than
just lifting
your arm.

a   b

As you perform the one-arm dumbbell row,

- ✔ **Do** remember that, although your arm is moving, this move is a back exercise. Concentrate on pulling from your back muscles (right behind and below your shoulder) rather than just moving your arm up and down.
- ✔ **Do** keep your abs pulled in tight throughout the motion.
- ✔ **Don't** allow your back to sag toward the floor or your shoulders to hunch up.
- ✔ **Don't** jerk the weight upward.

Variation: As you lift the dumbbell, rotate your arm so your palm ends up facing backward. This position gives the exercise a different feel and places extra emphasis on your biceps.

Dumbbell pullover

The dumbbell pullover is mainly a back exercise, but it also works your chest, shoulders, biceps, and abdominals.

If you have shoulder or lower-back problems, you may want to skip this exercise because the dumbbell pullover requires raising your arms overhead while stabilizing your spine.

Here's how to do the dumbbell pullover:

1. **Holding a single dumbbell with both hands, lie on the bench with your feet flat on the floor and your arms directly over your shoulders.**

   Turn your palms up so one end of the dumbbell is resting in the gap between your palms and the other end is hanging down over your face. Pull your abdominals in, but make sure that your back is relaxed and arched naturally. See Figure 4-4a.

2. **Keeping your elbows slightly bent, lower the weight behind your head until the bottom end of the dumbbell is directly behind your head.**

3. **Pull the dumbbell back up overhead, keeping the same slight bend in your elbows throughout the motion.**

   See Figure 4-4b.

4. **Repeat until you've done 10 to 12 reps.**

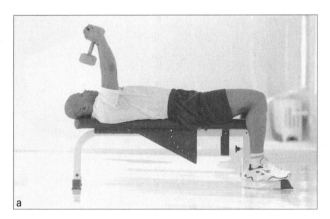

a

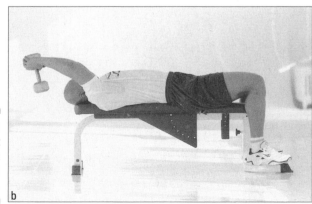

Figure 4-4:
Don't let
your back
arch off the
bench.

b

As you do the dumbbell pullover,

- ✔ **Do** make sure that you grip the dumbbell securely.

- ✔ **Do** concentrate on initiating the movement from the outer wings of your upper back rather than simply bending and straightening your arms.

- ✔ **Don't** arch your back up off the bench, especially as you lower the weight.

- ✔ **Don't** lower the weight too far behind you.

Variation: Do this same exercise with a bar, holding the bar in the center with your palms facing up. Another variation on the same theme: Hold a dumbbell in each hand with your palms facing in.

Book II

Focusing on Fairway Fitness

Dumbbell shrug

The dumbbell shrug is a small movement with a big payoff: It strengthens your shoulders and the trapezius muscles of your upper back. Be careful if you're prone to neck problems.

To do the dumbbell shrug,

1. **Stand tall and hold a dumbbell in each hand with your arms straight down and your palms in front of your thighs, facing in.**

   Pull your abdominals in, tuck your chin toward your chest, and keep your knees relaxed. See Figure 4-5a.

2. **Shrug your shoulders straight up toward your ears and then slowly lower your shoulders to the starting position.**

   See Figure 4-5b.

3. **Repeat until you've done 10 to 12 reps.**

When you perform the dumbbell shrug,

- ✔ **Do** keep your neck and shoulders relaxed.

- ✔ **Don't** roll your shoulders in a complete circle — a common exercise mistake that places too much stress on your shoulder joint.

- ✔ **Don't** move body parts other than your shoulders.

Variation: For a more difficult alternative, shrug your shoulders upward as in the basic version, squeeze your shoulder blades together, and then lower them back down. This version brings the rhomboids (back muscles) into the mix.

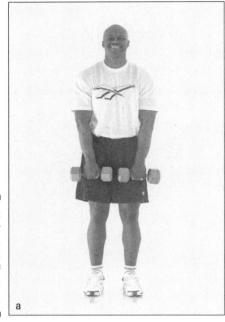

a   b

Figure 4-5:
Shrug your
shoulders
straight up
instead of
rolling them
in a circle.

Getting a Lower-Back Workout

Many people take for granted the role that their lower-back muscles play in their golf performance and even everyday mobility. Your lower-back muscles need to be not only strong but also flexible, which is why we're recommending two core-strengthening exercises covered in Chapter 3 of Book II: lying pelvic tilt and back extensions.

When you do a lower-back exercise, you should feel a mild pull or pressure build within the muscle, *not* a sharp pain. If you do feel a piercing pain, back off.

You may feel a dull ache in your back a day or two after you've worked your lower back. This sensation is normal. But if the pain is sharp and so debilitating that your most upright posture looks like you're trying to duck under a fence, you've either pushed yourself too far or you have a back problem.

Working Out Your Chest

Because your chest muscles are among the largest in your upper body, we suggest that you perform more sets of exercises with these muscles than with the smaller muscle groups of your arms. In addition to those exercises included in this section, your chest muscles also benefit from doing the kneeling push-up, which is covered in Chapter 3 of Book II.

All chest exercises should be done with strength in mind, not bulk. More repetitions with less weight help build muscle, not bulk. A very large chest will make it difficult to turn away from the golf ball.

Dumbbell chest press

This exercise works your chest muscles, along with your shoulders and triceps. You may want to modify or avoid this exercise if you have shoulder, elbow, or lower-back problems.

Book II

Focusing on Fairway Fitness

Here's how to do the dumbbell chest press:

1. **Lie on the bench with a dumbbell in each hand and your feet flat on the floor (or up on the bench if it's more comfortable).**

2. **Push the dumbbells up so your arms are directly over your shoulders and your palms face forward.**

   Pull your abdominals in without arching your back way up or jamming it into the bench. Tilt your chin toward your chest. See Figure 4-6a.

3. **Lower the dumbbells down and a little to the side until your elbows are slightly below your shoulders.**

4. **Push the weights back up, taking care not to lock your elbows or allow your shoulder blades to rise off the bench.**

   See Figure 4-6b.

5. **Repeat until you've done 10 to 12 reps.**

When you do the dumbbell chest press,

- ✔ **Do** allow your lower back to keep its natural arch so you have a slight gap between your lower back and the bench.

- ✔ **Don't** contort your body in an effort to lift the weight; lift only as much weight as you can handle while maintaining good form.

Variation: Perform this exercise on an incline bench and use less weight than when you perform a flat-bench press. You challenge the upper fibers of the pecs more.

Figure 4-6:
Don't lock
your elbows
at the
top of the
movement.

Incline chest fly

The incline chest fly primarily works your chest muscles, with lots of emphasis on your shoulder muscles. The exercise also places some emphasis on your triceps, although less than many other chest exercises.

Pay special attention to your form if you've had shoulder (especially rotator cuff), elbow, or lower-back injuries.

To perform the incline chest fly,

1. **Incline the bench a few inches.**

   Set the incline at 1 to 5 inches on the bench, depending on the bench.

2. **Holding a dumbbell in each hand, lie on the bench with your feet flat on the floor or on the bench, whichever feels more comfortable to you.**

   Press the weights directly above your chest, palms facing each other. Tuck your chin to your chest to align your neck with the rest of your spine; maintain your natural back posture, neither arched nor flattened. See Figure 4-7a.

3. **Spreading your arms apart so that your elbows travel down and to the sides, lower the weights until your elbows are just below your shoulders.**

4. **Lift the dumbbells back up, maintaining a constant bend in your elbows.**

   Imagine that you have a barrel lying on your chest and you have to keep your arms wide to reach around it. See Figure 4-7b.

5. **Repeat until you've done 10 to 12 reps.**

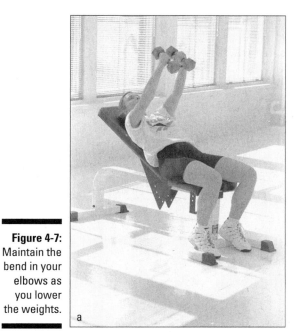 

a   b

Figure 4-7: Maintain the bend in your elbows as you lower the weights.

As you perform the incline chest fly,

- ✔ **Do** feel a stretch in the outer edges of your chest. Hold a moment in the lowered position to feel it even more.

- ✔ **Don't** forget to keep the bend in your elbows as you lower the weights. If your arms are too straight, you place excessive pressure on your elbows and shoulder joints.

- ✔ **Don't** move your elbows any lower than specified, or you risk damaging your shoulder and rotator cuff muscles.

Variation: Do the same exercise on a flat bench. The inclined version emphasizes upper chest fibers, while the flat version calls in the middle and lower fibers as well.

Getting a Great Shoulder Workout

You can strengthen your shoulder muscles through four main types of shoulder movements (although dozen of ways exist). In general, you lift the heaviest weights while *pressing* (straightening your arms up over your head) and the lightest weights while doing *back fly* movements (bending from the hips to align your lift against the pull of gravity).

Shoulder strength is important in the golf swing because the shoulder is the "hinge" that moves your arms through the swing.

As you get started, perform the following exercises in the order that they're listed. From time to time, though, you can vary the order of your exercises to target your weaker muscles first and to provide a variety of stimulation for the muscle group to optimize conditioning. You don't need to include all four types of exercises in each shoulder workout, but you should aim to perform each type on a regular basis so you develop evenly balanced shoulder muscles.

Dumbbell shoulder press

The dumbbell shoulder press targets the top and center of your shoulder muscles. This exercise also works your upper back and triceps. Use caution if you have lower-back, neck, or elbow problems.

Follow these steps to do the dumbbell shoulder press:

1. **Hold a dumbbell in each hand and sit on a bench with back support; plant your feet firmly on the floor about hip-width apart.**

2. **Bend your elbows and raise your upper arms to shoulder height so the dumbbells are at ear level.**

   Pull your abdominals in to create a slight gap between the small of your back and the bench. Place the back of your head against the pad. See Figure 4-8a.

3. **Push the dumbbells up and in until the ends of the dumbbells are nearly touching directly over your head and then lower the dumbbells back to ear level.**

   See Figure 4-8b.

4. **Repeat until you've done 10 to 12 reps.**

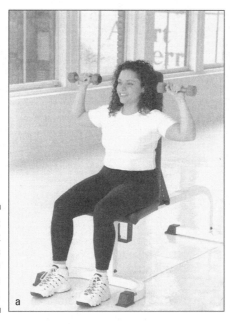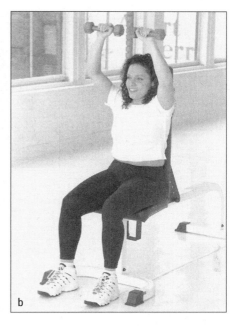

Figure 4-8:
Don't lock
your elbows
at the
top of the
movement.

As you do the dumbbell shoulder press,

- ✔ **Do** stop lowering the dumbbells when your elbows are at or slightly below shoulder level.
- ✔ **Don't** let your back arch significantly off the back support.
- ✔ **Don't** wiggle or squirm around in an effort to press the weights up.

Variation: Do this exercise with your palms facing each other. This position allows your wrists and biceps muscles to help execute the movement.

Lateral raise

The lateral raise works the center of your shoulder muscles. Make sure that you use stellar technique if you have neck or lower-back problems.

Here's how to perform the lateral raise:

1. **Hold a dumbbell in each hand and stand up tall with your feet as wide as your hips.**

   Bend your elbows a little, turn your palms toward each other, and bring the dumbbells together in front of the tops of your thighs. Pull your abdominals in. See Figure 4-9a.

2. **Lift your arms up and out to the side until the dumbbells are just below shoulder height; slowly lower the weights back down.**

   Imagine that you're pouring two pitchers of lemonade on the floor in front of you. See Figure 4-9b.

3. **Repeat until you've done 10 to 12 reps.**

Figure 4-9:
Don't raise the weights above shoulder height.

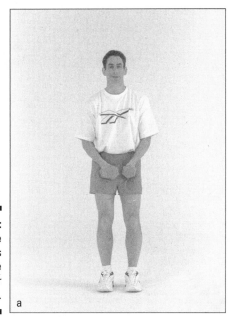

a

Keep your elbows slightly bent.

b

As you do the lateral raise,

- ✔ **Do** lift from the shoulders; in other words, keep your elbows stationary.

- ✔ **Don't** arch your back, lean backward, or rock back and forth to lift the weights.

- ✔ **Don't** raise the weights above shoulder height.

Variation: For an easier exercise, start with your arms bent at a 90-degree angle, your palms facing each other, and the dumbbells in front of your body. Keeping your elbows bent at 90 degrees throughout the motion, lift the weights until your elbows are at shoulder height.

Front raise

The front raise isolates the front portion of your shoulder muscles. Use caution if you have a history of lower-back or neck discomfort.

Here's what you need to know to do the front raise:

1. **Hold a dumbbell in each hand and stand up tall with your feet as wide as your hips.**

   Let your arms hang down at your sides — elbows relaxed and palms facing back. Stand up tall, pull your abdominals in, and relax your knees. See Figure 4-10a.

2. **Raise your right arm up to shoulder height and then lower it back down; repeat with your left arm.**

3. **Continue alternating for 10 to 12 repetitions with each arm.**

   See Figure 4-10b.

Book II

Focusing on Fairway Fitness

Figure 4-10: Don't lift your arm above shoulder height.

a

b

Keep these points in mind as you do the front raise:

- ✔ **Do** keep your elbows slightly bent as you perform the exercise.
- ✔ **Don't** arch, lean back, or wiggle around in an effort to lift the weight.
- ✔ **Don't** lift your arm above shoulder height.

Variation: For more of a challenge, do all your reps with one arm and then the other. You can also perform the front raise sitting on a bench with a back support; this position removes *any* possibility of cheating!

Back delt fly

The back delt fly is an excellent move for strengthening the back of the shoulders and upper back and for improving your posture.

To perform the back delt fly,

1. **Hold a dumbbell in each hand and sit on the edge of a bench.**

   Lean forward from your hips so your upper back is flat and above parallel to the floor (if you can, support your chest against your knees). Let your arms hang down so your palms are facing each other with the weights behind your calves and directly under your knees. Pull your chin back and in and draw your abdominals inward. See Figure 4-11a.

2. **Raise your arms up and out to the sides, bending your elbows a few inches as you go until your elbows are level with your shoulders.**

   Squeeze your shoulder blades together as you lift. Slowly lower your arms back down. See Figure 4-11b.

3. **Repeat until you've done 10 to 12 reps.**

As you perform the back delt fly,

- ✔ **Do** keep your chin tilted slightly toward your chest throughout the motion so your head and neck don't drop forward.
- ✔ **Do** lean forward from your hips instead of rounding your back.
- ✔ **Don't** allow the rest of your body to move as you do the exercise.

Variation: Use the same starting position, except orient your palms backward. As you lift the weights, you need to bend your elbows more than in the basic version.

Book II

Focusing on Fairway Fitness

Figure 4-11:
Keep the rest of your body still as you perform the exercise.

External rotation

External rotation focuses on your rotator cuff muscles, but these exercises also work your shoulder muscles.

To perform the external rotation,

1. **Holding a dumbbell in your right hand, lie on the floor on your left side.**

   Bend your right elbow to a 90-degree angle and tuck it firmly against your side so your palm faces downward. Pull your abdominals in. Bend your left elbow and rest the side of your head in your left hand or lie on your out-stretched left arm.

2. **Keeping your right elbow glued to your side, raise your right hand as far as you comfortably can (the distance depends on your flexibility); slowly lower the weight back toward the floor.**

   See Figure 4-12.

3. **Repeat until you've done 10 to 12 reps.**

4. **Flip onto your right side and repeat all steps with your left arm.**

Figure 4-12:
Imagine
that your
shoulder is
the hinge of
a door that's
opening and
closing.

As you perform the external rotation,

✔ **Do** perform the exercise gently and smoothly.

✔ **Don't** tighten up your neck and face.

✔ **Don't** throw the weight up.

✔ **Don't** force the weight farther than your natural flexibility allows.

Variation: For a more difficult option, hold a weight in each hand and stand with your feet as wide as your hips. Bend your elbows and raise your arms up to shoulder height (in the classic stick-'em-up position). Keeping your elbows still, rotate your forearms down until your palms are facing behind you and then rotate back up to the start.

Targeting Your Arms

Your arm muscles are smaller than your chest, back, and shoulder muscles, so you can spend less time training them and still get great results. If your goal is to increase your arm strength and develop some tone, one to three sets per arm muscle will suffice. The goal for you, as a golfer, is to build strength, not bulk, and to maintain or increase your flexibility.

Give your biceps and triceps equal time. Chances are, you'll enjoy training one of these muscle groups better than the other, but if one of them is disproportionately stronger than the other, you're more prone to elbow injuries.

Concentration curl

The concentration curl is especially good for targeting your biceps and excluding all other muscles. Be careful if you've had elbow injuries or are prone to lower-back discomfort.

Here's how to do the concentration curl:

1. **Hold a dumbbell in your right hand, and sit on the edge of a bench or a chair with your feet a few inches wider than your hips.**

   Lean forward from your hips and place your right elbow against the inside of your right thigh, just behind your knee. The weight should hang down near the inside of your ankle. Place your left palm on top of your left thigh. See Figure 4-13a.

2. **Bend your arm and curl the dumbbell almost up to your shoulder (see Figure 4-13b); straighten your arm to lower the weight back down.**

3. **Repeat until you've done 10 to 12 reps.**

4. **Repeat all steps with the other arm.**

Book II

Focusing on Fairway Fitness

Figure 4-13: Bend forward from your hips.

a

b

When you do the concentration curl

- ✔ **Do** bend forward from your hips instead of rounding your lower back to lean forward.
- ✔ **Don't** lean away from your arm as you lift the weight up to help get better leverage. (Hey, that's cheating!)

Variation: Hold a dumbbell in one hand. Stand alongside a flat bench, lean over, and place your other hand on top of bench. Let the arm holding the weight hang straight down to the floor. Bend your elbow so the weight moves up and in toward your armpit, and then slowly lower it back down.

Triceps kickback

The triceps kickback works — surprise! — your triceps. Use caution if you have elbow or lower-back problems.

To perform the triceps kickback,

1. **Hold a dumbbell in your right hand, and stand next to the long side of your bench.**

   Lean forward at the hips until your upper body is at a 45-degree angle to the floor, and place your free hand on top of the bench for support. Bend your right elbow so your upper arm is parallel to the floor, your forearm is perpendicular to the floor, and your palm faces in (see Figure 4-14a). Keep your elbow close to your waist. Pull your abdominals in and relax your knees.

2. **Keeping your upper arm still, straighten your arm behind you until the end of the dumbbell is pointing down (see Figure 4-14b).**

   Slowly bend your arm to lower the weight.

3. **Repeat until you've done 10 to 12 reps with each arm.**

Keep these points in mind as you do the triceps kickback:

- ✔ **Do** keep your abdominals pulled in and your knees relaxed to protect your lower back.
- ✔ **Don't** lock your elbow at the top of the movement; do straighten your arm but keep your elbow relaxed.
- ✔ **Don't** allow your upper arm to move or your shoulder to drop below waist level.

Variation: As you straighten your arm, twist it so your palm faces up at the top of the movement. Doing so makes the exercise more difficult.

Figure 4-14: Don't let your upper arm move or your shoulder drop below waist level.

a   b

Bench dip

The bench dip is one of the few triceps exercises that strengthen other muscles, too — in this case, the shoulders and chest. Be careful if you have wrist, elbow, or shoulder problems.

Here's how to perform the bench dip:

1. **Sit on the edge of a bench with your legs together and straight in front of you, pointing your toes upward.**

   Keeping your elbows relaxed, straighten your arms, place your hands so you can grip the underside of the bench on either side of your hips, and slide your butt just off the front of the bench so your upper body is pointing straight down (see Figure 4-15a). Keep your abdominals pulled in and your head centered between your shoulders.

2. **Bend your elbows and lower your body in a straight line; when your upper arms are parallel to the floor, push yourself back up.**

   See Figure 4-15b.

3. **Repeat until you've done 10 to 12 reps.**

Figure 4-15:
Don't lower
yourself
past the
point at
which your
upper arms
are parallel
to the floor.

We know this exercise is tough. Keep these pointers in mind:

- ✔ **Do** try to keep your wrists straight rather than bent backward.

- ✔ **Do** keep your hips and back (as you lower) as close to the bench throughout the motion.

- ✔ **Don't** simply thrust your hips up and down, a common mistake among beginners. Make sure that your elbows are moving.

- ✔ **Don't** lower yourself past the point at which your upper arms are parallel to the floor.

Variation: Instead of extending your legs out in front of you, bend your knees at a right angle so you're positioned as if you're sitting in a chair for an easier alternative.

Wrist curl and reverse wrist curl

The wrist curl and reverse wrist curl are great for strengthening your wrist muscles. Strong wrists allow you to maintain clubhead speed through impact, especially through deep rough. You also have better control of the clubface through the swing when your wrists are strong. Be careful while performing this exercise if you've had wrist or elbow problems.

Here's how to do the wrist curl:

1. **Hold a weight in your right hand with an underhand grip and sit on the edge of your bench with your knees as wide as your hips.**

   Lean slightly forward, and place your entire forearm on top of your thigh so your hand hangs over the edge of your knee. Clasp your left palm over your wrist to hold it steady (see Figure 4-16a).

2. **Curl your wrist up so the dumbbell moves toward your forearm and then lower the weight back down.**

3. **Repeat until you've done 10 to 12 reps with each wrist.**

Here's how to do the reverse wrist curl:

1. **Turn your palm down and secure your wrist in place with your other hand.**

   Bend your wrist up to raise the dumbbell to thigh height (see Figure 4-16b), and then lower the weight back down. (*Hint:* You may need slightly less weight to do the reverse wrist curl.)

2. **Repeat until you've done 10 to 12 reps with each wrist.**

As you curl your wrist

- ✔ **Do** curl straight up; try to avoid moving the weight to the side.
- ✔ **Don't** let your forearm lift off your thigh.

Variation: If you have weak wrists and find this exercise difficult, simply move the weight up and down a shorter distance.

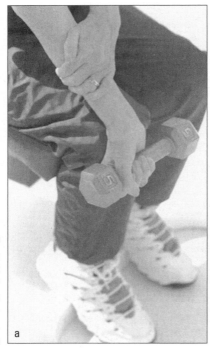

Figure 4-16:
Don't
let your
forearm
lift off your
thigh.

a   b

Working Out the Lower Body

In general, work your large lower-body muscles before moving on to your small ones. The only exception to this rule is if you specifically want to target a smaller muscle that's lagging far behind in its strength and is creating a too noticeable weak link. If that's the case, switch your exercise order around so you target the weakest muscle when it's fresh.

The lower body is the most important area to work out in relation to the golf swing. Your buttocks, upper legs, and lower legs are the frame for the swing, so these muscles have to be strong. They also start the downswing and provide the power for the golf swing.

Expect to feel sore and walk a little stiffly for a day or two after your first few lower-body workouts. Of course, any muscle that's new to weight training is likely to be sore after the first few sessions, but leg muscles seem particularly prone to this phenomenon. Start out with just your own body weight or light weights; otherwise, you may find yourself walking stiffly or wincing with discomfort when you get up from the breakfast table.

Squat

In addition to strengthening your butt muscles, the squat also does a good job of working your quadriceps and hamstrings. If you have hip, knee, or lower-back problems, you may want to try the variation.

Follow these steps to perform squats:

1. **Hold a dumbbell in each hand; stand with your feet as wide as your hips and with your weight slightly back on your heels.**

   Pull your abdominals in and stand up tall with square shoulders. See Figure 4-17a.

2. **Sit back and down, as if you're sitting into a chair; lower as far as you can without leaning your upper body more than a few inches forward.**

   Don't lower any farther than the point at which your thighs are parallel to the floor, and don't allow your knees to shoot out in front of your toes.

3. **When you feel your upper body fold forward over your thighs, straighten your legs and stand back up.**

   Take care not to lock your knees at the top of the movement. See Figure 4-17b.

4. **Repeat until you've done 10 to 12 reps.**

Figure 4-17: Don't shift your body weight forward so that your heels lift up off the floor.

a

b

You can easily do this exercise the wrong way, so here's our list of don'ts to make sure you perform squats correctly:

- ✔ **Don't** allow your knees to travel beyond your toes. We know we made this point before, but it bears repeating.
- ✔ **Don't** look down. Your body tends to follow your eyes, so if you're staring at the ground, you're more likely to fall forward. Instead, keep your head up and your eyes focused on an object directly in front of you.
- ✔ **Don't** shift your body weight forward so your heels lift up off the floor. When you push back up to the standing position, concentrate on pushing through your heels.
- ✔ **Don't** arch your back as you stand back up.

Variation: If you have trouble balancing or completing at least eight repetitions of the squat with good form, skip the weights. Instead, place your hands on your hips or the tops of your thighs as you do the exercise.

Lunge

The lunge is a great overall lower-body exercise: It strengthens your butt, quadriceps, hamstrings, and calves.

To perform the lunge,

1. **Stand with your feet as wide as your hips and your weight back a little on your heels, and place your hands on your hips.**

   Pull your abdominals in and stand up tall with square shoulders. See Figure 4-18a.

2. **Lift your right toe slightly and, leading with your heel, step your right foot forward an elongated stride's length, as if you're trying to step over a crack in the sidewalk.**

3. **As your foot touches the floor, bend both knees until your right thigh is parallel to the floor and your left thigh is perpendicular to it.**

   Your left heel will lift off the floor.

4. **Press off the ball of your foot and step back to the standing position.**

   See Figure 4-18b.

5. **Repeat until you've done 10 to 12 reps with each leg.**

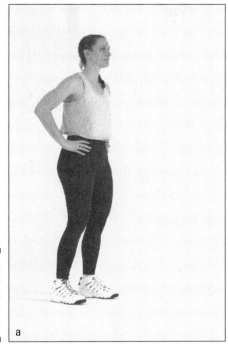

Figure 4-18: Keep your eyes focused ahead.

a   b

Don't let your knee shoot past your toes.

Follow these pointers when you do lunges:

✔ **Do** keep your eyes focused ahead; when you look down, you tend to fall forward.

✔ **Don't** step too far forward or you'll have trouble balancing.

✔ **Don't** lean forward or allow your front knee to travel past your toes.

Variation: For a more difficult exercise, hold a dumbbell in each hand with your arms down at your sides, or place a barbell behind your neck and across your shoulders.

Standing calf raise

The standing calf raise homes in on your calf muscles. Here's what you need to know to do this exercise:

1. **Stand on the edge of a step with the balls of your feet firmly planted on the step and your heels hanging over the edge.**

   If you have a step aerobics platform, place two sets of risers underneath the platform. Stand tall and rest your hands against a wall or a sturdy object for balance. Pull your abdominals in.

2. **Raise your heels a few inches above the edge of the step so you're on your tiptoes (see Figure 4-19a); hold the position for a moment and then lower your heels back down.**

   Lower your heels below the step in order to stretch your calf muscles. See Figure 4-19b.

3. **Repeat until you've done 10 to 12 reps.**

Figure 4-19: Lift as high as you can onto your toes.

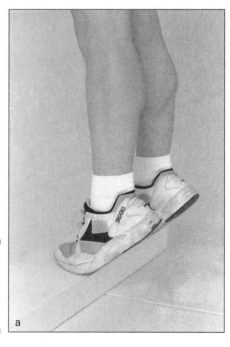 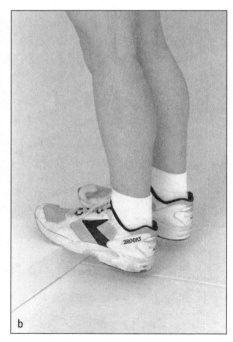

Keep these two do's in mind as you perform the standing calf raise:

- ✔ **Do** lift as high as you can on your toes.
- ✔ **Do** lower your heels down as much as your ankle flexibility allows.

Variation: Holding a dumbbell in one hand adds resistance to this exercise and also forces you to balance more because you can't hold onto something with both hands for stability.

Chapter 5

Calming Your Mind and Body for Better Golf

· ·

In This Chapter

▶ Controlling harmful stress with relaxation techniques

▶ Letting your breathing work for you

· ·

*Y*our body is strong and your clubs are willing, but you still have to contend with the mental aspect of golf. So many things can go wrong in the game of golf that you can easily start thinking negatively:

✔ "How will I mess up this *next* shot?"

✔ "This is embarrassing!"

✔ "This course is unfair."

✔ "I'll just hit it and hope for the best."

Keeping your cool can sometimes be your biggest challenge. Even the world's best players have "one of those days." Fortunately, this chapter discusses some tried-and-true ways to calm down, harness your inner mental strength, and cope with the situation at hand. (Chapter 2 of Book V covers more about the mental aspects of golf.)

Using Yoga for Mental Balance

Life in general is inherently stressful. And every golfer has his or her share of stressful moments on the tee and green. The question is whether that stress is helping you or hurting you.

Psychologists distinguish between *distress* (bad stress) and *eustress* (good stress). Many golfers have found that yoga can help minimize bad stress and maximize good, life-enhancing stress. Bad stress creates an imbalance in the body and the mind, causing you to tense your muscles and breathe in a rapid, shallow manner. Under stress, your adrenal glands work overtime and your blood becomes depleted of oxygen, a situation that starves your cells. Constant stress triggers the fight-or-flight response, putting you in a chronic state of alertness that's extremely demanding on your body's energies.

The good news is that you can control your negative stress through various yoga relaxation techniques. But don't get too excited. Relaxation isn't quite the same as doing nothing. Often, when you believe you're doing nothing, you're actually busy contracting unused muscles quite unconsciously. Relaxation is a conscious endeavor that lies somewhere between effort and noneffort. To truly relax, you have to understand and practice the skill.

Relaxation doesn't require any gadgets, but you may want to try the following:

✓ **Practice in a quiet environment where you're unlikely to be disturbed by others or the telephone.**

✓ **Try placing a small pillow under your head and a large one under your knees for support and comfort in the supine, or lying, positions.** Alternatively, fold up a blanket.

✓ **Ensure that your body stays warm.** If necessary, heat the room first or cover yourself with a blanket. Particularly avoid lying on a cold floor, which isn't good for your kidneys.

✓ **Don't practice relaxation techniques on a full stomach.**

Deep relaxation: The corpse posture

The simplest and yet the most difficult of all yoga postures is the corpse posture, also widely known as the dead posture. This posture is the simplest because you don't have to use any part of your body at all, and it's the most difficult precisely because you're asked to do nothing whatsoever with your limbs. The corpse posture is an exercise in mind over matter.

Here's how you do the corpse posture:

1. **Lie flat on your back, with your arms stretched out and relaxed by your sides, palms up (or whatever feels most comfortable).**

   Place a small pillow or folded blanket under your head if you need one and another large one under your knees for added comfort.

2. **Close your eyes.**

   Check out Figure 5-1 for a look at the corpse posture.

Ending relaxation peacefully

Allowing relaxation to end on its own is best — your body knows when it has benefited sufficiently and naturally brings you out of relaxation. However, if you have only a limited time for an exercise, set your mental clock to 15, 20, or however many minutes after closing your eyes as part of your intention.

If you need to have a sound to remind you to return to ordinary waking consciousness, make sure that your wristwatch or clock isn't so loud that it startles you and provokes a heavy surge of adrenaline.

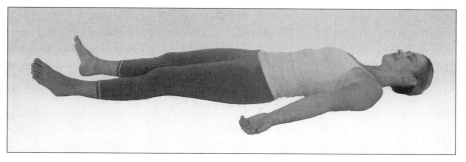

Figure 5-1: The corpse is the most popular of all yoga postures.

3. **Form a clear intention to relax.**

    Some people find picturing themselves lying in white sand on a sunny beach helpful.

4. **Take a couple of deep breaths, lengthening exhalation.**

5. **Contract the muscles in your feet for a couple of seconds and then consciously relax them.**

    Do the same with the muscles in your calves, upper legs, buttocks, abdomen, chest, back, hands, forearms, upper arms, shoulders, neck, and face.

6. **Periodically scan all your muscles from your feet to your face to check that they're relaxed.**

    You can often detect subtle tension around the eyes and the scalp muscles. Also relax your mouth and tongue.

7. **Focus on the growing bodily sensation of no tension and let your breath be free.**

8. **At the end of the session, before opening your eyes, form the intention to keep the relaxed feeling for as long as possible.**

9. **Open your eyes, stretch lazily, and get up slowly.**

Practice 10 to 30 minutes; the longer the duration, the better. But watch out! Relaxing for too long can make you drowsy.

Afternoon delight

The following exercise is a great stress-buster for golfers. You can practice it at home or in a quiet place at the office. Just make sure you can't be interrupted. For this exercise, you need a sturdy chair, one or two blankets, and a towel. Allow five to ten minutes.

1. **Lie on your back and put your feet up on the chair, which should face you (see Figure 5-2).**

   Make sure that your legs and back are comfortable. Your legs should be 15 to 18 inches apart. You can also put your legs and feet up on the edge of a bed. If none of the feet-up positions feels good, just lie on your back with your legs bent and feet placed on the floor. If the back of your head isn't flat on the floor, and your neck and throat feel tense, or if your chin is pushed up toward the ceiling, raise your head slightly on a folded blanket or firm, flat cushion to feel comfortable.

Figure 5-2:
Lie on your back and put your feet on a chair.

2. **Cover your body from the neck down with one of the blankets.**

   Don't let your body cool down too quickly, which can not only feel uncomfortable and interfere with your relaxation but also cramp your muscles and harm your kidneys.

3. **Place the towel folded lengthwise over your eyes.**

4. **Rest for a few moments and get used to the position.**

5. **Visualize a large balloon in your stomach.**

   As you inhale through your nose, expand the imaginary balloon in all directions. As you exhale through your nose, release the air from the balloon. Repeat this step several times until it becomes easy for you.

6. **Inhale freely and begin to make your exhalation longer and longer.**

   Think of it as "Inhale freely, exhale forever."

7. **Repeat Step 6 at least 30 times.**

8. **When you finish the exercise, allow your breathing to return to normal and rest for a minute or so, enjoying the relaxed feeling.**

   Don't rush getting up.

Magic triangles

The following relaxation technique uses your power of imagination. If you can picture things easily in your mind (like that ever-elusive hole-in-one), you may find the exercise enjoyable and refreshing. For this exercise, you need a chair and a blanket (if necessary). Allow five minutes.

1. **Sit up tall in a chair, with your feet on the floor and comfortably apart and your hands resting on top of your knees as shown in Figure 5-3.**

   If your feet aren't comfortably touching the floor, fold up the blanket and place it under your feet for support.

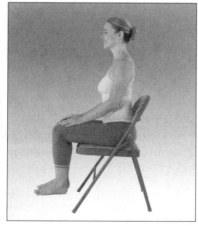

Figure 5-3:
Sit with your feet on the floor and your hands on your knees.

2. **Breathe through your nose, but allow your breath to move freely.**

3. **Close your eyes and focus your attention on the middle of your forehead, just above the level of your eyebrows.**

   Make sure that you don't crinkle your forehead or squint your eyes.

4. **Visualize as vividly as possible a triangle connecting the forehead point and the palms of both hands.**

   Register (but don't think about) any sensations or colors that appear on your mental screen while you hold the triangle in your mind. Do this visualization for eight to ten breaths and then dissolve the triangle.

5. **Visualize a triangle formed by your navel and the big toes of your feet.**

   Retain this image for 10 to 12 breaths. If any part of the mental triangle is difficult to connect, keep focusing on that part until the triangle fully forms.

6. **Keeping your eyes closed, visualize again the first triangle formed between your forehead and your two palms and then simultaneously visualize the second triangle (navel to toes).**

   This final step is more challenging. Picture both triangles together for 12 to 15 breaths and then dissolve them.

Breathing Your Way to a Better Mental State

In a given day, you take between 20,000 and 30,000 breaths. Most likely, barring any respiratory problems, you're barely aware of your breathing. Although the automatic nature of breathing is part of the body's machinery that keeps you alive, having breathing occur automatically isn't necessarily to your advantage; automatic doesn't always mean optimal. In fact, most people's breathing habits are quite poor. Poor breathing is known to cause and increase stress; stress shortens your breath and increases your level of anxiety (and most times, you don't need any help increasing your anxiety on the course).

You can help alleviate stress through the simple practice of *yogic breathing,* or breath control. Among other things, proper breathing loads your blood with oxygen, which nourishes and repairs your body's cells and maintains your health at the most desirable level. Shallow breathing, which is common, doesn't oxygenate the ten pints of blood circulating in your arteries and veins very efficiently. Consequently, toxins accumulate in the cells. Before you know it, you feel mentally sluggish and emotionally down. When that happens, your golf game is likely to suffer too.

Think about how you breathe — or don't breathe — while you're playing golf. Do you hold your breath or breathe faster while attempting a tough shot? Do you hyperventilate? The way you breathe affects the rhythm and tension of your swing.

Reaping the benefits of high-quality breaths

Before you jump right in and make drastic changes to your method of breathing, take a few minutes to assess your current breathing style. Check your breathing by asking yourself the following questions:

Book II

Focusing on Fairway Fitness

✔ Is my breathing shallow (my abdomen and chest barely move when I fill my lungs with air)?

✔ Do I often breathe erratically (my breathing rhythm isn't harmonious)?

✔ Do I easily get out of breath?

✔ Is my breathing labored at times?

✔ Do I hold my breath in stressful situations?

✔ Do I generally breathe too fast?

If your answer to any of these questions is "Yes," you make an ideal candidate for breath control. Even if you didn't answer "Yes," practicing conscious breathing still benefits your mind and body.

In addition to relaxing the body and calming the mind, regardless of whether you're playing golf, controlled breathing techniques offer an entire spectrum of other benefits that work like insurance, protecting your investment in a longer and healthier life. Here are some important advantages of controlled breathing:

✔ It uses muscles that automatically help improve your posture, preventing the stiff, slumped carriage characteristic of many older people. As we note throughout this book, proper posture is key for a solid golf swing.

✔ It tones your abdominal area. Head to Chapter 3 of Book II for information on how a strong core helps your golf game.

✔ It reduces your levels of tension and anxiety. Tension and anxiety keep you from playing in the subconscious; the more you can reduce these stress levels, the more confident you are in your golf game. See Chapter 2 of Book V for more on the mental golf game.

Relaxing with a couple of deep breaths

Think about the many times you've heard someone say, "Now just take a couple of deep breaths and relax." This recommendation is so popular because it really works! Pain clinics across the country use breathing exercises for pain control. Childbirth preparation courses teach yoga-related breathing techniques to both parents to aid the birthing process. Golfers, too, can benefit from controlled breathing exercises.

Yogic breathing is like texting your nervous system with the message to relax. One easy way to experience the effect of simple breathing is to try the following exercise:

1. **Sit comfortably in your chair.**

2. **Close your eyes and visualize a swan gliding peacefully across a crystal-clear lake.**

3. **Now, like the swan, let your breath flow along in a long, smooth, and peaceful movement, ideally through your nose.**

   If your nose is plugged up, try to breathe through your nose and mouth, or just through your mouth.

4. **Extend your breathing to its comfortable maximum for 20 rounds; then gradually let your breathing return to normal.**

5. **Afterward, take a few moments to sit with your eyes closed and notice the difference in how you feel overall.**

   Can you imagine how relaxed and calm you'd feel after 10 to 15 minutes of conscious yogic breathing?

Breathing through your nose

Yogic breathing typically occurs through the nose, both during inhalation and exhalation. We know at least two good reasons for breathing through the nose:

- It slows down the breath because you're breathing through two small openings rather than the one big opening in your mouth.

- The air is hygienically filtered and warmed by the nasal passages. Even the purest air contains dust particles.

Practicing safe yogic breathing

As you look forward to the calming power of breath control, take time to reflect on a few safety tips that can help you enjoy your experience.

✔ If you have problems with your lungs (such as a cold or asthma), or if you have a heart disease, consult your physician first before embarking on breath control.

✔ Don't practice breathing exercises when the air is too cold or too hot.

✔ Avoid practicing in polluted air.

✔ Don't strain your breathing — remain relaxed while doing the breathing exercises.

✔ Don't overdo the number of repetitions. Stay within our guidelines for each exercise.

✔ Don't wear any constricting pants or belts.

What if I can't breathe through my nose?

Some folks suffer from various physiological conditions that prevent them from breathing through their noses. If you have difficulty breathing when lying down, try sitting up. The time of day can also make a difference in your ability to breathe. For example, you may be more congested or exposed to more allergens in the morning than in the afternoon. You're probably already aware of when your breathing is better.

If you're still not sure how to settle on a comfortable breathing method, first try inhaling through your nose and exhaling through your mouth; if that doesn't help, just breathe through your mouth.

How about breathing through my nose all the time?

Many Americans participate in more than one kind of physical activity or exercise discipline. Each has its own guidelines and rules for breathing, which we suggest you follow. For example, the majority of aerobic activities — running, walking, weight lifting, and so on — recommend that you inhale through the nose and exhale through the mouth. The reason: You need to move a lot of air quickly in and out of your lungs. And breathing only through the nose while swimming can be very dangerous. In fact, we don't recommend underwater breath control exercises unless you enjoy a snootful of water making its way to your lungs.

Appreciating the complete yogic breath

Most people are either shallow chest breathers or shallow belly breathers. Yogic breathing incorporates a complete breath that expands both the chest and the abdomen on inhalation either from the chest down or the abdomen up. Both are valid techniques. (Figures 5-5 and 5-6 later in the chapter show you each of these techniques.)

If shallow or erratic breathing puts your well-being at risk, the complete yogic breath is your ticket to excellent physical and mental health. If you do no other yoga exercise, the complete yoga breath can still be of invaluable benefit to you, on the course and off.

Yogic breathing involves breathing much more deeply than usual, which in turn brings more oxygen into your system. Don't be surprised if you feel a little lightheaded or even dizzy in the beginning. If this happens during your practice, just rest for a few minutes or lie down until you feel like moving ahead.

Belly breathing

Before you jump into practicing the complete yogic breath, try out this exercise:

1. **Lie flat on your back and place one hand on your chest and the other on your abdomen as in Figure 5-4.**

   Place a small pillow or folded blanket under your head if you have tension in your neck or if your chin tilts upward. Place a large pillow under your knees if your back is uncomfortable.

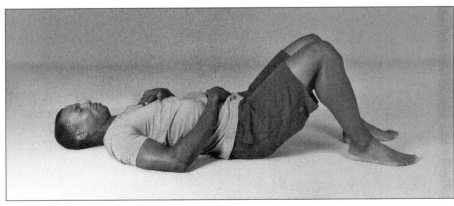

Figure 5-4:
Your hand position helps you detect motion during belly breathing.

2. **Take 15 to 20 slow, deep breaths.**

   During inhalation, expand your abdomen; during exhalation, contract your abdomen but keep your chest as motionless as possible. Your hands act as motion detectors.

3. **Pause for a couple of seconds between inhalation and exhalation, keeping your throat soft.**

Belly-to-chest breathing

In belly-to-chest breathing, you really exercise your chest, diaphragm, and lungs and treat your body with oodles of oxygen. When you're done, your cells are humming with energy, and your brain is very grateful for the extra boost. You can use this form of breathing whenever you feel so inclined throughout the day, whether on the course or off. You don't necessarily have to lie down as we describe in the following exercise. You can be seated or even walking. After practicing this technique for a while, you may find that it becomes second nature to you.

1. **Lie flat on your back, with your knees bent and your feet on the floor at hip width, and relax.**

   Place a small pillow or folded blanket under your head if you have tension in your neck or if your chin tilts upward. Place a large pillow under your knees if your back is uncomfortable.

2. **Inhale while expanding your abdomen, your ribs, and then your chest, as shown in Figure 5-5a.**

   Pause for a couple of seconds.

3. **Exhale while releasing your chest and shoulder muscles, gently and continuously contracting or drawing your abdomen in as shown in Figure 5-5b.**

   Pause again for a couple of seconds.

4. **Repeat Steps 2 and 3 six to twelve times.**

To help you experience this exercise, keep your eyes closed. Place your hands on your abdomen and feel it expand as you inhale.

Chest-to-belly breathing

Classically, yoga teachers taught yogic breathing from the abdomen up on inhalation (see the preceding section). This method works very well for many people. However, in the 1960s, yoga masters began to adapt the traditional yogic breathing to the needs of Western students, who sit and bend forward for most of the day in cars, at tables and desks, and in front of computers and TVs.

Chest-to-belly breathing emphasizes arching the spine and the upper back to compensate for all this bending forward throughout the day. Chest-to-belly breathing is also an excellent energizer in the morning; you can even do it before you hop out of bed. We don't recommend this exercise late at night, though, because it's likely to keep you awake.

Book II

Focusing on Fairway Fitness

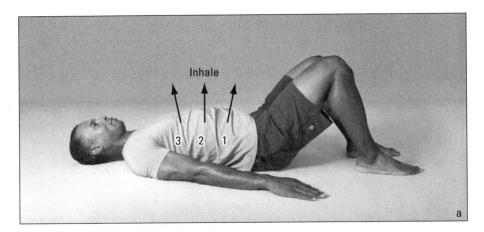

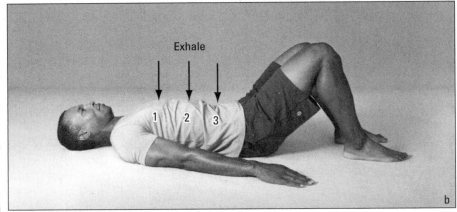

Figure 5-5:
The classic
yoga breath.

The following exercise complements the belly-to-chest breathing we cover in the preceding section. As with that technique, you can practice the following exercise lying down, seated, or even while walking to the next hole.

1. **Lie flat on your back, with your knees bent and your feet on the floor at hip width, and relax.**

   Place a small pillow or folded blanket under your head if you have tension in your neck or if your chin tilts upward. Place a large pillow under your knees if your back is uncomfortable.

2. **Inhale while expanding your chest from the top down and continuing this movement downward into your belly as shown in Figure 5-6a.**

   Pause for a couple of seconds.

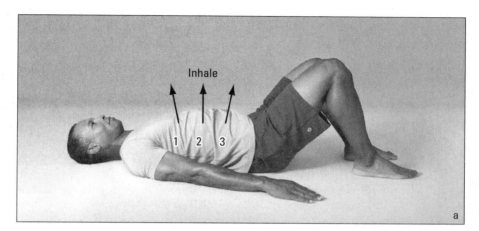

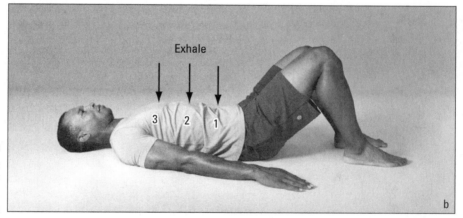

Figure 5-6:
The new yoga breath.

3. **Exhale while gently contracting and drawing your belly inward, starting just below the navel as in Figure 5-6b.**

   Pause for a couple of seconds.

4. **Repeat Steps 2 and 3 six to twelve times.**

Alternate nostril breathing

Newsflash: Humans don't breathe evenly through both nostrils. In a two-to-three-hour cycle, the nostrils become alternately dominant. It appears that left-nostril breathing is particularly connected with functions of the left cerebral hemisphere (such as verbal skills), and right-nostril breathing seems to connect more with the right hemisphere (such as spatial performance).

The following steps help you tackle basic *alternate nostril breathing*:

1. **Sit comfortably on a chair with your back straight.**

2. **Check which nostril has the most air flowing through it and begin alternative breathing with the open nostril.**

   If both are equally open, all the better. In that case, begin with the left nostril.

   You can check which nostril is dominant simply by breathing through one nostril and then the other and comparing the two flows.

3. **Place your right hand so your thumb is on the right nostril and the little and ring fingers are on the left nostril, with the index and middle fingers tucked against the ball of the thumb.**

4. **Close the blocked nostril and, mentally counting to five, inhale gently but fully through the open nostril — don't strain (see Figure 5-7).**

5. **Open the blocked nostril, close the other nostril, and exhale, again mentally counting to five.**

6. **Inhale through the same nostril to the count of five, and exhale through the opposite nostril, repeating 10 to 15 times.**

As your lung capacity improves, you can make your inhalations and exhalations longer, but never force the breath. Gradually increase the overall duration of the exercise from, say, 3 minutes to 15 minutes.

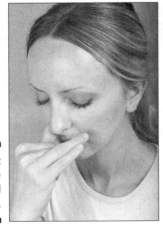

Figure 5-7:
Alternate
nostril
breathing.

Book III

Playing Golf: The Swing and the Short Game

"The book said I should place the ball opposite my left armpit. So I put it in my right armpit."

In this book . . .

How can the golf swing, something that takes a little over one second to perform, be so complicated to learn? Do you need to go back to school and study theoretical physics? No. Just enroll here, and we'll make it easy for you.

In this book we show you how to swing a golf club the simple, effective way. This book gives you pointers on how to build your swing and then how to do everything from knocking your drive off the opening tee to hitting bunker shots, pitches, chips, and putts. Of course, no game would be complete without a masterful short game, and this book discusses short-game strategies that can help you take your game to the next level.

Here are the contents of Book III at a glance.

Chapter 1

Understanding Swing Basics

- -

In This Chapter

▶ Examining different types of swings

▶ Preparing to get the ball airborne

▶ Achieving the correct position to create your swing

▶ Making a full, effective swing

- -

As the great golf expert Duke Ellington once said, "It don't mean a thing if you ain't got that swing." You can be the most stylish-looking golfer in the world, swinging the most expensive driver at the most exclusive country club, but without a sound fundamental swing, you're on the A-train to nowhere. This chapter helps you get into the swing of golf.

Making Sense of the Golf Swing

What is a golf swing? That's a very good question, one that has different answers for different people. For most folks, a golf swing means "body parts moving in an undignified manner."

In simple terms, though, a *golf swing* is a (hopefully) coordinated, balanced movement of the whole body around a fixed pivot point. If you do it correctly, this motion swings the club up, around, and down so that it strikes the ball with an accelerating blow on the center of the clubface.

Balance is the key to this whole swing thing. You can't play golf with consistency if at any time during your swing, you fall over. In contrast, when your swing consists of a simple pivot around a fixed point, the clubhead strikes the ball on the same downward path and somewhere near the center of the clubface every time. Bingo!

You're probably wondering where this fixed point in your body is. Well, it isn't your head. The idea that you must keep your head perfectly still throughout the swing is a myth (see the later sidebar "The myth of 'keep your head down'").

The fixed point in your golf swing should be in the middle of your chest, about 3 inches below the spot where your collarbones meet, as shown in Figure 1-1. Your swing rotates around that point. If you get that pivot point correct, your head swivels a little bit as you turn back and then through on your shots. If your head moves like Linda Blair's did in *The Exorcist,* you may have a career in the circus, but not in golf.

Your "fixed point" is 3 inches below the middle of your collarbones.

Your head swivels to the right as you swing back . . .

then through . . .

all the way to the finish.

Figure 1-1:
The proper swing pivot point.

Looking at Different Strokes

You can swing the club effectively in many ways. For example, there are long swings and short swings. Imagine that you've backed into a giant clock. Your head is just below the center of the clock. If, at the top of your swing, your hands are at 9:00 and the clubhead is at 3:00, you're in the standard position. The shaft is parallel to the ground. This setup is the standard, medium-length swing.

At the top of Jamie Sadlowski's much longer swing, his hands are at 12:00, and the clubhead is approaching 5:00. Other swings have a shorter arc. John Cook succeeded on the PGA Tour with a short swing. His hands go to only 8:00, and the clubhead goes to 1:00. Adam Scott stops short of parallel because he feels that his swing gets *loose* — more erratic — if he goes farther. Physical constraints dictate the fullness and length of your swing; the distance the club travels is unimportant. Any of these swings can work for a particular golfer, depending on his or her training, physique, and even personality.

Golf swings differ in other ways, too.

- ✔ Some players swing the club more around their bodies — the way you'd swing a baseball bat.
- ✔ Others rely more on their hands and arms to generate clubhead speed.
- ✔ Still others place that same emphasis on twisting and untwisting the body.

Physique and flexibility play a major role in how you swing a golf club. If you're short, you have a *flatter* swing — more around your body — because your back is closer to perpendicular at *address* (the motionless position as you stand ready to hit the ball). If you're tall, you either use longer clubs or bend more from the waist at address. Most tall players develop upright swings.

 The left arm always swings about 90 degrees to the angle of the spine. Stand straight up and put your left arm straight out in front of you. Now start bending at the waist. See how your arm lowers? It's staying 90 degrees to your back as you bend downward.

Book III

Playing Golf: The Swing and the Short Game

Getting the Ball in the Air

Although you can swing a golf club in many ways, all good swings have the same goals:

- ✔ You want to hit the ball.
- ✔ You want to get the ball up in the air and moving forward.
- ✔ You want to hit the ball a long way.

- You want to hit the ball toward your target.
- You want to hit the ball a long way toward your target while your friends are watching.
- You become obsessed, just like the rest of us.

Okay, maybe that last one shouldn't exactly be a goal, but if you spend much time at all playing golf, you may find yourself fixating on your ball's flight (or lack thereof). Lucky for you, the following sections give you the lowdown on getting the ball off the ground and moving in the right direction.

Hitting the ball

You'd think hitting the ball would be easy. But golf isn't tennis or baseball, where you can react to a moving ball. In golf, the ball just sits there and waits, beckoning you to make it go somewhere.

Here's your first thought: "I won't turn my body too much; I'll just hit the thing with my hands." That's natural — and wrong. You're worried about losing sight of the ball in your backswing and hitting nothing but air. You're not alone. All golfers have been through this sweat-drenched nightmare of flailing failure. But don't worry. You will evolve! You will make contact!

Getting the ball airborne

Okay, after a few fairly fruitless attempts, you're finally hitting more ball than air. Now you need to understand the aerodynamics of the game. The only time you want the golf ball to be on the ground is when you're close to the hole. To have any kind of fun the rest of the time, you want air under the ball; you need the ball to fly! Then you can stare with horrified fascination at the ridiculous places the ball goes, which is the essence of the game.

One of my *Golf For Dummies* secrets is that the only time you should lift something is when you rearrange your living-room furniture. *Never* try to lift a golf ball with your club. Hit down with every club except the driver and the putter, as shown in Figure 1-2. And when you do hit down, don't duck or lunge at the ball; hit down but keep your head up.

When you use your driver, the ball is set on a tee about an inch above the ground; if you hit down, the ball flies off the top part of the club and the shot is high and short — the dreaded pop-up! With the driver, you want the club-head moving into the ball on a horizontal path, slightly upward at impact.

When you putt, you don't want the ball airborne. A putter is designed to roll the ball along the ground, so you need a more horizontal hit with that club. (See Chapter 6 of Book III for information on putting.)

Figure 1-2:
Hit down to
make the
ball go up.

Generating power

As soon as the ball is in the air, your ego kicks in. Power with a capital *P* becomes your concern. Power intoxicates your mind. Power makes legends out of mere mortals. Power makes you want to get a tattoo. Power also sends the ball to bad corners of your little green world if you don't harness it.

Some professional golfers can create as much as 4½ horsepower in their swings. That's some kind of giddy-up. The ball leaves their drivers at speeds of more than 150 miles per hour. This power comes from a blending of the body twisting around a slightly moving pivot point with a swinging of the arms and hands up and around on the backswing, and then down and around in the forward swing. All this movement occurs in the space of about a second!

To optimize power, try to turn your back to the target on your backswing (see Figure 1-3). This move involves another must-do: On the backswing, turn your left shoulder under your chin until the shoulder is above your right foot. Make sure to turn your shoulders far enough. Don't just raise your arms. Turning your shoulders ensures that you have power for the forward move. The unwinding of the hips and the shoulders on the downswing creates a power surge.

TIP

More power for women!

Plenty of female golfers have tremendous power — women from Mickey Wright to Laura Davies to Michelle Wie. But for the most part, female golfers struggle to generate power. The average woman simply doesn't have the same upper-body, forearm, and wrist strength as a man. Much to her dismay, she finds it physically impossible to drive the ball 300 yards.

But with a few simple strengthening and conditioning exercises (see Book II), female golfers — or any golfers — can strengthen their upper bodies, wrists, cores, and forearms enough to boost the power in their swings.

Here's one simple exercise that improves wrist strength — and you can do it almost anywhere. Take a tennis ball in your hand and squeeze until it hurts. Then switch hands and do the same thing. You don't have to give yourself carpal tunnel syndrome — just repeat this exercise for at least five minutes with each hand. You'll notice gradual improvement in your wrist and forearm strength, which will help you avoid wrist injury and arm fatigue — and add precious yards to your drives.

Figure 1-3: On the backswing, turn your left shoulder over your right foot.

The same swing principles apply for women. However, to build momentum and swing speed, ladies generally rely less on muscle and more on a longer backswing. A long backswing allows full rotation in the left shoulder, which allows the left arm to extend and cocks the wrist to help release power.

Building Your Swing

To become a golfer, you must master the building blocks of your swing. How do you hold the club so you can give the ball a good whack? After you have a good grip, how do you align yourself to the target so the ball goes somewhere near where you aimed? What should your posture look like? How much knee flex should you have, and where in the world should the ball be in your stance? Should you look at the ball or somewhere near the sun? This section has the answers.

For natural left-handers, perfecting the golf swing can be tricky. In the past, not many clubs were designed for lefties, and most course designs put left-handed golfers at a disadvantage. As a result, many lefties learned to play right-handed. Today, however, technology has advanced to the point where left-handers have little trouble finding clubs.

Whether you swing left-handed or right-handed basically all comes down to which side has the stronger, most natural-feeling swing. To find out what works best for you, try swinging the club like a baseball bat from each side (keeping a safe distance from all breakable objects and small children). The muscles used in swinging a bat are similar to those used in a golf swing, so whichever side gives you a more powerful baseball swing is likely your best golf-swing side.

This section covers a lot, and it doesn't even have you take a cut at the ball yet. That's how important these preswing routines are. After you get yourself in position to move the club away from the ball, you can forget your address position and concentrate on your swing.

Getting a grip

Although the grip is one of the most important parts of the game, it's also one of the most boring. Few golfers who've played for any length of time pay much attention to hand placement. For one thing, your grip is hard to change after you get used to the way your hands feel on the club. For another, hand placement simply doesn't seem as important as the swing itself. That kind of neglect and laziness is why you see so many bad grips — particularly among bad players.

Book III

Playing Golf: The Swing and the Short Game

Your hands are the only part of the body that has contact with the club, so your grip controls the clubface and how it relates to solid contact.

Get your grip correct and close to orthodox at the beginning of your golfing career. You can fake just about anything, but a bad grip follows you to the grave.

Women tend to have smaller hands than men, so for them, having the right grip size on the club is important. *Grip size* means the width of the rubber (occasionally leather) handle on the club, which is generally smaller for women. Another tip for ladies is to use the closed-face grip position, which can help square the clubface during the swing.

Here's how to sleep well in eternity with the correct grip. Standing upright, let your arms hang naturally by your side. Get someone to place a club in your left hand. All you do now is grab the club and — *voilà!* — you've got your left-hand grip. Well, almost. The grip has three checkpoints:

1. **Place your left thumb and left index finger on the shaft.**

   Look for a gap of about ¾ of an inch between the thumb and index finger. To get that gap, extend your thumb down the shaft a little. If extending your thumb proves too uncomfortable, pull your thumb in toward your hand. Three-quarters of an inch is only a guide, so you have some leeway. But remember: The farther your thumb extends down the shaft, the longer your swing. And the opposite is also true: Short thumb means short swing. (See Figure 1-4 for a visual of these extensions.)

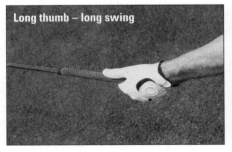

Figure 1-4:
Long thumb,
short thumb.

2. **Make sure the grip crosses the base of your last three fingers and the middle of your index finger, as shown in Figure 1-5.**

   This step is vital. If you grip the club too much in the palm, you hinder your ability to hinge your wrist and use your hands effectively in the swing. More of a finger grip makes cocking the wrist on the backswing, hitting the ball, and then recocking the wrist on the follow-through easy. Just be sure that the *V* formed between your thumb and forefinger points toward your right ear.

Figure 1-5:
Grip more in the fingers of the left hand than in the palm.

3. **Complete your grip by placing your right hand on the club.**

You can fit the right hand to the left in one of three ways: the overlapping (or Vardon) grip, the interlocking grip, or the ten-finger grip. We cover each of these grips in the following sections.

Vardon grip

The *Vardon grip* is the most popular grip, certainly among better players; probably 90 percent of tour players use this grip. The great British player Harry Vardon, who still holds the record for British Open wins (six) popularized the grip around the turn of the century. Old Harry was the first to place the little finger of his right hand over the gap between the index and next finger of the left as a prelude to completing his grip, as shown in Figure 1-6. Harry was also the first to put his left thumb on top of the shaft. Previously, players kept their left thumbs wrapped around the grip as if they were holding a baseball bat.

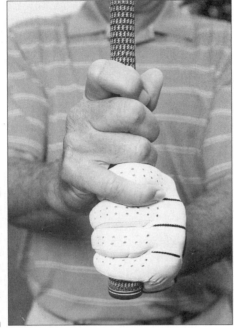

Figure 1-6:
In the Vardon grip, the right pinkie overlaps the left index finger.

Try the Vardon grip. Close your right hand over the front of the shaft so that the *V* formed between your thumb and forefinger points to your right ear. The fleshy pad at the base of your right thumb should fit snugly over your left thumb. The result should be a feeling of togetherness, your hands working as a unit.

Interlocking grip

The *interlocking grip* is really a variation on the Vardon grip (see the preceding section). The difference is that the little finger of your left hand and the index finger of the right actually hook together (see Figure 1-7). Everything else is the same. You may find this grip more comfortable if you have small hands. Jack Nicklaus, possibly the game's greatest player ever, used this grip for that reason. Many top female and junior players use this grip, too.

Ten-finger grip

The *ten-finger grip* is what the name tells you it is. You have all ten fingers on the club, like a baseball player gripping a bat. No overlapping or interlocking occurs; the little finger of the left hand and the index finger of the right barely touch (see Figure 1-8). The ten-finger grip used to be more common, and you still see it occasionally. Bob Estes has used it on the PGA Tour. Dave Barr — one of the best players ever from Canada — also uses this grip. If you have trouble generating enough clubhead speed to hit the ball as far as you want, or if you're fighting a slice, give this grip a try. Keep in mind that controlling the clubhead is more difficult with this grip because more cocking of the hands occurs.

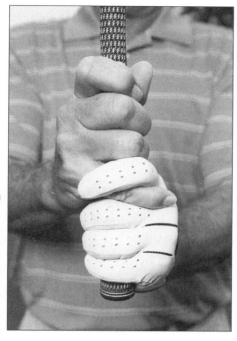

Figure 1-7:
An
alternative
is to
interlock the
right pinkie
and left
index finger.

Book III

**Playing
Golf: The
Swing and
the Short
Game**

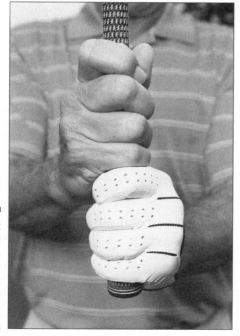

Figure 1-8:
You can
place all ten
fingers on
the club in
a baseball-
style grip.

Completing the grip

Put your right hand on the club, with the palm directly opposite your left hand. Slide your right hand down the shaft until you can complete whatever grip you prefer. Your right shoulder, right hip, and head lean to the right to accommodate the lowering of the right hand. Your right earlobe moves closer to your right shoulder.

Your grip pressure should never be tight. Your grip should be light — no clenching. You should exert only as much pressure as you would when picking up an egg.

A good way to check your grip is to hinge your hands and rest the club on your shoulders. Your knuckles should come close to being in line down the club.

Aiming

Aiming properly is difficult. Generally speaking, right-handed golfers tend to aim too far right of the target. Few aim left — even slicers, whose shots commonly start left and finish right. Invariably, people tend to aim right and swing over the top on the way down to get the ball started left. (For information on fixing common faults, see Book VI.)

What makes aiming so difficult? Human nature is part of it. Getting sloppy with your aim is easy when your mind is on other things. That's why discipline is important. Taking the time and trouble to get comfortable and confident in his alignment is one reason Jack Nicklaus was as great as he was. He worked his way through the same aiming routine before every shot. First, he looked at the target from behind the ball. Then he picked out a spot a few feet ahead of his ball on a line with that target. That spot was his intermediate target. Then he walked to the ball and set the clubface behind it so he was aiming at the intermediate point. Aligning the club with something 2 feet away is much easier than aiming at something 150 yards away.

How Nicklaus aimed is exactly how you should work on your aim. Think of a railroad track. On one rail is the ball and in the distance, the target. On the other rail are your toes. Thus, your body is aligned parallel with — but left of — the target line. If you take nothing else away from this section on aiming, remember that phrase. Cut out Figure 1-9 and tape it onto the ceiling over your bed. Stare at it before you go to sleep.

Figure 1-9:
Your feet
should be
parallel to
the target
line (left),
not aimed
at the target
(right).

Don't make the mistake that countless golfers make by aiming your feet at the target. Think about it: If you aim your feet at the target, where is the clubface aligned? To the right of where you want the ball to go! (Refer to the right-hand photo in Figure 1-9.) This point is important because misalignment is one of the most common errors in golf. So save yourself a lot of heartache and get your feet aligned a little to the left of the target line, *parallel* to it. It'll feel like you're aimed to the left — that's a *good* thing!

Nailing down the stance

Okay, you're aimed correctly. But your feet aren't finished yet. Right now you're just standing there. All the books tell you to turn your left toe out about 30 degrees. But if you have no clue what 30 degrees looks like or — more important — feels like, think of it this way:

You know what a clock looks like; if you can read a clock, you can build a stance. You want your left foot pointed to 10:00 and your right foot at 1:00. Forget about daylight saving time. Figure 1-10 demonstrates this stance. Keep it simple and always be on time.

Width of stance is easy, too. Keep your heels shoulder-width apart, as shown in Figure 1-11. Not 14 inches or 18 inches. Shoulder width. Let the shape of your body dictate what's right for you.

Book III

Playing Golf: The Swing and the Short Game

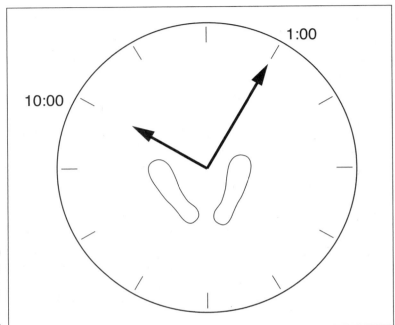

Figure 1-10: A clock-based stance.

With a driver, the gap between your knees should be shoulder width. Think "bow-legged."

Figure 1-11: Your knees should be as far apart as your shoulders.

Considering knee flex

After you've set your stance (see the preceding section), your next stop is at your knees. Again, you can read all sorts of books that tell you the precise angle at which your knees should flex at address. But that number doesn't do you much good when you're standing on the range without a protractor. What you need is a *feel*.

Think of knee flex as a "ready" position. You've got to set yourself so movement is easy. So, from an upright start, flex your knees and bend forward until your arms are hanging vertically, as shown in Figure 1-12. That's where you want to be. Just like a quarterback waiting for a snap. Or a soccer goalkeeper facing a shot. Or a shortstop ready for a ground ball. You're ready to move. Left. Right. Back. Forward. Whatever. You're ready. And remember, maintaining balance is the key.

Figure 1-12:
Flex your knees and bend forward until your arms hang vertically.

Book III

Playing Golf: The Swing and the Short Game

Deciding on ball position

Where is the ball positioned between your feet? You want it aligned with your left armpit with a driver. That means the ball is also aligned with your left heel. For other clubs, the ball moves steadily back with each club until you get to the middle of your stance with a wedge (see Figure 1-13).

For a driver, place the ball opposite your left armpit.

Figure 1-13:
Ball
position.

As we mention earlier in the chapter, you want to hit up on the ball with your driver — that's why the ball is forward in your stance (toward the target). You want to hit down with all other clubs, which is why you move the ball back in your stance (away from the target) as the loft of your clubs increases. When the ball is played back in your stance, hitting down is much easier.

Maximizing the bottom of the swing

The bottom of the swing is an important, often-neglected aspect of golf. After all, that's usually where the ball is! The arc of the swing has to have a low point; hopefully, that low point is precisely where your golf ball is as you swing an iron. If you don't know where the bottom of your swing is, how do you know where to put the ball in your stance? You can make the best swing in the world, but if the ball is too far back, you hit the top half of it. Too far forward is just as bad — you hit the ground before the ball.

Fear not; such shots aren't going to be part of your repertoire. Why? Because you're always going to know where the bottom of your swing is: directly below your head.

Think about it. The preceding section discusses how the ball is aligned with your left armpit when you use the driver. That position automatically puts your head behind the ball whenever you swing your driver. In other words, the ball is nearer the target than your head is, which means that you strike the ball with a slightly upward blow. The bottom of the swing is behind the ball, so the clubhead is moving up as it hits the ball, as shown in Figure 1-14. That's all right because the ball is perched on a tee. The only way to make solid contact (and maximize your distance) is to hit drives "on the up." (***Note:*** If you have a larger driver, be sure to tee your ball high enough; teeing the ball only an inch high may not be enough to get the proper trajectory of the driver.)

Figure 1-14:
Tee the ball about an inch high for an upward strike with the driver.

The situation for an iron shot from the fairway differs from that of the driver. Now the ball is sitting on the ground. Plus the club you're using has more loft and is designed to give best results when the ball is struck just before the ground. So now your head should be over the ball at address and impact. In other words, something has to move.

That something is the ball. Start from the middle of your stance, which is where the ball should be when you're hitting a wedge, one of the shortest and most lofted clubs in your bag. Move the ball steadily forward as the club in your hands gets longer. (See Figure 1-15.)

REMEMBER

Of course, you're not actually physically moving the ball until you hit it. What's moving in the stance is you — your setup in relation to the ball.

Figure 1-15:
The ball
"moves!"

When you use a wedge, place the ball in the middle of your stance.

As the club gets longer, the ball moves targetward.

Keeping your eyes on the ball

Too many players address the ball with their chins on their chests, probably because other golfers have said, "Keep your head down!" (For more on this point, see "The myth of 'keep your head down'" later in this chapter.) Or, if they've been warned not to do that, they hold their heads so high they can barely see the ball. Neither, of course, is exactly conducive to good play.

TIP

So how do you position your head? The answer is in your eyes. Look down at the ball, which is in what optometrists call your *gaze center*. Your gaze center is about the size of a Frisbee. Everything outside your gaze center is in your peripheral vision. Now lift or drop your head slightly. As your head moves, so do your eyes, and so does the ball — into your peripheral vision. Suddenly, you can't see the ball so well. But if you hold your head steady enough to keep the ball inside that Frisbee-shaped circle, you can't go too far wrong (see Figure 1-16).

Figure 1-16:
Stay
focused.

Observing the one-hand-away rule

One last thing about your address position: Let your arms hang so that the *butt* end of the club (the one with the handle) is one hand-width from the inside of your left thigh, as shown in Figure 1-17. You should use this position for every club in the bag except for your putter.

The butt end of the club is a useful guide to check the relationship between your hands and the clubhead. With a wedge, for example, the butt end of the club should be in line with the middle of your left thigh. For a driver, it should be opposite your zipper. Every other club is between those parameters.

Unleashing Your Swing

Now it's time to do what you've been wanting to do: Create some turbulence. Many people think the most effective way to develop a consistent swing is to stand on the range whacking balls until they get it right. But the best way to develop a consistent swing is actually to break the swing down into pieces. Only after you have the first piece mastered should you move on to the next one. In the sections that follow, we deal with each of those pieces and a few other swing considerations.

Making miniswings

Start the swing process with *miniswings*. Position yourself in front of the ball as described in "Building Your Swing" earlier in this chapter. Now, without moving anything but your hands, wrists, and forearms, rotate the club back until the shaft is parallel to the ground and the *toe* of the club (the part of the clubhead farthest from the shaft) is pointing up. The key to this movement is the left hand, which must stay in the space that it's now occupying, in its address position (see Figure 1-18). The left hand is the fulcrum around which the "swing" rotates. The feeling you should have is of the butt of the club staying in about the same position while your hands lift the clubhead.

The club should be one hand from your body.

Figure 1-17:
Your hands
and the
club.

The shaft of a wedge should point at the crease in your left pant leg (or the middle of your thigh).

A driver should point at your zipper.

Book III

Playing Golf: The Swing and the Short Game

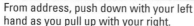
Figure 1-18: The miniswing.

From address, push down with your left hand as you pull up with your right.

Rotate the club back until the shaft is horizontal, the toe pointing up.

After you get the hang of that little drill, try hitting shots with your miniswing. Let the club travel through 180 degrees, with the shaft parallel to the ground on the backswing and then back to parallel on the through-swing; your follow-through should be a mirror image of the backswing. The ball obviously doesn't go far with this drill, but your hands and arms are doing exactly what you want them to do on a full swing: Cock the wrists, hit the ball, and recock the wrists.

After you have this move down, you can turn on the horsepower and get your body involved.

Testing your rhythm

One of the most effective ways for your brain to master something like the golf swing is to set the motion to music. Music plays a valuable role in the learning process. You learned your ABCs by putting the letters to song. When you start to move the club and your body into the swing, think of a melody. The golf swing should be a smooth motion, so your song should reflect that smoothness. Think Tony Bennett, not Eminem.

To begin adding body movement to your miniswing motion (see the preceding section), stand as if at address, with your arms crossed over your chest so your right hand is on your left shoulder and your left hand is on your right shoulder. Hold a club against your chest with both hands, as shown in Figure 1-19a.

Figure 1-19:
Turn your body.

Now turn as if you're making a backswing (see Figure 1-19b). Turn so the shaft turns through 90 degrees, to the point where it's perpendicular to a line formed by the tips of your toes. As you do so, let your left knee move inward so it points to the golf ball. The butt of the club also points at the ball.

The real key here is keeping your right leg flexed as it was at address. Retain that flex, and the only way to get the shaft into position is by turning your body. You can't sway or slide to the right and still create that 90-degree angle.

Your backswing should feel as if you're turning around the inside of your right leg until your back faces the target. That's the perfect top-of-the-backswing position.

Unwinding

From the top, you must let your body unwind back to the ball in the proper sequence. (Note that your spine angle must stay the same from address to the top of the backswing.)

Uncoiling starts from the ground up. The first thing to move is your left knee. That knee must shift toward the target until your kneecap is over the middle of your left foot, where it stops. Any more shifting of the knee, and your legs start to slide past the ball. An *alignment stick* (a flexible fiberglass stick used to help with alignment) poked into the ground just outside your left foot is a good check that your knee shift hasn't gone too far. (See Figure 1-20a.) If your left knee touches the stick (like in Figure 1-20b), stop and try again.

Next, your left hip slides targetward until it's over your knee and foot. Again, a stick in the ground provides a good test — a deterrent to keep your hip from going too far.

Pay special attention to the clubshaft across your chest in this phase of the swing (work in front of a mirror if you can). The shaft should always parallel the slope of your shoulders as you work your body back to the ball.

Swing through the impact area all the way to the finish. Keep your left leg straight and let your right knee touch your left knee, as shown in Figure 1-20c. Hold this position until the ball hits the ground — that way, you prove beyond a doubt that you've swung in balance.

Book III

Playing Golf: The Swing and the Short Game

Figure 1-20: Turn, don't slide.

An alignment stick at address

Bends if you slide forward (wrong)

But not if you turn (nice!)

The myth of "keep your head down"

How can you be target-oriented and not be overcome with anticipation about the result? Golfers blame many bad shots on "looking up," meaning that a player is so eager to see the result of the shot that he or she fails to complete the swing, which results in a mishit. As a cure or a precaution, people often remind themselves or others to "keep your head down." Not good advice. Seriously.

Technically, keeping your head down is improper form. Try swinging a golf club with your head down. Touch your chin to your chest

and see what happens to your shoulders. You notice that this posture is very uncomfortable. The more you keep your head down, the more you restrict your swing.

The phrase "keep your head down" isn't about literally keeping your head down; rather, it should remind you to keep your head still and follow though, making sure to finish the shot before you look up to see the result. You have to swing the golf club. And to swing the golf club, you can't be rigid. Keeping your head down makes you rigid.

Getting yourself together

Practice the exercises in the preceding sections. After you put them together, you'll have the basis of a pretty sound golf swing, one that combines hands/arms and body motion.

1. **Practice your miniswing.**

2. **Hum a mellow tune.**

3. **Turn your shoulders so your back is toward the target.**

4. **Turn, don't slide; sliding automatically takes your head off the ball.**

5. **At the finish, keep your left leg straight, with your right knee touching your left knee.**

Coordinating the parts into a golf swing takes time. The action of the parts soon becomes the whole, and you develop a feel for your swing. But knowledge, in this case, doesn't come from reading a book. Only repetition — hitting enough balls to turn this information into muscle memory — can help you go from novice to real golfer. So get out there and start taking some turf!

Key in on the rhythm of your swing. At a certain point in every golfer's life, he or she just has to "let it go." You can work on mechanics as much as you want, but then the moment to actually hit a ball comes. And when that moment comes, you can't be thinking about anything except, perhaps, one simple swing key, or swing thought. That's why top golfers spend most of their time trying to get into a focused, wordless, wonderful place they call the zone.

The *zone* is a state of uncluttered thought, where good things happen without any conscious effort from you. You know the feeling: The rolled-up ball of paper you throw at the trash can goes in if you just toss it without thinking. The car rounds the corner perfectly if you're lost in your thoughts. In golfing terms, getting into the zone means clearing your mind so your body can do its job. The mind is a powerful asset, but it can hurt you, too. Negative thoughts about where your ball may go don't help you make your best swing.

Of course, getting into the zone is easier said than done. So how do you get there? Perhaps the best way is to focus on the rhythm of your swing. By *rhythm,* we don't mean speed. We've seen fast swings and slow swings and a lot in between, and all can have good rhythm. For example, three-time major winner Nick Price has a fast swing. Blink and you miss it. In contrast, 1987 Masters champ Larry Mize has an extremely slow motion. Congress works faster. Yet Price and Mize both have perfect rhythm. You can still see it on the Champions Tour. And their rhythm is the key.

The rhythm of your swing should fit your personality. If you're a fairly highstrung, nervous individual, your swing is probably faster than most. If your swing is slower, you may be more laid back and easygoing. But the potential for great rhythm is within every golfer.

Selecting swing triggers: What's a waggle?

Good rhythm doesn't just happen. Only on those days when you're in the zone can you swing on autopilot. The rest of the time, you need to set the tone for your swing with your waggle. A *waggle* is a motion with the wrists in which the hands stay fairly steady over the ball and the clubhead moves back a foot or two, as if starting the swing. (Check one out in Figure 1-21.) In fact, a waggle is a bit like the miniswing drill described in the section "Making miniswings" earlier in this chapter.

Waggling the club serves three main purposes.

- ✔ **It's a rehearsal of the crucial opening segment of the backswing.**

- ✔ **It can set the tone for the pace of the swing.** In other words, if you have a short, fast swing, make short, fast waggles. If your swing is of the long and slow variety, make long, slow waggles. Be true to your species.

- ✔ **It gives your swing some momentum.** In golf, you don't want to start from a static position. You need a running start to keep your swing from getting off to an abrupt, jerky beginning. Waggling the clubhead eases tension and introduces movement into your setup.

Figure 1-21:
Get in
motion with
a waggle.

Your waggle shouldn't include a movement that puts your clubface or body out of position before you swing.

But the waggle is only the second-to-last thing you do before the backswing begins. The last thing is your *swing trigger,* which frees you up to get the club away from the ball. A swing trigger can be any kind of move. For example, 1989 British Open champion Mark Calcavecchia shuffles his feet. Gary Player, winner of nine major championships, always kicked his right knee in toward the ball. A slight turning of the head to the right was Jack Nicklaus's cue to start his swing. Your swing trigger is up to you.

Visualizing shots

As you practice your swing and hit more and more shots, patterns — good and bad — emerge. The natural shape of your shots becomes apparent. Few people hit the ball dead-straight; they either *fade* most of their shots (the ball flies from left to right, as shown in Figure 1-22) or *draw* them (the ball moves from right to left in the air). If you hit a ball that curves from left to right, aim far enough left to allow the curve of your ball to match the curve of the hole, and vice versa.

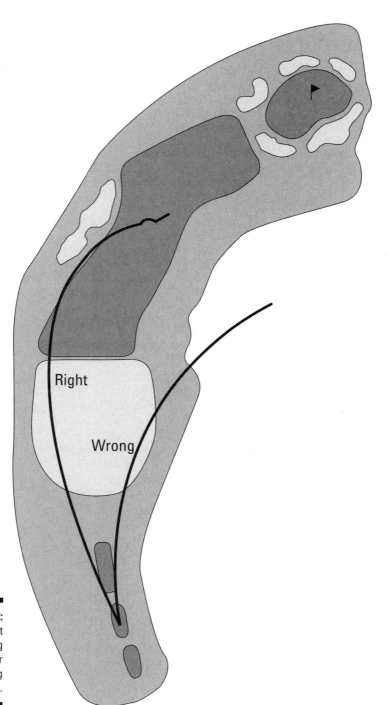

Right

Wrong

Figure 1-22:
The right
and wrong
paths for
correcting
a fade.

Book III

**Playing
Golf: The
Swing and
the Short
Game**

If either tendency gets too severe and develops into a full-blooded slice or hook (a *slice* is a worse fade, and a *hook* is a worse draw), you should stop playing. Go get a lesson. One session with your local pro should get you back on track. (Chapter 2 of Book I offers valuable information on golf lessons and golf schools.)

After you've developed a consistent shot shape, you can start to visualize how that shape fits the hole you're playing. Then, of course, you know exactly where to aim whether the hole is a *dogleg right* (turns right), *dogleg left* (turns left), or straightaway. This visualization helps free your mind and give you confidence to hit the correct shot. You're a real golfer.

Watching a near-perfect swing

When you put together all the connected parts discussed in this chapter, they should flow into a swing. The first time you see yourself swinging in a series of photos or a video/DVD clip, you'll swear that that person isn't you. What your swing feels like versus what really occurs can be deceiving.

If you can master the basic mechanics described in this chapter and apply them to your own personality, your swing should bloom into something unique. Work hard to understand your swing and watch how other people swing. The great Ben Hogan explained how he watched other golfers: If he liked something they did, he'd go to the practice tee and incorporate that particular move into his swing to see whether it worked. What finally came out was a mix of many swings blended to his needs and personality. A champion works hard.

My golf swing isn't the one that got me to the PGA Tour. In 1986, at the age of 38, I started working with Mac O'Grady to revamp my entire swing. Mac gave me a model that I blended with my existing swing, shown in the nine photos of Figure 1-23. What came out is a pretty good-looking golf swing, if I do say so myself. Thanks, Mac, for at least making me look good!

Address: The calm before the chaos. All systems are go and flight is imminent.

Monitor your swing speed at this time. Checking to see whether my seatbelts are fastened.

Turn and stay balanced over your feet. Feel the sun and breeze on your face.

I've reached the top. I'm in attack mode, my swing is growing teeth.

The start down is a slooooooow accumulation of speed. At this time, I've forgotten the sun and wind on my face.

I've organized my chaos. Liftoff is precise. My soul feels the ball.

Figure 1-23: Not a bad-looking golf swing!

The hit is relayed up from the shaft to my hands, through my arms into my command center. Post-impact, I feel I've been here forever.

My first glimpse at the sphere that is targetbound. The anxieties of flight and destination consume my brain.

Who cares where it went? I look good enough to be on the top of a golf trophy.

Book III

Playing Golf: The Swing and the Short Game

Chapter 2

Refining Your Swing

*T*his chapter comes with the golfing equivalent of a health disclaimer: The information on the next few pages isn't for everyone. That's not to say anything you read here is wrong; it isn't. But for many people — especially those at an early stage of development as golfers — it may be a lot to assimilate without little puffs of smoke coming from their ears.

So follow the wise man's advice: Golfer, know thyself. Are you the type who brings a new HDTV home and starts hooking this cable to that port and plugging this into that without looking at the instructions? Do you start punching buttons without taking the manual out of its wrapper? If so, skip this chapter. You already know all you need to know about the golf swing — at least for now.

But if you're the type who goes from page one to the end of the manual as you piece components together, you need to know more about the swing before you can unleash *your* swing with confidence. If that's you, read on, brave explorer.

Recognizing the Type of Golfer You Are

The renowned teacher Peter Kostis breaks golfers into four personas. When you know the basics of the game, you can probably recognize yourself as one of them:

✔ **Analytics** are organized. You can always spot their desks in the office — they're spotless.

✔ **Drivers,** as you'd expect, are driven to get the job done. They don't stop till they've reached their goal.

✔ **Amiables** are easy to deal with. They accept any advice you offer without questioning it.

✔ **Expressives** go with the flow; rather than rein in their feelings, they adjust to whatever comes their way.

In recent golf history, an analytic is someone like Nick Faldo or Bernhard Langer. Jack Nicklaus, Tom Watson, and Annika Sorenstam are drivers. Tiger Woods is a little of both. Correction: Make that *a lot* of both. Nancy Lopez, Fred Couples, Ernie Els, and Ben Crenshaw are amiables. And Phil Mickelson and Lee Trevino are classic expressives.

Drivers and analytics don't play like amiables and expressives. For a driver or analytic to score well, he needs confidence in his mechanics. An amiable or expressive doesn't — if he feels like he's playing okay, his swing must be okay, too.

At this stage of your development, your best bet is to be an amiable or an expressive. As a new golfer, you've got an enormous amount of information to absorb. Anything that limits confusion (such as a playing style where you roll with the punches) is a plus. Amiables and expressives may find more of what they need in Chapter 6 of Book III; this chapter is more tailored to the analytics and drivers out there.

To better illustrate the difference among the types, suppose four of history's greatest golfers plan to play an exhibition. Lee Trevino, Ben Crenshaw, Jack Nicklaus, and Nick Faldo are scheduled to tee off at Running Rut Golf Course precisely at 11 a.m. Because of a mix-up with the courtesy cars that deliver the players to the golf course (Nicklaus and Faldo don't like the color of their car; Trevino and Crenshaw couldn't care less about it), the players are late getting to Running Rut.

When they arrive with only ten minutes to tee time, the analytic (Faldo) and the driver (Nicklaus) hurry to the driving range. Faldo has to swing to gain confidence, and Nicklaus has to hit balls because he likes to work at his game.

The expressive (Trevino) and the amiable (Crenshaw) don't have to hit balls to get ready. They wake up ready and go from there. They're in the locker room putting on their golf shoes. Trevino is deep in conversation with the locker-room attendant about the virtues of not having to tune up his Cadillac for 100,000 miles because of the technologies of its good old Northstar system. Crenshaw is puffing a cigarette, telling a club member that he was flabbergasted yesterday when three 40-foot putts *lipped out* on him (touched the edge of the cup and didn't go in). By the way, the match never happens. Faldo and Nicklaus refuse to come to the tee because Faldo wants to keep hitting balls on the practice tee, and Nicklaus ends up redesigning the practice range. And the locker-room attendant buys Trevino's old Cadillac.

Establishing Your Swing Plane

The *swing plane,* at its most basic, is the path the club's shaft follows when you swing. Many factors affect your swing plane, including your height, your weight, your posture, your flexibility, the thickness of your torso, any physical limitations, and maybe even the magnetic field of your wristwatch. Swing plane can get complicated and for the beginner golfer must be simplified — especially if you want to cover all the possible variations in the plane from *address* (your stance over the ball) to the end of the follow-through.

The plane of your swing is dictated to a large extent by the shaft's angle at address. The swing you make with a wedge in your hands is naturally more upright — or should be — than the swing you make with a driver. The driver has a longer shaft than the wedge and a flatter *lie* (the angle at which the shaft emerges from the clubhead), so you have to stand farther away from the ball.

Book III

Playing Golf: The Swing and the Short Game

In this chapter, we're assuming that you maintain the plane and spine angle you establish at address throughout your swing. This scenario isn't always the case: If a player's favored shot bends a great deal in the air, the swing plane tilts to the right or left to compensate for the ball's flight. But if you're trying to hit straight shots — as most amateurs should — one consistent plane is the way for you. The following sections give you some pointers on getting your swing plane down.

Mastering checkpoints

The simplest way to keep your swing on plane is to use a series of checkpoints, as shown in Figure 2-1. For purposes of illustration, we're assuming that you're swinging a driver and that you're right-handed. Here are the checkpoints:

   ✓ **Checkpoint 1:** At address, the shaft starts at a 45-degree angle to the ground.

Start with the shaft at 45 degrees to the ground.

At the top, the shaft should be parallel with a line along your heels.

Impact should look a lot like address, except that the hips are opening to the target.

Figure 2-1: The swing plane.

✔ **Checkpoint 2:** Now swing the club back until your left arm is horizontal. At this point, the club's *butt end* (the end of the grip) points directly along the target line. (The *target line* is the line between the target and the ball that continues forward past the target and behind the ball in the opposite direction. What we're talking about in this case is one long, straight line.) If the end of the grip points along the target line, you're *on plane.* If the club's butt end points above the target line, your swing is too flat, or *horizontal;* if the butt end is below the target line, your swing is too upright, or *vertical.*

A good way to control the swing plane is to remember to move the club with your body to eliminate extra movements with your hands, which in turn will move the clubface. A good rule to follow when thinking about swing plane is "elbows to the ground."

✔ **Checkpoint 3:** At the top of your backswing, the club should be parallel with a line drawn along your heels, while your hands are positioned over your right shoulder. That's on plane. If the club points to the right of that line, you've crossed the line and will probably *hook* the shot from right to left. A club pointing to the left of that line is said to be *laid off.* In that case, expect a *slice* (which curves from left to right).

✔ **Checkpoint 4:** Halfway down, at the point where your left arm is again horizontal, the butt end should again point at the target line. This position and the one described in Checkpoint 2 are, in effect, identical in swing-plane terms.

✔ **Checkpoint 5:** *Impact* is the most important point in the swing. If the clubface is square when it strikes the ball, what you do anywhere else doesn't really matter. But if you want to be consistent, try to visualize impact as being about the same as your address position, except that your hips are aimed more to the left of the target than at address, and your weight is shifting to your left side.

Book III

Playing Golf: The Swing and the Short Game

To analyze your swing, use a camcorder, a series of still photos, or a mirror — or have someone watch you.

These checkpoints show a perfect-world situation. Your size, flexibility, and swing shape will probably produce different results. Don't be alarmed if you don't fit this model perfectly; no more than a dozen players on the PGA Tour do. As with anything else, there's room for deviation. Different folks make different strokes.

Taking it from the top

Take a closer look at the top of the backswing. If you can get the club on plane at the top, you'll probably hit a good shot.

Look for four things in your backswing:

- ✔ **Your left arm and your shoulders must be on the same slope.** In other words, your arm and shoulders are parallel to the target line.

- ✔ **The top of your swing is controlled by your right arm, which forms a right angle at the top of the swing (see Figure 2-2).** Your right elbow is about a dollar bill's length (around 6 inches) away from your rib cage.

- ✔ **Your shoulders are at 90 degrees to the target line.**

- ✔ **The clubface is parallel to your left arm and your shoulders.** Your left wrist controls this position. Ideally, your wrist angle remains unchanged from address to the top, making the clubface square at the top of the swing. That way, the relationship between the clubface and your left arm is constant. If your wrist angle does change, the clubface and your left arm will be on different planes, and that's a problem.

Figure 2-2: Your right arm should form a right angle at the elbow at the top of the backswing.

If your wrist angle changes, it's either bowed or cupped (check out Figure 2-3). A *bowed* (bent-forward) left wrist at the top makes the clubface "look" skyward in what is called a *closed* position. From that position, a hook is likely. A *cupped* (bent-backward) wrist makes the clubface more visible to someone looking you in the face. A cupped wrist leads to an *open* position, which probably results in a slice.

You *can* play good golf from an open or closed position at the top of the backswing, but it's not easy. To compensate, your swing must feature some kind of repeatable mechanism that squares the clubface at impact. And compensations take a lot of practice. Only if you have the time to hit hundreds of balls a week can you hope to play well with an inherently flawed swing. Even then, that compensated swing is going to be tough to reproduce under pressure. For classic examples, watch Corey Pavin (open) and Lee Trevino (closed).

GARY SAYS

Keep swinging, seniors

After 28 winless years as a touring pro, I finally broke through by winning the 1999 Toshiba Senior Classic. So when I address all you members of the Social-Security set, I know what I'm talking about!

And as I ponder the pitfalls of my maturing body and mind, I'm determined to enjoy this game right down to the last, desperate 210-yard drive. I'm not moving to Leadville, Colorado (elevation 11,000 feet), where the ball goes screaming for mercy through the alpine air. No, I'm using all my cunning (and lots of technology) to keep up with the kids right here at sea level.

I have brewed in my golf kitchen a recipe to keep my fellow seniors in the championship flight of their clubs' member-member tournament...from the back tees! And so, gramps and grannies, my two-stage plan to keep launching the long ball. Part one: the swing:

1. **Narrow your stance so that you can turn your torso without straining.**

   As we get older and less flexible, we tend to swat the ball with our hands instead of turning our bodies. Resist!

2. **Turn your left foot in.**

   This adjustment helps you make a bigger turn with your shoulders and hips.

3. **Turn your left knee behind the ball to ensure a bigger turn on the backswing.**

4. **Don't be afraid to lift your front heel off the ground on the backswing.**

   Jack Nicklaus did it, and he won the Masters at age 46 and played great golf into his 60s.

5. **Get the club parallel to the ground at the top of your backswing — even if you have to bend your left arm.**

   This strategy adds the clubhead speed you need to hit it a senior-citizen mile!

Okay, now that my pacemaker's smoking, here's part two, the easy stuff: high-tech help for great senior moments.

✔ **Get the lightest-possible shafts for your clubs.** As we get older, our egos can get in the way of good golf. But there's no shame in playing with the clubs that give you the best results. Manufacturers now make shafts as light as 45 ounces. Get a low *kickpoint* (the spot where the shaft bends the most) to help you get the ball into the air. The lower the kickpoint, the higher the *launch angle* (the angle at which the ball leaves the clubface). That's golf talk!

✔ **Go to the longest shaft on your driver that you can control and add the lightest grip and clubhead you can find.** You'll strike fear in your foes at Sun City with this fast-moving, lightweight beast! I use a 46-inch, 55-ounce driver shaft on the Champions Tour.

✔ **Use irons with stronger lofts.** Instead of starting with a 48-degree wedge and dropping four degrees per iron, some manufacturers start with a 43-degree wedge and go down from there. That's basically the same as using a longer-hitting club without doing anything. Add light shafts and today's superior golf balls and bingo — grandpa's revenge!

Book III

Playing Golf: The Swing and the Short Game

When your left wrist is "bowed," watch out for a hook.

When your left wrist is "cupped," watch out for a slice.

Figure 2-3: Bowed- and cupped-wrist swings.

Slow-motion swing sequences tend to show three very different methods. The legendary Sam Snead crossed the line at the top and came over every shot to make the ball go straight. Annika Sorenstam was the opposite: She laid the club off at the top. And 1995 PGA champion Steve Elkington stayed on plane. Make a swing like Elkington's your model, and you won't go too far wrong.

Mirroring Great Swings and Mindsets

Some of the latest sports science suggests that watching someone perform an action can be almost as helpful as doing it yourself. It activates "mirror neurons" in the brain that can help you imitate the action. When he was a toddler, Tiger Woods spent many hours watching his father hit golf balls — and when Tiger took his first whacks with a cut-down club, he already had a pretty good swing.

Phil Mickelson may be an even better example. A natural right-hander who was 18 months old when he began imitating his father, Phil literally mirrored what he saw — by swinging lefty!

Mimicking the moss bosses

If you want to follow some really fine putting, keep your eyes peeled for Champions Tour golfer Loren Roberts, who putts so well his nickname is "Boss of the Moss." Some of the best putters in the world today are Brad Faxon, Jim Furyk, and Steve Stricker. Nancy Lopez was another great putter in her heyday. (Head to Chapter 6 of Book III for more on putting.)

Grip can affect your putting stroke as well as your swing, so you may want to study the grips of various pros. Billy Casper was an all-time great putter who used his wrists to create momentum in the clubhead during his putting stroke. Fred Couples uses the cross-handed grip for putting. Chris DiMarco, who was once such a poor putter he almost quit the tour, made it big with a grip called "the claw."

Maybe you want to keep tabs on golfers who have modified their games to adapt to a situation such as the yips (also in Chapter 6 of Book III), like Bernhard Langer, who invented his own grip, and Sam Snead, who putted sidesaddle. Golfers also adapt to accommodate new tools, such as the long putter Tom Lehman switched to, or Vijay Singh's *belly putter* — longer than a standard model, shorter than a long putter.

No matter what your skill level, you can improve by observing good players, particularly those with some of the same characteristics that you have. Look for similarities in body size, pace, and shape of swing. You can also learn from the mistakes others make under pressure — just don't mirror those!

Start by identifying your goals. Do you want to emulate the game's big bombers, guys like Davis Love III, Bubba Watson, and Dustin Johnson, who regularly blast drives beyond 300 and even 350 yards? Or do you want to follow the short-game experts, such as all-time great Walter Hagen and tour veteran Brad Faxon? Phil Mickelson is long off the tee and has a great lob wedge. Tiger Woods, at his best, does everything well.

Maybe swing speed is your demon. Are you trying too hard to copy someone you admire, or is the pace you use as natural for you as tour golfers' swings are for them? Down through the years, Ben Crenshaw, Nancy Lopez, and Jay Haas have displayed slow-paced swings. Larry Mize's swing was so slow it looked like slo-mo. Ernie Els has a syrup-smooth motion that builds great power at impact. Jack Nicklaus, Sam Snead, and Annika Sorenstam all won with medium-paced swings. Ben Hogan, Lanny Wadkins, and Tom Watson swung fast. One of the quickest swingers of all is Nick Price. And those players have all had great careers.

Book III

Playing Golf: The Swing and the Short Game

Notice how the attitudes of famous players affect not only how they play but also how much they enjoy the game. Arnold Palmer was a master of special shots and a bold golfer. Other daring players include Mickelson and Ireland's Rory McIlroy, who are as fun and expressive as Lee Trevino in his prime. Fred Funk is a Champions Tour fan favorite whose love for the game is infectious. On the other end of the attitude spectrum, you find Hall of Famer Jackie Burke, who created intense drills for himself so that he knew all about pressure: His motivation was to win. Ben Hogan was another steely competitor, a perfectionist who surrendered not to any other player but only to the yips. Other perfectionists include Jack Nicklaus, Tom Watson, Annika Sorenstam, and many of the Asian players doing so well on today's LPGA tour — hard workers like Jiyai Shin and Song-Hee Kim of South Korea, and Japan's Ai Miyazato.

Whomever you choose to emulate, keep in mind that golf is an individualist's game. You can mix and match facets of great players' styles, or develop your own — whatever works for *you*.

Chapter 3

Defining the Art of the Short Game

Golf is a journey with no final destination — a series of trips up and down hills — but if you play long enough, you'll come to enjoy the ride. You discover nuances of the game as you go along, and sometimes you learn important lessons the hard way.

Players who seek improvement — and who tire of seeing three-digit numbers on their scorecards at the end of a round — often just want to have some consistency in their games. Who can blame them? What's worse than swinging a golf club and wondering where the ball will go or even worrying about making contact?

Five-time PGA champion Walter Hagen took one approach. As he stood on the first tee, the great Haig knew that he'd probably hit at least six terrible shots that day. So when he did hit one sideways, he didn't blow his top. Hagen simply relied on his superior *short game* (every shot within 75 to 80 yards of the hole) to get out of trouble.

Precision is never more important than when you get the ball close to the green or the hole, and as we convey in this chapter, the short game is the most complex and varied aspect of the game of golf. But lucky for you, the short game is also the area in which you can make the most immediate and significant improvement. Specific shots within the short game are covered in Chapters 4, 5, 6, and 7 of Book III: chipping, pitching, putting, and bunkers. Check out Chapter 8 of that book for a look at some short-game strategies.

Here, we take a look at the importance of the short game, the best way to approach it, and how to prepare yourself to hit the shots that can improve your scores. Improved scores give you a greater sense of enjoyment — and who could ask for more? Later in the chapter, we introduce the fundamentals so you can start developing your personal preferences based on those very same fundamentals. We show you, technically speaking, what to look for when you're sizing up the task at hand and considering which of the various types of short-game shots you need in your situation. And we make the case that, after you consider all the factors, you should forget everything and swing naturally — play in the subconscious.

Exploring the Short Game

Hang around golfers for a while and you inevitably hear one say something like, "I missed the third green but got up and down for my par." At this stage, you're probably wondering what in the world *up and down* means. Well, the *up* part is *chipping* (hitting a low, short shot) or *pitching* (hitting a higher, more airborne short shot) the ball to the hole (see Chapters 4 and 5 of Book III). The *down* half of the equation, of course, is holing the putt after your chip or pitch (see Chapter 6 of Book III). Thus, a golfer with a good short game is one who gets up and down a high percentage of the time (anywhere above 50 percent).

In the following sections, we explain why golfers who play good short games deserve just as much due as those who can hit the ball impressive distances. We also share insights about how a good short game improves your scores.

Respecting the short game

Now here's the weird thing: Although a good short game can erase your mistakes and keep a good round going, many amateurs tend to look down on golfers blessed with a delicate touch around the greens. They hate to lose to someone who beats them with good chipping and putting. Somehow a strong short game isn't perceived as "macho golf" — not in the same league as smashing drives 300 yards and hitting low, raking, iron shots to greens. Good ball strikers tend to look down on players with better short games. This attitude is more than a snobbery thing — it's also a missing-the-point thing.

In golf, you want to move the ball around the course in the fewest possible strokes. How you get that job done — great drives, expert chipping — is up to you. No rule says that you have to look pretty or hit picturesque drives when you play golf. Your scorecard won't be hung in an art gallery.

You can make up for a lot of bad play with one good short shot. As someone once said, "Three of them and one of those makes four." Remember that saying; even if you need three cruddy shots to get near the green, you can save par with a nice chip or pitch. Short-game master Walter Hagen won his matches without having hit his full shots too solidly. He proved that golf is more than hitting the ball well; it's a game of managing your misses.

You don't hear professionals downplaying the importance of a good short game. They know that the short game is where they make their money. Here's proof: If you put a club champion and a tournament pro on the tee with drivers in their hands, their drives don't look all that different. Sure, you can tell who the better player is, but the amateur at least *looks* competitive.

The gap in quality grows on the approach shots, again on *wedge play* (shorter approaches hit with wedges), and then again in the short game. In fact, the closer the players get to the green, the more obvious the difference in level of play. And the green is where a mediocre score gets turned into a good score, or where a good score gets turned into a great one. (Take a look at the sample scorecard in Figure 3-1, which pays special attention to short-game shots. Keeping that kind of record for yourself once in a while to monitor your short game doesn't hurt.)

Statistically speaking

According to the National Golf Foundation, a fine group of folks who make it their business to study the business side of golf, as many as 36.7 million people play golf in the United States. In a year's time, these golfers spend about $25 billion on golf equipment and fees. That's *billion,* with a *B.*

But like the old saying goes, money can't buy you love. And it can't buy you a 72 (the par score on almost all golf courses) either. Even with all the cash players currently spend, average scores have changed very little over the years. Only 22 percent of all golfers regularly score better than 90 for 18 holes; the overall average is an even 100.

Although critics and the media place a great deal of emphasis on how long a player can hit a golf ball (see the preceding section), you may use the driver from the tee something like 14 times on a golf course (not all tee shots necessarily call for the driver). By contrast, you use the putter and short irons for as many as 50 percent of the total strokes.

Book III

Playing Golf: The Swing and the Short Game

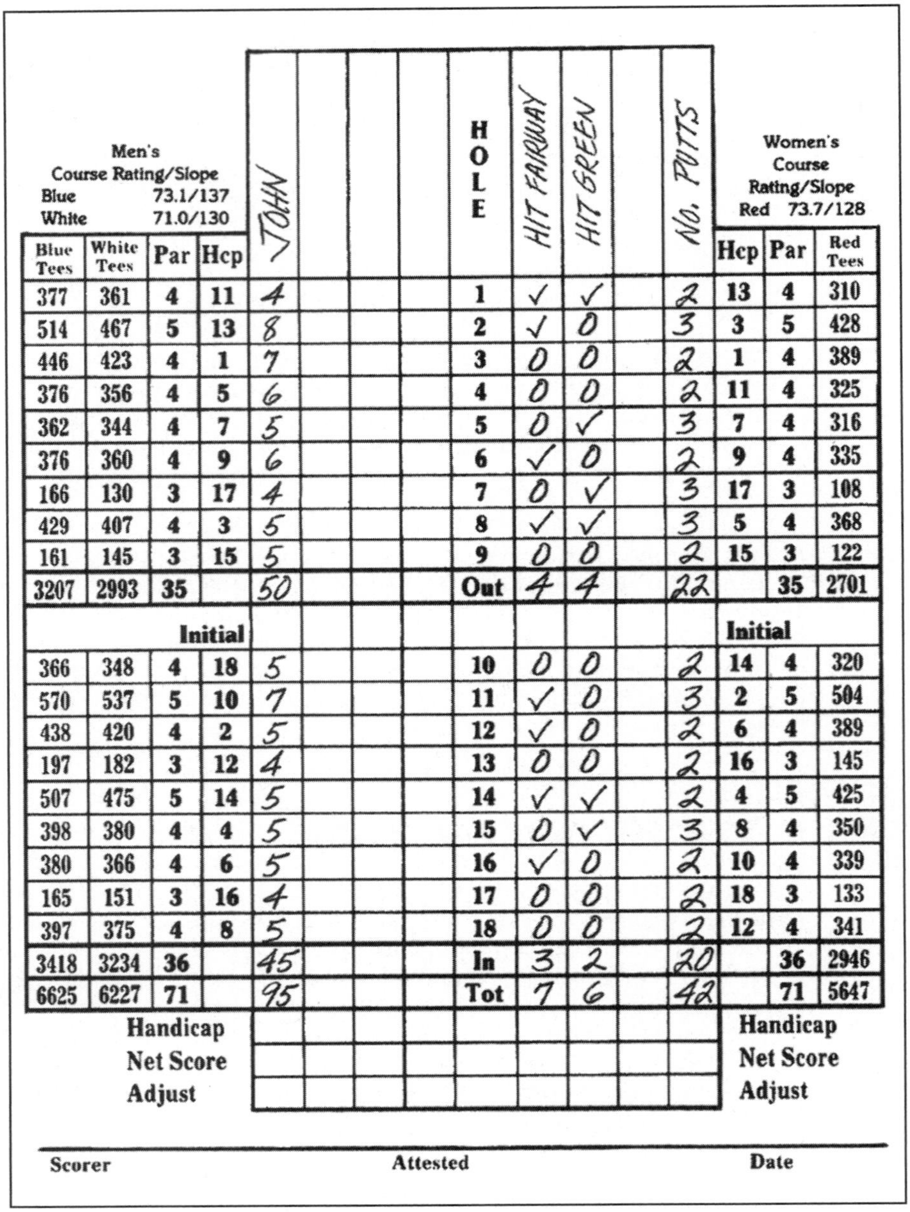

Men's Course Rating/Slope
Blue 73.1/137
White 71.0/130

Women's Course Rating/Slope
Red 73.7/128

Blue Tees	White Tees	Par	Hcp	JOHN			HOLE	HIT FAIRWAY	HIT GREEN	NO. PUTTS	Hcp	Par	Red Tees
377	361	4	11	4			1	✓	✓	2	13	4	310
514	467	5	13	8			2	✓	0	3	3	5	428
446	423	4	1	7			3	0	0	2	1	4	389
376	356	4	5	6			4	0	0	2	11	4	325
362	344	4	7	5			5	0	✓	3	7	4	316
376	360	4	9	6			6	✓	0	2	9	4	335
166	130	3	17	4			7	0	✓	3	17	3	108
429	407	4	3	5			8	✓	✓	3	5	4	368
161	145	3	15	5			9	0	0	2	15	3	122
3207	2993	35		50			Out	4	4	22		35	2701
				Initial								Initial	
366	348	4	18	5			10	0	0	2	14	4	320
570	537	5	10	7			11	✓	0	3	2	5	504
438	420	4	2	5			12	✓	0	2	6	4	389
197	182	3	12	4			13	0	0	2	16	3	145
507	475	5	14	5			14	✓	✓	2	4	5	425
398	380	4	4	5			15	0	✓	3	8	4	350
380	366	4	6	5			16	✓	0	2	10	4	339
165	151	3	16	4			17	0	0	2	18	3	133
397	375	4	8	5			18	0	0	2	12	4	341
3418	3234	36		45			In	3	2	20		36	2946
6625	6227	71		95			Tot	7	6	42		71	5647

Handicap
Net Score
Adjust

Handicap
Net Score
Adjust

Scorer   Attested   Date

Figure 3-1: A scorecard can tell you more than just your score.

Statistics prove that 50 percent of your score comes from shots within 75 yards of the green — whether you shoot 120 or you shoot 67. The percentage includes your putts, your chips, your pitches, and your bunker shots.

For instance, say you went out and shot that 67. You hit all 18 greens in regulation. You made five birdies with five 1-putts to shoot five under par. That means you hit 31 putts out of 67 shots. And to sink some of those 1-putts, you had to hit the ball close to the hole. You probably had a wedge or some type of short iron in your hand to do that. You didn't miss any greens, because you used your short game to get into position. Adding six more strokes to the putts, you have half your strokes accounted for.

If you shot 110, you surely didn't hit all the greens in regulation, because if you did, you would have used 70 putts (or four putts per hole) to shoot that 110 — a dismal result for even the worst of putters. More likely you missed some greens and needed to hit some short-game shots — all the more reason to improve your short game.

Singling out short-game shots

The short game, by definition, covers short shots. You hit short-game shots from 75 yards and in — which is also known as the *scoring distance.* The short game requires a shorter swing. A 100-yard shot, by contrast, is a full-swing shot.

The short game is all about scoring and precision — not distance and strength. You want to get the ball onto the green with a single approach shot and into the hole with two strokes. (See "Managing your goals and expectations" later in this chapter for how to set your goals and expectations for the short game.)

With this precision in mind, you can see why golfers use the term *approach shots* and not *bang it over the hole* shots. Think of an aircraft on approach to its final destination. To hit the runway and land safely, the plane has to travel at the right speed and at the proper angle of descent. It can't be short, and it can't be long. It has to, through a carefully made plan and proper execution, glide perfectly onto the runway and roll to a stop.

Your short-game swing options typically include the following shots, most of which you can read about in the corresponding chapters of Book III:

- ✔ **Chip shot:** A low running shot, measured in feet, that flies only a small percentage of its life before landing on the green or in front of the green and rolling toward the hole (see Chapter 4).

- ✔ **Pitch shot:** A shot that remains the air for about 70 percent of its life before hitting the green and rolling to the hole. You often use a pitch shot when you have an obstacle to fly over, such as a bunker, creek, or hill (see Chapter 5).

- **Putt:** A roll of the ball on the green. Putting the ball into the hole may seem like a simple act, and we have good news: It can be! Finding a way to roll the ball into the hole after you land the green is a matter of feel and preference, but good putters seem to have a bit of magic with the flatstick (see Chapter 6).

- **Bunker shot:** A shot needed to extract a ball from a bunker. You normally hit bunker shots with a sand wedge, which splashes through the bunker and sends the ball floating out on a pillow of sand. Bunker shots fly high and land softly near the hole (see Chapter 7).

- **Flop shot:** A high-flying, soft shot that lands near the hole and stops instead of rolling to the hole (see Chapter 2 of Book VI).

Giving yourself the best shot

The short game, and all its variables, offers golfers a multitude of options for playable shots. Although you hit some of your short-game shots from distances as far as 80 yards from the hole, you hit others from as close as a pace or two off the green. The variables include not only the distances of the shots but also the club you use, the terrain, the weather, the locale, and the competitive situation. We cover many of the variables you must consider later in the chapter and in the individual technique chapters that follow in Book III, but one piece of advice cuts through all the uncertainty:

If you want to play the percentages and improve your chances of having good results, you need to get the ball rolling. Get the ball on the ground as quickly as possible so that you max out the amount of time it spends traveling on the ground.

Trying to fly a ball to the hole invites too much possibility for error. For example, chipping and running the ball gives you more accuracy than sending the ball soaring through the air toward the hole does.

Think about it this way: If you have to hit a shot from 50 feet away from the hole, and you have an opportunity to putt the ball, you should choose to putt it most every time. When you putt,

- You stand directly over the *target line* (where the ball needs to roll to go in).

- Your eyes are over the line.

- You have an opportunity to make a simple backswing and follow-through.

So the only real challenge you have is judging your distance and speed. But if you line up for that 50-foot shot and put a 60-degree wedge in your hand, you allow additional variables in, such as

- How far the ball has to carry in the air
- The spin you generate by hitting right on or behind the ball
- The effect of the wind blowing the ball left or right, holding it up in mid-flight, or sending it soaring over the green
- Where you have to land the ball to stop it close

Do you really want to have to factor in all this technical stuff? Probably not. These variables make getting the ball into or near the hole much more difficult if you play the ball in the air. You have a much better chance of getting it close if you get the ball on the ground and moving.

Naturally, you face times when you need to hit a high-flying shot, such as when you need the ball to carry over a bunker, creek, or hill before landing on or near the green or when you don't have much room on the green for the ball to roll. These situations occur, but the more you can avoid them through careful course management, the simpler you make your short game. And a simple short game makes for lower scores.

Practicing for Short-Game Success

Although you can learn certain techniques and styles from watching the likes of Tiger Woods and Jack Nicklaus (and we point them out in Chapter 2 of Book I), trying to copy all their techniques isn't wise. Face it: The people who play competitive golf for a living are in a very, very small percentage. They don't show up on television for nothing.

They work at golf because it's their job. Their "office" is the golf course, the practice range, the practice green, or the practice bunker eight to ten hours each day. They play and they practice, and they practice by playing. You don't have that kind of practice luxury (we assume) because golf isn't your job. Lofting a ball in the air and stopping it within 3 feet of the cup is a shot best left to the professionals.

You can't spend eight hours each day practicing like the pros do, but you can, with whatever time you have, practice in a professional manner. People don't like to practice the short game, but the value of doing so is something you can learn from professional golfers.

Recognizing the importance of practice

What makes you go to the range and bang a driver? Sometimes you slice it. Sometimes it goes straight. But the results always intrigue golfers at some level. And what do you hear in television commercials about golf equipment? You hear almost exclusively about hitting the ball a long way!

Most people are competitive enough that they want to play golf to the best of their abilities. They want to realize their potential. They want to have their best scores. They forget sometimes that golf is a game that starts at the tee markers and ends at that little hole. If you don't care how many strokes it takes you, and you go out to the course for the enjoyment, that's great. Why bother to practice at all? But the point is that most golfers don't feel that way. And because you're reading this book, we assume you don't either.

Some people may really get a thrill out of banging the driver a long, long way, and they go out and hit all these prodigious, long drives, but when they look down at their scorecard after a round and see a big 100, they aren't so pumped anymore.

Maybe your goal is to shoot 90. Maybe you want to crack 80. You can shoot 80 or 90 consistently if you start spending half your practice time working on your short game.

Golf shots have much more value around the green, and the precision you need to display is much greater than on a drive or even an approach shot. A hole may be 400 yards, and you may be able to drive the ball 250 yards. You cover more ground, but your target, the fairway, is 35 yards wide. Your 150-yard approach shot is to a green that may be 60 feet wide. Your target when you chip, pitch, flop, or putt the ball is the hole — only a few inches wide — or a small circle around it.

If you shave five putts off your score because of improved chipping, or if you cut down on 3-putts by five per round, your handicap starts to reduce dramatically. Just these improvements take scores from 100 to 95 or from 85 to 80.

Developing a short-game practice plan

Practice should be an overview to everything. If you have 30 minutes in your busy schedule to run over to the practice range, you do yourself a huge disservice if you spend that entire half-hour hitting drivers and 5-iron shots. Every practice session, whether you take five minutes or five hours, needs to have a choreographed plan. Always include a specific amount of time that you devote to the short game: pitching, chipping, putting, bunker shots, and 50- to 75-yard shots.

Don't try this at home

Ben Crenshaw, a two-time Masters winner and one of the best putters ever, once had the honor of golfing with Ben Hogan late in Hogan's life. On one hole, Crenshaw found himself in a pickle and wanted to hit a low shot around a tree from a tangled, troubled lie. Crenshaw stood behind the ball contemplating the shot.

"What are you doing?" Hogan asked him.

"I'm going to hook this ball low around the tree to the green," said Crenshaw.

Hogan asked, "Have you ever played that shot before?"

"No," Crenshaw answered.

"Then why the hell are you trying to play it now? Chip the ball out."

The point is, whether you're a 30-handicap, a 15-handicap, or a *scratch* (0-handicap) player, why would you try to attempt a shot that you've never practiced and expect it to work?

You can't punch and run a ball or play any kind of shot effectively without knowing how, and knowing how comes with practice. When you assess different shots, you have more options in your repertoire. (To take a look at some of these options, including the punch shot, check out Chapter 8 of Book III.)

Because 50 percent of your score comes from strokes taken from 75 yards or closer to the hole, you should devote 50 percent of your practice time to the short game.

If you have two hours to practice, spend an hour of it on the short game. And make a plan to break down the hour. Divide the time however you feel comfortable, based on what part of your game needs the most work or on a new shot you want to practice. How much time will you spend chipping balls at a target or trying flop shots over a bunker? How many shots will you hit from the practice bunker? How many putts will you hit? From how many distances? In Chapter 3 of Book V, we help you answer these questions by customizing practice and preround warm-up routines to fit your needs.

Book III

Playing Golf: The Swing and the Short Game

Keeping practice fun

It's an unfortunate and unfair use of verbs to say that people "play" golf and "practice" golf. "Playing" anything is fun. "Practicing" anything is a drag. All work and no play makes golf a dull sport. So our goal is to show you how to be at play while you practice. In Chapters 3 and 4 of Book V, in particular, we give you some ways to have fun while you improve your short game.

When you start hitting really nice short-game shots and taking pride in the improvement you make, practicing becomes more fun and rewarding.

Facing the Peril and the Opportunity

Part of the joy of golf is that no two shots are alike, no two holes are identical, and the situations you face constantly challenge you. A round of golf contains many little decisions that compose a score.

Some folks say that the holes in a round of golf are like the links of a chain or a string of pearls — one bad link or pearl can render the chain useless and rob the necklace of its value. A round of golf is more than a chain of unique holes, however.

Think of a round of golf as a shot-by-shot test. The next shot you have to hit is what matters — not the previous shot (whether it was good or bad!) and not the putt that follows. Focus on the shot you're sizing up right now.

Some shots seem easy: a little chip to the hole from three paces off the back of green, for instance, or a chip-and-run up from 10 yards in front. Some shots seem very difficult, like a flop shot from high grass over a yawning bunker to a hole cut close to the edge. You need to recognize both the peril and the opportunity in these shots.

Reevaluating the easy

The easy shot has plenty of evident opportunity. You feel comfortable over the shot, and no real obstacles stand between your ball and the hole. You should be able to get your ball up and down with relative ease.

The peril of the easy shot may be minimal, but the peril remains. Be wise enough to take the shot seriously, no matter how easy it seems. Keep your mind focused: The greater the opportunity, the worse the disappointment if you misplay the shot. If nothing else, you can damage your confidence by blowing a good scoring chance!

Dissecting the difficult

In the case of the difficult shot, the peril is usually evident in the form of a bunker, a water hazard, or a narrow green that slopes away from you. (Not to mention the peril involved if you're competing in a match.) If you mishit the ball, it may end up in the bunker or the stream, fly across the green into the heavy rough, or run across the green into the woods. Dire consequences lie ahead! If you miss the shot, you may lose the hole to your opponent or even lose the match.

Less evident is the opportunity a difficult shot presents:

- ✔ **Put your practice to work:** A tough shot is an opportunity for you to test your skills and the techniques you've practiced. You have a chance to "show off." And, if you can pull the shot off, it may stun your opponent!

- ✔ **Build confidence:** Making a successful shot from a perilous situation helps you build confidence for the next time you face one. Tough shots present an opportunity to improve and gain experience.

Be aware of the hidden peril that each difficult shot presents. Notice the break of the green, the length of the grass, and any obstacles between your ball and the hole, and know the consequences of hitting the shot too short or too long.

Tackling Variables: Terrain and Conditions

Before you can decide what shot to play and how to play it, you need to make a full and honest assessment of the situation. You should pay attention to a number of variables when you consider your strategy, decide on a shot, and execute it.

The following sections cover some of the factors that the "computer of your mind" has to process when preparing for a shot. You factor some of these variables automatically or subconsciously with your instinctive awareness of your environment, but you should know that all the factors play a role in affecting your short game.

Shot variables demand your attention. Always take them into account when you analyze your situation, plan your strategy, and visualize the shot you're about to hit.

Accounting for the obvious

Outside of putting, where the surface of the green is typically uniform and the terrain subtle, your short-game shots become more complicated because of varying terrain and other variables, including the following:

- ✔ **The immediate lie:** What's the length of the grass? Is your ball lying flat on the ground? Or is it in a divot or a depression? Is the ball lying on an uphill, downhill, or sidehill lie?

- ✔ **Obstacles:** Do you have to maneuver around trees and bushes? Do you have to hit the ball over water or a bunker?

Book III

Playing Golf: The Swing and the Short Game

Sure, sometimes you can chip a ball from short grass off a flat lie to an unguarded green. But sometimes you have to pitch a ball off the side of a hill from deep rough and fly it over a bunker.

Much of the time, the mere fact that you need to play a short-game shot (chipping, pitching, or a bunker shot in this case) means that you missed the green with your approach shot, and missing the green almost always brings challenges — uphill, downhill, and sidehill slopes; bunkers; longer grass; and bushes and trees — into play.

Sensing the subtleties

In addition to obvious variables, you face subtle factors on the course that can affect the flight of the ball, its direction, and the distance it travels. You may be so caught up in your yardage, the hazards between you and the hole, and the target that you forget to consider how the more subtle conditions can affect your shot:

- **Grass variations:** If the grass is longer, factors such as the direction the grass grows affect your ball flight. Does the grass lean in the same direction as you intend to hit the ball, or is it growing against you? Grass growing against you fights your club as it passes through. Is the grass tangled? Is it wet? Is the ball sitting up in the grass near the tips of the blades or has it nestled down in? A good rule to keep in mind is that the more grass around the ball, the harder the shot becomes.

- **Firmness of the ground:** The ground may be soft or muddy because of rain, which can slow your ball when it lands. Or the ground may be hard and dry, which propels your ball forward faster when it hits the ground. Dry ground also affects ball-striking because a swing that brings the clubhead down too far behind the ball can bounce off hard ground and cause the blade to mishit the ball or even completely clear it.

- **Wind:** Are you hitting a shot with the wind blowing behind you? Is the wind blowing in your face? Maybe the wind is blowing from one side to another, which pushes the ball offline after it leaves the clubface. You know how the wind affects a high-flying, long drive from the tee, but your high-flying wedge shot, although it travels a shorter distance, spends a lot of time in the air and is therefore susceptible to the breeze. Check out the flag on the green. Is it dangling or whipping?

- **Lay of the land:** On some occasions, you may find yourself hitting a chip or a pitch uphill to an elevated green. Sometimes you can't see the hole or the green if the elevation is severe enough. And sometimes, especially on mountain courses, you may have to hit shots down to a green from an elevated position or a downhill lie. The lay of the land and where the ball lies in relation to your feet can force you to change your stance and, in some cases, affect your club selection. The ball reacts differently when coming off an uphill, downhill, or sidehill lie than it does from a flat position.

You should take all variables, even subtle ones, into account before you play a short-game shot.

Thinking through (But Not Overthinking) Your Play

After you recognize the peril and the opportunity of certain shots and consider the variables that affect the short game, consider your options. All the information you gather (by reading the previous sections in this chapter) should help you decide how you want to play the shot — what style of shot the situation calls for and what style of shot you're comfortable playing — and why.

As you consider your options for play within 75 yards of the hole, you also need to keep in mind your goals and expectations for short-game play. And after you've thought through your options, goals, and expectations, stop thinking! Let your subconscious mind and your body take over when you step up to the ball. Confused? Don't worry. We explain how all this psychobabble fits together for a top-notch short game in the following sections.

Understanding your options

For the short game, your options are typically a chip, pitch, bunker shot, putt, or flop, along with a handful of less-common specialty shots (which we outline in Chapter 8 of Book III). But the choices don't end there. You can play your many shot options with a variety of clubs. As we cover in more detail in Chapter 1 of Book I, you normally play short-game shots with a lob, sand, gap, or pitching wedge; a 9-, 8-, or 7-iron; or a putter.

You use these clubs because of the high lofts they provide, which make the ball travel a short distance. Highly lofted clubs are also easier to hit because they lift the ball off the turf and propel it forward.

You use your putter for the shortest shots because it offers no loft (or sometimes a tiny fraction of loft). Of the short irons and wedges, the 7-iron is the least lofted; it propels the ball the farthest on the lowest trajectory. Working up, each short iron produces more loft, less distance, and a higher trajectory.

REMEMBER

With each swing, you want to play the type of shot that gives you the most confidence and in turn the highest percentage of success.

Managing your goals and expectations

Setting goals and expectations is important for players who take the game seriously, but you need to set attainable goals and realistic expectations. If you're unsure of the difference between the two, check out the following list:

- **Goals:** Your short-game goals can be lofty. You may want to make more birdies, which means you want to 1-putt more often. That goal means you have to hit the ball closer to the hole consistently. Sometimes you achieve that goal; sometimes you fall short of the cup. Just remember that lofty goals often translate into hard work.

- **Expectations:** An expectation is something that you want to make happen all the time. For the average player, a good expectation is to make more pars or to improve your short game so that when you miss greens with your approach shots, you can occasionally save par or at least minimize the strokes needed to complete the hole.

Goals are important, but achieving reasonable expectations for each short-game situation builds the confidence necessary to strive for the goals. If your expectations are too high, you may be constantly disappointed, which wrecks your self-image and confidence. In Table 3-1, we outline suggestions for goals and expectations for the average golfer to keep in mind.

Table 3-1	Goals and Expectations for the Short Game	
Shot	*Expectation*	*Goal*
Chip	Get the ball on the green — anywhere on the green.	Sink the chip or get the ball close enough to the hole to need only one putt.
Pitch	Get the ball on the green — anywhere on the green.	Get the ball close enough to the hole to need only one putt.
Bunker shot	Get the ball out of the bunker in one shot.	Get the ball onto the green and as close to the hole as possible.
Putt	Use only two putts, and never more than three.	One-putt from time to time and never use more than two.

Work on your short game enough so that getting the ball on the green with one shot and then hitting no more than two putts is a reasonable expectation. If you consistently meet your expectations, holing a chip shot or hitting the ball close to the hole with one shot and needing only one putt becomes an attainable goal.

Problems arise when players think they have to get the ball close to the hole. They overanalyze, psych themselves out, and end up missing the green; now they have to chip it on or play a bunker shot and drill an 8-footer for par.

Relax and play within your abilities. Have a clear, concise, reasonable expectation of what you want to do. From 30 yards away, Tiger Woods can reasonably expect to get the ball up and in, but it may not be a realistic expectation for you. You should make getting up and down your goal, but your reasonable expectation is to get it on the green and 2-putt.

You can break down your goals and expectations depending on your distance from the pin. If you stand 50 yards away, your realistic goal may be to get the ball into the hole in three shots. But the closer your ball is to the green, the more you can realistically heighten your goals and expectations. For example, when faced with a short chip from just off the green, you may expect to get the ball into the hole in two strokes — a chip and one putt. (When you line up a short chip or short pitch shot, draw a mental five-foot circle around the hole.)

Short-game goals and expectations can also change as you play the hole. If you stand 50 yards away and your goal is to get the ball into the hole in three shots, flubbing your first shot into the bunker compromises your plan. You may make your goal to hit out of the bunker and close enough to the hole to 1-putt to keep on pace with your original plan, but that isn't a realistic expectation; if you miss that shot, you may end up adding more shots to your score than if you'd let your original goal go and worked with what you had. Make sure you minimize mistakes caused by unrealistic expectations. A reasonable expectation in this scenario is to hit your bunker shot and then 2-putt.

It seems simple, but breaking down the short game by setting goals and expectations illustrates why the short game is the best place to save strokes, and the best way to improve your scores is to aspire to improve your short game.

You can expect to land a ball onto the fairway far more often than you can expect to drop a shot within 10 feet of the cup from 50 yards. You can expect to hit the ball onto the green more often than you can expect to hit the ball close to the hole. You can expect to 2-putt more often than you 1-putt. Your goals may be to hit fairways, hit greens in regulation, and hit the ball close to the hole and 1-putt. But accomplishing reasonable expectations helps you build confidence and go a little easier on your psyche.

Book III

Playing Golf: The Swing and the Short Game

Playing in the subconscious

The game of golf, whether you're hitting a driver or a 75-yard sand wedge, is best played subconsciously. Let the game come to you. Trust the lessons you've taken and the skills that you've developed on the conscious side and then turn your mind off and make the shot subconsciously. The only thing you should think about during a swing is the target. After you perform all your analysis and consider the conditions, the variables, the perils, the opportunity, the percentages, the options, the statistics, and your goals for the shot, all your focus should be on the target.

You get too discombobulated if you play in the conscious mind. The golf swing is complicated, and the variables are many. All you can do is practice to develop a consistent swing and become confident with it. From there, golf is a matter of hitting a ball and walking after it. If you prepare yourself and don't take every second so seriously, you can enjoy the walk. Check Chapter 2 of Book V for all things mental.

Different people use different techniques to turn their minds off when the time comes to play the shot. Some folks use breathing techniques. Some use a repeating preshot routine, and others take a practice swing to relieve tension and reassure themselves about how they want to hit the shot. And some golfers choose to become very focused on the target.

The fundamental technique to quiet your mind during the swing that can serve you well in the long term is to build confidence through practice, which allows you to swing the club consistently and purposefully as opposed to a making a mechanical move toward the ball. You've hit the shot before countless times, so you know how to do it and you know how it feels; now let your body and sporting instincts take over.

Focusing on the Target Line

The object of golf is to propel the ball — via a putt, chip, pitch, or full shot — toward the hole. When the ball sits on a tee or lies at rest in the rough, fairway, or on the green, the hole is often the target. Sometimes, such as on par-5s, dogleg par-4s, or when the hole is tucked in a difficult spot on the green, you strategically aim at an area away from the hole.

According to simple physics, the shortest distance between two points is a straight line — in this case, the target line. The direction and distance between the ball and the target (which is usually the hole) is the *target line*. It extends from the ball to your target. (Actually, the target line should extend back through the ball 12 to 17 inches past the hole — or better, on to infinity — so that your putts are certain to reach the hole and not stop short.) The better you can visualize this imaginary line, the better chance you have of aiming properly and executing your shot with accuracy.

Visualizing the target line

Golfers use all sorts of techniques to visualize the target line. The key is to pick a visualization method, any method, and get into the habit of employing it each and every time. You want to visualize the line so you can draw your club back straight along the line. At the climax of your backswing, you swing the club forward, through the ball, and along the target line after contact.

The simplest way to help clearly "see" the target line is to stand behind the ball and position it directly between you and the target. Look at the ball and up the target line toward the target and draw yourself a mental path. When visualizing your target line, also visualize the speed of the ball on the green; that will affect how the ball rolls on the green.

For some extra mental reinforcement, some folks advocate picturing the target line as a blazing line of fire or dramatizing it as a trench dug in the ground. Some take their club and point it at the target as part of their pre-shot routine.

Standing close to the target line

The object of the short game is accuracy, and to be accurate, you have to get the club as close to the target line as you can. The farther you step away from your line, the more your swing and the clubhead begin to go around your body, which adds more power through centrifugal force. The longer the shot, the farther you have to step from the line. Therefore, the longer irons, like the 3-, 4-, 5-, and 6-irons, have longer shafts for more torque.

When your choice of iron gets shorter and your swing becomes more vertical, you need to step closer to the line. Not to worry: Short shots aren't about power.

The fundamental act of propelling the ball forward in a straight fashion is easier when you take the clubhead straight back and straight through. Think of playing horseshoes — you stand right on the target line and even face the target when tossing the shoe. Stand close to the line, and the swing becomes more vertical and straighter on that line.

Getting a Handle on Grip and Stance

Another important set of short-game fundamentals concern how to hold the club and where to stand in relation to the ball. When you understand what sort of grip to use and which hand should control the club, you can place more focus on your swing. The same goes for your stance; when you line up correctly with the ball, you can concentrate on the other variables that will come into play.

Grasping the importance of feel

Hold your club with a normal grip — the same one you use to hit full shots. Grip pressure on short-game shots should always be *soft,* or light. Hold the club lightly in your fingers to give yourself a better a judgment of your distance and direction. Tension in the hands and forearms can lead to firm shots that will travel too far. You may find having a good short game difficult if you choke the heck out of the club.

Loosening your grip helps you feel the weight of the clubhead because your fingers are more susceptible to the touch. You want to feel the weight of the club to improve your clubhead awareness. If you feel the clubhead, you can understand the mechanics of the swing, and in the short game, being aware of your swing leads to confident and controlled strokes. Your distance control improves, and you can experiment with different clubs and different shots knowing that as long as you can feel the clubface, you can hit any type of shot.

Allowing your front hand to lead

In all short-game shots, the face of the club needs to be square and straight to the target. If the face stays straight and contacts the ball straight, the ball can't go anywhere but straight.

What controls the face of the club? In chipping, pitching, putting, bunker shots, and in every other short-game variation imaginable, the hands run the show. More precisely, your nondominant hand controls the face: If you're a right-handed golfer, the left hand is in charge. (Vice versa if you're left-handed.) The back hand is only a guide — a supporter of the lead hand, who's the captain of the ship.

If you have trouble getting the feel for letting your front hand lead the swing, go to the practice tee and hit some chip shots with a 7-iron with your back hand firmly stuck in your pocket. You'll begin to see how the back hand is almost superfluous in the swing.

Centering on ball position

The average player should maintain a ball position in the center of the stance for normal short-game play. With as many variables as you face on a short shot — distance, speed of the green, loft of the clubface, length of the club, hazards, terrain, and wind, to name a few — keeping the ball in the center of your stance helps simplify and standardize at least one part of your technique.

Ben Hogan's real secret

The late, great American player Ben Hogan, who won every major championship and prided himself on practice and the search for perfection, was often asked what his "secret" was. The truth is debatable, but Hogan did offer those close to him one piece of advice that people rarely talk about and that certainly qualifies as a useful Hogan secret.

From time to time, as many people do, Hogan would awake in the morning for an early starting time with swollen or puffy hands. Hands in that condition are certainly a detriment to the short game, which requires touch and feel, so if you find yourself in this situation, you may try the same simple remedy Hogan used: drinking a pint of ginger ale, which reduces the swelling, before a morning round!

You need to move the ball up or back in your stance in some extreme situations caused by the terrain and wind, and we address those situations in Chapter 8 of Book III.

Coping With Common Misfires

Hitting the ball from the tee is easy compared to the short game. Heck, the ball sits up on a tee, you hit it with the same club almost every time, and you can swing away and hit it as far as you want. The short game, however, presents you with shots of different lengths and shapes from different lies. More possible shots mean more possible miscues. Don't be daunted, though: Every short-game shot has a common denominator of acceleration and simple mechanics. The shot isn't as difficult as it seems.

You can start improving your game this very minute simply by identifying and avoiding the common miscues that we cover in the following sections. And be sure to check out Book V and Chapter 8 of Book III, which offer concrete advice about how you can correct mistakes.

Playing without purpose

Without slowing up play, be sure to take the time to adequately check your lie, read the green, and clearly visualize a shot before you play it. Prepare for your shot while you walk to your ball or while other players hit their shots.

Despite what you see on television, you should golf at a brisk pace and not deliberately. Touring professionals play for hundreds of thousands of dollars and do so on closed golf courses in front of TV cameras. Although you should try to emulate their play, you shouldn't try to emulate their pace of play.

No matter what, don't hit a shot without having a crystal clear vision of it and deciding on a specific target. Play quickly, but don't just smack the ball around.

Being underprepared

Practice the various techniques and types of shots before you confront them on the golf course. Practice helps you build confidence and widen your array of options. Your self-confidence tells you when you're ready to try a certain shot on the golf course. Sometimes, just like with a rookie quarterback, you have to press a certain technique into service. Pressure presents the truest test, and you have to perform under fire — but make sure you prepare the shot enough times in practice to build up your confidence.

Using the wrong club

You can have a better short game, lower your score, and have more fun if you play shots you're comfortable hitting. If from 30 yards and in you feel comfortable hitting a 7-iron for every shot, and it works, do it. Tell yourself, "I'm comfortable doing this. I love hitting this club."

In the past, Tiger Woods has used a 60-degree wedge for every shot around the greens, whether that's a flop shot with a full swing where the ball goes only 20 yards or a shot that goes 50 feet by skipping along the ground knee high. He hasn't needed a bunch of different wedges; he's done it all with one wedge that he's felt very comfortable with.

Comfort and confidence contribute as much to short-game success as practice. After you get comfortable with a particular club and make it your go-to club, you can focus your practice sessions around shots hit with the club. Chapter 1 of Book I has more about stocking your bag for short-game success.

Aiming to displease: Shooting for the hole regardless of the conditions

Short-game shots are all straight shots. Unlike other shots in golf, you don't hit short-game shots with the intention of curving the ball. You don't need to hook it or fade it in there. Just knock it straight. This concept may seem simple to grasp, but remembering it can help you tremendously with your aim.

If you have a 10-foot break from right to left on the green, you still hit a straight putt to try to make it; you just have to aim 10 feet to the right of the hole because of the break. You don't aim at the hole and try to push the ball out with your putter. You pick a spot for your target line and aim so that the green takes care of the work for you.

The same goes for a 30-yard shot over a bunker, or any pitch or chip from off the green. You may determine that the uneven green will cause the ball to break 10 feet from the right to the left after you hit your target, so you have to allow for that, but all you want to do is hit the ball straight to your target landing area. Remove the curves and angles from your mind after you pick your line and focus on hitting the ball straight.

Ignoring textbook technique

In golf, you practice fundamentals and develop preferences. You have to adhere to the fundamentals to be successful; the preferences you can enjoy.

The trick is, you can't let a preference take over a fundamental because you reduce your chances of success. Standing a certain way when you putt may feel good, and being comfortable is great — but you can't be a good putter if your stance clashes with the fundamentals of putting.

For instance, you can't grip the putter with the toe in the air and stand far away from the ball and think you can be a good putter. If you do, the putter naturally comes off line. Your preference defies the fundamental that the blade should come straight back along the target line, come back down along the same line, and swing straight through toward your target.

Book III

Playing Golf: The Swing and the Short Game

Getting too far from your work

Fundamentally, if you put your eyes over your target line, keep your putterhead over the line, take the putterhead straight back on the line, and bring it forward straight through, you can be a good putter. The same goes for chipping. The closer you get to "your work," the easier it is to make good shots.

You won't find any magic that drives this premise, just simple physics and logic. Think of a dart thrower or a billiards player. Each faces his target and tosses the dart or slides the cue right on line toward the target or hole.

Golf's a little different from darts and billiards because you stand to the side of the ball, but you can improve your chances by getting as close to the line as you can.

Experiencing death by deceleration

Don't stop the club when it strikes the ball at impact. Never, on any shot in golf, should you decelerate. Let the club swing freely and through the ball to its natural completion, as if you're sweeping away dust with a broom or as the pendulum of a grandfather clock swings. Stopping at impact can only result in a flubbed shot that falls short of your target. Make sure you have confidence in the type of shot you want to hit and in the club you pull out of the bag. Most players decelerate because they don't want to hit the ball too far or because they don't have confidence in the shot. Commit . . . and hit!

Chapter 4

Chipping Away at the Short Game

The chip shot, which may seem like a little, unglamorous type of shot, is the foundation on which you can significantly improve your short game. Technically and literally speaking, you hit a *chip shot* when you're close to (but off of) the green. When we say "close", we're talking within 10 feet of the green.

A chip shot is shorter than a pitch shot. With a chip shot, you literally chip the ball off the old block like you're carving a wood chip. As you see in Chapter 5 of Book III, a pitch shot is more like throwing the ball up in the air — pitching it from farther out. You refer to chip shots in feet; if you're talking yards, you're talking about a pitch.

In this chapter, we show you how the chip shot is a hugely important skill to have and tell you how to play the shot effectively.

Discovering the Chip

Chip shots are shorter than pitches and stay mostly on the ground. Chips are also easier than pitches, or at least they should be. With the proper technique, you can chip the ball close enough to the hole to tap the ball in . . . unless, of course, you sink that chip!

Chips are played around the greens with anything from a 5-iron to a wedge. (Head to Chapter 1 of Book I for the lowdown on these and other clubs.) The basic idea is to get the ball on the green and rolling as soon as you can. If you get the ball running like a putt, you have an easier time judging how far it will go. The following sections show you some important chipping considerations.

Looking at the characteristics of chip shots

The following are the general characteristics of the chip shot:

- ✔ A chipped ball doesn't have much loft.
- ✔ The ball pops off the club, making a chipping or flicking sound.
- ✔ The ball streaks through the air but not in the arc of a high lob. It flies in a low, tight manner, propelled more forward than up.
- ✔ The ball covers only a short distance in the air. It should spend 20 percent of its duration in the air and 80 percent on the ground.

A chip is the best way to keep the ball low, keep it on the ground, and get it rolling as soon as possible. As we advise in Chapter 3 of Book III, you have a much better chance of getting the ball close to the hole if you roll it as opposed to hitting it through the air. You can lower your scores this way because judging the distance of a shot rolling on the ground is easier than estimating a shot that flies through the air.

Choosing the chip over the putt

A chip shot is the next best thing to putting because of the amount of time the ball spends rolling along the ground (and you don't always have the luxury of putting the ball). Consider using the chip shot when you miss the green with your approach shot and you're almost close enough to putt. Although you face occasions when you can use the putter from off the green (see Chapter 8 of Book III), you also encounter plenty of situations when putting your ball isn't strategically wise:

- ✔ Your ball may lie in longer grass around the green.
- ✔ Your ball comes to rest between a bunker and the green.
- ✔ Your ball must travel over a hill before it reaches the green.
- ✔ Your ball may be only a few feet off the green, but the hole may be a long way from your ball.

Evaluate your situation. On most courses, fairway grass gives way to an *apron* of longer grass that circles the green before you get to the fringe of shorter grass. If you have 20 feet between your ball and the hole and you want to try to putt, the chances of your 20-foot putt rolling through the fairway, over the collar, and finally onto the green and close to the hole aren't nearly as good as your chances of chipping it over that grass, landing it on the green, and letting it roll close to the hole. Chipping is often the best-case scenario for accuracy.

Choosing Your Chipping Tool

The club you use to chip the ball determines how the ball flies and rolls. If you're close enough to the hole to use a chip shot, you don't need to loft the ball into the air for a long time, so grab a less-lofted club to play the shot.

As long as you follow the fundamentals of execution (see the "Hitting a Solid Chip Shot" section later in this chapter), what club you use is a matter of preference. But keep in mind that hitting a chip shot with a highly lofted club reduces your chances of getting close to the hole. Getting a less-lofted clubface solidly on the ball at contact is easier, and a less-lofted club creates more roll after the ball lands on the green.

Players enjoy the highest percentage of success with a 7- or 8-iron. Those two clubs have less-lofted clubfaces, making them more accurate chipping tools, and they roll the ball nicely. Figure 4-1 illustrates this concept. You can use those clubs for every chip, no matter how many feet lay in front of you, by simply taking a longer backswing. Though we suggest that you practice with as many clubs as you can, if you forced us to pick, we'd say the best club to chip with is a 7-iron. Plus, choosing a 7-iron and sticking with it helps remove one variable from the chip shot — club selection.

Practice, and only practice, makes you better. Try all sorts of clubs for these shots. Sooner or later, you develop a feel for the short game. We can't stress this point enough: Use as many clubs as possible when practicing! Observing how different clubs perform in different situations is one of the secrets of a successful short game.

Contemplating the Chip

You'll likely need to chip at least once every time you go out on the course, so you need to know what you can achieve when you employ the chip shot. After you understand what you can accomplish, you can plan a strategy to meet your goals. The following sections help you reasonably evaluate what you can do with the chip and plan your shot.

Book III

Playing Golf: The Swing and the Short Game

From address...

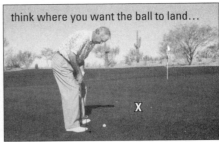

think where you want the ball to land...

then try to hit it...

so that the ball runs to the hole.

Figure 4-1:
Get the ball
rolling.

Chipping goals and expectations

For every golf shot you hit, you should have both goals and expectations for the result. Knowing the difference and how to push and prepare yourself for each shot allows you to start lowering your scores — and your blood pressure. What do you want to accomplish with each chip? What do you consider an acceptable result? A reasonable expectation?

- **Setting a goal:** Go for the green! An ambitious goal for your chip shots is that you chip every one close enough to the hole to tap in or need only one putt to finish the hole. Granted, you can hole a putt from anywhere if you get lucky, but a chip shot that results in a nice, comfortable, short putt is a great success and should be a goal you aspire to.

- **Meeting your expectations:** An easily attainable expectation for your chip shots, with reasonable practice, is that you hit the ball onto the green every time. Regardless of how close the ball is to the hole after your chip, you should expect to get the ball onto the green and hit no more than two putts every single time.

Mapping out a chip-shot strategy

Because a chip shot shouldn't cover much distance through the air, and because you use a less-lofted club such as a 7- or 8-iron, you want to run/roll the ball most of the way to the hole. The ball should pop over the grass between you and the green before rolling out. So you have to calculate the length of the shot, the speed of the green, and the direction the ball will roll after it lands. See the shot in your mind before you play it.

The quicker you get the ball onto the ground, the more it can roll to the cup. You should try to roll the ball for about 80 percent of the distance it travels. If your ball rests 20 feet from the hole, and you choose to chip the ball, you should try to land the ball about 4 feet in front of you to make it roll about 16 feet.

Hitting a Solid Chip Shot

Simply put, hitting a chip shot is a matter of physics. The following list breaks it down into easy steps. You can use this list as checklist for your setup and your chipping practice, along with Figure 4-2:

1. **Take out your club of choice.**
2. **Pick a suitable spot where you want to land the ball.**
3. **Stand close to your target line.**
4. **Keep your weight in the center of your stance.**
5. **Open your front foot and shoulders toward the target so that you can virtually face the hole.**
6. **Grip the club lightly.**
7. **Draw the club back low to the ground, keeping your wrists firm and turning by rotating your shoulders.**
8. **Keep your legs and lower body still and out of the swing.**
9. **Swing the club back along the target line and then forward through the ball.**
10. **Watch the ball hit the spot and roll toward the hole.**

Taking aim

Your first task is to pick an intermediate spot where you want to land the shot. The ultimate target, of course, is the hole, but first you have to deal with the initial 20 percent of the shot that flies through the air and lands on your target.

Figure 4-2:
When chipping, the clubface has to swing straight back along the line and straight through.

Pick a spot about 2 feet onto the green (see Figure 4-3). From that spot, I like to visualize the ball rolling the rest of the way to the hole. Visualization is a big part of chipping. Try to picture the shot before you hit the ball. Then be as exact as you can with your target. Don't aim for an area. Try to hit a blade of grass! You can't be too precise.

Figure 4-3:
Pick a
spot on
the putting
surface.

Book III

**Playing
Golf: The
Swing and
the Short
Game**

You consciously determine the spot that rests 20 percent of the way between you and the hole while you walk up to the shot, evaluate the situation, and read the break of the green. Is the shot uphill? Downhill? Will the ball roll to the left after it lands on the spot? To the right?

The spot you pick must allow for the unevenness and break of the green after the ball hits and rolls. If you think the green will break 10 feet from the right to the left, pick a landing spot ten feet to the right of the hole as your landing area. (Check out Chapter 6 of Book III for tips on reading greens.)

Don't try to curve the chip shot — you want to hit it straight to your landing spot and let gravity and the green naturally roll the ball toward the hole. (Take a look at Figure 4-2 to see how you hit straight toward the target, no matter whether you're aiming at the flag or off to one side.)

All you can do is pick a spot and hit it — the rest is up to the green and nature. You can't think about the hole. After you commit to the landing spot, turn off your brain and play in the subconscious. You've done your work! Hit the ball as if it were on a straight railroad directly to the spot.

Lies and secrets: Consider your ball placement

Next comes the problem of how your ball is lying on the ground. If it's in longer grass, you need to use a more lofted club and make a longer swing, no matter where the hole is. (**Remember:** Longer grass means a longer swing.) You need to get the ball high enough to escape the longer rough. If the ball is lying *down* (in a depression) and you can't get it out with a straighter-faced club, you have to go to more loft and move the ball back a little in your stance — closer to your right foot — to make the shot work. This part of the game calls for creativity.

Setting up your stance

One key to chipping is your setup. Creating the right positions at address is essential. Your stance should be similar to the one you use on pitch shots (which we cover in Chapter 5 of Book III): narrow, with about 12 inches from heel to heel, and open, with your left foot back from the target line (see Figure 4-4). Your shoulders should be open to the target as well.

During your stroke, focus on the back of your left wrist. That wrist must stay flat and firm, as in putting (see Figure 4-5). To keep your left wrist flat, tape a popsicle stick to the back of that wrist (slipping the stick under your watch-band works almost as well). You feel any breakdowns right away.

You hit a chip shot by taking a stance that puts you close to your line — close enough so that you can get your eyes almost directly over the target line, as you can see in Figure 4-2a (and see Chapter 3 of Book III for more on the target line). If you're close to the target line, you have a better chance of taking the club straight back along the line (see Figure 4-2b) and making it go straight through to the target (see Figure 4-2d).

Narrow your stance...

and keep your left wrist flat...

through impact...

and beyond.

Figure 4-4:
Chip with
your hands
ahead of
the ball.

Book III

**Playing
Golf: The
Swing and
the Short
Game**

Figure 4-5:
Keep your wrist flat and firm while chipping.

Put a pen inside your watchband.

That'll firm up your wrist.

Finding the stance that works for you

Your stance is largely a matter of preference (we detail fundamentals and preferences in Chapter 3 of Book III). What feels good to you? What makes you comfortable? As long as you're comfortable and in balance, you can let the club do all the work.

A preference that may make you feel more comfortable is to slightly open your stance. Opening your stance allows you to see down the target line and may make it easier for you to swing the clubhead at the target. Being comfortable enhances your confidence. If you're right-handed, you may want to drop your left foot back a few inches behind your right and point your left toe about 45 degrees out toward the direction of your target (see Figure 4-6). Instead of your feet being parallel and pointing out in front of you, your left foot should angle a bit outward.

Positioning the ball

Keep the ball in the middle of your stance for chip shots (see Figure 4-6a). This setup makes it simple for you to swing the clubhead along the target line, and the angle of attack at which the clubface comes through the ball holds true. Generally speaking, moving the ball back in your stance makes the ball fly lower (and moving it forward pops it higher), but you needn't move the ball back or forward for standard chip shots, no matter which club you use.

Figure 4-6:
Position the ball in the center of your stance, keep steady, and let your left wrist keep the clubface straight to the target.

Book III

Playing Golf: The Swing and the Short Game

Reviewing weight distribution

When playing a chip shot, put your weight in the center of your stance, right below your backside. This balanced position makes it easier to open yourself to the target — that is, to point your front toe and shoulder a little left or right of where they normally face when you address the ball.

In general, the higher you need the ball to fly, the more weight (as much as 80 percent) you should place on your front foot. The more weight you put on your left side (for righties), the more the club swings up rather than back and low to the ground. When a righty plants that left side, the club arch becomes more vertical, and swinging a club vertically makes the descending blow steeper, which makes the ball fly higher.

For most chip shots, you want the ball to fly low and run, so keep your weight in the middle of your stance throughout the swing. You don't really need leg power at all for the shot. Swing around your legs. If you have trouble with a too-active weight shift, hit some practice chips with your feet together to work on your balance. Or imagine that you're riding a horse and position your legs like you're in the saddle, which keeps them quiet and evenly weighted.

Setting your shoulders

Your shoulders will naturally open or angle just left of the target if your stance is open (see Figures 4-2a and 4-6c). You should be close enough to the ball so that you can almost look right over it and right down the target line (so you virtually face the hole).

If you have trouble visualizing this stance, stand in front of full-length mirror. Put a ball down, keep your eyes over your line, and then look up in the mirror and notice where your head position is, where your eyes are in relation to your line, and how your shoulders face slightly toward the target. See how close you are to the line. Imagine a target between you and the mirror, about 10 feet away. Chip a ball to the corner of the bedpost or the dresser. Seeing yourself and how you stand in relation to the ball and the target line gives you a good awareness of your body and the mechanics that go into the chip shot.

Gripping the club

A standard golf grip is fine for the chip shot (see Figure 4-6a). You may feel pressure to get the ball close to the hole, but be aware that pressure can produce tension. So try to resist. Keep a light grip on the club so that you can feel the ball hit the blade. A light grip lets you swing the club at a softer pace and gives you a better chance of propelling the ball the proper distance. The chip isn't a power shot — you need to focus on touch. Let your hands feel the shot by keeping a light grip.

Making your move

The distance of the shot and the velocity with which you need to swing the club to reach your target landing spot determine how far you take the club back. The chip shot relies on feel, and feel comes with practice. You're not born with feel. You're born with touch, perhaps, and vision.

Swinging the club to hit a chip shot is like drawing back the string on a bow to shoot the arrow (see Figure 4-6b). You must judge how far back you have to draw the club to shoot the ball over the fringe and onto the green, propelling it to the hole.

The chipper of days gone by

Golf club manufacturers used to produce and sell a club called a *chipper*. It looked like a putter, but it had the loft of a 4-iron. Why? Because in the olden days of Ben Hogan, Sam Snead, and Byron Nelson, players hit chip shots with 4- and 5-irons. The grass was firmer, dryer, and longer then; golf courses weren't as long and lush. Nelson, for instance, played on burned out, nonirrigated grass in Texas, so he could keep the ball very low without having grassy areas to carry. He also needed to propel the ball forward. In Scotland, course operators didn't irrigate until about ten years ago. Today's pros now play on lush, long grass, and so do you, in most cases.

Tracing the length and shape of the swing

The easiest way to understand the chip swing is to think of it like the hands on a clock. The bottom of your swing is 6:00. The top, above your head, is 12:00. If you swing the club back along the target line from a starting point of 6:00, and your backswing stops at 3:00, for example, the swing along the target line after you strike the ball shouldn't stop until the 9:00 position. In chipping, the appropriate times on the hands of the clock of your swing vary depending on the distance you need. (See Figures 4-6b and 4-6d for an illustration.)

Draw the club back low to the ground along the target line and then forward through the ball. Finish the swing pointing at the target, at the same distance that you took the club back. Don't stop when you hit the ball. Keep the club moving with your front wrist leading, which keeps the face on the target line (see Figure 4-6c). Players who stop the club when they hit the ball are left to wonder why the ball didn't make the green. You never see the professionals take a big swing and stop at the ball. They may take a big swing, but the follow-through is just as big after the ball sails away — and with good reason: simple physics!

Talking about speed

If anything, you should slightly accelerate your club through the ball. You can't take the club back at 10 miles per hour and then hit the ball at 5 miles per hour and expect to have success. You can take the club back at 10 miles per hour, swing it through at 10 miles per hour, and have a tremendous amount of success. You can even take the club back at 10 miles per hour and swing it through at 20 miles per hour for a successful shot. But you can't decelerate the club at impact.

Book III

Playing Golf: The Swing and the Short Game

Too Close for Comfort: Paul Runyan's Greenside Chip Trick

The late Paul Runyan is well known as a two-time PGA Championship winner (1934 and 1938) and revered for his short-game prowess. The Hall of Famer won more than 50 times on the PGA Tour despite being one of the shortest hitters of his time.

From time to time, Runyan gave short-game lessons and tips for PGA professionals to teach their students. One of the specialty shots he recommended is a shot that we'll call "the Runyan" because he deserves to have his name on it!

When you find your ball very close to the hole and just off the green, you don't want to putt the ball through a longer or grainy grass fringe. Trying to putt a ball through such grass is an unpredictable venture because the wiry or lush grass slows the shot and perhaps knocks your ball offline. But the prospect of chipping the ball through the long grass can also be daunting because the grass can grab the club and turn the face when you try to swing through it. And if the hole is cut close to your ball, an errant swing may send the ball much too far past the hole.

The Runyan is accurate because you stand over the ball like a putt, you use a putting grip, your eyes are over your line, and you take the club straight back and straight through. The loft of the club gets the ball out of and past the long grass, and the rest of the ball path rolls out like a putt.

If you face a tough situation and you aren't confident using the conventional chip shot, the time to use the Runyan has arrived. Here's how:

1. **Take your putting stance with your front foot open a bit.**

2. **Stand close to your target line.**

3. **Hold the club in a vertical fashion, like a putter, so the club stands up on its toe with the heel off the ground.**

   A 7-iron works best. See Figures 4-7a and 4-7b.

4. **Grip the club like you grip your putter (see Figure 4-8a).**

5. **Position the ball in the center of your stance or a little toward the back, which delofts the club (see Figure 4-8b).**

6. **Swing straight back and straight through in a pendulum fashion, as if you're putting, keeping the clubhead low to the ground.**

   Swing mostly with your shoulders and arms. (See Figure 4-8.)

Figure 4-7: With the heel of the club elevated, take the club straight back and straight forward to produce a Runyan roll.

The toe of the club, which is the only part that sits flush to the ground, makes contact with the ball (see Figure 4-7c). The toe deadens the hit a little bit. Because you employ little loft, the ball rides the face of the club slightly, giving the ball some overspin so it rolls forward.

The ball hops out of the grass low (see Figure 4-7d), just like a regular chip shot (depending on how hard you swing), and then rolls out softly to the hole. Just like with conventional chips, you want the ball to roll for about 80 percent of the shot. Putting imparts overspin — you want the ball to turn over and roll. With the Runyan, the ball rides up the face of the club, spins, hits the green, and skips a bit before it releases and starts to tumble and roll forward.

The advantage of playing the Runyan is that only the toe of the club goes through the grass. If you hit the shot normally, more of the blade would try to fight the coarse blades of grass. What happens when the grass grabs the blade? The clubface closes and knocks the ball offline. If the club catches in the grass, your shot goes kaput! But if you put only the toe through the grass, you reduce the chances that your club will catch.

Under certain situations, because of the long rough a few feet off the green and a close-cut pin, you face a very difficult shot. In this circumstance, you can try to hit the Runyan shot with a sand wedge. The ball comes out soft, bumps like a knuckleball, and trickles out. Because you hit it with only the toe, the ball comes out deadened and harmless. Just make sure to bring the club back far enough to get the ball close to the hole and accelerate through the swing.

As with every technique, be sure to spend time practicing the Runyan before you try to use it on the golf course.

GARY SAYS

Gary's approach to the chip

When I play a tour event, one of the first things I do is go to the putting green, where I hit putts and chips to get an idea of the speed of the greens. I find a flat spot on the green and drop some balls about 5 feet from the putting surface. Then I put a coin on the green 2 feet from the *fringe* (the collar of grass around the green — it's longer than the grass on the green but shorter than the grass on the fairway). Then I take an 8-iron, 9-iron, and wedge and chip balls onto the green, trying to bounce each ball off the coin so that it runs to the hole. This strategy gives me a good idea of how fast the greens are that week — and when you miss as many greens as I do, the practice comes in handy.

Figure 4-8: The Runyan resembles a lofted putt you hit with a 7-iron.

Book III

Playing Golf: The Swing and the Short Game

Chapter 5

Making the Pitch

The pitch shot is an exciting example of the precision and drama of golf. A pitch shot is fun to watch — especially if you're the one hitting it — because a well-struck pitch flies majestically through the air, hanging up until it lands on the green and hops near the flag. While in flight, a pitch shot provides suspense and gives you time to enjoy the view. Of course, you also have time to second-guess yourself and wonder whether the shot is as good as it seems. Will it reach the green? Will it carry the bunker? Will it stick or bounce off the back? "C'mon baby, be as good as you look!" Yeah, a pitch shot leaves you time to beg, too.

A pitch shot falling to the earth can cause you to gasp or curse: a gasp caused by the pleasant surprise of how close the ball falls to the hole, or the curse as the ball plummets into the front bunker.

In this chapter, we break down the pitch shot and tell you how to hit nice, controlled pitches that hit the green and stay there. Hitting these exciting, airborne flyers is simpler than you may imagine. Soon you'll be providing the drama shots on the golf course yourself!

Picking out the Pitch Shot

A *pitch* is a shot that you hit to the green from anywhere within 75 yards. By way of comparison, a pitch shot is longer than a chip shot, stays in the air for much more time, and, after it lands, rolls less. The techniques of both are similar. The best way to get a handle on the difference between a chip shot and a pitch shot, as we discuss in Chapter 4 of Book III, is to discuss the length of a chip in feet and the length of a pitch in yards.

Pinning down the traits of a pitch shot

The pitch is a vital shot to have in your repertoire because hitting the green from up to 75 or 80 yards out is essential to good scoring. You want to have confidence in both your pitches and chips, but you don't want to use them both on the same hole and put pressure on your putter.

The following are the general characteristics of the pitch:

✔ A pitch shot has a good amount of loft and flies through the air in the arc of a high lob.

✔ A pitch shot is a mini-version of the full swing and an extended version of a chip shot.

✔ The ball travels most of its distance (at least 70 percent) in the air and then stops near the hole with perhaps a little roll (no more than 30 percent of its total distance).

Even the best players try to avoid pitch shots. They're in-between shots. You can't just make your normal, everyday, full swing — that would send the ball way too far. You're stuck making a partial swing, which is never easy, especially when you're under pressure.

Knowing when to use a pitch shot

You need to pitch when your ball rests far enough away from the green that you have to fly the ball up and onto it because you can't chip it on — you have too much real estate to cover with a chip shot. And if you need to hit the ball high and have it land steeply without rolling much after it hits the green, the pitch shot is for you. In addition to distance and having a small amount of green to work with, you may face other troublesome features that stand between your ball and the cup:

✔ A bunker may loom between your ball and the green.

✔ You may have to carry the ball over a creek or pond.

✔ You may have to avoid a grass bunker.

✔ A hill or mogul may guard the green.

A pitch shot allows you to fly your ball high through the air, over the trouble, and onto the green.

Choosing the Pitching Club

The pitching stick you pull from your bag depends greatly on how much yardage lies between you, the green, and the hole. As long as you follow the fundamentals of execution when you hit the shot (see the "Hitting a Solid Pitch Shot" section later in the chapter), the club you use to hit a pitch is a matter of situation and preference.

Fundamentally, you want to choose a club that, when struck, sends the ball flying far and high enough to cover all the land and landscape features you need it to. You also need to bring the ball down with a suitable trajectory so it stops on the green or perhaps near the hole.

Your pitching wedge may seem to be the obvious choice, and fundamentally, it is. But the short game offers plenty of room for preferences. Some players may prefer to hit pitch shots with anything from a 9-iron to a sand wedge.

Practice pitch shots with your short irons on the range so when you get onto the golf course, you have a good sense for the trajectory and distance each short iron produces. Make sure you hit all types of pitches — low liners that stay under the wind or high flops that clear bunkers — with different clubs to account for any situation you may encounter.

Thinking through the Pitch

The pitch shot is one of the most pleasing and exciting shots in the game of golf when properly executed. A range of emotions can occur when you see that you've hit a good pitch shot. The best of them are sure to draw a smile from you and a grimace from your competitor. So how do you get that shot?

Before you make your pitch, you must think about what you want to achieve and how you want to achieve it. Think about your goals and expectations for your pitch swings and then take a minute on the course to plan how you can make the most of these swings.

Setting goals and expectations

For every golf shot you hit, you should have both goals and expectations for the result. The goal is the best-case scenario — the dream accomplishment for the pitch. The expectation is an acceptable result — what you'll be happy with if you can't meet your goal. Here are a couple of examples:

✔ **Establishing a goal:** Go for the green! An ambitious goal for your pitch shots is that you pitch every one of them close enough for a tap-in or 1-putt to finish the hole. Yes, you can hole a putt from anywhere if you get lucky, but a pitch shot that results in a nice, comfortable short putt is a smashing success and a great goal.

✔ **Meeting your expectations:** An easily attainable expectation for your pitch shots is that you hit the ball onto the green, *anywhere,* every time. Avoiding creeks, bunkers, or other hazards is a major part of this expectation because avoiding the trouble is more important than getting the ball close to the hole.

Planning your pitch-shot strategy

Visualizing and planning are vital to the success of your pitch shot. You need to consider the situation at hand before you pick your target line and your landing target. Ask yourself the following questions before you pitch and run (to the green):

✔ **Although your ultimate goal is getting the ball into the hole, should the hole really be your target?** Is the hole cut in a difficult spot, such as tucked behind a bunker or dangerously close to the edge of the green? Would aiming for the larger, middle part of the green be a safer, more sensible target?

✔ **How far do you need the ball to fly before it lands on the green?** This information is important for club selection, because you need to factor in the wind, the obstacles, and your desired ball trajectory.

✔ **Is the green tilted in such a way that your ball may roll off the green or toward the cup?** If so, pick your target line and target landing area accordingly.

✔ **Do you expect the green to be hard or soft? Will the ball hit and stick or will it bounce and roll?** Take into account the conditions of the greens you've seen on previous holes or on the practice-putting surface, the recent weather (wind hardening the surface or rain softening it), your shot trajectory (high shots may stick, lower liners may roll), and the slope of the green.

✔ **Will strong winds affect the ball while it sails through the air?** Pick your club, your target line, and your trajectory accordingly.

✔ **Do you have a good lie, or is the ball on an uneven spot, divot, or long grass?** Remember to swing accordingly. For right-handers, a ball above your feet tends to pull to the left *(draw),* and a ball below your feet fades to the right *(slice).* (Vice versa for lefties.) Be sure to stay down and swing through divots.

> ✓ **Where do you stand in your match? Are you in a situation that justifies taking a bold chance?** You may have to take on that tight pin placement if you come to the 18th one shot back, but if you're nursing a one-shot lead, pick a safe spot in the middle of the green and go for the 2-putt.

Consider all your options and available information before you choose a target, but when you do choose a target, make it very specific, like the flagstick, a ridge on the green, the line of a bunker, or the flat opening in front of the green. This exactness helps you focus your mind, gauge the length of the swing, and be precise with your aim.

Hitting a Solid Pitch Shot

Hitting a pitch shot is a matter of swinging the right club with the proper amount of force, allowing the loft of the iron and the speed of the clubhead to send the ball in the air toward the hole. As the old saying goes, "Let the club do the work." The following points break the pitch shot down into a "how to" list that you can come back to for reference, along with Figures 5-1 and 5-2 (and see the following sections for a detailed discussion of the pitch swing):

1. **Visualize the shot by picking a spot on which to land the ball.**

2. **Choose the club that can carry the ball through the air the proper distance.**

3. **Keep more of your weight on the front side of your body.**

4. **Open your front foot by withdrawing it about 6 inches from the target line.**

5. **Grip the club lightly.**

6. **Keep your head and body still.**

7. **Swing the club back along the target line and then forward through the ball in a smooth fashion.**

8. **Follow through straight toward the target.**

9. **Use the result of the shot to improve on your next pitch.**

   Where did the ball land in relation to your target? Did your highly lofted club put too much spin on the ball? Did the wind knock it down? Take all info into account.

Book III

Playing Golf: The Swing and the Short Game

Determining your flight plan and velocity

The peril in hitting a pitch shot is that you can't just swing away like you can with a driver or some of your long irons. Because the pitch shot places a premium on distance control within 75 yards, it requires you to hit the ball the proper length. You may have some wind to deal with, and you should account for that too. Unless you face a truly strong wind, however, you shouldn't be concerned with its effect on the distance or direction of the golf ball.

After you select the club you're comfortable with, the trick is to match the length of your backswing to the distance you want the ball to fly:

- ✔ If you don't take the club back far enough, your instincts can cause you to try to add some force on the downswing, which results in an uneven swing without a smooth or flowing motion.

- ✔ If you swing the club too far back, you may decelerate the club on the downswing in an attempt to feather the ball up to the hole. Deceleration, in any type of golf swing, is death.

Pick a suitable spot where you want to land the ball. Remember, you want the ball to fly over any trouble, such as a bunker or creek, and then land on the green near the hole.

Although pitch shots fly higher than chips, you still want to get the ball back to the ground ASAP so it doesn't sail too far. Pick out your landing area somewhere short of your final target and let the ball roll the rest of the way.

Setting up your stance

Your stance for a pitch shot isn't much different from the stance you use for a full golf swing. When you hit a pitch, however, you open up your stance a little bit by opening your lead foot about 6 inches forward from parallel (with your back foot), and you stand closer to the target line (see Chapter 3 of Book III for more on the target line). You should feel as though you're partially facing the hole. Your waist and shoulders should naturally follow that open toe (see Figure 5-1a). An open stance allows you to be target oriented (with your lead foot aiming at the target) and to finish your swing facing the target. Having your shoulders open to the target also helps you more easily sense the target and swing the club back closer to the intended flight line with your hands ahead of the ball, leading the clubhead. Stand so that the ball is about 2 inches to the left of your right big toe, as shown in Figure 5-2.

Figure 5-1:
With your
front foot
and body
properly
positioned,
swing along
the target
line with
good weight
balance.

Positioning the ball

The pitch shot fundamentals lie somewhere between the full swing and the
chip shot. Therefore, the ball position for a pitch shot is almost the same as it
is for any other shot — the longer the club, the more toward the front of the
stance the ball should be. For pitch shots, you're likely to use a sand wedge,
pitching wedge, 9-iron, or 8-iron, so you should play the ball in the middle of
your stance (see Figure 5-1b).

Figure 5-2:
When you pitch, your shoulders and feet must be aligned to the left of where you want the ball to go.

You can try positioning the ball about an inch farther back than normal, which puts your hands a little more forward and creates a steeper swing arc. This type of swing makes your clubhead come through the ball in a more downward fashion, creating a sharp blow that puts backspin on the ball. That backspin helps the ball stop quickly when it hits the green on the fly.

Distributing your weight

When playing a pitch shot, you should put your weight in the center of your stance or, if you prefer, shifted more onto your front leg. The more weight you put on your front side, the more the club swings up to provide a descending blow.

A steeper swing makes the ball fly higher, so the higher you need the ball to fly, the more weight you should place on your front foot.

Getting the right grip

As with most short-game shots, you need to grip the club lightly. If you're a right-handed golfer, put the club a little more toward the palm of your left hand, and keep the back of your left hand pointing at the target. Your left hand should always lead; you let the right go along for the ride and offer guidance to the swing (see Figures 5-1c and 5-3c).

Taking a swing

Club selection determines the length of your backswing. Because a pitching wedge is more lofted than a 9-iron, a ball pitched with a pitching wedge flies higher than but not as far as a ball stroked with a 9-iron. In order to cover the distance you need, your pitching wedge swing needs to be a touch longer than your 9-iron swing.

Take the club back as far as you need to (make your backswing proportional to the distance you need to cover), and then make a swing with a smooth, easy tempo, letting your lead hand carry the load. Draw the club back low to the ground, keeping your wrists firm and turning by rotating your shoulders. Swing the club back along the target line (see Figure 5-1b) and then forward through the ball (see Figure 5-1c). Make sure you accelerate through the ball and follow through (Figure 5-1d). If you decelerate, you'll flub the shot and leave it short of the green.

The distance you need to cover determines the length of your backswing. For a longer distance, swing back up to 11:00 (see Figure 5-3b) and forward up to 1:00 (see Figure 5-3d). Keep your legs and lower body still, but allow a small weight shift if you need distance.

Don't be so eager to see the result that you take your eyes off the ball and look up too early. You've chosen your club and made your strategic decision, so now you can swing confidently and follow through straight toward the target. (See Figure 5-3d.)

Book III

Playing Golf: The Swing and the Short Game

Making adjustments

The distance the ball travels is your point of reference for making adjustments to your pitch shot. Do you want to hit the next pitch 10 yards farther? Make your swing a little bit longer (see Figure 5-4). Shorter? Your swing follows suit. That way, your rhythm never changes. You want the clubhead accelerating smoothly through the ball. And you best achieve that acceleration if you build up the momentum gradually from _address_ (the point right before you swing to hit the ball).

Relax — and practice!

Poor pitchers of the ball do one of two things: Either they start their swings too slowly and then speed up too much at impact, or they jerk the club away from the ball and have to decelerate later. Both swings lead to what golf columnist Peter Dobereiner christened "sickening knee-high fizzers" — low, thin shots that hurtle uncontrollably over the green — or complete duffs that travel only a few feet. Not a pretty sight. The most common cause of both is tension. So relax!

Figure 5-3:
Making a
pitch swing.

From address…

swing the club with hands/arms only…

accelerate through impact to a relaxed finish.

Figure 5-4: Achieving the proper momentum.

Imagine that you're swinging with a potato chip — the thin, crispy American kind — between your teeth. Focus on *not* biting down on it. That'll keep you relaxed.

In golf, you get better by doing, *not* by doing nothing, so improve your pitching by practicing to get an understanding of how far back you need to draw the club in order to fly the ball to the green. Sure, some of the equation comes from touch, talent, and instinct, but if you spend time on the range hitting shots of varying lengths (75 yards, 50 yards, 25 yards, and so on), you know how far back you need to draw the club. When you face a 50-yard pitch shot on the golf course, you want to recall hitting that shot on the practice range. That way you can look at what may otherwise be a daunting shot full of indecision and say, "Yeah, I've got that shot."

Pitching a Fit: Complications

In the earlier section "Hitting a Solid Pitch Shot," we provide you with the fundamental building blocks for executing a classic pitch. But over the course of 75 yards, many additional issues and obstacles (manmade or natural) can make a difficult shot that much harder in terms of distance control. But don't get your knickers in a bundle just yet; we give you tips to overcome hazards and ball lies in the following sections.

Pitching over water hazards and bunkers

Sometimes you have to fly your ball over obstacles in order to reach the green. If you have to hit a pitch over a bunker, creek, or small hill, your shot may seem more daunting. The stakes are higher because a ball landing in a bunker or creek costs you precious strokes.

When facing a hazard or bunker between you and the hole, no matter how much you want to hit your pitch shot close to the cup, your most important priority is to make certain that the ball clears the obstacle.

Sometimes the hole is cut close to the edge of the green and you don't have much space between the obstacle and the hole to work with. You may be tempted to hit a very delicate, high-flying pitch shot that falls steeply, lands softly, and stops near the hole. As exciting as it is to successfully execute a shot like that, you feel even more disappointed when you watch your ball fall short and plug into a bunker or splash into a creek. (But you can check out Chapter 7 of Book III for all your sand needs and Chapter 8 of Book III for tips on when to pass on playing from a water hazard and when to take a stab at it.)

If the hole is close to the edge of the green, you have plenty of green to work with beyond the hole. Use it. After you become more skilled at hitting pitch shots, you can try to stop your ball close to the hole or to fly it beyond the hole and use backspin. But first and foremost, get your ball over whatever hazard you face.

If you're not comfortable playing your pitch shot over the hazard, or if you don't have enough green behind the hazard to stop your ball, don't be ashamed to play your pitch shot away from the trouble — even if it means playing away from the hole. If the cup is tucked on a small part of the green behind a water hazard, you can opt to play your pitch shot to the larger, unguarded part of the green — a much safer option with less risk. Let your maverick playing partner mock you; you can mock him when he's standing in a creek with his pants rolled up trying to save a shot.

Give the hazard its due, but at the same time, don't be too intimidated by the bunker or stream. Consider the lie, the shape of the land, the wind, the distance you need to carry the ball, the amount of land you have to stop it on, and the necessary height of the shot. After you analyze all the factors and make your decision, forget about the creek or bunker. Don't let fear restrict your swing or the obstacle intimidate you into making a timid pass. Of course, the more you practice, the more confidence you'll have in your ability, and the less intimidating obstacles and hazards will seem.

Pitching high and low

Although pitch shots are conventionally considered to have a standard, high trajectory, you may come across occasions when you need to craft a pitch of a certain height. You may need to hit a high pitch to fly over a tree, or you may need a low pitch to go under a tree branch or to keep the ball out of the wind. This kind of crafty control is sometimes called *creative shot-making,* and although creativity is good, make certain that you know how to play these types of shots by practicing them on the range.

The varied irons in your golf bag have different trajectories (the higher the number, the higher the shot), and the built-in loft of your club provides the desired trajectory and height of the shot. But you may find that you need to hit the ball the typical distance the given club provides with more or less loft than the club usually offers.

Being able to hit the ball at various trajectories with different irons is something you can work on after you feel you have a great grasp on fundamental pitch shots. Advanced players have mastered these types of shots, and you can too, but make certain you master pitch shots with your appropriate short irons before you begin experimenting with high and low trajectories with other clubs.

Book III

Playing Golf: The Swing and the Short Game

Here are some ways to alter the trajectory of a pitch shot.

Changing the ball's position

You can move the position of the ball in your stance:

- ✔ **Lower trajectory:** Put the ball farther back in your stance at address, nearer your back foot.
- ✔ **Higher trajectory:** If you put the ball closer to your front foot at address, near the front of your stance, you add more loft to the club.

Spinning the club

You can add more loft to the club or take away some of the loft by spinning the club in your hands and changing the angle of the iron's face:

- ✔ **Lower trajectory:** If you spin the clubhead more closed, you de-loft the club.
- ✔ **Higher trajectory:** If you spin the clubhead more open, you increase the loft.

In either case, keep your hands even with or slightly in front of the ball position and open or close the clubface as needed.

Getting hands on

Your hands can also affect the height of your shot:

- ✔ **Lower trajectory:** Keep your wrists firm and don't let them hinge until your follow-through after the ball is gone. The ball gets plenty of bounce off the clubface — you don't need to "help it" into the air by releasing your wrists.
- ✔ **Higher trajectory:** If your hands release or begin to flip through the ball early, you make the trajectory of the ball higher. If your hands stay in front of the ball when you pull the club down from the top, the clubhead doesn't catch up at impact and the ball flies on a low trajectory.

Pitching from a bare, tight lie

A pitch shot is challenging enough from a good fairway lie or from the light rough, especially when you have to carry a bunker or a water hazard and land the ball softly. But from time to time, you must face one of the toughest shots in golf — a pitch shot when the ball sits on a bare, tight lie or from any firm ground. In places like Texas or anywhere that endures a dry spell, the ground can become dry and cracked. On the short grass of links courses in Britain and Ireland, your lies may always be firm and tight.

The challenge in pitching from a bare, tight lie is that bad contact can add strokes to your score quickly. You can skull the ball if the club hits the ground first and bounces into the ball. Or, in an attempt to avoid such a fat strike, you may overcompensate and top the ball by trying to pick it off the hard surface.

Although you may be tempted to hold on for dear life, your best bet to hit a good pitch in this situation is to grip the club very lightly. Don't try to help the ball into the air. Let the club do the work; maintain a light grip pressure as you swing through impact. Let the weight of the clubhead fall through the ball under its own momentum by keeping your hands and arms soft and loosening your shoulders. Trust your swing and, as always, play in the subconscious.

Pitching from deep grass

If you regularly miss greens with your approach shots, you often find your ball in all types of lies and ground conditions. Long grass is one of the more common challenges you face, so you should be sure to practice hitting the ball from deep, grassy conditions.

When the ball rests down in the grass (see Figure 5-5), the lie requires a steeper swing (see Figure 5-6) than you use for a normal pitch, so take out one of your lofted clubs, such as the lob wedge, sand wedge, or pitching wedge.

Figure 5-5: Spin the face open to add loft and keep your hands forward.

Figure 5-6:
Not allowing your lead wrist to change keeps the face open and produces maximum loft on an already steep swing.

The steeper swing that lofted wedges automatically produce (because the clubs are shorter) lessens the amount of grass that can come between your clubface and the ball because the clubs come down at a steeper angle.

Don't short yourself. Use a long-enough club to be certain your ball can reach the green. Although you want to get the ball near the hole, your most important mission is to get the ball onto the green . . . anywhere on the green! A highly lofted club stops the ball quickly.

After you pick your pitching tool, follow these steps to escape the deep rough and get on in one:

1. **Play the ball in the center of your stance (see Figure 5-5.)**

   You want to give yourself enough loft, but the thick grass also requires some distance.

2. **Swing the club back smoothly (see Figure 5-6a) and let your wrists hinge up or bend if it feels like they naturally want to because of the weight of the clubhead.**

   Keep your lower body quiet — a pitch shot from rough requires "handsy-work," meaning that your clubhead falling through the ball propels the shot. You don't need the leg power a driver or long iron requires.

3. **On the downswing (see Figure 5-6b), shift your weight forward, which creates a steep descent and provides clean contact (see Figure 5-6c).**

4. **Follow through fully.**

   Turn through the ball so that at completion, you face the target (see Figure 5-7). A full finish with your body facing your target is an essential ending to a perfectly executed shot.

Figure 5-7:
A full pitch-
shot finish.

Pitching from uneven lies

Course designers like to present more challenges as you get closer to the pin, so within 75 yards of the green, you're likely to find your ball lying on an uneven lie from time to time. As scary as it may seem, you need to be able to hit effective pitch shots from sidehill, uphill, and downhill lies.

Staking out sidehill lies

If you find your ball on a sidehill lie in which the ball sits above your feet (see Figure 5-8), you can count on the ball drawing rather than flying straight. Gravity and the angle of the hill when the club makes contact conspire to pull the ball after impact. Account for this effect by adjusting your target line a bit more to the left or right than you may normally aim. You can also choke up on the club and try to keep your swing as level as possible.

Figure 5-8:
Adjust your normal aim for a sidehill lie where the ball sits above your feet.

If you find your ball sitting on a sidehill lie below your feet (see Figure 5-9), you can count on the ball slicing rather than flying straight. The same forces that pull the ball when it rests above your feet conspire to push the ball after impact. Account for this occurrence by adjusting your target line a bit more left or right than you may normally aim.

Figure 5-9:
Adjust your target line for a sidehill lie where the ball rests below your feet.

Dealing with downhill and uphill lies

The tricky part about hitting a pitch shot from a downhill lie is hitting the ball with the clubhead before it strikes the ground behind the ball. Make no mistake: This shot is tough!

When you come upon a downhill lie (see Figure 5-10), put most of your weight on your front side at address and keep it there throughout the swing. Because the hillside tilts you to your front, you naturally deloft the angle of the clubface. The ball will come off the club flying lower and perhaps longer, so you may want to take a more lofted club or shorten your backswing accordingly; position the ball more toward the back of your stance. Make certain you swing through the ball, and let the clubhead extend down the slope of the hill on its swing path to keep from topping the ball.

For uphill lies, you want to let the clubhead follow the ground contour, just as you do with downhill lies. Because the ball lies on an uphill slope (see Figure 5-11), the angle effectively increases the loft of the club, causing the ball to fly higher and shorter after impact. Choose a longer club than you would normally use and/or lengthen your backswing to account for the lost yardage. The angle of the hill, depending on its severity, also affects your balance by forcing your weight onto your back side and perhaps causing you to pull up or even fall back out of the shot. Guard against this effect by keeping your weight on your front foot and keeping the ball in the middle of your stance.

Figure 5-10: Adjust weight balance and ball position when you face a downhill lie.

Figure 5-11: Proper weight balance on an uphill lie helps keep you from falling back out of the shot.

Doing your repair duty

If you execute well and hit the green with your pitch shot, or any shot for that matter, be sure to find and repair the mark you make. Because a pitched ball flies high and lands on the green at a steep angle, it often leaves a quarter-sized indent in the green called a *pitch mark*. Soft greens after rains are especially susceptible to pitch marks.

Nobody likes to have a putt derailed by an ignored pitch mark. Pitch marks not only wreak havoc for putters but also take weeks to grow back. Most golf courses either provide or sell divot repair tools in the clubhouse, so you have no excuse for failing to carry one in your pocket!

To repair a pitch mark, put the sharp edges of the divot repair tool into the perimeter of the indentation and push the edge toward the middle. Don't try to push the ground in the middle back up. Just go around the perimeter a few times and push the sides toward the middle and then flatten the raised ground with the bottom of your putter.

Chapter 6

Putting: The Final Frontier

. . . .

. . . .

*P*layers at all levels of golf often overlook putting as an integral part of golf. Seems ridiculous, right? For most people, the mention of golf conjures up visions of long tee shots and powerful ball striking long before it provokes images of elegant putting.

But you can't score well if you can't putt — it's that simple. Putting is the culmination of every golf hole. You can hit a far, straight tee shot and then hit the green, even from the rough, with an expertly played approach shot, but if you can't master that funny-looking club to finish the job, your score will creep up.

Statistically, putting is 68 percent of the game of golf, so you may want to take notes. You'd be smart to keep a "reminder book" of putting tips from this chapter.

Appreciating the Putt

Putting is the most important part of the game of golf in terms of scoring. You need precision, speed, nerve, and confidence, along with an ability to handle misses (because they happen often). The challenge is to temper the enthusiasm for scoring with the soft touch you need to be accurate.

Doing the math

Think about it in logical terms: You can pull out your giant Big Bobby driver and sail the ball 300 yards, but that giant shot counts the same on the score-card as a lil' 1-foot putt! So, simple math tells you that putting is important. You need only one shot (assuming you can handle that Big Bobby with some success) to hit your drive 300 yards, but if you don't have confidence in your putting, it may take you three shots to end the hole. The numbers, in this case, don't lie.

Crunching another set of numbers, putting is important because it requires the most precision of any shot you hit. You typically bang your drives toward a fairway that measures about 40 or more yards wide and a playing corridor sometimes 80 yards wide. You have plenty of room for error when you drive the ball, and no one really expects you to hit your drive with laser precision. When you hit your approach shot, you aim for the green, a target that can be as big as 10,000 square feet. But when you putt, from no matter how long a distance, you aim at a circle that measures 4.25 inches wide. Now that's pressure! The margin for error in putting is comparatively tiny.

Preparing for putting's mind games

In putting, visualization is everything. You can visualize the hole in two ways: You see it either as a pinpoint or as a crater so big any fool could drop the ball in. The former, of course, is infinitely more hazardous to your mental health. When you picture a small hole, the ball doesn't seem to fit into it. You can keep telling yourself that the ball is 1.68 inches in diameter and the hole is 4.25 inches across, but the fact remains that the ball is too big.

And on other days, happily, the hole is so big that putting is like stroking a marble into the Grand Canyon. Simply hit the ball, and boom, it goes in. When this sensation happens to you, savor it. Drink in the feeling and bathe in it so you don't forget it, because you may not take another bath like that for a *long* time.

Getting in your opponent's head

Putting is just as important in a competitive sense. If your competitor in a match thinks of you as a good putter, that knowledge puts more pressure on her. She knows she can't make a mistake on the green because you'll surely seize the moment and take her down.

Using superior putting to apply direct pressure to your opponent is an invalu-able asset in competitive play. Say your ball is 30 feet from the hole, and your opponent's putt spans only 15 feet. She has the clear advantage, right? Well, that advantage may swing your way if you lag your long putt to inches from the hole for a certain 2-putt while she waits to putt her 15-footer (for more on lag putting, see Chapter 8 of Book III). Suddenly, she has something to think about. Should she try to make her 15-footer to win the hole? Should she be conservative and make sure she doesn't hit it too far by the hole, because a 3-putt means she takes a loss? She watched your ball break 2 feet. Will her ball break that much? Even though you didn't sink your long putt, your proficiency has tightened her collar a bit and stretched her putt out. Conversely, if you miss your putt by 6 feet, your opponent's job becomes much easier. She knows that she can safely (and rather easily) 2-putt from 15 feet and have a good opportunity to win the hole.

Setting Putting Goals and Expectations

For every golf shot you hit, you should have both goals and expectations for the result in mind. Knowing how goals and expectations differ and how to push and prepare yourself for each shot allows you to start lowering your scores (and maybe your blood pressure). What do you want to accomplish with each putt? What's an acceptable result? A reasonable expectation?

Book III

Playing Golf: The Swing and the Short Game

Holing putts in two: A good goal

If you want to lower your score to become a better player and have more fun, you need to avoid 3- or 4-putting a hole. You can hit good shots straight down the fairway and land the green in regulation, but if you take three strokes to hole the ball from a comparatively tiny distance, you'll forget your good shots instantly. This type of ending is positively criminal and will frustrate you endlessly.

Your initial *goal* — not your expectation — is to roll 36 or fewer putts in an 18-hole round of golf. That means hitting two or fewer putts on every green. Naturally, this goal becomes easy to achieve when you hit the ball close to the hole. But when you land it 40 feet away, 2-putting is a major feat. Accomplishing your goal requires you to focus on the first putt every time — especially the long ones.

It can be too easy to approach a long putt and not think about the consequences of your stroke. You may think that you can't possibly make the long one, so you get lazy and your mind wanders. You make a halfhearted pass at it. On the opposite end of the spectrum, you may get too aggressive with the long putt, trying to make a heroic bomber. Be smart and careful with the first putt. If your goal is to roll no more than two putts per green, 2-putting is a success and 1-putting is a smashing success!

You may be thinking that the goal of 2-putting every green doesn't sound terribly ambitious, but take a look at the PGA Tour professionals — the 200 or so finest players in the world. As of this writing, Andres Gonzales led the Putting Average category for 2011 with an average of 1.411 putts per green.

So if the greatest players in the world can beat the goal of 2-putting each green by just percentage points, you shouldn't hesitate to make it your goal to 2-putt each green. Your scores will improve and stay consistently good.

Meeting your expectations

In principle, you can raise your expectations the more you practice — to a point. Be excited by good results, but try not to fret over missed putts. You can control your performance when it comes to 2-foot putts, but you can only improve your performance with the 10-footers.

Sinking every 2-footer

You should never miss 1- or 2-foot putts — your "money-making" putts. They provide wiggle room as you try to reach the goal of two-putting over the entire round. If you practice 2-footers and focus on every putt during a round, you should make them every time. Sinking 2-footers is at first a goal, and if you put any amount of time into your short game at all, it becomes a realistic expectation. Missing a short putt is a terrible way to waste a stroke.

Many club golfers and weekend golfers, in the interest of speedy play and sportsmanship, concede 2-foot putts. Although conceding 2-foot putts is fine in match, skins, or casual recreational play (gimmes are against the rules in stroke-play tournaments), it means you may never have the opportunity to practice and make them consistently for when you really need to.

Whenever possible, hole out all your putts. And practice 2-footers, no matter how boring or remedial it may seem — especially if you often play with folks who treat them as gimmes on the course. Sometime, either in a stroke-play tournament or when your partners decide not to concede it to avoid losing a match, you'll need to make a 2-footer. Short putts are as valuable as the longest drive, and you should never, ever miss them. (Check out Chapter 3 of Book V for ways to insert a bit of variety into your putting practice.)

A subtle gamesmanship trick your opponent may employ is to concede 2-foot putts to you throughout the round and then make you take the putt when you need it and expect him to concede it. This trick affects you in two ways. First, it unnerves you and perhaps annoys you that he doesn't concede it. Second, it forces you to make a 2-foot putt when you haven't hit one all day and you haven't developed a rhythm for making them.

Looking at longer putts

You know you should make 1- and 2-foot putts all the time. But what's a reasonable expectation for longer putts? Consider that PGA Tour players make 10-foot putts 50 percent of the time. And though you may think tour players can make 3-footers all the time, the best players in the world make putts from 3 feet about 70 percent of the time. Surprised?

If you consider yourself to be an average player, you should be prepared to miss many long putts. If you're like most average Joes, though, your expectations are probably higher than reality allows. You may expect to make the longer putts as often — or more often — than the pros do. But by having extremely high expectations, you put added pressure on yourself to make hard, long putts. Don't beat yourself up mentally, or you may find your scores increasing and your confidence falling as the pressure mounts.

Now, you don't want to throw strokes away. Missing a 5-footer after you traverse 500 yards in 3 shots is disappointing, but you must be realistic. Statistically and realistically speaking, missing longer putts is a part of the game. When you miss, don't get angry and make a negative imprint on your self-image. If you beat yourself up for missing a putt, the next time you stand over a tough putt, you won't think you have a chance. You have a chance to make every putt, but even the greatest putters of all time didn't make them all.

Turn a missed-putt negative into a positive: If you miss, make sure that you miss by a little. Keep the ball close enough to the hole to leave yourself a tap-in putt — giving yourself a shot at achieving your goal of hitting only 36 putts per round (see the section "Holing putts in two: a good goal" earlier in this chapter).

Letting go of the misses

Longer putts are difficult to make regularly because despite your best efforts, sometimes putts just don't fall. And sometimes the miss just isn't your fault. You didn't mishit the putt. It just didn't go in. Many variables affect your putting, and you encounter factors that you may not be able to account for when you stroke a putt.

So sometimes you hit the absolute perfect putt, with a perfect grip, a perfect line, and the perfect speed, but when the ball approaches the hole, it takes an ungodly turn, hits the corner of the hole, or spins out. In the following sections, we cover some of the factors that can knock even the most perfectly struck putt off course. Find some comfort here (and turn to Chapter 2 of Book V for information on the mental aspects of the short game).

Book III

Playing Golf: The Swing and the Short Game

Blowin' in the wind

Wind is difficult to factor into your putting game. Putting requires such precision that a stiff wind can affect a ball's path toward the hole. Although you know how the wind affects a long-iron shot, most players don't think about how the wind affects their putting.

But can you realistically factor in the wind when you line up your putt? Not likely. Wind mainly gusts and blows, and you can't depend on it. The only thing that you can do is safeguard yourself against an inadvertent penalty. If you address the ball by resting your putter behind the ball, and the wind blows your ball before the stroke, you incur a one-stroke penalty. In heavy winds, therefore, don't dawdle when you ground your putterhead behind the ball. Wait to ground your putterhead until the last possible moment — when you're truly ready to make the stroke.

Grinding it out on the green

Other course players and the green itself provide some bumps in the road, literally, that you often can't factor in during putts:

- **Growing grass:** Although the slick and smooth surface of the green may seem constant and unchanging to you, you're still putting on grass, which is a living, growing organism. A crew mows the green before the day's play, and a green that no one has played on is much different than a green at 2:00 after 20 foursomes. The grass is cut so short that you can't see the growth, but it grows all the time.

- **Footprints:** Your fellow players should be polite and careful not to step in your line when you're on the green. But what about all the players who trotted across the turf before you? You may not see all the footprints of all the golfers that have played before you, but their impressions are there.

- **The unstepped-on zone:** When golfers walk on the green, read putts, talk, hit putts, walk to their next putt, and leave the green, they never (hopefully) step exactly right next to the hole. Even when players remove the ball from the hole, the closest they step is within 6 to 12 inches. So, after so many players have been on the green, the area within 6 to 12 inches of the hole ends up higher than the next 12 inches because people haven't stepped on it and pressed it down. And as you get away from the 6- to 12-inch area, the green begins to get lumpier.

- **Other imperfections:** Greens also fall victim to other imperfections that come from nature, players' spike marks, ball marks, and loose impediments (such as rocks and grass clippings) tracked on by golfers' shoes.

Picking Your Perfect Putter

Because putting is such a crucial part of golf, your putter is the most important weapon you've got. Club makers seem to have noticed: In recent years, they've brought out a dizzying array of high-tech putters. Some are as sleek as a sports car, while others look more like anvils or spaceships. One new model has been likened to "a fire hydrant on a stick." How can you choose the putter that's best for your game? It's not as tricky as you may think.

Your stroke shape dictates your putter

Although you have many putters to choose from (see Chapter 1 of Book I), you can eliminate most of them by knowing the type of putter you are. In other words, the shape of your stroke is the main factor in choosing a putter.

Noted teaching professional Peter Kostis explains that almost all putting strokes fall into one of two shapes. They either move "straight back and straight through," with the blade staying square, or "inside to inside," with the blade doing a mini-version of the rotation in a full swing. Conveniently, most putters are designed to suit one of those stroke shapes. The two main types (see Figure 6-1) are

✓ Face-balanced, center-shafted putters

✓ Putters that aren't face-balanced, such as heel-shafted blades

Book III

Playing Golf: The Swing and the Short Game

Figure 6-1: Heel-shafted and center-shafted putters.

If keeping the blade square throughout the putting stroke is your style, get a face-balanced, center-shafted model. You can test to see whether a putter is face-balanced by resting the shaft on your finger. If the putterface stays parallel to the ground, it's face-balanced. The inside-to-inside stroke is easier to make on a consistent basis with a heel-shafted putter. It hangs toe-down while resting on your finger. (The *toe* is the end of the putter, the part farthest from the shaft.)

Be warned, though. Some putters hang at an angle of 45 degrees. They're equally good — or bad! — for either stroke.

Thinking about fit

In the wide world of putters, choosing the flatstick that best suits you can be as daunting as courting a spouse. After all, you have to spend about as much time with your putter as you do your spouse if you want to get better. You use your putter for more strokes than any other club in your bag, so it must be dependable through the good times and the bad. Confidence is a hugely important aspect of your putting game, and you must have total confidence that the putter in your hand is capable of getting the job done.

We know of a fellow who had three putters in his bag that he rotated through, even during the round. He couldn't understand why his putting failed him on a regular basis. Every time he missed a putt he felt he should have made, he switched putters. In total frustration, he finally took all the putters out of his bag and bought the most expensive putter he could find at his local golf shop. Now, in his mind, he'd eliminated all the variables that hampered his putting performance. Because he'd bought an expensive, name-brand putter, he could no longer blame the putter. This mindset caused him to focus on the weaknesses in his technique and, perhaps more importantly, allowed him to putt with more confidence. His putting improved immediately.

Most people don't choose a putter based on the expense, but as the story illustrates, you should choose a putter (not three) that you're comfortable with and that you can count on. Commit and simplify.

But how to choose among the spectrum of bold mallets, shiny blades, and snazzy gunmetal putters? Try and try again. Many golf-specific retail shops have an artificial putting surface, and the larger ones may even have a real-grass outdoor practice green. The golf shop at your local public golf course or country club, often referred to as a *green grass shop,* is ideal because you can grab a handful of putters and spend an afternoon on the practice green trying each of them out. What should you look for during your practice sessions with probable putting weapons? Go through the following points:

✔ Decide which putters fit your look and idea of style (operating on the "look good, play good" theory).

✔ Give each putter a fair shake by making some long and short putts of similar lengths.

✔ Don't necessarily judge a putter by how many putts you sink. Don't even worry about making the putts — just get a feel for each of the putters and how the ball rolls.

✔ Hit some putts with your eyes closed to get a feel for the weight of the putter and how it feels when it makes contact with the ball.

Ultimately, choosing your putter comes down to a combination of physical and psychological factors: how the putter feels and how you feel about it. After you make your decision, run with it and don't look back. The best way to have confidence in your new putter and help it perform well is to spend as much time as possible practicing with it.

Meeting MOI

Don't be confused by all the high-tech (and high-priced) new putters on the market. Although they appear as colorful and as different as new cars, most offer only one or two features — features that may seem confusing at first.

One term that puzzles most beginners is *MOI,* which is short for *moment of inertia.* It sounds scientific, and MOI putters do in fact have a lot of science behind them, but don't worry about that. All you need to know is that MOI putters resist twisting on off-center hits. That means your bad putts turn out better than they would otherwise. How much better? That's hard to say, but a study cited in *Golf Digest* suggested that an MOI putter may make a 4-foot difference on a 22-foot putt. That's a massive difference — almost as massive as some of these putters.

Many modern putters also feature alignment aids, like the white circles behind the face of Odyssey's putters. Other manufacturers put bold lines or arrows on their weapons to help golfers start the ball on the target line. (For more on alignment, see "Addressing the Art of Aiming" later in this chapter.) Another new wrinkle is adding an insert to the face of the putter — often a panel of *urethane,* the same stuff golf balls are made of — for a softer feel when the putter strikes the ball.

As with other technological fixes, from titanium drivers to graphite shafts to super-comfy golf shoes, such features have their benefits — especially if you *believe* they can help your game. Because, as you know by now (or will soon figure out), this game is as much mental as it is anything.

Book III

Playing Golf: The Swing and the Short Game

Showing devotion to your putter

Superstition in sports is a time-honored tradition. Golf is no exception — especially when it comes to putting. Tales of golfers and their devotion to putters are legendary. Some clean and polish their putters regularly and lovingly. Some golfers cuddle with their putters in bed. And at the other end of the spectrum, some golfers punish their putters by removing them from the bag and banishing them to the darkness of the car trunk. One tale speaks of a golfer who tied his putter to the back bumper of his car, dragging it for miles at a high speed to teach it a lesson. Of course, more than one player has deep-sixed a putter in a greenside pond or broken it over a knee during a fit of rage.

Some of the great players in the history of golf have had long, warm relationships with their putters. Robert Tyre Jones Jr., possibly the greatest amateur ever (he's the only player to win the "grand slam" of the U.S. and British Amateur and both Open Championships in the same year), had a very successful partnership with his putter "Calamity Jane."

Jack Nicklaus made putters famous by winning major championships. He won with a putter he named "White Fang" and, in 1986, with a startling-looking putter called "Response" that had a massive black putterhead — one of the largest ever made! Sales of the Response soared after Jack's win.

Scott Hoch surely helped sales of his futuristic putter by winning the PGA Tour event at Doral with it, despite the fact that he laughed about the bizarre appearance of the putterhead by saying that it looked like a potato masher.

 Still, the best feature of all is sound fundamentals. Without them, all the tech support in the world can't do you much good.

Building Your Putting Stroke

You can putt well using any number of methods or clubs. But at this stage, you should putt in as orthodox a manner as possible. That way, when something goes wrong — which it will — the fault is easier to fix. The trouble with being unorthodox is that finding order in the chaos is more difficult. The following sections help you set up your putting foundation.

Getting a putting grip

The putting grip isn't like the full-swing grip (which we cover in Chapter 1 of Book III). The full-swing grip is more in the fingers, which encourages your wrists to hinge and unhinge. Your putting grip's purpose is exactly the opposite.

Grip the putter more in the palm of your hands to reduce the amount of movement your hands make. Align the end of the putter in a straight line with your forearm. Although you may putt well with a lot of wrist action in your stroke, taking the wrists out of play as much as possible is a good idea. Unless you have incredible touch, your wrists aren't very reliable when you need to hit the ball short distances. You're far better off relying on the rocking of your shoulders to create momentum in the putterhead.

Not all putting grips are the same — not even those grips where you place your right hand below the left in conventional fashion. But what almost all putting grips have in common is that the palms of both hands face each other so that your hands can work together. The last thing you want is your hands fighting one another. Too much of either hand, and your ball has a bad experience. If your left hand dominates, your right hand sues for nonsupport. Both hands need to work together.

In the conventional grip, your hands can work together in one of two ways, as shown in Figure 6-2. Start by placing the palms of your hands on either side of the club's grip. Slide your right hand down a little so that you can place both hands on the club. You should feel like you're going to adopt the ten-finger grip (refer to Chapter 1 of Book III). Then do one of the following, depending on which grip you prefer:

- **Place your left index finger over the little finger of your right hand.** Known as the *reverse overlap*, this putting grip is probably the most popular option on the PGA and LPGA tours.

- **Extend your left index finger past the fingers of your right hand until the tip touches your right index finger.** Call this grip the *extended reverse overlap*. The left index finger, when extended, provides stability to the putting stroke.

Go with the grip that feels most comfortable. We describe other methods of gripping the putter in the following sections.

Your grip pressure on your putter needs to be consistent and comfortable. You shouldn't squeeze the putter grip too tightly. You can sense the weight and position of the clubhead better this way, and developing a feel for the putterhead is essential to keeping putts around the hole. You can grip the putter any way you like, but keep the grip pressure light and your left wrist still through impact.

Left hand low

This method is commonly referred to as *cross-handed*. The left hand hangs below the right with the putter (or vice versa if you're a lefty). Many players use this method today because it helps keep the lead hand (the left, in this case) from bending at the wrist as you hit the ball. (See Figure 6-3.)

Book III

Playing Golf: The Swing and the Short Game

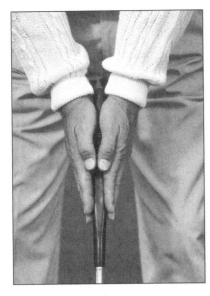

Place your palms on opposing sides of the grip.

Slide your right hand down and place your left index finger over your right pinkie.

Or extend your left index finger over the fingers of your right hand.

Figure 6-2:
A gripping start.

One of the biggest causes of missed putts is the breakdown of the left wrist through impact. When the left wrist bends, the putter blade twists. This twisting causes the ball to wobble off-line, even if you've got an MOI putter. That's why you should maintain the bend of your left wrist from the address position all the way through the stroke.

A left-hand-below-right putting grip helps stop left-wrist breakdown.

Figure 6-3:
Keep that
left wrist
firm.

Book III

**Playing
Golf: The
Swing and
the Short
Game**

The cross-handed grip can make maintaining that wrist position easier. PGA Tour stars — including Jim Furyk and Stuart Appleby — have won with this type of grip.

Another reason you see many of today's pros using a cross-handed grip is that, with the left arm lower on the shaft, you pull the left shoulder more square to your target line. Pulling your left shoulder happens automatically with this grip.

The claw

This weird-looking grip got a boost at the 2005 Masters, where claw-gripper Chris DiMarco took eventual winner Tiger Woods into a thrilling playoff. To try the claw, start with a standard putting grip. Turn your right palm toward you and bring it to the putter's handle so the handle touches the spot between your thumb and index finger. Now bring your index and middle fingers to the shaft, leaving your ring finger and pinkie off, as shown in Figure 6-4.

Removing your glove

If you watch professional golf on television, you see PGA Tour players removing their golf gloves before they putt. This act seems to have become fashionable among many recreational golfers, too. Perhaps players feel that removing their glove helps them have better feel when they putt.

If removing your glove makes you feel more confident, and you don't hold up play when you're next to putt, go ahead. But Jack Nicklaus, for one, never removed his glove to putt. He said he just didn't want to be bothered to take his glove on and off so many times during a round of golf. And Jack Nicklaus is considered one of the greatest clutch putters of all time.

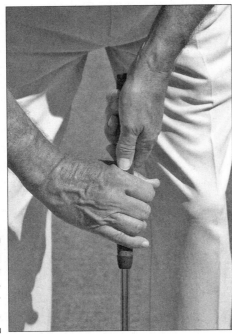

Figure 6-4: The claw grip — another option.

DiMarco had gone through a spell of such terrible putting that he nearly gave up hope; with this grip, he rejuvenated his career and clawed his way to the top.

Putting posture: Stand and deliver

As you crouch over the ball to putt, your knees should flex slightly. If your knees are locked, you're straining your back too much. Don't bend those knees too much, though, or you may start to look like a golf geek!

Bend from your waist so your arms hang straight down. This position allows your arms to swing back and forth from a fixed point in a pendulum motion. Hold your arms straight out from your body. Bend down with those arms outstretched from the waist until your arms are pointing to the ground. Now flex your knees a little, and you're in the correct putting posture.

You can break a lot of rules in how you stand to hit a putt (see Figure 6-5). Ben Crenshaw, one of the best putters ever, always stood open to the target line, his left foot drawn back. Gary Player did the opposite: He set up closed, his right foot farther from the target line than his left. But that's their style.

Toeing the line

As in a full swing (see Chapter 1 of Book III), the line of your toes is the key. Regardless of which stance you choose, your toe line should always be parallel to your target line. Be aware that the target line isn't always a straight line from the ball to the hole — if only putting were that simple! Few greens are flat, so putts *break* or bend from right to left or from left to right. (See "Reading the Break of the Greens" later in this chapter.) So sometimes you aim, say, 5 inches to the right of the hole, and other times maybe a foot to the left. Whatever you decide, your toe line must be parallel to your target line.

On breaking putts, aim your feet parallel to the line you've chosen, not toward the hole (see Figure 6-6). In effect, you make every putt straight. Applying a curve to your putts is way too complicated and affects your stroke. Imagine how you'd have to adjust if you aimed at the hole and then tried to push the ball out to the right because of a slope on the green. You'd have no way to be consistent.

Standing just right

Okay, now what about width of stance? Again, you have margin for error, but your heels need to be about shoulder-width apart at address, as shown in Figure 6-7.

To putt, you can stand open.

Or closed.

Or square.

Figure 6-5:
Putting
stances
vary.

Figure 6-6:
Place your
feet parallel
to your
putting line.

Book III

**Playing
Golf: The
Swing and
the Short
Game**

Figure 6-7:
While
putting, your
heels should
be shoulder-
width apart.

You have to bend over to place the putter behind the ball. How far should you bend? Just far enough to get your *eye line* (the direction of your gaze — a much-neglected part of putting) directly over the ball. To find that position in practice, place a ball against your forehead between your eyes, bend over, and let the ball drop, as shown in Figure 6-8. Where does the ball hit the ground? That's where the ball should be in relation to your body. It shouldn't be to the inside, the outside, behind, or in front of that point. It should be right there, dead center. This alignment places your eyes not just over the ball but also over the line that you want the ball to ride.

Drop the ball from a point between your eyes.

Where the ball lands is where it should be positioned in your stance.

Figure 6-8: Your eyes should be over the ball.

Perfecting Your Putt

In putting, you practice fundamentals and incorporate personal preferences. Your putting style is the most personal of your golf swings, but players who execute the putting stroke according to the proven fundamentals experience better results. How you make yourself feel comfortable and confident enough to get the putterhead through the ball is a matter of preference.

More than having technique, putting is all about having feel. Success comes with developing a feel for the weight of the putter, the speed of the green, and the roll of the ball. How do you develop feel? Practice, practice, and more practice.

You can find helpful tips and advice on long putts, short putts, and yips in Chapter 8 of Book III, which covers a host of short-game strategies.

Matching your putt to your full swing

One basic rule for a beginning golfer is to match the length of your golf swing to your putting stroke. That is, if you have a *short swing* (your left arm, if you're right-handed, doesn't get too far up in the air on your backswing), make sure that your putting stroke is a short one, too. If your full swing is *long,* make your putting stroke long. This way, you're not contradicting yourself.

Look at two of the greatest putters in history: Ben Crenshaw and Phil Mickelson. Both have long, slow swings, and their putting strokes are — you guessed it — long and slow. On the other hand, major champions Nick Price and Lanny Wadkins have quick swings and quick putting strokes.

Your swing tells a lot about your personality. If your golf swing is long and slow, you're probably an easygoing person. If your swing is short and fast, you're probably the type who walks around with his hair on fire.

Getting up to speed

In my decades in pro golf, I've seen players of all shapes and sizes with a lot of different putting methods. Some putted in what could be termed mysterious ways, and others were totally conventional. So analyzing different putting methods is no help. The best way to look at putting is to break it down to its simplest level. The hole. The ball. The ball fits into the hole. Now get the ball into the hole in the fewest possible strokes.

You want to get the ball rolling at the right speed. That means hitting a putt so that if the ball misses the cup, it finishes 14 to 18 inches past the hole, as shown in Figure 6-9. This distance is true no matter the length of the putt. Two feet or 40 feet, your aim must be to hit the ball at a pace that has it finish 14 to 18 inches beyond the hole. If it doesn't go in, that is.

You're probably wondering why your ball needs the right speed. Well, the right speed gives the ball the greatest chance of going into the hole. Think about it: If the ball rolls toward the middle of the cup, you don't want it moving so fast that it rolls right over the hole. If it touches either side of the cup, it may drop in. Your goal is to give the ball every chance to drop in, from any angle — front, back, or side. You want that hole to seem as big as possible.

Book III

Playing Golf: The Swing and the Short Game

Figure 6-9:
Hit your putt
hard enough
to get it
just past
the hole.

The only putts that *never* drop are the ones you leave short of the hole. If you've played golf for any length of time, you've heard the phrase "never up, never in." The cliché is annoying but true. As the Irish say, "Ninety-nine percent of all putts that come up short don't go in, and the other 1 percent never get there." Remember that saying! Also remember that you should try to sink every putt from ten feet or closer.

Targeting a line

Every putt you hit should be a straight putt. "You wish," you say? We mean that you should stroke every putt straight down a target line, in the direction of the amount of break you need to play to make the putt roll into or near the hole (see the section "Reading the Break of the Greens" later in this chapter). You read the break of the green and determine the line the putt needs to go on and roll the ball straight on that line. You don't try to hook or bend a putt or put English on it. Choose your line. Keep it straight and simple.

To hit a straight putt, imagine a straight line that goes from the back of the ball straight down your target line. The straight line should stretch to the hole or to a point you selected so the ball breaks to the hole (see Figure 6-10). (Check out Chapter 3 of Book V for a straight-line putting drill.)

Figure 6-10: Playing the break.

Sometimes your target isn't the hole.

Sometimes you have to allow for the ball to bend on a sloping green.

To increase your chance of success, pick a spot on the target line to aim for. The target isn't necessarily the hole; the target is the point you need to focus on in order to get your ball rolling down the proper target line and toward the hole. The spot may be a few feet in front of you, or it may be 10 feet in front of you. It depends on the length of your putt. Choose a spot somewhere between your ball and the hole on the target line.

Imagine a bowling lane, which has a foul line and arrows that serve as aiming devices. Same concept (but without the curves or embarrassing gutter balls).

Swinging the flatstick

After you read the break of the green (see the section "Reading the Break of the Greens" later in this chapter), find your target line, pick a spot, and get your eyes over the line, you need to concentrate on swinging the putter back and forward along the line, keeping the following fundamentals in mind:

- **Keep your putterhead on line through its entire movement.** The putter needs to travel straight back on the target line and then straight forward on the target line. Keeping your legs, head, and shoulders still helps you swing the putter with your arms and hands.

- **Keep the putterhead square and aimed straight to the target.** The face of the blade should be perpendicular to the target (see Figure 6-11) and remain so throughout the stroke. The direction the blade faces shouldn't wobble; it should remain true to the arc of the putterhead. Keeping your wrists solid and firm helps you maintain the direction of the putterface.

- **Never decelerate the putter during the swing.** This putting-scared style kills your putting stroke and your score. Accelerate an equal amount through the backswing and the downswing.

Book III

Playing Golf: The Swing and the Short Game

Figure 6-11:
Keep your clubface square to the target line.

Putting is about rolling the ball, not hitting the ball. You want to think about tumbling the ball end over end.

You could be anyone and go out on that putting green with Tiger Woods or Brad Faxon or the best putter in the world and putt 10-footers competitively. You can be 100 years old and frail as can be and still have enough strength to make the putter go back and through at the right speed to roll the ball. That's really all putting is about. You shouldn't do anything that takes away from the simple act of making the putter swing.

Playing in the subconscious is the best way to enjoy success, especially in putting. You practice and prepare in the conscious state, and you can turn it all off and go to the subconscious during your round.

Staying low and level

When you swing the putter back and forward along the target line, keep the putter as low to the ground as you can without scraping the grass. It should feel more like you're letting the putter hang; you don't want to push it down. If you swing the blade close to the ground, you can stay level.

When wrists ruled

If you watch old films, you can see that golfers, from the era of Bobby Jones and even up to the time of Billy Casper, were a lot "wristier" with their putting style. In the olden days, putters had more loft because the greens were much slower. The grass on the greens was longer because greenskeepers didn't cut the grass at the low level you enjoy today. When players putted, they used a flick of the wrist to get the ball airborne with enough "oomph" to get to the hole. It was much like chipping with a 7-iron to get the ball over longer grass and onto the green.

You don't face the same problems today. The greens you putt on are flat and fast, and your putter has very little loft. Keep your wrists firm and inactive during the putting the stroke.

Awareness of the putterhead helps you keep the putter low throughout the stroke, and a light grip helps you get a sense for the size and the weight of the putterhead. Let the putterhead swing through the ball like the bottom of a pendulum on a grandfather clock. The pendulum swings as low as it physically can in the arc, and so too should your putterhead. Keeping the blade low helps you concentrate on *rolling* — not hitting — the putt.

You need to stay level. When you hit your driver, your shoulders should stay level when you turn. The same thing goes for putting. After you take your stance and put your eyes over the target line, you want to keep the putterhead close to the ground and level. Take it back as low to the ground as you can, using your level shoulders to propel the club, and follow through as low to the ground as you can.

Stilling your legs

Your legs should stay quiet throughout the putting stroke. Putting is about moving the putterhead at a specific speed to allow the ball to die within 18 inches of the hole. In order to do that, you need to feel the putterhead as you swing it. You don't need to make a bunch of shoulder and body turns or use any powerful leg action.

Stiffening your wrists

Another key to rolling the ball, bringing the putter back on line, sweeping the club low to the ground, and maintaining good speed is keeping your wrists firm and inactive during the putting stroke. You want your arms and hands working as one unit rather than independent of each other.

If your wrists get ahead of your arms as they guide the putter through the stroke, the direction of the putterhead or angle of the face can change.

Think of creating an upside-down triangle with your body when you hold the putter and stand over the ball. Your shoulder line, parallel to the ground, is the base of the triangle, and your two arms, which lead to the putter, are the sides of the triangle. Your triangle should simply pivot as one unit as you take the putter back and through the ball. (See Figure 6-12 for the shape of this setup.)

Freezing your head and eyes

After you complete the putting stroke and send the ball toward the hole, keep your eyes focused on the spot the ball occupied (see Figure 6-12c). If you keep your eyes trained on the spot where the ball was, you're more likely to let the putter swing through to its completion and not interrupt it or swing it offline by looking up too early and decelerating.

You don't need to watch the ball go into the hole or miss the hole, other than to satisfy your curiosity and excitement. Instead, try listening for the sound of the ball falling into the hole. What a wonderful sound to hear! Try it and see immediately how much more solidly you roll the ball.

Following through and holding your finish

After your putter strikes the ball, the follow-through is extremely important. You wonder, "What sense does it make to follow through when the ball has already left the putterface?" Letting the putterhead follow through and swing naturally ensures that you'll accelerate through the ball. The natural "fall" of the putterhead into the ball initiates the ball's forward roll along the target line. Any effort to slow the putterhead or stop it after the ball is gone causes the putterhead to wobble off-line, pulling or pushing the putt awry.

As the putterhead follows through toward the conclusion of the stroke, let it swing freely through and then hold your finish with the putterhead pointing toward the hole as if you're posing for a picture.

Mediocre and poor putters recoil their blade after the stroke. We've all done it. To recoil, you need to slow down your putter as it comes through the ball, and if you do that, your blade wanders off-line and hits the ball at the wrong speed.

You can't recoil without slowing down. Finish with the putterhead low to the ground on the target line and hold the finish — you become a better putter because you give the putterhead the opportunity to roll the ball end over end.

Figure 6-12:
Form a
triangle
with your
shoulders,
arms, and
grip, and
keep your
sight line
directly over
the ball.

Book III

**Playing
Golf: The
Swing and
the Short
Game**

Addressing the Art of Aiming

Golf requires an assortment of physical skills and techniques. It also requires you to use your mind, which makes the final decisions and tells your motor system where and when things will happen, hopefully in some sort of harmony. For putting, all that stuff starts with alignment.

Some golfers aim at a spot a few feet in front of the ball. When they place their putters behind the ball, they aim the face of the putter or the lines on the putter at that spot. Aligning to a spot a foot or so in front of the ball is easier than aligning to the hole, which may be much farther away.

You can also use other strategies to help with alignment. One is to take the logo of the golf ball and set it along the line that you want the putt to follow. This method can help you get a better visual reference to the line. Some players, such as Tiger Woods, use a permanent marker to make a line about an inch long on the ball (see Figure 6-13) for the same reason: to achieve a better visual reference for directing the ball down the intended path. When you stand over the putt, the ball is already aimed.

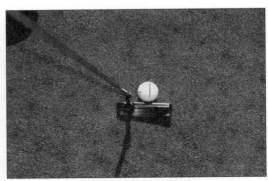

Make a line on the ball with a permanent marker.

Figure 6-13: Aim the logo of the ball or a drawn line toward the target.

The eyes like lines

Players say they putt better when they "see the line" of the putt. Sometimes this visualization is easy, but most of the time golfers have to concentrate to see the line.

Another set of lines that can help your optics are the lines of your feet, knees, and shoulders. By keeping them *square* (at a right angle) to the target line, you help your eyes appreciate what is straight — and keep your stroke on line.

To help you keep the clubface square to your target line, use tape or a yardstick on the floor. Aim the tape at a distant target, like a baby grand piano at the far end of your ballroom. Now set up at the end of the tape as if you were going to hit an imaginary ball straight down the tape line. You're practicing visual alignment. Give this drill a chance — it can really help your perception of straight lines.

When I'm having alignment problems, I take some of the gum that I've been chewing for the last three days and attach a tee to the putter with the fat end flush to the face, as shown in Figure 6-14. Then I aim that tee at the hole from about 3 feet away.

Figure 6-14: Stick a tee to the face of your putter to help align with your target.

Book III

Playing Golf: The Swing and the Short Game

This drill trains your eyes to square the clubface. You can use this exercise to visually process what a square clubface looks like as you look down the attached tee to the hole. Spend a couple of minutes appreciating this perspective. If it looks okay to you on your first try, you're in line for your Bachelor of Alignment degree. If not, repeat the drill daily until it looks okay the first time you place the club down.

The need for speed

One of the best ways to develop a touch for the speed at which putts should roll is to imagine things happening before they really do.

You must optically preview the putt's roll from its stationary point to a resting place near the hole — a tap-in is really nice. This optical preview activates the motor system to respond with the right amount of energy to hit the putt. You'd do the same thing if we told you to throw a ball over a bush and make it land no more than 5 feet beyond the bush. You'd decide at what arc and speed to toss the ball, and your mind's eye would relay this information to your muscles.

View a putt from a point off to the side of the target line, midway between the ball and the hole, as shown in Figure 6-15. This technique can give you a better feel for the distance. Some professionals swear they can visualize the proper speed of a putt twice as well from the side.

Figure 6-15: Viewing a putt from the side can help you judge distance and speed.

A good rule of thumb: Don't change your mind while you're over a putt. For one thing, putts look different from above than from the side! For another, the ground you stand on may not be sloped the same as it is near the hole. And unless the putt is all downhill, the ball does most of its curving during the last third of the putt. (That's another reason to stand to the side of the putt — assessing the last third of the putt is easier from there.)

Some quick tips you may want to scrawl in your reminder book:

- ✔ **Fast greens break more, so don't hit the ball too hard.** But keep in mind that hitting the ball softly means that the slope affects it more.

- ✔ **Downhill putts act like fast greens because the slope affects the roll of the ball for more than the last few feet.**

- ✔ **Slow greens break less, so you have to hit the ball harder.** That initial burst of speed keeps the ball from breaking as much.

- ✔ **Uphill putts act like putts on slow greens.** Your challenge is to figure out how much uphill slope you're dealing with, and adjust your putt accordingly — the steeper the slope, the more power it takes. Try imagining that the hole is farther away than it really is.

Points of the roll

This chapter covers some complicated stuff, so keep in mind some key points:

- ✔ **Keep your alignment parallel to the target line.** All the following parts of you stay parallel to that line:

  - Feet
  - Knees
  - Shoulders
  - Eye line

- ✔ **Know what your putter blade looks like when it's square to the line.**

- ✔ **Use the ball's logo or a line marked on the ball to help you align putts.**

- ✔ **Follow the line of your intended putt with your eyes at the speed that you think the ball will roll.**

- ✔ **Stare at the line of your putt longer than you look at the golf ball.**

Good putting takes practice. And then more practice. The boys at the club practice their putting less than anything else, and then they wonder why they lose bets!

More than half the strokes you make in this silly game may be putts. Create games on the putting green to make putting practice more fun. Your scorecard will thank you.

Book III

Playing Golf: The Swing and the Short Game

Reading the Break of the Greens

After you have the distance control of your stroke, you can work on the second half of the putting equation: reading the break. The *break* is the amount a putt moves from right to left or left to right. Slope, the grain of the grass (see this chapter's "Reading the grain"), topographical features such as water and mountains, and, perhaps most important, how hard you hit the ball dictate the break. For example, an aggressive player who routinely hits putts 5 feet past the cup isn't going to play as much break as someone with a softer touch. (**Remember:** You should hit your putts no more than 14 to 18 inches past the cup.)

The more firmly you hit a putt, the less the ball breaks on even the steepest gradient. So don't be fooled into thinking that you can hole a putt one way only. On, say, a 20-footer, you probably have about five possibilities. How hard you hit the ball is one factor.

The first thing I do when I arrive at a golf course is to find the natural slope of the terrain. If the course is near mountains, finding the natural slope is easy. Say the mountains are off to the right on the first hole. Any slope on that hole runs from right to left. In fact, the slope on every green is going to be "from" the mountain (unless, of course, a particularly humorless architect has decided to bank some holes toward the mountain). So I take that into account on every putt I hit.

Look at each green in detail. If you're on an older course, the greens probably slope from back to front to aid drainage. Greens nowadays have more humps and undulations than ever and are surrounded by more bunkers. And the sand tells a tale: Most courses are designed so that water runs past a bunker and not into it. Take that insight into account when you line up a putt.

Reading the break of a green is an art and a gift. It all seems so simple — you look at the ground and decide which way the surface of the green tilts, and then you adjust the line of your putt accordingly.

Sometimes, however, the break and slope can be tricky to see. Sometimes you may face more than one break in a putt. It takes patience and imagination to envision the path the ball may naturally take as it rolls along. We do have, however, a few ways that you can help yourself read the break — clues that help you forecast the way the ball will roll. (Check out Chapter 8 of Book III for more in-depth putting strategies, including ways to deal with particularly difficult breaks.)

An ode to miniature golf

The clown's nose, the windmill, the waterfalls — ah, the joys of miniature golf. Also known as putt-putt, miniature golf is considered child's play in the golf world. Although players attend the big-money championships of miniature golf, most golfers turn their noses up at 18 little par-1s or 2s with a snack bar at the end.

However, a trip to the miniature golf course can do you some good. You can use your own putter and your own ball — rather than a rubber red one — and in addition to getting a little putting practice in, you may even have fun and remember that fun is what the game is really about! (Just don't hit your ball down the hole on the 18th . . . it won't be your ball anymore, although you may win a free game!)

Examining all angles

Don't hold up play, but do look at the putt from all angles. As you walk up to the green or while the other players putt, move discreetly around and look at your putt from behind the ball and from behind the hole back toward the ball. Look at the putt from the side. If you can, get down low and look at the ball from a worm's-eye view. (You can do so easily on raised greens or from bunkers.) The more information you can process, the better the result.

Closing your eyes

If you have trouble seeing the break, close your eyes and stand at the hole or behind your ball with your hands at your sides. Closing your eyes causes your other senses to come alive to maintain your sense of balance. You feel yourself being pulled by gravity one way or another and your body naturally corrects that pull. Take these clues to heart.

Spilling a bucket of water

To help yourself read the break of a green, you can stand at the hole and imagine that you've spilled a huge bucket of water on top of the hole. Which way would all that water run after you fill up the hole and it overflows? Would it run off the front of the green? Would it stream to the back or off the side? Adjust your line accordingly. If you have trouble imagining, don't go for realism and dump water in . . . unless you think you can outrun the greenskeeper and the cops.

Book III

Playing Golf: The Swing and the Short Game

Reading the grain

Golf is played on different grasses (ideally, not on the same course). Climate usually dictates the kind of grass you find on a course. When dealing with grasses, architects try to use the thinnest possible blade, given the climate, and then try to get that grass to grow straight up to eliminate *grain*, or the tendency of grass to lie horizontally to the sun. Grasses in hot, tropical areas have to be more resilient, so they typically have thick blades. *Bermuda grass* is the most common. Its blades tend to follow the sun from morning to afternoon — in other words, from east to west. Because the blade is so strong, Bermuda grass can carry a golf ball according to the direction in which it lies. Putts *downgrain* (with the grain) go faster than putts *into* (against) the grain. All that, of course, has an effect on your putt.

Look at the cup to find out which way the Bermuda grass is growing. Especially in the afternoon, you may see a ragged half and a smooth, or sharp, half on the lip of the cup — that shows the direction in which the grass is growing. The ragged look is caused by the grass's tendency to grow and fray. If you can't tell either way, go to the *fringe* (the edge of the green). The grass on the fringe is longer, so you can usually see the direction of the grain right away. The grain of the fringe is the same as on the green.

Another common type of grass is *bent grass*, which has a thinner blade than Bermuda grass. You see this strain mostly in the northern and northeastern United States. Many golf-course builders use bent grass because it allows them to make the greens fast, and the recent trend for greens is to combine slope with speed.

Looking into the hole

Looking down into the hole can provide a sloping clue. Because a plastic cup lines the actual hole after the greenskeeper cuts it, you can see the discrepancy in the earth that rings around the top of the cup if the hole sits on a rise or a hill. The side with more dirt is the lower side of the hole, and the side with less dirt is higher. Therefore, if you putt the ball toward the higher side, it rolls and slides down toward the lower side.

Watching other players' putts

The break of another player's putt isn't proprietary information. Pay attention to your playing partners and competitors when they putt and watch how their putts react to the break of the green. Sometimes you get lucky and someone has the exact same line as you. In the 2004 Masters, Phil Mickelson caught a break when Chris DiMarco's bunker shot rolled behind Mickelson's ball, giving him a great view of the break of his winning putt. But even putts stroked from another angle can tell you something about the beak of the green.

Although standing directly behind or in front of another player (beyond the hole) on the line of his putt isn't against the rules of golf, players consider doing so to be bad form and inappropriate. The player may ask you to move so you don't distract him. If you want to look from directly on the line, wait until the ball leaves his putterhead to step into the line.

Sidesaddling Up: Face-on Putting

Here's another alternative that's starting to surface in the wonderful world of golf. It's called *face-on* or *sidesaddle putting.* If you've been struggling with your putter, this stroke may be the cure.

It starts with common sense: Think about how you'd putt without a putter: You'd roll the ball into the hole. Everyone, from Ben Crenshaw to the greenest golf novice, would face the hole and roll the ball underhand. *Nobody* would turn sideways first. Why? Because facing your target is more natural. Impractical for full swings, but perfectly practical for putting, if you know how to do it.

If you adopt the face-on method shown in Figure 6-16, you need a putter designed for it. (They're becoming more common but can still be hard to find. For information on ordering putters and other equipment from websites, see Chapter 1 of Book I.) You can get a feel for this putting with a regular long putter, but remember: To do it right, you need a face-on putter.

Book III

Playing Golf: The Swing and the Short Game

Figure 6-16: Face-on putting.

Here's how to try face-on putting:

1. **Use the same posture as if you were rolling a ball by hand: Face the target, knees flexed, with the ball slightly to your right, just ahead of your right foot.**

2. **Place your left hand at the top of your putter's grip; keep the face of your putter square to the line of your putt.**

   The left hand acts as the fulcrum for your putting stroke.

3. **With your eyes on the ball, bring the putter straight back with your right hand, and then straight through along your putting line.**

4. **Let your head come up naturally as you follow the ball on its merry way into the hole.**

For more on face-on putting, check out `Puttmagic.com`.

Chapter 7

Bunkers: Playing in Golf's Sandbox

They lurk, yawning like hungry monsters and gleaming in the sun like happy beaches. Their long, delicate fingers, sweeping faces, and geometric balance belie the trouble they can cause your scorecard. Bunkers add both artistry and complexity to the golf course.

Bunkers guard the fronts, sides, and backs of greens, catching the timid, the bold, and the off-line shots of players who miss the target. Flagsticks hide behind them, tempting players to hit shots over the bunkers or provoking enough fear to have them steer shots away from the hole to vacant portions of the green.

Some bunkers are deep and some shallow; some are simple and some complex. Make no mistake, however: Bunker play is an art as refined and as thoughtful as the very design of the splashy hazards themselves. This chapter helps you to both appreciate the danger of bunkers and demystify their desperate, desert spell.

Tackling the Bunker

Bunkers, hazards filled with sand, provoke an extraordinary amount of "sand angst" among golfers. (You may also know them as *sand traps,* but many golfers and commentators shy away from this term, and so do we.) But sometimes, *aiming* for a bunker actually makes sense — on a long, difficult approach shot, for example. The pros know that the *up and down* (getting onto the green and then into the hole) from sand can actually be easier than from the surrounding (usually gnarly) grass.

Bunkers began as dips in the ground on the windswept Scottish linksland. Because such areas were sheltered from cold breezes, sheep would take refuge in them. Thus, the dips expanded and got deeper. When the land came to be used for golf, the locals took advantage of what God and the sheep left behind and fashioned sand-filled bunkers. (No word on what the sheep thought of all this.) On these old courses, the greens were positioned so as to maximize the bunkers' threat to golfers' shots, which is why they came to be named *hazards* in the rules of golf. Later, course architects placed these insidious "traps" so as to penalize wayward shots. That's why you generally don't see bunkers in the middle of fairways — they're mostly to the sides.

Few amateurs have ever aimed at a bunker. Mired in sand is the last place they want to be. The saga the late Tip O'Neill endured years ago during the Bob Hope Chrysler Classic, a *pro-am* tournament (where professionals play with amateurs), is a great example of how amateur golfers look at bunkers. The former Speaker of the House, admittedly not the strongest golfer (even among celebrities), found himself in a very deep bunker. He then spent the next few hours (okay, it just *seemed* that long) trying to extricate first the ball and then his hefty, honorable self from the trap — all on national television. You could almost hear millions of viewers muttering, "Been there, done that."

Getting your mind out of the bunker

Why do bunkers scare most amateurs to death? Just what is it about sand play that they find so tough? Simple: It all comes down to lack of technique and/or a lack of understanding.

Faced with a bunker shot, many golfers are beaten before they start. You can tell by their constipated looks, sweaty foreheads, and hesitant body language. Their reactions when they fail are also interesting. After a couple of shots finish up back in the bunker, most players don't focus on technique. They merely try to hit the shot harder, making more and more-violent swings. Wrong! Swinging harder only makes them angrier, and then the ball sure isn't going to come out. They wind up digging a nice, big trench perfect for burying a small animal but not much good for anything else.

Part of the reason for this all-too-human reaction is that long stretches of failure resign you to your fate. In your mind, you've tried everything, and you *still* can't get the damn thing out. So you trudge into the bunker expecting the worst, and that's what you usually get.

Building a better bunker shot

So how do you go from digging for buried treasure to ejecting your ball from the bunker? Golf, and especially bunker play, is mainly in creating the proper angle that the clubhead must take into the ball. Most golfers address the ball in a way that makes creating the correct angles in their golf swings all but impossible. Ball position is the root of many duffs, hacks, slashes, and other misbegotten shots. If you have the ball positioned way back toward your right foot, as so many people seem to do, you'll never get it out of the trap. You can't hit the ball high enough, for one thing. For another, the clubhead enters the sand at too steep an angle. In other words, the clubhead digs into the sand instead of sliding through it. When that happens, the ball usually stays in the bunker, sucking sand.

Another trap (pun intended) is the idea that the stroke out of the bunker should be an "explosion shot" Although it may look like a blast to you when the clubhead hits the sand and the ball flies out, thinking of a bunker shot as an explosion is a harmful comparison.

Explosion means "bang!" It means a bomb went off. Rather than explosion, think "splash." Splash says, "Hey, I'm having fun here playing in the sand. Sand is my friend. I'm just splashing around." It may seem like a minor issue, but as we discuss throughout this book, short-game success is all about the mental. Splash takes the aggressive, violent connotation out of your mind and therefore out of your swing.

The later section "Hitting Effective Bunker Shots" gives you more information on avoiding these pitfalls and improving your bunker success.

Setting your bunker goals

Well-executed bunker shots are a beautiful sight. The sand bursts up in all directions, looking like a splashy fireworks show, and from this cloud emerges the ball, which soars high to its apex and lands softly on the green, checking up and stopping near the hole.

If you're an average player, your expectation and goal should be one in the same: Get the ball out of the bunker and onto the green in one shot. From there, make two-putting your new expectation and consider the outcome a success. If you happen to hit it close to the hole and make your putt — a lofty goal — enjoy your wild success.

If you play golf long enough, you'll hit some splendid, beautiful shots from time to time, and you'll feel great. Hitting a ball from a bunker onto the green and then making the putt is characterized in statistics as a *sand save*. Your pals in a friendly game may call this occurrence a "sandy." Enjoy sand saves when they happen because they rarely occur for the average player.

Book III

Playing Golf: The Swing and the Short Game

Special beach rules apply

Bunker play boasts its own set of rules. A bunker is considered a hazard, and a ball is in a bunker when it lies in or touches any part of the bunker. Before you make your stroke from a bunker, you can't

✔ Test the condition of the hazard

✔ Touch the sand with your hand or your club

✔ Touch a loose natural impediment in the bunker

In other words, you must be very careful not to let your club touch the ground when you take your stance. If you take a practice swing, don't hit the sand. The penalty for violating this rule is the loss of the hole in match play or two strokes in stroke play.

Some golf courses have large, sandy areas defined as *waste bunkers.* These scrubby areas aren't raked or maintained, and they often have shells and pebbles in them. You can ground your club and take practice swings in waste bunkers, which aren't considered hazards, just as you normally do anywhere outside a hazard on a golf course.

Check your scorecard, which typically identifies these waste areas, or ask the PGA professional in the clubhouse before your round to alert you to waste bunkers. When in doubt, consult with your competitor before you ground your club in what you think is a waste bunker.

Exploring the Sand Wedge's Bounce Effect

To be a competent sand player, you must take advantage of the way your sand wedge is designed. The bottom of the club is wider than the top (see Figure 7-1). The *bounce* is the part of a wedge that hangs below the *leading edge*, the front part of the *sole*. (The sole, like the bottom of a shoe, is the bottom of the clubhead.) Trust us, if you can make the best use of the bounce, you can take bunker play off your list of phobias.

The bounce is the part of the clubhead that should contact the sand first. This approach encourages the sliding motion that's so crucial to good bunker play. Think about it: The sand is going to slow the club as you swing down and through, which is okay. But you want to keep the slowdown to a minimum. If the club digs in too much, the ball probably won't leave the bunker. So *slide* the clubhead; don't use it to dig.

Take note, however, that not every sand wedge has the same amount of bounce. The width of the sole and the amount that it hangs below the leading edge varies. The lower the *trailing edge* (the rear part of the sole) hangs below the leading edge, the more bounce your sand wedge has. This point, of course, begs another question: How do you know how much bounce your sand wedge needs? The determining factor is the type of sand you play from. The bigger the bounce or the wider the sole on your sand wedge, the less the wedge digs into the sand.

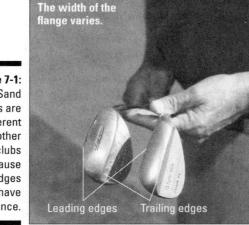

The width of the flange varies.

Leading edges   Trailing edges

Figure 7-1: Sand wedges are different from other clubs because wedges have bounce.

If the sand at your home course is typically pretty firm underfoot, you need a sand wedge with very little bounce. A club with a lot of bounce does just that — bounce. Hard (or wet) sand only accentuates that tendency, so using that club leaves you hitting a lot of shots *thin,* as the clubhead skids off the sand and strikes the ball's equator. Thin shots fly too low. Either you hit the ball into the face of the bunker and don't get out at all, or the ball misses the face and zooms over the green. Neither result is socially acceptable. The first is hazardous to your mental health, the second to your playing partners.

At the other end of the scale is soft, deep sand. For that sort of stuff, you need plenty of bounce. In fact, because the clubhead digs so easily when the sand is soft, you can't have enough bounce.

Book III

Playing Golf: The Swing and the Short Game

Hitting Effective Bunker Shots

Although you can easily be intimidated by the complexity of a bunker shot, it isn't unlike hitting a pitch shot or a flop shot (see Chapter 5 of Book III and Chapter 2 of Book VI). The key is to splash the sand with your club before it makes contact with the ball. Of course, the ball isn't technically trapped because you have plenty of methods to help it escape after you plot your exit strategy. The following sections help you do just that.

Assessing the sand variables

Not all bunkers are alike, and neither is the sand that forms them. You need to make a perceptive, smart assessment of the type of bunker your ball lands in, the lie you have to deal with, and the bunker's sand type.

Determining the shape you're in

The size of every bunker is different. But, generally, you encounter two extremes:

- ✓ **Sand scrapes:** Some bunkers may be shallow but expansive, so although you may not need to fly the ball extremely high, you have to hit it a longer distance forward to escape the bunker. In this case, be certain to use the proper amount of clubhead speed to propel the ball forward and not just up and out. A longer backswing and a closed clubface can propel the ball farther.

- ✓ **High lip:** Some bunkers are small, circular pot bunkers that may be deep but not large in circumference. If you have to negotiate a big lip between the ball and the green, make certain that the ball gets up quickly: Take the club back steeply and follow through. Open the clubface and maintain that position through the shot. (See the "Facing steep situations" section later in this chapter and the accompanying figure for more information.)

Regardless of the bunker shape you're in, you have to account for the variables of height and distance:

- ✓ How far does the ball have to fly in order to escape the bunker and land on the green?

- ✓ How high does the ball have to fly in order to clear any high side or rising lip that extends up in the bunker?

The more upright your swing, and the more open the clubface becomes, the higher and shorter the ball travels.

Adjusting to the sand

The sand that one golf course uses in its bunkers may be very different from the sand another course uses. Some courses have bunkers with fine, soft sand, and others put in firm sand. You see some bunkers with more sand than others, and the sand can be fluffy or wet and hard-packed.

Although the rules dictate that you can't test the nature of the sand before you play a shot from a bunker, take the time to be aware of whether the sand looks wet and hard or light and fluffy. Different conditions call for different techniques:

✔ **Soft sand:** If the sand in the bunker is soft and fluffy, you need to put a bit more speed in your swing because cushy sand slows the club down as the clubhead goes through. So feel free to be aggressive and make a strong swing.

✔ **Hard sand:** When the bunker sand is firm or wet, you need to slow your swing speed down, which means not taking the club back as far. The ball comes out more quickly because you don't have as much cushy sand between your ball and the clubhead. But make sure you don't decelerate your swing and leave the ball in the sand.

Checking out your lie

Examine the ball and the way it lies in the sand. Is it sitting on top of the sand or is it buried? If you have a clean lie, consider yourself lucky that the ball isn't buried or lying in a footprint. A ball partially buried is to be expected, but if it looks like you need a shovel, the "Coping with Troubled Lies" section later in the chapter can help. Figure 7-2 features a perfect lie in a bunker with seemingly soft sand that calls for a bigger swing.

Choosing your club

Greenside bunker shots often require you to fly your ball high through the air over a short distance. The height you have to fly your shot in order to escape the bunker is more important than the distance you need to cover; therefore, to play an effective bunker shot, you should use the shortest, most lofted club in your bag. The most lofted club in your bag is likely your sand wedge; you may also have a 58- or 60-degree club. Note the amount of loft of the wedge in Figure 7-2a.

Raising clubface awareness

To be an effective sand player, you must be aware of what's going on with the face of the club. You select a highly lofted club to play the shot, and the clubface needs to remain lofted as it slides through the sand and sends the ball skyward. In other words, when you take your grip and swing the club, you shouldn't do anything that could deloft the clubface or change its angle, such as trying to help the ball into the air. In Figure 7-2, you can see that the clubface doesn't change from the address (Figure 7-2a) through impact (Figure 7-2c) — a product of the lead wrist position at impact, which isn't broken.

Your grip shouldn't be tight, either, in an effort to keep the loft. The harder you grab, the more tension you put into your arms and hands, and if you have tension in your grip, you can't feel the clubhead. You always want to feel the clubhead and maintain its lofted state, so keep your grip relaxed.

Figure 7-2:
Dig your feet in with an open stance and splash through the sand with your natural swing.

Taking your stance

When you set up to hit a bunker shot, you stand virtually the same way you stand to hit a pitch shot (see Chapter 5 of Book III). When you take position over the ball, your lead foot should point open 45 degrees, and your body and shoulders should open to that same 45-degree angle facing down the target line and toward the target (see Figures 7-3b and 7-4a). Put more of your weight on your front foot to keep from swaying and make sure to keep your knees flexed.

Figure 7-3: Open your stance and wedge face until they feel vaguely ridiculous.

Digging in and staying level

You do have to deal with one major difference between your pitch stance and your bunker stance, and it stems from the conditions of the shots. Unlike a pitch shot, when you hit the ball off the ground and brush the grass with the clubhead, a bunker shot requires you to make contact with the sand *behind* the ball on the downswing at impact, forcing the ball in front of a cushion of sand. You don't strike the ball. Because the clubhead needs to splash through the sand below the ball, you naturally have to get lower.

To make splashing the sand easier, when you open your lead foot and take your stance, dig yourself down into the sand (see Figure 7-2b). You should bury the soles of your shoes. If you stand level, you have to reach down unnaturally during your swing to make proper contact with the sand. You want your swing to stay consistent, and the only way to do that is to lower yourself by digging your feet in. This way, you can take your natural swing.

Choosing your ball position

Generally, when you stand over the ball, you should position it in the middle of your stance (see Figure 7-2a). As an average player, you should keep the ball in the middle of your stance for all bunker shots — a way to go about playing the shot that allows you to develop your touch and feel by keeping it simple.

Advanced players do some creative things with ball position, but you should play the ball in the middle, and practice with it there, until you feel as though you've mastered the bunker shot — to the extent that it can be mastered, that is. When you step into a bunker without fear and are confident that you can get the ball out of the bunker and reasonably close to the hole with one shot under any conditions, you've come as close to "mastering" the sand as you can.

Sometimes, however, the circumstances you find your ball in dictate that you move the ball from the center of your stance no matter what your skill level is:

- ✔ **Uphill bunker shot:** Move the ball a little bit forward of center to make certain you hit the sand in front of the ball.
- ✔ **Downhill bunker shot:** Move the ball a little behind center in your stance to make certain the ball flies up, because gravity naturally pulls it down.

Read more about particularly troublesome lies in the "Coping with Troubled Lies" section later in this chapter.

Picking a target and taking aim

Because your ball comes out higher as a result of the highly lofted face of the club you use for bunker shots, it doesn't roll as far. If you never deloft your open clubface and splash the ball out, your ball comes out high; lands in a soft, vertical fashion; and rolls only a short distance after it hits the green.

In numerical terms, your ball should roll for only about 40 percent of its life — so 60 percent of the shot takes place in the air. After you become an efficient bunker player, you can pick a spot to aim at, but if you're an average player, don't concentrate on a particularly small spot. Your expectation should be to get the ball out of the sand and onto an area of the green. You don't want to have to hear any lame beach jokes from your partners as you scrape sand all day.

As we note in the section "The shape of the backswing" later in this chapter, your bunker swing should be steeper than your natural swing, so you can't go straight back along the target line (see Chapter 3 of Book III for an introduction to the target line). And because your clubhead comes across the target line, you have to aim a little bit to the left of the target when you set up (see Figure 7-4b).

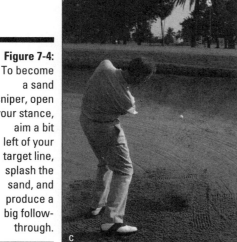

Figure 7-4:
To become
a sand
sniper, open
your stance,
aim a bit
left of your
target line,
splash the
sand, and
produce a
big follow-
through.

Book III

**Playing
Golf: The
Swing and
the Short
Game**

Taking a sand-sweeping swing

As odd as it sounds, you have to understand that you don't try to hit the ball
during bunker shots. As we indicate earlier in the chapter, a well-executed
bunker shot sends the ball flying out of the bunker on a platform of sand (see
Figure 7-4c). The impact the club makes on the sand, and the reaction of the
sand, is what propels the ball out of the bunker.

Pick a spot 2 inches behind the ball. Concentrate on that spot and swing the club through it. When you practice your bunker shots, imagine the ball sitting on an area of sand that you want your club to sweep — or splash — through.

Imagine another golf ball lying in the sand directly behind yours — that's about how far behind the ball your clubhead should enter the sand. Attempt to hit the second imaginary golf ball in order to move the real one.

Don't "help" the ball out of the bunker and into the air. Anytime you try to do so, your weight transfers to your back leg, and you raise up as you try to scoop the ball. The more your weight stays on your back side, the more likely you are to belly the ball by hitting it with the bottom of the club and skulling it across the green or into the side of the bunker. Keep your weight in the center of your stance and minimize any leg action or transfer of weight.

The shape of the backswing

The shape of your takeaway and backswing should be a very upright, vertical motion. Your backswing should be steeper because the angle of attack needs to be steeper in order to get the ball up sooner and higher than normal. (For an example of a really upright vertical backswing, check out Figure 7-9 later in the chapter.)

The angle down, when you swing a golf club through a ball, actually translates as up in terms of the ball's response. If you swing down with your club, the ball goes up.

But also consider that the more steeply you take the club back, the shorter the distance the ball can travel because of the emphasis on height. Your club goes vertical, you swing slowly, and the clubhead is lofted, so the ball simply can't go very far.

To swing the club back more vertically, use your hands to swing the club more than your arms. To get the backswing steeper, you need to get wristier by cocking your wrists a little more than you normally do. When you cock your wrists, the club may wander off the target line some, but you should stay focused on the face and keep your grip loose. You swing the clubhead though the ball just as you normally do, but you swing at a steeper angle.

The length and speed of the backswing

We're talking distance control here. With a bunker shot, the length of your backswing determines how far the ball flies after it leaves the bunker.

If you just have to get the ball out of the bunker and the flagstick is cut close to your side of the green, you can't take the club very far back or you'll send the ball a long way. But no matter how far you judge that you need to take the club back, be sure to swing all the way through and follow through to a complete swing (see Figure 7-4d). Take it back halfway if you need to, but be sure to finish fully! (Check out the next section for more on the follow-through.)

Depending upon your lie and the density of the sand, the speed of your swing is also a factor. Think of this concept like driving your car: The faster and harder you swing, the farther the ball goes. But you also have more margin for error — just like driving too fast!

Try to maintain a consistent swing speed all the time to achieve success. The speed should be smooth and slow enough so you can feel the clubhead. If you play a course with harder sand, you can swing easier (or harder in the case of softer sand), but always keep the clubhead speed the same during the round. To vary the distance of a bunker shot, vary how far back you take the club. The speed takes care of itself.

The follow-through

One of the biggest mistakes players make during a bunker shot is failing to follow through after they make contact with the sand and begin to move the ball forward.

A bunker shot requires a big finish. No matter how short your greenside shot is, it requires the *chorus line finish* — a big, full follow-through, not the *9:00 to 3:00* finish of a chip shot or pitch shot (see Chapters 4 and 5 of Book III, respectively).

The reason for the big follow-through is that the sand slows your clubhead down at impact. Metaphorically, if this swing is 10 miles per hour, the clubhead can go through the ball at 12 or even 15 miles per hour, but it shouldn't go through at 5 miles per hour. Your goal is to get your downswing to go the same speed as your backswing — or a bit faster. You slow the downswing by decelerating the clubhead, which kills the momentum of the swing.

Hitting off grass is different. The club goes through the grass easily, so you can swing the club more easily. Shorter grass doesn't really catch on the blade too much. But the minute you try to hit through the sand, the clubhead slows down. Therefore, you have to make sure that you constantly maintain good clubhead speed, and in order to maintain good speed, you need that big finish. Concentrating on making that finish ensures that you don't inadvertently slow down the clubhead on the downswing or at impact. The bigger the finish, the better your chances of escaping the bunker.

You may be tempted to quit on a bunker shot and not make the big finish out of hesitation or lack of confidence. If you stop the club just after you hit the ball, you've decelerated — and you never want to decelerate! Deceleration is the short-game kiss of death, no matter the shot.

Focusing on a full, uninhibited follow-through helps. Forget the ball; all you're trying to do is throw sand out of the bunker (see Figure 7-5). If you can throw sand, the ball gets carried along for the ride. And that's why better players say that bunker play is easy: The clubhead never actually contacts the ball. (*Remember:* The more sand you throw, the shorter the shot is. So if you need to hit the shot a fair distance, hit maybe only 2 inches behind the ball.)

Form a firm, balanced foundation...

slide the clubhead under the ball...

throwing some sand and the
ball onto the green.

Finish with a big follow-through.

Figure 7-5:
Make sure
to follow
through
when hitting
from a
bunker.

Coping with Troubled Lies

As if bunker shots aren't difficult enough, sometimes you encounter a situation where the ball doesn't lie on perfectly flat sand. The following sections give you some pointers on succeeding from these problematic positions.

Negotiating uphill and downhill lies

One of the most intimidating and difficult bunker shots you encounter occurs when you find your ball halfway up the face of the bunker or halfway down the back of a bunker.

If you think logically about an uphill or downhill lie in a bunker, you understand that

- When you have an uphill lie, the ball comes out higher.
- When you have a downhill lie, the ball comes out lower.

So, what to do about it? When you have an uneven level, you must adjust your shoulders at address to mimic the slope of the hill:

- **Uphill shot:** Your shoulders need to tilt until they rest parallel to the ground (see Figure 7-6). If you don't make your shoulders level to the hill, your swing smashes into the hill. You also make it difficult to get through the hill into your big follow-through; you end up with the clubhead stopping and a ball that can't go anywhere. You don't want the club getting caught in the sand because you swing right smack into the hill. The clubface should square, not open, because the incline already adds loft. Play the ball forward in your stance.

- **Downhill shot:** Your shoulders need to tilt again, this time so they mirror the downhill slope of the bunker (see Figure 7-7). Tilting back on a downhill bunker shot causes you to bury the club in the sand too far behind the ball or top the ball. The angle becomes unnaturally severe and inappropriate. Keep your weight on your front side and swing the club vertically. Put the ball to the back of your stance.

If you tilt your shoulders to match the hill, you make plenty of room for your swing. Tilting for the downhill or the uphill lie naturally allows you to swing normally, splash through the sand, and rotate into your finish because you swing with the slope of the hill. Simple physics, we suppose, but you don't need a physics course to improve your sand game.

Book III

Playing Golf: The Swing and the Short Game

Figure 7-6:
Positioning
yourself for
an uphill
shot.

Figure 7-7:
Setting
up for a
downhill
shot.

Extracting the fried egg: Buried lies

Unfortunately, not every lie in a bunker is perfect. Sometimes the ball *plugs,* or embeds itself in the sand so that only part of it is visible. Some golfers call this lie a *fried egg,* but don't reach for a spatula. Instead, after you're through cursing your bad luck, try a different technique.

To exhume your ball from a buried lie, follow these steps:

1. **Set up your stance and clubface.**

   You need to open your stance as you do for any sand shot (see the earlier section "Taking your stance"). But this time, don't open the clubface. Keep it a little *hooded.* In other words, align the clubface to the left of your target. Shift nearly all your weight to your left side, which puts you ahead of the shot (see Figure 7-8), and play the ball back in your stance. This situation is the one time you *want* the leading edge of the club to dig. The ball, after all, is below the surface of the sand.

2. **Swing the club up and down.**

   And we mean *up* and *down* like you're chopping wood with a dull ax. Hit straight down on the sand a couple of inches behind the ball as shown in Figure 7-9. A full follow-through isn't necessary. Just hit down. Hard. The ball should pop up and then run to the hole. With little or no backspin, that sneaky little escapee runs like it just stole something. So allow for extra roll.

   Just how hard you should hit down is difficult to say — it depends on the texture and depth of the sand and on how deep the ball is buried. That old standby, practice, tells you what you need to know.

Second-to-last point: Practice with clubs of various lofts, and then use whatever works for you. Especially consider the pitching wedge (which has less bounce and a sharper leading edge than a sand wedge, and therefore digs more) for buried-lie escapes. (See the earlier section "Exploring the Sand Wedge's Bounce Effect" for more on bounce.)

Last point: Always smooth out your footprints when leaving a bunker — that's golf etiquette. If no rake is nearby, use your feet.

Put the ball back in your stance...

but don't change your posture.

Close the clubface at address.

Figure 7-8:
A buried lie
in a bunker:
Can you
dig it?

Facing steep situations

You may stumble upon occasions when you find your ball up against a severely steep sod face or lying under an extremely high, looming lip. If you stand over your ball, look up at the wall or lip of the bunker, and think, "I can't get this ball up fast enough to get it over that lip and land the green," you're almost always right! You probably have such a bad lie that the ball can't physically come off the club at a sharp enough launch angle to allow it to clear the bunker's face/lip.

"Bury" the club in the sand...

which shortens your follow-through.

Figure 7-9: Hit down hard!

Book III

Playing Golf: The Swing and the Short Game

What are your options? Check out the following pointers:

- ✔ In the face of overwhelming odds, you may want to take a swing at the ball anyway, which can lead to terrible repercussions. The ball may hit the lip or wall and fall back into the bunker in the same spot or in an even worse position; you may plug the ball into the face of the bunker or the lip; or, even worse, the ball may bounce back off the wall or lip and hit you, putting you in danger and causing you to incur a two-stroke penalty. (This situation happened to Jeff Maggert at the Masters.)

- ✔ You can declare the ball unplayable, take a one-stroke penalty, and drop the ball within two club-lengths of where it lies but no nearer to the hole. The downside of this option is that the ball must remain in the bunker.

- ✔ Perhaps the least desirable but wisest option is to play the ball out of the bunker — backward. Play the ball out of the bunker at the easiest point of escape, and then play it to the green with your next shot. Such defeatism is against the nature of every golfer; you don't want to hit the ball backward up a fairway or away from the hole, but sometimes you have to take your medicine and go the smartest, safest route.

If you decide to give it a go in the face of the odds, open your clubface as much as you can (see Figure 7-10a); take a very vertical, upright backswing (see Figure 7-10b); and then let your lead hand take the clubhead through the sand (see Figure 7-10c) at a consistent speed. Try to ignore the result so you can swing the clubhead all the way through to a big, full finish (see Figure 7-10d).

Figure 7-10:
Shooting
to clear
a steep
bunker face.

Blame the sheep for that pot bunker

Although you may feel like bunkers were created specifically to complicate your trip around the golf course, that bit of Machiavellian self-pity isn't always warranted. The original golf courses — treeless, seaside links courses in Scotland — only featured bunkers because the resident sheep dug the holes to escape the wind and "bunker down" at night. Indeed, caddies and sometimes even roustabout golfers have been known to seek refuge in the bunkers of the Old Course at St. Andrews.

Because the sheep cared little about golf strategy, the shape and placement of their bunkers on golf's original courses had no real rhyme or reason; they often weren't even visible to the golfers who hit shots into them. These pot bunkers were deep and deadly, and therefore course managers gave them names such as the famous "Hell Bunker" or "Principal's Nose," "Coffin," or "Sahara."

Modern golf course architects have been much more strategic in their placement of bunkers, although some still end up with dastardly names, such as the "Church Pew" bunkers at Oakmont CC and "Hell's Half-Acre" at Pine Valley. But architects don't merely place bunkers in precarious spots to make golf holes tougher. Knowing what the designer had in mind can help you play the course more effectively. Listen to the language of a golf course when you play and take time to notice how the bunkers are positioned. Most architects repeat their styles and philosophies on each hole on a given course, and recognizing what the designer had in mind can help improve your strategy.

Architects design bunkers to frame the hole or give it style. Bunkers also serve as aiming points or directional devices to show the player where to aim the ball. In some cases, bunkers are designed to "save the players from themselves," in which case the bunkers may catch a wayward ball that would otherwise roll into a pond or down the side of a cliff. You may find that a short hole has many bunkers defending the green. Only fair, wouldn't you say?

Chapter 8

Short-Game Strategies

You need to do more than keep your eye on the ball to improve your short game. This chapter reveals strategies that can take your performance to the next level. The pitch and run, the Texas wedge, the yips, and the flop aren't dance moves; they're short-game terms we explain in this chapter.

Waging a Ground Campaign

Is golf a game of vertical darts? Or is it more like lawn bowling over long distances? You most likely view and play the game somewhere between these two ends of the spectrum. You face times during a round when shots from both extremes are required and advisable. But as an overall philosophy, are you better off adopting a high-flying air attack or a low-to-the-earth ground campaign? This section makes the case for going low to have lower scores.

For some reason, most golfers seem to enjoy hitting majestic, high shots that stick into the green. Maybe it's seeing nature's backdrop as the ball flies through the sky or experiencing the thrill of seeing the ball land and stop close to the pin. Maybe players want to emulate a PGA Tour player's often-high trajectory. Truly, a great high shot is fun to watch, but television can distort reality.

Sometimes, hitting a high shot just isn't practical: You don't always face the obstacles that call for a flop shot (see "Flipping the Flop" later in this chapter), and sometimes, such as during heavy winds or when hard ground makes using a more lofted club tougher, trying to get a ball high in the air isn't advisable.

Knowing when to go low

Keeping the ball low is an effective strategy that you can easily adopt. A famous football saying notes, "When you pass the ball, three things can happen . . . and two of them are bad." That's why many coaches embrace the safe, effective, "three yards and a cloud of dust" philosophy that fans dislike because of its boring nature. Golf is much the same way; although less flashy, doing the golf equivalent of running the ball (playing it low) is often the safest option.

The following circumstances encourage the ground game in golf:

- ✔ **You're close to the green:** You can judge how far a ball will roll much more easily than you can judge how far it will fly. Therefore, if no impediments block your path to the hole, keeping the ball low and getting it rolling on the ground as soon as possible makes sense when you're close to the green. From 30 yards and closer, popping the ball high up in the air can only introduce problems. Instead, use the natural contour of the green to roll the ball to the hole.

   Hitting a chip shot or pitch shot at a low trajectory can help you become much more precise with your short shots. Imagine you have a baseball in your hand and a steel bucket sits 30 yards away. Which seems easier: landing the ball in the bucket through the air or rolling the ball so that it hits the bucket or stops near it?

- ✔ **You have wind to deal with:** The higher you hit the ball, the more susceptible it is to the vagaries of the wind. The wind can blow your ball to the left or right when you hit it up high. If you hit your shot into the wind, breezes can knock a high ball down short of the target, and if the wind is at your back, a high ball may balloon over the green and into trouble.

   On the other hand, a low, firm shot can bore through the wind and hold its line much better than a high ball. Keeping the ball low in the wind is an easier, safer, and ultimately more effective shot.

Playing the ball low also gives you helpful options when you find your ball under a tree or behind branches that can block a high shot. Even if you can't reach the green, you can play a sensible, low-running lay-up shot to a suitable spot in the fairway. Practicing these types of shots helps you better understand the distance control involved around and away from the greens.

Choking down for a knockout knock-down

The dreaded C word . . . choking! But in golf, choking doesn't *always* mean screwing up a gimme shot at the worst possible moment. Oh, sure, you have plenty to get nervous about when you're in a tight match or trying to put the finishing touches on a career-best round. But here, we're just talking about how you grip the club (so relax!).

Choking down . . . not choking . . . is a valuable fundamental for keeping a ball low to the ground. *Choking down* on a club simply means placing your hands lower on the grip than you normally do. You take your normal grip, but you position your hands halfway down the club's grip and nearer to the club's exposed shaft.

Reviewing the benefits of choking down

You choke down on a club when you want to hit a low-flying, hard, straight shot such as a *punch shot,* or *knock-down shot.* These swings are called punch shots because of the abbreviated, controlled swing and the manner in which the ball seems to punch through the air. You don't have to use the word *punch* or think of it as a punch shot, however, because that word may cause you to tense up or swing the club in a violent, punchlike fashion.

Choking down on the club also lets you stand very close to the target line, which allows you to look at the shot almost as if you're putting. And although you effectively shorten the club and reduce the distance the ball can travel, the lower trajectory can make up for that lost distance through control and feel.

Executing a successful choke-down shot

You can, if the situation dictates, punch a shot on a lower trajectory than normal with more lofted clubs. You may find that you like hitting a knockdown-style shot, for instance, if you find your ball at a distance from the green that puts you between clubs — too long for the pitching wedge but too short for the 9-iron. Choke down and hit a knock-down 9-iron.

Even a shot that requires abbreviated movements and causes a hard-driving ball, such as a punch shot, should come from a fluid, relaxed motion.

Follow these steps to get your ball flying lower and straighter:

1. **Choke down on the handle of the club.**

    Use your normal grip, but slide your hands farther down on the handle. The farther down your hands go, the shorter and lower the shot flies.

2. **Position the ball slightly back of center in your stance.**

3. **Make your backswing.**

   How far you take the club back depends on how far you want to hit the ball, but a three-quarter-length swing often does the trick.

4. **Keep your swing speed consistent and hit down and through the ball on the target line.**

   Keep your hands ahead of the ball at impact to send the ball darting on a low path. Make sure you keep your hands and wrists firm to avoid any collapse (flipping) that may cause you to change the loft or direction of the clubface.

A small physics lesson may help. The length of a club governs the arc and plane of a golf swing. Choking down shortens the club, shortens the arc, and makes the plane flatter, which makes the ball fly on a lower trajectory.

Some instructors teach that an abbreviated follow-through should follow the choked-down punch shot. The technique is sound, but only advanced players with a mastery of short-game fundamentals should attempt it. Typically, an abbreviated follow-through results in a natural deceleration at impact in an attempt to slow the club down in time to stop it quickly. Deceleration in any golf swing is a recipe for disaster: It almost always causes the ball to go offline or results in a poor swing. You don't want to inadvertently train yourself to decelerate your swing and ruin your short-game fundamentals. Work on your fundamentals before you experiment with an abbreviated follow-through.

Staying Low: Pitching and Running

The *pitch and run* shot, sometimes called a *bump and run,* is a good way to play the ball low around the greens and to keep it out of the wind on longer shots. The pitch and run acts just like its name suggests — you pitch the ball and it runs on the ground toward the hole. (See Chapter 5 of Book III for more on the pitching portion of the shot.)

Say you're standing 20 to 40 yards from the green and mulling over your options. A little wind is in the air, and you don't have bunkers or water hazards in your way; nothing but short grass lies between you and the hole. A pitch and run shot is an effective and even fun option.

Taking aim

With a pitch and run, you have a few more mental calculations to consider than you do when dropping a lob shot onto the green from the air. You must imagine the entire life of the shot before you hit it and then re-create your vision. It can be a fun and effective shot if you envision and line it up properly:

- ✔ **Decide on the shape and length of the "pitch" portion of the shot.** Decide how far you want the ball to fly before it starts rolling. Consider how hard you must hit the ball to get it to fly that far and pick a target to set up your target line (see Chapter 2 of Book III for more on the target line).

- ✔ **Figure out how far the ball has to roll to reach the green or the hole after it touches down.** You also have to take the roll into account when deciding on your backswing. You may have to hit the ball hard to get it to roll across the green. Take the thickness of the grass and other variables into account as well.

- ✔ **Factor in the break and slope of the green.** Look at the green and predict what direction the ball will roll after it reaches the green. What's the break and slope of the green? Use this info to pick a target and target line. Essentially, you approach this aspect of the pitch and run as you do a putt, which we cover in Chapter 6 of Book III.

Decide on a target line that will steer the ball in the proper direction. Stand behind your ball and envision this imaginary line from your ball to the spot you want the ball to initially land on. You now have a target line that you can use for aiming purposes.

Selecting your club

To land your target, you have to grab a stick from your bag. A 7-iron is a perfect choice to hit the bump and run, but you can play this shot with any iron you prefer — even a 3-iron! We recommend the 7-iron because the face of the club is lofted enough to help the ball into the air but not lofted so much that it sends the ball too high. A 7-iron can get the ball easily off the turf and propel it forward.

Of course, you may face occasions when you want less loft and more distance, such as running a ball from outside 50 yards or trying to keep it under a tree branch. In these cases, a less-lofted club, such as a 5-iron, may suit you. Practice with all your irons so you get comfortable with them and know how far each sends the ball and on what type of flight.

Getting into your stance

After you select your club, address the ball by turning your front toe to point 45 degrees between the target line and an imaginary line perpendicular to the

Book III

Playing Golf: The Swing and the Short Game

target line. Open your shoulders an equal amount so that your body is open to and nearly facing the target. Keep the ball in the middle of your stance. Your stance is the same as it is for a standard pitch shot (see Chapter 5 of Book III).

Taking your swing

The swing here is largely the one you make for a pitch shot (see Chapter 5 of Book III); only the style of the shot differs. Design it in your head to land the ball in front of the green and run up. Imagine you have a clock behind you, with 12:00 at the top and 6:00 between your feet where your club rests behind the ball. Swing the club no farther on the clock in your follow-through than you do on the backswing. If you take the club back to 4:00, follow through no farther than 8:00, the corresponding number on the other side of the dial.

How far back you swing the club determines how far the ball flies, just as with a standard pitch. But in this case, you want to aim for the front of the green or just off the front of the green to give the ball enough room to run, so you want to take the club only far enough back to land the ball on the desired spot and let it bounce and run up to the hole.

Remember to take the club straight back on the target line and follow through along the target line. Don't decelerate the clubhead as it strikes through the ball. And keep your head down.

The best way to master the pitch and run is to spend time hitting the shot on the practice range or at a short-game practice area. Try hitting the shot at varying lengths and with different clubs until you find an iron that you're comfortable with at different distances. Take pride in your ability to imagine these shots; you can enjoy consistent success with the shot after you get a feel for it.

Discovering the Famed Texas Wedge

If you've ever heard the term *Texas wedge* bandied about by golfers before, you may have wondered what the heck a Texas wedge is. You use the Texas wedge when you hit a shot with your putter from any spot off the green where you traditionally use a wedge. The Texas wedge can refer to both the putter and the strategy/improvisation of using the putter around the greens.

Why Texas? Because the plains of Texas are well known for their sweeping, whipping winds, which make keeping the ball low a necessity for golfers. And no club keeps the ball lower than a putter!

Using a putter from off the green can be a very effective strategy if the conditions and the situation warrant it. For example, consider the Texas wedge in these circumstances:

✔ If the ground is firm, dry, and fast

✔ If the grass leading to the green is short

✔ If no bunker or other hazard lies between you and the hole or along the target line

✔ If the target line doesn't run too severely uphill, although moderate elevation is fine as long as you compensate for it in your shot

✔ If strong winds make the shot a more attractive option than a pitch into the air

Playing this shot effectively requires imagination and practice on your part. Spend a little time around the practice green working it into your repertoire. After you become proficient at very long putts, you may be surprised at how much easier the short ones feel!

Don't be embarrassed to putt from off the green, and don't be swayed by players who tease your strategy by mocking it with the phrase "Texas wedge." Not everyone has this effective and unique shot in the bag, but we know that the best players in the world do.

Holding the Green

Keeping the ball on the green with your approach shot, whether you pitch or chip, is obviously your goal. And, after you practice your short game enough to get comfortable, sticking the green can become an expectation.

Sometimes, you have to be crafty to get the ball to stay on, or *hold,* the green because holding may be more difficult in certain situations:

✔ Hard greens, from maintenance practices or a lack of rain, may cause the ball to bounce over.

✔ Fast, short-cut greens tend to run balls into the fringe.

✔ Crowned greens, which slope off every side from every angle, can be difficult to hold, especially if a greenskeeper or the weather makes them hard and/or fast.

✔ Greens with severe undulations or moguls can be tough to hold because of the angles the ball encounters when it hits the slopes and how it rolls afterward.

Book III

Playing Golf: The Swing and the Short Game

So how can you get your ball to stop on the green during these conditions? Get creative. Sometimes you may have to aim for a target away from the hole and visualize how the ball will roll after it hits that spot on the green.

Sometimes, with pitch shots especially, you may choose not to aim at the green at all. You may be better off landing the ball in front of the green and letting it roll onto the putting surface so it can run out of speed. Hitting the longer grass or a mound in front of the green can help to slow the ball down enough so that it trickles toward the hole and stops instead of skipping, sliding, rocketing, or rolling over the back of the green or off the side.

You may also consider hitting the ball high and dropping it down onto the green. A high, spinning ball falls in a vertical fashion and doesn't roll very far. Even a high pitch shot (see Chapter 5 of Book III) struck with a light grip can land in a soft and deadened fashion and stop or check up before rolling out a bit or spinning back.

Pulling the Pin . . . or Leaving It In?

According to the rules of golf, when you play shots from on or near green, you must decide whether you want to leave the flagstick in the hole, remove it, or have it tended by your caddie or playing partner. We outline the factors that go into making such a decision in the following sections.

From off the green

When your ball comes to rest off the green, including that closely mown area around the edge of the green called the *fringe* or the *collar,* you have the option of leaving the flagstick in the hole. Whether to pull or leave the pin is an age-old debate among golfers. When you have to play a short shot and you have flagstick options, what should you do?

The debate, as you may have guessed, features pros and cons for both approaches.

- ✔ **Pull the pin:**
  - **Pros:** Taking the flagstick from the hole clears the pathway to the bottom from any obstruction. Without the pin in, the ball can fall freely into the hole.
  - **Cons:** If you pull the pin, a ball moving too fast can roll right over the hole.

🗸 **Leave it in:**

- **Pros:** The advantage of leaving the pin in the hole is that your ball may hit the flagstick and fall in. In addition, if you hit your chip too aggressively, the ball may hit the flagstick and slow down. The flagstick can serve as a "backstop" for chip shots — especially downhill chip shots on fast greens, the type of shot that can run away from you in a hurry.

- **Cons:** Not taking the pin out can keep the ball from falling in, causing it to ricochet away from the cup. And if the green is speedy or downhill on the sides of the cup, your ball may roll quickly off the green.

And now we're back to the question at hand: Pull the pin or leave it in? Everyone has an opinion on this matter. "The pin never helps a good shot" is one mantra, and some professionals say that they pull the pin when they want to make the shot and leave it in when they hope to get the ball close. Experts have conducted scientific research, but it proves inconclusive.

Ultimately, whether to pull the pin or leave it in is a matter of personal preference. But the following bits of advice may help you make your decision based on the situation you're in:

🗸 You may consider leaving the flagstick in on slippery downhill chips and taking it out in uphill situations.

🗸 Check the angle on which the hole is cut. If the hole is cut into the green at a severe angle, the flagstick may unevenly block one side of the hole.

If you decide to leave the pin in, always check (without slowing up play) before you hit any short-game shot to be certain other players have properly inserted the flagstick into the cup so it doesn't lean to one side or impede the hole.

From on the green

According to the rules of golf, a ball played from on the green must not strike the flagstick. If it does, a two-stroke penalty, or loss of the hole in match play, is assessed.

When your ball is on the green and you can see the hole from where your ball lies, remove the flagstick. But if you're putting from far enough away that you can't clearly see the hole, your caddie or playing partner can tend the flagstick by standing beside the hole and removing it after you stroke your putt and before the ball reaches the hole.

Book III

Playing Golf: The Swing and the Short Game

Good caddies, and hopefully fellow playing partners, know that when tending the flagstick during putts, you should twist the pin and pull it from the bottom of the hole before the player strokes the putt. Sometimes the sand that builds up in the bottom of the cup can get wet or dry like paste and make the pin stick in the hole. You don't want this sticky situation to happen when the ball is in motion, because if you can't remove the flagstick in time and the ball strikes it, the putter incurs a penalty. We've also heard of occasions when people tending the pin have attempted to remove it and pulled the entire plastic cup liner out of the hole, which impeded the ball from rolling into the hole (obviously) and forced the putter to take a costly two-stroke penalty.

Pulling Out Your Putting Strategies

Putting is a skill you perform with an innate sense of touch and feel. A sense of the speed and the break of the green is a gift that the best putters seem to be born with — a gift of skill mixed with steely nerves. But no great putter just walks onto a green and sinks every putt he looks at without carefully thinking over the situation, reviewing his options, considering the circumstances, and strategizing about how to sink the ball or get it close.

Of course, a great putter practices a great deal to become comfortable with his knowledge of the options and ability to assess the situation. Practice builds the confidence to implement whichever strategic approach is necessary.

In this section, we build on the putting mechanics we introduce in Chapter 6 by focusing on a number of putting strategies you can incorporate into your game. We suggest that you try out these strategies when you practice. If you get comfortable with them, don't slack off; continue to practice and become proficient enough to use them during play. When you play, concentrate on putting in the subconscious after you consider all your tried and tested strategies. You want your putting to become an effortless, Zen-like activity that happens through natural skill, not through mechanical technique. Practice your mechanics and technique well enough to shut off those thoughts. We also give you a hand if the wheels have fallen off your putting game by examining the causes of and providing some possible corrections for the dreaded yips.

Settling on a style

Some golfers are so confident, or trick themselves into feeling so confident, that they convince themselves they can make any putt they look at, no matter the length or the severity of the break. Without reservation, they size up every putt, walk it off, read the break, figure the speed, and then, with squinty eyes and ice water in their veins, they fire at the hole like a gunslinger.

Becoming a great putter

You can always see something special in a great putter. And "great putter" can describe both the piece of equipment and the person doing the putting.

You can go out and spend hundreds of dollars on a great putter, but your flatstick is really only as great as you think it is. If you need to spend a lot of money to convince yourself that something is great, by all means, dole out the cash! (But check out Chapter 6 of Book III, where we discuss the ins and outs of picking a putter, before you do.) But regardless of your equipment's cost or technology, if you really believe that the piece of metal you carry to the green is a great putter, it will be! Heck, you can make putts with a table leg.

The key to becoming a great putter is confidence. If you believe that you're a great putter, you will be. Ask any good putter, and the confident Joe will tell you that he believes he has

a chance to make any putt he looks at. You can spot good putters a mile away: They look over a putt almost with grins on their faces, as if they're working on the Sunday morning crossword puzzle. They approach their balls and line up over them like a gunslinger, cocked and ready to draw.

When a putt goes into the hole, they act humble and nonchalant; after all, they expect to make every putt. When they miss, the flatstick masters always have a ready-made, ego-protecting reason: The ball hit a stone or a spike mark. Sometimes you see them look at the hole as if it moved while the ball rolled toward it. Often, you hear them say things such as, "There's no way that putt can break that way" or "I hit a good putt, it just didn't go in." Your goal is to become as confident and witty as these rulers of the green.

Book III

Playing Golf: The Swing and the Short Game

Maybe your mindset doesn't boast the bravado required to putt like a gunslinger. But that doesn't mean you can't be effective. Your approach to becoming a good putter may be to stalk the hole like a predator and sneak up on it like a stealth cat. Yes, you guessed it: We're talking about lag putting, which can make you a formidable opponent on the greens.

Adopting, practicing, and perfecting either approach is a viable route to lowering your score. Your personality or experience on the golf course may steer you toward one mindset or the other.

In fact, you needn't even settle on one putting personality forever or on every putt. Maybe you like to feel cautious on long putts and adopt the gunslinger mentality on the shorter putts. Maybe on a given day you feel more confident with your putting, so you go for it more. If you don't have the confidence just yet, you may spend the round in a putt-lagging mindset. Conditions can also dictate the style of your putting. Are the greens dangerously fast enough to inspire caution? Are they flat and slow enough to encourage boldness? Whatever makes you comfortable and allows you to putt in the subconscious, go with it!

Make it or break it

So you've decided that the best way to get a putt close to the hole and win the showdown with your opponent is to try to make it. If you want to be a putting gunslinger, however, you need to heed a few factors to make certain you don't get yourself gunned down!

If you want to hit firmer, more aggressive putts, you should do so by simply lengthening your backstroke, not by swinging the putter harder or faster. Just like shooting an arrow from a bow, draw the string (club) back more to make the arrow (ball) go farther. And be sure that your putterhead accelerates through the ball during and after contact.

You need to be aggressive if you want to knock down putts from all over the green, and throwing some muscle behind your putts can be tricky: Be careful not to make unusually firm, strong strokes that restrict your putterhead from moving smoothly along the target line. Here are some other drawbacks of ramming the ball home:

- ✔ Aggressively stroked, hard putts can speed right through the break. Speed may be the most important factor for a putt, but you can't become so concerned about the speed that you forget about the line. You can try to will the ball into the hole, but don't force it in.

- ✔ Faster, firmer putts are more likely to hit the hole and spin out (ride along the lip and, with centrifugal force, flip back up out of the hole) or hop over.

The only merit of firm, fast putting is that you never leave the putt short. But if you keep running putts three feet beyond the hole, you're likely to three-putt more often.

Try to stop your putts no more than 18 inches beyond the hole. If you consistently leave yourself a one-foot comebacker, you can watch your scores lower and brag about your perfect speed control.

Learning from your putts

It sounds simple, but you have to spend as much time as you can trying to sink putts from as many different lengths and on as many different breaks as possible. Practice sinking long putts and short putts; spend time holing out straight putts; hit putts that break right-to-left or left-to-right; and roll balls both uphill and downhill. By practicing every type of putt, you get comfortable with almost any mindset.

You get better and gain confidence with each putt you sink, but you also get better after you analyze the ones you miss:

- ✔ Did you misread the break? (See Chapter 6 of Book III and the "Conquering speedy breaks" section in this chapter.)

- ✔ Did you hit the putt too hard or too soft?

- ✔ Did you pull the putt or push it with an uneven or angled stroke? (See Chapter 3 of Book V for drills that help you with this problem.)

- ✔ How far past the hole did the ball go? Was it farther than you expected when you lined up the shot? Did you hit it too hard to sink it even if it hit the hole?

- ✔ Are you comfortable with the length of putt you left yourself?

- ✔ Did you hit the hole? Was the ball online? Was it fast enough to reach the hole?

- ✔ How did the ball react when it hit the hole? Was the speed too fast to allow the ball to tumble in? Did the ball hop over the hole or ride along the rim? Did you putt it too hard, or did it just wander offline?

Going for preround precision

If you want to spend your round trying to make everything you look at, you should make certain you arrive early enough to spend time on the practice green. This make-it-or-break-it approach can pay off big, but the costs can also be huge. Hitting the practice green helps you

- ✔ **Get a feel for the conditions:** You need to get a sense for the speed of the green, the type of grass you have to play on, and the grain, if the greens have any. (Grainy Bermuda grass, for instance, leans one way or another; usually, the blades lean toward the position of the sun.) Most of the time, the practice green represents the conditions you face on the greens during your round. Now's the time to get comfortable with the conditions and lay of the land.

- ✔ **Build some confidence:** Get used to the feeling of making putts. Frank Sinatra used to say that he felt a little nervous before his live performances. Even the Chairman of the Board felt uncertain about being "in voice" on a given evening! You don't want to step onto the first green of an important match wondering whether your putting touch will show up that day. Hit some high notes before your performance. Work out the kinks and build up some confidence by sinking some on the practice green. Find your voice!

Lag it or flag it

Lag putting is a kinder, gentler technique with the flatstick than the more aggressive philosophy of make-it-or-break-it is (see the earlier section "Make it or break it"). The term *lag putt* provokes images of long putts that take their time drifting along a sweeping line toward the hole, where the ball eventually finishes with just enough speed to "die" at the hole.

A great lag putt is a beautiful thing; although a lag putt may occasionally stop just short of the hole, it should never run too far past. You should have a comeback putt of a comfortable, makeable length.

Most lag putters create a mental circle around the hole to use as an aiming tool. For instance, if a player feels confident that she can always make a 2-foot putt, she creates a circle that allows for 2 feet all around the hole. Instead of putting at the 4¼ inches of cup, she can aim at a 4-foot target. Sounds easier than jarring it, right? It is, and when you stop your ball in that imaginary circle, you virtually assure yourself of taking no more than two putts to complete the hole. (If you've practiced making 2-footers consistently, that is. See Chapter 6 of Book III for more on the fundamentals of putting and Chapter 3 of Book V for a putting drill that can help you sink 2-footers in your sleep.)

Revisiting the defensive label

Lag putting isn't necessarily as defensive a strategy as it may seem. Sure, on the long putts that have a lower chance of going in, lagging to a safe area near the hole seems like a conservative strategy. And although going that route may test your hard-nosed reputation, doing so makes a lot of sense. But taking a conservative stroke doesn't mean that the lag putt doesn't have a chance to go in. If it does drop in, it trickles in softly in instead of ramming into the back of the cup.

Hitting shorter lag putts has its advantages, too. A soft, lagged putt rides the natural break of the green better than a burner. Lagged putts that finish close to the hole are more likely to tumble into the front or side of the cup, even if they veer a little bit off-line. If you think of the hole as the face of a clock, a lag putt can fall into the hole anywhere in between 3:00 and 9:00, as opposed to an aggressive putt, where you probably have a window from 5:00 to 7:00.

Taking the teeth out of long lag putts

You can make a long lag putt less daunting and give the ball a better chance of finishing near the hole by following these steps to break the putt into two pieces:

1. **Take a look at your target line and walk along the line to the hole.**

   Make sure not to step in another player's line along the way.

2. **Determine the widest or highest spot on the target line between the ball and the hole where the ball will begin its turn toward the cup; stand at that spot and look at the line.**

   You may even take a few practice strokes from that spot in order to get a feel for the break and the gravity.

3. **Go back to your ball.**

   You have a new sense for the break, and you can easily visualize how the ball will roll over the course of the long lag putt.

Watching your speed

Sometimes players concentrate too much on the target line they see for the putt and don't pay attention to the speed needed to get the ball close to the hole. The target line can easily vex you, especially if you have to putt on a highly contoured green with two or three tiers or *swales* (depressions) and bumps. Standing over a ball and determining that the line of the putt has two breaks can be intimidating. You may start thinking, "Where do I begin? The ball breaks right and then left and then right again!" Even a simple breaking putt, such as a right-to-left bender, can challenge your mind.

To simplify your challenge, read the break and then pick an intermediate spot between your ball and the hole to aim at. The spot can be a spike mark, a piece of sand, or perhaps a discolored spot on the green, but you should choose something that you can easily see.

After you determine a line, you need to clear your head so that you can pay attention to the speed. You've broken up the complicated putt into pieces, which helps you with the line and the speed. How fast do you need to hit the putt to get it to your initial spot, and what do you expect the putt to do after it hits that spot? In terms of speed, will the ball roll more quickly downhill or toward the break?

If you can pick an initial target spot that sits close to where your ball lies, it makes quick putts much easier to handle. If you have to put some muscle behind the ball, you may want to pick a target farther from your ball that you can still clearly see. Picking a target allows you to concentrate on getting it close with the correct speed.

Conquering speedy breaks

Some courses have greens that feature severe slopes. Donald Ross-designed courses, for instance, are known for their undulating greens, which, depending on maintenance standards, can be very speedy. Sometimes, such as on crowned greens, you can easily see the breaks. But other times, such as when you play in the mountains or near bodies of water, you may have difficulty seeing the break.

Uncertainty is a certain way to mishit a putt. Make sure, even if you have to convince yourself, that you make a good, informed decision on the break and stick with it. Use all your powers of analysis (see Chapter 6 of Book III) to make a judgment on the line of the putt and the speed you need to get it close, and don't look back. Stroke the putt with conviction and confidence.

In some unfortunate incidences, you stare down a quick and hard-breaking putt. On some short, downhill putts, it seems like all you have to do is breathe on the ball and it will go rocketing past the hole. Science tells you that objects in motion tend to remain in motion, and a speedy green cut to run very fast, coupled with gravity, doesn't help matters much when you're on a downhill slope facing a pronounced right-to-left break.

You may be tempted to hit the ball as softly as you can in this situation or even in speedy downhill situations without much break. The danger in hitting the ball too softly is that you may, consciously or subconsciously, wind up decelerating the putterhead during the down-stroke, and deceleration can cause a jerky motion that pulls the club off-line or a stab that pushes or pulls the ball. Nerves can also take their toll on a hair-raising putt, causing the same types of mistakes.

You can take some of the speed, break, and fear-induced shakes out of a putt by hitting the ball off the toe of the putter. Line up for the putt with your putter behind the ball in its normal place. Slide the putterhead back toward your inseam until the far end of the blade, the *toe,* sits behind the center of the ball. Stroke the putt.

Because you strike the ball with less mass when the putterhead makes contact, you deaden the blow and take some speed off the putt. This crafty move also takes some of the break out of the putt and causes it to roll straighter. Try it on the practice green for yourself and see. Amaze your friends and opponents alike with this strategy!

Defeating the yips

Golfers who suffer from a putting malady known as the *yips* are a pitiful sight. They may have a brilliant tee to green game, driving the ball long and straight with brilliant, confident approach shots onto the green. But with the putter in their hands, they suddenly become whimpering, simpering basket cases — unable to sink even the shortest of putts.

The yips, although prevalent from anywhere on the green and in any putting situation, are most evident during short putts. Imagine standing over a perfectly makeable 2-foot putt and feeling completely unable to sink it. Now imagine hitting the putt with a stabby, jabby, fearful, timid stroke and watching the ball skid by the hole without even grazing the lip. You've yipped it.

The first words you may utter after a putt like this one are, "I knew it!" The yips are an evil ailment that perpetuates itself by demolishing your confidence and thus leading to self-fulfilling putting prophecies. In the following sections, we outline some causes and solutions to this common putting malady. (And be sure to check out Chapter 2 of Book V, where we provide a ton of tips on staying mentally strong even when you face adversity.)

Cataloguing the causes

What causes the yips? If some pharmaceutical company could come up with a pill to guard against them, similar to a flu shot, every golfer would want it, because the yips can appear without warning and for no apparent reason. After you miss a few makeable putts and your confidence starts to falter, the yips spread like a quick virus and infect your entire stroke, destroying what confidence remains. However, here are a few common culprits:

- **Anxiety:** If you look up too quickly to see the ball falling into the hole, you may not complete the stroke properly, pulling or pushing with your hands. Your hands may even shake and wobble.

- **Steering:** Instead of letting the putterhead freely swing through the ball and propel it toward the hole, you may find yourself trying to steer the ball into the hole. Steering is typically a tension-filled attempt to guide the ball into the hole, but it can cause you to push the putterhead toward the hole and mistakenly get your wrists or legs into the act.

- **Alignment:** If you line up improperly before you hit the putt, and you misalign your putterhead, your body may subconsciously cause you to alter the swing path in midstroke in an attempt to make a correction.

- **Wrist breakdown:** A breakdown in your right wrist (if you're a right-handed player) can result in the yips. Often, a breakdown or flick of the wrist happens just before impact — a mechanical flaw that can send the putt off-line.

- **Overanalysis:** You may get so caught up in the mechanics of your stroke that you paralyze your natural movement. You become so self-conscious of your body position, putting stroke, and movements that you can barely take the putter back in any simple, straight fashion along the target line.

Book III

Playing Golf: The Swing and the Short Game

✔ **Lack o' confidence:** Sweating over a putt, especially a shorty, is a sure way to miss it. Without confidence, you allow all manner of negative thoughts to enter your head and your play. What can you do to make the putt? Will it go in? Can you lose the hole or the match by missing it? What will your playing partner think of you missing such a short putt? How embarrassing!

Tackling some solutions

Pro golfers Johnny Miller, Tom Watson, and Mark O'Meara have suffered from the yips. But each of them found a way to overcome the yips enough to win again — at least temporarily. If you find yourself, as many golfers do at some point, suffering from the yips, don't panic. The condition doesn't need to last forever. How can you overcome a putting meltdown?

✔ **Fuggedaboudit.** Because the major contributors to the yips are tension, anxiety, and a lack of confidence, one way to help rid yourself of the yips is to empty your mind. Play in the subconscious. Forget about the stroke, the result, and the circumstances. Just play, in the literal sense of the word.

✔ **Don't look now.** Looking up or peeking to see whether the ball goes into the hole is a sure way to miss a putt. Resist the temptation to watch the ball. Keep your head still over the ball and stare down at the empty spot the ball used to occupy long after you hit the putt. Don't allow your eyes to follow the putterhead during the stroke. *Note:* Though we note elsewhere in the book that having to keep your head still during shots is something of a golf myth, when you're suffering from the yips, restricting this movement anyway can be helpful.

✔ **Check your alignment.** Pick a hole on a flat spot on the practice green and drop your ball a few feet from the hole. Stand behind the ball and line up the putt; use the printed brand name on the ball as a helper. Position the ball so that the name points straight at the hole. When you get over the ball with your putter, match the aiming line on the top of your putter to the line of the logo on the ball. Put the putterhead flush behind the ball on this line. Now take notice of your feet. Are they perpendicular to the line created by the logo? How about your shoulders? Finally, are you taking the putterhead straight back and straight through during the stroke?

✔ **Take the hole out of your head.** Take the hole out of the equation. Pick a spot on the practice green that has no hole. You can drop some balls and putt to a colored imperfection on the green or to a tee you stick in the ground. Removing the hole from the equation may take away any tension or concern you have about the result. It causes you to focus more on the stroke than on whether the ball goes into the hole.

Solving your yip situation with drills

In your quest to defeat the yips, go to the practice green and try creating your own remedy. Here are a few drills to get you started:

✔ **Hit some putts with your eyes closed.**

✔ **Hit some putts while looking at the hole.**

✔ **Try different putting grips, including a cross-handed grip or a claw-style grip (see Chapter 6 of Book III).**

✔ **Hit putts while making certain that you keep your wrists firm and that your arms, shoulders, and hands work as one solid triangle-shaped unit.** (See Chapter 3 of Book V for more putting drills.)

✔ **Ram some putts into the back of the hole with some speed.**

✔ **Lag some putts to the hole by hitting the middle of the ball with the bottom, leading edge of the putter blade.** Don't hit real putts with this technique. You want to use this drill as a sort of shock therapy to get your mind off the yips. You can develop a better feel and awareness of the putterhead with this drill, and that feel helps you gain confidence.

✔ **Hit some putts while gripping the putter with only your leading hand.** Try neutralizing your other hand by sticking it into your pocket. If you find that you hit putts more solidly this way, it may be a clue that when your back hand is on the putter, your back wrist may be breaking down or flipping before impact.

Never panic when you have a case of the yips. The best way to fight the yips is to practice enough to putt in the subconscious.

Book III

Playing Golf: The Swing and the Short Game

Flipping the Flop

An impressive component of the short game is the *flop shot,* which sends a golf ball high into the air without much distance. Flopping the ball became *en vogue* with the advent of the 60-degree wedge and square grooves. With a highly lofted club, players can lay the clubface open, creating even more loft, and pop the ball almost straight up into the air. The ball comes down with backspin and sticks or draws back a tiny bit.

Backspin happens when the ball rides the face of the clubhead after it makes contact during the swing. The ball goes up the grooves on the clubface, the dimples catch, and it starts to revolve into a backspin. Because the clubhead moves softly as it cuts under the ball and through the grass with the flop, the ball doesn't "suck back" with much backspin when it hits the green, which is how a longer pitch shot with more clubhead speed behaves.

Choosing to hit a flop shot

Because a flop shot flies through the air almost all the way to its target and doesn't roll very far, most good players use the flop shot around the green. Typically, you should attempt the shot when you need the ball to fly over an obstacle and stop quickly. You can use the flop to clear a bunker, the top of a hill, long grass, or water.

Here's a textbook scenario for when to play the flop shot: Say you miss the green with your approach shot, and you find your ball off the green to the right, lying in medium to long grass. When you assess the shot, you see that the green is elevated above the ball, and a bunker stands between your ball and the green. In addition, the hole is cut close to the edge of the green nearest to your ball, meaning that if you fly the ball very far over the top of the hill and onto the green, you leave yourself a long comeback putt. A chip shot flies too low and runs too long. A pitch shot flies longer but still may run out too much. A flop shot is the answer. The ball flies high for a short distance and doesn't roll very much after it lands.

Anytime you need to put the ball in the air but have only a short distance and little green to work with, the flop shot is a possible option.

Playing a flop shot

The fundamentals of hitting a flop shot are as follows:

- **Club:** Use a highly lofted club, such as a 60-degree wedge.

- **Stance:** Taking a basic pitch stance (see Chapter 5 of Book III), move your target line a little bit to the left and open up your stance. Because you add more loft to the face and open the face angle, you can expect the ball to come out to the right (for righties). Lay open the face of the club at address to create even more loft. Hold the club lightly. Position the ball in the center of your stance. Put your weight a little more on your front leg.

- **Hand position:** As in every golf shot, your lead hand must do just that at all times. Therefore, your hands should be slightly ahead of the ball through impact to maintain the open clubface swinging down the target line.

- **Swing:** Swing the club steeply up and outside the target line.

  - **Take the clubhead back as far as you think you need to.** Use your feel. It seems nonsensical that you have to swing fully on this shot, but the angle of the clubface lofts the ball; it doesn't give the shot distance. You take the distance out of the shot with the loft and the opening of the face. The steeper you swing, the higher the ball flies with a minimal gain in distance.

- **Don't break your wrist position through impact to keep the clubface open and lofted.** You can hit this shot with a lot of wrist movement and hand flipping, but you shouldn't expect success. If you look at the guys who hit the best flop shots, you can see that their clubface remains constant.

- **Be sure to follow through with a big, high finish.** The clubface should still be open and lofted after impact.

You can make the ball pop even higher if you take the swing back outside the target line (meaning the clubhead doesn't go straight back on the line; it goes back on an angle away from you, as opposed to back around you, which would be inside the target line). This change makes your swing steeper.

Seeing the flop shot's dark side

The flop shot is handy to have, but the only way to use it with success is to practice it. The average player often tries to use the flop shot after he sees it on television, but he doesn't really know how to play it because he hasn't practiced with the proper technique. He tries the shot once or twice a round, and then he wonders why he shanks it or skulls the ball across the green.

It takes maximum practice time to master the flop shot to the point that you can rely on it. If you're an average, recreational player or even an intermediate player who occasionally competes, consider how much time you really have to devote to practicing the flop shot and whether you can better spend your time refining other areas of your game that have a more immediate impact on your short-game success.

Take time to ponder the downsides to playing the flop shot:

- ✔ The higher the ball goes up in the air, the more susceptible it is to the elements — especially the wind.

- ✔ To be effective, you have to strike the flop shot more precisely than a chip or pitch, because a mishit from close range with a full swing can be catastrophic.

- ✔ You have almost no margin of error when it comes to hitting the flop shot the proper distance. The ball travels so high and comes down so steeply that it almost has to land on top of the target, because it doesn't roll very much. If you want to hit a flop shot over a bunker out of long grass and have it end up right at the hole, you have to land the ball within a foot of the hole.

Sounds tough, right? It is. But if you spend enough time practicing and perfecting the shot, being able to land the ball near the hole consistently can help reduce your scores.

Considering your other options

You may be asking, "But if I don't play the flop shot, how can I get the ball close when I'm faced with a tight pin or a carry over a bunker or grassy hill?" The answer is simple.

If you want to improve your game, lower your handicap, and shoot better scores, when you're faced with this kind of shot — and most players without single-digit handicaps face extreme situations often — *don't get cute*. And a flop shot is getting cute. When you have to shoot to a tight pin or you face a delicate carry from just off the green, your expectation should be to get the ball on the green and two-putt. Your realistic goal isn't to stick it close to the hole and tap it in.

If you get the ball onto the green in one shot and two-putt, pat yourself on the back and move on! If you hit it on the green and hole out a putt, jump for joy. But don't try to get cute.

If you expect to pitch the ball over a bunker and onto the green from 25 yards and two-putt (which is realistic), you feel much better when you do, and you score much better in the long run. Conversely, if you stand over your ball and expect to flop it close to the hole and make the putt on a consistent basis, you feel disappointed more often than not. Even if you do pull off the flop shot and hit it to 6 feet, missing the short putt leaves you disappointed.

Play the percentages. Get the ball on the green safely with a shot you're comfortable with and two-putt. Make that your expectation and goal. After you become comfortable with the flop shot because you've given it a good amount of practice, you can expect your scores to gradually lower as you use discretion by picking your spots to put it to effective use.

Going With an Unconventional Strategy

Golf is a staid and traditional game. Players tee off according to honor, compliment each other's shots, and shake hands at the end of a round. The game of golf is more than 500 years old and built around time-honored traditions, musty as some of them may be.

From time to time, however, certain traditions give way to practicality. For instance, men used to play golf in wool jackets, overcoats, and ties, and women played in ankle-length skirts. Now some players wear collarless, form-fitting shirts and some of the loudest pants you'll see in just about any sport! Somewhere along the line, golfers realized that, despite its elegance, playing golf in stiff formalwear made the game more difficult than it had to be, and they broke with tradition and wore resortwear in keeping with the dress code of the time.

But changing times aren't the only reasons golfers deviate from the norm; necessity is often the mother of invention. Gene Sarazen, a Hall of Famer who won tournaments (including the Masters) two generations ahead of Tiger Woods, devised the sand wedge when he imagined he could improve his chances of escaping from deep bunkers with a lofted, heavy-bottomed club . . . and he was right! Bunker play immediately became a fairer challenge. Nowadays, the loft of the blade on some short game clubs is 60 degrees — even more loft than a sand wedge.

Clubmakers and players continue to improvise. At the 2004 PGA Tour Championship, Ernie Els damaged his putter in a fit of temper and was forced to play the last few greens by using a sand wedge in place of his putter. On the golf course, you may find that, either by necessity or out of preference, you have to discard the traditional short-game shots and get creative. The following sections show some of the unconventional options.

Chipping with a 3-wood

The object of chipping is to quickly get the ball rolling on the ground and keep it rolling until it rolls into or near the hole. (See Chapter 4 of Book III for more on chipping.) One good way to accomplish these goals is by using your 3-wood.

Some players prefer to hit chip shots with a 7-iron, 8-iron, or 9-iron. But sometimes you may want to put a little more heft and a little less loft behind the ball than the blade of an iron offers. The traditional loft of the face of a 3-wood is about 15 degrees. The traditional loft of a 4-iron is about 24 degrees. Putter lofts are about 5 or 6 degrees and less. So chipping with a 3-wood propels the ball lower than an iron can (see Figure 8-1), but it gives the ball more immediate hop than a putter does. In addition, the heft of the head of a 3-wood gives more oomph (that's a technical term) when it strikes the ball, making the ball go farther with the minimal effort and touch you need in the short game.

Figure 8-1:
Using a
low-lofted
3-wood
to chip
gets the
ball rolling
farther
and more
quickly than
irons can
without as
much effort.

When, exactly, does this situation arise? Well, the following conditions beg for you to grab your 3-wood out of the bag:

✔ **The ball rests on hard, firm, dry ground and short grass.** In this situation, you have less margin for error when you try to hit the ball with the blade of an iron. The more loft the club has, the more perfectly the clubhead or blade must strike the ball, and hitting a chip off a tight lie on hard, dry ground or shaved grass can be very tricky.

✔ **The green is above the ball, so you have to chip up.** If your ball comes to rest on hard ground, you may opt to use a putter to putt the ball onto the green instead of chipping it. But if the shot is uphill to the green or perhaps over a ridge, and striking a putter hard enough to get your ball up the hill and beyond the ridge feels a bit too unnatural, you have good chance to chip it hard enough with a 3-wood.

✔ **No bunkers or terribly long patches of grass block your way to the hole.** Either impediment quickly stops a ground-hugging 3-wood chip.

✔ **You have an opening to the green over which to chip and roll your ball.** Some greens have natural, unprotected pathways to the hole. Take advantage of these opportunities!

The only disadvantage to chipping with your 3-wood is that because the shaft is so much longer than that of a short iron, you need to stand farther away from the target line than you normally do. Therefore, be sure to stand behind the ball before you take a swing and carefully line up the shot.

Otherwise, you use the 3-wood to chip in the very same way you use an iron — keeping a light grip and making certain the clubface goes straight back on the target line and comes straight through (see Chapter 4 of Book III). The face of the wood is steeper and less lofted than that of an iron, so you can expect the ball to stay a great deal lower. The heft and size of the head makes the ball pop off the clubface with more energy, so temper your swing a bit (you discover just how much you need to tone the swing down through practice).

Chipping with a 3-wood is a valuable shot to have in your repertoire — if you practice it enough. You need to feel comfortable with this shot before you can use it effectively.

Putting from bunkers

Sometimes, if the sand is hard and no lip of grass rises up between your ball and the green, you can consider the option of putting from a bunker rather than hitting a traditional bunker shot. Anytime you can put the putter in your hand, your chances of a good, precise shot improve, and putting from a bunker is no different. One old adage, often attributed to Arnold Palmer, is that "your worst putt is better than your best chip."

Assessing the situation is very important. The following conditions must exist if you want to consider putting from a bunker:

- ✔ The sand should be firm, hard, and well-packed.
- ✔ The green shouldn't be behind a high lip of grass or landform that may hamper the ball from rolling up and out of the bunker and onto the green.
- ✔ The bunker shouldn't have a hairy collar of grass between it and your ball; such grass can stop the ball or drag it down.
- ✔ The ball shouldn't have to roll over more than 5 feet or so of sand because, in most cases, rolling a ball over sand can be tougher than rolling it over long grass.
- ✔ The hole should be fairly close to the bunker so that the ball doesn't have to roll a long way to get to the hole after it rolls out of the bunker.

Book III

Playing Golf: The Swing and the Short Game

Putting from a bunker requires that you keep your head down, follow through with the putterhead, and have just the right amount of touch, feel, and imagination. Line up the shot just as you do a long putt: by examining the break of the green and choosing an appropriate target line (see Chapter 6 of Book III). As with all putts, speed is also a very important part of the shot (see this chapter's "Conquering speedy breaks").

In addition to properly sizing up the situation and deciding whether a putt from the bunker is the best course of action, spend time practicing the shot at some point before you try it. More and more golf courses or practice ranges with short game practice areas offer practice bunkers. When you practice hitting bunker shots, spend a little time dropping some balls in a part of the bunker you find suitable for putting. Bunkers on some golf courses have very soft, beachlike sand, but some regions, such as Texas and Georgia, have firmer, earthier sand. Often, so do courses that have taken a lot of rain. If you live and play in a region with firm, hard sand or play on courses that have this type of sand and bunkers without high lips and faces, this unconventional shot can be a common option for you.

Putting without a putter

Okay, all golfers lose their tempers from time to time — especially on the golf course, where your play can get pretty frustrating. Sometimes the flatstick bears the brunt of the anger. Even PGA Tour players have broken putters over their knees or bent them on trees. Woody Austin, winner of the 2004 Buick Championship, once bent the shaft of his putter on his head after missing a crucial putt. Players who don't want to put their head through that kind of trauma normally toss their putters into trees or ponds.

According to the rules, if your putter becomes damaged in the normal course of play, you can replace it. How exactly a putter can get broken during the course of play is a mystery, but imagine that your putterhead happens to fall off. In that case, you can have someone get you another putter, or you can call the golf shop and ask someone to run you out a putter on loan.

More likely, though, you've altered (shall we say) your putter though some action other than the normal course of play and, according to the rules, you have to quit using it and can't replace it. Now you have a problem: What can you putt with to finish the round?

Assuming that your putter has met an unnatural end, you need to find a replacement. When you putt the ball on the green, you're not looking for loft. You want to roll the ball. So what club, other than the putter, can roll the ball into the hole? Some players left without a putter prefer to putt with a wedge. The advantage of using a wedge is that the shaft length is very similar, and that length allows you to use your normal putting stance and get your eyes over your line.

The trouble with using a wedge to putt is that you have to strike the middle of the ball with the very thin bottom leading edge of the blade. To do that, you have to have plenty of precision and confidence, which can be hard to come by when you've broken your putter because of a mishit shot.

In this situation, some guys on the PGA Tour choose to putt with their drivers because, second to the putter, the driver is the least-lofted club in the bag; the face is angled anywhere from 5 degrees to 10.5 degrees. Although the driver's shaft is typically a great deal longer than your putter's, the driver's large face and small amount of loft make contacting the ball the easy part. The trickier part is standing so far from your target line, because standing the driver upright makes the large head of a driver awkward and decreases your sweet spot. Try choking down as much as you can on the driver, and keep the driver's head as close to the target line as possible when swinging the clubhead back and through the ball. Be aware, too, that the ball pops off the driver's face with more energy because of the mass of the clubface.

In any case, be sure to spend some time practicing putts with your driver or wedges just in case your putter goes awry and suffers your angry dismissal some day!

Playing from a cart path

You get free relief, normally, when your ball lies on an artificially surfaced road or cart path, according to the rules of golf. Sometimes, however, the free relief you receive, which must be no nearer to the hole than where the ball came to rest on the path, is at an undesirable position — perhaps in long, tangled grass or behind a tree. And sometimes you can't receive relief from a road, particularly one unpaved or deemed to be an integral part of the golf course, such the road along the 17th hole — known as the Road Hole — on the Old Course at St. Andrews in Scotland.

What shouldn't you do when you have to play a ball from a road or cart path? Here are two options that may spring into mind that you should leave unexplored:

- ✔ **Pulling out the putter:** The road at St. Andrews, for instance, is made up of many little pebbles. In this type of situation, putting makes the ball roll immediately, and if you roll a ball through pebbles, it faces a number of opportunities to waver and wobble off-line.

- ✔ **Getting some air:** Conversely, using a highly lofted club off the firm or rocky conditions of a road surface brings many different negative variables into play. Trying to use a wedge to hit a ball from a firm surface requires an almost impossible amount of precision, and the club is likely to bounce off the surface wildly and into the ball.

Book III

Playing Golf: The Swing and the Short Game

The best-case shot option when playing the ball on a road is to chip the ball with a 7-iron so that the club can clip the ball, loft it off the path, and get it to tumble over and roll out after it clears the road. (See Chapter 4 of Book III for more on chipping technique.)

The ball jumps much faster off a road surface, so be sure to account for that when you judge how far back to take your backswing. You become eager to see the outcome and nervous about how it will feel when the blade hits the road, so be sure to force yourself to keep your eye on the ball, accelerate through the shot, and follow through. Maintaining fundamentals increases your chances of making the best of this bad situation.

Bellying the wedge

Sometimes you find your ball lying in a tough spot — perhaps up against a collar of long, thick grass on the edge of the green or, on a Pete Dye-designed course (see Chapter 3 of Book I), up against a railroad tie. It may be to your advantage in these situations to hit the ball by bellying your wedge. Up against deep grass, when the club comes back toward the ball with a straight face, it catches on the tangled grass. Bellying the wedge can eliminate that hindrance.

To *belly* your wedge is to lay the face of the club open so much that you strike the ball with the only the leading edge (or *bounce*) of the bottom of the blade. Sort of like striking a billiard ball with a pool cue, only you use the thin bounce of your wedge. If you open up the wedge so much that the bounce (or *flange*) hits the ball, the club doesn't drag on the grass, and the leading edge hits the ball like a putter. Because the ball doesn't ride up the face of the wedge, it comes off with plenty of overspin and tumbles forward.

Open your stance as you do when making a standard chip shot (see Chapter 4 of Book III). Grip the club normally after you open the face of the wedge. Take the clubhead back and bring it through the same distance; if you take the club back to 4:00, follow through to 8:00. Make sure you take the club along the target line and bring it through the ball and forward along the target line.

A bellied wedge is a nifty shot to have when you just need to nip the ball and send it forward. This shot takes real concentration and precision, so be certain to practice it before you try it on the golf course.

Splishing after you splash

Finding your wayward golf ball in a greenside creek or pond is a bit of a mixed blessing. Oh, you can be happy about locating the ball and knowing for certain that you dunked it in the water hazard, but sometimes that ball is just close enough to the edge, sitting up so nicely that it tempts you to try to hit from the water.

Playing from the water is sheer madness. The rules of golf offer you some very civilized options to keep you from soaking yourself with folly-filled swipes, and in every case we can imagine, you should take the penalty shot and avail yourself of the drop alternatives. (Depending on the hazard's shape and whether course officials mark it as lateral, red-lined, or yellow-lined, the drop options vary greatly and give you plenty of smart choices. Flip to Chapter 1 of Book IV for more on rules regarding hazards.) Live to fight another day.

But sometimes sensibility just isn't your cup of tea, and you want to let 'er rip by hitting a ball from the water.

If more than half the ball is below the water line, return to our previous suggestion: Forget about hitting the ball, take the penalty stroke, and drop. Always.

If you see a good portion of the ball above the water line, get ready to go wading (see Figure 8-2). If you have a rain suit in your bag, put it on. You get wet hitting this shot. Take these steps to try to avoid aquatic doom:

1. **Open your stance and grip the club normally, keeping the ball in the middle of your stance if you can do so without sinking or stumbling into deeper water.**

2. **Swing the club back very steeply and try to hit the ball cleanly.**

   Unlike a bunker shot, you don't want to hit the water behind the ball. When the club makes contact with the water, the clubhead significantly slows down and the water tries to alter the swing path. Swing hard and do the best you can to get the club through the water. Be wary of rocks!

3. **Try your best to follow through — and hope.**

   Completing your swing can be very difficult because the water tries to bring your club to a screeching halt. But swing bravely and fully. Any hint of fear or deceleration doesn't allow you to punch your ball out of the water, which is the least you can hope for.

Book III

Playing Golf: The Swing and the Short Game

Figure 8-2:
Make sure
you can see
at least half
the ball on
water shots.

Hitting lefty (or righty)

If you miss the green often enough with your approach shots, especially on wooded courses, you eventually find your ball snuggled up against a tree or under a bush. As if your shot isn't complicated enough already, you may find that your ball is snookered on the wrong side of the tree or bush, making your normal stance or a true swing at the ball impossible.

You have options in this situation, and you should carefully consider them before you act:

- ✔ **Declare it unplayable.** According to the rules of golf, declaring the ball *unplayable* allows you, with one penalty stroke added, to move the ball one club length from its current position or return it to the spot where you played it before it landed up against the tree or bush.

- ✔ **Play it where it lies.** Your other option is to attempt to hit the ball and advance it from where it lies.

Try not to allow your emotions to enter into your decision. You're disappointed and frustrated that your ball got into such trouble in the first place — don't let anger or impatience propel you into making a rash decision to take a wicked swipe at the ball. Although blowing off some steam by taking a good chop at the ball may feel good, you have a good chance of compounding your problems by wasting a stroke: You may miss the ball or smack it into an even worse position.

You should also give yourself a bravado check. Feeling ironically heroic, you may plan to step up to the ball and show off your magic by making an astounding, par-saving trick shot. Again, the results of a foolhardy attempt can be embarrassing and damaging to your scorecard.

In this case, an old adage holds true: Discretion is the better part of valor. If you can't significantly advance the ball from its position with little to no risk of whiffing or knocking the ball into another unplayable lie, take your medicine, invoke the unplayable lie option, take the one-stroke penalty, and drop the ball in the best possible spot the rules allow.

If, on the other hand, you've prepared yourself for a shot such as this one by practicing and think the advantages of hitting a well-played left- or right-handed shot outweigh the risks, you can try playing a wrong-sided pitch. Understand that precision is difficult to achieve with a wrong-sided attempt and that a certain amount of luck is involved in the following methods.

Taking a backhand swing

Ever looked at life from a different direction? You may have to if your ball comes to rest against a tree or a hedge. In this case, you simply have to mimic the technique of an opposite-handed player. The forgiving loft of a 7-iron probably gives the best results if you have to try this switch-hitting swing off the back of the blade. So grab the club, head over to the unknown, and follow these steps as a road map to back to the fairway:

1. **Take a stance over the ball with a 7-iron as if you're playing with your normal dominant hand.**

2. **Reverse your hands on the club's handle so that you have the grip of a player with the opposite dominant hand.**

   Just as when hitting a normal shot, grip the club lightly and stay aware of the clubface. The grip and the swing will obviously feel awkward, unless, that is, you give this shot a little practice from time to time.

3. **Swing the club as normally as possible and hit the ball with the back of the blade.**

4. **Make certain that you follow through as best you can.**

   Your goal is to propel the ball toward the green or the fairway and, at least, out of the trouble. Don't try to be a hero at the expense of missing the ball completely.

Book III

Playing Golf: The Swing and the Short Game

Flipping the blade

If you want to get a little bat on the ball and have the clubface make (almost) normal contact with the ball, you have to do a little flip-flop with your wedge or a short iron you feel comfortable with. Take out your club and run through the following steps:

1. **Take a stance over the ball with your wedge or short iron as if you're playing with your normal dominant hand.**

2. **Reverse your hands on the club handle so that your grip is that of a player with the opposite dominant hand.**

3. **Flip the blade of the iron over and upside down so that when you take your swing, the true clubface, although it points toe-down, strikes the ball (refer to Figure 8-3).**

   Make sure that you adjust your aim to correspond to the new angle of the clubface.

4. **Swing the club as normally as possible and hit the ball with the clubface.**

5. **Make your best follow-through to propel the ball toward the green and, at least, out of trouble.**

Figure 8-3: If you have a favorable lie and a clear path to shorter grass, you can flip the club over and take a shot from your opposite side.

Looking away

Many golfers try to heed the advice "keep your eye on the ball" or "keep your head down" when they find themselves eager to lift their head for a peek at the result. The shot we outline in this section makes peeking very difficult because you actually face away from the hole. Craig Stadler and many other PGA Tour players have used this method in competition when they've found their balls lodged against a tree, shrub, or fence. For a truly adventurous and effective trouble-escaping shot, follow these steps:

1. **Stand to the left of the ball if you're a righty or to the right of the ball if you're a lefty, facing away from the target.**

   It feels awkward at first to be looking away from the target, but try to relax and keep your body loose.

2. **Hold whatever club you deem appropriate extended down from your dominant hand, with the blade pointing toward your feet.**

   You aim the clubface toward the target. See where we're going with this setup yet?

3. **Put the blade of the club behind the ball and turn your head back to properly aim the shot.**

4. **Pull the club up and extend it forward, and then swing it down along the target line as best you can; follow through as far as your body position allows you to.**

5. **Try to resist the urge to turn too quickly to see the result.**

   Concentrate on following through and sending the ball out of trouble and toward the green.

Carrying an opposite-handed club in your bag

If you play heavily wooded golf courses regularly, you may want to consider picking up a left- or right-handed 7-iron to carry in your bag to prepare for tough spots. If you practice enough with it, you can make fairly normal, successful shots out of awkward situations.

The rules of golf allow you to carry no more than 14 clubs in your bag, so you may have to take one out of play if you want to carry an opposite-handed club, especially if you carry a number of wedges. Which club can you do without? Do you have a club in your standard set that you almost never use or are wary to hit because you don't have confidence with it? If so, you can identify that problem club and pull it out in favor of an opposite-handed iron.

Rehearsing the unconventional

Most of the time when you need to improvise or conjure up some unconventional shot on the golf course, you can point to a rare situation that you're unprepared for as the cause. So why not practice for some of the situations and ready yourself for the inevitable slings and arrows of outrageous fortune, as Billy Shakespeare would say? If nothing else, practicing rare types of shots varies your practice sessions and livens things up a bit from time to time.

Practically speaking, don't go hitting shots off a busy road. But, if you have a road or cart path on the course that you play regularly, you can make practicing off this road or path a regular part of your practice sessions. Hit a few 5-irons back into play so that if you're ever faced with the shot, you've been there before. People who play golf for a living practice like this.

Find an old iron similar to the ones you play or pick up an inexpensive or used club at a golf retail store so you can practice these shots without repeated damage to your regular clubs. In addition to the shots we cover in the preceding sections, here are some unconventional shots you may want to try practicing to lighten the mood and prepare for rare situations:

- Playing from a road
- Playing from up against a fence or wall
- Playing from behind a tree
- Playing from a *fried egg* (partially buried) lie in a bunker (see Chapter 7 of Book III)
- Playing from hardpan-type ground or dried out grass
- Putting with a 3-wood
- Playing from your knees when the ball is far below you in a bunker

Book IV
Rules and Etiquette

The 5th Wave   By Rich Tennant

©RICHTENNANT

"What exactly do the rules say about giving and receiving advice?"

In this book . . .

You've got your clubs, you're getting in shape, and you've got a handle on your swing. In this book, we discuss the written and unwritten rules of golf. This book isn't long enough to cover all the rules in *The Official Rules of Golf,* but we cover the ones you need to know to make it through a course without getting in trouble. We also take the mystery out of the scorecard and the handicap system.

Not sure whether you should replace that divot, use a cart, outplay your boss, or place a bet on a game? Wondering whether you should ask that pro for another autograph? Read on. This book also discusses some important nuances of golf etiquette.

Here are the contents of Book IV at a glance.

Chapter 1

Understanding Penalties, Handicaps, and Scorekeeping

In This Chapter

▶ Surviving penalty shots

▶ Decoding the handicap system

▶ Scorekeeping with confidence

*G*olf is a beautifully structured game, rife with rules of play, etiquette, and scoring that have evolved through its long history. Take a look at a rulebook (you can pick one up from almost any professional's shop, or order one directly from the USGA), and you find a seemingly endless list of clauses and subclauses — all of which make the game sound very difficult and complicated.

 In my opinion, the Rules are too complex. For a smart, enjoyable look at them, pick up a copy of *Golf Rules & Etiquette For Dummies* (Wiley) by John Steinbreder. You can also check out an excellent book by Jeffrey S. Kuhn and Bryan A. Garner, *The Rules of Golf in Plain English,* 2nd Edition (University of Chicago Press).

Even if you're too busy to track down those two fine tomes, you can get by with about a dozen simple rules. Common sense can help, too. You can't go too far wrong on the course if you

✔ Play the course as you find it.

✔ Play the ball as it lies.

✔ Do what's fair if you can't do either of the first two things.

This chapter gives you a quick overview of the rules and explains how to deal with penalty shots, understand golf handicaps, and keep score.

Reading the fine print

The book is innocent-looking enough, but it can be a couple hundred pages of procedure, confusion, heartbreak, logic, clarity, and imperatives. It is *The Official Rules of Golf,* as approved by your friends at the United States Golf Association and the Royal and Ancient Golf Club of St. Andrews and updated every four years. (Call the USGA at 800-336-4446 to order your copy. And believe me, anyone who plays golf should have one.)

In actuality, golf has only 34 rules, so you have to wonder why a book that contains them ends up being so long. But golf does have its complications, and the book contains countless definitions, notes, subsections, interpretations, and other important information on how to play the game the right way.

And if *The Official Rules of Golf* isn't enough, you can also get a companion publication known as *The Decisions of the Rules of Golf.* This collection of official rulings on more than 1,000 golf situations is a must-read — and a must-have — for rules officials or anyone who's overseeing a tournament or match. (You may call the USGA to order a copy.) This manual was developed simply because the governing bodies of the game receive thousands of calls and letters each year seeking clarification of the rules — and the hope was that this book would help answer most of those questions.

Dealing with Penalty Shots

Penalty shots are an unfortunate part of every golfer's life. Sooner or later, you're going to incur a penalty shot or shots. Although we can't cover all the possible penalty situations, we outline some of the most common scenarios in the following sections.

Taking a drop

Part of taking a penalty shot often involves dropping the ball into a new place to hit it from. Here's how to make the drop:

1. **Lift and clean your ball.**

2. **Find the nearest spot where you have complete relief from the problem and mark that spot with a tee.**

   You have to get not only the ball but also your feet away from the obstruction. So find a spot where your feet are clear of the obstruction and then determine where the clubhead would be if you hit from there. This spot is the one you want to mark. The spot you choose can't be closer to the hole.

3. **Measure one club length from that mark.**

4. Drop the ball.

Stand tall, holding the ball at shoulder height and at arm's length, as shown in Figure 1-1. Let the ball drop vertically. You aren't allowed to "spin" the ball into a more favorable spot. Make sure the ball doesn't end up nearer the hole than it was when you picked it up. If it does, you have to pick up the ball and drop it again.

Every golf course has places where you're allowed to take a free drop. A cart path is one — you can move your ball away from the path with no penalty. *Casual water* (such as a puddle) is another.

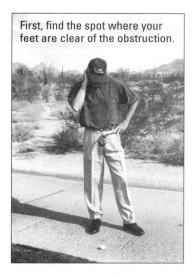

First, find the spot where your feet are clear of the obstruction.

You get one more club length from there.

Now drop your ball.

Figure 1-1:
Dropping your ball.

Book IV

Rules and Etiquette

Out of bounds

Out of bounds is the term used when you hit your ball to a spot outside the confines of the golf course — over a boundary fence, for example. Out-of-bounds areas are usually marked with white stakes that are about 30 yards apart. If you're outside that line, you're out of bounds (often abbreviated with the dreaded initials *O.B.*).

Okay, so it's happened; you've gone out of bounds. What are your options? Limited. First, you're penalized *stroke and distance.* That means you must drop another ball (or tee up if the shot you hit out of bounds was from a tee) as close as possible to the spot you just played from. Say that shot was your first on that hole. Your next shot counts as your third on that hole. Count 'em:

- The shot you hit
- The stroke penalty
- The distance

So now you're *playing three* from the original spot.

Unplayable lies

Inevitably, you're going to hit a ball into a spot from which further progress is impossible. In a bush. Against a wall. Even buried in a bunker.

Keeping lost balls to a minimum

How can you keep lost balls to a minimum? Here are a couple of suggestions:

- **When your ball is in midair, watch it like a hawk.** That sounds pretty obvious, but not watching the shot is perhaps the number-one reason (after bad technique) why balls get lost. Temper gets the better of too many players. They're too busy slamming the club into the ground to watch the ball. Don't make that mistake.

- **Pay attention when the ball lands, too.** Give yourself a reference point — like a tree — near the landing area so you can easily remember the location. You should also put an identifying mark on your ball before you begin play so you can be sure that the ball you find is the one you hit.

Avoiding advice: Double trouble

The advice issue has two sides in golf. First, you can't give advice or receive it from anyone but your caddie. That means you can't ask your playing companion what club he or she hit. Neither can you say anything that may help in the playing of his or her next stroke.

This rule is a toughie, and even the best have been caught breaking it. In the 1971 Ryder Cup matches in St. Louis, Arnold Palmer was playing Bernard Gallacher of Scotland. Arnold hit a lovely shot onto a par-3, whereupon Gallacher's caddie said, "Great shot, Arnie. What club did you hit?" Arnold, being Arnold, told him.

Gallacher never heard the exchange, but the referee did. Arnold, despite his own protestations, was awarded the hole. That was in match play; in stroke play, it's a two-shot penalty. So take care!

Second, you're going to find yourself playing with people, *lots* of people, who think of themselves as experts on every aspect of the golf swing. These know-it-alls may mean well, but they're dangerous to your golfing health. Ignore them. Or, if that proves too difficult, listen, smile politely, and then go about your business as if they'd been speaking Martian.

When the unplayable lie happens (and you're the sole judge of whether you can hit the ball), you have three escape routes.

- ✔ You can pick up the ball and drop it — no nearer the hole — within two club lengths (take your driver and place it end-to-end on the ground twice) of the original spot under penalty of one shot.

- ✔ You can pick up the ball, walk back as far as you want (keeping that original point between you and the hole), and then drop the ball. Again, it's a one-stroke penalty.

- ✔ You can return to the point where you hit the original shot. This option is the last resort because you lose distance as well as adding the penalty shot. Believe us, nothing is worse than a long walk while you're burdened with a penalty stroke!

Water hazards

Water hazards are intimidating when you have to hit across one. "Watery graves," the English TV commentator Henry Longhurst used to call them.

Whenever you see yellow stakes, you know the pond/creek/lake in question is a water hazard. If you hit into a water hazard, you may play the ball as it lies, with no penalty, if the ball's only half-submerged or otherwise hittable. (If you do, you may not *ground your club* — touch it to the ground or water before swinging.) Or choose from these options:

Book IV

Rules and Etiquette

✔ Hit another ball from the spot you just hit from.

✔ Take the point where your ball crossed into the water hazard and drop another ball (you can go back as far as you want, keeping that point between you and the hole).

Either way, it's a one-shot penalty.

Lateral water hazards

If you're playing by the seaside, the beach is often termed a *lateral water hazard*. Red stakes indicate a lateral hazard. Your options are to play the ball as it lies (no penalty, but risky) — as with regular water hazards, you may not ground your club — or as follows, with a one-stroke penalty:

✔ Drop a ball at the point where the ball last crossed the boundary of the hazard — within two club lengths, no nearer the hole.

✔ Drop a ball as close as possible to the spot on the opposite margin of the water hazard, the same distance from the hole.

✔ Hit another ball from within two club lengths of the spot you just hit from.

✔ Take the point where the ball crossed the water hazard and drop another ball as far back as you want, keeping that point between you and the hole.

Strike one! The dreaded whiff

It's the beginner's nightmare: You make a mighty swing and miss the ball. The penalty? None, actually. But you must count that swing as a stroke.

If you swing at a ball with intent to hit it, that's a shot regardless of whether you make contact. You can't say, "That was a practice swing." If you meant to hit the ball, your swing counts as a stroke.

Airballs can be highly embarrassing, but they're part of the journey of golf.

Making Sense of Golf's Handicap System

If you, as a beginner, are completing 18-hole rounds in fewer than 80 shots, you're either a cheat or the next Jack Nicklaus. In all probability, your scores are considerably higher than par. Enter the handicap system.

The USGA created a handicap system in 1912, and the idea was to make the game more enjoyable by enabling players of all abilities to compete with each other on an equal basis. By examining the number of strokes a golfer takes to complete an 18-hole round and making allowances for the layout and difficulty of the course, the USGA can determine with remarkable fairness and accuracy how many shots a player should get. What the system does, in essence, is compare a player's scoring ability to that of an expert amateur (who is expected to shoot par) on a course of standard difficulty. The higher your handicap, the more strokes you need to complete that course. The lower the handicap, the better a golfer you are.

The handicap system is one reason I think that golf is the best of all games. Handicapping allows any two players, whatever their level of play, to have an enjoyable — and competitive — game together. Try to compete on, say, a tennis court. I can't go out with Rafael Nadal and have any fun. Ditto for poor, bored Nadal, who may at least get the excitement of doing CPR on me. The disparity in our abilities makes competitive play impossible. But in golf, if you play a little better than usual, your handicap may help you beat Phil Mickelson and Tiger Woods.

The following sections explain how to figure out your handicap and how it impacts your game.

Getting a handicap

You probably don't have a handicap yet. No worries — you've got plenty of time. When you can consistently hit the ball at least 150 yards with a driver, you're ready to play a full 18-hole round of golf.

When you reach the stage where you can hit the ball a decent distance on the range, you're ready to do the same on a real course. You want to test yourself and give your progress a number. Make that two numbers: your score and your handicap.

The first thing to do is keep score. Get a golfer friend to accompany you for 18 holes. This person must keep score and sign your card at the end of the round. To be valid, a card needs two signatures: your own and that of the person you're playing with. That way, all scores are clearly valid, and nobody fudges his or her total.

You need to play at least ten rounds before you're eligible for a handicap. Don't ask why; those are the rules. After ten rounds in a prehandicap cocoon, you emerge as a beautiful, full-fledged, handicap golfer.

At first, your handicap will probably drop quite quickly. Most new golfers improve by leaps and bounds at first. After that, the real work starts.

Book IV

Rules and Etiquette

Of course, the handicap system is easy to abuse, and some people do. Interestingly, most abuse occurs when players want their handicaps to be higher. They either fabricate high scores or don't record their better rounds so their handicaps rise. Thus, they get more strokes from other players in betting matches. A few golfers go the other way; they want a lower "vanity" handicap to make people think they're *sticks* (championship-level golfers). Find these vanity handicappers and gamble with them for everything they own!

Don't get too cynical, though. Any abuse of the system is confined to a tiny minority of players. That's another reason golf is such a great game: Golfers can generally be trusted. The few cheats are soon identified and ostracized.

Calculating your handicap

Okay, you're wondering how you get a handicap. It's easy: All you do is report your scores at the course where you normally play. Then you're off and running. Your handicap at any one time is the average of the best 10 of your previous 20 scores (see Figure 1-2). Technically, it's 96 percent of that number — another wacky golf quirk — but we'll let the math whizzes handle that wrinkle.

Most country clubs and public courses make things easy for you. They have computers that take your scores and do all the work to update your handicap throughout the golf season, about twice a month.

Suppose your ten scores average out at exactly 100. In other words, for your first ten rounds of golf, you hit 1,000 shots. If par for the 18-hole course you played is 72, your average score is 28 over par. That figure, 28, is your handicap.

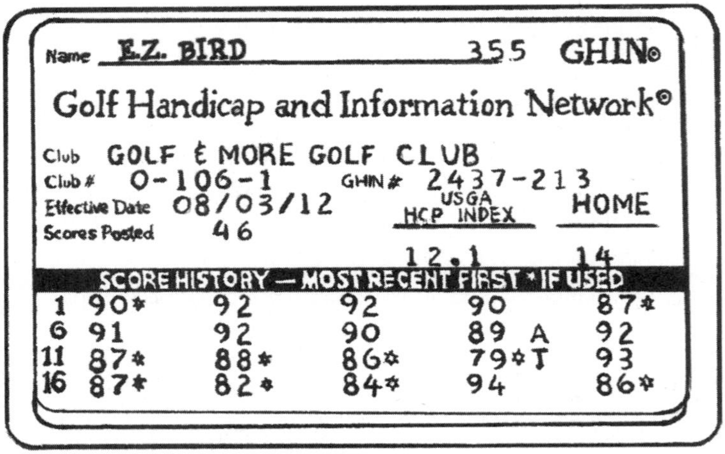

Figure 1-2:
Your
handicap
card.

Name **E.Z. BIRD**			355 **GHIN®**	
Golf Handicap and Information Network®				
Club **GOLF & MORE GOLF CLUB**				
Club # **0-106-1**		GHIN # **2437-213**		
Effective Date **08/03/12**		**USGA HCP INDEX**		**HOME**
Scores Posted **46**			**12.1**	**14**
SCORE HISTORY — MOST RECENT FIRST * IF USED				
1 **90***	**92**	**92**	**90**	**87***
6 **91**	**92**	**90**	**89** A	**92**
11 **87***	**88***	**86***	**79*T**	**93**
16 **87***	**82***	**84***	**94**	**86***

Every time you play from then on, your handicap adjusts to account for your most recent score. Suppose your 11th round is a 96. That's only 24 over the par of 72. So your *net score* — your actual score minus your handicap — is 68, four under that magic number of 72. Nice round! When you feed that 96 into the handicap computer, you'll probably find that your handicap drops.

In order for the handicap system to work properly, the handicaps have to be accurate. That means you have to turn in exactly what you got during a round. You can't turn in a higher or lower score you've fudged for betting or ego-inflating reasons (see the preceding section), and you can't turn in a score if you haven't adhered to the rules of golf. In other words, if you kick your ball out of the rough a couple of times during a round, if you use nonconforming equipment, if you play a round with more than 14 clubs in your bag, or if you play 2 balls, you cannot use that score for handicap purposes.

Understanding what your handicap means

The lower your handicap is, the better golfer you are. Thus, if your handicap is 6 and your partner's is 10, you're a better player. On average, 4 strokes better, to be exact.

Assume that par for the 18-hole course we're going to play is 72. You, as someone with a handicap of 6, would be expected to play 18 holes in a total of 78 strokes, 6 more than par. Your partner, on the other hand, being a 10-handicapper, would on a normal day hit the ball 82 times, 10 more than par. Thus, your handicap is the number of strokes over par you should take to play an 18-hole course.

When you're just starting out, you don't want to team up with three low-handicap players — that's just discouraging. Play with golfers of your own ability at first. After you get the hang of the game, start playing with people who are better than you so you can learn from them.

Keeping Score Without Fear

Scoring is another unique part of golf, and it comes with its own set of rules and regulations.

Every course has a scorecard that tells you each hole's length, its par, and its rating relative to the other holes (see Figure 1-3). You can easily see how you're doing because your score is in black and white on the scorecard.

Book IV

Rules and Etiquette

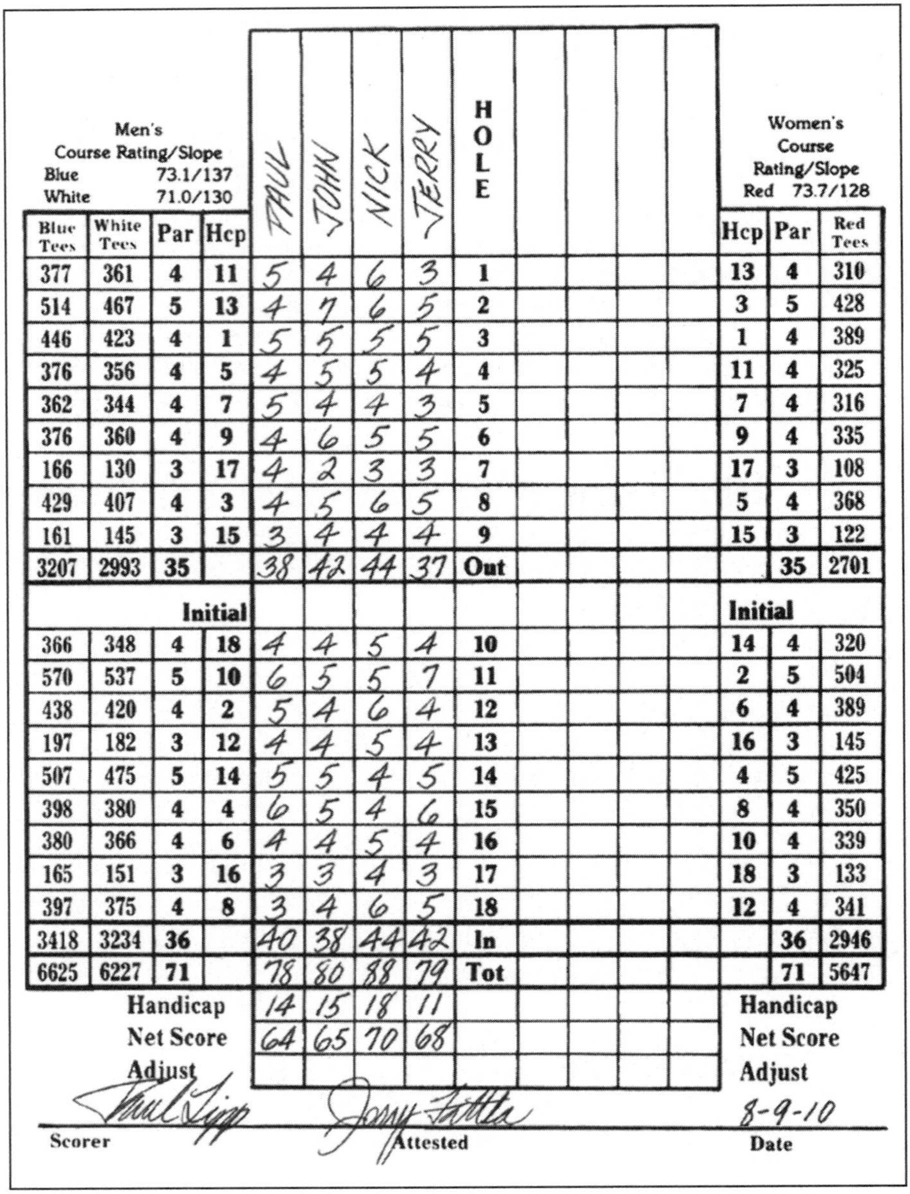

Blue Tees	White Tees	Par	Hcp	PAUL	JOHN	NICK	JERRY	HOLE					Hcp	Par	Red Tees
377	361	4	11	5	4	6	3	1					13	4	310
514	467	5	13	4	7	6	5	2					3	5	428
446	423	4	1	5	5	5	5	3					1	4	389
376	356	4	5	4	5	5	4	4					11	4	325
362	344	4	7	5	4	4	3	5					7	4	316
376	360	4	9	4	6	5	5	6					9	4	335
166	130	3	17	4	2	3	3	7					17	3	108
429	407	4	3	4	5	6	5	8					5	4	368
161	145	3	15	3	4	4	4	9					15	3	122
3207	2993	35		38	42	44	37	Out						35	2701
		Initial											Initial		
366	348	4	18	4	4	5	4	10					14	4	320
570	537	5	10	6	5	5	7	11					2	5	504
438	420	4	2	5	4	6	4	12					6	4	389
197	182	3	12	4	4	5	4	13					16	3	145
507	475	5	14	5	5	4	5	14					4	5	425
398	380	4	4	6	5	4	6	15					8	4	350
380	366	4	6	4	4	5	4	16					10	4	339
165	151	3	16	3	3	4	3	17					18	3	133
397	375	4	8	3	4	6	5	18					12	4	341
3418	3234	36		40	38	44	42	In						36	2946
6625	6227	71		78	80	88	79	Tot						71	5647

Men's Course Rating/Slope — Blue 73.1/137, White 71.0/130

Women's Course Rating/Slope — Red 73.7/128

Handicap	14	15	18	11		Handicap
Net Score	64	65	70	68		Net Score
Adjust						Adjust

Scorer *Paul Lipp*   Attested *Jerry Tottla*   Date 8-9-10

Figure 1-3: Keeping score.

The relationship of the holes is important when you're playing a head-to-head match. Say your partner has to give you 11 shots over 18 holes because of your handicap difference (check out the earlier section "Making Sense of Golf's Handicap System" for more on handicap). In other words, on 11 holes during our round, you get to subtract 1 shot from your score. The obvious question is, "Which holes?" The card answers that question. You get your shots on the holes rated 1 through 11. These holes, in the opinion of the club committee, are the hardest 11 holes on the course. The 1-rated hole is the toughest, and the 18-rated hole is the easiest.

Most of your golf will typically be matches against others. That's why each hole's rating is important.

Marking a scorecard

Scorecards can be a little daunting when you first look at them (see Figure 1-3). All those numbers and little boxes. But fear not — keeping score is actually simpler than it looks.

Say your handicap is 9 and your partner's is 14. That means you're going to give him 5 strokes over the course of the round. He gets those strokes at the holes rated the most difficult. That's logical. Equally logical is the fact that these holes are handicapped 1 through 5. So mark those "stroke holes" before you begin. (We explain handicaps earlier in this chapter.)

After the match begins, keep track of the score with simple pluses or minuses in a spare row of boxes.

In stroke play (which we cover later in the chapter), you're expected to keep and score your playing companion's card. His name is at the top of the card, his handicap in the box at the bottom. All you have to do is record his score for each hole in the box provided. You don't even have to add it up because you're only responsible for the hole-by-hole score, not the total.

Match play

In *match play,* you don't have to write down any score. The only thing that matters is the state of the game between you and your opponent.

In match play, the score is recorded as holes up or holes down. Say your partner's score on the first hole was 4, and your score was 5, and you received no strokes on that hole. He's now one up. Because each hole is a separate entity, you don't need to write down your actual score; you simply count the number of holes you've won or lost. In fact, if you're having a particularly bad time on a given hole, you can even pick up your ball and concede the hole. All you lose is that hole. Everything starts fresh on the next tee. Such a head-to-head match ends when one player is more holes up than the number of holes remaining. Thus, matches can be won by scores of *four and three.* All that means is that one player was four holes ahead with only three left, the match finishing on the 15th green.

Stroke play

Stroke play (or *medal play*) is different. It's strictly card-and-pencil stuff. Now you're playing against everyone else in the field — or against that elusive standard, par — not just your playing companion. All you do is count one stroke each time you swing at the ball. If it takes you five strokes to play the first hole, you write 5 on your card for that hole. Well, your opponent does — your playing partner keeps your official score, although you can track it as well if you want. The card in your pocket has your playing companion's name on it. At the end of the round, he signs his name to your card and gives it to you; you do the same with his card. After you've checked your score for each hole, you also sign your card. Then, if you're in an official tournament, you hand your card to the scorers. If you're playing a casual round, you record your score on the computer.

Take care when checking your card. One *Rules of Golf* quirk is that you're responsible for the accuracy of the score recorded under your name for each hole — your companion isn't. Any mistakes are deemed to have been made by you, not him. And you can't change a mistake later, even if you have witnesses. Take the case of Roberto DeVicenzo at the 1968 Masters. Millions of spectators and TV viewers saw him make a 3 on the 17th hole in the final round. But the man marking his card, Tommy Aaron, mistakenly marked a 4. Checking his score after the round, DeVicenzo failed to notice the error and signed his card. The mistake cost him the chance to win in a playoff with Bob Goalby. DeVicenzo had to accept a score one higher than he actually shot and lost by that one stroke. Tragic. After realizing his mistake, poor DeVicenzo said, "What a stupid I am!"

DeVicenzo's misfortune shows what can happen when the score on your card is higher than the one you actually made on the hole. You're stuck with that score. If the opposite is the case and the score on the card is *lower* than it should be, the result is even worse: You're disqualified.

One last thing: Don't worry about the addition on your card. You aren't responsible for that part. As long as the numbers opposite each hole are correct, you're in the clear.

Chapter 2

Comprehending Course Etiquette

*T*o some people, the topic of golf etiquette seems about as huge as quantum physics. Although nowhere near as complicated as the Theory of Relativity, the game of golf has many nuances that extend far beyond the actual rules of play, and knowing as much about them as you can is important. Don't worry, no one expects you to have an encyclopedic knowledge of golf etiquette after only a few years in the game. Picking up all the relevant do's and don'ts takes a lot of time — and a lot of rounds. Even the most experienced players find that they learn new things about manners and behavior on the golf course all the time.

What's important, then, isn't so much a complete and total comprehension of golf etiquette but rather a respect for what is and isn't acceptable, a willingness to learn as much as you can about those unwritten rules, and a basic common sensibility when it comes to playing the game and deciding what is — and isn't — right to do.

This chapter introduces you to the world of golf etiquette and lets you know how to carry yourself on a course with ease. We begin with the basics — a list of do's and don'ts for the game of golf, no matter where you're playing or with whom. Then we move on to the specifics, like playing in tournaments and using caddies.

Using Your Manners: Knowing the Right Way to Play

Golf has its own code of etiquette: semiofficial "rules" of courtesy that every player is expected to follow. Knowing why a rule is in place isn't as important as just making sure you obey it — at least when it comes to etiquette. So here's a list of do's and don'ts for the game of golf. If you know nothing else about golf etiquette, make sure you're at least familiar with the following.

Minding your mouth and your movements with your foursome

Golf is a social game, but it's also a game that requires concentration. As you probably know (or will find out), focusing on your shot is hard when your buddies are talking smack or walking around in your line of vision. Show them the same respect that you expect them to show you. Here are some tips to help you be a courteous competitor:

- **Don't talk while someone is playing a stroke.** Give your partners time and silence while they're analyzing the situation, making their practice swings, and then making their swings for real.

  Easygoing types may not mind if you gab away while they're choosing a club, but that isn't true for everyone. When in doubt, stand still and shut up. If you're a problem more than once, you'll hear about it.

- **Be careful where you stand while others are hitting their shots.** Standing away to the side of a player is not only safe but also unobtrusive. Don't stand near them or move about, especially on the greens. Never stand behind someone's ball, even if you're out of range of his swing. That can be terribly distracting to the person making the shot. Even be mindful of your shadow.

- **Don't walk way ahead of the group while someone is hitting (or getting ready to hit).** Peeling off to the sides to find and then hit your own ball is acceptable. In fact, that is *de rigueur* for golfers who want to maintain a reasonable pace of play (by being ready to hit when their turns are up). But everyone should be roughly the same distance from the hole. If you wander up ahead of everyone, that can be distracting for the rest of your group (not to mention unsafe).

- **Don't walk across someone's putting line on the green.** If you do, you can give her what some golfers call a *bigfoot,* and that may affect the direction and speed of her putt. The *line* of a putt — the path it must follow to the hole — is holy ground. Walking across someone else's putting line is less of a problem than it used to be because most players these days wear soft-spiked golf shoes. But it's still a no-no.

✔ **Don't stand behind someone who's hitting a putt.** Some people like to stand here to get a good read of the line, but it's very bad form. The exception: Your match partner is putting, and he allows you to do that as his teammate. It's also good form to stay out of your companion's peripheral vision while he's putting. Don't stand near the hole or walk between your partner's ball and the hole.

✔ **Refrain from giving "lessons" to other members of your foursome when you're out on the course.** Doing so is obnoxious and holds up play. Offer tips only if asked. (And the best tip may be, "Go see a real golf pro.")

✔ **Establish the bet for the day, if any, on the first tee and make sure all aspects are agreed upon before you head off.** You don't want someone trying to change things up partway through the round. Especially if you're beating him. See Chapter 3 of Book IV for more on betting.

✔ **Keep in mind that a little verbal abuse of your playing partners and opponents is well within the realm of good golf course decorum.** But go easy on bosses, coworkers, and people you don't know very well. Feel free, however, to be a little rougher on those childhood friends you play with every week. Ask the broker in your group about that lemon stock he sold you a few years ago. Tell the magazine publisher how much you like his competitor's most recent issue. Inquire as to whether your opponent has been able to cure his incessant snap-hook just as he gets ready to tee off. After all, this game is supposed to be fun, and if you can't take a little heat. . . .

Showing courtesy to other players

Golf, unlike the trash-talking sports you see on TV, still prizes sportsmanship. In addition to respecting the other players in your foursome, you need to show some common golf courtesies to other players you encounter on the course. Here are the basics:

Book IV

Rules and Etiquette

✔ **The _honor_ (that is, the first shot) on a given tee goes to the player with the lowest score on the previous hole.** If that hole was tied, the player with the lowest score on the hole before that retains the honor. In other words, you have the honor until you lose it.

✔ **Always be sure that the person in your group who is farthest from the hole is allowed to hit first.**

✔ **A _mulligan_ (a do-over) is fine on the first hole if everybody in your group agrees.** But take only one. Some folks like to "hit 'til they're happy," but that just holds everyone up. Be sure you treat it on your scorecard the way *The Official Rules of Golf* say you should.

✔ **Make sure everyone in your foursome is behind you when you hit.** You don't hit every shot where you're aiming it. When in doubt, wait for your playing partners to get out of your line of play.

✔ **Ensure the group in front of you is well out of range before you hit your shot.** Few things are more aggravating than some yahoo crunching a 3-wood onto a green that you're still occupying and then trying to excuse it (and the ball that has just bounced off your leg) by saying, "I'm sorry, I just hit my career shot. I had no idea it would go so far." Have better sense than that — and better manners. If you see any chance that you may be able to hit someone in front of you, don't take the swing or the risk.

✔ **Pay attention to the group behind you, too.** Are they waiting for you on every shot? Is there a gap between you and the group ahead of you? If the answer to either or both is "yes," step aside and invite the group behind you to play through. This move is no reflection on your ability. All it means is that the group behind plays faster than you do.

The best place to let a group behind play through is at a par-3 (it's the shortest hole and, therefore, the quickest way of playing through). After hitting your ball onto the green, mark it, and wave to them to play. Stand off to the side of the green as they hit. After they've all hit, replace your ball and putt out. Then wait for them to finish, and let them go to the next tee ahead of you. Simple, isn't it?

Sadly, you see this piece of basic good manners ignored time and again by players who don't know any better. Do what's right: Let a faster group play through.

✔ **If you must play with a golf cart, park it well away from greens, tees, and bunkers.** To speed up play, park on the side of the green nearest the next tee. The same is true if you're carrying your bag: Don't set the bag down near any of the aforementioned items; leave it in a spot on the way to the next tee.

✔ **Know the rules.** Read the USGA's *The Official Rules of Golf*. Enough said.

Respecting the pros and course staff

The pros and the employees at your local golf course are more familiar with the course than anyone else, and they want to help you have the best game you can have. Respect these folks and listen to them; you'll have a better experience on the course as a result.

✔ **Always check in with the pro shop before you go out on any course.** Courses want to keep records of who is playing, and your checking in gives them a chance to tell you about specific problems or issues you need to be aware of.

✔ **Listen to what the pro says.** He is in charge of the golf program, so heed his word. If he tells you to go off (start from) the back nine rather than the front, go off the back. If he tells you that you can't do something, don't. A good pro knows how to manage a golf course and understands what's what. He knows it better than most of his members, and he deserves their undivided attention and respect.

✔ **Keep your complaints to a minimum.** Anyone able to go out and play golf is pretty lucky, and no one really wants to hear a lot of whining about everything you perceive to be wrong with the course or the club you're playing. Sadly, more and more people seem to be complaining these days, demanding greater services — and perfection — from their golf courses than at any other time in memory.

That's too bad, because most of the gripes are ridiculous and cause enormous grief for the people running the course or club, making it tougher for the players who have to listen to that nonsense to enjoy their day. We've heard guys rail about seeing too many leaves on the greens — during a late fall day in New England. If something really is wrong with the course you're playing, bring it to the manager's or pro's attention. Otherwise, be thankful for what you have and keep quiet.

✔ **Be on your best behavior.** Be humble and respectful. Too many people strut around with the most remarkable arrogance and attitude, all because their families have been members of this club for years and they think that they can therefore do no wrong. They berate caddies and pro shop workers. They refuse to follow the rules. They act loudly and like to show off. Bad ideas, one and all. No one needs to act that way, and no one in their right mind wants to be around people who do. That sort of behavior has no place anywhere, especially not in the game of golf.

Playing It Safe

Sometimes the etiquette of golf has more to do with preventing someone from getting beaned by a ball than it has to do with upsetting a golfing tradition. Check out the following safety-related tips:

✔ **Watch where you swing your clubs.** Make sure you don't inadvertently clock someone on the head.

✔ **Don't throw your clubs.** It's bad manners, it can upset your playing partners, and it can be dangerous to your fellow golfers.

Book IV

Rules and Etiquette

✔ **Yell "Fore!" — quickly and loudly — if it looks like you may hit someone with your ball.** Any chance you can give someone to protect himself is appreciated. (And try not to laugh too hard at the reactions some players have when they hear that word. We've watched people hit the deck as though they were dodging a cruise missile, tap dance around like Savion Glover, run for daylight like Adrian Peterson, or freeze like a popsicle. It can be very amusing.)

✔ **Help the superintendent and his workers by making sure they're out of the way when you hit (or are at least aware that you're hitting into them).** We've watched people pound approach shots into greens while guys are still mowing the grass, and they don't even try to alert them. Show those workers the same courtesy you show others and make sure they know the balls are coming.

Timing Is Everything

Sadly, most golfers don't have an unlimited amount of time to spend playing a round of golf. Here are a host of ways you can help keep things moving on the course:

✔ **Don't take too many practice swings before a shot.** Two should be the maximum. This limit keeps the game moving at a comfortable pace.

✔ **Don't prowl around the green for five minutes trying to line up your putts and discern every undulation.** Take a look at what you have before you, and then make the shot. Just because the pros take forever around the green doesn't mean *you* have to; it's their livelihood.

✔ **Be ready when it's your turn — especially when your ball lies farthest from the hole.** Make your decisions while you're walking to your ball or while waiting for others to hit. Obviously, don't pull clubs out of your bag while your partner is in the middle of his back swing. But do try to accomplish as much as possible as far as shot preparation is concerned so you're ready to go when it's your turn. And when it's your turn, don't delay. You don't have to rush; just get on with it.

✔ **Line up your putt while others are doing the same so you're ready when it's your turn to make a run at the hole.**

✔ **Don't tell stories at the expense of holding up the group.** Stop your tale when it's time for you — or others — to play a ball, and then pick up your story later. You don't want to keep people standing around the fairway listening to your story while others are waiting to play.

✔ **Keep up with the group in front of you.** That really is your best gauge of pace of play. As long as the group in front of you is no more than a hole ahead, you're doing fine.

Playing solo or as part of a twosome

Single players really have no standing on a golf course, especially if they go out at peak times. So don't expect to fly through group after group if you're solo. Doing so is not only disruptive but also rude. Twosomes are only moderately more acceptable in that regard, and most times they should be allowed to play through slower and larger groups. But we have no sympathy for the pair who goes out on a Saturday or Sunday morning and tries to force its way around at prime time.

Our advice is simple: If you want to play as a single or in a twosome, be among the first or last ones out on a given day, and don't feel it's your right to bull your way through the course.

- ✔ **If you can't keep up with the group in front of you, let the folks behind you play through.** Stand aside, preferably on the tee or green, and allow them to hit their shots and move ahead. Some people consider allowing others to play through to be a completely humiliating experience, but it's really the only option for slow players. And if you keep a proper pace, you should never have to do that in the first place.

- ✔ **Leave the green as soon as everyone has finished putting.** You see this situation a lot: You're ready to play your approach shot to the green, and the people in front are crowding around the hole marking their cards. That's poor etiquette on two counts: It delays play, and the last thing the greenskeeper wants is a lot of footprints around the cup. Mark your card on the way to the next tee!

- ✔ **Keep your round of golf to four hours or less.** We have played 18 holes in less than three hours on plenty of occasions, without rushing. Yes, avoiding the monster round at busy public courses is difficult. But golf really should not be an all-day affair.

- ✔ **Hold an extra ball or two in your pants pocket so you can reload quickly if you need to hit a second shot or a provisional ball.** Anything to save time and ensure a faster round, right? (Flip to Chapter 1 of Book IV for info on provisional balls.)

- ✔ **Keep an eye on where the balls of your partner and opponents go.** You can help maintain a good pace of play by knowing exactly where to look for errant shots. And many eyes mean less work for all involved.

- ✔ **Remember that you have only five minutes to look for a ball before you have to declare it lost.** Some schools feel you should cut that time down to three minutes if people are waiting to play behind you.

- ✔ **Play only one ball while on the course and leave the practicing for the driving range.**

Book IV

Rules and Etiquette

Caring for the Course

Common sense says that you should treat all golf courses with respect and care, but some golfers assume that someone else will pick up after them, fix their mistakes, and so on. Show the world that you're a class-act golfer by following some guidelines for taking care of the course.

✔ **Help out the greenskeeper.** A busy course takes a major pounding — all those balls landing on greens, feet walking through bunkers, and divots of earth flying through the air. Do your bit for the golf course. Repair any ball marks you see on the greens. (You can use your tee or a special tool called a *divot fixer,* which costs about a dollar in the pro shop.)

Here's how to repair ball marks:

1. **Stick the repair tool in the green around the perimeter of the indentation, starting at the rear, and gently lift the compacted dirt.**

2. **Replace any loose pieces of grass or turf in the center of the hole and then take your putter and tap down the raised turf until it's level again (see Figure 2-1).**

When a ball lands on a soft green, it often leaves a *pitch mark.*

Lift the back edge of the hole... and then flatten it out.

Figure 2-1: Take care of the green.

You also want to smooth out or rake any footprints in bunkers, as shown in Figure 2-2 (but only after you play out). And replace any divots you find on fairways and tees.

✔ **Pick up any broken tees you create — or find — on the teeing area.** Doing so helps out the superintendent and his crew and not only makes the tee look better but also protects the mowers when the grass is cut.

Figure 2-2:
Be rakish
and restore
the bunker.

✔ **Never leave your tee in the ground after you've hit.** Tees left in the ground can be rough on the mower and be a real pain to other players, who have to dig the tee out before they hit. Never, ever pound your tee into the ground with your club after a bad shot (or after a good shot, for that matter). It's bad sportsmanship — and besides, someone's going to have to pull it out.

✔ **Don't lean on your putter while on the green.** That move can leave a divot in the ground that may damage the green and affect the roll of someone else's ball.

✔ **Don't drag your feet on the green.** Even if you aren't wearing metal spikes, you can damage the green that way and mar the putting surface.

✔ **Don't litter, and pick up after people who do.** The credo to live by is this: Leave the course in better shape than you found it.

Book IV

Rules and Etiquette

Playing Well with Others

At some point in your golf career, you'll find yourself in a new group or perhaps faced with some changing dynamic in your current group. This section gives you some survival tips for making the most of situations where you're not as good as your partners and dishes out some pointers about coping with other players.

When you're the worst in your group

Early in your golfing existence, almost everyone is better than you. So you'll probably spend some rounds as the worst player in your foursome. What do you do?

Pick it up!

The worst thing you can do is delay your playing partners. After you've hit the ball, oh, nine times on a given hole, pick it up and quit that hole as a courtesy to your playing partners. There's always the next hole.

Another option for players who are constantly scoring worse than their partners is to ask to move up a tee — even to the start of the fairway — just to keep it fun for everyone.

When you're actually scoring a game, you're required to finish out every hole — that is, you must post a score for each hole. But beginners should feel free to skip that technicality. While you're learning, don't worry about scores.

Find your own ball

This idea comes under the "don't delay" heading. If you happen to hit a shot into the highest spinach patch on the course, don't let your companions help you look for it. Tell them to play on and that you'll catch up after a "quick look." They'll see you as someone who, though having a bad day, would be worth playing with again. (If you don't find the ball within a couple of minutes, declare it lost — put an *X* on your scorecard for that hole.)

Never moan, never analyze

Don't be a pain in the you-know-what. Most golfers gripe and moan when they're playing poorly. That's bad — and boring for the other players, who don't want to hear about your woes. All they care about is the fact that you're slowing things up. So grit your teeth and keep moving.

Analyzing your swing is another common crime: You hit a few bad shots — okay, more than a few. Then you say, "Maybe if I just turn a little more through the ball. . . ." That's the *last* thing your playing partners want to hear. Repeat: *They don't care about your game.* So don't analyze, and don't ask them for swing tips. If one is offered, try it, but keep it quiet.

When you're not the worst

How do you behave when another golfer in your group can't get the ball above shin height? Here are some pointers:

- ✔ **Zip that lip.** Whatever you do, don't try to encourage your pal as his or her game implodes. After a while, you run out of things to say, and your friend gets annoyed with you.

- ✔ **Never give advice or swing tips to the other player.** The other person will only blame you for the next bad shot he or she hits.

- ✔ **Talk about other stuff.** The last thing you should discuss is your pal's awful game. Find some common interest and chat about that. Try football, movies, or the stock market. Even politics and religion are safer topics than that 20-yard drive your friend just dribbled off the tee.

When you're stuck with a jerk

Most golfers are princes — tall, smart, and handsome. The game not only tests character but also builds character. We're willing to bet that you find fewer louts and scoundrels in golf than in any other major sport. But with more than 25 million American golfers out there, you're bound to encounter a few bad apples. Here's how to avoid a rotten matchup and deal with one that comes along despite your best efforts.

Who not to play with

Most foursomes are made up of players of roughly equal ability. That's what you want. In fact, the best scenario is to find three golfers who are just a little bit better than you. By trying to keep up with them, you'll probably improve your game.

Those are the sorts of people you should be playing with. The people you shouldn't be playing with are those who play a "different game." That means anyone who shoots more than 20 shots lower than you on an average day. All someone like that does is depress you, and your slower, less-expert play may irritate him or her. Such a situation can bring out the jerk in both of you. So stay away from the best golfers at your course — at least for now. When you get better, playing with them can help you improve.

How to endure

Sometimes you can't help it — you're stuck with a loud, cursing lunkhead who talks during your swing, jabbers on his or her cellphone, and gives everyone unsolicited advice. How to deal:

- ✔ **At first, ignore the jerk.** It's a beautiful day, and you're out on the course playing the best game in the world. Play your game and be glad you're only spending a few hours with Golfzilla. If the jerk's behavior annoys the other members of your group, let them be first to call him or her on it.

✔ **If the jerk keeps it up, speak up.** Being firm but polite often works with jerks. Say, "You walked on my putting line — please don't." Or, "You're distracting me by talking on your cellphone."

✔ **Treat the jerk as a hazard.** If all else fails, think of Golfzilla the way you think of a strong wind or a lousy lie in a bunker. Golf is all about dealing with adversity. If you can keep your wits and make a good swing despite the jerk, you'll be a tougher, better golfer next time out.

Knowing How to Play Different Courses

Although golf etiquette is golf etiquette wherever you go, the particular venue you're playing does make a difference. In this section, we provide tips about golf etiquette as it relates to public or municipal courses, high-end daily fee tracks, private clubs, and practice facilities. So no matter where you're playing, read on.

Mastering municipal course basics

In this section, *municipal golf course* or *muni* actually means any facility that is open for public play (with the exception of those high-end daily-fee tracks known as "country-clubs-for-a-day" that we cover later in this chapter). Some municipal courses are owned by towns and counties; others are held and operated by individuals or corporations. As a rule in these spots, the prices are low, the course conditions only fair, the variety of players extensive, the good tee times tough to come by, and the hours needed for a round on the long side.

At municipal courses, golfers generally pay minimum attention to basic golf etiquette, mainly because many of them either don't know how best to handle themselves on a course or simply don't care. That's not to say all public layouts are madhouses. But you can pretty safely assume that people you find on the public courses aren't as concerned about following all those do's and don'ts we list earlier in the chapter as other golfers may be. The environment is less structured in that way, and you find very little peer pressure to moderate. Plus, public courses are the sort of venues where newcomers begin to work on their games, and unless they have read a book like this, they really don't know any better.

The dress code is looser at public layouts as well and pretty much anything goes. You get all sorts of odd combinations out there that would surely make any worst-dressed list — tank tops and cutoffs, sweat pants and halter tops. You name it, and you'll probably see it on one municipal course or another.

In general, betting is much heavier at public courses. The money got so big at the putting green at Griffith Park in Los Angeles at one time, for example, that the police set up a sting operation and busted a dozen people or so to tone it down.

You can expect to see more beer carts at public courses as well — and more liquor consumed during the round. It's simply part of the deal.

Here are a few other tips to remember when you go out to the local course:

- **Be on time.** People jump through hoops to get tee times at many of these places, and they can lose them if everybody in the group hasn't shown up on time. So be there.

- **Treat the golf course as your own.** Sure, it really isn't yours, and it's not like a club where you have some vested financial and emotional interest in its condition. But following the unwritten rules about leaving a golf course in better shape than you found it still applies, no matter what course you're playing. See the earlier section "Caring for the Course" for more on how to take care of the course.

- **Don't assume that just because you tee it up at a muni that you should play as slowly as everyone else.** Keep pace the way you're supposed to, and maybe that steady play will help speed things up all over.

Playing at a high-end course

As a rule, the courses we're referring to here cost up to $200 or so for a round of golf, cater to a lot of business outings, have fantastic facilities, and are open to all comers. The layouts are generally very high quality, designed by big-name architects, and kept in prime condition. Service is terrific, and so is the food and drink. In many ways, these locations give golfers country-club facilities and treatment for a daily fee price, and in many cases, they have really improved the quality of golf available to the public.

Along those lines, expect that the demands for etiquette and dress code at these facilities are higher than they are at most public spots, which means you should act accordingly:

- **Wear traditional golf clothes.** Slacks and collared golf shirts are best. No blue jeans, no cutoffs, and no tank tops.

- **Plan on having soft spikes on your golf shoes.** The vast majority of these courses now require that.

- **Stick to the unwritten rules of etiquette listed in this chapter.** The vast majority of the quality daily-fee tracks demand this adherence. They want to provide "country-club-for-a-day" facilities, and they want their players to act like they're playing at such an upscale facility.

Teeing it up at a private club

Of all the places you can play golf, the private club is the one that puts the greatest emphasis on the unwritten rules of etiquette and behavior — especially the really exclusive private clubs. They expect people, whether members or guests, to act in certain ways, and they're often pretty tough on those who don't toe the line.

Yes, the folks who frequent private courses can be a little ridiculous about what does and doesn't matter from an etiquette standpoint. But remember, the course is theirs, and if you want to play there, either as a member or a guest, you have to play by their rules.

However, for all the nonsense you sometimes have to put up with at big-time golf or country clubs, a pile of benefits awaits you. Many private clubs don't have tee times, so you can play pretty much when you want. They spend substantial amounts of money on course maintenance, so the conditioning is generally superb. Most keep the numbers of members fairly small, so the courses are rarely crowded. A number of them also have caddie programs, so you can play golf the way it was meant to be played. They are, all in all, very good places to tee it up.

So how should you handle yourself at a private club? Keep in mind that the many tips provided early in this chapter apply to private courses, too. But here are a few more:

✔ **If you're invited to a private club as a guest, be careful not to embarrass your host.** Follow your host's lead, and always ask before you do anything that may be considered even the least bit tacky. Don't, for example, pull out your cellphone at the first tee unless you know that cellphones are allowed on the course (and that your host doesn't mind your using one). As a rule, be subtle and unobtrusive. Clubs like people to blend into the background, and you can't go wrong if you do that yourself.

✔ **Check in with your host for a little advance guidance before you show up at his club.** Ask whether jackets and ties are required for lunch. Is wearing shorts on the golf course allowed? Is the course spikeless? Take care of these issues beforehand, and you don't have to worry when you show up to play.

✔ **If you're invited to join a club and you decide to sign on, be a quiet member for a while and just observe the way the club works.** As a new member, take the time to get a sense of the club's history, if you haven't already, and the type of place it wants to be. Get to know more of the members and understand the general feel and ambience. Don't start making a lot of suggestions. Don't tell people what to do. You joined the club because you liked what it was all about, right? So why would you immediately try to change things?

✔ **Never, ever, change your shoes in the club parking lot.** Few things rile a good club membership more than that. Bring your shoes into the locker room and change there instead.

✔ **If your golf equipment isn't very good, consider renting.** One story tells of a friend showing up at a fancy member-guest tournament one year with a pair of golf shoes that not only hadn't been cleaned or shined in weeks but also had long cuts on the sides. And his golf bag had such a gaping hole in the bottom that clubs and balls started dribbling out of it as the caddie master hauled it down to the pro shop. Some people thought the scene hysterical, especially the caddies who were infinitely amused by the balls that were bouncing down the asphalt cart path and the pro shop workers who were rushing trying to collect them. But the host member wanted to hide.

✔ **Know the tipping culture.** Get the lowdown on gratuities before you start handing out sawbucks like Rodney Dangerfield in *Caddyshack*. Most private clubs don't allow tipping, and if they do, they expect it to be done in a discreet fashion. Pay heed. This chapter's "Tipping Gracefully" covers more on tipping.

✔ **Dress appropriately.** Golf and country clubs generally insist on collared shirts for men; women may wear collarless ones. Men and women may wear Bermuda-length shorts as well as slacks (but no blue jeans). Tank tops, cutoffs, and t-shirts are prohibited, and so is anything that makes you look like a skateboarder rather than a golfer. You see the guys on tour on TV? That's more or less how you should look at a private club.

✔ **Know how to work with a caddie.** Help out your caddie on the course when you can. Yes, your caddie is technically supposed to be working for you. But lend a hand if the occasion calls for it. If he has to hustle a club over to your playing partner right after you have hit out of a bunker, rake the sand yourself, and give him a small break. For more information on caddies, check out the section later in this chapter.

✔ **Always write a thank-you note to your host when the day is done.** Things like that mean a lot, and they're a particularly good idea if you want to get invited back.

Book IV

Rules and Etiquette

Doing it right at driving ranges

The driving range is where golfers go to warm up before a round, correct mistakes in their swings afterward, and work on their games in between golf outings. It's typically a place where people talk easily, tell jokes, toss barbs back and forth, and catch up with each other, all while they try to smooth 9-irons and crush 3-woods.

You guessed it: Proper range play has unwritten rules, and making sure you're aware of them is one way you can ensure that you're a welcome sight for your fellow golfers at the range rather than the person they groan about when they see you walking up.

- ✔ **Watch where you're aiming.** Be mindful of your line on the driving range. Take care where you aim. Be considerate of the pro who is buying those range balls, and of the people playing the course around the range. The practice areas are often shoehorned into tight spots surrounded by different golf holes, so certain shots can pose something of a hazard on occasion for golfers on the course. Take the time to know where those spots are, and do your best to avoid them.

- ✔ **Leave the range balls on the range.** We're constantly amazed by how many golfers actually put range balls in their golf bags and use them on water holes (instead of using the ones they bought in the pro shop). Everybody should buy the balls they use on the course, and leave the range balls where they belong — on the range.

- ✔ **Pay for your range balls.** Many clubs and facilities leave bags or buckets of balls down at the range for golfers. The only thing they ask is that you sign a chit for those double-stripers when you use them. If you're not sure whether the balls are complimentary, ask at the clubhouse if you need to pay for what you play.

- ✔ **Hit your balls between the ropes.** Most driving ranges have a pair of ropes that the golf course superintendent uses to show the areas a player may hit balls from on the tee during certain days. Do what he asks, and stay between those lines. Yes, the quality of the turf outside them can look pretty tempting at times, what with the complete lack of the divots usually found in the well-worn areas (and a busy driving range can get well-worn in a hurry). But the super has the area sectioned off in a certain way for a reason, and he wants to give the other areas a rest. So don't purposely hit outside the ropes. It is, quite simply, bad form. And it doesn't help the grass out much, either.

- ✔ **Stay behind the hitting area when the range is open.** Believe it or not, we've seen golfers actually walk off the tee and onto the range itself to collect balls when they only want to hit a few more and don't feel like paying for another bag. Balls are whizzing by their heads, yet they're so determined to save money that they don't seem to notice. They should, because they could really get hurt. A range can be a very dangerous place.

Staying on course at putting greens

Putting greens are located near the first tee at most golf courses. They're a place where you can hone your putting stroke and get a feel for the greens at that particular layout. (They're also the site of some unbelievably feverish betting at many municipal tracks, but more on that in Chapter 3 of Book IV.) As is the case with driving ranges, putting greens have some basic tenets of behavior that are important for all golfers to abide by.

- ✔ **Treat the putting green as you would any green on the course.** Don't drag your feet across the putting green as you walk; doing so creates spike or scuff marks. And don't make any marks or indentations in the turf with your putter, either by leaning on it or by swinging at the ground when you miss a shot. If for some reason you do mar the surface, be sure to fix it so the next person using the green finds its shape as good as you did.

- ✔ **Don't use more than a couple of balls when you're practicing.** Limiting the number of balls you use is simply a courtesy to other golfers who may be using the green at the same time you are. That way, you don't crowd them out by rolling your equipment all over the place. The exception, of course, is if you're the only one on the putting green. Then you should feel free to putt as many balls as you want.

- ✔ **Pay attention to which pin you're putting at.** Putting greens usually have at least half a dozen holes with small flagsticks at which golfers can aim. Try to avoid stroking your ball at the same pin that some other players may be aiming for. Pick one of your own.

- ✔ **Don't assume chipping around the putting green is allowed.** Most facilities have a rule against chipping around a putting green, mostly because they're afraid someone will inadvertently line an errant shot into the forehead of a fellow golfer. Be sure to check with the pro to make sure chipping is all right before you pull out your wedge around the putting green. And if it's allowed, use the club carefully.

- ✔ **Use practice greens as a way to introduce the game to your kids.** Practice greens are a great place to introduce the game to your children. It's an easy place for kids to get initiated — and interested — in the game. It's also a fun place to hold little parent/child competitions, as one club we know does a couple of times each summer. These events are always well attended and always a lot of fun.

Book IV

Rules and Etiquette

Visiting other practice facilities

Essentially, practice facilities are comprised of driving ranges and putting greens, but we're adding this brief section here because some also include what are known as *short-game areas,* which have bunkers from which players can hit sand shots, and small greens up to 75 to 80 yards away to which golfers can hit different wedges. The idea here is pretty much the same as with the other areas you find at a practice facility: Take care to keep the greens, bunkers, and tees that you use in excellent shape for the next players, and watch out for your fellow golfers so nobody gets hit by one of your balls.

Taking Part in Tournaments

You don't have to be a *scratch* (0-handicap) player with a deadly draw and a strong putting stroke to enjoy tournament golf. Men and women of all ages and abilities can enter tournaments at clubs or facilities, play with people of their same level, and have a fantastic time going at it on the course.

But you need to keep some important things in mind, etiquette-wise, when you play events. Consider the following do's and don'ts as you get ready to win your silver:

- **Always shake hands at the start of a match and wish the other player or team good luck.** Being nice to the person or people you're about to do battle with is sometimes difficult, especially if they're folks you don't particularly care for. But get over it. Respectful gestures like a handshake set a good tone for the match. And frankly, they're the right thing to do.

- **Show up on time.** You're disqualified from most tournaments if you miss your tee time. And even if you're allowed to continue competing despite your tardiness, you're not off the hook. In all likelihood, you've upset your playing partner and opponents by being late. And you just may cause a rift that lingers throughout the round and makes play much less enjoyable than it otherwise could have been.

- **Acknowledge a well-played shot.** You don't have to give your opponent a high-five, but a quick "Good shot" or even a smile and a nod is an appropriate and sportsmanlike response to a solid hit. At the same time, don't patronize your opponent with false praise when he has hit a bad or mediocre ball. He doesn't want to hear that from you, and he shouldn't have to.

- **Stand in the right place when the other player is hitting.** Head to the earlier section "Minding your mouth and your movements with your foursome" for more on staying out of the way. Also, don't be afraid to ask a player to move, or refrain from moving, if he is bothering you with his position while you're trying to hit the ball.

- **Play at a reasonable pace.** Fast play is great, but tournaments take a bit longer than your regular recreational rounds because more is generally at stake. Still, you don't have to line up a putt from ten different angles or take five practice swings for each shot. Concentrate hard and think about your strokes, but keep moving.

- **Drop the running commentary.** Some people like to give you a full recap of every shot from address to follow-through, as well as all the things that went wrong in the process. Most people really don't care, especially if they're playing a match. Making remarks that may influence your opponent's decision-making when it comes his time to hit (for example, commenting on the speed and grain of the green or perhaps the direction of the wind) is distracting. Keep those thoughts to yourself. If you have to vent, do so with your playing partner or caddie, not with your opponents.

✔ **Don't lash out.** Okay, so you've been playing horribly and having terrible luck. Part of you wants to throw your club into the lake. Resist that impulse to lash out; behaving like a madman is very bad form and something that may really disturb your opponent. Take a deep breath. Count to ten. Do whatever it takes to control your frustration.

✔ **Go easy on the attempted psych-out.** Plenty of golfers consider themselves to be master manipulators of the mind when it comes to playing competitive golf, and they do lots of little things to try to psych out their opponents. Some of that is fine, to a degree. But unless you're playing on the PGA Tour or competing in the U.S. Amateur, keep your gamesmanship to a minimum. After all, the main idea of the sport on the club or municipal course level is to have fun, and nothing can be more aggravating than some clown who tries to take the psychological edge in your match by making you, for example, hit all the short putts that most others would concede or start talking about the divorce and child custody battle you just went through.

Some people evoke some obscure bylaw of the rule book just as you're about to hit a shot, wondering whether you may be in danger of violating some sacred edict. And others ask you whether you inhale or exhale when you swing, just to get you thinking about anything but your swing. The ploys are numerous, and they can be effective and even funny if done humorously. But looked at seriously, that sort of behavior really is nothing more than nonsense. As a player and a person, you don't want to be like that because you don't want to ruin the game — and the day — for all involved.

✔ **Shake hands when the match is done.** Look your opponent in the eye; say, "Good match;" and walk off the green together. If you have a hat on, take it off before you shake.

Good sportsmanship is a pillar of golf, and no matter how you do in a tournament, you have to play with class.

Book IV

Rules and Etiquette

Going with Tradition: Utilizing Caddies

Nothing is quite like playing golf with a caddie, and to skip the caddie is to miss out on a very important and pleasing element of the game. Caddies are a tradition that has been a part of the sport for centuries. Whether it's a grizzled, brusque Scotsman guiding you around one of the classic links courses across the pond or a young college student carrying bags during the summer to make some money for school, caddies offer comfort and companionship as well as a sense of how the game really should be played.

More than a strong back: Respecting the caddie's role

A caddie does far more than just carry your golf bag. A good caddie gives you yardage, cleans your clubs after each shot, and wipes off your ball after you've made it to the green (and marked it properly). He can tell you exactly how far you'll hit a ball with each club in your bag (after watching you swing only a few times), and he reads a green as easily as you can read *See Spot Run.* He helps you find balls, and if you're playing a new course, he makes sure you know where and where not to hit your shots.

A caddie also gives you a sort of companionship on the golf course unlike the relationship than you have with anyone else on a course, or probably anyone else in sports, for that matter. A caddie is your teammate and rooting section, your confidante. A good caddie makes you laugh at the right time and makes you think very clearly about your next shot. He's your midround therapist and knows just how to keep you from getting too high or low with each good or bad shot. He helps build your confidence and keeps you from falling apart. And he also allows you to play golf in a very reasonable amount of time. Some people swear you can play a round quicker in a golf cart. But a good caddie can get you around just as fast. And sometimes even faster.

Following the trends

Many of the best and fanciest clubs in the United States — and in the United Kingdom — have truly professional caddies. These are people who make their living at the game, and generally they're very good, though you do get some fellows who think they know it all and forget that they're supposed to work with their golfer and not show off. The people who carry your bag at Augusta National, Pine Valley, or Seminole (three of the finest private golf clubs in the world) are at the top of their field, and, as the old saying goes, they have forgotten more about golf than most will ever know. Many of them can really play, too.

Once upon a time, caddie programs thrived throughout the golfing world. But as the electric cart became more and more popular among a public who decided it would rather ride than walk, the use of caddies fell off dramatically. By the early 1980s, finding caddies had gotten harder and harder at most places, and many resorts banned walking altogether. They wouldn't even let you go out cartless if you carried your own bag.

Caddie scholarships

The revival of caddie programs is helping bring back another of the great traditions of golf: caddie scholarship funds. You think you feel good about giving a kid $40 for a morning round and knowing that you're helping him make a living for the summer? Try being part of a group that split $30,000 in caddie scholarship money among eight caddies in one year and realizing that you're making it that much more possible for them to get ahead in life. That may sound corny, but it's a wonderful sensation and a very worthwhile thing to be involved with.

Many clubs start their own caddie scholarship funds. One, called Sankaty Head on Nantucket Island in Massachusetts, actually has a caddie camp and has boarded as many as 60 youths during the summer. In addition to getting at least one loop (round) in a day, they're given instruction in golf and trained how to caddie.

A number of organizations have been giving out scholarships to worthy caddies for decades.

✔ The Western Golf Association's Chick Evans Foundation, named for the great amateur golfer (and former caddie) who won the 1916 U.S. Open, has provided about 7,000 men and women with college tuition and housing assistance since 1930.

✔ The Francis Ouimet Scholarship Fund in Massachusetts (also named after a one-time caddie who won the U.S. Open) has provided scholarships for some 3,500 students since 1949.

✔ The Westchester Golf Association Caddie Scholarship Fund operates out of offices in suburban New York City and is currently helping to support 250 area caddies in schools around the country. Its four-year commitment tops $2 million.

If you have an opportunity to get involved with or contribute to organizations like these, do it. They're great causes, and as an added bonus, they help promote golf.

Fortunately, that is starting to change, and golfers are increasingly trending toward walking in general and using caddies in particular. More private clubs are starting caddie programs or reviving ones that have fallen on hard times. Consider, for example, the East Lake Golf Club in Atlanta, which is most famous for being the home course of Bobby Jones. That club, which didn't have many caddies to speak of and was actually in danger of closing completely some years ago, has become a caddie's dream. Currently, it puts some 250 caddies a year to work on its magnificent grounds, and they're good. The Secession course in Beaufort, South Carolina, only opened in 1992, but it has the caddie traditions of an old-line club. The only way you take a cart there is if you have a letter from your doctor. Otherwise, you're walking.

If you get the opportunity to play with a caddie, be sure to follow some very simple tips:

- **Always take a caddie if one is available.** Some places require golfers to take a caddie if one is around, whereas others mandate caddie use at designated times. None of that should really matter. If the club has a caddie for you, take one.

- **Ask the caddie's name early on, preferably at the first tee.** And then introduce yourself as you want to be addressed during the round.

- **Let your caddie know whether you like to chat a lot or prefer to keep quiet when you play so that the caddie can act accordingly.** The good ones pick up on this preference right away. Others don't, though many of them are usually quite deferential and speak only when spoken to.

- **Let a caddie know whether you want him to read greens and provide yardage or whether you want do that yourself.** At your own club, you may generally prefer to read the greens and club yourself. When playing an unfamiliar course that has good caddies, however, you may choose to defer to them (unless, of course, their advice turns out to be lacking, at which point you should gently let them know that you'll take on those tasks yourself).

- **Help the caddie out.** If your caddie is carrying bags for you and another player, for example, and you have hit your drives on opposite sides of the fairway, take a couple of clubs from your bag to your ball and let your caddie take care of your partner. Your caddie shouldn't have to walk all over creation.

- **Treat your caddie with respect and consideration.** A caddie isn't your serf or lackey, so don't lord over him like he is. He's also not the person who hit that drive into the water or 3-putted on the last green. Don't abuse him or blame him for your errors.

- **Work with younger caddies.** These folks are out there in most cases because they're interested in golf and want to learn. Give them a hand by providing a little guidance and advice. If they do something wrong, don't berate them. Talk to them about their mistake the next time you're walking down the fairway together and let them know how they can correct it. They'll appreciate it, and so will the next golfers who take them.

- **Try to avoid taking out a club when the caddie still has your bag slung on his shoulder.** Wait until he has put your bag down before you grab your weapon.

- **Praise your caddie if he does a good job.** Give him some credit for a good read on the green or for having the right yardage.

- **Buy him a drink and a snack at the halfway point or if a beverage cart comes by.** He's working hard for you, usually in warm weather, and deserves a little something for the effort. Don't feel compelled to buy him a six-course meal, though.

- **Take a little time to get to know the person who is carrying your bag.** Ask some questions; be interested in who he is and what he does. That, quite simply, is good manners. He will appreciate the effort, and you'll likely enrich yourself by taking the time to get to know him.

Tipping Gracefully

Tipping can be a tricky business at times because so much is contingent on where you're playing and what the general rules are at the facility. At some municipal layouts, no one tips anyone, and if you did, you'd get laughed off the place. Then you find private clubs and high-end daily-fee courses where it seems like you're handing out greenbacks all day: to the kid who opens your car door and takes your bag when you arrive, to the guys who shine your shoes and clean your spikes in the locker room, and to everyone in between. Other places have strict prohibitions against tipping, and you never see any money changing hands between players and workers.

Your best bet is to find out what the accepted behavior is regarding gratuities at the track you're playing and follow that to the letter, especially if you're a guest at a private club. Ask your host, preferably beforehand, so you know what to expect (and whether you should put a lot of $1 bills in your money clip). If you find yourself at a club or resort still not knowing quite what to do, talk to the pro or one of his assistants. They should be able to set you straight without causing anyone any embarrassment.

When in doubt, follow these simple guidelines:

- ✔ **Tip the fellow taking care of your shoes in the locker room a couple of bucks.** Give him more if he does a bang-up job and sends you home with clean, polished golf shoes.

- ✔ **Tip your caddie if he does a good job.**

- ✔ **Don't worry about gratuities for anyone else.** For the most part, they're expecting — and expected — to be working on salary.

- ✔ **When you do tip people, do so as discreetly as possible.** Even if the practice is allowed, it's best not to make a spectacle of it.

Book IV

Rules and Etiquette

Chapter 3

Gamesmanship, Sportsmanship, and Special Golf Outings

*N*ot all the golf you play is going to be weekend rounds with your usual group, especially now that the game has become such a popular business, entertainment, and fundraising tool. Business and celebrity outings, as well as charity events and tournaments, are as big a part of golf these days as friendly matches. And knowing what to do — and what not to do — is important.

One inevitable part of golf is betting. To be sure, gambling can be a touchy subject. Golf, being the type of game that it is — easy to handicap, played at a leisurely pace — lends itself to betting. So you'll probably find yourself playing for money before long. At first the money isn't much — if you have any sense, that is. But money games can get out of hand if you're not careful.

Fortunately, this chapter covers the rules for gambling on the course and for handling other sportsmanship situations that golfers encounter. We also discuss many of the unspoken rules of playing with business associates — even your boss — as well as how to handle yourself when you play in a pro-am tournament.

You Bet: Gambling on Your Golf Match

Golfers typically come in two types: those who want an even match and those who want to give you an evil beating. We recommend playing with the first group, at least in your early days. Those folks won't take advantage of your inexperience. They want a good, close match, so they give you the shots you need to make a good showing. The winner is the one who plays his or her best that day. Nothing wrong with that, of course. If someone is going to win, someone has to lose, and sometimes that loser is you.

Unfortunately, the nice people we just described sometimes seem as rare as four-leaf clovers. That second group constitutes the majority of gambling golfers. They don't play for the sunshine, the exercise (unless getting in and out of a cart qualifies as exercise), or the relaxation. They play golf for one reason: to bet and win. The following sections guide you through the golf bets you may encounter and help you keep from getting a raw deal when the betting begins.

Never play for more than you can afford to lose. Keep the bets small when you're a new golfer learning the ropes. Golf is a great game to bet on, but if you lose so much money that it starts to hurt, the game's no fun. Be careful and bet at your own risk.

Knowing common bets and how to win them

Following are the most common types of golf bets and what you can do to increase your chances of winning:

✔ **Nassau:** This bet was named for New York's Nassau Country Club, where it's said to have originated. Players bet a certain amount on the front nine, the same on the back nine, and the same on their overall score. So if you play a $5 nassau and win every hole, you pocket $15. The tricky part comes when players *press,* conceding the bet and doubling it for the rest of the round. You can even find an *aloha press,* in which you press everything on the last hole. By pressing, you can lose the first 17 holes and still come out ahead by winning the 18th.

Even pros are familiar with nassaus. Lee Trevino, in his early days as one of golf's great hustlers, once said, "Pressure is $5 on the front nine, $5 on the back, and $5 for the 18 when you've got $2 in your pocket."

✔ **Skins:** Players bet a certain amount each hole — a *skin* — but if two tie, all tie, and the money is added to the pot for the next hole. If a foursome plays skins and no golfer beats the other three on any hole, you can wind up with five, six, or even more skins riding on a later hole. To win at skins, relax early in the round and focus on playing your best when the chips (well, skins) are down. And don't be afraid to take risks. Remember, you have to win the hole outright to claim the skin.

✔ **Wolf:** Golfers take turns being the wolf, who takes on everyone else in the group. For a set price at each hole, the wolf can either choose one of the others as his partner (before anyone tees off) or *go wolf* and try to win the hole himself. If a wolf partners up and his team wins, he and his partner split the money on that hole. If he goes wolf and wins, he gets it all for himself, but if he loses, he has to pay everyone else. In this game, you're smarter to partner up if you're a consistent player and to be the lone wolf if you're the type who can make a pressure putt.

✔ **Snake:** *Snake* is a fun side bet that makes putting more pressure-packed than ever. The first player who 3-putts a green gets a snake that sticks with him until somebody else 3-putts. If the snake is worth $5 and no one 3-putts for five holes, he owes each other player $25. To win snakes, remember that most players leave their first *lag putts* (long putts meant to end up close to the hole) short. Hit your lag putts hard enough to reach the hole, and you'll dodge more snakes.

✔ **Sixes:** *Sixes* are a *best-ball match* (where players partner up and take the best score) with a twist: Golfers switch teams every six holes. That means that a foursome features three different best-ball battles in an 18-hole round. In sixes, every member of the foursome plays six holes with every other member. Try to play the first six with your group's best golfer as your partner. That way, you can establish momentum — and relaxation — that can last all day.

✔ **Bingo Bango Bongo:** Three points are up for grabs on each hole. One goes to the first golfer on the green (bingo), one to the golfer closest to the hole after everybody's on the green (bango), and one to the first in the cup (bongo). If a point's worth $5, you can win $15 on a good hole. Or steal a bango on a bad hole by chipping your sixth shot close.

Many golfers add bets for *greenies* (anyone hitting the green in one shot wins a predetermined sum from everyone else) or *sandies* (ditto for anyone who gets from a bunker into the hole in two shots). Such wagers are called *junk,* but everyone agrees they're fun. You can add *barkies* — you win if you hit a tree and still make par or better on a hole — or even bets of your own invention. Years ago, an Arnold Palmer fan invented a bet to honor his hero's talent for saving par from under trees, behind snack bars, and so on; you win an *Arnie* if you make par on a hole without ever hitting the fairway.

If you think all those wagers make golf betting seem dizzying, you're not alone. We've seen scorecards so marked up with bets and presses that they looked like modernist paintings. Fortunately, modern technology can help. Apps such as GolfMoolah for the Apple iPhone keep track of all your bets and side bets — all you have to do is hit the ball.

Book IV

Rules and Etiquette

Betting games for practice facilities

Practice facilities have a series of betting games all their own; they're especially popular at municipal courses, where longer waits for tee times leave you with more time to kill. Here are some favorites:

✔ **Take Ho:** One player selects a target cup 30 feet or so away, and everyone putts to that hole from the same spot on the putting green. If someone sinks his putt, he wins two points from each of the other players (and the points can be worth any amount you want). The remaining players (or all of them if no one has sunk his ball) determine who's still farthest away. That player then has two options. He may try to sink his putt, and if he misses, he must pay two points to the remaining players. If he makes it, he loses nothing, and the game starts over at a new hole. Or he can simply pick up and pay one point to each of the other players. The game is great fun for those who have a little accountant in them because it requires a lot of bookkeeping.

✔ **Shoot-out:** Named after the tie-breaker system used in some soccer and hockey games, this game entails having players hit five shots each from a predetermined distance, usually 3 to 6 feet. Count the number of putts that go in, and whoever has the most wins. If things are still tied up after five, the game goes into sudden death, and the first one to go ahead is the victor. The game makes for a good time; it's also a good way to work on relaxing over those short putts.

✔ **Targets:** Each player hits to three imaginary range greens at various distances. The closest one to each one wins a point. Then comes the fourth leg of this game, the drive; the longest ball to land between two predetermined points wins that point. Run it for three cycles, and the person with the most points wins.

✔ **Sandies:** Working out of practice bunkers, hit five shots each to the pin on the adjoining green. Whoever has the most balls closest to the pin wins a point. Play as long as you have time (or until you've hit all the sand out of the bunker). *Note:* This sandies game is different from the sandies bet on the regular course. See the nearby section "Knowing common bets and how to win them" for info on that wager.

Negotiating strokes at the first tee

Common convention says that most golf bets are won on the first tee — the *arena of negotiation,* we call it. This spot is where golfers fight over and agree upon bets. The key to first-tee negotiations is determining the number of strokes you give or receive over the course of a round.

As a beginning golfer, you typically play with people whose handicaps are lower than yours, which essentially means they spot you some strokes to make the game a little more even. Say your handicap is 30 and your opponent's is 18. (Check out Chapter 1 of Book IV for more on handicapping.) That's 12 strokes to you, right?

How to spot a golf hustler

As a relatively new golfer, you're going to be a prime target for hustlers. They'll figure you're not talented or savvy enough to beat them. And they'll be right — at least until you've played a while. So avoid them. Here's what to look for:

- **Does he have a 2-iron in his bag?** If so, don't play him. Only good players can hit those things. (And in these days, when even expert players have traded long irons for hybrid clubs, you may wonder about anyone with a 3-iron, too.)

- **If a stranger wants to bet serious money, beware.** If you do make the bet, make it a straightforward nassau (see the "Knowing common bets and how to win them" section in this chapter for more on nassau bets). Don't get bamboozled with lots of side bets.

- **If he uses a ball that isn't new, say good-bye.** Bad players don't have old balls; they lose them too quickly.

- **As legendary teacher Harvey Penick used to say, "Beware of the golfer with a bad grip."** Why? Because he's found a way to make it work.

- **Another thing about the grip — look at your opponent's left hand.** If he has calluses, he's either played or practiced a lot. *Adios*.

- **If that left hand is less tan than the right, the same applies.** Anyone who's spent that much time wearing a golf glove has probably practiced more than you have.

Not if Mr. Cutthroat has his way. He's not interested in improving your win chances when money is on the line. He'll moan that his wife just left him. Or that he hasn't played in weeks because of his workload at the office, that his old football injury is acting up again, or that he's worried sick about the value of the euro. In any case, he'll try to cut your strokes down by at least three. That, he figures, is the edge he needs to beat you.

You have a couple of options here: You either (a) nod sympathetically or (b) spin more tall tales than he just did. What you do *not* do is give up even a single stroke. Not one. European economy aside, you don't owe him anything; do you think he'd help you if you were the one with the excuses?

If you find yourself in the position of giving strokes to a player with a higher handicap, never *net* the strokes so that you're playing with 0. For example, if your handicap is 12 and your opponent's is 18, netting gives you 0 strokes and your opponent 6. Take all your strokes because they're on the toughest holes.

Book IV

Rules and Etiquette

Choosing up sides

As with betting, picking partners for a round of golf can be as cutthroat or as casual as you like. If you're just playing for fun or for a few dollars, who your partners are doesn't really matter. If you play with the same people every time, everything pretty much evens out in the end, anyway.

But if things are a little more serious, you need to put some thought into your partners. Here are some rules to follow in "money" games:

✔ Look for a partner who always has a perma-tan and callused, leathery hands.

✔ You want your partner to have more than 37 tags hanging from his bag — preferably from Pebble Beach, PGA West, TPC Sawgrass, Harbour Town, and other famously difficult courses.

✔ If caddies treat him like royalty, take notice.

✔ Snag the guy who has used the same putter since he was 5 years old.

✔ If a guy tells you about his marital problems on the practice range, he's out!

Conceding putts: "That one's good"

The green is one place where a little tactical planning can pay dividends when you're playing for money. No one, from a first-time beginner to the most famous pro, likes short putts, especially when they mean something. That's why they're called *knee-knockers*. For this reason alone, you shouldn't be too generous in conceding short putts to your opponents. Always ask yourself whether you'd fancy hitting the same putt. If the answer is "no" or even "not really," say nothing and watch.

That's the hard-nosed approach. If you're playing a friendly round or you're with your boss, you can be a bit more generous. The conventional rule has long been that any putt *inside the leather* — that is, any putt closer than the length of the grip on your putter (or in some places, between the grip and the clubhead) to the hole is deemed to be unmissable and therefore a *gimme*. Such a policy is still applicable today, although those long putters some players use have pretty long grips, so watch out!

If, like Goldilocks, you don't like either of the extreme approaches in this section, you can consider the middle ground favored by the great Walter Hagen, the best match player of his day. In the 1920s, when the PGA Championship was a *match-play* event (in which each hole is a separate contest), "The Haig" won it four times in a row. So he had to know a thing or two about psychology. One of his ploys was to concede a few shortish putts early in the match. That way, two things happened: His opponent got used to being given putts and, perhaps more importantly, was deprived of the practice of knocking a few in. Then later in the round, old Walter wasn't so generous. The opponent would suddenly be faced with a knee-knocker, the sort of putt he hadn't hit all day.

I don't really recommend Walter's strategy. You can lose friends in a hurry if they miss that short one on the 17th. And your strategy may not work. *Remember:* A short putt missed on the 3rd green counts the same as one on the 17th or 18th.

Showing Off Your Match-Play Smarts

Stroke play has a simple premise: Score the best you can over 18 holes. Match play is equally simple: Win more holes than the other golfer. As you can probably guess, match play generally involves more strategy and thinking than stroke play. Here are some match-play tips:

- ✔ **Don't be too bold too soon.** Play conservatively on the first few holes to avoid making big numbers at the outset. Handing a couple of early holes to your opponent only hurts your confidence and boosts his.

- ✔ **Never lose your temper.** Nothing gives your opponent more heart than watching and listening as you blow a gasket.

- ✔ **Pay attention to where your opponent's ball is at all times.** Your opponent's situation dictates your tactics on any given shot. For example, if he's deep in the woods, you may want to play it safe.

- ✔ **Figure that your opponent will hole every putt he looks at.** Then you aren't disappointed if he does make one. And if he misses, you get a boost.

- ✔ **Observe and contradict your opponent's patterns.** Watch how fast he walks, for example. If he's slow, go fast; if he's fast, slow down. Anything to break his natural rhythm.

- ✔ **Try never to hit two bad shots in a row.** Easier said than done, of course! But trying to hit a great shot to make up for a bad one is tempting. Instead, try to follow up a clunker with a *decent* shot — you avoid more train wrecks (golf talk for disasters) that way. Sometimes mediocrity pays.

- ✔ **Never second-guess yourself.** If you're playing it safe, don't suddenly get aggressive halfway into your downswing. And if you're going for it, don't hold back. Even if you miss, you'll feel better because you tried!

- ✔ **Only concede a hole when the situation is hopeless.** Make your opponent win the hole instead of gift-wrapping it for him. The more shots he has to hit under pressure, the more likely he is to make a mistake.

Book IV

Rules and Etiquette

Being a grinder

Here's the exception that proves the rule: In the 1972 British Open at Muirfield, Lee Trevino and Tony Jacklin were tied standing on the 17th tee in the final round. Distracted by a spectator, Trevino hooked his drive on the par-5 into a deep bunker, while Jacklin drove perfectly. After splashing out only a few yards, Trevino then hooked his third shot into heavy rough to the left and short of the green. Jacklin hit his fairway wood into the perfect spot, about 50 yards from the hole.

At that point, Trevino gave up. He quit. He told Jacklin that the championship was all his and did everything but shake his hand right there.

Trevino's fourth shot flew right over the green halfway up a grass bank. Jacklin hit a so-so pitch to about 15 feet.

Barely glancing at the shot, Trevino then hit a lazy, give-up chip that rolled right into the cup for par! Jacklin then 3-putted for a 6. Trevino won.

We tell this story because it's so unusual — quitters never win! The moral: Never give up, as Lee did that day. Don't be a quitter, because anything can happen in this game. Be a *grinder* — that's what golfers call a player who gives his all on every single shot of every round.

Minding Your Manners When Golf is All Business

Golf is not only a game of fun and recreation but also, to many players, a critical business tool for building relationships with their customers and coworkers and developing deals. Think about it: The setting is comfortable and relaxed, and you have a captive audience with the person for a few hours, a scenario that's hard to duplicate any other way (well, any other legal way). And watching someone compete is a great way to gauge what kind of person and businessperson he or she is.

Golf outings have become a staple of doing business in the United States, but they don't necessarily attract the most stringent followers of golf rules and etiquette or always induce participants to adhere to those codes. In fact, business-related golf outings often have a bit of the Wild West in them, simply because not all the invitees know a lot about the game of golf. And the host may have a hard time doing anything when someone behaves badly — whether intentionally or not — because he's trying to schmooze the very people he has asked to the outing. Even Emily Post would admit that chastising someone for various breaches of rules or etiquette on the golf course isn't the best way to advance your entertainment goals.

The following bits of advice apply to all games of golf you may play, but they're especially important to those rounds that have a business bent.

Playing golf with your clients

If you play business golf, your most likely companions are going to be clients or people you want to have as clients. Follow the simple guidelines in the following sections, and you should increase your chances of nailing that big deal.

Go all out for your clients, even if doing so means a day of hell on the golf course. You invited them; now you should take care of them. And who knows, your fortitude may even work out for you in the long run.

Make sure your clients like golf before inviting them

You never want to put someone in the awkward position of doing something he or she doesn't really want to do. A quick inquiry can pay a lot of dividends here and should let you know whether golf is a good idea.

Inform your partners of the dress code and other rules

Letting your playing partners know what to expect helps put them at ease and ensures that everyone will be able to focus on the game and have a good time. Even if you know your clients have played golf before, don't assume they know the rules at the course where you're taking them. Some places, for example, don't allow men to wear shorts. Others insist that men don jackets — and sometimes ties — in the clubhouse. If that's the case, tell your clients that beforehand to avoid any chance of embarrassment or inappropriate attire.

Alert your guests to things like tipping policies (most clubs don't allow tipping, but the daily-fee facilities do) and whether soft spikes on golf shoes are mandatory (they usually are). Remember, these folks are your (potential) clients, and you want to take good care of them and make them as comfortable as possible.

Compliment your clients on their games

Even if he hasn't had that great a shot, offering a client a compliment can't hurt. You don't want to overdo it, but you can find genuine ways to praise even the ugliest drives or chips. "That'll play" usually works. If someone is putting, you may want to holler, "One time!" if his putt looks like it has any chance of falling into the hole. Doing so makes you sound supportive and into the game. Another innocuous but effective bit of encouragement is to ask with a certain amount of incredulity, "How did that stay out?" if a putt does just that.

Beauty is in the eye of the beholder, and if, as the beholder, you're trying to get — or keep — someone's business, your standards as to what truly constitutes a good shot are bound to go down. But hey, you have to do what you can.

Help your clients look for lost balls

Few things can be as frustrating as searching fruitlessly for a ball in the rough while the other members of the foursome are off chatting. If you don't lend a hand to a client who has just put his drive in the deep rough, what kind of a partner are you going to be if something goes wrong in a business deal?

Don't talk business every minute

The idea of a business round is to have fun and build a relationship. Oftentimes, a golf game is your first and best chance to get to know each other. Be patient and let things flow naturally from your game. Don't fret if you haven't cut the big deal by the end of the day. In reality, very few business sales are actually closed on the course, but an effective and efficient round can ensure that those sales happen shortly afterward.

We recommend that you don't even broach the subject of business until you're well into the first nine. And after that, do it sparingly. Every rule has exceptions, of course, including this one. Be aware of what your clients really want businesswise out of the round and follow their lead. If they seem to want to talk business with greater intensity and regularity and possibly wrap up some sort of agreement on the course, by all means, go for it.

Don't be a teacher

Nothing is worse than having some know-it-all start handing out midround playing tips. This presumption is both obnoxious and patronizing and shouldn't happen.

Be careful about making any unsolicited comment or reference to anyone's swing. Saying something like, "I'm amazed you can get so much distance with such a short backswing" only causes your guest to think about his backswing the next time he stands up to a drive. Maybe he tries to lengthen it, and invariably he hits the worst drive of the day at that very moment.

Walk whenever possible

In addition to having a general disdain for golf carts (except for those who have a medical excuse), we find them to be particularly unhealthy for business golf because they break up the foursome. If you're all walking, you can stride down the fairway together and split off into different twosomes any time you want. This strategy gives everyone a chance to be with each other. Carts inhibit good interaction between players. If you have two carts, the social aspect of the game is interrupted because you have two separate vehicles tooling down the paths.

Look the other way if your client breaks a rule here or there

Golf is a game governed very strictly and appropriately by rules, and following them whenever you play is important. But when you're playing with clients, you may need to overlook a few things — especially if you're playing with a good customer. We're not talking about actively cheating here (such as purposely misrecording scores); cheating is wrong, of course, and it sends the wrong message. Do you want potential business partners to see you as a corner-cutter or, worse, a dishonest person? Don't cheat even if no one else can possibly know. You'll know.

However, you may encounter a client who likes to use the so-called *foot wedge* to kick his ball out of the rough. Rather than call him out for his fancy footwork, you may need to let that little infraction slide to keep the mood light and make the sale.

Keep the jokes G-rated

Go easy when it comes to telling jokes. The golf course is a great place for classic storytelling and bawdy jokes. But when you're playing for business, be sure to stay away from any jokes that may offend people in your group. An offensive joke or story can easily ruin an otherwise good round, to say nothing of what it may do to the business relationship.

Don't go overboard with the booze

Drinking is another area of concern, and with good reason. Too many drinks before, during, or after a round can cause significant problems at the workplace. And it doesn't do your driving home any good either.

The best advice is to follow the lead of your client. Wait to see what he does, and then go from there. That doesn't mean you have to toss down one shot after another just because the potential client you really want is doing it. But if your client has a beer after a round, don't be afraid to have one yourself if you want to. If, however, your client sticks to plain old lemonade, hold off on the booze. You never know whether he's a teetotaler offended by any alcoholic consumption or perhaps has a drinking problem and is uncomfortable around drinkers. Plus, if you're the only one drinking, you may end up yapping too much after a drink or two and saying something you may regret later.

As the host, offer your guests a drink as a matter of courtesy. But don't push the booze on anyone, and don't make them feel uncomfortable if they do or don't partake.

Playing golf with your boss

The golf you play with the boss can be the diciest of rounds. You may be a little nervous, and your game may very well reflect that. The key here is to relax and try to enjoy yourself.

Book IV

Rules and Etiquette

What golf tells you about a person

In his best-selling book, *What They Don't Teach You at Harvard Business School* (Bantam), the late Mark McCormack, the founder and chairman of the enormously successful International Management Group (IMG) and the father of modern sports marketing, wrote about the insights he garnered about people on the golf course over the years. A former collegiate player who represented Arnold Palmer for years and counted Tiger Woods among his other clients, McCormack advised countless Fortune 500 chief executives on growing their companies through sports. McCormack often said that he could tell more about how someone was likely to react in a business situation from one round of golf than he could from a hundred hours of meetings.

One of McCormack's key markers was the *gimme* putt, a short and very makeable putt that one opponent concedes to another. Some people, he observed, refuse all gimmes and insist on putting everything in the hole and accurately recording their hole. McCormack's business translation: It's hard to do a favor for people like that. Other golfers don't even wait for the gimme offer from their opponent; they assume a putt is a gimme even when it's a good distance from the cup. The business translation here is that those folks won't ask for a favor either; they'll expect one. And then you have the people who half-try to sink the putt by sweeping at it with one hand. It's fine if it goes

in, and if it doesn't, well, they weren't really trying. According to McCormack, these people are hard to pin down in business, have a capacity for self-deception, tend to exaggerate, and may give you a rounded-off version of what they originally said.

Another way to peer into the mind of your business friend or foe is to ask the very simple question, "What did you shoot?" and see how he or she responds. In his book, McCormack told the story of a CEO he had played golf with several times who always gave the same answer whenever he'd had a bad round: "I had a 79." But that 79 included a few gimme putts that rimmed the hole and a couple of memory lapses in counting up strokes. And what intrigued McCormack most of all was that this person really believed he shot a 79. "This kind of individual makes me nervous in a business situation," McCormack wrote. "He has the capacity for creatively interpreting facts, then sticking to them until they become gospel."

The moral of these stories: Pay attention. Your golfing partner may actually be telling you quite a bit about himself or herself when the two of you play a business round, and what you gather may have a real impact on whether you want to end up working with that person. In addition, be careful about how you act. The person you're playing with may have also read McCormack's book, or this one, and may be watching just as closely.

When playing with your boss (or with anybody, really), you want to do your best. If you're just starting to play golf, you don't have to worry about beating the boss and feeling bad. He or she has probably played a lot longer than you have and just wants to get to know you on the course. The golf course is a great place to find out a person's true personality. The game leaves you psychologically naked in front of your peers. See the nearby sidebar "What golf tells you about a person."

Being competitive is okay, but not to the point at which you're embarrassing the person who signs your paychecks. Be subtle with your celebrations, fair with your rulings, humble with your successes, and reasonable with your behavior.

As your game develops and you become a better player, your boss may recognize your golf game as an asset to the company. Millions of dollars in business deals have been negotiated on the golf course.

Playing golf with your coworkers

If you're playing a round with your coworkers, follow the same general tips for playing with clients. The hope is that your coworkers are your friends, and the occasional round of golf should be a good way to solidify those relationships. If you don't know each other, golf can be a great way to break the ice and develop that friendship.

Be careful about engaging in office gossip with coworkers you don't know very well, and don't say anything that may offend them (and get you in trouble with others). And because you're playing with people from your office, you need to be on your best behavior, especially with folks you aren't that close to. You never know how some faux pas may affect you at work.

Surviving a Pro-Am

One tradition in pro golf is called a *pro-am* (short for *professional-amateur tournament*), where professional players partner with amateur golfers as teams (though some do include rounds that actually count for the pros). If you're armed with a sizable amount of cash (as little as $500 or more than $10,000, but often around $5,000), you can tee it up with Tiger Woods, Phil Mickelson, Karrie Webb, or Rory McIlroy and tell your friends for the next 300 business lunches how you enthralled these pros with your prowess on the course and your witty banter between shots.

Pro-ams provide one of the great thrills in sports because what other game allows amateurs to play with professionals? Ever hear of any of your friends shooting hoops with Michael Jordan or running pass patterns for Tom Brady? No, because that sort of thing doesn't happen in basketball, football, hockey, or baseball. But it does in golf, thanks largely to a handicap system that makes it possible for rank amateurs to play with tour stars.

Most pro-ams take place on Wednesday, the day before the professional tournament begins and a time when the folks on tour are mostly concerned with getting in a little practice. But some events, like the AT&T Pebble Beach

Book IV

Rules and Etiquette

National Pro-Am and the Bob Hope Chrysler Classic, last longer. Each team consists of four amateurs and a pro. Corporations pay handsomely for the opportunity to put their names on tournaments and entertain their clients. This setup is unique in sports, and it's the pros' duty to see that corporate clients have a good time and want to come back for more.

Since 1998, the *Saturday Series* has been a pro-am for the budget-minded. It pairs amateurs with pros who have *missed the cut* (failed to score well enough to continue) in the current week's PGA Tour event, on a course near that week's tour venue. Entry fees are often less than half than those at traditional pro-ams. To find out more about the Saturday Series, check out www.saturday series.com.

The following sections spell out tips for pros and amateurs alike — a few do's and don'ts of playing with a pro and a road map through the purgatory of the pro-am. We hope these guidelines help both you and your pro enjoy the day.

- **Know your skill level.** Make sure you're a good enough golfer and know enough about the game to play a decent round and not cause anyone any problems or embarrassment on the course. No one is asking for you to play at *scratch* (0-handicap). But you should at least have played enough to have a handicap, some tournament experience, and a good understanding of the rules and etiquette of the game before entering a pro-am. Otherwise, the experience simply won't be a pleasant one for all involved. (Flip to Chapters 1 and 2 of Book IV for details on getting a handicap and mastering etiquette, respectively.)

- **Get a caddie.** Having a *caddie* to carry your clubs is the only way to play the pro-am game. You can walk free of hindrance and have clubs handed to you clean and dry. If possible, get one of the tour caddies whose player isn't in the pro-am. For $50 to $100, you can hire someone who is used to being screamed at and blamed for the weather, the rate of inflation, and some of those hard-to-explain skin rashes.

  Mind you, the caddie can't help you choose clubs very well at first because he or she isn't familiar with your play. But as your round progresses, he or she catches on and helps you more and more. Your caddie can also regale you with bizarre caddying stories, or *looper legends.* These tales are worth the price of admission. You can find more information on working with caddies in Chapter 2 of Book IV.

- **Be ready to hit.** You need to be ready to swing even if it isn't your turn. Discuss with your partners the concept of *ready golf* before you tee off. This setup means forgetting who earned the right to tee up first from the last hole — if you're ready, hit the ball. Pro-am play can be hideously slow, and your pro really appreciates it if you keep things going.

- **Respect your pro.** Make sure that you, your caddies, and your partners don't move or talk when your pro is playing, and keep out of his way as he hits his shots. Show the pro the utmost respect out on the course.

Remember that this arena is where the pros make their livings, and even if it's a practice round, they're still trying to concentrate on things that can make the difference in winning or losing thousands of dollars of prize money.

✔ **Forget your cellphone.** Don't bring cellphones out to the golf course. They don't belong there, and neither do you if you can't get through a round without putting one to your ear. The only two exceptions we can think of are if you're a doctor on call and may have to respond to an emergency or if your wife is pregnant and about to have your child. Otherwise, leave the phones at home.

✔ **Get a yardage book.** A *yardage book* (a booklet showing distances from various landmarks on each hole that you often find for sale in the pro shop) can help you contribute to your pro's mental health by being the first "ammy" in the history of his pro-am career not to ask the question "How far have I got from here?"

✔ **Don't insist on holing out a doomed ball.** If you're up to seven or so strokes on a particular hole, pick up your ball instead of hacking away for several more strokes. And be sure to tell your pro that you've done so. Not only do you contribute to the pace of play by picking up, but you also avoid the awkward situation of having the pro wait, expecting you to hit. The general rule is, if you can't make better than a *net par* (the maximum score for the hole), put the ball in your pocket and move on, marking that maximum score on your card.

This tip doesn't contradict the earlier advice in this chapter telling you never to give up (see "Being a grinder"). You should *not* pick up your ball if you have any chance to help your team. But the moment that chance disappears, pocket that ball. In a pro-am, the only thing worse than waiting around for no apparent reason is waiting around for a very bad apparent reason — for example, somebody who's holing out for a 9.

✔ **Don't sweat your score or whether your pro sweats the score.** Don't be upset if your pro doesn't know how your team stands. It's a Wednesday. He probably doesn't even know his own score, and, quite honestly, after the 26th pro-am of the year, he may not remember what his gender is.

✔ **Watch your step.** Yes, you're wearing soft spikes and it shouldn't matter, but stepping on somebody's putting line, regardless of what's on the bottom of your soles, is an invitation to a hissy fit. Even soft spikes leave indentations in the green that can send a putt veering off-line. Be very, very mindful of the line of your pro's putt. Look at TV coverage of a golf tournament and see how respectful the pros are of each other's lines. Stepping on another pro's line is close to stepping on Old Glory.

Simply ask the pro where his line is, and he'll show you.

✔ **Don't coach the pro.** If you're still interested in playing in a pro-am ever again, do *not* give the pro any advice on how to play the course, even if you can wander it in the dark without bumping into anything.

The four best pro-ams

Almost every professional golf tournament has them, but our friends in the game say these are the pro-ams you really want to play:

- **AT&T Pebble Beach National Pro-Am:** The crème de la crème of this kind of golf outing, the AT&T Pebble Beach National Pro-Am, first gained its fame as Bing Crosby's Clambake, and the crooner's Hollywood buddies would all show up. Started in San Diego in 1937, the event moved to the Monterey Peninsula in 1953 and has been there ever since. Crosby's name hasn't been attached to it since 1985, but the tournament is still a must-play. Why? Its history, for one thing. Also, amateurs get at least three days of golf and play on some fabulous courses, including Pebble Beach. No event has such a flashy group of celebrities ("You're away, Mr. Costner"), and the parties are pretty good, too.

- **Bob Hope Chrysler Classic:** This great tournament features four days of golf on some of the best courses in the Palm Springs area. The Hope has history, beautiful weather in the winter, lots of parties, and a good complement of celebrities from both the sports and entertainment worlds. In addition, it always attracts a very strong field of touring pros at a time when they're fresh and the new season is just starting up.

- **Kraft Nabisco Championship:** One of the things that make this two-day, LPGA pro-am so good is that it's one of that tour's Grand Slam events. The best players in the world show up to compete at Mission Hills in Palm Springs, and that means good pairings for the amateurs. It also means plenty of topflight stargazing because celebrities flock to this event, not only to play but also to entertain. One year, for example, Celine Dion sang at the big pro-am dinner, and years ago, when the tournament bore singer Dinah Shore's name, she used to coax people like Frank Sinatra into stopping by for a song. The prizes are deluxe, the social events happening, and the desert setting first-rate. Plus, many amateurs say that players from the women's tour are better than their male counterparts at relating to weekend golfers and making sure they have a great time, so playing with them is an added bonus.

- **Hassan II Trophy:** This pro-am is easily the most exotic — and certainly one of the most exclusive in the world. Started by the late King Hassan II of Morocco in 1971 and staged on the superlative Red Course at the Royal Dar Es Salaam Golf Club in the capital city of Rabat, it attracts pros from both the American and European men's and women's tours and includes a couple of black-tie dinners and ten days of fun in the North African kingdom. Participants get to eat, drink, play, and travel with the pros; rub elbows with Moroccan royalty; and experience everything from the souks in Marrakech to the ancient Roman ruins at Volubilis. Locals feel that anyone who plays in the Hassan II Trophy is a guest of the King (now the late monarch's eldest son, Mohammed VI), and competitors are treated royally at every turn.

Let the pro's caddie advise him. Even giving the occasional line off the tee ("Aim for the church steeple") can be dangerous because you don't normally play from where the pro tees off.

✔ **Go easy on the autographs.** Don't badger your pro with dozens of photograph and autograph requests. You can ask for some (it's expected), but too many can get very, very tiresome. Pros sometimes talk about being *ammed out* (sick of playing with amateurs). Try not to be the one who does that to your guy. (And if you see one of your playing partners starting to get that way, tell him to back off as well.)

✔ **Relax and have fun.** Playing with someone who drives the ball 60 yards past you or never misses a green with his irons (while you miss every one) can be a bit intimidating. Don't worry; that's why they're pros. Just play your game and do what you can to help the team.

Pros are people like everyone else, and some are better at this pro-am game than others. Unfortunately, some players on the tour just can't let loose enough to have fun with their amateurs. It's "Hello" on the first tee, "Goodbye" on 18, a few "Nice shots" in between, and that's it. But the vast majority of the pros are extremely good at making their amateurs feel welcome. They tell jokes, dole out playing tips, give you high-fives, and help you read putts. The key is this: Treat your pro with consideration and respect, and the pro will likely do the same for you.

Book IV

Rules and Etiquette

Chapter 4

Fan Etiquette

. . . .

In This Chapter

▶ Deciding which events to attend

▶ Knowing how to act at golf tournaments

▶ Enjoying your day as a fan to the fullest

▶ Interacting with pro golfers

. . . .

Some golf-lovers spend years, even their whole lifetimes, without ever attending a live golf event. Of course, we can understand wanting to play the game rather than watch others play. And when you find yourself in a spectating mood, tuning in to a telecast can be easier than trekking to the event itself. But not every tournament is covered on television, and not all coverage is worth watching!

Seriously, every golfer and golf fan should try to see live competition at least once a year. It doesn't have to be a PGA Tour or LPGA event. It doesn't have to be a professional tournament of any kind. You can find exciting golf action in your neck of the woods if you know where to look.

Previous chapters in Book IV outline some basic rules of etiquette for golfers. But keep in mind that golf etiquette isn't limited to the players. There are also lots of do's and don'ts for the folks who watch tournaments in person, whether it's a Grand Slam event for one of the three major professional tours in the United States or a local amateur contest. And these events demand a more moderate kind of behavior than is generally found, say, in the stands of a professional baseball game, where blowing air horns and heckling athletes are an accepted part of the fun.

Searching for Live Golf

Where should you go to watch golf action live? The short answer: It doesn't matter. You can have a great day on the course and glean important information by witnessing golf at any level. Just pay close attention. You pick up more that way, and you can duck any dimpled missiles that may be headed your direction.

High school golf

It's fun, dramatic, and accessible. Your local high school team tees it up at a nearby public or country club course. If you go to watch, you're part of a very small gallery, along with a few parents and girl- or boyfriends, with no gallery ropes to keep you away from the action. You're close enough to see the terror and excitement in the players' eyes — and their appreciation if you clap politely after an excellent shot.

Ask at your home course to see whether local teams play there; the professional can tell you. You can also check the local school's website to see when and where the golf team plays or call the school and ask for the golf coach. Be sure to ask the coach whether you can come out and watch. He or she will probably be delighted to hear that you're interested. Explain that you're learning the game and ask whether you can learn from a certain player's swing (or whether you should avoid following a particular person because some youngsters get unnerved by spectators). Before you know it, you may be an honorary assistant coach!

College tournaments

Collegiate competition is a big step up from high school golf (see the preceding section). You may be surprised by how well (and how far) college players hit the ball. But don't just gape at the collegians' power. Study how precise they are around the greens. How _deliberate._ This meticulousness should drive home the crucial importance of the _short game_ (chipping, pitching, and putting; see Book III). With rare exceptions, the best players are the ones who chip and putt better than the others.

College websites generally post schedules for their men's and women's golf teams. At the course, pairings are posted in or near the clubhouse. Galleries aren't much larger than at high school matches, so don't sneeze at the wrong time! Pick a calm moment to introduce yourself to the coach (invariably a focused-looking person wearing a cap with the school logo). Praise one of his or her players, and you may make a new friend.

USGA events

Each year the United States Golf Association stages the prestigious U.S. Open, one of golf's four major championships (along with the Masters, British Open, and PGA Championship). The USGA also runs championships for women, seniors, amateurs, public-course players, and juniors. See www.USGA.org for details.

Galleries at these events are larger than at high school and college events, but except for such premier tournaments as the U.S. Open, the Women's Open, and the U.S. Amateur and Senior Opens, you can still get up close and personal with the golfers.

Here's a great chance to test your eye for the golf swing. What makes the typical player at a USGA event better than a good college golfer? Size, strength, power? Maybe. Maturity (that is, the ability to forget a bad bounce or bad hole and instantly refocus)? Probably. Consistency? Certainly! Consistency is the essential difference between good golfers and expert golfers. Watch closely, and you notice that competitors in USGA tournament play hit fewer bad shots than high school and college players, and the bad ones they hit don't miss by as much.

Professional tours

If you live in Florida or Southern California, you can see professionals try to make a living the hard way, by teeing it up on the Gateway Tour, Emerald Coast Tour, NGA Hooters Tour, and other *minitours*. Minitours offer limited schedules and don't pay much compared to the riches on the PGA Tour. Tour leaders often earn decent money, but most minitour golfers struggle to make expenses. That's why these circuits are also called *developmental tours;* the players are developing their games under intense pressure.

Farther up golf's ladder, you find the Nationwide Tour, where future stars hone their craft just one rung below the PGA Tour. Nationwide Tour pros can earn more than $100,000 for a victory, and each year the top 25 on the money list (led in 2011 by J.J. Killeen with $414,273) earn their *PGA Tour cards:* membership on the "big tour" for the following year. The women's version of the Nationwide Tour is the Duramed Futures Tour, led in 2011 by Kathleen Ekey's $66,412. Each year, the top ten Futures Tour players advance to the LPGA.

Book IV

Rules and Etiquette

Then you have the Champions Tour for players 50 and older. What can you discover from following graying veterans? Everything! These elder golfers still drive the ball farther than 99.9 percent of the golfing population, but more important, they know their limitations. Follow a group of senior pros and you see plenty of strategy: drives on the favorable side of the fairway and lay-up shots that stay out of trouble. (See Chapter 3 of Book VI for more on course management.)

The older golfers stage their share of thrilling finishes, though they may not celebrate them quite as vigorously as the young pros do. You can throw your back out that way! But as good as seniors are when they bring their A-games

(*A* for ageless), they're not the main event. That's the PGA Tour, which we cover in the following section.

The PGA Tour

The world's best golfers. The most beautiful courses. Golf's most dramatic moments. The PGA Tour can be expensive to watch — count on $100 a day for tickets, parking, and refreshments (kids 15 and under usually get in free with a paying adult) — but what you see is priceless. When the Tour with a capital *T* comes to a venue near you, you get to feast your eyes on the world's finest as they make a cruelly difficult game look easy. At least until the old game jumps up and bites them, of course. And then you get to enjoy the world's finest trouble shots!

Check out pgatour.com for the current year's schedule. (You can also find homepages for the Nationwide and Champions tours there.) Then pack up the car and get ready for a day you'll never forget. You may not get close enough to hear the players breathe at a PGA Tour event, but the level of play will leave you breathless at least once or twice.

Behaving Appropriately at Golf Tournaments

Nothing in sports is quite as enjoyable as attending a professional golf tournament, or even a tournament that pits top amateur players against each other. Doing so gives you the chance to observe the best players in the world up close and personal and see exactly how they're able to crush 300-yard drives and drain 30-foot putts. You can get so near the action that you can actually hear the golfers talk to their caddies, to each other, and even to their balls as they try to coax a bit more fade or draw from their shots. You can follow your favorite golfers around the course or watch them hit balls on the practice range or work on their strokes on the putting green. No other athletic pursuit gives you access like that in such an accessible and enjoyable fashion. So if you have the chance to attend a tournament, we have only one word for you: Go!

But if you do go, you have to understand that fans are expected to act in certain ways at golf tournaments so as not to disturb the competitors or the spectators around them. Unlike many sports, golf has a code of etiquette for spectators that you need to be aware of. And although the exact guidelines may vary from event to event, you'll never go wrong if you adhere to these simple edicts:

How they do it at Augusta

The people who run the Masters like to remind those who go there each April that a certain kind of behavior is expected at Augusta National. And they publish a message from the club's cofounder and its president in perpetuity, Bobby Jones, that was written in 1967 and sums up the way they feel about conduct on a golf course:

> "In golf, customs of etiquette and decorum are just as important as rules governing play. It is appropriate for spectators to applaud successful strokes in proportion to difficulty but excessive demonstrations

by a player or his partisans are not proper because of the possible effect upon other competitors.

> "Most distressing to those who love the game of golf is the applauding or cheering of misplays or misfortunes of a player. Such occurrences have been rare at the Masters, but we must eliminate them entirely if our patrons are to continue to merit their reputation as the most knowledgeable and considerate in the world."

How could anyone say it better?

✔ **Be quiet when players are addressing their balls and swinging their clubs.** And watch the noise even when they've completed their shots. Sounds carry easily on a golf course, especially if it's windy and the course is relatively treeless. What you say on one fairway may be heard quite clearly on another one 100 yards away. The group you're watching may have finished, but someone on the next hole may be getting ready to hit.

✔ **Don't move when a player is addressing or hitting a ball.** Always make sure to look around carefully before you do move so you know you won't disturb someone in the process. Movement can be terribly distracting to players, and they really appreciate fans who are extra careful about that issue.

✔ **Wait for all the players to finish hitting before you move.** This point is a very big problem these days with all the people following certain players, such as Tiger Woods, around the course. Spectators are sometimes inclined to leave the green or tee after Tiger has hit his shot instead of waiting for the other members of Tiger's group to play. Give every golfer the same respect, and make sure he doesn't have to hit his next shot while you and dozens of other spectators are fleeing to another spot.

✔ **Don't run around a golf course.** That's a big no-no at Augusta National and other venues. You're not trying to evacuate from a fire, so move at an orderly pace, even if the skies open up and a downpour ensues.

✔ **Leave your cellphone and camera at home.** Cellphones are a general nuisance, and they're prohibited at most golf events, with good reason. They beep in the middle of backswings and just before clutch putts. And nothing is more obnoxious than listening to some self-important jerk

Book IV

Rules and Etiquette

bark at an underling on the phone while you and others are trying to figure out how Nick Price is going to hit a certain shot. Our view on cell-phones is quite simple: If you absolutely can't be without yours for a few hours or are simply too busy to be gone from work for so long, attending a golf tournament isn't for you.

✔ **Don't, under any circumstances, holler "You da man!" after someone has hit his drive.**

In general, the behavior of golf fans is far and away better than that of spectators of most other sports. But the game has recently been undergoing some dramatic changes in that regard, in large part because of a great influx of new fans. Their emergence is part of what is called the *Tiger factor,* and it has mostly benefited golf. Attendance of PGA Tour events, for example, has never been higher, and more people than ever before seem to be interested in the game. The problem is that many of the newcomers don't know or understand the nuances of the game, even as it relates to being a spectator; they're more accustomed to sports where rowdiness is a crowd virtue. Sadly, that lack of knowledge has led to some unfortunate incidents, so make sure you have the right spectator mindset before you head out to the course.

Making the Most of Tour Spectating

Before you make plans to spend a great day at the course in the festive atmosphere that attends any Tour stop, decide what you want to get out of your day. Do you want to find out more about the game? Do you want to get close to the players? Or do you want to feel the unfolding drama of a top-tier sporting event? In this section, we give you some pointers to enhance your experience.

Deciding what day (or days) to attend the event

If you've watched a Tour event on television, you've likely seen the weekend play. However, a lot of action goes on before the national broadcasts, and the early practice and play rounds are open to the public for viewing.

If you're after a learning experience, take in a Tuesday practice round. You save on your ticket and avoid the big weekend crowds. You can also take your camcorder on practice days — a definite no-no during tournament rounds. Go to the range, watch players warm up, and get a feel for how focused and disciplined they are. To see even tighter focus, stop by the practice putting green. Watch for a putting drill or two that you may want to try yourself.

The best-behaved crowd

You find the best behaved crowds at Augusta National. For one thing, many of those attending the Masters have been going to golf tournaments for years, so they know the game and they know the ways they're supposed to act around it. It's a very traditional golf crowd.

Secondly, other fans at Augusta exert a great deal of peer pressure to behave well because minding your manners is extremely important to so many who attend the event. If you break into a run between holes or pull out a cellphone, you get severe stares and sometimes even an admonishment from other fans.

Finally, the people who run the tournament are very clear that they take golf course behavior seriously. Spectators lose their badges (tickets) if they act badly, and the powers at Augusta aren't the least bit shy about enforcing the rules. That, perhaps, is the greatest deterrent because people know that if they step the least bit out of line, they'll lose what is considered one of the toughest tickets in sports. But it's also one of the things that makes the Masters a lot of fun to attend. The crowds there are always good.

On the course, film a few swings. When you get home, compare your own swing to the pros' swings. Not to make you feel inadequate, but to see where you can improve!

Wednesdays are *pro-am* days, when the pros team up with amateurs, and are generally best avoided. Play often slows to a crawl, and the pros are itchy for the next day's action to start.

After the tournament begins, Thursdays and Fridays offer better views because the crowds are smaller. You can also be sure to see your favorite player (assuming he entered the tournament) because the cut isn't made until the first two rounds are complete. The *cut* removes about half the players from the tournament after two rounds of play. They're considered too far behind to contend on the weekend, and they earn $0 for their efforts that week. Players who make the cut get a paycheck; those who don't, don't.

For those who survive the cut, Saturday is often called *moving day* because a good round can move them into position to win on Sunday. If you don't mind the bigger crowds, Saturday can be a great choice. You can follow your favorites in the flesh and then see them on TV the next day.

Whatever day you choose, be sure to spend some time watching the top 20-somethings: young stars such as Rickie Fowler, Dustin Johnson, and Rory McIlroy. They're fearless!

Books like this one can advise you all day about the importance of strategy and caution on the course. Never forget it! But sometimes seeing these youngsters going full-throttle, firing at flags, and playing like their hair is on fire is good. They prove that even at the highest level, golf's supposed to be fun!

Book IV

Rules and Etiquette

Eight ways to max out your day at a PGA Tour event

You'd be surprised how many spectators — particularly rookie spectators — are unprepared for their sojourn at a Tour venue. Take these tips, and you can be a superfan.

✔ Don't leave home without sunscreen, a hat, a portable chair, and binoculars.

✔ If you want to work inside the ropes, contact the tournament committee and offer to volunteer. The best volunteer jobs are walking scorer (keeping track of players' scores) and standard-bearer (carrying the sign that shows the scores). Either way, you're almost as close to the pros as their caddies are.

✔ Spend some time at the practice range, watching good swings.

✔ The best day for autographs is Wednesday, during the pro-am, when the pros sign between holes. Remember to bring your own pen! Check out this chapter's "Actively seeking autographs" for more on scoring signatures.

✔ Arrive early on tournament days (usually Thursday through Sunday). Pick up a map of the course (you can usually find one on the pairing sheets you get free at the gate, as well as in souvenir programs). Choose a spot that's sure to see plenty of action, like a green guarded by water, and set up your portable chair right behind the gallery rope.

✔ Most tournaments offer XM PGA Tour radios for rent; they're a must for keeping track of what's going on.

✔ If you choose to walk along with a particular group, stay one shot ahead of the players; that way you can see their shots land.

✔ Be a proud host: Wear something that represents your city or local team.

Knowing how to interact with players

Professional golfers love their jobs, and who makes pro golf possible? That's right: golf fans! Most professionals recognize this crucial truth, and they try their best to be courteous to the thousands of gallery members they meet in the course of their jobs.

Want to have a great moment with a tour pro? It's as easy as one, two, three:

1. **Choose your moment.**

   Between holes during a Tuesday practice round can be a good time to say hello. Another is in the designated Autograph Area, which is usually behind the 18th green, after a tournament round. Players expect to meet fans and sign autographs at these times and places. Read the following section for more on the sport of getting golf autographs.

2. **Remember your manners.**

You wouldn't shout "You da cop!" at a police officer, would you? You wouldn't demand a movie star's autograph, shoving a cap or program at her face. Fortunately, most golf fans would never do that stuff, either, but a few bad apples can spoil a great day for players and fans alike. Ask nicely, and you'll probably get that autograph you want.

3. **Make a connection.**

It's easy. All you have to do is say something the pro hasn't already heard 100 times. Maybe you saw him or her pull off a great shot: "That was a beauty from the rough at 16." Maybe you read about him online or in the newspaper: "I hope your wrist is feeling better." Or maybe you just want to share the moment: "I like the way you play and just want to shake your hand."

What do pro golfers *really* think of the fans — at least the polite fans who approach them the right way? They think of them as friends.

Actively seeking autographs

Autograph-hunting has long been a part of the tournament golf scene, and a lot of spectators like to clamor for the signatures of their favorite players. That's fine, with plenty of caveats.

Be considerate, not demanding, when you ask a golfer for his or her autograph. "Players are usually more than happy to oblige," says a longtime tournament director from one of the professional tours. Provide a pen and an item that you'll hang onto for years; players don't like signing items that a fan may sell online for personal profit. And remember to say thank you, too.

After you decide you want to get your favorite player's autograph, you need to find out when and where you can ask for it. At many tournaments, such as the Masters, spectators aren't allowed to ask for autographs on the course, and players aren't allowed to give them there. Instead, special places are set up for just such an exchange, usually off by the locker room or practice area. (At the Masters, it's on the parking lot side of the clubhouse, near the range.) Find out the policy of the place you're visiting and adhere to it.

As for *when,* the tournament director thinks the practice days (Tuesday and Wednesday) are best because players are most relaxed then (though homing in on the player during the pro-am, when he is supposed to be entertaining his amateurs, may not be ideal). During the actual event, wait until the players have putted out on 18 and are walking off the course, assuming, of course, that this approach fits in with tournament guidelines. Remember that

Book IV

Rules and Etiquette

the golf course is where the players do their work, and to compete on any of the professional tours is an enormous accomplishment that requires the utmost concentration. One or two strokes can make the difference between a big payday and nothing. So wait until the players have punched their clock before hitting them up for their autographs.

Be aware of what the pros you're approaching have shot. "It is not a good idea to go up to some guys right after they have posted a 78," the tournament director says. "They usually don't want to be bothered by anyone at that point, and you can understand that. As for the guy who just shot 66, he'll usually sign for an hour."

Finally, be careful about jabbing your pens and markers at the pros you want to have sign your items. Too many times, the players feel that they're about to be skewered like a piece of meat for a shish kabob when they see those things being shoved at them. Many have taken to wearing dark shirts when they know they're going to be besieged so that the ink that invariably ends up on their shirts isn't quite so noticeable.

Avoiding fan faux pas

Interfering with a ball in play is a capital crime at any tournament. (But we know you'd never do that.) Getting struck by one is just a pain. Sometimes, especially at PGA Tour events where fans are packed like toothpicks along fairways and around greens, a shot gets away and a fan gets plunked.

This incident can leave the fan with a bump or bruise, as well as a few potential benefits, such as a moment on national TV, a handshake from the embarrassed pro who hit the ball, and an autographed cap and ball from said pro.

Just remember: The pros are playing for their livelihoods out there. Don't ask the Tour player whose ball hit you — or the one you spot in the parking lot or near the practice green — to shake hands with all your buddies and wave to your cousins watching at home.

A few more reminders:

- ✔ **Don't ask for autographs before or during a tournament round.** See "Actively seeking autographs" for more on this topic.

- ✔ **Don't try to sneak a cellphone through the gate.** You'll get caught and either lectured or kicked out.

- ✔ **Don't get dehydrated.** Following the pros can entail miles of walking in heat and blazing sun. Drink plenty of water!

Book V
Hitting the Course

The 5th Wave   By Rich Tennant

Okay, that's one way to address the ball. Now, let's try it again without the postage meter.

In this book . . .

Book V takes you through the steps of getting on the course, from warming up the right way to keeping your head in the game when the going gets tough. In this book, we show you techniques for warming up your body and your swing. You may also need some help with teeing off, and this book outlines helpful first-tee tactics as well as guidelines for coping with the pressures of the mental game.

Even though practice isn't likely to make you play a perfect game of golf, it is a golfer's best friend. In this book, we also offer tips and ways to make a game out of the chore of practicing. Plus, Chapter 4 tells you how to step your game up from the beginner's level to something even better.

Here are the contents of Book V at a glance.

Chapter 1

Step Right Up: Prepare to Play!

*Y*ou know the basics of the game. You've got the right equipment, you know your way around different sorts of courses, and you've developed a swing that suits your body and soul. At this point, you could possibly hit a terrific bunker shot from a bad lie during a tornado! But the idea of actually getting out on the course may give you a case of nerves. Relax; this chapter covers a few more steps that will make your feel like a pro.

Like a good warm-up, for instance. Baseball pitchers get an opportunity to throw warm-up pitches before each inning, and basketball players always have a shoot-around before tip-off. The same needs and opportunities exist in golf. Just as a symphony orchestra before a performance, you need a little time before every golf round to sharpen your touch and tune your instrument, and we show you how to do so in this chapter.

Limbering Up Before You Play

Before you hit the driving range, practice green, or course, you need to stretch your golf muscles. In the following sections, we cover a number of warm-up exercises for each of the muscles you use throughout your golf practice or round. If you devote at least five minutes to warming up without even hitting a ball, you'll be ready to start swinging. You can knock out all these warm-ups in five minutes.

Never confuse practice with warming up. Practicing golf and getting ready to play a round of golf are two decidedly different activities. Practice is what it is: practicing specific areas of your game to increase your skill and technique. Head to Chapter 3 of Book V for all you need to know about practicing.

Loosening the legs

Your legs (including your ankles and feet) are very important to your golf swing. Your legs give you foundation, balance, and power. Before you walk over to the practice tee or green, stretch your hamstrings, which are the most powerful muscles in your legs and the ones most featured in the swing.

Simply put your heel on the back of the cart and slowly lean forward to grab your toe (or as close as possible) with the opposite hand, keeping your leg straight (see Figure 1-1). You should feel your hamstring on the back of your leg stretching. Hold still when you grab your toe, count to five, and repeat a few times with both legs. Of course, if you're walking (and we hope you are), you don't have a golf cart; in that case, a bench or raised landscaped area like a flower box does the trick. Bonus: This exercise also stretches your ankles.

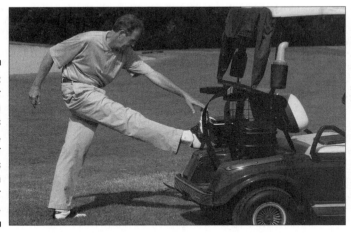

Figure 1-1: Using your cart or a bench as a spotter, reach for your toes to stretch out your hamstrings.

Working the upper arms and shoulders

You also need to stretch the muscles in your shoulders and upper arms, including your rotator cuffs. Stretching out your shoulders and your arms is easy, but you should perform the stretch deliberately and with patience and care.

First, take a club (or two) — a wedge works nicely — and hold it in one hand by the grip. Using a club gives this activity some weight for resistance. Now work those rotator cuffs:

1. **With your off-hand at your side, gently begin to swing the arm holding the club forward and back alongside your body without bending your elbow.**

2. **When you're comfortable, swing your arm forward, keeping it relatively straight, all the way above your head and back behind you, making a large circle (see Figure 1-2).**

   You may find it difficult to go backward and around, so try going forward and around.

3. **Stretch with each arm until your shoulders feel loose.**

Figure 1-2:
Make a circle with a club to stretch out your rotator cuffs.

The next exercise stretches your shoulders and your back. Take out the shortest club in your bag — your putter or sand wedge — and follow these steps:

1. **Point the grip end of the club into the palm of one of your out-stretched hands and the blade of the club into your other palm, with your arms extended straight out in front of you.**

The shaft of the club should be at arms' length in front of you, parallel to the ground.

2. **Keeping opposing pressure to hold the club in place, bring your left arm up and over your right until your arms are crossed and you feel pressure on your shoulders and back, as shown in Figure 1-3.**

   Hold the position for five to ten seconds.

3. **Perform the same movement in a counterclockwise fashion.**

   Again, hold the position for five to ten seconds.

4. **Repeat Steps 2 and 3 a few more times.**

Figure 1-3:
Rotate your arms in front of you, using the pressure of a golf club to stretch your shoulders and back.

Don't feel ready yet? Here's another shoulder, arm, and back stretch:

1. **Hold your shortest club between your palms at arms' length in front of your body, applying pressure on the ends of the grip and blade.**

2. **Keeping your left arm firm and straight, with a little resistance, push the club with your right hand toward the left side of your body, rotating the back of your shoulder blades, as shown in Figure 1-4.**

   This activity stretches out your biceps and shoulders. Hold the finish for five to ten seconds.

3. Do this pushing exercise a few times in both directions.

Figure 1-4:
Push one of your arms away from your body with your shortest club to apply pressure to the shoulders and biceps.

Finally, if you don't like any of the preceding warm-ups, or you just want to make sure you're really loose, try this stretch for your arms, shoulders, and back:

Holding a club by the head, place the grip end in your armpit so the shaft runs the length of your arm (use a club that's the same length as your arm for this one, as shown in Figure 1-5). This action stretches your arm and shoulders. Now bend forward until your arm is horizontal. The forward movement stretches your lower back, one of the most important areas in your body when it comes to playing golf (see the following section). Hold this position for a few seconds and then switch arms; repeat this stretch until you feel loose enough to swing.

Stretching out your back and torso

Your back needs to be loose for the twisting that the proper golf swing requires. If your back is stiff, you have a hard time making a full turn on the backswing. In the preceding section, we give you some stretches that work your shoulders and back. This section covers an exercise that focuses on the back and torso. Grab a longer club (your driver or 3-iron; see Figure 1-6) and follow along:

Holding the club like this, bend forward.

Then switch arms and do it again.

Figure 1-5:
Stretch
before you
swing.

1. **Put the club behind your back and across your body and thread it through the crooks of your bent elbows (see Figure 1-6a).**

2. **Assume your golf stance as if you're standing over the ball.**

   Keep some flex in your knees, with a straight spine and your butt stuck a bit out.

3. **Mimic your backswing with your upper body by making a level turn back; hold this position.**

   Feel that motion and that weight on your back hip. Your belt buckle should point directly to your right (for righties), as shown in Figure 1-6a. Hold the position for ten seconds or so.

4. **Turn back the other way, up off your back side and onto your front, into your follow-through as you normally finish your swing.**

   Hold that position for about ten seconds.

5. **Repeat the exercise slowly, holding at both ends.**

You can also slide the club up behind your shoulders, grasping each end, as shown in Figure 1-6b. Repeat the swing motions, again holding the position for ten seconds or so at the end of the backswing and your finish.

Figure 1-6: Mimic your normal swing to stretch the back and torso.

Another method of loosening up is more traditional. Instead of practicing your swing with one club in your hands, double the load by swinging two clubs (see Figure 1-7). Go slowly, trying to make as full a back-and-through swing as you can. The extra weight soon stretches away any tightness.

Swing two clubs back...

and through.

Figure 1-7: Double up for a smooth practice swing.

Readying your wrists and forearms

Your wrists and forearms play a key role in the golf swing — especially in the short game — so you shouldn't overlook them in favor of the larger muscles. Here's a quick stretch: Hold your right arm straight out in front of you and arch your palm outward as if you're signaling someone to "stop!" (See Figure 1-8.) With your left hand, reach over and grab the tips of your fingers, pulling them back toward you. This move stretches your wrist, and you should feel a stretch of the muscles in your forearm. Hold it for five to ten seconds, release, and pull again. Do this exercise with both hands.

Figure 1-8:
Make a stop sign with your hand and pull back your fingers to stretch the wrist and forearm muscles.

Preparing before a Round

Getting ready to play a round involves preparing yourself mentally and physically (starting with the stretches earlier in the chapter). Give yourself at least 40 minutes before your tee time if you can. Arrive at the golf course with plenty of time to unload your clubs, change your shoes, pay your fees, greet your fellow players, and warm up.

Keep in mind that you don't want to do anything that could negatively impact your mood or psyche, such as trying to fix a problem club at the last minute. And don't head to the practice range and say, "I can't hook a 5-iron. I want to try to figure out how to hook a 5-iron because not being able to is bugging the heck out of me," and then keep hitting 5-iron after 5-iron to try to work the problem out. Doing that before a round sends you to the first tee frustrated and unprepared.

In the sections that follow, we provide a perfect pregame preparation for a round of golf and some suggestions for an abbreviated routine if you don't have the time for a full warm-up.

Warming up your swing

Go to any pro tournament, and you'll see that most players show up on the practice range about an hour before they're due to tee off. Showing up early leaves them time to tune their swings and strokes before the action starts for real.

Although some players like to schedule about an hour for preround practice, half that time is probably enough. You really need to hit only enough balls to build a feel and a rhythm for the upcoming round. Don't make any last-minute changes to your swing.

Before you hit a ball, do five minutes of the full stretching exercises we describe in the earlier section "Limbering Up Before You Play." Start your warm-up by hitting a few short wedge shots. Don't go straight to your driver and start blasting away. That's asking for trouble. You can easily pull a muscle if you swing too hard too soon. Plus, you probably aren't going to immediately hit long, straight drives if you don't warm up first. More than likely, you'll hit short, crooked shots. And those are hazardous to the golfer's mental health.

The following steps and Figure 1-9 lead you through a good swing warm-up. ***Remember:*** You're just warming up. Focus on rhythm and timing — not on the ball.

Before each round, hit a few wedge shots...

and then a few 6-irons...

Figure 1-9:
A sensible
warm-up.

and then a few drivers...

and finish up with a few long putts.

1. **Start with the wedge.**

   Focus on making solid contact. Nothing else. Try to turn your shoulders a little more with each shot. Hit about 20 balls without worrying about where they're going. Just swing smoothly.

2. **Move to your midirons.**

   Try to hit your 6-iron at this point. You're just about warmed up, and the 6-iron has just enough loft that you don't have to work too hard to get the ball flying forward. Again, hit about 20 balls.

3. **Hit the driver.**

   Now you're warmed up enough for the big stick. We recommend that you hit no more than a dozen drives. Getting carried away with this club is easy, and when you go overboard, your swing can get a little quick. Don't worry if you hit a few bad ones. Concentrate on what you want to do and focus.

4. **Before you leave the range, hit a few more balls with your wedge.**

   You're not looking for distance with this club, only smoothness. That's a good thought to leave with.

5. **Finally, spend about ten minutes on the practice putting green.**

   You can break your green time down into three main parts:

   A. Hit a few putts and get a feel for the speed of the green. Focus on rolling the ball, staying quiet and relaxed, and not worrying about the outcome. Do this activity for five minutes, and after you're comfortable, hit six or seven two-foot putts in a row into the hole. Stroke them nicely into the hole without even thinking about it. Get accustomed to the sound of the balls landing in the bottom of the cup. Get your confidence.

   B. Hit a few 10-foot putts. Get a good read with a couple of balls and really concentrate on trying to make them. Take the balls to the other side of the hole and give yourself a different break and green speed. Focus on pace rather than direction.

   C. After you have a feel for the green, you may want to pull out your favorite chipping club, whether you prefer a 7- or 9-iron or one of your wedges, and hit some chip shots from off the green for five minutes. Hit the shots to different parts of the green with the same relaxed, quiet attitude you had when you hit your putts. Get a feel for the blade making contact with the ball and the speed of the green. Chapter 4 of Book III can show you how to hit effective chip shots.

   Now, go to the tee — you're ready to roll! You should be on the tee five minutes before your time.

Warming up under the gun

If you come running to the golf course late and you have to race to the tee, you need to change your strategy to find a way to prepare yourself. How can you best use the ten minutes you have left?

If you're running late, take the few minutes to just slow down. Stop and relax. Forget about hitting any balls. Depending on your time situation, practice the following exercises:

  ✔ **If you have ten minutes:** Take five of the minutes to stretch and get loose (see the section "Limbering Up Before You Play" earlier in this chapter). Warm up right next to the putting green so you can take your putter and calmly hit a few ten-foot putts after you finish. Follow those with a series of two-footers. Stretching and putting help you get loose and calm down, which is far better than racing out to the range not fully stretched because you have to hit balls.

  ✔ **If you have five minutes:** If you're really running late, just work on the stretching exercises. Forget the putting. The key is to get rid of as much of the real-life baggage — stress, frustration, and anger — as you can.

If you're running late to the first tee, don't hit your driver (the club or the car-pool leader who made you late). Hit something comfortable that you don't feel you have to overpower. Don't be concerned about anything but making a nice, soft swing and getting the ball safely in play. Your body will warm up and get loose as you move along.

Trying Out First-Tee Tactics

The best players start each round with a plan for how they'll play the course. They know which holes they can attack and which holes are best to play safely. So should you.

Many people say golf is 90 percent mental. You're wise to take that statement to heart. The fewer mental errors you make, the lower your score is. And the great thing about bad thinking is that everyone at every level of play can work on eliminating it. (Chapter 2 of Book V goes into more depth on this topic.)

Think of golf as a game of chess. You have to plan two or three moves in advance. Over every shot, you should be thinking, "Where do I need to put this ball in order to make my next shot as easy as possible?"

You can find yourself in countless situations on the course. It's too many to cover in one book, and you don't need all that information yet. So what follows is a brief overview of tactical golf. We've selected three common situations; you'll come across each one at least once in almost every round you play. You can apply your approach for each one to many other problems that you encounter. So don't get too wrapped up in the specifics of each scenario — think big picture.

Tactic 1: Don't be a sucker

You're playing the 170-yard par-3 hole in Figure 1-10. As you can see, the hole is cut toward the left side of the green, behind a large bunker. If your first inclination is to fire straight at the flag, think again. Ask yourself

1. What are my chances of pulling off such a difficult shot?

2. What happens if I miss?

3. Is the shot too risky?

If the answers are 1. Less than 50 percent; 2. I may take 5 to get down from the bunker; or 3. Yes, you want to play toward the safe part of the green (shown by the solid line in Figure 1-10). Only if you happen to be an exceptional bunker player should you go for the flag (using the dotted path in Figure 1-10).

Think of it this way: Golf is a game of numbers. If you shoot at the pin here, you bring the number *2* into play: If you hit a great shot, you have a great opportunity for a deuce. That's the upside. The downside is that missing the green makes the numbers *5, 6,* and maybe even *7* possibilities, especially if you aren't too strong from sand or if you're unlucky enough to get a really bad lie. You want to eliminate your chances of making anything worse than a bogey.

If, on the other hand, you play for the middle of the green, your range of likely results is narrower. Say you hit the putting surface with your first shot. In all likelihood, the most you'll take for the hole is 4, and that's only if you 3-putt. You'll get a lot of 3s from that position, and once in a while you'll hole the long putt — so a 2 isn't impossible.

Even if you miss the green on that side, you'll probably be left with a relatively simple chip or pitch. So unless you mess up terribly, 4 is again your worst score for the hole. Those numbers are better, right?

You should follow this policy more often than not. If you decide to be a middle-of-the-green shooter, practice your long-putting a lot. You're going to have a lot of 30- to 40-foot putts, so be ready for them.

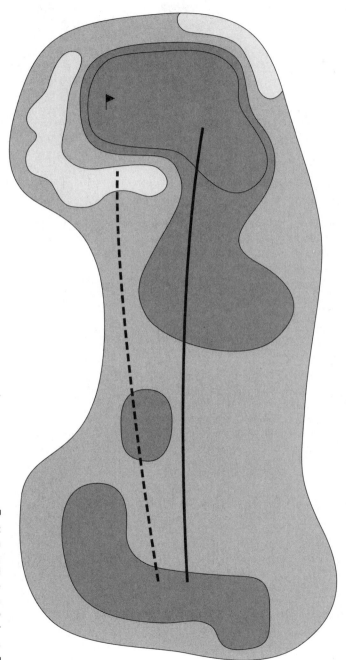

Figure 1-10:
Don't aim
for the flag
(dotted
line); the
safer path
(solid line)
is farther
right.

Tactic 2: Think before you drive

You're on the par-4 hole of just more than 400 yards shown in Figure 1-11. But the actual yardage isn't that important. All you have to do is pay attention to the layout of the hole and plan accordingly. The key to this hole is the narrowing of the fairway at the point where your drive is most likely to finish. When this situation comes up, tee off with your 3-wood, 5-wood, or whatever club you can hit safely into the wide part of the fairway. Even if you can't quite reach the green in two shots, that's the best strategy. Like in the preceding section, it's a question of numbers. If you risk hitting your driver and miss the fairway, you'll probably waste at least one shot getting the ball back into play — maybe more than one if you get a bad lie. Then you *still* have a longish shot to the green.

Now follow a better scenario: You hit your 3-wood from the tee safely down the fairway. Then you hit your 5-wood, leaving the ball about 25 yards from the green. All you have left is a simple chip or pitch. Most times, you'll make no more than 5 on the hole. Indeed, you'll nearly always have a putt for a 4. Most golfers don't follow this path, but it makes sense, doesn't it?

Tactic 3: It's easy as one, two, three

This par-5 hole is long, just more than 500 yards (see Figure 1-12). Your first inclination is again to reach for your driver. Most of the time, that's probably the correct play, but not always. Look at the hole: You can break it down into three relatively easy shots with a single club! Say you hit your 4-iron 170 yards. Three of those 4-irons can put you on the green. To us, that's easier for the beginning player than trying to squeeze every possible yard out of the driver and getting into trouble. (***Disclaimer:*** We know some of you won't consider this strategy. You'd rather flail away. But flailing often leads to failing.)

No law says that you must use your driver from the tee. If you don't feel comfortable with your driver, go with your 3-wood. If your 3-wood doesn't feel right, go to the 5-wood. And if you still aren't happy, try your 3-iron or a hybrid club. Don't swing until you're confident that you can hit the ball into the fairway with the club that's in your hands. Most golfers would rather be 200 yards from the tee and in the fairway than 250 yards out in the rough.

Being in a spot where you can hit the ball cleanly is better than being in a tough spot, even if the clean shot is longer. If you don't believe us, try this test. Every time you miss a fairway from the tee, pick up your ball and drop it 15 yards farther back but in the middle of the fairway. Then play from there. Bet you shoot anywhere from five to ten shots fewer than normal for 18 holes.

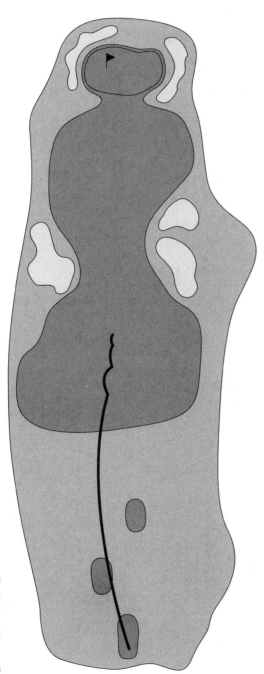

Figure 1-11:
Safety first:
Go for the
wide part of
the fairway.

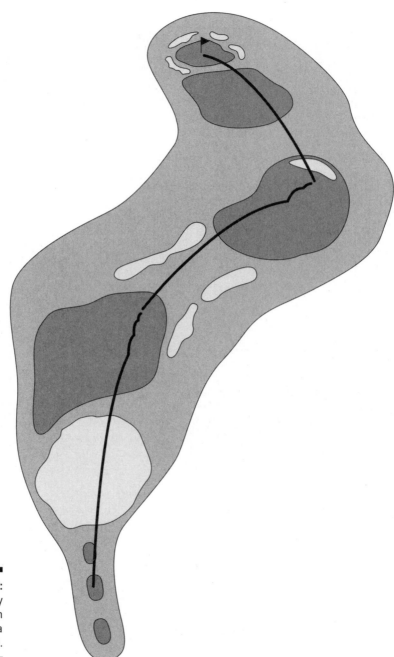

Figure 1-12:
Three easy
shots can
tame a
long hole.

Knowing your strengths and weaknesses

To really employ good strategy, you have to know your tendencies. For example, on the par-4 hole described earlier in this chapter (see "Tactic 2: Think before you drive"), a really accurate driver of the ball can take the chance and try to hit the ball into the narrow gap. She's playing to her strength.

But how do you know what your pluses and minuses are? Simple. All you have to do is keep a close record of your rounds over a period of time. By "a close record," we don't simply mean your score on each hole. You have to break down the numbers a bit more than that.

Keep a record of your scores that details various aspects of your game: how many fairways you hit, how many times you hit the green, and how many putts you take on each green. That record can tell you which parts of your game you should work on. (You can see an example of such a card in Chapter 2 of Book I.)

Beating the first-tee jitters

The opening shot of any round is often the most stressful. You're not into your round yet. Even the practice shots that you may have hit aren't the real thing. And people are almost always nearby watching when you hit that first shot. If you're like most golfers, you're intimidated by even the thought of striking a ball in full view of the public.

How a player reacts to first-tee jitters is an individual thing. You just have to get out there and do it and see what happens. Common symptoms: Blurred vision. A desire to get this shot over and done with as soon as possible. Loss of reason.

The most common mistake, however, is doing everything twice as fast as you normally would: looking down the fairway, standing up to the ball, swinging — the lot. Your increased pace is because of the misguided notion that if you get this swing over with really quickly, no one will see it. It's the hit-it-and-go syndrome, and you should avoid it.

I remember when my golf swing wasn't where I wanted it to be. I had a bad grip, a bad takeaway, and a bad position at the top. I wasn't comfortable with myself, so how could I be comfortable with others watching? I'd get up there, hit the ball as soon as I could, and get out of the way. After I understood the mechanics of my swing, that dread went away. All of a sudden, I stood over the ball as long as I wanted to. I thought about what I was doing, not about what others were thinking. I *wanted* people to watch, to revel in the positions in my golf swing, because they were good positions. I didn't mind showing off.

Being too concerned about your audience is really a social problem. Rather than taking refuge in your preshot routine, you're thinking about what others may be thinking. The secret to overcoming this problem is to immerse yourself in your routine. Say, "Okay, I'm going to start behind the ball. Then I'm going to look at my line, take five steps to the ball, swing the club away to the inside and turn my shoulders." Whatever you say to yourself, just remember to focus internally. Focus on *you* and forget about *them*.

Deciding which Format You Should Play

Perhaps the best format for the beginning golfer is a *scramble*. In that format, you're usually part of a team of four. Everyone tees off, and then everyone plays another shot from where the best shot lies. And so on. A scramble is great for beginners because you have less pressure to hit every shot well. You can lean on your partners a bit. Plus, you get to watch better players up close. And you get to experience some of the game's camaraderie. Scrambles are typically full of rooting, cheering, and high-fives. In short, they're fun.

You can also play in games where the format is *stableford*. In this game, the scoring is by points rather than strokes. You get one point for a *bogey* (score of one over par); two for a par; three for a *birdie* (one under par); and four for an *eagle* (two under par). Thus, a round in which you par every hole reaps you 36 points. The great thing is that in a stableford, you don't have to complete every hole. You can take your 9s and 10s without irreparably damaging your score. You simply don't get any points for a hole in which you take more than a bogey. That's with your handicap strokes deducted, of course. (For more on golf handicapping, see Chapter 1 of Book IV.)

You may well find that you play most of your golf with three companions. That's known as a *foursome* in the United States (a *four-ball* elsewhere). The format is simple. You split into two teams of two and play what is known as a *best-ball* game. That is, the best score on each team on each hole counts as the score for that team. For example, if you make a 5 on the first hole and your partner makes a 4, your team scores a 4 for the hole.

Chapter 2

Keeping Your Head in the Game

*Y*our mind is undeniably a big part of your golf game — especially the short game. In golf, the mind can be overactive and distracted. You walk a fine line between being mentally engaged and being overly analytical. Although your goal should be to reach a point where you can play the game in the subconscious, you also have to be aware of your situation and the options available to you, not to mention the way playing conditions can affect your performance.

Taking all the factors and options into account at once can make you mad! But listen to the old contrary adages, both of which contain good advice: "Look before you leap" and "He who hesitates is lost."

In this chapter, we explore the mental gluts that can destroy an otherwise poetic and effective game, and we give you ways to combat your own mind.

Regrouping When the Wheels Come Off Your Game

It happens to all golfers. You have a nice, pleasant round cooking along when, suddenly, you're all thumbs. It seems to happen in an instant. You can't play golf effectively. You miss some short putts. You fumble around with your short irons or *foozle* (that's golf-speak for *bungle*) pitch shots. You blade your chip shots over the green because of an ugly mishit or leave the ball short of the green with a chunky, fat shot. (*Fat* shots occur when you hit the ground before you hit the ball.) Your confidence abandons you faster than your enjoyment level, which is also quickly heading downhill.

Consider the case of Jean Van de Velde, who experienced an infamous meltdown as he tried to put the finishing touches on what looked like a certain victory at the 1999 British Open at Carnoustie. Despite having a comfortable lead, he suddenly found himself hanging on to make a 7 on the final hole just to get into a playoff (which he lost). A bad bounce, and suddenly things can start happening fast.

Often, the more you try to pull yourself from this downward spiral, the farther into the mire you slip. So relax and quit fighting it so hard. Recognize that these helpless, hapless spells of uselessness strike every amateur golfer (and even the pros). Don't panic; just try to laugh it off, or at least grin and bear it. Remind yourself that you're not alone, and recognize that you've hit good shots before and can hit them again. And beware of opponents who want to make double-or-nothing bets.

In this section, we cover the steps you can take to get your mind right when you encounter some of the more common mental mishaps that occur on the course.

Regaining your tempo

You can sense when you start to lose your tempo. Your golf swing feels quick and jerky rather than slow and fluid. You become aware of the fundamental disconnect between your upper body and lower body, and maybe even between your hands and arms.

If you lose your tempo, you've lost your focus and, as it slips away, you get more fearful. With increasing fear comes a rising tension level. The more you think about it and the more you fight and struggle with your golf game, the higher your tension and anxiety levels rise. You stand over every shot and think

> "Can I hit this one correctly? Will I hit this putt too far past the hole? Don't leave this short of the green! I'm about to hit this shot in the bunker . . . again! Dear God, I made a 7 on the last hole. Don't 3-putt again! Could I possibly miss this 1-foot putt? Why is this happening?"

When this situation happens, you need to lower your tension and anxiety levels to get your groove back!

So how can you regain your tempo? The more air you take into your system, the more you can relax. The more you relax, the faster you begin to regain your tempo. Try the following techniques:

- ✔ **Start breathing.** Take big, deep breaths that go all the way down to your diaphragm. The more oxygen that comes into your body, the more your heart rate begins to go down. Breathe deep and don't get caught up in the moment!

- ✔ **Fake a yawn.** Look at some of the greatest Olympic sprinters and track athletes. When they get ready to run, they seem relaxed because they start taking big yawns. You may think those athletes are about to fall asleep! The truth is that they become tense and want to get some air.

Overcoming analysis paralysis

Golf games often go awry during a round because players get too focused on the conscious part of the swing. You need to stay focused on playing in the subconscious. Smell the flowers, hear the music, and calm down. Don't over-think every situation or overexamine your swing; trust it and the work you've put toward it on the range. Take aim at the target and let it go. *Play* golf.

The middle of a golf round is no time to fix a swing flaw or experiment with a new grip. Let it flow. Focus on the target. Talk with your playing partners. Do anything that stops you from overanalyzing your swing or breaking it down into small parts. Can you imagine the flood of swing thoughts and the number of mental checklist items you could clutter your mind with if you wanted to? Playing such a round may take forever, and it'd certainly be a mechanical, grueling affair. Unless you round the course for a living, golf is still just a game.

Getting out of the blame game

When it comes to putting, many factors are out of your control. You have too many variables to consider around the greens to always shoulder the blame. Remind yourself of this fact from time to time when the ball doesn't break the way you read it and your frustration level starts rising.

GARY SAYS

The power of positive excuse-making

Even if you aren't a pro, no matter what goes wrong on the course, it's never — I repeat, *never* — your fault. You must always find someone or something else to blame for any misfortune. For example, I once fired my caddie after I played to the wrong green as I was trying to qualify for the U.S. Open (even though I knew the course like the back of my hand). Sometimes, though, you have to be creative in the excuse department.

Golfers have come up with some great excuses over the years. My favorite came from Greg Norman. He once blamed a miscued shot on a worm popping up out of the ground next to his ball as he swung. Poor Greg was so distracted that he couldn't hit the shot properly! Then you have Jack Nicklaus's gem at the 1995 British Open at St. Andrews. In the first round, Jack hit his second shot on the 14th hole, a long par-5, into what is known as Hell Bunker. It's well named, being basically a bottomless sand-filled crater. Anyway, seeing his ball down there came as a bit of a surprise to Jack. He apparently felt that his shot should have flown comfortably over said bunker and chalked the problem up to having his ball deflected by seed heads!

These two examples are extreme, of course, but you should apply the same principle to your game. You can often tell a good player from his reaction to misfortune. He blames his equipment, the wind, whatever. On the other hand, less-secure golfers take all responsibility for bad shots. Whatever they do is awful. In fact, they really stink at this stupid game. That's what they tell themselves — usually to the point that it ruins their next shot. And the next. And the next. Whatever they perceive themselves to be, they become.

So be sure that you err in the former way rather than the latter. To play this game well, you gotta believe — in yourself!

First of all, remember that the green beneath your feet is a living, growing organism. The grass grows and changes all the time as you play on it. And like any Saturday at any golf course, a number of foursomes have teed off in front of you (unless you're a part of the early-bird crew loaded with coffee and pancakes). One foursome takes as many as 140 steps on a green. If you play in the tenth foursome of the day, you putt on greens that have endured more than 1,000 steps! Steps in your line, scuffed grass from someone who drags his feet, pitch marks, and general wear and tear concentrated around the hole prevent your ball from rolling on the pristine line you see in your head.

Did we forget to mention that mower lines, uneven grass, grass clippings, dew, fertilizer, pebbles, and sand can also contribute to even the best-stroked putts going off-line and missing the hole? How do you like your odds now?

The margin of error is very small when putting to a hole. Take your best read, concentrate on your smooth and controlled stroke, and give the ball your best roll. Sometimes, missing a putt just ain't your fault. (Check out Chapter 6 of Book III for putting tips.)

Coping With the Pressure

From time to time, the shot you want to play may be simple, but the environment and situation you face may make it seem more difficult. Pitching a ball over a bunker and onto the green, for instance, may be something you normally pull off with no trouble. But pitching a ball over a bunker and onto a green when you're one stroke ahead of a competitor on the last hole of a tournament or a $10 match against a buddy makes the shot seem worlds more difficult.

Pressure and nervousness over the result of the shot can make you second-guess your strategy or stifle your technique. Suddenly, the pitch shot that seemed second nature on the third hole is life or death on the last hole.

Ken Venturi, who won the 1964 U.S. Open and went on to enjoy a long career as a CBS golf analyst, often talked about the thrill of competition and how exciting it was to come down to the last hole with your heart beating and a chance to win. In your case, the situation may be the chance to shoot your best round ever, to break 90 for the first time, or to impress your boss during a round. In any case, golfers find ways to deal with stress and nervousness in varied ways.

Accepting the fear

The more competitive you are, the more opportunities you face for fear to take over, and the more you have to be able to manage your fear. Fear controls the mind. Fear causes you to top your drive off the first tee because you're not thinking about making a comfortable, fluid golf swing and just rolling with it. You think about who's watching your shot; you feel the eyes of all the people around.

If you're a 30-handicapper and you just play to hit and giggle and get exercise, you don't have any fear. You just want a walk in the park to enjoy the scenery. That's terrific, but because you're reading this book, you probably don't represent this type of player.

If you are or want to become competitive, however, you constantly try to get better. And the harder you try and the more you press, the more opportunities you face for fear to enter in.

Some sports psychologists, stress management experts, and hypnotists suggest that you make a conscious effort to recognize that you are, indeed, in a stressful situation. Tell yourself something like, "Heck yes, I'm nervous. What a tough spot. I need to get this ball over the bunker and onto the green to have any chance to win. I have good reason to be nervous. I should be nervous."

You recognize the situation for what it is and allow yourself to take your nervousness into account when you prepare for the shot. Knowing that you have to carry the bunker and get the ball onto the green, and that you have to do it with frayed nerves, is important information.

After you size up your situation, and perhaps even embrace it, you can put the fear aside and control it. Just as you recognize a patch of long grass, the wind, or airplane noise from above, recognize the drama and marginalize it just as you do the other factors.

Take some deep breaths. Shake your hands out. Roll your head around. Think happy thoughts. In the golf movie *Happy Gilmore,* Adam Sandler's title character mentally takes himself to a "happy place." Your happy place may be different from Happy's, but the idea isn't as silly as the movie makes it seem.

You can also cope with a tough situation by distracting yourself for a few minutes. Talk to someone in your group about something besides golf until it's your turn to hit. That way, you can skip over the two minutes of nerves and focus on your shot when your turn comes around.

If you can't completely let go of your fear, you can make it work for you by turning it into something less scary: caution.

You often hear risk-taking golfers described as fearless. Arnold Palmer played that way, and so did Phil Mickelson — especially early in his career. But Mickelson didn't win so much early in his career, when he often tried to pull off low-percentage miracle shots. He was bold, he was dashing, and he was famous as the "best player never to have won a major championship." Fearlessness can get you in as much trouble as playing scared.

But Phil changed. He was still bold, still willing to go for a miracle when that was the only way to win, but as he got a little older he took fewer foolish chances. Mickelson finally bagged his first major, the 2004 Masters, at the age of 33. Now he's got four majors (as of this writing), and he's not finished yet.

Phil didn't suddenly start playing scared. He started playing smarter. Rather than go for broke, he sometimes *laid up* — hit his ball short of trouble, in good position for the next shot.

Ignoring the result

Forget about the outcome. Forget that a chip can set up a par-save, or that your putt is for birdie, or that if you hit the green you can 2-putt for your best round ever. Forget that your opponent is watching and that you need this putt to tie the hole.

Zero in on the simple physics of the matter. The club goes back on the line . . . the club swings through . . . the ball goes toward the hole. The ball either goes in the hole or it doesn't. Simple as that.

If you want to be fatalistic about it, wouldn't you rather miss boldly than cowardly? You can live with making a confident swing and missing the shot or putt, but a weak, trembling, terror-provoked yip is a haunting indignity.

Pacing your swing with a phrase

Golf is a mental challenge, but you have to play in the subconscious to achieve success. To "lose" your mind, you may consider coming up with a little phrase, ditty, or song that can occupy your thoughts while you swing. Some PGA Tour players whistle to relieve tension and maintain their tempo. Some golf teachers advocate mental catchphrases such as "super fluid," "golden laddie," or even "hamburger," where you think of the first word/syllable on the backswing and the rest of the word/phrase on the downswing: ham — burger.

Giving yourself some kind of magic phrase — something fun — can help you ease your mind into the subconscious when you swing the club. If you think about that little key word or ditty every time you hit a shot and the result goes well four or five times, you feel pretty comfortable the next four or five times you try it. You can count on doing the same thing — with the key being the hypnotic phrase, a phrase you can rely on under pressure, becoming part of your routine.

Visualizing the Shot

Many psychologists say that the subconscious mind can't tell the difference between a real event and an imagined one. If you can clearly visualize a shot and its result, it may be easier to implement and achieve.

Whether you're in the boardroom dreaming of your round to come later that day or standing in front of the ball preparing for a shot you're about to hit, taking the time to imagine your shots can help you emulate your vision — to literally live your dreams! Just follow these steps:

1. **Stand directly behind the ball, keeping it between yourself and the hole.**

   Of course, if you're doing some daydreaming visualization off the course, you'll have to do this step mentally.

2. **Envision the journey you want the ball to take.**

   Is the shot a pitch or a chip? Do you want the ball to fly high or hop low? Where do you want the ball to land? Will it roll a long way after it lands, or will it hit and stop quickly . . . or even immediately?

   Is the shot a putt? Will the ball break right, break left, or roll straight? Is the putt downhill or uphill? Have you watched the way the ball rolled when your playing partner or opponent putted from a similar line or distance? Do you want your ball to behave similarly?

   One sports psychologist advocates imagining that you can burn a fiery pathway to the hole with your eyes. Whatever colorful vision works for you and gives you confidence, use it!

3. **Regardless of the shot type, see the ball roll into the hole.**

4. **Go ahead and hit the shot!**

Your execution may not always match your imagination, but you can certainly give yourself a better chance by imagining a good "flight plan." A good mental road map helps you steer the plane in the most efficient manner without getting lost.

Staying Positive

As the old adage says, "Attitude is everything." A positive attitude can do wonders for your golf game; even if you're having a bad day on the course, staying positive can at least help you enjoy it more. The following sections help you keep from becoming your own worst enemy.

Before every swing, picture a great result. This practice is more than optimism; it's science! Sports psychologists teach visualization for one simple reason: It works. Just as negative thoughts can derail your swing, positive thoughts — and images — can and do help you hit the ball better.

Don't be too hard on yourself

Ten feet isn't that far, is it? When you stand behind a 10-foot putt and look at the space between the ball and the hole, it really doesn't look that far. How many times out of ten attempts do you think you can sink a 10-foot putt? Six times? Eight? Every time?

What's a reasonable expectation? Your mind may tell you that you can make a 10-footer all the time. Statistics, however, say that PGA Tour players — the guys who play golf every day, practice all day long, and hit thousands of putts; the best players in the world — only make 10-footers half the time!

If PGA Tour players make only 50 percent of their 10-foot putts, why should you expect to make them 60 to 80 or even 100 percent of the time? You're expecting an impossible level of consistency! So don't beat yourself up and tell yourself that you're a lousy putter when you miss a 10-footer. Have you ever made an expression of angst after *lipping out* a putt (rimming it around the cup without holing it)? Don't do that. You damage your ego and your short game (and, depending on the outburst, quite possibly your putter).

How close to the hole do you expect to chip the ball every time? Two feet? Four feet? Less? More? Remember the difference between a goal and an expectation (see Chapter 4 of Book III for info chipping goals and expectations). Just because you didn't chip the ball to within 3 feet of the hole doesn't mean you're a lousy player!

The minute you tell yourself you're a lousy putter or a crummy chipper as you walk off a green, you make a huge negative imprint on your psyche. Killing your confidence is a big mistake; the next time you come up to a putt, you tell yourself that you can't make the putt because you missed the last one. You make yourself aware that you're a lousy putter, and that's what lousy putters do — miss putts.

When describing a putt he missed, Tiger Woods has often said, "I hit a good putt; it just didn't go in." Use similar positive self-talk to turn a positive into a negative.

Keep your confidence

Self-doubt can turn the best golf swing into a mess of flying knees and elbows. This point is especially true when you're facing the wide variety of unsavory situations waiting to strike on the course: divots, high winds, trees, and so on. (See Book VI for more on these troubles.)

How can you beat those nagging feelings of self-doubt? Practice. The idea may sound obvious, but too many golfers rely on hope to keep them out of trouble. They say, "I hope this works," and flail away, trying to hook a shot between trees, over a lake to a postage-stamp green. But if you've never hooked a ball on purpose before, what hope have you got?

Your chances are far better if you can say these magic words: "I've hit this shot before." That means working on your techniques — not just a couple of times, but until they feel familiar. That way, you're not guessing and hoping when it counts there. You're trying to repeat past successes.

Say you have a 40-yard shot over a stream. You know you can hit the ball that far. After all, you just hit the ball 225 yards off the tee; therefore, you can certainly hit the ball 40 yards with just about any club in your bag! You can easily carry the ball 40 yards. No way you should dunk it in that stream.

But unless you practice that type of shot and feel comfortable with the club that you put in your hand, the shot can give you trouble. The minute you start having doubts about making proper contact with the ball and lofting it up and over the pond, you have a problem. Mishits happen when the mind starts wavering.

If, on the other hand, you remain confident and no doubt clouds your mind, you can execute the shot because you know you can, without a doubt; you know you've hit this club and this type of shot before. Let the clouds of doubt blow from your mind and see the sunny, clear skies of confidence. Get comfortable and free up your mind so you can play subconsciously: target, swing, green. Instead of looking at the stream, find the spot on the green where you want to land your ball. The stream all but disappears.

Chapter 3

Finding Creative Ways to Practice Golf

*I*n the 1984 film *The Karate Kid,* Mr. Miyagi teaches his pupil Daniel the fundamental secrets of martial arts by putting the boy through his paces. Miyagi has him do chores, such as sanding the deck, painting the fence, and waxing the car, which frustrates Daniel until he finds out how the chores apply to karate; they actually strengthen his techniques for fighting! You don't have to get so menial in your training, but you can utilize some simple devices that help you train on and off the golf course.

You can find a plethora of practice gadgets and trinkets in retail golf shops, magazines, or on television infomercials, but before you do that, check out our recommendations in this chapter. You may end up buying some devices, but you can make many of them yourself. One trip to a hardware store to buy a rubber band, a chalk line, two 2-x-4s, and a dowel, and you can build yourself five training devices for less than $20.

Another step to take before you shell out your hard-earned cash for the latest gadget is to pay a visit to a PGA professional at your club or your course. See what he or she uses to teach. The devices golf professionals use to teach likely are time honored and tested and focus on the key, fundamental points.

In this chapter, we give you some easy tricks to try to improve your golf game, particularly the *short game* (everything within 75 to 80 yards of the hole). The treat is the fun you have on the golf course when you begin to notice the results!

Understanding the Importance of Practice

It's amazing, but nearly half of golfers who score poorly don't practice. Are you one of them? You can't expect to improve if you don't put some time in. Now, we can already hear you griping, "I don't have time!" Well, stop whining, because this section features a sample practice schedule that you can easily work into your weekly routine.

Practice can be fun. If you don't want to take strokes off your game, skip this part, but if you're a weekend warrior who wants to improve, here's a shortcut to success:

- ✔ **Practice your swing whenever possible.** You can practice most of your swings in your basement, living room, or backyard. Place old clubs in various locations around your house so you're prepared to swing when the spirit (or schedule) moves you.

- ✔ **Make imaginary swings in front of a mirror or window with your arms and hands in the proper position (see Chapter 1 of Book III).** If you don't have a club handy, that's okay. Visualize and feel the correct position.

- ✔ **Grip a club when you watch television.** You're not doing anything else! Try swinging a club during commercials.

- ✔ **Build a practice area in your house or office where you can work on your short game.** Use those plastic practice balls. Set up a small obstacle course in your yard. (Your kids can help you with this part.)

- ✔ **Where and when possible, hit a bucket of balls during lunch**. If it's a hot day in July, you may want to hit the showers before you head back to the office.

Fitting your life into your busy practice schedule

Here's a sample practice schedule. You may want to tone it down at the office (you look bad if your boss walks in while you're practicing your putting), although you may be able to multitask during those long conference calls.

✔ **Monday:** Health-club workout (1 hour); putt on rug (15 minutes).

✔ **Tuesday:** Swing a club in front of a mirror or window (30 minutes).

✔ **Wednesday:** Health-club workout (1 hour); read a golf magazine or golf book or watch a golf DVD (30 minutes). Chapter 2 of Book I gives you some good options for study materials.

✔ **Thursday:** Swing a club or chip (1 hour).

✔ **Friday:** Health-club workout (1 hour); practice range, including golf drills (1 hour).

✔ **Saturday:** Practice range (1 hour); play 18 holes.

✔ **Sunday:** Watch golf on TV; practice range (30 minutes); play 9 holes.

Practicing like you play

No one outside of Vijay Singh likes to practice. The very word conjures up images of drudgery. Some golfers even refer to the practice range as "the rock pile."

For improvement, however, practice is unavoidable. When you can't get to the golf course, and the practice tee is your only option, try to make the best of the situation. And the way to really make the best of it is to practice like you play — that is, make your practice session as important and varied as an experience on the golf course can be.

You won't improve your game if you stomp out there and pound away ball after ball with a driver. Golf practice isn't a purely quantitative endeavor. Quantity doesn't equal quality. Vijay Singh may hit hundreds of balls a day, but he hits every ball like he's standing on the 18th hole with a chance to win a tournament.

Think of a football coach. He may have his team hit blocking sleds or run drills from time to time, but the most vital part of any football practice is the scrimmage in which the team tries its plays out against a mock opposing team. The scrimmage is designed to simulate the real game situation as closely as possible. You can do the same in golf.

You should conduct goal-oriented, organized practice sessions. Before you begin your session, break down your practice time so that your routine mimics an actual round — instead of falling into the grip-it-and-rip-it pattern — so you can practice the specific aspects of your game that need work. Say you have one hour to practice. That means you spend the first five minutes stretching out (as we cover in Chapter 2 of Book V). After you stretch out, you can start hitting short shots and putts for 30 minutes. Spend the final 25 minutes hitting range balls with your longer irons and drivers. Set the schedule in your head and stick to it!

Getting older — and better

We all age, and our games change as we do so. If you've recently become a senior golfer, you need to know some things to keep your game young. As you may know already (or will find out soon enough), you just don't hit the ball as far as you used to. Four basic problems cause this discrepancy:

- **Poor posture:** Bad posture can stop you from turning properly. Be careful how you hold your head; keep it off your chest. Maintain good posture by standing in front of a full-length mirror and holding a club out in front of you. Keep looking in the mirror as you lower the club into the hitting position. Don't let your head tilt or move forward. When you master this technique, you can make that turn and swing your arms.

- **Lack of rotation on your backswing:** You probably aren't turning your hips and shoulders enough on the backswing. You can increase your range of motion by increasing your flexibility. See Chapter 2 of Book II for stretching exercises. They can be a huge help! Then review the elements of the swing in Chapters 1 and 2 of Book III, get out to the driving range, and work out those kinks.

- **Lost strength:** As you grow older, you lose strength in your hands and forearms, which makes keeping your wrists in the proper position on the downswing harder. This weakness reduces clubhead speed, so the ball doesn't go as far. Simple drills to combat loss of strength include squeezing a tennis ball, doing forearm curls with light barbells, and Harvey Penick's drill: Swing a club back and forth like a scythe 20 or 30 times a day. Just don't do this drill anywhere near your new flat screen TV.

- **Lack of rotation in the follow-through:** You may be so intent on hitting the ball that you're not finishing your swing. This short shot causes the club to stop 3 or 4 feet beyond the ball and your arms to stop somewhere around your chest, with your belt buckle pointing to the right of your target. As you can imagine, this swing results in an unsightly shot. The ball flies to the right and is, well, weak.

To correct such a problem, repeat the following drill each day until it feels natural: While looking in a full-length mirror, go to the top of your backswing (see Chapter 1 of Book III) and then mirror-image that position on the follow-through, with your belt buckle facing to the left of your target. To make this happen, you must transfer 90 percent of your weight from your right foot to your left foot.

Finally, we can't stress this point enough: If you don't exercise, start (see Book II). Consult your local golf pro for suggestions, too. A good program coupled with a stretching routine improves your flexibility and strength, your golf game, and your life in general.

When you plan to practice, set a method for yourself, but try varying it every time. Don't get stale because practice gets boring.

Shoring Up Your Short Game

When you arrive at the course, the putting green, or the edge of your backyard to practice, you should remember that 50 percent of your score comes from 50 yards and in; therefore, you should devote 50 percent of your practice time to improving your short game. If you do that without fail, you can become a better player.

The best players in the world don't go into their "office" for an eight- or nine-hour day for nothing. They want to practice all aspects of their game, but they need to spend a lot of time on the aspects that make up 50 percent of their score. That work ethic and dedication is what makes them what they are — stars! You, however, can't devote an eight-hour block to practice. But you can divvy up your practice time in the same manner. And if you do, you get better and your scores start to drop.

Having a game plan for your short-game practice

Variety rules the range, even when you're focusing on your short game. Use the entire practice range — and your entire range of shots. Check out the following list to organize your time:

- **Start with the short irons and work your way up.** If you haven't been driving the ball well lately or you've been watching John Daly play, your first thought upon hitting the range may be to reach for your driver. But don't spend all your allotted time on the range on your driver. You may hit the driver something like 14 times in a round (not all drives actually call for that club), so your skill with the club is important. But you have to prepare to hit *all* your irons, too.

  Work your way up to the driver by practicing your technique with short irons. Working through the clubs gives your short game the attention it deserves. Plus, nothing says that you can't take a break from the big stick after you have it going. Hit a few 9-irons. Find a specific target. Hit a few fades and a few draws, and then go back to the driver.

- **Vary your targets.** It doesn't matter where you position yourself on the range or in the hitting bays because you don't have to smack every practice shot straight out into the field from your spot on the range. Although the tee markers, mats, and sidewalls tend to point players straight out, you should avoid mechanical, rote ball striking.

Practicing with the wind

If you have the luxury of hitting balls on a large range with many options, always practice into the wind. It makes you extend your swing a little bit more, because you naturally sense the need for more follow-through and power. It makes you hit more driving, low shots that don't balloon up into the air. Having a good follow-through is important on every shot after you get on the golf course, no matter which way the wind is blowing when you approach a shot.

Hitting shots downwind is the next-best option, because it allows you to try to hit straight shots and get pure feedback as to whether you hit them straight. A right-to-left wind can be beneficial as well. Sometimes you're stuck with it, but if you can avoid it, you never want to practice into a left-to-right wind if you're a right-handed player (and vice versa for lefties). You have a harder time controlling the ball in a left-to-right wind. The easiest mistake to make is a slice. Most people cut the ball and make it fade a little, and if you face a left-to-right wind, you have to fight to get the ball straight, which can mess up your swing.

Sure, go ahead and hit some shots straight out, especially at the beginning of the session when you want to get a feel for the ball and find your alignment. But after you get comfortable, hit three shots to the right. Aim 40 yards to the left and hit some balls. Pick out a target — a tree, flag, or green — on the left and then pick out some aiming points on the right.

✔ **Vary your shot selection.** You don't need to swing for the fences all the time. Take your practice time to work on your bump and runs to improve your scores around the greens; your punch shots for windy weather; or shots between your club distances. (Head to Chapter 8 of Book III for more on punch shots and bump and runs.)

One routine you need to avoid during your practice session is grabbing ball after ball and whacking them without a target. Many players just hit ball after ball. They hit a bad shot and, sometimes while that ball is still in the air, they grab another. These firing squad players don't have a routine to focus on. They go to the golf course to play with no plans for practice or improvement. If you get into a routine of practicing the way you play, you become a far better player.

Go at each ball as if you're standing on the tee or in the fairway in the middle of a round and you need to come up with an accurate shot. Pick your alignment and your target and know what you want to do with every shot. Get your mind set before every swing like you do before a shot on the golf course and turn off your conscious mind. Hit each shot and watch it finish before dragging another ball over and preparing for the next swipe.

Spending time on the green

Variety is also the keyword when working around the greens. If you putt first to start practice one day, try chipping first in your next session. Vary the types of shots you hit during a practice session and the locations you hit them from.

Chip some balls in one direction, and then walk over and chip a few from another spot in another direction (see Chapter 4 of Book III for chipping instruction). Don't make the same putt over and over; save that drill for a putting-specific practice session (we cover putting mechanics in Chapter 6 of Book III and drills later in this chapter). Move around the hole and vary the lengths. Hit some bunker shots in the middle to spice things up (see Chapter 7 of Book III for instructional info). Choose a different target, flag, or hole to hit pitches to.

You can try to make every one of your practice shots, and we could tell you to grind over every one as if you're facing your final shot to win the U.S. Open, but you can't realistically expect that from yourself. Try to remain focused and result oriented, but don't be afraid to experiment with your swing and stance until you're comfortable and confident. Try hitting shots lower, higher, longer, and shorter. Play while you practice. For some drills to help you remain focused, turn to this chapter's "Tuning your swing with music."

On the golf course, you get a different look on every hole and on every shot, so you should practice with that in mind. You never get the same shot. It never happens. So don't keep hitting the same chip over and over. After you successfully master a chip shot from a specific lie, move on to another lie or distance from the hole and go about practicing that one until you feel comfortable with it.

Riding the Range

Going to the practice range doesn't have to be like a punishment. You can make the experience useful and fun by experimenting with different ways to practice. Use some of the following tricks to make practice more like play.

Standing up for balance

Good balance aids your golf game because it helps you swing smoothly and evenly — you have a better chance of taking the club back along the target line and through the ball with good tempo and rhythm. Rather than a choppy or forced feeling, you want an even, fluid swing, and good balance helps you do just that. Hitting shots or taking swings with your feet placed together improves your balance and gives you a good sense of the physics involved in the golf swing (see Figure 3-1).

Figure 3-1:
Hit some balls with your feet together to get a feel for balance and the physics of the golf swing.

It may feel a bit awkward at first, but you can discover a lot about the turn of your body and the release of your hands by swinging with your feet together. Hitting shots with a condensed base gives you a good sense for the weight and power of the clubhead and how it shoots the ball virtually on its own without the aid of your body.

When you have time on the practice range, hit 10 or 15 balls with your feet squarely together. Try using a pitching wedge and position the ball back in your stance, off your back foot (see Figure 3-1). Swing along the target line, keeping your hands ahead of the ball at all times. Stand closer to your line than on most other shots. You're not looking for distance here; you just want to make good contact without falling over.

Becoming a one-armed bandit

A brilliant way to develop your sense for the swing and for ball striking is to hit golf shots with one hand. Here's how:

1. **Stand over the ball at the practice range and take your normal stance with a wedge or a 9-iron.**

2. **Remove your dominant hand from the club and leave it to dangle at your side.**

   You don't need it for this drill.

3. **Start by hitting some one-handed chip shots.**

   Hitting these little chips helps you develop a feel for getting the club on the ball and lets you see how the ball comes off the clubface.

4. **Work your way up to three-quarter-swing pitch shots, using only your nondominant hand.**

   Your confidence with one arm begins to improve, and your shots become stronger and fly farther.

   If you find that your dangling arm gets in the way of your swing, try stuffing your hand into your pocket before you make the swing.

It may seem difficult to hit one-handed shots, but hitting them without your dominant hand guiding the swing helps your short game in a number of ways:

- ✔ It proves to you that, in the short game and in the full golf swing, the non-dominant hand truly is the leader, and the dominant hand serves only as a guide. You discover after a few swings that you can hit the ball a long way and in an effective fashion with your nondominant hand. This psychologically frees up your mind and your sense of the swing, helping you rely on the nondominant hand and arm. (See Chapter 3 of Book III for the importance of letting your nondominant hand lead the way.)

- ✔ You're forced to practice pulling your nondominant hand and arm through the shot and letting that arm truly captain the swing because it has no first mate to help.

- ✔ You develop a greater awareness of the face of the club. Using only one hand heightens the sensation of feel with that one hand.

Tuning your swing with music

More often these days, players, especially the young ones, show up on the practice range wearing headphones. They hit practice balls while they listen to music. And the youngsters aren't the only ones. PGA Tour player Vijay Singh has admitted that he has a little ditty he sings in his head when he swings a golf club. No rule prohibits this extra piece of equipment, but is playing to music a good idea? We think so. The following sections tell you why.

Playing in the subconscious

If you listen to music while you hit golf shots, you play in the subconscious. The activity trains you to play the game from a mentally suspended state. Think about it. When you're driving a car down the road and listening to music on the radio, do you consciously think about every move you make while you drive? Keep my foot on the gas pedal . . . check the rear view mirror . . . turn on my right turn signal . . . check the right lane . . . turn the steering wheel to the right . . . merge to the right to change lanes . . . move my foot to the brake to decrease my speed.

No, you probably don't drive that way. Although driving demands concentration and attention to ensure safety, more often than not, the actual motions just kind of happen without much thought. You use your instincts and force of habit to drive mile after mile.

If you listen to the music, you don't think about the literal components of your swing: Is my face square . . . take the club back slowly . . . gotta keep my elbow tucked . . . okay, pause at the top and shift my weight to the left side . . . don't decelerate. These types of thoughts can paralyze you.

It may seem like a mystical phrase, but *playing in the subconscious* improves your game. You want to get to the point where you can grab the club and just swing it naturally, instead of stepping over the ball with a series of running thoughts. (See Chapter 3 of Book III for more on the power of the subconscious.)

Talking about tempo

Music can also help one of the most important characteristics of the golf swing: your tempo. Your ideal tempo as you swing isn't a fundamental set in stone; it's really a matter of preference. Some may think of tempo as smooth and rhythmic, conjuring up images of Fred Astaire and Ginger Rogers. Good tempo to others may be more like the jitterbug.

Choosing music to accentuate your tempo is a "what's right for you" part of the golf game. Hard rock is terrible for a slow, rhythmic swing, but another guy may benefit from hard rock because it makes him feel like his fast swing has rhythm and balance. Probably the best choice for music, if you have no preference, is a waltz. In Chapter 2 of Book V, we cover tips for regaining your tempo.

Surf and Turf: Practicing in the Sand and on the Green

Not all practice takes place on the driving range. Really. Anytime you're at a facility that has a practice bunker, short-game area, or practice green, take advantage of the situation to try some of the following tricks. You can even use some of them in your own living room.

If you plan to try some of these DIY devices, read through each section to figure out what materials you need for your desired exercises. That way, you make only one trip to the hardware store.

Bunker board

Hitting sand shots is dry and dirty work. Who wants to spend time in a bunker? Well, you do if you want to lower your golf scores by improving your bunker game. But another, less obvious advantage to swinging a mean sand wedge is confidence. If you're confident about how you play a bunker shot, that confidence spills over to shots outside of the bunker, like flop shots over bunkers and short shots out of high rough. Confidence breeds success, which equals lower scores and a lower handicap.

But instead of just dropping practice balls into a bunker and thrashing about, approach bunker practice with a plan. One way to teach yourself to handle bunker shots is to practice with a bunker board.

The goal of the bunker board exercise is to train yourself to hit through the sand positioned under the ball and splash it out at the right depth. The setup is simple: Buy a wooden 2-x-4 board at the lumberyard or hardware store and take it to the course with you. Place the board in a practice bunker along your target line and perpendicular to your feet. Put 2 to 3 inches of sand on top of the board, and carefully leave the ends of the board uncovered so you don't hit the end when you swing. Put a golf ball on the middle of the board.

Set up for a bunker shot with your sand wedge and hit the ball from its position on the sand above the board, trying not to hit down on the board. As we explain in Chapter 7 of Book III, if you take more than 2 inches of sand on your bunker shots, you hit too many heavy, short shots. If you splash the club through the inch or two of sand you put on the board, you shouldn't hit it. A proper shot may skim the board with the wedge, but that's about it.

The board prevents you from digging in any farther than the 2 inches of sand. The club should glide through the sand and reveal the board lying underneath (see Figure 3-2). If you do hit the board, you feel it. If you hit the board, you're digging too low. The presence of the board helps you, consciously at first and then subconsciously, not to dig the club too deep and leave your shots in the bunker or short of the green.

Figure 3-2:
Pick the ball cleanly out of the few inches of sand to sweep the board dry.

Conversely, if you bring the clubface in too high, you hit the shot *thin* — you hit the top of the ball and send a line drive — and the ball may stay in the bunker or bound across the green, possibly into another bunker!

Chalk talk

After you line up a putt and determine the target line that can sink the putt or get it near the hole, your task is to swing the putter back and bring it forward along the target line.

When the ball doesn't go where you expect it to, you're left to wonder what went wrong. Did it leave the target line? Did your putter wobble off the target line? One way to get immediate feedback as to why your putts go astray is to make the target line visible.

Buy a powder chalk line normally used for carpentry work. The device contains a string loaded with blue or white chalk; when you lay the string down on the ground and snap the line, it creates a straight chalk line on the surface of the green (see Figure 3-3).

Figure 3-3:
Make like a carpenter and snap a chalk line to help you with your putting.

Take the chalk line and go out to the practice green at your golf course, to your carpet at home, or to the office. Pick a flat area and a line that you want to roll the golf ball on (which may or may not end at a hole). Pull out the chalky string and snap it down on the ground. Let the green or the carpet pick up the chalk so when you remove the string, it leaves an exact line on the ground.

Put the golf ball on the line you marked and stand over the putt. You have an immediate visual feel for your putting line as you stand with your eyes directly over the ball and the putting line. Now you don't just focus on the ball and a hole — you literally see the line.

Hit putts down the line and into the hole. Notice the blade on the takeaway:

✔ Does the blade stay on the line as you take it back?

✔ Does the blade stay on the line during the follow-through?

✔ Does the ball roll nicely along the line toward the hole or toward the end of the line?

✔ When does the ball leave the line?

You can look for a number of possible reasons why a ball leaves the target line when putting:

- ✓ **The blade doesn't go straight back along the target line.** This occurrence means you have to somehow correct the path of the putterhead in midstroke, which causes an unnatural, forced flow to the putt.

- ✓ **The blade doesn't come straight forward and through the ball along the target line.** Anticipation of the shot or anxiety about the result can cause you to let your eyes wander toward the hole or to hurry the putterhead through the ball. A push or a pull can result, sending the ball right or left of the target line.

- ✓ **You decelerate the blade at impact.** The putterhead veers off the target line as it slows instead of moving confidently, like a pendulum, through the ball.

Trench warfare

Need more than just an imaginary target line or a chalked line to keep your putterhead on target during the stroke? Try a little practice in the trench to develop a repeating putting stroke that goes straight back and straight through the ball every time.

Take two 2-x-4 boards to the practice green (or the carpet in your home or office); one of them can be the board from the earlier "Bunker board" exercise if you try that drill. Lay the boards down flat, parallel to each other and pointing at the target, as shown in Figure 3-4. Leave just enough room between the boards for your putterhead to swing parallel to the boards. They should be far enough apart so your putter has room to swing freely, but they need to be close enough that you get immediate feedback if your putter sways and bangs into either or both of the boards.

To train your putting stroke, stand over the boards with your putter in the trench. Try to swing your putterhead down the putting line without banging the toe or the heel of the putter into the boards.

Repeatedly swinging the putter between the boards helps you clearly see the backward and forward path of the putterhead, and it also trains you to pivot at your shoulder, using your arms and hands to take the putterhead straight back and straight through the ball. Do this drill often enough, and you'll start taking your putter back and forth with your eyes closed. Awareness of the putter helps you putt with great precision.

Figure 3-4:
Employ two wooden boards to help you keep your putterhead online throughout the stroke.

You can put a ball in the trench and putt it out of the opening if you like, and you can combine the trench drill with the chalk line drill we discuss in the preceding section to really create a straight and steady putting stroke (see Figure 3-4). You don't need the ball or the chalk line, however, because you can use the boards alone to discover the nature of your swing.

Dowel drill

Accurate putting starts with rolling the golf ball straight to your target. Being one degree off can cause the putt to be several inches off. The dowel drill is a good way to get a feel for hitting through the ball on the intended line. Buy an inch-wide dowel and have it cut to about 8 inches long. (A *dowel* is a piece of solid wood shaped like a rod or a cylinder.)

Put the dowel on the practice green (or your carpet) and choose a putting line; place the dowel perpendicular to the line. Put your putterhead flush behind the dowel. Make your stroke and hit the dowel. The rolling dowel should resemble the rolling golf ball.

When you hit the dowel, you want to hit it flush with the blade (see Figure 3-5). The rolling dowel gives you immediate feedback on the movement of your putterhead when it hits the ball. If you hit it on the money, the dowel rolls straight, end over end. But if you hit it with an errant stroke, you don't get the intended roll:

✔ If the heel of your putter comes in first, even at the slightest percentage angle, and your putter doesn't hit the dowel flush, you push the dowel instead of rolling it down the line.

✔ If the toe comes through first, you pull the dowel off-line.

Figure 3-5:
You can use
a dowel to
help you roll
your putts
on-line with
a proper
putting
stroke.

If the misdirected dowel veers right or left, your putterhead isn't coming squarely through the ball on the target line. You can try to correct the path of your putter on your own or try the drills we cover in the "Chalk talk" and "Trench warfare" sections earlier in this chapter to straighten the swing path of your putter.

Home Improvement: Working on Your Game off the Course

The phrase "don't try this at home" doesn't apply to improving your golf game. Anytime you can get a little practice in or do some drills to improve your technique, do it! Some of the following tricks and drills can help you at home when your golf course is under winter's snow or when you just can't get out of the office.

Stretching your putting skill

The following stretching exercise is designed to help you build your sense for letting your putterhead fall through the ball, swing to completion, and hold at the finish — as great putting strokes do. It trains your muscles — and your mind — to make sure that your putterhead extends forward along the target line after the ball leaves the face.

Get a strong, 6-inch rubber band and put one end around the thin table leg or any piece of furniture — something heavy and stable that won't move under minimal pressure. Put your putterhead through the space in the middle of the band. Take your putting stance, with your putter on the left side of the table leg if you're a righty and on the right side if you're a lefty. Stretch the blade and rubber band forward, as if you're putting away from the table toward an imaginary hole, and hold the finish, as shown in Figure 3-6.

The band tries to pull your putter back, but keep stretching out the band. Stop after you complete a normal follow-through. Hold the finish, and then stretch it out again. Maintain a nice, soft grip. You don't want to break the rubber band; you just want to stretch it out. All you want to do is train your muscles.

You also see that trying to use your wrists to pull the putter forward doesn't work as well as keeping your wrists firm and having them work in concert with your arms and shoulders. Wristy putting isn't solid, and it complicates matters, as you can tell by trying to pull the putter forward with your wrists. Your hands, arms, and wrists should pull the rubber band as one triangular unit, which is what they should do during a real putting stroke.

Now take the rubber band off and go hit some real putts on a practice green or on your carpet. Without the rubber band, you feel so much freer to accelerate through the ball, which is what you want to do on every putt you hit. Keep the same light grip, and let the muscles you've trained do the dirty work.

Figure 3-6: Train your muscles to accelerate through your putts by practicing with a strong rubber band and a piece of furniture.

Weighing in on weights

In any golf shop or in most sporting goods stores, you can buy a small, lead, donut-shaped weight. You typically use a donut to add weight to a golf club for loosening up and swinging. But in this case, you should take the club home with the weight.

You can sit in your chair watching television or be in any room in the house to perform this drill. Drop the donut weight around the shaft of your club so it falls all the way down and stops at the *hosel* (where the shaft connects to the blade). If you push the donut against the hosel, the rubber coating around the weight sticks and holds the donut in place. With your forearm on the chair's armrest, grip the club with your nondominant hand first.

With the club extended out in front of you, slowly lift the club up to a 90-degree angle, using just your wrist; slowly, using your wrist and forearm for resistance, lower the club back down so it points directly outward. Repeat — from flat to a 90-degree angle and back.

Now, instead of going up and down, use your grip and wrist to maneuver the club from side to side — to the right and back to the middle and to the left and back to the middle — on a flat plane. Repeat.

This drill builds up your forearm and wrist strength, which helps you swing the club firmly and fully on pitch shots and approach shots. Strong wrists and arms are also useful when hitting full wedge shots from long grass and tangled rough, or when you need to pitch a ball a long way. Building these muscles also benefits your mental game because while you build up your wrist and forearm strength, you can see the face of the club and increase your conscious and subconscious awareness of the clubface. You train your hand into the grip, and you see the face of the club . . . all while you watch the news or read a magazine.

If you're a righty, do more lifting with your left hand and arm than you do with the right. If you're a lefty, concentrate on your right side. The nondominant arm is the one that provides the power and direction of the club.

Mirror, mirror: Checking your alignment

Awareness of the clubface is vital when you try to swing the club along the target line (see Chapter 3 of Book III for more on the target line). Overall awareness of your alignment and the position of your body are also important. Are you actually aiming where you think you're aiming? Are you swinging your clubhead along the target line? Are your shoulders aligned parallel to the target line?

Your PGA professional, or even a friend, can check your swing on the practice range, but you're on your own during a round, so you need to be able to sense good alignment and have an awareness of the proper positioning of your body. As with many aspects of self-awareness and introspection, you need to look no further than the mirror for answers!

Stand in front of a floor-length mirror with one of your short irons. Without looking into the mirror, take your golf stance — the position you take for chipping or putting — as if you're aiming to hit a ball into the mirror. After you get comfortable, look at yourself in the mirror and consider the following points:

- ✔ **Your stance:** Are your feet open to the target line?

- ✔ **The face angle of the blade on the club:** Is it square to the target line?

- ✔ **The angle of the shaft:** Do you have the club properly positioned in a vertical fashion in the middle of your stance, with perhaps a slight forward lean?

- ✔ **The position of your head over the ball:** Can you see down the target line?

✔ **The distance between your feet:** Are they shoulder-width?

✔ **The position of your hands:** Are they close to your body and gripping the club lightly?

Now take your stance with your chest facing the mirror, as if you're hitting a ball to the side. Get set and then look up at the mirror and evaluate the same areas. Looking at yourself in the mirror gives you immediate pieces of important feedback. Seeing is believing, and recognizing where your body is as opposed to where you think it is helps train your mind and muscles.

The Games People Play: Keeping Practice Interesting

Ben Hogan is credited with saying that "for every day you miss practicing, it will take you one day longer to be good." But practice, practice, practice is like work, work, work. Who needs it?

One way to keep your head in the game when you practice is to banish the term "drill" by creating exciting scenarios and playing games with yourself and others. Whether you want to hone your skills alone or enjoy the company of a fellow short-game wizard, the practice drills we disguise as challenge games can get you started in your love affair with practice.

Pitching for Dollars

Pitching for Dollars is a one-on-one, closest-to-the-pin contest that can make you more aggressive with your pitch shots (see Chapter 5 of Book III for more on pitching). Hitting chips and pitches to a flagstick without competition often results in a lack of focus. Remember, you want to practice like you play. Putting $1 on each swing and a competitor's ball on the green simulates competition and builds confidence.

The more individual battles you edge your opponent out in, the more dollars you earn; therefore, this game also teaches you not to let up on your opponent when you're ahead and not to give up when you're down. Some folks say that the best way to get a shot close to the hole is to try to sink it, and this game provides you plenty of incentive to hole shots.

Here's the deal: You and a friend grab a small bucket of practice balls (40) and meet at the chipping green. Upon arrival, follow these steps:

1. **Pick a grassy spot about 20 paces off the green and divide the balls between the two of you.**

2. **Taking turns, pitch the balls to the hole one at a time.**

3. **After you each pitch one, keep track of whose ball stops closer to the hole.**

   Whoever's pitch is closer to the hole goes up 1 point. Wager $1 for each point — and $5 for holing a shot — and keep a running tally of the score.

4. **Keep the game going until you pitch all the balls.**

5. **Loser pays up!**

   Of course, you don't have to play for money. Try substituting a hot dog in the clubhouse or a drink after the session for the winner. Anything that keeps you competitive and driven to win!

 After you hit and retrieve the first 20 balls and you figure the totals, try a different club. If you used a pitching wedge for the first round, try crafting less-lofted shots with an 8-iron in the second round. This variety helps you develop a strong sense of distance, feel, and touch — the key to shots around the greens. You can also create certain types of golf shots for subsequent rounds by

   ✔ Pitching from a bad lie

   ✔ Placing the ball in heavy rough

   ✔ Pitching over a bunker

   ✔ Blasting out of the sand

   ✔ Rehearsing other on-course conditions, such as chipping balls from behind a tree or hitting balls over a branch

Horse-ing around

Consistency wins this game and rounds on the golf course. Being able to sink 5-footers under pressure isn't a talent; it's a gift — and a skill that you can improve through a game such as *Horse*.

Saddle up for a game of Horse by following these steps:

1. **You and an opponent take one golf ball each to the practice green.**

2. **Just as in the basketball version of Horse, one player picks a spot around the hole and attempts to sink a putt from there.**

   • **If player one sinks it:** His opponent must sink it too. If the opponent fails to duplicate the putt, he picks up an *H,* the first letter of H-o-r-s-e. If player two sinks it, player one conjures up another challenge.

   • **If player one misses it:** Player two chooses a putt of his own design and attempts to make it.

You can shorten the game word to *Pig* if you're short on time; for that matter, you can really pick any word that tickles your fancy.

3. The first player to get stuck with all five letters spelling "Horse" loses.

Just as in the basketball game, your first temptation may be to choose wild, long, downhill, or sidehill shots with swinging breaks in them. These tough putts are fun and useful to practice, so keep your opponent guessing by mixing in the occasional cross-country slider. But making your opponent sink a straight-in 5-footer right after you make yours is a sure way to give him fits, too. (For more on putting fundamentals, head to Chapter 6 of Book III.)

Bingo Bango Bongo (Jingles)

Bingo Bango Bongo is a short-game competition that you can play on the golf course during a round. Also known as *Jingles,* the game works best with a foursome. Bingo Bango Bongo is great fun because players of varying strength and age can compete because of the game's focus on the short game. Now you have a fun way to see how your short game stacks up against others'.

The fun begins at the first tee by following these steps:

1. Starting at the tee, each player plays a ball.

You must remember to execute your shots according to the etiquette of golf, which dictates that the player farthest from the hole plays first.

2. Three points are awarded on each hole:

- One point for the *first on* (the first ball on the green)

- One point for the *closest to* (the closest ball to the hole) after everyone is on the green

- One point for the *first in* (the first ball in the hole)

Although getting the ball on the green and close to the hole is obviously the goal, strategy should enter in from time to time. For instance, if a player has no chance of reaching the green to win the first-on point, she may carefully lay up her ball into a good position from which to chip for the closest-to point. (You can also turn this practice exercise into a betting game; see Chapter 3 in Book IV for details.)

The game sounds simple, but it can become a dramatic and complex strategic match. Here are a few sample scenarios to help explain the game:

✔ **First on:** Assume that all four players hit their drives on a par-4 and Johnny rests the farthest from the hole at 170 yards out. Johnny has the first chance to win the first-on point — if he hits the green! If he misses the green, the next farthest player to the hole has a chance to win the point for first on, and so forth.

✔ **Closest to:** You also have incentive to get the ball not only onto the green but also close to the hole because you can gain a point for that. Johnny misses the green by 5 yards to the right with his second shot. Maggie, who stands at 160 yards out, plays next. She hits the green, so Maggie wins the first-on point. The other two players, Harrison and Julie, hit the green in turn with their shots. All three players who hit the green are various distances from the hole, but Johnny still has to play up. If he can get the ball closer to the hole than anyone on the green, he wins the closest-to point. The point is awarded to whoever lands closest to the pin after all players are on the green, no matter how many shots it takes, as long as the players hit in turn.

✔ **First in:** After all four players land the green, the putter decides the first-in point. Johnny wins the closest-to point by hitting his chip shot to within 5 feet of the hole. Harrison's ball is farthest from the hole — 20 feet away — so he gets the first chance to putt. If he holes it, he wins the first-in point.

Bingo Bango Bongo requires golfers to play in turn, based on who is *away,* which is the traditional manner of play in standard, competitive golf. But many golfers, in the interest of speedy play, subscribe to playing *ready golf,* meaning any ready player can hit. If you want to play Bingo Bango Bongo, each player, in the interest of maintaining speedy play, should always be ready to hit in turn and be aware of where the other players are at all times.

Snake

Throughout the ages, the sinister snake has symbolized evil. On the golf course, nothing is more evil, more heartbreaking, and more maddening than a 3-putt. You play *Snake* on the golf course to punish the 3-putt.

Snake sharpens your putting by forcing you to pay closer attention to your first putt. Many players hit their first putts during a round carelessly and without real purpose. Snake teaches you to be more precise with your putts — not running them too far by or leaving them woefully short — because the punishment for a 3-putt means more than just another stroke on your scorecard. It means hearing it from your partners.

Holing out all your putts is a good habit to get into. Although you may find it sporting to concede small putts to each other in the interest of speedy play, you encounter times, particularly when you play in stroke-play tournaments, when you need to make 2-footers. The slightest lack of attention to a 2-foot tap-in can result in a hideous miss, as you find out playing Snake.

Follow these steps, and the game of Snake is on:

1. **Purchase a rubber snake at any toy store — the uglier the snake, the better.**

2. **As soon as the round of golf begins, pull the reptile from your golf bag.**

3. **The first player to 3-putt takes possession of the snake, and the other players hang it from his golf bag or cart.**

   Be sure to putt in turn based on who's away — more than one player may 3-putt on a given green.

4. **The 3-putter suffers the indignity of carrying the snake until another player 3-putts.**

5. **The player who carries the snake when the round ends loses the match.**

You concede no gimmes or inside the leather putts in Snake. *Gimmes* are putts so short that the players assume they're unmissable and concede them in a friendly match. *Inside the leather* means that if a putt is shorter than the length of your putter grip (a throwback to when grips were made of leather, not rubber), you count it as a gimme putt. Because of the pressure the Snake game induces, you must hole all putts, no matter how short.

If you want to make Snake more interesting, put a friendly wager on the outcome. Flip to Chapter 3 in Book IV for the lowdown.

Snake provides some natural opportunities to tease your opponents mercilessly. But be warned: You may be on the receiving end of some ribbing as well. Three-putts resulting from missing little tap-ins that players normally concede during friendly rounds can be embarrassing and frustrating. Go easy on the needle, unless you can handle the other players applying it to your backside!

Eight in a Row

Do you believe that you can make eight 8-foot putts in a row? You may be able to.

Eight in a Row is a fantastic putting game that you can play all by yourself. The immediate improvement of your putting may astound you after you play the game. Putting consistently is a huge confidence builder. The knowledge that you can hole eight 8-footers in a row in practice takes the teeth out of a knee-knocking 4-footer on the golf course.

Take these steps toward putting success:

1. **Pull eight balls from your golf bag.**

2. **Find a fairly flat hole on a practice green and pull the flag from the hole.**

3. **Set yourself up 2 feet from the hole and try to make all eight putts consecutively.**

   If you miss one, start over until you make all eight putts.

4. **Back up one foot and try to make all the 3-foot putts consecutively.**

   If you miss one, begin again until you make all eight putts consecutively. If you fail to make all the 3-footers again, go back to 2 feet and start over.

5. **Repeat the process, increasing the distance by 1 foot every time you make eight consecutive putts.**

   Keep going until you stand 8 feet from the hole. Don't be startled when you find yourself repeatedly draining 8-footers.

6. **After you master the flat putt, try the same game on a sidehill, uphill, or downhill putt.**

Making a bunch of 2-foot putts consecutively isn't difficult. It may seem easy, as may the 3-footers, after you get into a rhythm. But this game tests your focus and attention span. If you allow your mind to wander, you quickly find out how easy it is to miss a 3-footer.

You also find that the pressure increases as you back up. After you take the time and energy to hole eight consecutive putts from 2, 3, and 4 feet, that eighth putt from the 5-foot range is important. After all, who wants to go back to 2 feet and start all over again?

First to Make Five

Arriving late at the golf course with only a limited time to warm up on the practice green? The best way to roll as many putts as possible is to join forces with another player. Instead of taking four or five balls to the practice green and chasing them around, pick a partner and grab one ball each.

After you each have a ball in hand, follow these steps to quickly get up to speed:

1. **Choose two holes on the practice green cut about 10 to 15 feet apart.**

2. **Position yourself to the side of one hole while your partner stands at the other.**

   Keep your ball between your feet and the hole closest to you.

3. **At the same time, or in a quickly alternating fashion, putt to the opposite hole.**

4. **When the ball arrives at or in your hole, rake it up and putt it to the other hole.**

5. **The first player to sink five putts wins.**

You can switch sides to continue the game.

Although the name *First to Make Five* implies a race, don't hurry yourself. The speed of this game isn't important. You can hit putt after putt in rapid fashion, but concentrate on making good strokes and trying to hole your putts. Think of the alternating putts as baseball innings.

Because you don't have to retrieve your putts (a fresh ball your opponent putts instantly arrives at your feet), you can roll countless putts and build a solid, repeating, confident stroke in a short time. After you and your practice partner find a rhythm, you don't have to move your feet to keep putting — you begin to read the break and the speed so well that the 10- to 15-foot putt seems easy, so you start to putt without fear. Your only goal is to consistently make that putt.

Subconsciously, when you go onto the golf course, you find yourself confidently attempting 15-foot putts because you know the speed and develop a hunger for sinking them.

The practice prowess of Se Ri Pak

At the age of 14, a high-school track star named Se Ri Pak took up golf. Six years later, in 1998, Pak was named the LPGA Rookie of the Year! By the end of her 2003 season, she became a virtual lock for the LPGA Hall of Fame, having won 21 times, including four LPGA major championships.

Talk about the fast track. Pak was an overnight success, right? How did she do it? "I really love golf. I love to play, so I spend most of my time at the golf course. I always like to spend time on my game," she said before the 2002 U.S. Women's Open.

You can relate, right? Yeah, you can relate . . . if, like her, spending time at the golf course means nine-hour practice sessions. Se Ri, on her "off days," practices all aspects of her game, including myriad short-game shots, over a nine-hour session (with a one-hour lunch break).

But how can she possibly keep her mind engaged while she hits practice shots for nine hours? She squints with confusion when asked the question. "It's my job," she finally answers.

Chapter 4

Stepping Up Your Game

In This Chapter

▶ Challenging yourself to play better

▶ Saving strokes by thinking ahead

▶ Taking notes from the game's greats

After you have a good sense of what kind of golfer you are, know your strengths and weaknesses, and get to the point where you can usually keep the ball in play with more 4s, 5s, and 6s on your scorecard than 8s, 9s, and Xs, you're ready to take the next step: improving your game. In this chapter, we show you how to set reasonable goals for your improvement, make smart stroke-gaining decisions, and emulate the attitudes of some great golfing pros.

Shifting from Novice to Greatness

Golf is hard. Few master the game, and nobody perfects it. But one of the great things about this game is that it rewards a little effort almost as much as a lot of blood, sweat, and blisters. After you get over *the hump* — the initial period when everything is new and the club feels weird in your hand — your improvement can be rapid. Some beginners can go from shooting 120, 130, or more for 18 holes to shooting around 100 in a matter of months.

Of course, the better you get, the harder you have to work to whittle away the next ten strokes. Did we say ten strokes? How about one, or even less than one? Touring pros would gladly work like maniacs to save half a stroke off their per-round statistics. Matt Kuchar led the PGA Tour in 2010 with an average score of 69.59, while Charlie Wi tied for 12th with an average of 70.09, exactly half a stroke worse. Kuchar raked in $4.9 million, and Wi earned $1.5 million, or less than a third as much! That's an extreme example — Kuchar played more rounds and played his best at the right moments, winning $1.35 million for a single tournament victory. But it goes to show you how valuable each stroke can be at the game's highest level.

Keep in mind that you don't have to *break* 70 like Kuchar — that is, shoot 69 or better — to have a breakthrough on the course. You don't have to break 80, 90, or even 100. Depending on your experience and physical abilities, breaking 120 may be the achievement of a lifetime.

What matters more than the number is setting goals. If you set out to make par on every hole, you're pretty much guaranteed to spend the day grumbling. The great Annika Sorenstam had an approach she (and coaches Pia Nilsson and Lynn Marriott) called Vision 54. The idea was to birdie every hole. Because most courses have a par of 72, that would give her a "perfect" round of 54.

Annika got within five shots of that number, firing a historic 59 in a tournament in 2001. But don't shoot for perfection, at least until you're playing in front of thousands of fans. Give yourself a goal that's challenging but reachable:

- ✔ I'm going to break 110 (or 100) this year.
- ✔ I'm going to play a whole round without 3-putting.
- ✔ I'm going to shoot my best score yet.
- ✔ I'm going to keep the ball in play and finish a round with the same ball I teed off with.

We know one player who was so focused on improving that he taped the words *Break 100 — and celebrate* on his golf bag. He was 13 years old, and doing it took him all summer. One day, he finished a round of 98, tore the message off his bag, and set a match to it. He's enjoyed the game for 40 years since then but still calls that his favorite day on the course.

Surveying Strategic Stroke-Savers

If your dream is to progress from beginner to intermediate golfer, remember one word above all: practice. May we reiterate the most important tip any golfer ever got? *Practice!*

Thank you. And if you promise to heed that crucial bit of advice, following the methods outlined in this book, we'll offer some tips that can help you get to the next level.

Minimizing trouble

Picture a hole with danger on the right: dense rainforest, with volcanoes, swooping pterodactyls, machine-gun nests, and probably vampires. That's an exaggeration, but you get the picture. And on the left, clean green fairway as far as the eye can see.

GARY SAYS

The reds, whites, and blues

Just as you start to feel ready to advance in this game, it often grabs you and drags you, kicking and screaming, back to where you were last month — or last year.

So don't get ahead of yourself. Too many golfers hit a few good shots in a row or shoot a career round and believe they've reached a new level of play. They're often the ones you see at your local course, playing from the blue tees . . . and dribbling worm-burners that never reach the fairway. You'll be better off playing to your level of skill — and gaining confidence.

I mention the various tee boxes in Chapter 3, Book I. Closest to the green are the junior and/or women's tees. They're often red. Next come the regulation tees, often called the men's tees. They're usually white. Then come the blue tees

for better players. Still farther back, you find the championship tees, often reserved for tournament play and black or gold in color. They're often called *the tips,* as in "I shot 66 from the tips today."

The blues are widely abused. And believe me, you don't want to be the drive-dribbling impostor in the blue-man group. That makes you unpopular with others in your foursome as well as those in groups behind you because you're the one holding up the pace of play. The *marshal,* whose job it is to keep each group moving at a reasonable pace, may even ask you to pick up your ball.

So unless you consistently shoot in the low 80s, stick to the white tees. It's healthier for your score, your psyche, and the pace of play.

Now watch your typical amateur set up to hit his drive. Does he adjust? Noooo, he aims right down the middle, as if this hole were just like any other. And two times out of three, he slices his drive into the vampires.

TIP

When danger lurks, shirk it. On a hole where all or most of the trouble is on one side, change your aim. You should choose a target that keeps your shot safe even if you miss toward the trouble.

The same is true for shots with your irons. If you see a pond or bunker in front of the green but no trouble behind it, shift your target. Take more club and try to hit the ball to the back part of the green. (See the later section "Taking one more club" for more on this suggestion.) You may be surprised how often you come up a little short — and the shot turns out to be perfect! You may even begin to notice how architects often bank the back of such a green to favor the smart shot.

If you tend to leave sand shots short, like most players do, quit trying to land the ball short of the hole. Visualize a longer shot, with the ball landing beyond the flagstick. You double your margin for error and wind up escaping more bunkers. (After you get more proficient, of course, you need to do that less and less.)

The putting surface offers its own danger. If the hole is cut near a drop-off in the green, the greenskeeper may be inviting you to 3-putt. Outsmart him by leaving your lag putt a few inches shorter than usual for a safe tap-in.

The safer side of the hole is almost always the side below the hole. You'd much rather have an uphill 2- or 3-footer than a downhill slider of the same length.

Knowing when to be a hero

Golf is a game of risk and reward. It usually rewards those who limit risk, playing "within themselves." As Socrates once said (or was it Snead?), the race doesn't always go to the swift, or the golf match to the smart player, but that's the way to bet. That said, sometimes the smart golfer embraces risk. And those can be some of the most exciting, *fun* times of all.

Suppose you're playing a best-ball match, and your partner's ball is safely on the green. Or you're in a scramble, and one or more of your three partners has struck a good shot. (For information on various team formats, see Chapter 1 of Book V.) You've got a next-to-impossible shot over water, trees, and a barn to a green the size of a sticky note. Or maybe it's only a tricky flip from rough to a slippery green, as in Figure 4-1. Now's the time to go for it! If you splash the shot or even *chili-dip* it (hit behind the ball), it's no loss. But if you succeed, you're a hero to your partners and yourself. What's more, you gain confidence for the next time you face such a shot.

The same goes for a less glorious situation. In match play, if you're down by two holes with two to play, for example, and your opponent is safely on the green, you can't just match his or her score on the hole. You've got to win it. So hitch up your courage and fire at the flag.

When you encounter the occasional must-make putt, whether it's a 3-footer or a 20-footer like the one in Figure 4-2, don't forget the one cardinal rule: *Don't leave it short!*

Taking one more club

Do yourself a favor and *take more club*. Pro golfers are pessimists, or at least realists. That's because it's a humbling game. They know how easily things can go wrong on the course, so they guard against disaster — or even bogey — and usually aim for the wide side of the fairway or the fat part of the green.

Figure 4-1:
In some tricky cases, you can go for the heroic shot.

Figure 4-2:
If it's a do-or-die putt, it absolutely, positively has to reach the hole.

Your typical amateur is the exact opposite. After he bombs one 250-yard drive, the longest of his life, he's convinced they're all going to go that far. After she hits a 6-iron to a green 150 yards away, she reaches for the same club every time she's got a 150-yard shot.

May we be diplomatic here? All right, please attend to these words of wisdom: *Don't be an idiot!* Smart golf is more about typical shots than career shots. That's why the pros spend so much time determining precisely how far they *usually* hit a particular club. It's why you should pay more attention to your average shot than to the laser beam you blasted over the dogleg at 15.

Say you're *between clubs* — a little closer to the target than you want for a shot with one of the clubs in your bag, a little farther than you want for a shot with a different club. For example, many players hit an 8-iron about 140 yards and a 7-iron about 150. What should they hit from 145?

You're way ahead of us here. As a rule of thumb, hit the longer club. You come out ahead in the long run because your less-than-perfect shots will turn out better. In fact, most amateur golfers score better when they try a simple test: Each time they'd usually hit a 7-iron, they hit a 6-iron, and each time they'd usually hit a 6-iron, they hit a 5-iron. Try it yourself, and you can see what we mean.

Just don't get discouraged if you catch one pure and knock it over the green. Enjoy the feeling of solid contact; store it in your muscle-memory bank. But remind yourself: This game is all about typical shots.

Seeking help from the pros

The time when you're setting new goals may be the perfect time for a lesson. A PGA professional can spot flaws that may have crept into your swing and offer tips to help you reach your next level. He or she can also provide invaluable advice on your equipment. Ask these questions (and check out Chapter 2 of Book I for more on lessons):

- ✔ Can I keep improving without major swing changes?
- ✔ Is my practice routine appropriate to my current game and to the level I want to reach?
- ✔ Are my clubs appropriate to my current game and to the level I want to reach?

As golf's glorious road leads you to lower scores, you may seek more technological assistance through launch monitors and high-tech swing analysis. It's all part of the never-ending pursuit of happiness, or at least a half-stroke improvement.

Channeling the Golf Champions

If you're a weekend basketball player, you're probably not doing your own game much good to watch Kobe Bryant soar to the hoop for a thunderous dunk. As hard as you may try, you couldn't match that feat without a ladder or a jetpack.

Just as you likely can't dunk like Kobe, slug homers like Albert Pujols and A-Rod, or crush an overhead smash like Serena Williams, you'll probably never play a full round of golf like Tiger Woods or Phil Mickelson. But you can apply aspects of great golfers' games to your own as you work to improve.

If you're looking to step up toward the promised land where drives soar out of sight and putts disappear, emulate these exemplary players:

✔ **Ernie Els:** Ernie has been swinging like syrup for more than 20 years on tour. Despite some recent physical woes, he has one of the smoothest moves the game has ever seen. And under the most intense pressure, with the world watching, he seems to relax even more. A competitive fire lurks under that calm exterior, and probably at least some of the same terrors that beset all golfers. But the Big Easy doesn't show it, and that helps keep his swing nice and easy when it counts.

Before your next really important shot, step back. Take a deep breath and picture Ernie's smooth, unhurried swing.

✔ **Tiger Woods:** Tiger went through a personal and professional crisis in 2010, but many still expect him to come back in a big way, winning more majors as he chases Jack Nicklaus's record of 18. That's due in part to his track record. Unlike most great athletes, Woods wasn't satisfied with being the best. Earlier in the decade, the already-top-ranked golfer decided he had to improve. So he rebuilt his swing and played even better. At his best, he's been both the game's best player and its greatest *grinder* — a golfer who gives his absolute all on every shot whether he's tied for the lead or ten strokes behind.

During your occasional bad rounds, grind out a bogey that could have been a double- or triple-bogey. Even if your score that day is terrible, you'll have something to be proud of.

✔ **Phil Mickelson:** Phil was the modern Arnold Palmer, always taking chances and never laying up, until he realized he wasn't going to win majors that way. By banking his fires a little and choosing discretion over valor, he took a step to the very forefront of the game. Phil can still hit the heroic miracle shot when he has to; he just doesn't feel he always has to.

Play a practice round with two balls. Play it safe with one ball, and go for broke with the other. Compare your scores. And whatever happens with your hero ball, enjoy giving it a ride.

✔ **Christina Kim:** Christina is an LPGA star who wears her emotions on her colorful sleeves. A sharp dresser and fan favorite, she treats golf as a joy, not a job. Through 2010 she had two tour victories — no majors yet, but keep an eye on Christina and an ear out for her next highly quotable quip.

Try playing a round as if you didn't have a care in the world, as if just hitting the shot were the whole point, regardless of the outcome. You'll probably have a blast out there, and you may even play better.

✔ **Jim Furyk:** Jim had a weird swing when he was a kid, and he still does. Commentator David Feherty describes it as "like an octopus falling out of a tree." And Jim still has that unique swing because he and his father, Mike, resisted every attempt to change it when Jim was growing up. Jim actually delivers the club to the ball in near-perfect, classic fashion (that's why his swing works), and he plays with a belief in himself that owes a lot to the way he and his dad stuck to their guns.

When you play with golfers whose swings are prettier than yours, remind yourself that it's *how many* that counts in golf, not *how*. Picture 40-year-old Furyk playing with all those guys with picture-perfect swings in September 2010. All he did was win the season-ending Tour Championship and its first prize of $1.35 million. Plus a little bonus for claiming the FedEx Cup: another $10 million.

✔ **Jack Nicklaus:** Jack was a master at just about everything, really, with six Masters championships among his all-time-record 18 major titles, but he was particularly brilliant at minimizing danger and at *course management* — moving the ball around the course in a way that optimized his chances. The Golden Bear *faded* the ball from left to right with great consistency, so he seldom had to worry about trouble on the left. And although the weakest part of his game was wedge play ("weak" only compared to the rest of his genius game), that didn't matter much: Jack would bomb the ball all the way to the green, or lay up so that he had a 9-iron shot.

Strategize like Jack by laying up once in awhile, leaving yourself a full shot to the green.

✔ **Erik Compton:** Erik, a Florida pro, has spent much of his career on the minor-league Nationwide Tour, one rung below the PGA Tour. Not bad for a former college star who has endured two heart transplants. His health and strength are always a worry, but he doesn't complain, saying he's lucky to be playing the game he loves. Few people in any walk of life have shown more heart than Erik.

Step up, swing hard, and smile. Isn't it great to be alive?

Book VI

Easy Fixes for Common Faults

"My golf teacher is also a psychiatrist. I still play as badly as I always have, but now I blame my mother and father for it."

In this book . . .

Have you ever had one of those days when nothing goes right? You hit one ball fat, the next one thin, and when you do hit the thing solidly, it slices into the parking lot! This book is about the many maladies that can afflict your golf game and how to cure them. We've got remedies for what ails you.

In this book, we also tell you how to play in all sorts of weather and how to deal with the bad breaks you're sure to encounter. We even give you tips on playing through the cold and the rain. Finally, we include a glossary that contains all sorts of golf-specific terms.

Here are the contents of Book VI at a glance.

Chapter 1

Solving Common Problems

· ·

In This Chapter

▶ Coming to terms with everyday swing flaws

▶ Conquering errant tee shots

▶ Focusing on ball contact and direction

▶ Dealing with the scary shank

· ·

The old saying is true in golf, as in life: Nobody's perfect. In golf, nobody's even close. Even the best players have some little hitches in their methods that bedevil them, especially under pressure. Greg Norman once had a tendency to hit the ball well to the right of the target on the closing holes of big tournaments. Phil Mickelson and Tiger Woods have gone through periods when they drove the ball crookedly at the worst possible times. Watch your playing companions when they get a little nervous; you can see all sorts of unfortunate events. They leave putts short and take longer to play even simple shots. Conversation all but stops. Any flaws in their swings are cruelly exposed.

No matter how far you progress in this game, you're going to develop faults of your own. They're a given. The trick is catching your faults before they get worse. Faults left unattended often turn into major problems and ruin your game. In this chapter, we show you how to head off (pun intended) many faults by controlling your head position. Then we discuss the most common faults you're likely to develop, with cures for each one. After you figure out what you tend to do wrong, you can refer to this chapter regularly to get help.

Using Your Head for Better Golf

The root cause of most faults is your head position. Your noggin's position relative to the ball as you strike it dictates where the bottom of your swing is. If you don't believe that, try this: Shift your weight and your head toward the target onto your left side while leaving the ball in its regular position. Now make your normal swing with, say, a 6-iron.

The divot the club makes is more in front of the ball. The bottom of your swing moves toward the target along with your head. The opposite is also true. Shift your weight and head to the right, and the bottom of your swing moves that way.

The bottom line: If your head moves too much during the swing, you have little chance to correct things before impact, and the result is usually poor contact — and a poor shot.

But don't get the idea that excessive head movement is responsible for absolutely every bad shot. Other poor plays can stem from improper use of your hands, arms, or body. But try to keep your head as steady as possible.

Swinging Into Action: Swing Faults

Most bad shots result from a handful of common swing errors. Fortunately, they're fixable. Here's how to beat back the gremlins that can creep into your game.

Slicing and hooking

Most golfers *slice* the ball, which means that it starts moving toward the left of the target and finishes well to the right. Slices don't go very far. They're horrible, weak shots that affect your DNA for generations to come.

In general, slicers use too much body action, especially upper body, and not enough hand action in their swings. Slicing likely stems from the fact that most players tend to aim to the right of their target. When they do so, their swings have to compensate so the resulting shots can finish close to the target. In most cases, that compensation starts when your brain realizes that if you swing along your aim, the ball will fly way to the right. The resulting flurry of arms and legs isn't pretty — and invariably, neither is the shot. Soon this weak, left-to-right ball flight makes your life a slicing hell.

If you're a slicer, you need to get your hands working in the swing. Here's how:

1. **Address a ball as you normally do.**

   Address is the position of your body just before you begin to swing.

2. **Turn your whole body until your butt is toward the target and your feet are perpendicular to the target line.**

3. **Twist your upper body to the left so you can again place the clubhead behind the ball.**

   Don't move your feet, however. From this position, you have in effect made turning your body to your left on the through-swing impossible (see Figure 1-1).

If you slice, try this drill:
Stand with your back to the target.
Then turn your whole body until
your butt is to the target and twist
your upper body to address the ball.

Swing back…

Figure 1-1:
Extra hand
action cures
the slice.

and then swing your
hands and arms through…

to finish. The ball should fly from
right to left.

Try it. The only way you can swing the club through the ball is by using
your hands and arms.

4. **Hit a few balls.**

Focus on letting the toe of the clubhead pass your heel through impact. Quite a change in your ball flight, eh? Because your hands and arms are doing so much of the rotating work in your new swing, the clubhead is doing the same. The clubhead is now closing as it swings through the impact area. The spin imparted on the ball now causes a slight right-to-left flight — something you probably thought you'd never see.

After you've hit about 20 shots by using this drill, switch to your normal stance and try to reproduce the feel you had standing in that strange but correct way. You'll soon be hitting hard, raking *draws* (slight hooks) far up the fairway.

Golfers prone to *hooks* (shots that start right and finish left) have the opposite problem of slicers — too much hand action and not enough body. Here's a variation on the earlier drill if you tend to hook the ball:

1. **Adopt your regular stance.**

2. **Turn your whole body until you're looking directly at the target.**

3. **Twist your upper body to the right — don't move your feet — until you can set the clubhead behind the ball (see Figure 1-2).**

4. **Hit some shots.**

Solid contact is easiest to achieve when you turn your body hard to the left, which prevents your hands from becoming overactive. Your ball flight will soon be a gentle *fade* (slight slice).

After about 20 shots, hit some balls from your normal stance, practicing the technique in the exercise. Reproduce the feel of this drill, and you're that much closer to a successful swing.

Hitting from the top

When you start cocking the wrist in your golf swing, the thumb of your right hand (if you're a right-handed golfer) points at your right shoulder on the backswing. That's good! When you start the downswing, try to keep that thumb pointing at your right shoulder for as long as you can, thus *maintaining the angle*. That's golfspeak for keeping the shaft of the club as close to the left arm on the downswing as possible. If your right thumb starts pointing away from your right shoulder on the downswing, not good! That's known as *hitting from the top*. In essence, you're uncocking the wrist on the downswing.

If you hit hooks, try this drill:
Stand with both feet facing the target. Then turn your upper body until you are facing the target.

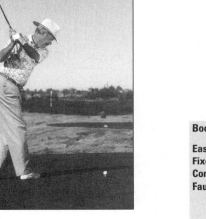

Swing back...

Figure 1-2:
Extra body action straightens your hook.

and then turn your body in concert with the club...

to finish. The ball should fly from left to right.

To stop hitting from the top, reduce your grip pressure. Too much tension in your hands makes you throw the clubhead toward the ball, causing you to hit from the top. After you've relaxed your grip pressure, place an alignment stick (flexible fiberglass stick used to aid alignment) or an old 2-by-4 on the side of the ball away from you, parallel to the target line. The ball should be about 2 inches from the stick. If you keep pointing your right thumb at your right shoulder on the downswing, you don't hit the stick with your club. If you point your thumb away from your shoulder on the downswing, you may just chop that stick in half. (See Figure 1-3 for a visual of this stroke.)

The reverse pivot

A *reverse pivot* occurs when you put all your weight on your left foot on the backswing (shown in Figure 1-4) and all your weight on your right foot during the downswing. That's the opposite of what you want to do!

Picture a baseball pitcher. Pitchers have all their weight on the right foot at the top of the windup, the left foot is in the air (for a right-hander), and on the follow-through, all the weight goes to the left foot. (The right foot is now in the air.) That's the weight transfer you need. Here's how you can achieve it:

1. **Start your backswing; at the top of your swing, lift your left foot off the ground.**

   Now you can't put any weight on that foot! You'll feel your whole body resist placing your weight over your right foot.

2. **Take your time and let your weight transfer to your right foot.**

3. **Start the downswing by placing your left foot back where it was and then transfer all your weight over during the swing.**

4. **When you've made contact with the ball (hopefully), put all your weight on your left foot and lift your right foot off the ground.**

5. **Stand there for a short time, feeling the balance.**

This rocking-chair transfer drill lets you feel the proper weight shift in the golf swing. Take it easy at first. Practice short shots until you get the feel, and then work your way up to your driver.

Another good way to avoid a reverse pivot is to keep the right knee flexed through the swing. This tweak will help keep weight on the right side.

On the downswing, try to point your right thumb at your right shoulder (if you're right-handed).

Keep trying!

So this is how the big bombers do it!

Figure 1-3: Don't hit from the top!

Figure 1-4:
The dreaded
reverse
pivot.

Swaying off the ball

In a *sway,* your hips and shoulders don't turn on the backswing but simply slide back in a straight line, which moves your head away from the ball, as shown in Figure 1-5. Here's a good drill to help you stop swaying:

1. **Find a bare wall.**

2. **Place a 5-iron on the ground with the clubhead touching the wall and the shaft extending straight into the room.**

3. **Place your right foot against the end of the shaft with the little toe of your right shoe hitting the end of the club.**

   Now you're standing exactly one club length from the wall.

4. **Put your left foot in the normal address position for the 5-iron and, without moving your feet, bend over and pick up the club.**

5. **Take a backswing.**

   If you sway with your hips 1 inch to the right on your backswing, you hit the wall immediately with the club.

Figure 1-5:
The
sway ain't
the way.

TIP

Practice this setup until you can do it without hitting the wall.

We suggest practicing this drill in your garage at first to save the walls at home. You may want to use an old club, too.

The belly-button twist

Another common fault is doing the *belly-button twist:* sliding your hips too far toward the target at the start of the downswing. How far should your hips slide before they start turning left? They must slide until your left hip and left knee are over your left foot. Then those hips turn left in a hurry!

Here's how to improve your hip position at the downswing:

1. **Get a broken club that has just a shaft and a grip on it.**

   You can find broken clubs in lost-and-found barrels, or just ask somebody at a driving range. Your golf pro can also help you find one. You can also use a broom handle or alignment stick — any stick you can plant in the ground.

2. **Stick the broken club into the ground just outside your left foot; the top of the grip should be no higher than your hip.**

3. **Now hit a few shots.**

When you swing, your left hip should not hit the club stuck in the ground. It should turn to the left of the shaft. The key here is to straighten the left leg in your follow-through. To help you stay balanced, try to "hold" your finish at the end of the follow-through.

A swing that's too short

In most cases, a short swing comes from too little shoulder turn. Turn your left shoulder over your right foot at the top of your backswing. If you can't, lift your left heel off the ground until you can. Many players with short swings also keep their right elbows against their rib cages at the top of the swing. The right elbow should be 6 inches away from the rib cage to allow some freedom in the swing and give the needed length to your swing arc.

A swing that's too long

If your swing is too long and sloppy (going beyond parallel to the ground at the top of the swing), here are two positions to work on:

- ✔ The right arm in the backswing (for a right-handed golfer) must not bend more than 90 degrees. It must stay at a right angle (see Figure 1-6).

- ✔ The right elbow must not get more than 6 inches away from your rib cage at the top of the backswing.

If you can maintain these two simple positions at the top of your swing, you don't overswing.

Figure 1-6: Do the right (angle) thing in your backswing.

Your right arm should form a right angle at the elbow.

Tackling Tee Trouble

What's worse than starting a hole with a pitiful bloop or a screamer into uncharted lands? That's trouble with a capital tee! To get well off the tee, you need to avoid the common blunders in the following sections.

Popping up your tee shots

One of the most common sights on the first tee of a pro-am or member-guest tournament is the *skied* tee shot — the ball goes higher than it goes forward. The golfer usually hits the ball on the top part of the driver, causing an ugly mark to appear, which is one reason a tour player never lets an amateur use his driver. If the amateur hits such a *fountain ball* (a skied tee shot that has the same trajectory as one of those fountains in Italy) with another player's driver, he has a lot of apologizing to do.

If you're hitting the ball on the top side of your driver, you're swinging the club on too much of a downward arc. What's that mean, you ask? It means that your head is too far in front of the ball (toward the target side of the ball) and your left shoulder is too low at impact.

Here's what to do:

1. **Go find an upslope.**
2. **Stand so your left foot (if you're right-handed) is higher than your right.**
3. **Tee the ball up and hit drivers or 3-woods until you get the feeling of staying back and under the shot.**

   The uphill lie promotes this feeling.

Here's a secret: People who hit down on their drivers want to kill the ball in front of their buddies. These golfers have a tremendous shift of weight to the left side on the downswing. If you hit balls from an upslope, you can't get your weight to the left side as quickly. Consequently, you keep your head behind the ball, and your left shoulder goes up at impact. Practice on an upslope until you get a feel and then proceed to level ground. You'll turn your pop-ups into line drives.

Suffering from a power outage

Every golfer in the world wants more distance. Tiger Woods and Michelle Wie want more distance. We want more distance, and we're sure you do, too. For that, you need more power. Here's how to make it happen:

✔ **Turn your shoulders on the backswing.** The more you turn your shoulders on the backswing, the better chance you have to hit the ball longer. So really stretch that torso on the backswing — try to put your left shoulder over your right foot at the top of your swing. Thinking that you're turning your back to the target may help.

If you're having difficulty moving your shoulders enough on the backswing, try turning your left knee clockwise until it's pointing behind the ball during your backswing. This setup frees up your hips, and subsequently your shoulders, to turn. A big turn starts from the ground up.

✔ **Get the tension out of your grip.** Hold the club loosely; you should grip it with the pressure of holding a spotted owl's egg. If you have too much tension in your hands, your forearms and chest tighten up, and you lose that valuable flexibility that helps with the speed of your arms and hands.

Turning your hips to the left on the downswing and extending your right arm on the through-swing are trademarks of the longer hitters. Here's a drill to help you accomplish this feat of daring:

1. **Tee up your driver in the normal position.**

2. **Place the ball off your left heel and/or opposite your left armpit.**

3. **Now reach down, not moving your stance, and move the ball toward the target the length of the grip.**

4. **Tee up the ball there; it should be about a foot closer to the hole.**

5. **Address the ball where the normal position was and swing at the ball that's now teed up.**

To hit that ball, you have to move your hips to the left so your arms can reach the ball, thereby causing you to extend your right arm.

Practice this drill 20 times. Then put the ball back in the normal position. You should feel faster with the hips and feel a tremendous extension of your right arm.

Getting Solid Ball Contact

Less-than-solid contact is the payoff you get for a bad day's work on fundamentals. It happens to everyone. The cure is to review — and apply — a few reliable swing basics.

Topping the ball

Topping isn't much fun. Plus, it's a lot of effort for very little return. *Topping* is when you make a full-blooded, nostrils-flaring swipe at the ball only to tick the top and send the ball a few feeble yards. Topping occurs because your head is moving up and down during your swing. A rising head during your downswing pulls your shoulders, arms, hands, and the clubhead up with it. Whoops!

To whip topping, you must keep your head from lifting. The best way to do that is to establish a reference for your eyes before you start the club back. Stick an umbrella in the ground just beyond the golf ball, as shown in Figure 1-7. Focus your eyes on the umbrella throughout your swing. As long as you stay focused on the umbrella, your head and upper torso can't lift, which ends topped shots.

Focus on the umbrella while you swing.

Figure 1-7: The umbrella drill can help you avoid topped shots.

Avoiding the worm burner

Do worms fear your dreaded worm-burner drives? Does your drive look like a scared cat skittering along the ground? If you're having this problem with your driver, make sure your head stays behind the ball at address and at impact. Moving your head back and forth along with your driver can cause too low a shot.

Drivers come in different lofts. If you're hitting the ball too low, try a driver that has 11 to 12 degrees of loft.

If you're having a problem with low iron shots, you're probably trying to lift those golf balls into the air instead of hitting down, as we cover in Chapter 1 of Book III.

Duffing and thinning chip shots

Duffing and thinning are exact opposites, yet, like the slice and the hook we describe earlier in the chapter, they have their roots in a single swing flaw (see Figure 1-8).

When you *duff* a chip (also called a *chili-dip*), your swing is bottoming out behind the ball. You're hitting too much ground and not enough ball (also called *hitting it fat*), which means that the shot falls painfully short of the target and your playing partners laugh outrageously. Duffing a chip is the one shot in golf that can get you so mad that you can't spell your mother's name.

If you continually hit duffs, jam an alignment stick or old club shaft into the ground. Get your nose to the left of the stick, which moves the bottom of your swing forward. Doing so allows you to hit down on the ball from the right position. Make sure that your head stays forward in this shot. Most people who hit an occasional duff move their heads backward as they start their downswings, which means that they hit behind the ball.

Thinned chips (skulls, as they call it on tour) are the opposite of duffs. You aren't hitting enough ground. In fact, you don't hit the ground at all. The club strikes the ball above the equator, sending the shot speeding on its merry way, past the hole into all sorts of evil places. You need to hit the ground slightly so the ball hits the clubface and not the front end of the club.

If you're prone to hit an occasional skull, set up with your nose behind or to the right of the ball, which moves the bottom of your swing back. When you find the right spot, you hit the ball and the ground at the same time, which is good. We've found that most people who hit their shots thin tend to raise their entire bodies up immediately before impact. Concentrate on keeping your upper torso bent the same way throughout the swing.

Neutral position, head over the ball.

If you tend to hit it thin, place your head behind the ball.

If you tend to hit it fat, place your head ahead of the ball.

Figure 1-8: The cure for chipping nightmares.

Double the chip, double the trouble

One shot you rarely witness is the *double chip,* where you hit the chip fat, causing the clubhead to hit the ball twice — once while it's in the air. You couldn't do that if you tried, but sometime, somewhere, you'll see it performed and will stand in amazement.

I was playing a tournament when one of the amateurs, standing near the condos surrounding the course, hit a chip shot. He had to loft the ball gently over a bunker and then have it land on the green like a Nerf ball on a mattress. He hit the shot a little fat, the ball went up in the air slowly, and his club accelerated and hit the ball again about eye level. The ball went over his head, out of bounds, and into the swimming pool. The rule says that you may have only four penalty strokes per swing maximum, but I think he beat that by a bunch with that double-hit chip shot. When I saw him last, he was still trying to retrieve his ball with the homeowner's pool net.

Worrying about backspin

How can you back up the ball like the pros on the tour? People ask this question all the time. The answer: The more steeply you hit down on the ball and the faster you swing, the more spin you generate. People who play golf for a living hit short irons with a very steep angle of descent into the ball, which creates a lot of spin. Their swings get the clubhead moving quickly, creating force that adds more spin. They also tend to play three-piece golf balls with relatively soft covers — balls that spin more than the two-piece ball most people play. (Chapter 1 of Book I explains the different types of golf balls.)

They also play on grass that's manicured and very short so they can get a clean hit with the club off these fairways. All these considerations help when you're trying to spin the ball.

The good news: You don't *need* to spin the ball like the pros. Spin is simply a way of controlling the distance a ball goes. All you need is a consistent swing that hits the ball predictable distances. Whether the ball backs up or rolls forward to get to the target doesn't matter.

So there: Do you like how we made that swing fault disappear?

Missing the Target

Why doesn't the ball go where you aim it? Maybe it *wants* to, but you're giving it bad directions like a busted GPS. Here are three common directional maladies, with remedies.

Pushing

The *push* is a shot that starts right of the target and just keeps going. It's not like a slice, which curves to the right (see "Slicing and hooking" earlier in the chapter); the push just goes right. This shot happens when the body doesn't rotate through to the left on the downswing and the arms hopelessly swing to the right, pushing the ball in that direction.

Hitting a push is like standing at home plate, aiming at the pitcher, and then swinging your arms at the first baseman. If this scenario sounds like you, here's how to hit one up the middle: Place an alignment stick or a wooden 2-by-4 parallel to the target line and about 2 inches beyond the golf ball. If your arms go off to the right now, splinters are going to fly. Naturally, you don't want to hit the stick, so you swing your hips left on the downswing, which pulls your arms left and cures the push.

Pulling

The *pull* is a shot that starts left and stays left, unlike a hook, which curves to the left. (Check out the earlier section "Slicing and hooking" for more on fixing hooks.) The pull is caused when the club comes from outside the target line on the downswing and you pull across your body.

Hitting a pull is like standing at home plate and aiming at the pitcher but swinging the club toward third baseman, which is where the ball would go. This swing malady is a little more complicated than a push, and picking out one exercise to cure it is more difficult, so stay with us.

Pulls happen when your shoulders open too quickly in the downswing. For the proper sequence, your shoulders should remain as close to parallel to the target line as possible at impact. Here's a checklist that can help you cure your pull:

- **Check your alignment.** If you're aimed too far to the right, your body slows down on the downswing and allows your shoulders to open at impact to bring the club back to the target.

- **Check your weight shift.** If you don't shift your weight to your left side on the downswing, you spin your hips out of the way too quickly, causing your shoulders to open up too quickly and hit a putrid pull. So shift those hips toward the target on the downswing until your weight is on your left side after impact.

- **Check your grip pressure.** Too tight a grip on the club causes you to tense up on the downswing and come over the top for a pull.

- **Check your distance from the ball.** If you're too close, you instinctively pull inward on your forward swing — which means pulling to the left.

Spraying the ball

If your shots *spray* (take off in more directions than the compass has to offer), check your alignment and ball position. Choose the direction you're going and then put your feet, knees, and shoulders on a line parallel to the target line. Be very specific with your alignment.

Ball position can play a major part in spraying shots. If the ball is too far forward, you can easily push it to the right. If the ball is too far back in your stance, you can easily hit pushes and pulls. The driver is played opposite your left armpit. (Flip to Chapter 1 of Book III for more on ball placement.)

Here's a check-up for your ball position: Get into your stance — with the driver, for example — and then undo your shoelaces. Step out of your shoes, leaving them right where they were at address. Now take a look: Is the ball where it's supposed to be in your stance? Two suggestions: If it's a wet day, don't try this exercise. And if your socks have holes in them, make sure nobody is watching.

Avoiding Shanks and Point-Blank Misses

They're two of the most-feared mishaps in the game: the short putt and the shank. Shanks can strike when you least expect, sending the ball squirting sideways while you shake your fist at the golf gods. Short, point-blank putts that somehow miss the hole can be just as aggravating — or more aggravating, if you just lost a match by missing one.

But don't despair! The following sections offer simple fixes to these vexing visitations.

Shanking

Flash back a few centuries: Alone with his sheep in a quiet moment of reflection, a shepherd swings his carved crook at a rather round rock toward a distant half-dead, low-growing vine. The rock peels off the old crook, and instead of lurching forward toward the vine, it careens off at an angle 90 degrees to the right of the target. "Zounds! What was that?!" cries the shocked shepherd. "That was a shaaank, you idiot!" cries a sheep. "Now release the toe of that stick, or this game will never get off the ground!"

This story has been fabricated to help with the tension of a despicable disease: the shanks. A *shank* (also called a *pitchout,* a *Chinese hook, El Hosel,* a scud, or a snake killer) occurs when the ball strikes the hosel of the club and goes 90 degrees to right of your intended target. (The hosel is the neck of the club, where the shaft attaches to the clubhead.) The shanks are a virus that attacks the very soul of a golfer. They come unannounced and invade the decorum of a well-played round. They leave with equal haste and lurk in the mind of the golfer, dwelling until the brain reaches critical mass. Then you have meltdown. The shanks sound like one of those diseases Hollywood folks make movies about. And to a golfer, no other word strikes terror and dread like shank.

Can you cure the shanks? Yes!

Shankers almost always set up too close to the ball, with their weight back on their heels. As they shift forward during the swing, their weight comes off their heels, moving the club even closer to the ball, so the hosel hits the ball.

When you shank, the heel of your club (the closest part of the clubhead to you) continues toward the target and ends up right of the target. To eliminate shanks, you need the toe of the club to go toward the target and end up left of the target.

Book VI

Easy Fixes for Common Faults

Here's an easy exercise (shown in Figure 1-9) that helps cure the shanks:

1. **Get a 2-by-4 and align it along your target line.**

   You can also use a cardboard box.

2. **Put the ball 2 inches from the near edge of the board and try to hit the ball.**

   If you shank the shot, your club wants to hit the board. If you swing properly, the club comes from the inside and hits the ball. Then the toe of the club goes left of the target, the ball goes straight, and your woes are over (the shanking ones, at least).

Missing too many short putts

Some people argue that putting is more mental than physical. But before you resort to séances with your local psychic, check your alignment. You can often trace missed putts to poor aim.

You can work on alignment in many ways, but my colleague Peter Kostis invented a device called The Putting Professor to help straighten out troubled putters. It's similar to an old, tried-and-true putting aid, the string between two rods, which helped golfers keep the putter going straight back and straight through impact toward the hole. Straight as a string, get it?

Release the toe and don't hit the board.

Figure 1-9:
Just
say, "No
shanks!"

But Peter had a better idea. The Putting Professor features a plexiglass panel and a metal bar that attaches to your putter (see Figure 1-10). Keep the bar in contact with the plexiglass as you practice, and you groove a smooth stroke that keeps the face of your putter square to the target. This stroke is particularly important on those knee-knocking short putts.

Figure 1-10:
The Putting
Professor
keeps a
putter's face
square to
the target.

Of course, you can't use such a device during a round of golf. But after you develop the right stroke on the practice green, you can repeat it on the course — and watch those putts roll straight and true.

An important lesson you can learn with devices like The Putting Professor is the crucial relationship between the putter's face and the target line. Putting takes imagination: If you can picture the line and keep the face of your putter square to it, stroking the ball along that line to the hole is easy.

Book VI

Easy Fixes for Common Faults

Chapter 2

Recovering from Bad Breaks and Bad Weather

. . . .

In This Chapter

▶ Making shots that save your day

▶ Coping with Mother Nature's moods

▶ Becoming a golfer for all seasons

. . . .

*I*f you break golf down into its primal form, it's simple. All you have to do is hit a ball from a flat piece of ground (you even get to tee the ball up) to, say, a 40-yard-wide fairway. You find the ball and hit it onto a carefully prepared putting surface. Then the golf gods allow you to hit not one but two putts. And even after all that stuff, you still get to call your score par.

However — you knew there had to be a catch, didn't you? — golf often isn't so straightforward. For one thing, you're going to make mistakes. Everyone does. Usually the same ones over and over. (That doesn't change, by the way. Even the best players in the world have glitches in their swings that give them fits.) Everyone has a bad shot that he or she tends to hit when things go wrong. You may not hit that fairway with your drive or that green with your approach shot, or you may miss both. You may take three putts to get the ball into the hole now and again.

And golf doesn't often take place on a level playing field. Very seldom is the ball lying enticingly on a perfectly flat carpet of grass. Sometimes you play three or four holes into the teeth of a howling gale and reach a hole going the other way — just in time for the wind to change direction. And then it starts to rain.

This chapter's all about how to deal when the golfing gets tough.

Overcoming the Scenery

As if trying to hit a tiny ball into an only-slightly-bigger hole that's hundreds of yards away weren't hard enough, you've got nature's natural beauty to overcome. Long grass and trees may add visual interest to the course, but that's little comfort when you literally can't see the hole for the trees. The following sections explain what to do when you have to play from these unfortunate spots.

Getting out of a rough spot

Rough is the grass on the golf course that looks like it should be mowed. It's usually 2 to 3 inches high and lurks everywhere but the tees, fairways, and greens.

When you try to hit a ball out of long grass, the grass gets between the clubface and the ball. The ball then has no backspin and flies off like a bat out of heck, and direction can be a concern. But the real problem is that, with no backspin, the ball can take a longer voyage than you expected. The lack of backspin means less drag occurs while the ball is in the air. When that happens, you've hit a *flyer*. That's never been a problem with the driver off the tee, but it's a concern when you're trying to hit the ball a certain distance.

If the lie is bad enough, just get the ball back into the fairway. If you can hit the ball, the technique for this shot is much the same as the shot out of a divot: Play the ball back in your stance and put your hands forward. A chopping-down motion allows the club to come up in the backswing and avoid the long grass; that way you can hit down on the ball. Swing hard, because if you don't, the grass will wrap around the club and twist it, giving the ball an unpredictable trajectory.

The more you play this game, the more you hit these shots and understand how to play them. Keep your sense of humor and a firm grip on the club.

Tackling tree trouble

A walk in the woods can be a serene, soul-enhancing, mystical journey, blending one's spirit and body into nature and all her beauty. But when you're walking into the trees to find your golf ball, you may feel like you're in a house of mirrors with branches and leaves. The trees seem to be laughing at your predicament, and you end up talking to them in a less-than-flattering dialogue. It happens to everyone.

When I'm in the trees, the trees play games with me. And so, to extract my ball from this maze of bark, I play a game with the trees. Usually, one lone tree is in my way as I try to exit this forest. All I do is take dead aim at that tree and try to knock it over with the ball. The key here is to not be too close to the tree in case you score a direct hit. You don't want to wear that Titleist 3 as a permanent smile.

My reasoning is that I got into these trees with something less than a straight shot. So if I now try to hit something that's 30 yards away from me and only 12 inches in diameter, what's the chance that I'll hit it? If I do hit it, what a great shot it was! I can congratulate myself for that, turning a negative into a positive. I'm still in the trees, but now I'm proud of my accuracy. Now you probably know why I'm on TV and not on the regular tour anymore.

Making Special Shots

Because golf is a game of mistake management, you're going to get into trouble at least a few times in every round. How you cope with those moments and shots determines your score for the day and, ultimately, your ability to play well. Never forget that even the greatest rounds have moments of crisis. Stay calm when your heart tries to eject through the top of your head.

Trouble lurks everywhere on a golf course. You have to know how to hit shots from the rough, and others that go around, between, or over trees. Long shots, short shots, and, perhaps most important, in-between shots. You may be faced with a shot from 200 yards where a clump of trees blocks your path to the hole. Or you may be only 50 yards from the hole and have to keep the ball under branches and yet still get it over a bunker. Whatever the situation, the key is applying the magic word (drumroll): *imagination.*

Visualization strikes again: If you can picture the way a shot has to curve in the air in order to land safely, you're halfway to success. All you have to do is hit the ball. And the best way to accomplish both things is through practice — practice on the course, that is. You can't re-create on the range most shots that you encounter out on the course. The range is flat; the course isn't. The wind constantly blows the same way on the range. On the course, the only constant about the wind is that it changes direction. That's golf — a wheel of bad fortune.

The best way to practice these weird and wonderful shots is to challenge yourself. See how low you can hit a shot. Or how high. Practice hitting from bad lies and see how the ball reacts. Play from slopes, long grass, and all the rest. Or play games with your friends. The first player to hit over that tree, for example, gets $5. The trick is to make practice competitive and fun — and also beat your friends out of five bucks. Check out Chapter 3 of Book V for more ways to take the sting out of practicing.

Wait a minute, though. We're getting a little ahead of ourselves. We'd be remiss if we didn't tell you that many of the trouble shots hit by the pros are not only very low-percentage plays but also way, way out of most people's reach. Even the pros miss the tough shots now and again. And when they do miss, the result can be a *triple bogey* (a score of three over par for one hole — for example, a 7 on a par-4) or worse. So admire the pros who go for broke like the old, even bolder Phil Mickelson. But never, ever try to copy them — if you've got a choice.

The good news is that at this stage of your development, all you really need is a couple of basic shots. Leave the fancy stuff for another time, another book. All you need to know to score well is how to hit the ball low or high back onto the fairway. That's enough to cover 99 percent of the situations that you encounter. Better to give up one shot than risk three more on a shot that you couldn't pull off more than once in 20 tries.

Altitude adjustment

Because golf isn't played in a bubble, you're going to come across situations where a higher or lower shot is required. For example, when you have a strong wind in your face, a lower shot is going to go farther and hold its line better. The great thing is that you make all your adjustments before you begin. Then after you start your backswing, you can make your regular swing. You don't have to worry about adding anything else. Figure 2-1 illustrates the shots in the following sections.

Hitting the ball lower

Hitting the ball low is easy. All you have to do is subtract from the effective loft of the club. The best way to do that is to adjust your address position. Play the ball back in your stance, toward your right foot. Move your hands toward the target, ahead of the golf ball, until they're over your left leg.

Now take your usual swing, focusing on re-creating the positional relationship between your hands and the clubface as the ball is struck. In other words, your hands should be "ahead" of the clubface at impact, thus ensuring that the ball flies lower than normal.

Golfers commonly employ this sort of technique when playing in Florida, Texas, and Hawaii, where they often have to deal with strong winds. When you play the ball back in your stance with your hands ahead, you come down into the ground with a more abrupt angle that takes more turf.

For a lower shot, move the ball back in your stance, with hands forward.

Then return your hands, at impact, to your address position. Hands ahead of ball at impact.

Book VI

Easy Fixes for Common Faults

For a higher shot, move the ball forward in your stance.

Your head should be behind the clubhead when the ball is struck.

Figure 2-1: The downs and ups of golf.

I remember one good story about a low shot. It happened years ago during the Bing Crosby tournament on the 7th hole at Pebble Beach (a downhill par-3 of 110 yards). From an elevated tee, you can just about throw the ball to the green. On this particular day, the wind was howling from the coast (the green sits on the ocean), and the 7th hole was impossible. Water was erupting from the rocks; wind was blowing water everywhere; seals were hiding; and seagulls were walking. Definitely a bad day for windblown golf balls.

Billy Casper arrived on the tee and surveyed the situation. Many players were using *long irons* (irons that go 200 yards) because the wind was so fierce. Billy went to his bag and got his *putter!* He putted the ball down a cart path into the front bunker. From there he got the ball in the hole in two for his par-3. Now that's keeping it low into the wind and using your imagination!

Hitting the ball higher

As you'd expect, hitting the ball higher than normal involves making the opposite adjustments at address. Adjust your stance so the ball is forward, toward your left foot. Then move your hands back, away from the target. Again, hitting the ball is that simple. All you have to do is reproduce that look at impact, and the ball takes off on a steeper trajectory.

Uneven lies

No golf course is totally flat. So every now and again, you need to hit a shot off a slope. The ball may be below or above your feet. Both positions are *sidehill lies.* Or you may be halfway up or down a slope.

When you're faced with these situations, you need to make an adjustment. And as we note in the preceding section, if you can make most of your changes before starting your swing, the shot gets easier. The common factor in all these shots is the relationship between your shoulders and the slope. On a flat lie, you're bent over the ball in a certain posture. You should stand about 90 degrees to the ground.

But if the ball is above your feet, you have to lean a little into the hill to keep your balance. If you stand at your normal posture to the upslope of the hill, you may fall backward. You're close to the ball because of the lean, and you need to *choke up* on the club (hold it farther down the handle on the grip).

The reverse is also true. With the ball below your feet, lean back more to retain your balance on the downslope. Because you're leaning back, you're a little farther away from the ball; grip the club all the way at the end and use the whole length of the shaft.

The main idea for sidehill lies is to stay balanced. We don't want you falling down any hills.

For uphill and downhill lies, the setup is a little different. Imagine that your ball is halfway up a staircase, and you have to hit the next shot to the top. Because your left leg is higher than your right, your weight naturally shifts to your right leg. On a downslope, your weight shifts in the opposite direction, onto your left leg. Let that weight shift happen so your shoulders stay parallel to the banister. Keep your shoulders and the imaginary banister parallel, as shown in Figure 2-2.

On an upslope, leave your weight on your right side.

On a downslope, shift your weight to your left side.

Figure 2-2: Keep shoulders and slope parallel.

Finally, follow these three rules:

- ✔ **Adjust your aim when you're on a slope.** Off a downslope or when the ball is below your feet, aim to the left of where you want the ball to finish. Off an upslope or when the ball is above your feet, aim right.

- ✔ **Play the ball back toward the middle of your stance if you're on a downhill lie, or forward off your left big toe from an uphill lie.**

- ✔ **Take *more club* (a club with less loft) if you're on an uphill lie because the ball tends to fly higher, and use *less club* (a club with more loft) from a downhill lie because the ball has a lower trajectory in this situation.** For example, if the shot calls for a 7-iron, take your 8-iron instead. ***Remember:*** From these lies, swing about 75 percent of your normal swing speed to keep your balance. Practice with different clubs from different lies to get a feel for these shots.

Digging out of divots

Unfortunately for your blood pressure, your ball occasionally finishes in a hole made by someone who previously hit a shot from the same spot and forgot to replace the grass. These holes are known as *divots*. Don't panic. To get the ball out, first set up with the ball farther back in your stance to encourage a steeper attack at impact. Push your hands forward a little. You need to feel as if you're really hitting down on this shot. A quicker cocking of the wrists on the backswing helps, too. Some pros like to swing a little more upright on the backswing with the club (take the arms away from the body going back). This method allows a steeper path down to the ball. (See Figure 2-3.)

Depending on the severity and depth of the divot, take a club with more loft than you'd normally use. Extra loft counteracts the ball's being below ground level. Don't worry — the ball comes out lower because your hands are ahead of it. That makes up for the distance lost by using less club.

Remember that a shot from a divot comes out a lot lower and runs along the ground more than a normal shot. Aim accordingly.

You have little or no follow-through on the downswing of your shot from a divot. Because the ball is back in your stance and your hands are forward, your blow should be a descending blow that chops the ball toward the green.

The best swing thought for this situation is *Don't swing too hard*. If you swing hard, your head tends to move — you don't hit the ball squarely. And when the ball is lying below the ground, you *must* hit it squarely. So take a smooth, downward swing.

Hang Onto Your Hat: Handling High Winds

When conditions are rough because of wind or rain, scores go up. Adjust your goals. Don't panic if you start off badly or have a couple of poor holes. Be patient and realize that sometimes conditions make golf even harder. And remember that bad weather is equally tough on all the other players.

When the ball is in a divot, move your hands forward.

Cock your wrists more than usual...

Book VI

Easy Fixes for Common Faults

and then hit down and through.

Figure 2-3: Escaping a divot.

I've played professional golf for 40 years, and I've played in some bad conditions. Because I'm not a patient person, my scores in bad weather have been high. If I got a few strokes over par early in my round, I'd take too many chances trying to make birdies. I'd then boil as I watched my score rise with my blood pressure. A calm head and good management skills are just as important as hitting the ball solidly when you're trying to get through tough days in the wind and rain.

I remember playing the TPC Championship at Sawgrass in the late 1980s on one of the windiest days we'd ever seen. J. C. Snead hit a beautiful downwind approach to an elevated green. Somehow the ball stopped on the green with the wind blowing upward of 50 miles per hour. J. C. was walking toward the green when his Panama hat blew off. He chased it, only to watch the hat blow onto the green and hit his golf ball! That's a two-shot penalty — and rotten luck.

If the wind is blowing hard, try these tips:

- **Widen your stance to lower your center of gravity.** This change automatically makes your swing shorter (for control) because turning your body is more difficult when your feet are set wider apart. (Figure 2-4 illustrates this stance.)

- **Swing easier.** Try taking a less-lofted club than normal and swinging easier. This way, you have a better chance of hitting the ball squarely. By hitting the ball squarely, you minimize the wind's effects.

- **Use the wind — don't fight it.** Let the ball go where the wind wants it to go. If the wind is blowing left-to-right at 30 miles per hour, aim left and let the wind bring your ball back. Don't aim right and try to hook it back into the wind. Leave that to the airline pilots and the guys on the PGA Tour!

- **Choke down on the club.** You don't have to keep your left hand (for right-handed golfers) all the way at the top end of the grip. Move it down an inch. This grip gives you more control. Keeping your left hand about 1 inch from the top of the grip gives you more control over the club and the direction of the shot it hits. But more control comes with a cost: The ball doesn't go as far as it would if you used the full length of the shaft.

- **Allow for more run downwind and shorter flight against the wind.** You have to experience this part of the game to understand it. The more you play in windy conditions, the more comfortable you become.

A wide stance helps you keep your balance in a breeze.

Figure 2-4: Windy means wider.

Swingin' in the Rain

If you're from Southern California, you may not have much experience playing in the rain. Those of you from the Pacific Northwest may already know a bit about how to swing in the rain. Regardless of your climate, the following sections give you some pointers on playing in wet conditions.

Packing the right equipment

The best advice we can give you for playing in the rain is to make like a Boy Scout and *be prepared*. For starters, pack the right all-weather gear:

- ✔ **An umbrella:** Pack one of those big golf umbrellas. And never open it downwind; you end up like Mary Poppins, and the umbrella ends up looking like modern art.

- ✔ **Rain gear:** That means jackets, pants, and headwear designed to be worn in the rain. If you play in wet weather all the time, get yourself some good stuff that lasts a long time, not a garbage bag with holes cut out for your head and arms. Good rain gear can cost between $100 and $700, but if you're on a budget, you can get decent gear for less — see Chapter 1 of Book I for tips on that.

- ✔ **Dry gloves:** If you wear gloves, keep a few in plastic bags in your golf bag. They stay dry even if the rain comes pouring in.

- ✔ **Towels:** Keep several dry towels in your bag because the one you have outside will get wet sooner or later. Keep one dry towel hanging from the rib on the underside of your umbrella and another inside your side pocket. When the weather gets really wet, you can wipe your club off on the closest caddie.

- ✔ **Dry grips:** Having dry grips is one of the most important components of wet-weather golf. You really don't want to have a club slip out of your hands on the driving range and fly through a snack-shop window.

- ✔ **Waterproof shoes:** Keep an extra pair of dry socks in your bag, too, in case the advertiser lied about those "waterproof" shoes.

Wet course conditions

A golf course changes significantly in the rain. You need to adjust your game accordingly:

- ✔ On a rainy day, the greens are slow. Hit your putts harder and remember that the ball doesn't curve as much. You can also be more aggressive on approach shots to the greens.

- ✔ If you hit a ball into a bunker, remember that wet sand is firmer than dry sand. You don't have to swing as hard to get the ball out.

- ✔ A wet golf course plays longer because it's soft — a 400-yard hole seems more like 450. The good news here is that the fairways and greens become, in effect, wider and bigger, because your shots don't bounce into trouble as much as they would on a dry day. That means you can afford to take more club — and more chances.

✔ Try not to let the conditions affect your normal routines. The best rain players always take their time and stay patient.

✔ Rainy days result in soft green conditions. Even if you normally don't make a ball mark on the green, you may when it's raining. Be sure to fix them.

✔ Playing in the rain is one thing; playing in lightning is another altogether. Here's our tip on playing in lightning: *Don't.* When lightning strikes, your metallic golf club (along with the fact that you tend to be the highest point on the golf course, unless a tree is nearby) can make you a target. So when you see lightning, don't take chances — take cover.

Weathering the Seasonal Elements

If you live in Florida, California, or Arizona, you only notice the change of seasons when 40 bazillion golfers from colder climes flood the area trying to get the seven tee times that are still available. If you live in an all-season climate and prefer to enjoy the changing weather without giving up your golf game, this section offers some tips.

Swinging into spring

Golfers anticipate spring like no other season. You've been indoors for most of the winter and read every book pertaining to your golf game. You've watched endless hours of golf on TV and ingested everything the announcers have told you not to do. It's spring — time to bloom!

One of the first things you need to do is decide your goals for the upcoming year. Is your goal to be a better putter? Become a longer driver? Simply want to get the ball off the ground with more regularity? Establish what you want to do with your game and then set out to accomplish that feat.

Here's some more springtime advice:

✔ **See your local golf professional for a tune-up lesson.** All golfers pick up bad swing habits during the off-season. Get off to the right start!

✔ **May is free lesson month.** Find a local PGA professional who participates in this program, and he or she will give you a free 10-minute tune-up.

✔ **Practice all phases of your game.** Don't neglect weak areas of your game, but stay on top of your strengths, too. Spring is a time of blossoming — let your game do the same.

✔ **Map out an exercise program.** Did you avoid exercise during the winter? Spring is a good time to map out a game plan for your physical needs. Are you strong enough in your legs? Does your rotator cuff need strengthening? Does your cardiovascular system short out later in a round? Book II details how to develop a golf-specific fitness program.

✔ **Dress for the weather.** Spring is the cruelest time of year to figure out what to wear. It can be hot. It can be cold. It can rain. It can be blowing 40 miles per hour. It can be doing all these things in the first three holes. If you're carrying your bag, it can get heavy with all the extra gear in it, but you don't want to get caught without something you need. Take along your rain gear, a light jacket, hand warmers (we discuss these amazing creations in "Winterizing your game" later in the chapter), your umbrella, and an extra towel. And take along some antihistamines — it's spring, and the pollen is everywhere.

✔ **Learn about yourself and your golf game.** Remember, spring is the time of year to be enlightened. In the words of Spanish philosopher Jose Ortega y Gasset, "To be surprised, to wonder, is to begin to understand."

Heading into hot summer swings

Hopefully, you've been practicing hard on your game, working toward those goals you set forth in the spring (see the preceding section). But practicing and playing are two very different animals. The more you practice, the easier you should find it to play the game well. Summer is the time to find out whether your game has improved.

These tips help you make the most of your days in the sun:

✔ **Work on course management.** How can you best play this particular golf course? Sometimes, for one reason or another, you can't play a certain hole. Figure out a plan to avoid the trouble you're having on that hole. Do you have the discipline to carry out your plan? That's why summer is great for playing the game and understanding yourself. You can regularly go out after work and play 18 holes before it gets dark.

✔ **Tailor your equipment for the conditions.** During the summer, consider getting new grips on your clubs. The grips are called *half cord* because they have some cord blended into the underside of the grip. New grips give you a better hold on the club during sweaty summers. You can also use a driver with a little more loft to take advantage of summer's drier air (which makes the ball fly farther).

✔ **Practice competing by playing in organized leagues.** You play a different game when your score counts and is published in the local paper.

✔ **Dress for fun in the sun.** Take along sunblock of at least SPF 15 and put it on twice a day. Not everyone wants to look like they fell asleep in a tanning bed. And wear a hat that covers your ears.

- ✔ **Play in the morning.** Afternoons are often too darned hot.

- ✔ **Drink plenty of fluids during those hot days.** You don't want to dehydrate and shrivel up like a prune, so keep your liquid intake constant. Try to drink water on every tee during the heat of summer. One hint: Alcoholic beverages can knock you on your rear end if you drink them outdoors on a hot day. Stick with water and save the adult beverages for the 19th hole.

Having a ball in the fall

Without a doubt, fall is the best time of year to play golf: The golf courses are in good shape, the leaves are turning in much of the country, and the scenery is amazing. The weather is delightful, and all sorts of sports are on TV. Both you and your game should be raring to go.

If you have the time and the money, make travel plans to the Northeast and play golf there. The colors are astounding. Colorado is also breathtaking in the fall. Some vacation planners specialize in golf trips. Get a bunch of friends you enjoy and start planning one now.

Here are four fall golf tips:

- ✔ **Dress for the fall much like you do for the spring.** Take a lot of stuff with you because the weather can change faster than you can swing. (Flip to the earlier section "Swinging into spring" for more on packing for spring golf.)

- ✔ **Keep a close eye on your shots.** Especially if you live where trees lose their leaves in the fall; you can easily lose your ball in the leaves.

- ✔ **Assess everything you did with your game this year.** Did your techniques work? If not, were your goals unrealistic? Was your teacher helpful? Take a long, hard look and start to devise a game plan for next spring.

- ✔ **Look at new equipment as your game progresses.** Fall is a great time to buy equipment, because all the new stuff comes out in the spring. By fall, prices are lower for last year's clubs.

Winterizing your game

Get out there and work on your game — you don't have to mow the grass until April!

Book VI

Easy Fixes for Common Faults

Preparing for brisk weather

If you're brave enough to venture onto golf's frozen tundra, we have three musts for you:

- ✔ **Take a jumbo thermos with something warm to drink.** You may think that bourbon chasers make the day much more fun, but alcohol makes you feel colder. Coffee or hot chocolate works better.

- ✔ **Dress warmly.** Silk long johns work well on cold days. Women's seamless long johns work best, but if you're a guy, the salesperson looks at you funny when you ask for a women's size 14. That kind of request may lead to the wrong conclusions.

  - • **Wear waterproof golf shoes and thick socks.** Some hunting socks have little heaters in them. You can also wear wool pants over silk long johns and then use rain pants as the top layer when it's really cold. A turtleneck with a light, tightly knit sweater works wonders under a rain or wind jacket made of Gore-Tex or one of those other miracle-fiber, space-age fabrics like Under Armour. A knit ski cap tops off this cozy ensemble.

  - • **Get some hand warmers.** Among the great inventions of all time are those little hand warmers that come in plastic pouches. You shake them, and they stay warm for eight hours. You can put them *everywhere* on cold days. Let your imagination run wild. Hand warmers can keep you toasty on a cold winter's day when you're three strokes down to your worst enemy.

  - • **Keep your hands warm by using *cart gloves*.** These oversized fingerless gloves have a soft, warm lining and fit right over your hand, even if you're already wearing a glove. Put a hand warmer in each one.

- ✔ **Walk the course if you can.** Walking isn't just good exercise; it keeps you warmer than taking a cart. Besides, you really feel cold when your face collides with an arctic blast of winter. If you must take a cart, make sure that it has a windshield. Some courses have enclosed carts with heaters in them.

Adjusting your swing for a cold day

When you swing a club with all these clothes on, you probably won't have as long a swing as normal. The clothes restrict your motion. Try taking your jacket off to swing the club and then put it right back on. Because of the restriction of winter clothes, make your swing a little slower than normal, which puts it in a slow rhythm on a cold day. While you're at it, take more club to offset your slower swing than you'd normally use. If you usually hit an 8-iron for the 140-yard shot you're facing, take a 7-iron instead.

Here are a couple of other points to keep in mind when you're playing winter golf:

- ✔ **Lower your expectations.** When you're dressed for the Iditarod, don't think that you can pull off the same shots that you normally do. Good *short-game* skills (chipping, pitching, putting, and sand play) and game management are the most important aspects of winter golf. (Chapters 3 through 8 of Book III give you the lowdown on the short game.)

- ✔ **If you usually play in extreme conditions — colder than 40 degrees Fahrenheit — seek professional help.** Golf may be too much of a priority in your life. You may be crazy — or you may be the perfect host for a new reality show on Golf Channel.

Indoor golf: Practicing at home

Winter is a great time to become one with your swing and fix all those faults you accumulated during the preceding year. Here's how:

1. **Place a large mirror behind you.**

2. **Pretend you're hitting away from the mirror, and check your swing when your shaft is parallel to the ground in your backswing.**

   Is your shaft on a line that's parallel to the line made by your toes? If it is, that's good. If not, that's something to work on during your offseason.

3. **Continue to swing and go to the top.**

   Is your shaft on a line that's parallel to the line made by your heels? If it is, that's good. If it isn't, put that on your list of things to improve.

These two positions are crucial to the golf swing. Repeat this exercise until you can do it in your sleep.

Have someone videotape your golf swing. Play the tape over and over until you have a really good picture of what it looks like. *Feel* your own swing. Then work on those areas that you need to improve — an instructor can help (see Chapter 2 of Book I for more on working with a teaching pro).

Next, make your changes and make another tape of your swing. Not only should you be able to see the changes, but you should also feel them. Visualization strikes yet again: Seeing your swing can help you understand your movements and get your body and brain on the same page — ready to turn to the next page.

Appendix

Golf Talk

· ·

*G*olf has a language all its own, so if you're going to be a golfer, you need to sound like one. Here are the phrases, terms, and slang of that language.

These terms are written with right-handed golfers in mind. Lefties will have to think in reverse!

A

A-game: The best a golfer can play. Sometimes you can shoot a good score with your B- or even C-game, but you always hope to bring your A-game to the first tee.

ace: A hole-in-one. Buy a round of drinks for the house.

address: The positioning of your body in relation to the ball just before starting your swing.

airball: When your swing misses the ball. Blame it on an alien spacecraft's radar.

albatross: British term for *double eagle,* or three under par on one hole.

amateur: Someone who plays for fun, not money. Playing golf for fun? What a concept!

angle of approach: The degree at which the clubhead moves either downward or upward into the ball.

approach: Your shot to the green made from anywhere except the tee. Sounds dangerous; really isn't.

apron: The grass around the edge of a green, longer than the grass on the green but shorter than the grass on the fairway. Often called the *fringe*.

attend: To hold and remove the flagstick as another player putts, usually from some distance.

away: Term used to describe the ball farthest from the hole and, thus, next to be played.

B

back door: The rear of the hole.

back lip: The edge of a bunker that's farthest from the green.

back nine: The second half of your round of golf.

backspin: When the ball hits the green and spins back toward the player. Galleries love backspin.

backswing: The part of the swing from the point where the clubhead moves away from the ball to the point where it starts back down again.

baffy: Old name for a lofted wood; short for *baffing spoon*.

bail out (hang 'em high): When you hit the shot, for example, well to the right to avoid trouble on the left.

balata: Sap from a tropical tree; the most popular cover for balls until high-tech plastics came along.

ball at rest: The ball isn't moving. A study in still life.

ball marker: Small, round object, such as a coin, used to indicate the ball's position on the green.

ball retriever: Long pole with a scoop on the end used to collect balls from water hazards and other undesirable spots. If the grip on your ball retriever is worn out, get some lessons immediately.

ball washer: A device for cleaning balls; found on many tees.

banana ball: See *slice.*

bandit: See *hustler.*

barkie: Bet won by a player making par or better on a hole after hitting a tree.

baseball grip: To hold the club with all ten fingers on the grip.

best ball: A game in which two or more players form a team; the best net score for each team is recorded on the scorecard.

birdie: Score of one under par on a hole.

bisque: Handicap stroke given by one player to another. Receiver may choose which hole to apply it to.

bite (also vampire, bicuspid, overbite): A spin that makes the ball tend to stop rather than roll when it lands.

blade: Shot where the leading edge of the club rather than the clubface strikes the ball, resulting in a low, ugly shot that tends to travel way too far. Also a kind of putter or iron. See also *thin* or *skull.*

blast: Aggressive shot from a bunker that displaces a lot of sand.

blind shot: Shot where you can't see the spot where you want the ball to land.

block: See *push.*

bogey: Score of one stroke over par on a hole.

borrow: The amount of curve you must allow for a putt on a sloping green. Or what you need to do if you play a hustler.

bounce: The bottom part of a sand wedge, designed to slide through sand. Or what a ball does (usually in the wrong direction) when it hits the ground.

boundary: Edge of the course; it confines the space/time continuum. Usually marked by white stakes.

brassie: Old name for a 2-wood.

break: See *borrow.*

British Open: National championship run by Royal and Ancient Golf Club of St. Andrews — known in Britain as "the Open" because it was the first one.

bulge: The curve across the face of a driver or fairway wood (or fairway metal).

bump and run: See *run-up.*

bunker: Hazard filled with sand; should not be referred to as a *sand trap.*

buried ball/lie: Lie where part of the ball is below the surface of the sand in a bunker.

C

caddie: The person carrying your clubs during your round of golf. The person you fire when you play badly.

caddie master: Person in charge of caddies.

carry: The distance between a ball's takeoff and landing.

cart: Motorized vehicle used to transport some golfers around the course.

casual water: Water other than a water hazard on the course (such as a puddle) from which you can lift your ball without penalty.

center-shafted: Putter in which the shaft is joined to the center of the head.

character builder: Short, meaningful putt; only builds character if you make it.

charting the course: To walk each hole, noting distances from various land-marks, so you always know how far you are from the hole.

chili-dip (Hormel, lay the sod over it, pooper scooper): A mishit chip shot, the clubhead hitting the ground well before it hits the ball.

chip: Very short, low-flying shot to the green.

chip-in: A holed chip.

choke: To play poorly because of self-imposed pressure.

choke down: To hold the club lower on the grip. *Choke up* means the same; don't ask us why.

chunk: See *chili-dip.*

claw: An innovative grip that takes wrist action out of the putting stroke.

cleat: Spike on the sole of a golf shoe.

cleek: Old term for a variety of iron clubs.

closed face: Clubface pointed to the left of your ultimate target at address or impact. Or clubface pointed skyward at the top of the backswing. Can lead to a shot that goes to the left of the target.

closed stance: Player sets up with the right foot pulled back, away from the ball.

clubhouse: Main building at a golf club.

club length: Distance from the end of the grip to the bottom of the clubhead.

collar: See *apron.*

come-backer: The putt after the previous putt finishes beyond the hole. Tends to get harder to make the older you get.

concede: To give an opponent a putt, hole, or match.

core: The center of a golf ball.

country club: A golf club open only to members and their guests.

course rating: The difficulty of a course, measured with a formula by the USGA.

cross-handed: Grip with the left hand below the right.

crosswind: Breeze blowing from right to left or from left to right.

cup: Container in the hole that holds the flagstick in place.

cuppy lie: When the ball is in a cuplike depression.

cut: Score that eliminates a percentage of the field (or players) from a tournament. Usually made after 36 holes of a 72-hole event.

cut shot: Shot that curves from left to right.

D

dance floor: Slang for *green.*

dawn patrol: The players who tee off early in the day.

dead (body bags, cadaver, on the slab, perdition, jail, tag on his toe, wearing stripes, no pulse — you get the idea): No possible way to pull off this shot!

deep: High clubface from top to bottom.

deuce: A score of 2 on a given hole.

dimple: Depression on the cover of a golf ball.

divot: Turf displaced by the clubhead during a swing.

dogleg: Hole on which the fairway curves one way or the other.

dormant: Grass on the course is alive but not actively growing.

dormie: In match play, being ahead by the same number of holes as there are holes left to play — for example, five up with only five holes left, or four up with four left.

double bogey: Score of two over par on a hole.

double eagle: Score of three under par on a hole. Forget it, they're nearly impossible. See also *albatross.*

down: Losing.

downhill lie: When your right foot is higher than your left at address.

downswing: The part of the swing where the clubhead is moving down toward the ball.

DQ'd: Disqualified.

drain: To sink a putt.

draw: Shot that curves from right to left.

drive: Shot from teeing ground other than par-3 holes.

drive for show, putt for dough: Old saying implying that putting is more important than driving. It happens to be true.

drive the green: When your drive finishes on the putting surface. Can happen on a short par-4, or when the brakes go out on your cart.

driving range: Place where you can go to hit practice balls.

drop: Procedure by which you put a ball back into play after it's been lifted and/or replaced in accordance with a rule.

dub: Bad shot or player.

duck hook (shrimp, mallard, quacker): Shot curving severely from right to left.

duffer: Bad player.

dying putt: A putt that barely reaches the hole.

E

eagle: Score of two under par for a hole.

embedded ball: Portion of the ball is below ground.

etiquette: Code of course conduct.

explode: To play a ball from a bunker by moving a large amount of sand. Or what you do if the ball *doesn't* get out of the bunker.

extra holes: Played when a match finishes even (is tied).

F

face: The front of a club or bunker.

face-on: A style of putting that may cure the yips.

fade: Shot that curves gently from left to right.

fairway: The closely mowed turf running from tee to green.

fairway wood: Any wooden club that's not your driver. Nowadays, saying *fairway metal* is more accurate.

fat: To strike the ground before the ball.

feather: To put a delicate fade on a shot.

first cut: Strip of rough at the edge of a fairway.

first off: Golfers beginning their round before everyone else.

flag: Piece of cloth attached to the top of a flagstick.

flagstick: The stick with the flag on top, which indicates the location of the cup.

flange: Projecting piece of clubhead behind the sole.

flat: Swing that is less upright than normal and more around the body than up and down.

flatstick: Slang for a putter.

flex: The amount of bend in a shaft. Also the amount of bend in your knees during a swing.

Golf All-in-One For Dummies

flier: Shot, usually hit from the rough, that travels way too far past the target.

flub: To hit the ball only a few feet.

fly the green: To hit a shot that lands beyond the putting surface.

follow-through: The part of the swing after the ball has been struck.

foozle: To make a complete mess of a shot.

fore: What to shout when your ball is headed toward another golfer.

forged irons: Clubs made one by one, without molds.

forward press: Targetward shift of the hands, and perhaps the right knee, just prior to takeaway.

foursome: Group of four golfers. In the United States, it's a group of four playing together. In Britain, it's a match between two teams of two, each hitting one ball alternately.

free drop: Drop for which no penalty stroke is incurred, generally within one club length of where the ball was.

fried egg: When your ball is partially buried in the sand.

fringe: See *apron.*

frog hair: Slang for *apron, fringe,* or *collar.*

front nine: The first half of your round of golf.

full swing: Longest swing you make.

G

gallery: Spectators at a tournament.

gimme: A short putt that your opponent doesn't ask you to hit, assuming that you can't possibly miss the shot.

G.I.R: Acronym for *greens in regulation* (greens hit in the regulation number of strokes).

glove: Usually worn on the left hand by right-handed players to help maintain grip.

Golden Bear: Jack Nicklaus.

golf widow(er): Your significant other after you get addicted to the game!

go to school: To watch your partner's putt and learn from it the line and pace that your putt should have.

good-good: Reciprocal concession of short putts. See also *gimme.*

grain: Tendency of grass to lie horizontally toward the sun.

Grand Slam: The four major championships: Masters, U.S. Open, British Open, and PGA Championship.

graphite: Lightweight material used to make shafts and clubheads; the same stuff that's called *lead* in pencils.

green: The shortest-cut grass, where you do your putting.

green fee: The cost to play a round of golf.

green jacket: Prize awarded to the winner of the Masters Tournament in Augusta, Georgia.

greenies: Bet won by player whose first shot finishes closest to the hole on a par-3.

greenside: Close to the green.

greensome: Game in which both players on a team drive off. The better of the two is chosen; then they alternate shots from there.

grip: Piece of rubber/leather on the end of a club. Also your hold on the club.

grooves: *Scoring* (the set of shallow notches) on the clubface.

gross score: Actual score shot before a handicap is deducted.

ground the club: The process of placing the clubhead behind the ball at address, generally touching the bottom of the grass.

ground under repair: Area on the course being worked on by the grounds-keeper, generally marked by white lines, from which you may drop your ball without penalty.

gutta percha: Material used to manufacture golf balls in the 19th century.

H

hacker: Poor player.

half: Tied hole.

half shot: Improvised shot with ordinarily too much club for the distance.

halve: To tie a hole.

ham-and-egging: When you and your partner play well on alternate holes, forming an effective team.

handicap: Number of strokes over par a golfer is expected to score for 18 holes. For example, a player whose handicap is 16 is expected to shoot 88 on a par 72 course, or 16 strokes over par.

hanging lie: Your ball is on a slope, lying either above or below your feet.

hardpan: Very firm turf.

hazard: Can be either sand or water. Don't ground your club in hazards — it's against the rules!

head cover: Protection for the clubhead, usually used on woods.

heel: End of the clubhead closest to the shaft.

hickory: Wood from which shafts used to be made.

high side: Area above the hole on a sloping green.

hole: Your ultimate 4¼-inch-wide target.

hole-high: Level with the hole.

hole-in-one: See *ace.*

hole out: Complete play one hole.

home green: The green on the 18th hole.

honor: When you score lowest on a given hole, thus earning the right to tee up first on the next tee.

hood: Tilting the toe end of the club toward the hole. To hood a club lessens the loft and generally produces a right-to-left shot.

hook: Shot that curves severely from right to left.

horseshoe: When the ball goes around the edge of the cup and comes back toward you. Painful!

hosel: Curved area where the clubhead connects with the shaft.

hustler: A golfer who plays for a living. Plays better than he claims to be. Usually leaves your wallet lighter.

hybrid: A club similar to a fairway metal, designed to get the ball airborne quickly; many players prefer hybrids to 2-, 3-, and 4-irons.

I

impact: Moment when the club strikes the ball.

impediment: Loose debris that you can remove from around your ball as long as the ball doesn't move.

Impregnable Quadrilateral: Slang for the Grand Slam.

improve your lie: To move the ball to make a shot easier. Illegal unless local rules dictate otherwise.

in play: Within the confines of the course (not out-of-bounds).

in your pocket: After you've picked up the ball! (Generally after you finish a hole without holing out.)

inside: Area on your side of a line drawn from the ball to the target.

inside-out: Clubhead moves through the impact area on a line to the right of the target. Most tour players do this. See also *outside-in*.

intended line: The path on which you imagine the ball flying from club to target.

interlocking: Type of grip where the little finger of the right hand is entwined with the index finger of the left.

investment cast: Clubs made from a mold.

J

jail: Slang for when you and your ball are in very deep trouble. In golf jail, the bars are often made of bark.

jigger: Old term for a 4-iron. Also a great little pub to the right of the 17th fairway at St. Andrews.

jungle: Slang for heavy rough. See also *rough.*

junk: Enjoyable golf wagers on such things as hitting the green in one shot, getting up and down from a bunker, or making par after hitting a tree.

K

kick: See *bounce.*

kickpoint: The spot on a club's shaft that twists the most during the swing.

kill: To hit a long shot.

L

ladies' day: Time when a course is reserved for female golfers.

lag: A long putt hit with the intent of leaving the ball close to the cup.

laid off: When the club points to the left of the target at the top of the backswing.

lateral hazard: Water hazard marked by red stakes and usually parallel to the fairway.

lay-up: Conservatively played shot to avoid possible trouble.

leader board: Place where the lowest scores in a tournament are posted.

leak: Ball drifting to the right during flight.

lie: Where your ball is on the ground. Also, the angle at which the club shaft extends from the head.

lift: What you do before you drop.

line: The path of a shot to the hole.

line up: To stand behind a shot to take aim.

links: A seaside course. Don't expect trees.

lip: Edge of a cup or bunker.

lip out: When the ball touches the edge of the cup but doesn't drop in.

lob: A short, high shot that lands softly.

local knowledge: What the members know and you don't.

local rules: Set of rules determined by the members, rules committee, or course professional.

loft: The degree at which a clubface is angled upward.

long game: Shots hit with long irons and woods.

loop: Slang for *to caddy*. Also a round of golf or a change in the path of the clubhead during the swing.

low handicapper: Good player.

low side: Area below the hole on a sloping green.

LPGA: Ladies Professional Golf Association.

M

make: Hole a shot.

makeable: Shot with a good chance of being holed.

mallet: Putter with a wide head.

mark: To indicate the position of the ball with a small, round, flat object, such as a coin, usually on the green.

marker: Small, round object, such as a coin, placed behind the ball to indicate its position when you lift it. Also the person keeping score.

marshal: Person controlling the crowd at a tournament.

mashie: Old term for a 5-iron.

mashie-niblick: Old term for a 7-iron.

Masters: First major tournament of each calendar year. Always played at Augusta National Golf Club in Georgia.

match of cards: Comparing your scorecard to your opponent's to see who won.

match play: Game played between two sides. The side that wins the most holes wins the match.

matched set: Clubs designed to look and feel the same.

medal play: Game played among any number of players. The player with the lowest score wins (also called *stroke play*).

metal wood: Driver or fairway "wood" made of metal.

miniature course: Putting course.

misclub: To use the wrong club for the distance.

misread: To take the wrong line on a putt.

miss the cut: To take too many strokes for the first 36 holes of a 72-hole event and be eliminated.

mixed foursome: Two men, two women.

model swing: Perfect motion.

MOI: Abbreviation for *moment of inertia;* in putters, it means resistance to twisting at impact.

mulligan: Second attempt at a shot, usually played on the first tee. It's illegal.

municipal course: A course owned by the local government and, thus, open to the public. Also known as *munis,* municipal courses generally have lower green fees than privately owned public courses.

N

nassau: Bet in which a round of 18 holes is divided into three — front 9, back 9, and full 18.

net score: Score for a hole or round after handicap strokes are deducted.

never up, never in: Annoying saying coined for putts that finish short of the hole.

niblick: Old term for a 9-iron.

nine: Half of a course.

19th hole: The clubhouse bar.

O

O.B.: Slang for out-of-bounds.

off-center hit: Less than a solid strike.

offset: Club with the head set farther behind the shaft than normal.

1-putt: To take only a single putt on a green.

one up: Being one hole ahead in match play.

open face: Clubface aligned to the right of the target at address, or to the right of its path at impact. Can lead to a shot's veering to the right.

open stance: Player sets up with the left foot pulled back, away from the ball.

open up the hole: When your tee shot leaves the best possible angle for the next shot to the green.

order of play: Who plays when.

out-of-bounds: Area outside the boundaries of the course, usually marked with white posts. When a ball finishes out of bounds, the player must return to the original spot and play another ball under penalty of one stroke. He or she thus loses stroke and distance.

outside: Area on the far side of the ball.

outside-in: Swing path in which the clubhead moves into the impact area on a line to the left of the target. See also ***inside-out.***

over the green: Ball hit too far.

overclub: To use a club that will hit the ball too far.

overcooked: An approach shot that zooms onto — and over — the green.

overlapping: A type of grip where the little finger of the right hand lies over the index finger of the left hand.

p

pairings: Groups of two players.

par: The score an average player would expect to make on a hole or round.

partner: A player on your side.

penal: Difficult.

persimmon: A wood from which wooden clubs were made before the age of metal woods.

PGA: Professional Golfers' Association.

piccolo grip: A very loose hold on the club, especially at the top of the backswing.

pigeon: An opponent you should beat with ease.

pin: See *flagstick.*

pin-high: See *hole-high.*

pin placement: The location of the hole on the green.

pitch: A short, high approach shot. Doesn't run much on landing.

pitch and putt: A short course. Or getting down in two strokes from off the green.

pitch-and-run: Varies from a pitch in that it flies lower and runs more.

pitching-niblick: Old term for an 8-iron.

pivot: The body turn during the swing.

plane: The arc of the swing.

playoff: Two or more players play extra holes to break a tie.

play through: What you do when the group in front of you invites you to pass.

plugged lie: When the ball finishes half-buried in the turf or a bunker.

plumb-bob: Lining up a putt with one eye closed and the putter held vertically in front of the face.

pop-up: High, short shot.

pot bunker: Small, steeply faced bunker.

practice green: Place for working on your putting.

preferred lies: Temporary rule that allows you to move the ball to a more favorable position because of abnormally wet conditions.

press: Way to get your bet money back after you've lost your match. This new bet takes place over any remaining holes.

private club: See *country club.*

pro-am: A competition in which professional partners team with amateurs.

professional: A golfer who plays or teaches for his or her livelihood.

pro shop: A place where you sign up to start play and can buy balls, clubs, and so on.

provisional ball: You think your ball may be lost. To save time, you play another from the same spot before searching for the first ball. If the first ball is lost, the second ball (the provisional ball) is in play.

public course: A golf course open to all.

pull: A straight shot that flies to the left of the target.

punch: A low shot hit with the ball back in the stance and a shorter-than-normal follow-through.

push: A straight shot that flies to the right of the target.

putter: A straight-faced club generally used on the greens.

Q

Q-school: An annual tournament in which aspiring players try to qualify for the PGA Tour. The ultimate grind: six rounds of fierce pressure.

quail high (stealth, skull, rat-high): Low.

quitting: Not hitting through a shot with conviction.

R

rabbit: A poor player.

rake: A device used to smooth the sand after you leave a bunker.

range: Practice area.

range ball: Generally, a low-quality ball used on a driving range. Range balls often have stripes painted on them; these are called *stripers*.

rap: To hit a putt firmly.

read the green: To assess the path on which a putt must travel to the hole.

regular: A shaft with normal flex.

regulation: The number of strokes needed to reach the green and have two putts left to make par.

release: The point in the downswing where the wrists uncock.

relief: Where you drop a ball that was in a hazard or affected by an obstruction.

reverse overlap: Putting grip in which the index finger of the left hand overlaps the little finger of the right hand.

rhythm: The tempo of your swing.

rifle a shot: To hit the ball hard, straight, and far.

rim the cup: See *lip out.*

ringer score: Your best-ever score at each hole on the course.

Road Hole: The 17th hole at St. Andrews — the hardest hole in the world.

roll: The distance a shot travels after landing.

rough: Area of long grass on either side of the fairway or around the green.

round: Eighteen holes of golf.

Royal and Ancient Golf Club of St. Andrews: The organization that runs the British Open.

rub of the green: Luck.

run: How far a golf shot travels after landing.

run-up: A type of shot to play when the ground is firm. You bounce the ball onto the green and let it roll to the hole.

S

sandbagger: A golfer who lies about his or her ability/handicap to gain an advantage.

sand trap: Undesirable term for a bunker.

sandy: Making par after being in a bunker.

scorecard: Where the length, par, and rating of each hole is recorded. Also holds your score.

scoring: The grooves on the clubface.

scramble: To play erratic golf but still score well. Also a game in which several players tee off, pick the best shot, and then all play their balls from that spot; play continues that way until the team holes the ball.

scratch play: No handicaps used in this type of game.

scratch player: A golfer with a 0 handicap.

second cut: Second level of rough, higher than first cut. Some courses have three cuts of rough.

semiprivate: A course with members that is also open to the public.

setup: See *address.*

shaft: The part of the club that joins the grip to the head.

shag: To retrieve practice balls.

shag bag: To carry practice balls.

shallow: Narrow clubface. Also a flattish angle of attack into the ball.

shank: Shot struck from the club's hosel; flies far to the right of the intended target.

shooting the lights out: To play very well.

short cut: Cut of grass on the fairway or green.

short game: Shots played on and around the green (within 75 to 80 yards of the hole).

shut: Clubface aligned left at address or impact; looking skyward at the top of the backswing. Results in a shot that goes to the left of the target.

sidehill lie: Ball either above or below your feet.

sidesaddle: Putting style where a player faces the hole while making the stroke. See also *face-on.*

sink: To make a putt.

sit down (full flaps, pull a hamstring, develop a limp): A polite request for the ball to stop.

skins: Betting game where the lowest score on a hole wins the pot. If the hole is tied, the money carries over to the next hole.

skull: A low shot. See also *blade* or *thin.*

sky: Ball flies off the top of the clubface — very high and short.

sleeve of balls: Box of three golf balls.

slice: Shot that curves sharply from left to right.

slope: A measure of the difficulty of a golf course.

smother: To hit the ball with a closed clubface, resulting in a horrible, low, hooky shot.

snake: Long putt.

snap hook: Severe hook.

sole: Bottom of the clubhead.

spade-mashie: Old term for a 6-iron.

spike mark: Mark on the green made by a golf shoe.

spin-out: Legs moving too fast in relation to the upper body on the downswing.

spoon: Old term for a 3-wood.

spot putting: Aiming for a point on the green over which the ball must run if it is to go in the hole.

square: Score of a match is even. Equivalent to "all square." Also indicates the clubface and stance are aligned perfectly with the target.

square face: Clubface looking directly at the hole at address/impact.

square grooves: USGA banned them from clubfaces.

St. Andrews: The home of golf, located in Fife, Scotland.

stableford: Method of scoring by using points rather than strokes.

stance: Position of the feet before the swing.

starter: Person running the order of play from the first tee.

starting time: When you tee off at the first tee.

stick: The pin in the hole.

stiff: A shaft with reduced flex. Also a shot very close to the hole.

stimpmeter: Device used to measure the speed of greens.

stroke: Movement of club with the intent to hit the ball.

stroke hole: Hole at which a player either gives or receives a shot, according to her handicap.

stymie: Now-obsolete term for a ball obstructing your route to the hole.

sudden death: Form of playoff in which the first player to win a hole wins the match or tournament.

superintendent: Person responsible for the upkeep of the course.

surlyn: Material from which golf-ball covers can be made.

swale: Depression or dip in terrain.

sway: To move excessively to the right on the backswing without turning the body.

sweet spot: Perfect point on the clubface with which to strike the ball.

swing plane: Angle at which the club shaft travels around the body during a swing.

swing weight: Measure of a club's head weight relative to its length.

T

takeaway: Early part of the backswing.

tap-in: Very short putt, considered unmissable.

tee: Wooden peg on which the ball is set for the first shot on a hole. Also, the area from which that initial shot is hit.

teeing ground: Area in which you must tee your ball, between the tee markers and neither in front of them nor more than two club lengths behind them.

tee it up: To start play.

tee time: The time golfers start a round; a difficult thing to get at premier courses like Pebble Beach.

tempo: The rhythm of your swing.

temporary green: An alternate putting surface used when the permanent green is being renovated, or used in winter to save wear and tear on the permanent green.

Texas wedge: Term for a putter when used from off the green.

that'll play: A kind reference to a mediocre shot.

thin: To hit the ball around its equator — don't expect much height.

three-putt: To take three putts on the green, which is undesirable.

through the green: The whole course except hazards, tees, and greens.

Tiger tee: Slang for the back tee.

tight: Narrow fairway.

tight lie: The ball on bare ground or very short grass.

timing: The pace and sequence of movement in your swing.

titanium: Metal used in lightweight shafts, clubheads, and even inside a few golf balls.

top: Ball is struck on or above the equator.

torque: Twisting of the shaft at impact.

tour: Series of tournaments for professionals.

tradesman's entrance: Ball goes in the hole from the rear of the cup.

trajectory: Flight of the ball.

trap: See *bunker.*

triple bogey: Three over par on one hole. Not good.

turn: To make your way to the back nine holes. Also the rotation of the upper body during the backswing and forward swing.

U

uncock: See *release.*

underclub: To take at least one club less than needed for distance.

unplayable lie: Lie from which you can't hit the ball. A one-stroke penalty is your reward.

up: Ahead in the match. Also the person next to play or reaching the hole with a putt.

up and down: To get the ball into the hole in two strokes from off the green.

upright: To swing with a steep vertical plane.

urethane: Synthetic material used in making golf balls, including covers.

USGA: United States Golf Association. The ruling body for golf in the United States.

U.S. Open: National men's golf championship of America.

U.S. Women's Open: National women's golf championship of America.

V

Vardon grip: See *overlapping.*

W

waggle: Movement of the clubhead prior to the swing.

water hazard: Body of water that costs you a shot to escape.

wedge: Lofted club (iron) used for pitching.

whiff: See *airball.*

whipping: The string that fixed the head of a wooden club to the shaft in the old days.

whippy: A shaft more flexible than normal.

wind-cheater: Low drive.

winter rules: See *preferred lies.*

wood: Material that long clubs used to be made of.

wormburner: Low mishit.

Y

yips: When a golfer misses short putts because of nerves, reducing the afflicted unfortunate to jerky little snatches at the ball, the putterhead seemingly possessing a mind of its own.

Index

• **G** •

• H •

hackers, 606
Hagen, Walter, 273
hamstrings
  flexibility self-test, 124–125
  stretch, 144–145
handicap
  abuse of, 433
  calculating, 434–435
  defined, 432, 606
  getting, 433
  meaning of, 435
  net score, 435
  scorecard signatures for, 433
  system, 432–435
  vanity, 433
hanging lies, 606
hard sand, 375
Hassan II Trophy, 478
Hazard icon, 5
hazards. *See also* bunkers; water hazards
  defined, 370, 606
  pitch shots over, 324–325
  respecting, 325
  treating jerks as, 450
head position
  checking in mirror, 539
  problem, solving, 557–558
high school golf, 482
high-trajectory shots, 584
hip extension, 174–175
hip flexion, 175–176
hip lifts. *See also* core training
  defined, 158

illustrated, 159
importance, 159
steps, 158
hip position at downswing, 565–566
hitting from the top. *See also* problems
  defined, 560
  high-trajectory shots, 584
  illustrated, 563
  low-trajectory shots, 582–584
  solving, 562
hitting the ball, 236
Hogan, Ben, 281, 291
holding the green, 397–398
holes
  defined, 606
  facing away from, 423
home improvement. *See also* practicing
  alignment, 539–540
  putting, 537–538
  weights, 538–539
honor, 441
hook
  defined, 260, 607
  duck, 602
  problem, solving, 560, 561
  top of backswing checkpoint and, 267
Horse, 541–542
hosel, 21, 607
hustlers, 467
hybrids
  defined, 11, 607
  recommendations, 27

• I •

icons, explained, 5
imagination, 581
impact
  checkpoint, 267
  stopping at, 294
impediments, 607
improving lies, 607
Indian Creek Country Club (Miami Beach, FL), 81
indoor golf, 595
injuries
  overcoming, 188
  RICE for, 188
  sprain, 187
  strain/pull, 187
  stretching correctly to prevent, 109–113
  weight training, 187–188
inside-out, 607
instruction. *See also* lessons
  books, 50
  DVD, 53
  gadgets, 51–52
  Internet, 53–55
  magazine, 50–51
  options, 39
  sources of, 49–55
  TV golf, 55–61
integrated performance enhancement, 88
interlocking grip, 242, 243, 607
introductions, 74
investment-cast clubs, 12
irons. *See also* clubs
  bottom of swing with, 249–250
  defined, 11